böhlau

A. Tül Demirbaş & Margret Scharrer (Eds.)

Sounds of Power

Sonic Court Rituals In- and Outside Europe
in the 15th–18th Centuries

BÖHLAU

Die Druckvorstufe dieser Publikation wurde vom Schweizerischen Nationalfonds
zur Förderung der wissenschaftlichen Forschung unterstützt.

Die Publikation wurde inhaltlich vorbereitet mit Unterstützung der Fondation Johanna Dürmüller-Bol, der Burgergemeinde Bern sowie des Instituts für Musikwissenschaft der Universität Bern.

Bibliographic information published by the Deutsche Nationalbibliothek:
The Deutsche Nationalbibliothek lists this publication in the Deutsche
Nationalbibliografie; detailed bibliographic data available online: https://dnb.de.

© 2024 by Böhlau, Lindenstraße 14, 50674 Köln, Germany, an imprint of the Brill-Group
(Koninklijke Brill BV, Leiden, The Netherlands; Brill USA Inc., Boston MA, USA;
Brill Asia Pte Ltd, Singapore; Brill Deutschland GmbH, Paderborn, Germany,
Brill Österreich GmbH, Vienna, Austria)
Koninklijke Brill BV incorporates the imprints Brill, Brill Nijhoff, Brill Schöningh,
Brill Fink, Brill mentis, Brill Wageningen Academic, Vandenhoeck & Ruprecht,
Böhlau, and V&R unipress.

Unless otherwise noted, this publication is licensed under the Creative Commons
Attribution-NonCommercial 4.0 International License (CC BY-NC 4.0);
see https://creativecommons.org/licenses/by-nc/4.0/deed.de
DOI https://doi.org/10.

All rights reserved. No part of this work may be reproduced or utilized in any form
or by any means, electronic or mechanical, including photocopying, recording,
or any information storage and retrieval system, without prior written permission
from the publisher.

Cover image: İbrahim Pasha's entrance to Vienna, 1700: https://gdz.sub.uni-goettingen.de/id/
PPN476413826?tify=%7B%22pages%22%3A%5B67%5D%2C%22pan%22%3A%7B%22x%22%3A0.67
%2C%22y%22%3A0.699%7D%2C%22view%22%3A%22export%22%2C%22zoom%22%3A0.612%7D
Cover design: Guido Klütsch, Köln
Typesetting: Bettina Waringer, Vienna
Printed and bound: Hubert & Co, Ergoldingen
Printed in the EU

Vandenhoeck & Ruprecht Verlage | www.vandenhoeck-ruprecht-verlage.com
ISBN 978-3-412-52898-0 (Print)
ISBN 978-3-412-52899-7 (OpenAccess)

Contents

Foreword 9

Preface 11

Part I
Introduction & General Reflections

Introduction
Margret Scharrer & A. Tül Demirbaş 15

What's All this Noise?
Exploring the Sounds of Power at Early Modern Courts
Harriet Rudolph 25

Acoustic Agencies in the Early Modern European City
A Conceptual Approach
Jan-Friedrich Missfelder 49

Part II
Ottoman Court Culture

Music Theory Sources in Ottoman Urban Culture and the Court Space
Between the 14th and 15th Centuries
Using the Science of Music for Providing a Cultural Authority
Cenk Güray 63

Sensing the Sultan's Power
The Sound of the *Mehter* and other Sensorial Elements in the 1582 Festival
A. Tül Demirbaş 79

"… quando il Gran Signore vuole la musica"
17th-Century Europeans on Music and the Ottoman State
Judith I. Haug 103

An Untold Battle of Music and Banners
Ambassadorial Entrance Ceremonies between the Ottoman and Habsburg Empires
Gamze İlaslan Koç 123

Traces of Modern Ideas in the Music of the Ottoman Empire
Songül Karahasanoğlu & Suleyman Cabir Ataman 147

The Discovery of Life's Pleasures in the Tulip Era
The Rise of City Life and a Worldly Perception in the Ottoman Empire
Ali Ergur 161

Part III
Habsburg-Burgundian Court Culture

Une symphonie de faveurs
Les dons aux musiciens, entre communication politique et expression du pouvoir
à la cour de Bourgogne (1404–1467)
Baptiste Rameau 175

Images sonores des rituels politiques dans les manuscrits enluminés des ducs Valois
de Bourgogne Philippe le Bon et Charles le Téméraire (1419–1477)
Des musicalités pour "une bibliothèque monde"?
Martine Clouzot 191

Courts in Motion
Burgundian Court Sounds between Daily Life and Celebration
Margret Scharrer 217

Marian Devotion as an Expression of Power
Aspects of Repertoire at the Court of Margaret of Austria with a Special Regard to
Her "Court Composer" Pierre de la Rue
Daniel Tiemeyer 237

The Soundscape of the Imperial Diet in the Age of Emperor Maximilian I
Moritz Kelber 261

Part IV
Expanding the Scope: Rituals and Sounds Across Borders

Ad sonum campanæ et tubæ
Power-Reflecting Sonic Elements of Early Modern Republic of Dubrovnik
(1358–1667)
Tin Cugelj 281

Durch Klang zur Harmonie
Koreanische Hofmusik der Joseon-Dynastie zur Zeit von König Sejong
Jieun Kim 299

The Soundscape of the Popes
Music, Sound and Communication Strategies of Early Modern Papacy
Tobias C. Weißmann 319

The Power of Silence
What Came Before and After Morales' Music in Mexico City in 1559?
Grayson Wagstaff 343

Commanding Sounds and Sights
A Case Study of State Processional Music in Late Ming China (1572–1644)
Joseph S. C. Lam 361

Setúbal Soundscapes
Performing Power in a Portuguese Urban Environment During the
Early Modern Period
Ana Cláudia Silveira 381

The Sound of Victory
The Triumphant Entry of King Sigismund III Vasa into Vilnius in 1611
Aleksandra Pister 397

The Soft Sounds of Power
The *Rebecchino* in the Kunsthistorisches Museum Vienna
Thilo Hirsch & Marina Haiduk 417

Appendix

Biographies 437

Online Workshop I
Sonic Rituals: Ottoman, Habsburg & Burgundian Festivities (15th–17th Centuries)
from an Intermedial Perspective 445

Online Workshop II
Between Court and City: Soundscapes of Power in East and West
(15th–17th Centuries) 447

International Conference
Sounds of Power: Sonic Court Rituals In- and Outside Europe in the 15th–17th
Centuries 449

Foreword

Anyone who has experienced the big bells of the main churches in a town ringing all at once, a lavish fireworks display at a public festival, the national anthem played at a sporting event, or a sound document of any meeting held by a fascist ruler has experienced the potent impact of music and sound. It is the sound of power. The borders between noise, sound, and music are blurred, because all of these elements are taking place at the same time. During the coronation of a king or queen, bells ring, cannons are fired, the choir sings, and the organ plays to emphasize a miraculous transformation.

During my training as a musicologist, such manifestations of meaningful organized sound were not part of the curriculum. Music was represented by a certain corpus of canonical works – most of them composed by German men – documented in scores and performed at concerts. Being able to lead the Swiss National Science Foundation (SNSF) project "Sound of Power" was a privilege I could compare to studying anew, learning to think about music as a lived experience that does not differentiate between centres and peripheries, good and not-so-good music, I and they. Rulers in all parts of the world used the power of music and sound to convey their supremacy, to present themselves as legitimate kings, queens, or emperors.

The papers collected in this volume deal with a great variety of acoustic manifestations of power all over the world between the 15th and 18th centuries. They were originally presented at two workshops and a conference organized by the "Sound of Power" project's researchers, Margret Scharrer and A. Tül Demirbaş.

Today's society is accustomed to the ubiquity of music, so it takes some abstraction to understand the effect of the noise, light, and music that was used to represent power in earlier times. And we also have to take into consideration the multi-mediality of the events described. The effect of the "Sound of Power" relied on its contextualization in performances involving all the senses: seeing, hearing, smelling, feeling, and tasting. Moreover, even the absence of sound, politically imposed silence, is relevant because it emphasized the power that rulers exerted over the acoustic sphere. The interdisciplinary and international approach to the "Sound of Power" in this collection opens a window onto past experiences of fascination, overwhelming impact, persuasion, and mass manipulation that might be instructive for the present.

Cristina Urchueguía

Preface

We are delighted to present this volume *Sounds of Power: Sonic Court Rituals In- and Out-side Europe (15ᵗʰ–18ᵗʰ Centuries)* in Open Access format. This publication is one outcome of a four-year academic project that brought together two researchers in Bern, Switzerland, where they found a flourishing and inspiring academic environment and were guided by a highly supportive director. Throughout our collaboration within the SNSF project "The Sound of Power: Sound as an Intermedial Category of Courtly Festive Rituals in an Intercultural Perspective in the 15ᵗʰ–17ᵗʰ Centuries", we, the editors of this book, have had a mutual enthusiasm for the interdisciplinary study of music and sound, despite our work being focussed on two different cultures. All but one of the contributions to this volume originated from presentations at two workshops and a conference, convened in 2020 and 2021, that focused on court cultures and the sonic environments of court celebrations and/or rituals. The main goal of these events was to expand the perspective beyond our own research fields, the courtly sonorities of Burgundy and of the Ottoman Empire, to encompass different cultures and engage with the work of esteemed scholars from other disciplines. With the publication of this book, we are now very pleased to present this diverse research to others. We believe it will make an important contribution to the fields of historical musicology, sound, and late medieval and early modern court studies.

The publication was prepared under the auspices of the Institute of Musicology at the University of Bern, in an environment of highly prolific and open-minded scholars. We have always felt very fortunate to be part of this warm intellectual atmosphere created by our colleagues. As mentioned above, none of this would have been possible without our wonderful project supervisor. We thus would like to express our enormous gratitude to Cristina Urchueguía for her tremendous and continuous support at every step of this journey.

We are very grateful to the Swiss National Science Foundation (SNSF) for generously funding both our project and the publication of this volume. We would also once again like to express our great appreciation to the sponsors who provided financial support to organize and convene the international conference and workshops: the Burgergemeinde Bern, the Fondation Dürmüller-Bol, the Schweizerische Musikforschende Gesellschaft (SMG), the Schweizerische Akademie der Geistes- und Sozialwissenschaften (SAGW), various organizations of the University of Bern, including the Promotion Fund and the committee for research and young academics support of the Faculty of Humanities, as well as those institutions not wishing to be named. Some of these institutions and organizations also provided support for the preparation of this volume.

There are a few other people we would like to mention and to whom we would also like to express our gratitude for their contributions to the project and related events: our cooperation partners, especially Songül Karahasanoğlu, Wolfgang Behr, Joseph Lam, Martine Clouzot, Grayson Wagstaff, François Picard, as well as, particularly, Judith I. Haug, Martin Greve, and the Orient-Institut Istanbul for their collaboration and "virtual" hospitality during the first workshop, Selina Gartmann and Yves Chapuis for their assistance during the conference, Tuğçe İşçi Özen for her support in the preparation of the conference booklet, and all the other technical helpers in the background. We would also like to thank those who, during the conference, enriched the creation of this volume with their advice. This applies in particular to the speakers at the round table, including among others Britta Sweers, Karolina Zgraja, and Markus Koller.

Moreover, we are indebted to the entire staff of Böhlau Verlag for their diligent work during the production process. Our endless thanks go to Stephen Ferron, the "hidden hero" of our book, for months of detailed and highly nuanced proofreading support. His contribution to the success of this volume is enormous. We thank our reviewer for a conscientious and critical reading and valuable advice. And finally, we owe a great debt of appreciation to all of the authors for their meticulously prepared papers, as well as for their patience during the editorial and publication process.

Bern, June 2023
A. Tül Demirbaş & Margret Scharrer

Part I
Introduction & General Reflections

Introduction

Margret Scharrer & A. Tül Demirbaş

The present volume brings together contributions originating from an international interdisciplinary conference, as well as from two workshops that preceded it. The conference and workshops were made possible by the generosity of various foundations and donors. The volume is an integral part of the research project "The Sound of Power: Sounding as an Intermedial Category of 15th–17th Century Court Festivity Rituals in an Intercultural Perspective". The project is being conducted at the University of Bern under the direction of Cristina Urchueguía and funded by the Swiss National Science Foundation (SNSF). This is also where the above-mentioned conference took place from 17 to 19 June 2021. Entitled "Sounds of Power: Sonic Court Rituals In- and Outside Europe in the 15th–17th Centuries", the conference focused on the phenomena of intermediality as well as the multi- and transculturality of court rituals and ceremonies across borders. The three central questions were: Does power have its own specific sound? How did sounds in combination with other media function specifically in courtly rituals of the pre- and early modern eras? What reactions and associations did they trigger in ritual communities?

The two workshops, "Sonic Rituals – Ottoman, Habsburg & Burgundian Festivities from an Intermedial Perspective" (4–5 September 2020) and "Between Court and City: Soundscapes of Power in East and West" (5 February 2021), were convened online due to the pandemic. For the first workshop, we enjoyed the virtual hospitality of the Orient-Institut Istanbul; the second workshop was hosted online at the University of Bern. The two workshops aimed above all at preparing the conference and discussing the main issues of the "Sounds of Power" project. The participants of the first workshop reflected on the project's central questions of Ottoman and Burgundian-Habsburg rituals between the 15th and early 18th centuries and the sounds involved in them. The second was focussed on interactions between courts and cities, as well as the interplay between sound, ritual and ritualization in everyday life and festivals. In both workshops, we questioned and reflected on our methodological-theoretical approaches. Since contributions to the two workshops covered topics and methods that were not only important for the conference, but also for the broader research project and its two sub-projects, we decided to include them in this conference proceedings volume as well.

The diversity of the topics and approaches at these events is reflected in this volume's structure. We should emphasize that by no means should the arrangement of the various sections and the respective contributions be considered a hierarchical ranking. All three events, as well as the work presented here, aimed at contributing to the subject of cross-cultural forms in the interplay of courtly rituals and their sonic dimensions.[1] Thus, not only do we consider specific characteristics and forms, but also anthropological constants and comparative phenomena. Covering, in a purely geographical sense, "European", "Asian" and "South American" forms of sounding rituals, the scope may seem rather broad. In fact, we would have liked even greater variety. Not all the papers presented at the conference and the workshop were designed to become written papers, as for example the round table discussions.[2] Thus in order to map the multiplicity of topics and approaches that were covered, in the appendices to this volume we include the conference and workshop programmes. Due to the focus of our project and its individual sub-projects, several of the contributions deal with the courtly cultures of the Ottomans and of Habsburg-Burgundy.

Courtly rituals were not only concentrated on the narrow construct of the court. In many respects they also included surrounding urban spaces and required the participation of the city with its diverse institutions as organizers and audience.[3] This is tangible in the transcultural phenomenon of ceremonies conducted on the occasion of the entrance of rulers and diplomats, or in the circumcision ceremonies of the sultans' sons.[4] Both rituals crossed social boundaries, leading to complex processes of expressions of power and transfers of meaning. This was pronounced at various sonic levels. There were overlaps and correspondences between city and court in how symbolic capital or power was demonstrated, in the sonic expressions of festive or everyday situations. Courtly events extended to the city for the very reason that rulers and their spouses resided in cities. Thus, at the second workshop we addressed urban spaces and have included the topic in this volume. There are also overlaps with the sacred sphere, obviously because many rituals are closely connected with it, often owing their motivation and form to it.

Indeed, our conference proceedings can only provide some initial insights into this broad field, as a first step in an intercultural and interdisciplinary dialogue that includes

---

1   The fact that rituals were intermedial and theatrical events transcending borders has been confirmed many times by research. See for example: Köpping, 1997; Dücker, 2007, pp. 2–3; Walsdorf, 2013; Hayden, 2014, passim.

2   We are happy to include a paper by Aleksandra Pister, not presented at the conference, on sounding Vilnius at the entrance of King Sigismund III Vasa. See pp. 397–415, below.

3   See, e.g., the numerous publications within the framework of the project "Residenzstädte im Alten Reich (1300–1800)" of the Residenzen-Kommission der Niedersächsischen Akademie der Wissenschaften zu Göttingen: https://adw-goe.de/forschung/forschungsprojekte-akademienprogramm/residenzstaedte/. Date of Access: 24.01.2024.

4   See especially the contributions to this volume by Cenk Güray, A. Tül Demirbaş, Judith I. Haug, Gamze İlaslan Koç, Harriet Rudolph, Moritz Kelber and Margret Scharrer.

other "cultures" beyond "Europe". This cross-border and interdisciplinary exchange calls for a willingness to leave known territory, to engage with other cultures and traditions, and sometimes to question one's own scholarly standards, not seeing them as the only possible way to "the truth". Thus, the chapters in this volume vary in terms of research contexts and states of knowledge, depending on the questions being asked and how these are being approached. Due to the cultural dominance of the "West",[5] scholars of different cultural backgrounds have only discovered in recent years that they have their own music history. One example of this is Korea, whose sounding court rituals are also represented in this volume with a special study. According to Hyesu Shin, "[…] it can be assumed that the Korean population of today understands music primarily as Western music and no longer as that of their own culture" (2013, p. 256). It is clear that for this reason, the main questions and problems of Korean researchers concerning their own music history are very different from some of the Western music histories that have been a continuous object of study since the 19th century.

In addition, how sounds are approached and analysed – and we understand sounds in a broader sense than currently discussed in various debates in sound studies – varies depending on the discipline. In recent years, certain turns have led to a reorientation and rethinking in the humanities and in cultural studies.[6] Only recently has this been joined by the so-called "sonic" or "musical turn", which is expanding, not surprisingly, at different speeds in the various disciplines and scholarly cultures.[7]

---

5   A legitimate question is what is meant by "Western culture". See, e.g. (with thanks to Ulf Scharrer for references), Sen, 1999, pp. 232–248; Bavaj, 2011; Harrison, 2011, pp. 122–126; Sen, 2009, pp. XIV, 228, 330–334; Geulen, 2018. Here, too, hierarchical views and particular perspectives can be identified. In musicological research on the late Middle Ages and the early modern period, the focus is clearly on Italian, French, English or Dutch music history. While some attention has been paid in recent years to Eastern Europe, excluding Russia, very little interest has been devoted to other continents. However, there are signs of a change. This is evident, e.g., in individual study groups at the IMS, but especially in the "Global History of Music" (https://www.musicology.org/index. php. Date of Access: 26.01.2024). This rethinking is also visible in some recent conferences, such as MedRen 2022, which focused on the global histories of early music as one of its main topics, and the conference "Between Ulm and Jerusalem – Sound and Hearing Cultures in Mutual Perception (500–1500)" held the same year at the Orient-Institut in Istanbul. See also Strohm, 2018, and the research of Judith I. Haug and her contribution to this volume, pp. 103–122.

6   There is a lot of literature on this topic. A good overview can be found in Moebius, 2012; on sound studies, see specifically Morat & Ziemer, 2018.

7   While scholars of early modern history have been discovering the world of sound for some time, medieval historical scholarship is only now beginning to explore it. In February 2020 the cultural theorist Jan Söffner (2020) stated in the *Neue Zürcher Zeitung* that it is "time for the musical turn". It has long since reached us. We will not list all the research literature of the last decades here, since it is highly variable depending on research traditions and thus requires a differentiated view. In the German-speaking world alone, much has been happening recently. Reference is therefore made here

*

Let us now turn to the contents and structure of our volume. It is divided into four sections. The first section, with chapters by Harriet Rudolph and Jan-Friedrich Missfelder, is dedicated to conceptual approaches, methodological questions, and general reflections. The first examines sounds of power in the intersensory and -medial texture of courtly festive cultures in the early modern period. The author proposes seven categories for analysing courtly sounds according to their functional contexts and processes: competitive power-political and legitimization, social order, military sovereignty, pleasure, religion, patronage, and interculturality. The bridal entry of Renata of Lorraine in Munich in 1568 serves here as an exemplary case study. The second opening chapter discusses the connection between sound practices and acoustic agency with a view of urban cultures of the pre- or early modern period as "ear-to-ear societies" (following Rudolf Schlögl's concept of early modern cultures as "face-to-face" or "Anwesenheitsgesellschaften"). He reflects on concepts and analyses of Brandon LaBelle, Judith Butler and Hannah Arendt, and Jacques Rancière with regard to the political dimensions of sounds, the senses, and their perception. The focus is on the impact and vocal power of sounds, the multiplicity of meanings sounds can have, and the interplay between noise and the public sphere.

Following these theoretical and methodological inquiries, the chapters of each section of the volume are arranged chronologically based on their thematic focus. The second section is devoted to Ottoman court culture. The first chapter of this section deals with the connection of power to music and sound in the context of music theory. Cenk Güray focuses on Ottoman urban culture, the palace, and orders by examining music manuscripts of the 14th and 15th century, as well as the function of Ottoman music theory as an element of power. In the next chapter, we move from theory to the practice of music and sound.

---

only to Morat & Ziemer, 2018; Clauss et al., 2020; Clauss & Mierke, 2022, the conference volume of the Konstanzer Arbeitskreis für mittelalterliche Geschichte (Constance Working Group for Medieval History) "Klangräume des Mittelalters" (Sound Spaces of the Middle Ages), Jaspert & Müller 2023, as well as a wide variety of other research initiatives, such as the DFG network "Lautsphären des Mittelalters" (Sound Spheres of the Middle Ages). In addition, there are some DFG-funded projects on this topic, such as "Lärm vor Dezibel" (Noise before Decibel) at RWTH Aachen University: https://www.ma.histinst.rwth-aachen.de/cms/HISTINST-MA/Forschung/Projekte/~vreuc/DFG-Projekt-Laerm-vor-Dezibel/, and: "Der laute Krieg und die Laute des Krieges" (The loud war and the sounds of war) at Chemnitz University of Technology: https://www.tu-chemnitz.de/phil/iesg/professuren/gdma/dfg-netzwerk_belliphonie.php. Date of Access: 24.01.2024. For research being done in Switzerland, see especially the work of Jan Friedrich Missfelder and the research project he is conducting at the University of Basel "Macht der Stimme – Vocal Power" (Power of the Voice – Vocal Power): https://dg.philhist.unibas.ch/de/bereiche/fruehe-neuzeit/snf-professur-macht-der-stimme/. Date of Access: 24.01.2024. See also his contribution to this volume on pp. 49–59. For a French perspective, see, among others, the research of Martine Clouzot and her contribution to this volume on pp. 191–216.

A. Tül Demirbaş analyses the circumcision festival organized in Istanbul in 1582 to understand the relationship of power to music and sound. Using both Ottoman and European sources, Demirbaş concentrates on sensorial aspects of the celebrations. In this context, she examines the Sultan's power based on the example of the military music ensemble known as *mehter*. The contribution of Judith I. Haug gives us a deeper insight into the Ottoman court and its music based on a compilation and comparison of written accounts by 17th-century Ottoman courtiers. At the centre of Haug's analysis is one of the most important of these sources to our subject, an account containing observations about the soundscape of the Ottoman state. Focusing on the passages on military music in Ali Ufkî's *Serai Enderun*, the author compares and examines different translations of this 17th-century Italian source. In the next chapter, Gamze İlaslan Koç brings together the Ottoman and Habsburg courts to discuss the diplomatic side of sound or the sound of diplomacy. The chapter discusses the sounds that accompanied ambassadorial exchanges, welcoming ceremonies, and other diplomatic missions, as well as how silence was used as a powerful tool in both cultures. The focus of the following chapter, by Songül Karahasanoğlu and Süleyman Cabir Ataman, returns to music theory. As in the chapter by Güray, Karahasanoğlu and Ataman trace reflections of Western ideas in Ottoman music theory from the beginning of the 17th century. Accordingly, we discover theoretical changes in Ottoman music: the abandonment of the early *Edvâr* tradition, and the emerging of new directions with the introduction of "modern" ideas. The last chapter of this section deals with the changes in culture, specifically in the area of music, during the 18th-century Tulip Period of the Ottoman Empire. In addition to the changes in music theory related to the idea of "modernization" as discussed in the chapter by Karahasanoğlu and Ataman, Ali Ergur investigates the music practices, poetry, and public performances of the period, focusing on concepts of urban life, public space, individualism, and worldly pleasures. In this context, the chapter also discusses imperial events organized by the sultans.

The third section of the volume, on Burgundian-Habsburg court cultures, is opened by Baptiste Rameau with a study on the relationship between the Burgundian dukes and their musicians as reflected in princely gift practices. From the types of gratuities that changed hands, Rameau concludes that these often went beyond official remuneration and were an expression of the dukes' gratitude to their musicians. In particular, trumpeters benefitted from princely allowances. The next chapter, by Martine Clouzot, turns to the world of book illuminations, which she analyses with regard to the information they hold about Burgundian rituals and their sounds. Essential to her analysis is Zrinka Stahuljak's concept of a "littérature connectée" and the "bibliothèque monde" resulting from it. By referring to the "hétérochronies", the plurality of discourses and the interconnections of courtly societies in Burgundy, she simultaneously deconstructs the oft-invoked myth of Burgundy and places the sounds of power within symbolic, historical, mythological, biblical, and literary motifs. Margret Scharrer also examines the Burgundian soundscape, in her case with regard to everyday court rituals. She shows that the court was surrounded by a special "sound cocoon", various sound spaces whose sonic presence demonstrated and exercised power. Daniel Tiemeyer then deals with the special sound and devotional worlds of Marian worship at the court of Margaret of Austria. His study focuses on the Marian masses of Pierre de la Rue, including their compositional nature and how they were used in both every day and festive liturgies. The closing contribution of this section by Moritz Kelber looks at the soundscape of the Imperial Diet under Emperor Maximilian I, in particular the extent to which power was staged and exercised through sounds.

The fourth and final section of the volume is devoted to regions beyond the Ottoman, Habsburg, and Burgundian courts, examining imperial festivities and ceremonies in various other parts of the world. The section is opened by Tin Cugelj with a chapter on the early modern Republic of Dubrovnik (Ragusa) and its soundscape. Cugelj's semantic analysis of the sounds' different meanings and functions shows the effectiveness of power. In Dubrovnik, as in many other early modern urban areas, various ceremonies, festivals, and funerals were scenes of sonic reflections of power. The next contribution focusses on a different part of the world, the court culture of the Korean Joseon Dynasty. Jieun Kim presents the contributions made to court music by King Sejong, examining the idealized Confucian idea of Ye-Ak: ceremony (Ye) and the performing arts, which are a combination of music, song, and dance (Ak). Through various examples of these two concepts and their role in historic events and performances, she examines how one balanced the other. Tobias C. Weißmann's chapter investigates papal rituals in early modern Rome. In particular, he examines communication strategies in these rituals and the role played by planned and organized sound, in particular how this related to the papacy's power. The next chapter explores the cross-continental impact of the sound of power, with Grayson Wagstaff investigating the influence of "Habsburg sound" in colonial Mexico of the 16th century. He shows how the music of Cristobal de Morales was used to ritually symbolize Emperor Charles V. By looking at both sound and silence, Wagstaff addresses power in the context of the monarchy as well as the Catholic Church. Through his analysis of illustrated scrolls from the Ming court, Joseph S. C. Lam focuses on the 1583 trip of Emperor Shenzong to the imperial tombs and how this event was reflected in 16th-century Chinese music. Lam discusses the performance of military music and how sound accompanied imperial power. The contribution by Ana Cláudia Silveira looks at another culture, the Portuguese port city of Setúbal. She explores the representation of political power through cultural symbols in Setúbal, its urban environment, and sound in civic and religious ceremonies. In particular, she examines the connection of the House of Aveiro with festivities and processions that functioned as political tools. The chapter by Aleksandra Pister is devoted to the glorious entry in 1611 of the Grand Duke of Lithuania and King of Poland into Vilnius on the occasion of the recapture of Smolensk from the Russians by the Polish-Lithuanian army. Analysing the sonic atmosphere of the ceremony, the chapter considers the performance of various kinds of music in the interior and exterior spaces of the Lithuanian capital, explaining the role of music in the celebration of this military achievement within the power-sound relationship. The book ends with the only organological essay, dedicated to the rebecchino in the Collection of Historic Musical Instruments at the Kunsthistorisches Museum in Vienna. Thilo Hirsch and Marina Haiduk discuss the relationship of this 15th-century instrument to political and social power, its use in musical performances, and especially its meaning as a symbolic element.

While the contributions to this volume are quite diverse, a common thread runs through them all: sounds constituting an essential element of rituals. Whether in daily life or in special rituals, no prince, ruler, or religious authority of the early modern era made an appearance without sounds. Even when these authorities were absent, their presence could be imagined through sounds. Sounds were not only used for publicity or for staging external representations, they were also used for shaping and transforming places and people, indeed, all kinds of living beings. They created order and transported meaning, they evolved into the most diverse of effects. As part of a sensory atmosphere created by various mediators, sounds triggered and guided the senses. The power they produced can be seen at multiple levels. Spaces and people could be dominated through sounds, in both a positive and negative sense. Since sounds channelled emotions, they could be used to manipulate. But sounds could also invoke an ideal realm or a reign of harmony. Depending on a ruler's cultural orientation or predilection, sounds played various roles in political-philosophical attitudes and concepts. For example, the Korean King Sejon attributed extraordinary importance to music for harmony in his kingdom, presenting himself as the creator of new melodies and compositions. And the Ottoman ruler Murad III attempted to confirm his role as an exemplary ruler – as a man and as a powerful and ideal representative of his dynasty and religion – by means of sounds and festivities.

It was not only by means of sounds that rulers regulated rituals temporally, spatially, and emotionally. Silence also played an essential role as an important element of the soundscape (Breitsameter, 2018). Even though rather less attention is given to this concept, in this volume, some of the contributions do mention silence within the context of power. Not only is the function and aim of silence important to consider, but also how silence has been interpreted in different cultures, practices, and rituals. Moreover, silence can be perceived differently by persons of different cultural backgrounds. Ottoman–Habsburg diplomatic encounters were an important example in this regard, where not only sound but also silence was influential. Silence could also characterize a loss of power or a lower status in a hierarchical order, as demonstrated by Byzantine imperial ceremonies, where the emperor deliberately used rhythms of silence and sound (Grünbart, 2023). For a more comprehensive and deeper knowledge about sounding rituals, the element of silence still needs further investigation.

There are other aspects that should be investigated further, such as, for example, the question of gender: How did sounding rituals and court societies differ between male and female rulers and their relatives (children, brothers/sisters, or widows)? Other questions might include: What specifically constituted the soundscape of a spiritual ruler? What role did musicians and other artists play in processes of creating soundscapes? How have sounding rituals varied and developed over time? Many other questions could be mentioned. The following contributions must be seen as a starting point for this multifaceted panorama of questions, a panorama we hope in future will continue to be explored.

Bibliography

Bavaj, R. (2011). "The West": A Conceptual Exploration. *European History Online*. http://www.ieg-ego.eu/bavajr-2011-en. Date of Access: 23.01.2024.

Breitsameter, S. (2018). Soundscape. In D. Morat & H. Ziemer (Eds.), *Handbuch Sound. Geschichte – Begriffe – Ansätze* (pp. 89–95). Metzler.

Clauss, M., Mierke, G. & Krüger, A. (Eds.) (2020). *Lautsphären des Mittelalters. Akustische Perspektiven zwischen Lärm und Stille*. Böhlau.

Clauss, M. & Mierke, G. (Eds.) (2022). *Akustische Dimensionen des Mittelalters*. Heidelberg University Publishing.

Dücker, B. (2007). *Rituale. Formen – Funktionen – Geschichte*. J.B. Metzler.

Geulen, C. (2018). Test the West: Bemerkungen über ein Raumkonzept – und seinen Geltungsraum. In R. Bavaj & M. Steber (Eds.), *Zivilisatorische Verortungen. Der "Westen" an der Jahrhundertwende (1880–1930)* (pp. 150–161). De Gruyter. https://www.degruyter.com/document/doi/10.1515/9783110529500-011/html. Date of Access: 23.01.2024.

Grünbart, M. (2023). Die Macht des Klangs: Akustische Dimensionen des griechischen Mittelalters. In N. Jaspert & Harald Müller (Eds.), *Klangräume des Mittelalters* (pp. 161–198). Thorbecke.

Harrison, T. (2011). *Writing Ancient Persia*. Bristol Classical Press.

Hayden, B. (2014). *The Power of Feasts: From Prehistory to the Present*. Cambridge University Press.

Jaspert, N. & Müller, H. (Eds.) (2023). *Klangräume des Mittelalters*. Thorbecke.

Köpping, K.-P. (1997). Fest. In C. Wulf (Ed.), *Vom Menschen. Handbuch Historische Anthropologie* (pp. 1048–1065). Beltz.

Moebius, S. (Ed.) (2014). *Kultur. Von den Cultural Studies bis zu den Visual Studies. Eine Einführung*. Unpublished transcript.

Morat, D. & Ziemer, H. (Eds.) (2018). *Handbuch Sound. Geschichte – Begriffe – Ansätze*. Metzler.

Sen, A. (1999). *Development as Freedom*. Knopf.

Sen, A. (2009). *The Idea of Justice*. Belknap.

Shin, H. (2013). Parallelwelten? Das Eigene und das Fremde in der Musik Koreas. In S. Ehrmann-Herfort & S. Leopold (Eds.), *Migration und Identität. Wanderbewegungen und Kulturkontakte in der Musikgeschichte* (pp. 256–273). Bärenreiter.

Söffner, J. (2020). Es ist Zeit für den „Musical Turn" – von mehr Musikalität könnten die Kulturwissenschaften nur profitieren. *Neue Zürcher Zeitung*, 24 Feb. 2020: https://www.nzz.ch/feuilleton/musical-turn-mehr-musenkunst-fuer-die-kulturwissenschaften-ld.1541055. Date of Access: 23.01.2024.

Strohm, R. (Ed.) (2018). *Studies on a Global History of Music: A Balzan Musicology Project*. Routledge, Taylor & Francis Group.

Walsdorf, H. (2013). Performanz. In Brosius, C., Michaels, A. & Schrode, P. (Eds.), *Ritual und Ritualdynamik: Schlüsselbegriffe, Theorien, Diskussionen* (pp. 85–91). Vandenhoeck & Ruprecht.

What's All this Noise?

Exploring the Sounds of Power at Early Modern Courts

Harriet Rudolph

We are looking at a dark study chamber. A man is sitting at a desk. He is declaiming, lamenting, calling out. Suddenly, a voice: "What's all this noise?" asks Mephisto. What Mephisto is referring to, however, is not only noise in the sense of sound. It is human effort; it is an effort related to the idea of power. By addressing an imagined transcendental force, Faust is aiming at the power of the mind and, in addition, at a state of contentment as well as fulfilment. In vain he had tried to silence the growling, barking, howling poodle that was allegedly drowning out all the "sacred sounds" encompassing Faust's soul while he was trying to translate the Bible.[1]

What does this scene have to do with the sound of power at European courts in the early modern period? Sound in every outward appearance was a means of princely effort to gain legitimisation, to secure rule over a prince's subjects, to claim dominance in an ostentatiously self-staging European "society of princes" (Bély, 1999), to assert cultural refinement, to attract political as well as cultural actors, etc. Early modern Germans used to call exuberant effort *Lärm/Lärmen* (noise/making noise). This derived from the term "alarm", which in turn referred to the Italian phrase *al arme* (to weapons); thus the origins of the term were in a military context.[2] *Lärm* as a means of sonic warfare was used to frighten the enemy, bolster one's own courage, and banish evil spirits (Žak, 1979, pp. 8, 79). In a figurative sense, *Lärm* marked various situations in which people were asked to be attentive or to act, even if the term was increasingly linked to the idea of disorder, social unrest, and indecent showing off.

---

1   The scene of the "study room" is full of references to sound. Johann Wolfgang von Goethe: Faust: Der Tragödie erster Teil, Studierzimmer; cf., for example, verses 1186, 1193, 1202–1209, 1238–1242, 1322. https://faustedition.net/print/faust.6#scene_1.1.3. Date of Access: 26.01.2024.

2   "LÄRM, m.", Deutsches Wörterbuch von Jacob Grimm und Wilhelm Grimm, digitalisierte Fassung im Wörterbuchnetz des Trier Center for Digital Humanities, Version 01/21. https://woerterbuchnetz.de/?sigle=DWB&lemid=L01684. Date of Access: 26.01.2024. See here also the numerous compound terms such as "noise fire" that people were supposed to see, not to hear: https://woerterbuchnetz.de/?sigle=DWB#1; cf. also "Lärm", in DWDS: https://www.dwds.de/wb/L%C3%A4rm. Date of Access: 26.01.2024.

In this sense, making noise represented all sorts of strategies used to attract people's attention by appealing to human senses, not only hearing, sight, smell, touch and taste, but also to the sense of place.[3] This reminds us of the simple fact that while sound at early modern courts was certainly one means of princely effort, hearing was only one of various human senses that court actors addressed at the same time in one and the same performance. While listening to court music, for example, people were eating, sniffing, talking, laughing, moving around, dancing, and watching – not necessarily the musicians, but primarily other people of the same or higher rank present at the occasion. And even if the audience had to stay in place and remain silent, they might have focused on various matters other than music and experienced all kinds of senses. We must ask, therefore, how intended and unintended sensory effects of court performances were interrelated. We must also examine how contemporary actors arranging court festivals and other kinds of public spectacles made a priori allowances for the multi-sensory quality of whatever staging they had in mind or were implementing.

My argument, however, is that *in actu*, sound was one of the most significant communication tools overall, though not necessarily of every festival element, and certainly not with regard to the medialization and memorialization of such events afterwards. It was the irretrievable and multi-sensory experience of sound, for example, that was used at solemn entries, not sight, taste, smell, or touch. Moreover, at such events, it was probably not sight that followed sound in importance, as most people seem to presume, but the sense of place. Indeed, there was a strong relationship between these two senses: the aural sense and the spatial sense.[4] This applied particularly to court festival cultures in Europe in the first half of the early modern period, since they primarily addressed societies in attendance,[5] despite increasing numbers of festival books and other handwritten and printed media containing verbal and visual representations of court performances.[6]

---

3   Most modern studies on the history of the senses, however, only refer to the five "classical" senses. Cf. for example the relevant studies by Smith, 2007; Nichols et al., 2008; Howes, 2021. This applies even more to the vast number of studies addressing the historical dimensions of one individual sense, such as hearing, touch, or smell.

4   The sense of place was not reflected upon theoretically in the early modern period, even though the entire social order was based not only on the idea of knowing exactly where one was positioned in relation to others, but in fact to feel this position. For the relevance of place, though here not always differentiated from space, cf. Edensor et al., 2020.

5   The term *Anwesenheitsgesellschaft* was coined by Rudolf Schlögl (2004, pp. 9–60).

6   For this reason, some European princes ordered their court kapellmeisters and other musicians to arrange not only musical performances, but other festival elements and sometimes the whole event as we know of it, as for example, the occasion of the 1568 Bavarian–Lorraine wedding (Orlando di Lasso, Massimo Troiano), or the emperor's visit to Dresden in 1617 (Heinrich Schütz). For the former, see section two of this chapter, for the latter, Rudolph, 2011, pp. 164–185.

There are at least three reasons why the sense of sight has been strongly overrated in relation to other senses addressed in court performances. First, there is an unprecedented predominance of pictures today. We have access to a vast and ever-increasing number of visual messages (Levin, 1993). We research current and past visual cultures to a much greater extent than other sensory cultures. Secondly, the complex multi-media and multi-sensory reality of early modern court spectacles is transmitted to us solely by media addressing the sense of sight: paintings, drawings, sketches, and various kinds of text to be read, clearly by using the sense of sight. Even if we analyse the limited number of noise-producing objects that have survived and try to reconstruct sounds of the past by using them, we neither produce the same sounds nor hear what early modern people might have heard. The "audible past" (Sterne, 2003; cf. also 2012) is, in fact, often not very audible. No vital element of court performance is more ephemeral than sound. The design of a costume or triumphal arch can be handed down in a drawing, and despite all the methodologically more-or-less subtle reflections we could consider about the source value of such works, these are visual phenomena represented by using visual media (Rudolph, forthcoming/b). However, contemporaries were never able to transmit sound via a sonic medium. They preserved musical tones in music books by using a combination of signs.[7] This is a fundamental difference. Thirdly, we must deal with an overwhelming human speechlessness regarding acoustic phenomena. Many early modern people "translated" sound experiences into text by using stereotypical phrases such as "thunder that made the ground tremble",[8] or words like "heavenly", "sweet", "coarse", "discordant", etc. But what exactly do these phrases or words mean? Most European languages do not come even close to doing justice to the highly diverse nature of musical tones or of other sound phenomena and the various ways these might have been perceived by people. In addition, there are decisive differences between European languages regarding the available options to describe the infinite variety of sounds.[9] There are different visual "languages", too, but the interpretative challenges that arise from analysing these are very different from those we encounter with texts.

---

7   In spite of a performative turn in musicology in the last two decades, the idea of music as an element of complex sensual regimes at court and as a means of courtly power politics is still rather underrepresented in research. Cf. Riepe, 2003; Wasserloos et al., 2012; Ramel et al., 2018; Rudolph, 2021a; Natour et al., forthcoming.

8   That enormous noise was able to make "the ground tremble" is, on the one hand, a classical topos in early modern festival books; on the other, it is a phenomenon that people could in fact experience. They might tremble themselves because certain kinds of noise were able to pervade the human body as well as to invade it, reminding us of the haptic dimension of sound.

9   Until the first half of the 17th century, festival books were also written and published in Latin. In this case, we must also consider the familiarity of a certain author with the Latin language while describing specific sound phenomena.

To bypass some of these interpretative dilemmas, it has become commonplace to argue in accordance with literary studies and culturalist approaches: well, we are not interested in what happened in early modern "reality"; we are seeking to analyse how media producers represented court performances, how they constructed representations of rule, how they perpetuated such events "by other means" (Rahn, 1993),[10] how certain media of representation are interrelated, etc. Some authors – including me – used to differentiate between levels of performance, as for example, primary performances that are lost, and secondary performances established by simultaneously produced festival media. These media flanked, commented on, attempted to preserve and – at the same time – to disambiguate ephemeral events that often contained complex and confusing messages and were marked by conflicts and failures completely omitted in festival books.[11] Constructivist approaches such as these are legitimate, and at a certain point were even considered innovative, but the latter is no longer the case. Now seems like the time to go beyond the idea of merely (de-) constructing constructions of the past.

Having said this, I would like to come back to the high relevance of sound, which leads me to the question of why this might have been the case: What were sonic experiences able to achieve as reflections of princely power that other sensory impressions could not or, at least, not to the same extent? To examine this, I differentiate between several kinds of sound in which power could take shape at European courts. In the first section below, I introduce seven categories of the sound of power that are suitable for investigating the functions and impact of sound at princely courts, particularly in relation to court festivities.[12] In addition, they might be used to compare the soundscape of different types of festivals at the same court, as well as the soundscape of such performances at different courts. In the second section, I illuminate the potential for knowledge these categories allow by presenting a case study. However, I do not consider the explanatory potential of my approach to be limited to specific elements of festival culture, or to the Holy Roman Empire or Europe as research areas.

---

10   According to Helen Watanabe-O'Kelly, printed festival reports should be understood as "not so much a report of the festival but simply another aspect of it", even though they were supposed to be used as reports memorializing ephemeral events (Watanabe-O'Kelly, 1988, p. 197). For court music, cf. also Bowles, 2000.

11   See Rudolph, 2011, pp. 332–427. In literary studies, constructivist approaches have strongly shaped the analysis of festival books, which are considered to have been highly influenced by already established narrative structures. See, for example, the fundamental study by Rahn, 2006. However, this approach can lead to a failure to adequately reflect on the specificity of particular texts, and thus to underestimating their potential source value for particular events.

12   Cf., among many others, Strong, 1984; Braun et al., 1993; Watanabe-O'Kelly et al., 2000; Mulryne et al., 2002; Maurer, 2004; 2010; Mulryne et al., 2018.

The Various Sounds of Power at European Courts in the 16th Century

The everyday soundscape of early modern courts in Europe consisted of various sounds, including those of daily activities, music heard in church service (if there was music; daily services often did not have it), and sounds made by musical instruments, such as in court ceremonies. But this soundscape was certainly not limited to or even dominated by music, although we observe an increasing frequency and variety of musical performances at European courts from the 17th century onwards. It included the sounds of household activities such as those coming from kitchens or stables, or the sounds of people and carriages coming to the court. By soundscape[13] I am referring to all auditory experiences that early modern courts offered to contemporary receivers, who, both consciously and unconsciously, created individual versions of the soundscape of court life: by listening to sound, imagining sound, ignoring sound, producing sound themselves, and perhaps by disturbing sound.[14] The court soundscape can be seen as the interplay between the totality of human-made/modified sounds (intended and unintended) and the perception of these sounds by people, both individually and collectively, which is significantly influenced by external conditions such as spatial structures, distance relationships and background noise.

The complex soundscape of European courts interacted with the soundscape of residential towns,[15] which in everyday life must have dominated the former by far: sounds caused by handicrafts, traffic, trade, human and animal voices, sounds associated with religious practices, sounds of weapons, etc. On the occasion of exceptional court festivities, many rulers enforced certain measures which, taken together, resulted in a sound regime that emphasised their own dominance at court, in the royal residence and in the surrounding countryside. The most effective measure consisted in declaring a festival a Feast Day, a day on which all working activities had to cease and, accordingly, were silenced (Barbet, 2013; Corbin, 2016). This applies particularly to court festivities related to dynastic *rites de passage*, such as princely weddings or a new ruler's accession to the throne. In cases like these, we observe a clear distinction between everyday court life and the *curia solemnis*.[16] At mi-

---

13 Cf. Murray, 1993. In one way or another, the vast number of *sound studies* have dealt with this term while applying various meanings to it. For critical reflections, cf., for example, Kelman, 2010; as well as several papers in Pinch et al., 2011; Bull, 2018; Bull et al., 2020.

14 Thus, soundscape is considered here both more and less than "the acoustic cover that surrounds the human being" (Breitsameter, 2010, p. 15).

15 Cf., among others, Howard et al., 2010; Atkinson, 2016; Knighton et al., 2018; Hammond, 2019. Most sound studies focusing on early modern times do not refer to courts (other than court music and selected festivals), but rather to the sounds of towns or rural regions.

16 In this case, the princely court was expanded by hiring additional staff and summoning the nobility of the territory with an appropriate retinue to the residence. For the *curia solemnis*, see also Rudolph, 2021, pp. 15–16.

nor festivities, this was not necessarily the case. The imagined festive community included all the inhabitants of a prince's realm and often even beyond it. Ritualized activities – and not solely ceremonial ones – represented vital elements at such events.[17]

Enforcing sonic dominance to effectively exert princely power was based on factors such as volume, frequency, and reverberation, but also on the affective and emotional reactions of the recipients, which may have varied considerably between different social groups and even within the same group. Human beings tend to feel sounds in their bodies to different degrees and in different ways. In addition, the relevance a particular individual or social group ascribes to certain kinds of sound governs their perception not only of sonic but of all sensory effects. Courtiers and people working at courts must have been very sensitive to the complex political messages offered to them by various court sounds. Thus, we should also consider auditory intelligence[18] related to living circumstances as having had a decisive impact on the function and effect of sound on early modern people's minds. While examining the sound of power at courts, I therefore differentiate between seven dimensions in which sound could take shape.[19] There was not only a single sound of power but, in fact, various sounds of power in the early modern period.[20]

1) The *sound of dynasty* refers to the various ways courts tried to distinguish themselves from other courts through a specific sound setting. This was influenced by local sonic traditions as well as by personal preferences of the princely family. There were noisy courts but also quiet ones, musical courts and less musical ones. A common way for a prince to distinguish his own court from other European courts was through the size, composition, and repertoire of the court chapel, especially if its members were particularly accomplished, famous, and expensive musicians. Substantial investment in a court music ensemble could signify that a prince needed to legitimate his rule, or that he aspired to being elevated in rank, a desirable goal of many princes. This was the case, for example,

---

17 Even though the terms ritual and ceremony are sometimes used interchangeably, it makes sense to distinguish between them, especially when investigating the sound of power. Rituals derive their legitimacy from real or constructed traditions, whereas ceremonies could be held *ad hoc*, despite often referring to an alleged tradition as well. For example, while *rites de passage* are aimed at creating community, ceremonial acts are focused primarily on displaying social difference. These (and other) differences between ritual and ceremonial acts are mirrored by specific manifestations of sound. For an in-depth discussion and further literature, see Rudolph, 2011, pp. 28–30.

18 The expression auditory intelligence is generally defined as the ability not just to hear sounds, but to attach complex meanings to them as relevant to one's own life. Cf., for example, Baldwin, 2012, p. 53.

19 There are, of course, overlaps between these categories depending on the subject of consideration. Nonetheless, it seems to make sense to differentiate and categorize various sounds of power at an analytical level.

20 This point is highlighted, for example, by Garrioch, 2003.

for the Sforza court in the second half of the 15th century and the Wittelsbach court from the 1550s onwards. Both courts aimed at displaying their cultural superiority by promoting highly sophisticated court music, in order to counteract the inferiority of their political power compared to other princes and dynasties in Europe.

2) The social order of early modern societies was not only to be seen but also to be heard. At court, the *sound of order* consisted of oral announcements and commands, public speeches such as the ritualized reading of court orders, tones meant to signal the beginning of certain acts such as meals, masses, hunts, receptions, etc., and the structuring of these. Sound signals during a specific festival element sometimes announced an increase in splendour intended to astonish the audience. Very often, the sound of order coincided with the sound of hierarchy, not surprising in an estate-based society where public performances represented and confirmed existing social hierarchies. Such sounds were even able to create new hierarchies, as can be seen in the many conflicts over precedence accompanied by shouting, "sabre rattling", sometimes even shooting, or appealing to legal courts.

3) There were certain sounds in early modern times that only sovereign entities were entitled to produce. The European concept of sovereignty was only taking shape in the first half of the early modern period, but it is certainly no coincidence that a well-known sound-based ritual of sovereignty emerged simultaneously: the reception with military honours. It is a ritual still applied and observed, with the same connotations and performative qualities, around the world today. Because the notion of external sovereignty was increasingly linked to the right to wage war, the *sound of sovereignty* was characterized by a distinctly military quality, such as the thunder of guns on the occasion of a solemn entry. It was not limited to the sounds of weapons, however, but included the sounds of trumpets, timpani, etc., which also signalled notions of sovereignty to all listeners.

4) The idea of a *sound of pleasure* is largely absent in historical research. As a result of the impact of concepts such as "civilization" (Norbert Elias), "social control", and "social discipline" (Gerhard Oestreich), historians of the early modern era have long tended to underestimate the relevance of pleasure. In the meantime, critical research has put these concepts into perspective. The ability of early modern princes to provide abundant pleasure and entertainment for their subjects and guests was not only vital for festival cultures as such, but an important means for increasing the acceptance of princely rule. Sounds of joy and fun were intended at creating positive emotions towards the ruling dynasty.

5) The *sound of transcendence* encompassed various noise-creating practices: from religiously connoted messages and sonic practices of worship appealing to the spirituality and devotion of all listeners, to highly formalized rituals of sacralization with their own sublime sound, that one could, however, hear primarily in selected interior spaces. This type of sound was not limited to sophisticated sounds, as we are reminded by the ringing of church bells, one of the most prominent and multi-functional sounds. In the early modern period, the

sound of transcendence was not only made *for* heaven but sometimes seemed to be made *by* heaven. From the 1520s onwards, it included confessional messages. Most sound studies related to religion have focused on confession due to the high impact of the confessionalization paradigm, at times hardly taking into account that religion involves more than displaying and enforcing one's own confession.

6) The privilege of speaking, singing, or playing an instrument at a court festival was granted by the prince, or on his behalf by holders of certain court offices. This fact was particularly relevant if the sonic performance in question went beyond the specific office held in the princely household by the respective performer, or if the performer did not formally belong to the court. That meant that by listening carefully, it was possible, in fact, to hear networks of patronage and clientelism at court adding up to a *sound of patronage*. It was shaped not only by the ruling prince as a patron, but also by other members of the ruling dynasty or selected officials acting as patrons at the respective court. In oral societies, information was spread by speaking and listening. It was therefore necessary to listen to "key speakers" (or key players and key singers), who were willing to share their political knowledge in this way.

7) In early modern times, large colonial empires emerged. These political entities developed specific soundscapes that were characterised by certain features reflecting the enormous reach of imperial rule, often spanning several societies, cultures, religions, and even continents. The *sound of empire* was therefore marked by a particularly high variety and hybridity of sound actors, sound-producing tools, and sound effects. In important political rituals, the performance of sonic otherness may not only have been accepted, but often ostentatiously staged to demonstrate an empire's cultural diversity, or to display the participation of various social groups, including indigenous groups having their own sonic traditions and modes of perception.

Solemn Entries on the Occasion of the Bavarian-Lorraine Wedding in 1568

To elucidate the first five of these categories, I will focus on the ritual of solemn entries on the occasion of the wedding between William V of Bavaria and Renata of Lorraine in 1568, for which we have unusually elaborate contemporaneous descriptions of the sound effects that were used.[21] A solemn entry was granted to a new ruler in towns of his own realm, to rulers

---

21   See Rudolph, 2020a; for comparisons to other Bavarian Wittelsbach weddings, see Rudolph, 2020b, Stand, Rang und Status. Among other sources, three printed festival books are extant, one by the sonic expert and alto of the Bavarian court music ensemble Massimo Troiano, one by the court chancellery official Johann Wagner, and one by the Swiss-born Pritschenmeister Heinrich Wirrich (Wirri, Wirre), who, however, does not elaborate on many details in this regard.

(and gradually also their ambassadors) visiting a foreign court, and to the bride of a future or already reigning prince.[22] It represented one of the most distinguished performances of sovereignty in the early modern era. On the occasion of a dynastic wedding, several solemn entries often had to be organized, beginning with the entries of high-ranking guests into the residential town of the prince hosting the wedding celebrations – in this case Duke Albrecht V of Bavaria – and ending with the bride's entry one day before or on the day of the wedding mass.[23]

In Munich, these entry spectacles began with the entry of Archduke Ferdinand of Tyrol and his large retinue of 749 horses on 15 February 1568.[24] Two days later, the Pope's representative, Otto Seneschal of Waldburg, Cardinal and Bishop of Augsburg, entered the town, followed a day later by Archduke Charles of Inner Austria. On 19 February 1568, the Administrator of the Grand Master's Office of the Teutonic Order,[25] representing the emperor, was ceremoniously led into the town. On 19 February 1568, Eberhard of Württemberg, on behalf of his father Duke Christoph of Württemberg, and the Archbishop of Salzburg, representing the Holy See, entered Munich. In this entrances, there were likely sounds of trumpets, because both princes were accompanied, respectively, by three and two of their own trumpeters, and the Princes Ferdinand and William of Bavaria, who formally received them, were accompanied by Bavarian trumpeters. The envoys of the Kings of Spain and Poland, the Duke of Tuscany, the electors of Saxony and the Palatinate, as well as the Dukes of Baden and Julich-Cleve were received with less ceremony and, therefore, without any noise worth mentioning (Wagner, 1568, fols. 21v.–29v.).[26]

Only three princes had a large number of trumpeters and timpanists in their entourage: the Archdukes Ferdinand and Charles of Austria, who brought their own musicians to Munich, and Duke Albrecht V of Bavaria.[27] In the Holy Roman Empire, the right to carry

---

22   In the meantime, there are a vast number of studies concerning the ritual of solemn entry in early modern times; see, including older literature, Rudolph, 2011; see also, for example, the newer anthologies by Canova-Green et al., 2013; Mulryne et al., 2015.

23   This was preceded by a few smaller entry spectacles on the way to Munich. In Ingolstadt, for example, the Duchess Christine of Lorraine and her daughter Dorothea were announced on 12 February 1568 with a *Kreidenschuss* and greeted with a gun salvo as well as fireworks. Some days later, Christine of Lorraine refused a solemn entry into Munich, however, because she was ill. Four days after her mother, the bride was received by the citizens of Ingolstadt with two salvos and a lot of rifle-shooting (Wagner, 1568, fols. 7r., 11v., 26r.).

24   For this and the following, see Wagner, 1568, fols. 8–21.

25   Noted by Wagner as "Herrn Walther Administrator" (Wagner, 1568, fol. 20v.). From the imperial diet of 1566 onwards, this was actually Georg Hund von Wenkheim.

26   The same applies for the reception of the representatives of the imperial cities of Nuremberg and Augsburg, and of Dorothea of Denmark, the widowed Countess Palatine.

27   Wagner gives the following numbers: archduke Ferdinand *summariter* 16 "trumpeters, timpanists, and musicians, for archduke Charles 11 trumpeters, 1 timpanist, 2 cornet blowers, all with names, and the court kapellmeister Haimrolt Baduwan" (Annibale Padovano) (Wagner, 1568, fols. 10r., 17v., 18r.).

Fig. 1–4: Reception of Renata of Lorraine, engraving by Nikolaus Solis, 1568.

timpanists at solemn entries had formerly been an imperial prerogative that challenged high ranking and politically influential imperial princes. Since both archdukes were members of the imperial family, they could use timpani. And in his own territory, the Duke of Bavaria could do as he pleased, thus ostentatiously displaying his internal sovereignty. Therefore, timpani were only heard during the entries of the archdukes representing Emperor Maximilian II, and during the entry of the bride, which identified her not as the Princess of Lorraine but as the future Duchess of Bavaria.[28]

In every regard, particularly concerning sound effects, the ritual of solemn entry culminated in the entry of Renata of Lorraine into Munich on 21 February 1568. Two shots fired by single guns – which could be heard from afar – announced the imminent entry not only to everyone present, but also to the inhabitants of the town and the surrounding areas. Here, the guns served as ceremonial signals representing the sound of order, which structured the complex entry ritual consisting of several stages. The first stage was the bride's reception half a mile outside of town by selected male princes.[29] Shortly thereafter, the Bavarian *Obersthofmarschall* arranged the procession order. In the next stage, the bride passed the city gate and proceeded through the streets of Munich to the Church of Our Lady. In front of the church, she was received again, this reception followed by particular religious acts in the church. Afterwards, the bride proceeded to the *Neuveste,* where she was formally received for the third time and the entry day ended with a banquet. In theory, all these stages were marked by a specific soundscape. In practice, the various soundscapes overlapped each other, partly enhancing each other, partly drowning each other out.

Massimo Troiano begins his detailed description of the bride's entry by highlighting that on this morning: "[…] one was able to hear – although the heavy air and the fierce north wind had covered mountains and plains with snow – in the streets only trumpets, horns, pipes, timpani and drums. The air shaken with joyous sounds rang in everyone's ears […]" (Troiano, 1980, p. 57, my translation). Although these musical instruments were also used to signal social status and dynastic affiliation during the entry ritual, this was not the sound of order. The author uses an enthralling image to describe the effect of these musical sounds: Although snow usually tends to muffle every sound, even the snow was no match for the overpowering sounds of joy, which caused the air to shake. The male citizens of Munich, equipped as foot soldiers with rifles (*Hakenbüchsen*), moved into the field accompanied by the sounds of drummers and town pipers; the princes and their noble retinues on horses had trumpeters and timpanists with them.

---

28 Accordingly, timpanists are explicitly mentioned only in the context of the entries organized for the archdukes as representatives of the emperor, and for the bride (Wagner, 1568, fol. 20v.).

29 In fact, if we count all receptions in Bavarian territory organized for Renata of Lorraine, this reception near the Bavarian village of Neuhausen represented already the fourth: the first was at the border, the second in Ingolstadt, and the third in Dachau, where she stayed one night.

A hand-coloured steel engraving by the Augsburger engraver Nicolaus Solis shows the reception of the bride half a mile outside of Munich (Fig. 1–4).[30] Most of the space in this "giant" engraving is taken up by the large Bavarian and Austrian retinue, including six units (*Fähnlein*) of four hundred citizens equipped with armour and weapons and arranged in battle formation. Two gunshots announced the approaching bride to the multitude of five to six thousand people who had gone to meet her in the field (Wagner, 1568, fol. 31r.; Troiano, 1980, p. 59). Solis, who seems to have been present at the event, is clearly less interested in the ceremony of the reception (Fig. 2), but more in its imposing soundscape, with its rifle salvos, cannon and gunshots, the sound of trumpets and timpani, as well as the direct effect this enormous noise had on people and animals nearby. In some scenes in the image, we see horses shying (Fig. 3), with their riders trying to stay in the saddle and using riding crops to subdue the mounts gone wild. In the centre, there is one Bavarian timpanist and eleven Bavarian trumpeters on horses (Fig. 2–3) – as in fact there were on this occasion. One is blowing his trumpet for no recognizable reason, the others are waiting, watching, and listening. The first sections of the pageant are already moving in a seemingly endless procession in the direction of the Neuhäuser Tor (Fig. 4).

The citizens of Munich, who had already waited for an hour, "again and again fired shots of joy" (Wagner, 1568, 30v., my translation)[31] when they felt like shooting, not only to pass the time and to have fun, but also to display their privilege to carry arms.[32] The sonic chaos is mirrored by the chaotic ways the artist depicts the shooting citizens (Fig. 3). Although this common practice always carried the danger of disorder, they were allowed to shoot by Duke Albrecht V of Bavaria, because the soundscape of this public spectacle was not only related to the idea of sovereignty reflected by military power, but also to the idea of pleasure and fun. The soundscape of pleasure was enhanced by the many nobles and citizens greeting the bride "with great rejoicing" (Wagner, 1568, fol. 31r.; Troiano, 1980, p. 67). In deliberate contrast to these disordered and spontaneous sounds of joy, Count Charles of

---

30 Solis' depiction of this episode is quite traditional; cf. the woodcut that he surely knew by Hans Sebald Beham and Niklas Meldemann "Ankommen und Einreytten Kayserlicher Majestat [...]" (entry of Emperor Charles V in Munich 1530), coloured *Riesenholzschnitt*, Nürnberg 1530, StadtA München HVBS-E-01-10. Although Beham depicts fireworks, which were not part of the entry spectacle in 1568 in Munich, we see here the Bavarian cavalry, the "infantry", the artillery with a long line of firing guns, tents erected, etc., although they are depicted in a more orderly fashion than in the image by Solis. Visual representations of solemn entries produced a few decades later focused mostly on procession orders, which are portrayed quite stereotypically. See Rudolph, 2011, pp. 394–400. On Solis, see O'Dell, 1977.

31 For the relevance of military actors in such spectacles, see Rudolph, 2017.

32 According to Troiano, municipal foot soldiers moved into the city at the end of the procession "[...] in good order. And every now and then, one or the other, or even ten or twenty at a time, would put the fuse on the powder pan, as they pleased." Troiano, 1980, p. 71.

Zollern held a formal reception speech in French on behalf of Albrecht V (Fig. 2). Only a small number of people standing near the reception tents decorated with the Bavarian and Lorraine coats of arms would have been able to hear this speech, however, and even fewer would have understood what was said.[33]

In fact, the guns were not fired simultaneously as depicted by Solis (Fig. 3), but one after another. Not only did the people hear these gunshots, they also smelled them, saw their bursts of fire and clouds of smoke,[34] and they must have felt the sound waves in their bodies. Wagner even specifies the exact number and type of cannons (64) and guns (11)[35] that had been placed on bastions and city walls, and the precise number of shots fired (2, 18). Troiano's literary voice reads as follows: "And while they [the princes] were exchanging tokens of eternal brotherhood, ninety cannons were fired twice, which had been set up not far from the tents. (One cannon burst at the first shot and shattered, but without – praise be to God – causing any damage). The noise was heard with great astonishment, and I believe that even Jupiter with all his thunder never caused such a violent earthquake as this one, where in an instant the heavy clouds [...], shaken by the roar, burst apart as the fury of the fiercest wind could not have done in such triumph, and the spectators were presented with a serene, calm sky" (Troiano, 1980, p. 69).[36] The metaphorical contrast between noise/violence (war) and triumph/tranquillity (peace) made the Bavarian duke appear to be a prince who not only controlled his people and the entire festival staging, but the weather as well. The author even added mountains to the flat landscape surrounding Munich to help visualize the particularly impressive sound effects, such as the reverberations produced by gunshots.

Within the procession, trumpets announced the various social groups and the representatives of the dynasties taking part in the event (Wagner, 1568, fols. 30r.–v.).[37] The manner in which the musicians structured the pageant is mirrored perfectly in Wagner's

---

33 The speech was answered by the Duke of Vaudemont, who represented the absent Duke of Lorraine, the bride's father, also in French. The reception speech ("zierliche schöne Oration") is translated into German in: Wagner, 1568, fol. 31r.

34 These are only visible in the coloured version of the etching, however. Cf. the non-coloured version, without bursts of fire, held in the Bavarian State Library: http://daten.digitale-sammlungen.de/~db/0008/bsb00085154/images/. Date of Access: 26.01.2024.

35 Wagner specifies the kind of guns and their exact placement: large "Schlangen", "Mauerbrecher", and "Cartaunen" were lined up in the field; "Feldschlangen", "Falckenetel", and "Doppelhacken" stood on the bastions (Wagner, 1568, fol. 31v.). All of them caused individual types of noise.

36 Bursting cannons hurting or not hurting people are a literary motif in quite a few entry accounts. In our case, the reference mainly serves to illustrate the destruction that these weapons could cause, as well as the protecting hand of God, which would also protect the wedding couple as well as the entire Wittelsbach dynasty.

37 This is not illustrated in Solis' engraving. Cf. also Rudolph, 2011, pp. 131, 173–174, 193.

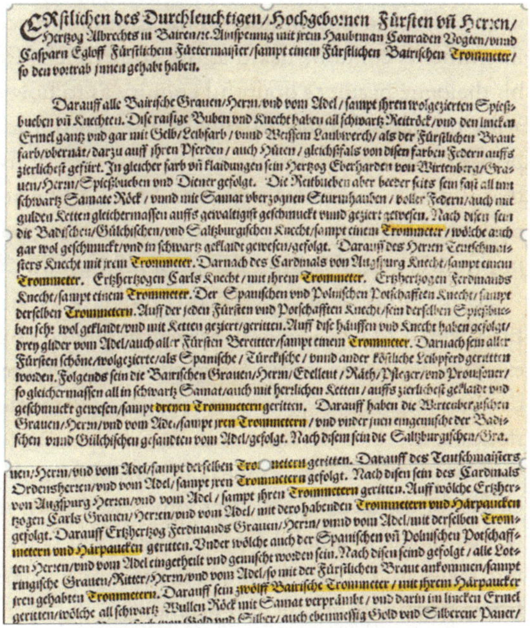

ERstlichen des Durchleuchtigen/Hochgebornen Fürsten vñ Herren/ Hertzog Albrechts in Bairen/rc. Ainspennig mit jrem Haubtman Conraden Vogten/vnnd Casparn Egloff Fürstlichem Füttermaister/sampt einem Fürstlichen Bairischen Trommeter/ so den vortrab jnnen gehabt haben.

Darauff alle Bairische Grauen/Herrn/vnd vom Adel/sampt jhren wolgezierten Spießbueben vñ Knechten. Dise raisige Buben vnd Knecht haben all schwartz Reitröck/vnd den lincken Ermel gantz vnd gar mit Gelb/Leibfarb/vnnd Weissem Laubwerch/als der Fürstlichen Braut farb/obernät/darzu auff jhren Pferden/auch Hüten/gleichsfals von disen farben Federn auffs zierlichest gefürt. In gleicher farb vñ klaidungen sein Hertzog Eberharden von Wirtenberg/Grauen/Herrn/Spießbueben vnd Diener gefolgt. Die Reitbueben aber beeder seits sein fast all inn schwartz Samate Röck/vnnd mit Samat vberzognen Sturmhauben/voller Federn/auch mit gulden Ketten gleichermassen auffs gewaltigist geschmuckt vnnd geziert gewesen. Nach disen sein die Badischen/Gülchischen/vnd Saltzburgischen Knecht/sampt einem Trommeter/wölche auch gar wol geschmuckt/vnd in schwartz geklaidt gewesen/gefolgt. Darauff des Herren Teutschmaisters Knecht mit jrem Trommeter. Darnach des Cardinals von Augspurg Knecht/sampt einem Trommeter. Ertzhertzogen Carls Knecht/mit jhrem Trommeter. Ertzhertzogen Ferdinands Knecht/sampt einem Trommeter. Der Spanischen vnd Polnischen Potschafften Knecht/sampt derselben Trommetern. Auff der jeden Fürsten vnd Potschafften Knecht/sein derselben Spießbueben sehr wol geklaidt/vnd mit Ketten geziert/geritten. Auff dise häuffen vnd Knecht haben gefolgt/drey glider vom Adel/auch aller Fürsten Bereitter/sampt einem Trommeter. Darnach sein aller Fürsten schöne/wolgezierte/als Spanische/Türckische/vnnd ander köstliche Leibpferd geritten worden. Folgends sein die Bairischen Grauen/Herrn/Edelleut/Räth/Pfleger/vnd Prouisoner/ so gleichermassen all in schwartz Samat/auch mit herrlichen Ketten/auffs zierlichest geklaidt vnd geschmuckt gewesen/sampt dreyen Trommetern geritten. Darauff haben die Wirtenbergischen Grauen/Herrn/vnd vom Adel/sampt jren Trommetern/vnd vnder jnen eingemischt der Badischen vnnd Gülchischen gesandten vom Adel/gefolgt. Nach disem sein die Saltzburgischen/Gra.

uen/Herrn/vnd vom Adel/sampt derselben Tro[…]etern geritten. Darauff des Teutschmaisters
Ordensherren/vnd vom Adel/sampt jren Trommetern gefolgt. Nach disen sein des Cardinals
von Augspurg Herren/vnd vom Adel/sampt jhren Trommetern geritten. Auff wölche Ertzhertzogen Carls Grauen/Herren/vnd vom Adel/mit dero habenden Trommetern vnd Härpaucken
gefolgt. Darauff Ertzhertzog Ferdinands Grauen/Herrn/vnnd vom Adel/mit derselben Trom-
meteren vnd Härpaucken geritten. Vnder wölche auch der Spanischen vñ Polnischen Potschafften Herren/vnd vom Adel eingetheilt vnd gemischt worden sein. Nach disen seind gefolgt/alle Lot-
ringische Grauen/Ritter/Herrn/vnd vom Adel/so mit der Fürstlichen Braut ankommen/sampt
jren gehabten Trommetern. Darauff sein zwölff Bairische Trommeter/mit jhrem Härpaucker
geritten/wölche all schwartz Wullen Röck mit Samat verprämbt/vnd darin im lincken Ermel
[…] auch ebenmessig Gold vnd Silberene Paner/

Fig. 5: Description of the procession order in Wagner's festival book, 1568.

description (Fig. 5). The increasing number from one Bavarian trumpeter at the beginning to several trumpeters from various dynasties to finally twelve Bavarian trumpeters and a Bavarian timpanist in front of the highest-ranking participants also made clear by means of sound that the procession order was organized according to social rank, dynastic affiliation, and political power.[38] The musical instruments were played by members of the princes' households using certain tone sequences as a kind of ringing heraldic sign (Žak, 1990). This simple version of the sound of dynasty required sonic knowledge, which most recipients are unlikely to have had, had it not been mirrored by the heraldic flags decorating the instruments (Fig. 3). Since many such tone sequences would have been played at the same time, it would have been necessary to listen carefully to decipher sonic messages such as these.

The next acoustic highlight marked the moment when the bride passed the city gate: "And no sooner had the gentry reached the city gate than the serpents, falconets, and mortars roared from the walls, towers and bastions and made the air tremble. Trumpets, cornets, timpani and drums of the town and the mounted men rang together with all the signs of joy, and the whole thing lasted for half an hour. You can imagine what a din

38 In fact, the Duke of Bavaria had only 11 trumpeters, as is correctly shown by Solis, although Wagner mentions 13. Maybe Albrecht V hired additional trumpeters, or used city trumpeters.

it was when, to the thunder of the cannons, more than a hundred wind and percussion instruments could be heard at the same time" (Troiano, 1980, pp. 71–72). In response to his dialogue partner's doubtful enquiry as to how such a large number of trumpeters and army timpanists could actually be assembled, the narrator inaccurately asserts that every prince or Bavarian landlord had at least four or five musicians among his horsemen, and that the Archdukes of Austria and Duke Albrecht alone had a total of 63 trumpeters and timpanists.[39] Troiano exaggerates here as well; nevertheless, the soundscape must have been impressive, even though it had been raining and snowing for quite a while.[40]

As the procession proceeded through the Kaufinger Strasse and Augustinerstrasse to the Church of our Lady, the spectacle offered constantly changing sonic experiences for everyone lining the streets, looking out their windows, or staying in their homes, depending on their respective positions in relation to the various sources of noise. There were moving noises at the street level, such as the trumpets and timpani within the pageant. There were immovable noises, such as the bells ringing from the church towers. There were spontaneous cheers for the bride and bridegroom as well as for the House of Wittelsbach, which intensified considerably when people saw Renata of Lorraine in her splendid golden carriage decorated with four golden lions and drawn by six white horses (Fig. 1).[41] The cannons and guns, firing alternately at different locations in the open fields and on the city walls, must have produced a kind of Dolby surround effect, which should have been all the more impressive due to the large buildings and narrow rows of house facades disrupting and echoing both single and compound sounds. It must have seemed as if the sounds came from everywhere.

In front of the church, the Bishop of Augsburg, the clergy, and male as well as female members of the Wittelsbach and visiting dynasties greeted the bride. After a blessing of the bridal couple outside the church, the procession moved "triumphantly" (Wagner, 1568, fol. 33v.) into the church "to the ringing of bells and the blaring of twenty trumpets and four booming timpani" (Troiano, 1980, p. 75).[42] These multiple sounds of earthly power reverberating from the high church walls and its vaults may have reminded the listeners, however, that it was God the Almighty who granted all earthly rule. Near the entrance, the bride and groom knelt for a silent prayer of thanksgiving. After that, the Cardinal said some prayers in a low voice, blessed the couple again, and sprinkled them with holy water.

---

39 In fact, the two archdukes had only 28 trumpeters and timpanists at their disposal; Duke Albrecht V had 12, and the Bavarian lords, very likely none at all. For Salzburg, Württemberg, and Lorraine, Wagner reports two to three trumpeters and no timpanists (Wagner, 1568, fols. 23r., 24v.).

40 Wagner speaks of "Regen, Schnee und ander übel Wetter" (Wagner, 1568, fol. 31r.).

41 Cf. the descriptions of the carriage in Wagner, 1568, fol. 31r.; and in Troiano, 1980, p. 69.

42 As a member of the Bavarian court music ensemble, Troiano describes the musical procedures in detail, ostentatiously demonstrating his professional knowledge. While he could not have been an eyewitness to the events outside of town and on the streets, he surely attended the acts in the Church of our Lady and most of the following events. See Rudolph, 2019.

Fig. 6: The Bridal Mass on 22 February 1568, steel engraving by Nikolaus Solis.

These actions could only be heard by a few people nearby, however, especially since the disorderly, joyful shooting of guns continued. The bishop and the clergy then made their way to the inner sanctum, followed by princes and princesses in ceremonial order. Then the clergy sang the antiphons *Posui adjutorium* and *Orta est speciosa* with powerful voices (Troiano, 1980, p. 77). Because the church doors were still open, the people outside would have been able to hear these chants to a certain extent.

Inside the inner sanctum, the political elite that had been ceremoniously exalted in the open space just a moment earlier gathered in ostentatious humility before God (Fig. 6), submitting themselves to a religious ritual designed by the Cardinal, not by the Duke of Bavaria.[43] A solemnly performed *Te deum laudamus* that embodied one version of the sound of transcendence reinforced these political-religious messages.[44] Composed by the highly acclaimed Bavarian court kapellmeister Orlando di Lasso (1532–1594) and intoned in antiphony by the bass voice of Cardinal Otto Seneschal of Waldburg, the clergy, and

---

43   The engraving depicts the inner sanctum during the bridal mass the following day. The clergy next to the main altar and the Bavarian court music ensemble on an elevated stage to the left of the altar are shown in exactly the same position as in the service during the solemn entry, however. The image demonstrates the exclusive nature of the events performed in the inner sanctum, which were attended solely by members of the high nobility.

44   On the *Te deum* in general, see Žak, 1982. According to Horst Leuchtmann, di Lassos' *Te deum* may have been composed especially for this wedding (Troiano, 1980, p. 394). Cf. the highly stereotypical description by Wagner: "allda man dann den nechsten Te Deum laudamus mit der Musicen zum zierlichsten gesungen" (Wagner, 1568, fol. 32v.).

the multiple voices of the famous court chapel, for which the Duke had hired additional singers and musicians prior to the wedding, the powerful sound of the *Te deum* may have reached beyond the church walls, although the church doors were now probably closed due to the multitudes of common people in front of the building.[45]

Troiano describes the musical liturgy of the *Te deum* in a highly differenciated manner, stating that "the most reverend and serene Cardinal intoned prayers and verses in a low voice, as taught in the Holy Scriptures. He was answered by the musicians of the most illustrious Duke Albrecht. Afterwards, the illustrious Cardinal intoned the *Te deum laudamus* in a louder voice, and with strong, cheerful voices, the singers continued with *Te deum confitemur* and sang the six-part composition by Mr Orlando di Lasso, which begins with *Te aeternum Patrem*. All listened attentively, the more so as this composition contains elaborate three-part[46] and splendid four-part passages and was performed by good voices and experienced singers. [...] When the *Te deum* had ended in all solemnity, the most venerable cardinal intoned in a low voice: *Sit nomen Domini benedictum*, and the singers responded. Then he gave his blessing. All the people then left the church in the same order in which they had arrived" (Troiano, 1980, p. 79). This marks the end of Troiano's description of the events in the Church; he omitted the following service, even though it included another composition by the admired Orlando di Lasso.[47]

The liturgy of this service, in combination with the wedding masses on the next two days and the regular services at court that continued as long as the festivities lasted,[48] aimed not only at securing God's blessing for the wedding, but at sacralizing the Bavarian-Lorraine marriage and the Bavarian Wittelsbach dynasty as one of the preeminent dynasties of the Holy Roman Empire. As for confession, however, the Bavarian-Lorraine wedding of 1568 was surely not as ostentatious a demonstration of confessionalism as might have been expected.[49] Even though Duke Albrecht V enforced the Counter-Reformation behind the scenes in Bavaria during this decade (Ziegler, 1989), he almost scrupulously avoided anti-

---

45 The extant sources suggest that the Munich court music ensemble played a decisive role throughout the wedding festivities. See, with further literature, Rudolph, 2019; Rainer, 2021.

46 Translated by Leuchtmann as "two-part", correcting an alleged error of the author (Troiano, 1980, p. 384).

47 In contrast to Troiano, Wagner reports this in a stereotypical and rather lacking style, which I deliberately do not translate here: "Darauff ist der Gottsdienst mit Lobpsalmen und künstlichen Figurieren auch allerley Instrumenten gar verricht und zu end desselben der Psalm Beati qui timent Dominum zierlich gesungen worden." (Wagner, 1568, fol. 33r).

48 Troiano mentions three regular services every day: "due messe basse & una cantata con celeste harmonia" (Troiano, 1980, p. 14).

49 Not surprisingly, a great deal of scholarly literature on Bavaria has focused on confessional conflicts; cf. Fisher, 2014, who hardly mentions the wedding for exactly this reason; in general, see also Thomas, 2010.

Protestant statements during the whole of the wedding festivities. On one hand, he had invited an interconfessional festive community to Munich;[50] on the other, the entire event was meant to epitomise the idea of peace and unity between the dynasties assembled in Munich, as well as between the Duke as sovereign and the Bavarian people as his subjects.

The third and final reception of the bride at the *Neuveste* was marked by a final salute of the guns, signalling the official end of the entry, even though the shooting by citizens continued for some time. The entry was followed by a banquet meant to prepare the Bavarian court and the wedding guests for many sumptuous banquets in the following two weeks. The sonic framework of these banquets corresponded to a principle already established at the Bavarian court, namely, the representative effort and complexity of staging successively increasing (Rudolph, 2019). As was customary, each course of the meal was announced by the sound of trumpets and by the voice of the Bavarian *major-domo*.[51] The various meal courses were accompanied by sophisticated musical performances, with the number of musicians increasing with every course. Moreover, the kinds of instruments played varied with each course.[52] Let us listen to Troiano one last time: "And during the two hours that the dinner lasted, the loyal musicians of the Bavarian Duke, whom he keeps constantly in his service, performed various compositions with wind instruments, string instruments, and with a choir of singers, and they presented the music in such a way that I could justifiably have sworn that I believed myself staying in an earthly paradise on that blissful evening" (Troiano, 1980, p. 83).[53]

---

50 Protestant princes such as the electors of Saxony (Lutheran) and the Palatinate (Calvinist) had sent representatives, and Lutheran princes like Eberhard of Württemberg were also present.

51 The image illustrates the wedding banquet the following day, but again, what is depicted here is largely the same as the events of the first day, even if the material effort and the number of people attending had certainly increased. For details about these banquets, see Rudolph, forthcoming/b.

52 First there was only the sound of wind instruments, then of strings, then also of plucked instruments and a harpsichord, and finally of singers performing for the festive community. In another engraving by Solis, musicians and singers of several ages can be seen in the left foreground. The prominent position of the Bavarian court musicians in this image reflects the high relevance of table music on occasions such as these. Nikolaus Solis, The Wedding Banquet in the Neufeste 1568, coloured steel engraving, 35,2 x 57,3 mm cm, in: Wagner, 1568, s.p., online at: http://www.ubs.sbg.ac.at/sosa/bdm/bdm1010.htm. Date of Access: 26.01.2024.

53 "Earthly paradise" is again a *topos* serving to illustrate not only the heavenly quality of music, but also the particularly cultivated state of the Bavarian court music ensemble. Troiano does not mention plucked instruments or the harpsichord we see in the image (Fig. 6), maybe because less effort was put into the first meal on the arrival day, or because he later describes the wedding feast it in more detail, only referring to it in passing in this context.

Conclusions

The sound of power could take very different forms in early modern times. Accordingly, we should speak not of one sound of power, but of various sounds of power. I have classified these into seven categories: the sound of sovereignty, the sound of dynasty, the sound of order, the sound of pleasure, the sound of transcendence, the sound of patronage, and the sound of empire. All were manifested in certain sound effects produced by various sound actors and characterized by specific sound spaces overlapping each other in many ways. In this paper, I have exemplified the first five categories by analysing the solemn entries that took place on the occasion of the Bavarian-Lorraine wedding in 1568. The various sounds of power that were audible at this event created auditory communities that might be interpreted as sub-communities within the entire festive community. These communities were delimited by the technical reach of sound, as well as the privilege of certain social groups gain to access, their ability to understand the sonic messages, and the largely similar scale of relevance these people attached to the messages they were able to hear. While the sound of power and the sound of order, for example, were meant to resound throughout the town, the sacralizing dimensions of the sound of transcendence could be heard primarily in the exclusive space of the church, with the cheers, laughing, and joyful gun shooting outside possibly drowning out some of the religious sounds.

Despite all social differentiation by means of sounds, it was sound in particular that was able to create a ritual *communitas* across social classes and between local and foreign people as a vital element in every *rite de passage*, such as, for example, weddings and the festivities linked to them. In contrast to sight, sound was able to transcend walls and spaces and to invade the bodies of listeners, and in so doing, to produce positive reactions that princes, as festival organizers, intended to create. More than other sensory effects, the cacophony of loud and soft sounds, fixed and moving sounds, simple and refined sounds, temporal and eternal sounds aimed to overwhelm the senses of everyone present through sheer abundance and emotional overload. They also focussed attention on the main actors. With regard to solemn entries, the overall aim of any sound "design" was to create a tremendous roar in which various social groups could participate. It might be described as the thunder of power meant to amaze and arouse awe among all the listeners.

In actu the auditory experience of a ruler's entry very likely exceeded all other sensory experiences. Such an event could be heard by people who were not able to see, smell, taste, or touch anything related to the public performance in question. By sensing, by partly sensing, or by not sensing sound, by understanding that sound, partly understanding it, or not understanding it at all, people could, in fact, sense their own place within society – as well as outside that society. The auditory experience of a ruler's entry, however, was largely limited to early modern societies of attendance. It was not possible for producers of contemporary festival reports to adequately transfer the experience of the ephemeral sounds of individual festival elements into contemporary media of information and memorialization. It is precisely due to early modern societies being largely societies of attendance, however, that the sounds of power must be considered to a much greater degree by research than they have until now. Power had to be heard and rulers had to be listened to.

Bibliography

Printed Sources and Source Editions

Deutsches Wörterbuch von Jacob Grimm und Wilhelm Grimm, digitalisierte Fassung im Wörterbuchnetz des Trier Center for Digital Humanities, Version 01/21. https://www.woerterbuchnetz.de/DWB?lemid=L01684. Date of Access: 26.01.2024.

Wagner, J. (1568). *Kurtze doch gegründte beschreibung des [...] gehalten Hochzeitlichen Ehren Fests [...]*. Adam Berg. https://daten.digitale-sammlungen.de/~db/0008/bsb00085154/images. Date of Access: 26.01.2024.

Troiano, M. (1980). *Die Münchner Fürstenhochzeit von 1568. Dialoge (Dialoghi). Zwiegespräche über die Festlichkeiten bei der Hochzeit des bayerischen Erbherzogs Wilhelm V. mit Renata von Lothringen, in München, im Februar 1568. Ein ausführlicher Bericht über die geistlichen und weltlichen Zeremonien und Feiern [...]*, transl. and ed. by H. Leuchtmann. Katzbichler.

Scholarly Literature

Atkinson, N. (2016). *The Noisy Renaissance: Sound, Architecture, and Florentine Urban Life*. University Park.

Baldwin, C. L. (2012). *Auditory Cognition and Human Performance: Research and Applications*. CRC Press.

Barbet, D. & Honoré, J.-P. (Eds.) (2013). *Le silence en politique*. ENS éditions.

Bély, L. (1999). *La société des princes. XVIe–XVIIIe siècle*. Fayard.

Bowles, E. A. (2000). Music in Court Festivals of State: Festival Books as Sources for Performance Practices. *Early Music* 28, 421–443.

Braun, R. & Gugerli, D. (1993). *Macht des Tanzes – Tanz der Mächtigen. Hoffeste und Herrschaftszeremoniell 1550–1914*. Beck.

Breitsameter, S. (2010). Hörgestalt und Denkfigur – Zur Geschichte und Perspektive von R. Murray Schafers Die Ordnung der Klänge. Ein einführender Essay. In R. Murray Schafer (Ed.), *Die Ordnung der Klänge. Eine Kulturgeschichte des Hörens* (pp. 7–28). ed. and transl. by S. Breitsameter. Schott.

Bull, M. (Ed.) (2018). *The Routledge Companion to Sound Studies*. Routledge.

Bull, M. & Cobussen, M. (Eds.) (2020). *The Bloomsbury Handbook of Sonic Methodologies*. Bloomsbury Academic & Professional.

Canova-Green, M. C. & Andrews, J. (Eds.) (2013). *Writing Royal Entries in Early Modern Europe*. Brepols.

Corbin, A. (2016). *Histoire du silence: de la Renaissance à nos jours*. Albin Michel.

DWDS. Der deutsche Wortschatz von 1600 bis heute. https://www.dwds.de. Date of Access: 26.01.2024.

Edensor, T., Kalandides, A. & Kothari, U. (Eds.) (2020). *The Routledge Handbook of Place*. Routledge, Taylor & Francis Group.

Fisher, A. J. (2014). *Music, Piety, and Propaganda: The Soundscape of Counter-Reformation Bavaria*. Oxford Univ. Press.

Garrioch, D. (2003). Sounds of the City: The Soundscape of Early Modern European Towns. *Urban History* 30, 5–25.

Hammond, N. (2019). *The Powers of Sound and Song in Early Modern Paris*. University Park.

Howard, D. & Moretti, L. (2010). *Sound and Space in Renaissance Venice: Architecture, Music, Acoustics*. Yale Univ. Press.

Howes, D. (Ed.) (2021). *Empire of the Senses: The Sensual Culture Reader*. Berg.

Kelman, A. (2010). Rethinking the Soundscape: A Critical Genealogy of a Key Term in Sound Studies. *Sense & Society* 5, 212–234.

Knighton, T. & Mazuela-Anguita, A. (Eds.) (2018). *Hearing the City in Early Modern Europe*. Brepols.

Levin, D. M. (Ed.) (1993). *Modernity and the Hegemony of Vision*. Univ. of California Press.

Maurer, M. (Ed.) (2004). *Das Fest. Beiträge zu seiner Theorie und Systematik*. Böhlau.

Maurer, M. (2010) (Ed.). *Festkulturen im Vergleich. Inszenierungen des Religiösen und Politischen*. Böhlau.

Mulryne, J. R. & Goldring, E. (Eds.) (2002). *Court Festivals of the European Renaissance. Art, Politics and Performance*. Ashgate.

Mulryne, J. R., Aliverti, M. I. & Testaverde, A. M. (Eds.) (2015). *Ceremonial Entries in Early Modern Europe: The Iconography of Power*. Ashgate.

Mulryne, J. R., De Jonge, K., Morris, R. L. M. & Martens, P. (Eds.) (2019). *Occasions of State. Early Modern European Festivals and the Negotiation of Power*. Routledge, Taylor & Francis Group.

Nichols, S. G., Kablitz A. & Calhoun, A. (Eds.) (2008). *Rethinking the Medieval Senses*. Johns Hopkins Univ. Press.

O'Dell, I. (1977). *Kupferstiche und Radierungen aus der Werkstatt des Virgil Solis*. Steiner.

Pinch, T. & Bijsterveld, K. (Eds.) (2011). *Oxford Handbook of Sound Studies*. Oxford University Press.

Rahn, T. (1993). Fortsetzung des Festes mit anderen Mitteln. Gattungsbeobachtungen zu hessischen Hochzeitsberichten. In J. J. Berns & D. Ignasiak (Eds.), *Frühneuzeitliche Hofkultur in Hessen und Thüringen* (pp. 233–248). Palm und Enke.

Rahn, T. (2006). *Festbeschreibung: Funktion und Topik einer Textsorte am Beispiel der Beschreibung höfischer Hochzeiten (1568–1794)*. Niemeyer.

Rainer, B. (2021). *Instrumentalisten und instrumentale Praxis am Hof Albrechts V. von Bayern 1550–1579*. Hollitzer.

Ramel, F. & Prévost-Thomas, C. (Eds.) (2018). *International Relations, Music and Diplomacy: Sounds and Voices on the International Stage*. Palgrave Macmillan.

Riepe, J. (Ed.): *Musik der Macht – Macht der Musik. Die Musik an den sächsisch-albertinischen Herzogshöfen Weißenfels, Zeitz und Merseburg*. Verlag Karl Dieter Wagner.

Rudolph, H. (forthcoming/a). Musikalische Politik und politische Musik – Anmerkungen aus Sicht einer Historikerin. In E. Natour & A. Zedler (Eds.), *Musik und Politik im Europa der Frühen Neuzeit*. Böhlau.

Rudolph, H. (forthcoming/b). De arte culinaria. Repräsentationswissen und Tafelkulturen im höfischen Fest unter Albrecht V. von Bayern. In R. Dauser, M. Mutz & L. Schilling (Eds.), *Herzog Albrecht V. von Bayern – Wissenshorizonte eines europäischen Dynasten*.

Rudolph, H. (2021). Was ist höfische Repräsentation? Aktuelle Forschungsansätze zu einem alten Thema. *Schütz-Jahrbuch* 42, 7–18, 162–167.

Rudolph, H. (2020a). Die Münchner Fürstenhochzeit von 1568. Politische Rahmenbedingungen und Medialität eines 'Jahrhundertereignisses'. *Troja. Jahrbuch für Renaissancemusik* 15, 51–79. https://journals.qucosa.de/troja/issue/view/196. Date of Access: 26.01.2024.

Rudolph, H. (2020b). Stand, Rang und Status. Feste als Medium höfischer Repräsentation in reichischen und europäischen Hierarchiegefügen. *Jahrbuch der Stiftung Thüringer Schlösser und Gärten* 23, 73–93.

Rudolph, H. (2019). Kommentar. In W. Fuhrmann (Ed.), *Musikleben in der Renaissance: zwischen Alltag und Fest*, vol. 1: *Orte der Musik* (pp. 411–424). Laaber-Verlag.

Rudolph, H. (2017). Heer und Herrschaftsrepräsentation. Militärische Dimensionen der Selbstinszenierung bei Herrscherbesuchen (1550–1800). In M. Müller & P.-M. Hahn (Eds.), *Zeichen und Medien des Militärischen am Fürstenhof im frühneuzeitlichen Europa* (pp. 53–72). Lukas Verlag für Kunst- und Geistesgeschichte.

Rudolph, H. (2011). *Das Reich als Ereignis. Formen und Funktionen der Herrschaftsinszenierung bei Kaisereinzügen, 1558–1618*. Böhlau.

Schafer, R. M. (1993). *The Soundscape: Our Sonic Environment and the Tuning of the World*. Inner Traditions/Bear (first ed. Destiny Books, 1977).

Schlögl, R. (2004). Vergesellschaftung unter Anwesenden. Zur kommunikativen Form des Politischen in der vormodernen Stadt. In R. Schlögl (Ed.), *Interaktion und Herrschaft. Die Politik der frühneuzeitlichen Stadt* (pp. 9–60). UVK Verlags-Gesellschaft.

Smith, M. M. (2007). *Sensing the Past: Seeing, Hearing, Smelling, Tasting, and Touching in History*. Univ. of California Press.

Sterne, J. (Ed.) (2012). *The Sound Studies Reader*. Routledge, Taylor & Francis Group.

Sterne, J. (2003). *The Audible Past. Cultural Origins of Sound Reproduction*. Duke University Press.

Strong, R. (1984). *Art and Power: Renaissance Festivals 1450–1650*. Boydell.

Thomas, A. L. (2010). *A House Divided. Wittelsbach Confessional Court Cultures in the Holy Roman Empire, c. 1550–1650*. Brill.

Wasserloos, Y. & Mecking, S. (Eds.) (2012). *Musik – Macht – Staat. Kulturelle, soziale und politische Wandlungsprozesse in der Moderne*. V & R unipress.

Watanabe-O'Kelly, H. (1988). Festival Books in Europe from Renaissance to Rococo. *The Seventeenth Century* 3, 181–201.

Watanabe-O'Kelly, H. & Simon, A. (2000). *Festivals and Ceremonies: A Bibliography of Works Relating to Court, Civic, and Religious Festivals in Europe 1500–1800*. Mansell.

Žak, S. (1990). Luter schal und süeze doene. Die Rolle der Musik in der Repräsentation. In H. Ragotzky & H. Wenzel (Eds.), *Höfische Repräsentation. Das Zeremoniell und die Zeichen* (pp. 133–148). Niemeyer.

Žak, S. (1982). Das Te Deum als Huldigungsgesang. *Historisches Jahrbuch* 102, 1–32.

Žak, S. (1979). *Musik als "Ehr und Zier" im mittelalterlichen Reich. Studien zur Musik im höfischen Leben*. Päffgen.

Ziegler, W. (1989). Art. Bayern. In W. Ziegler & A. Schindling (Eds.), *Die Territorien des Reiches im Zeitalter der Reformation und Konfessionalisierung. Land und Konfession 1500–1600*, vol. 1: *Der Südosten* (pp. 56–71). Aschendorff.

Illustration Credits

Fig. 1–4: Nikolaus Solis: The Reception of Renata of Lorraine 1568 outside of Munich, coloured steel engraving, 26,8 x 149,8 cm, in: Wagner, 1568, s.p., Graphische Sammlung München, Inv. 1910:226-01 B.

Fig. 5: Description of the procession order in Wagner's festival book, in: Wagner, 1568, fols. 30r.–v., markings by the author.

Fig. 6: Nikolaus Solis: The Bridal Mass in the Church of our Lady Munich 1568, coloured steel engraving, 39,2 x 60,5 cm, in: Wagner, 1568, s.p., Universitätsbibliothek Salzburg, Sign. R 11.240 III: http://www.ubs.sbg.ac.at/sosa/bdm/11240III03.jpg. Date of Access: 26.01.2024.

Acoustic Agencies in the Early Modern European City

A Conceptual Approach

Jan-Friedrich Missfelder

The aim of this chapter is to develop a conceptual approach to sound practices in early modern urban societies. To do so, I will advance the concept of "acoustic agency" in order to grasp the inherent power dynamics invested in sound practices. For this, I will discuss three variants of contemporary agency theory from history, philosophy, and critical sound studies and evaluate their value for early modern sound history and historical musicology. Secondly, I will offer some possible connections to existing historical and musicological research in the sound history of power in an urban context. This chapter is by no means intended to give a comprehensive overview of what has been done in the field of early modern sound history and musicology during the course of the last decades. Its humbler goal is to investigate if and how this research might profit from embracing the concept of acoustic agency – or, for that matter, how some of it may already have been done without having been noticed.[1]

Whose Agency? (LaBelle)

What exactly does "agency" as a concept mean? Ever since the British social historian E.P. (Edward Palmer) Thompson introduced the concept of agency into the discourse among sociologists and historians in the late 1950s, the question has been raised as to who precisely is to be granted agency in a particular historical situation. For Thompson, the concept of agency served as an antidote against orthodox Leninist and even Stalinist readings of the Marxist tradition that championed the "objective logic of economic evolution" (Stalin) over any kind of human factor in history. Consequently, Thompson established a "crucial distinction between determinism and agency", opening up the field for an acknowledgement of human choices in political reasoning and acting and to "conscious

---

1   This chapter expands and elaborates on my more empirical take on the subject in Missfelder, 2019, pp. 87–106.

human agency in the making of history" (1958, pp. 89–106). The emphasis on choice and consciousness has proved particularly influential in the theoretical development of agency. By attributing and tracing agency, historians have stressed the historical specificity of an allegedly unquestionable human universality and set out to investigate those social situations in which the very possibility of political choice and human consciousness was questioned or even denied. This is why the concept of agency has proven especially fruitful in debates on slavery, subalternity, and marginality in history (Johnson, 2003, pp. 113–124). It has drawn attention towards constellations in which choice and human consciousness were far from self-evident as a precondition of human interaction.

Thus, agency increasingly has become a quality that could be ascribed to various "agents" by historians. On the one hand, the resulting "humanity/agency circuit" (Johnson, 2003, p. 113) reserves agency for those agents who were able to prove their humanness by enacting choice and consciousness in historical contexts adverse to those enactments (e.g., slavery). On the other hand, within the concept of agency itself lies the inherent tendency of expansion beyond consciousness and choice. This becomes evident in recent debates on animal agency and Latourian symmetrical anthropology, as well as through terminological innovations like "interagency" focusing on interdependencies between various human and non-human agents (Shaw, 2013, pp. 146–167; Despret, 2013, pp. 29–44). Consequently, debates have evolved around questions concerning whether animals, Berlin keys or, for that matter, sounds have agency or not (Schiel et al., 2017, pp. 17–48). Whereas in some ways the attribution of agency keeps its original emancipatory impetus by implicitly or explicitly claiming dignity and rights for women, workers, slaves, or animals in other contexts, the critical emphasis shifts towards specific practices that engage with certain agents in an emancipatory manner. And this is where sound and sonic practices come into play. For instance, in his reflections on "sonic agency", sound artist and theorist Brandon LaBelle defines having agency rather broadly as the "capacity to affect the world around us" (2018, p. 8). In his view, it is not the inherent conceptual characteristics of agency as such that establish a close connection to the politics of subalternity addressing, in LaBelle's words, "the asylum seeker and the refugee, the expatriated and the disenfranchised, the erased and the disappeared" (p. 6), but the ontological qualities of sound itself. Sound, he argues, "is political by extending or restricting the limits of the body, in the desires and needs announced in the cry, through the care and compassion listening may yield, and in acts of rupture and fragmentation, improvisation – the rapturous and violating noises that return us to the base materialism of bare life" (p. 7). Ultimately, LaBelle identifies two related practices of sonic agency with particular political potential: listening and making noise. Whereas listening in his account is conceptualized as an activity associated with connectivity and solidarity within subaltern individuals and groups, making noise engages more directly with power. Building upon the seminal work of Jacques Attali (2011), La-

Belle conceives of noise as fundamentally relational: "Noise, in this regard, is the force of the marginal and the different; a strange sound from a strange body which threatens the social order" (LaBelle, 2018, p. 69). Noise and order are mutually constitutive since, in this perspective, there is nothing that qualifies a particular sound as noise beyond social negotiations based upon political, economic and cultural power relations. Put simply, sounds socially marked as noise are always "unwanted" (Keizer, 2010) by certain social actors and at the same time "out of place" within a particular socio-spatial order.[2] For LaBelle and other protagonists of sonico-political activism like Marie Thompson or Holger Schulze (Schulze, 2016, pp. 68–81; 2018), it is precisely the potential of irritation, disturbance and rupture that offers the "productive, transformative" (Thompson, 2017, p. 3) opportunities that noise (and sound in general) provides in order to "challenge the tonalities of social community [and] enrich the vitality of its shape and form" by "amplifying the shuddering vibrancy of shared joys and political imagination" (LaBelle, 2018, p. 69).

Although LaBelle convincingly contributes to the debate on agency and its applicability to acoustic constellations, by presenting sonic agency as partisan tactics to subvert the reifying, distancing, and dividing rule of the modern empire, his argument runs the risk of falling back into what Canadian sound historian Jonathan Sterne called the "audiovisual litany" (Sterne, 2003, pp. 14–19). Inherently, sonic characteristics like vibrancy and resonance gain political and even metaphysical qualities "deliver[ing] into the social order a force of desire and festivity" (LaBelle, 2018, p. 69), providing acoustic remedies against the violations of humane coexistence and, at the same time, weapons for resistance: "[V]ibrancy […] may […] unwittingly fulfill our desires for cultural diversity – for what we may secretly desire: the wish to be disturbed, that is, to love and be loved: a love at first hearing" (LaBelle, 2018, p. 72). To my ears at least, this sounds more like cloudy sound metaphysics and politico-academic kitsch than historical analysis. To link the vibrational qualities of sound almost exclusively to politics of productive disturbance and resistance tends to overlook precisely the dynamics of power invested in acoustic practices always oscillating between sonic affirmation of power and acoustic subversion.

On a methodological level, though, LaBelle's argument resonates with recent theoretical accounts of early modern societies as fundamentally characterized by bodily interaction, face-to-face communication and presence. According to German historian Rudolf Schlögl, social integration in early modern society was essentially achieved through rituals and performances requiring the personal presence of the actors involved (Schlögl, 2009, pp. 2–28; 2019, pp. 23–40; 2014). Because political and administrative practices primarily based on writing and impersonal media were only gradually introduced during the course of the

---

2   Cf. Pickering et al. (2017) investigating the links between Mary Douglas' work on dirt and sound studies research, and referring to Douglas, 1966.

later early modern period, politics was always in need of some kind of "mediation" that allowed for communicative stability in the political process. Performative action in "presence societies" (Schlögl, 2009, p. 25) directed at the senses of both the authorities and their subjects served this target very effectively (Missfelder, 2016, pp. 131–134). Within this setting, sound media and listening techniques hold a peculiar position by sonically organizing and negotiating proximity and distance, presence and absence. Historically, however, this form of sonic agency does not exclusively apply to the marginal and subaltern strata of society. On the contrary, tracing the agency of sound in early modern history means accounting for the plurality of claiming and enacting agency through sound practices. Thus, it's not the ontological qualities of sound itself that ensure the agency of sound, but its appropriations and political implementations.

Spaces of Sonic Appearance (Butler/Arendt)

In recent years, studies in early modern sound and urban history as well as in the cultural history of music have amply shown how various groups and individuals applied sound to reach diverse political ends. But what does "apply sound" actually mean? Early modern politics, Schlögl has argued, crucially depended upon a sensorially mediated presence within a common space of public perception. Projecting sonic power in this early modern public sphere required dealing with the acoustic conditions of urban spaces, with hearing ranges, reverberations, echoes, and counter-sounds presenting the danger of diverting the audience's acoustic attention. Sonic occupations of urban space, like princely entries, religious processions, and other forms of political ritual thus used any opportunity to widen the range of sensory perception. Drums, trumpets, and other *capella alta* instruments were capable of expanding the time span of presence beyond visual appearance (Rudolph, 2013, pp. 19–48, 46–47). To contemporary audiences in early modern cities, political power quite literally could be heard long before and long after its bearers actually appeared in person. Representational sounds functioned as temporal "stand-ins" and, to paraphrase Canadian media theorist Marshall McLuhan, as extensions of bodies of power whose presence was urgently required in early modern presence societies. This representational logic applied to powerful individuals like kings, princes, nobility, and magistrates, as well as to communities and, eventually, crowds. Collective singing of psalms, hymns, and chants in religious processions not only created a confessional attitude, but staged religious conflict and confessional strife as a struggle over dominance of the urban space (Fisher, 2017, pp. 187–203; 2014). Moreover, in religiously contested cities, confessionally infused sounds could serve as "aural memory vectors" (van der Linden, 2019, p. 19) of past experiences of suffering, persecution, or triumph in religious conflict and war.

This applies particularly to the acoustic mass-medium of the period *par excellence*: bells. Early modern listeners were perfectly capable of identifying and distinguishing the sonic characteristics of particular bells and associating them with their often-contentious histories. Bell-ringing had a temporal as well as a spatial dimension (and still has) (Missfelder, 2018, pp. 329–331). On the one hand, bells structured everyday life. They punctuated the day by drawing listeners' attention to religious requirements, signalled the opening and closing of gates, or announced extraordinary events. Spatially, bells created a common space of listening that usually surpassed the limits of face-to-face communication. Bell sounds addressed larger collectives and forged them into a community of simultaneous listeners. By the centripetal sound of bells "[u]rban spaces", argues Argentinian historian Gisela Coronado Schwindt (2021), "were resignified in the process of subjectivation" (pp. 60–77, 68). On the other hand, it was exactly this capacity that could spur different acoustic agencies. Early modern and medieval urban societies abounded with violent conflicts over bell towers.[3] Controlling the toll of the bell meant wielding power over communities that were politically and socially united and divided by its sounds. As Niall Atkinson (2016) has shown in his pioneering sound history of Renaissance architecture, bell towers not only shaped the skylines of early modern communes, but also created webs of social identities and sonic allegiances. In his book, Atkinson proposes a rereading of the 1378 Ciompi rising in Renaissance Florence as an act of acoustic communication. Bell towers were seized by discontented wool workers and their allies; crowds were gathered from the city's *campanili* and assembled before the Palazzo Vecchio. "Two days of sustained screaming" (Atkinson, 2013, p. 82) reminded the city's authorities of the weavers' presence in the urban social fabric and sonically testified to their political agency. How can this particular kind of acoustic agency be theorized? The one feature all of the examples cited above have in common is the sonic appropriation of urban space, either by filling the air with loud music, loud screams, or even louder bell sounds, or by simply occupying urban spaces with resonating bodies.

In all of these instances there is relatively little interest in the articulation of concrete political concerns or even the formulation of political agendas or ideas. Instead, they testify to what Judith Butler termed politics as "embodied performance" beyond what she calls the "vocalization" of particular claims (2015, p. 19). In her 2013 *Notes toward a Performative Theory of Assembly*, Butler accounts for the multisensoriality of political action and acknowledges the significance of sound as a marker of presence and solidarity: "We are not simply visual phenomena for each other – our voices must be registered, and so we must be heard" (2015, p. 76). By insisting on the vocality of politics without resorting too quickly to articulately voiced political demands, Butler echoes the metaphorical language

---

3   Cf. the essays in Clauss et al., 2020; Marsh, 2010; Hahn, 2015, pp. 525–545.

of "voices of the people" that haunts so many studies on popular grievances, petitions, and gravamina in the early modern period.[4] But instead of joining the choir of the language of *vox populi* as a political metaphor, she takes the expression seriously and literally links it to its corporeal foundations. Echoing the performative practices of the Occupy movement as well as the Arab Spring, Butler draws attention to the mere factuality and corporeality of bodies within public spaces articulating sheer presence and enacting political agency even before and beyond discursive arguments: "Although the bodies on the streets are vocalizing their opposition to the legitimacy of the state, they are also, by virtue of occupying and persisting in that space without protection, posing their challenge in corporeal terms, which means that when the body 'speaks' politically, it is not only in vocal or written language" (Butler, 2015, p. 83). Political bodies in Butler's account are always exposed and vulnerable, threatened to be violated by state authorities. In order to grasp their specific agency, Butler resorts to Hannah Arendt's notion of a "space of appearance". In her seminal *The Human Condition*, Arendt argues that the "space of appearance" predates and precedes the public sphere organized by political discourse and deliberation, enabling the creation of the political and the public as a kind of performative space open to all (Arendt, 1998, p. 199).

Still, in many ways Butler's re-reading of the concept presents it as an exclusive tactic of "the stateless, the occupied, and the disenfranchised" (*pace* LaBelle), thereby running the risk of reproducing the ideological restrictions of the agency concept outlined above. Yet, making noise was by no means a timeless tactic of the subaltern (whoever that may have been) but, rather, a flexible strategy of assuring political presence (or "appearance") within a society based upon ear-to-ear interaction and communication (Missfelder, 2019). Acoustic agencies that aimed at occupying a particular space of appearance were available to almost all strata of society, from the prominent individual making his solemn entry, to the drunken day labourer disturbing it by raising his voice in protest. Sound media beyond the human voice obviously played a significant role. Bells not only served to silence oppositional noise, but also forced listeners into a common space of audibility shared by everyone within earshot. Conceiving of sonic agency as a form of politics of appearance thus analytically privileges performance over content and media over message. Somewhat paradoxically, it always goes even beyond the mere "indexical force of the body" (Butler, 2015, p. 9). In Arendt's understanding, "space of appearance" is by no means a fixed state of political interaction or even organization but is rather a flexible and endlessly unstable potentiality of publics and political action. The *polis*, she writes, "is the organization of the people as it arises out of acting and speaking together, and its true space lies between people living together for this purpose, no matter where they happen to be." For Arendt, there

---

4   Cf., for example, Dumolyn et al., 2014; Hébert, 2018.

is no established Habermasian public sphere that frames legitimate political discourse, but instead there are concrete situations "where I appear to others as others appear to me, where men exist not merely like other living or inanimate things but make their appearance explicitly" (1998, pp. 198–199).

There is an intrinsically theatrical dimension to Arendt's concept of public sphere that resonates with early modern political practices based upon collective visibility, audibility, and sensorial display. As Schlögl and others have argued, early modern politics were essentially performative insofar as they were confined to temporally and spatially delimited constellations of bodies in which power relations were rendered sensorially perceptible. In this sense, making an appearance in a public space served to create ephemeral and "tactical" publics by transforming acoustic agency into political agency.[5] Yet, historically, spaces of appearance were not equally accessible but themselves subject to struggle and strife over who was legitimately supposed to make a bodily and, for that matter, sonic appearance. Early modern societies were characterised by explicit, but more often implicit understandings of the legitimacy of various sound practices. Tracing the agency of sound in early modern societies requires, accordingly, a deeper understanding of who was entitled to raise his or her voice, to claim silence and attention, or to be heard and accounted for, and where and how. Acoustic agency as a concept thus raises further questions concerning access to sound media and resounding spaces. To account for acoustic agency in terms of access requires considering the political and social distribution of sound media and the acoustic constitution of political power.

Distribution of the Audible (Rancière)

The concept of the "distribution of the sensible", advanced by the French philosopher Jacques Rancière, links the Butlerian/Arendtian theory of "appearance" to questions of aesthetics and sensory studies (2010; 2004). Rancière conceives of aesthetics in a decidedly Kantian way as structuring and directing sense perception and, consequently, regulating the space of appearance as a space of sensory agency. The distribution of the sensible is defined as "a system of self-evident facts of sense perception that simultaneously discloses the existence of something in common and the delimitations that define the respective parts and positions within it" (2004, p. 12). By attributing political power to sensory perceptions, Rancière aims at de-ontologizing the senses and rendering them socially "distributable" and politically productive, i.e. subject to power relations and social hierarchies. In his view, the distribution of the sensible does not refer to the realm of sensorially perceptible

---

5   For the concept of tactical publics, cf. Fumerton, 2020.

as such, but rather to the current sensory economy of visibility and, for that matter, audibility: "[I]t defines what is visible or not in a common space, endowed with a common language etc. [...] It is a delimitation of spaces and times, of the visible and the invisible, of speech and noise, that simultaneously determines the place and the stakes of politics as a form of experience. Politics revolves around what is seen and what can be said about it, around who has the ability to see and the talent to speak, around the properties of spaces and the possibilities of time" (2004, p. 13). In determining the hegemony of political visibility, audibility, touchability, etc., at a given point of time, the distribution of the sensible proves to be an essentially historical category of thinking. It refers to the current state of what Rancière calls "police": "Its essence lies in a certain way of dividing up the sensible. [...] A partition of the sensible refers to the manner in which a relation between a shared common and the distribution of exclusive parts is determined in sensory experience" (2010, p. 36).

Rancière distinguishes "police" very sharply from "politics", with the extremely rare, unlikely, and mostly violent re-organization of "police" certain distribution of the sensible. Historically speaking, the Rancièrian category of "police" bears theoretical resemblance to early modern conceptions of *bonne police* or *gute Policey* referring to a common understanding of the order of things that determines the legitimacy of social and political practices and, thus, distributing agency (Iseli, 2003). Therefore, the agency of sound may be traced in the particular state of "police" regulating and distributing sonic utterances or the legitimacy of being heard. Rancière's concept draws attention not only to an epistemic field that renders some utterances socially audible and others not, but also to the individual and collective actors who are entitled to them or not. Power, in other words, makes itself heard as a historically specific entanglement of discourses, norms, and privileges which together produce acoustic agency within the framework of a certain historically specific distribution of the audible.

Analytically, sound historians may take Rancière's distinction between speech and noise as a starting point for an examination of the current state of *police* in terms of distribution of the acoustically sensible. The attribution of certain sonic utterances as (intelligible, discursive, socially relatable) speech or (incomprehensible, chaotic, politically threatening) noise is both a political act in its own right and a testimony to the valid normative order of acoustic legitimacy (Hahn, 2013, pp. 355–367). While, for example, the authorities in early modern Zurich took harsh measures against nocturnal sonic disturbances in the name of public tranquillity and silence, it didn't prevent them from ordering the city's trumpeters to announce the time by playing edifying religious tunes from the church tower of St Peter's all through the night. Within the framework of the Zurich sonic *police*, the hourly trumpet sounds by no means contradicted the official norms of quiescence, but instead unmistakably reminded the population of the authorities' constant vigilance and, thus, acoustically reinforced its claim of political sovereignty. On the other hand, itinerant journeymen in particular were considered the usual suspects guilty of disturbing the urban peace and civic sleep by noisy behaviour at night and were policed accordingly.[6] Silence, legitimate sound production, and noise proved historically contingent and relational categories, rather than merely physical qualities of the urban space.

Conclusion

In conclusion, the three concepts of acoustic agency discussed here refer to three rather different ways of examining political sounds in urban history and beyond. Whereas LaBelle's rendering of sonic agency as a vibrational force runs the risk of reification of sound devoid of social and political context, the Butlerian/Arendtian idea of politics as a performative creation of spaces of appearance presents a model to analyse concrete sound practices as enactments of power relations. Rancière's notion of "distribution of the sensible" offers a theoretical means to capture how power relations historically limited the space of appearance and established a taxonomy of sonic legitimacy. In short, acoustic agencies reveal who was entitled to perform which acoustic practices under which social and political conditions. And this might be precisely what the sound history of power is about.

Bibliography

Arendt, H. (^{2}1998). *The Human Condition*. University of Chicago Press.

Atkinson, N. (2016). *The Noisy Renaissance. Sound, Architecture and Florentine Urban Life*. Pennsylvania State University Press.

Atkinson, N. (2013). The Republic of Sound. Listening to Florence ant the Threshold of the Renaissance. *I Tatti Studies in the Italian Renaissance* 16, 57–84.

Attali, J. (2011). *Noise. The Political Economy of Music*. University of Minnesota Press.

Butler, J. (2015). *Notes toward a Performative Theory of Assembly*. Harvard University Press.

Clauss, M., Mierke, G. & Krüger, A. (Eds.) (2020). *Lautsphären des Mittelalters. Akustische Perspektiven zwischen Lärm und Stille*. Böhlau.

Coronado Schwindt, G. (2021). The Social Construction of the Soundscape of the Castilian Cities (15th and 16th Centuries). *Acoustics* 3, 60–77.

Despret, V. (2013). From Secret Agents to Interagency. *History and Theory* 52, 29–44.

Douglas, M. (1966). *Purity and Danger. An Analysis of the Concept of Pollution and Taboo*. ARK paperbacks.

---

6   For details, see Missfelder, 2019.

Dumolyn, J., Haemers, J., Herrer, H. R. O. & Challet, V. (Eds.) (2014). *The Voices of the People in Medieval Europe. Communication and Popular Politics.* Brepols.

Fisher, A. J. (2017). 'Mit singen und klingen'. Urban Processional Culture and the Soundscapes of Counter-Reformation Germany. In D. Filippi & M. Noone (Eds.), *Listening to Early Modern Catholicism. Perspectives from Musicology* (pp. 187–203). Brill.

Fisher, A. J. (2014). *Piety, and Propaganda. The Soundscapes of Counter-Reformation Bavaria.* Oxford University Press.

Fumerton, P. (2020). *The Broadside Ballad in Early Modern England. Moving Media, Tactical Publics.* University of Pennsylvania Press.

Hahn, P. (2015). The Reformation of the Soundscape. Bell-Ringing in Early Reformation Germany. *German History* 44, 525–545.

Hahn, P. (2013). Sound Control. Policing Noise and Music in German Towns, ca. 1450–1800. In R. Beck, U. Krampl & E. Retaillaud-Bajac (Eds.), *Les cinq sens de la ville: Du Moyen Âge à nos jours* (pp. 355–367). Presses universitaires François Rabelais.

Hébert, M. (2018). *La voix du peuple. Une histoire des assemblées au Moyen Âge.* Presses universitaires de France.

Iseli, A. (2003). *"Bonne police". Frühneuzeitliches Verständnis von der guten Ordnung eines Staates in Frankreich.* Bibliotheca Academica Verlag.

Johnson, W. (2003). On agency. *Journal of Social History* 37, 113–124.

Keizer, G. (2010). *The Unwanted Sound of Everything We Want. A Book about Noise.* Public Affairs.

LaBelle, B. (2018). *Sonic Agency: Sound and Emergent Forms of Resistance.* Goldsmiths Press.

Marsh, C. (2010). *Music and Society in Early Modern England.* Cambridge University Press.

Missfelder, J.-F. (2019). Sound Politics. Sonic Agency and Social Order in Early Modern Zurich. *Annali dell'Istituto storico Italo-Germanico in Trento* 45(2), 87–106.

Missfelder, J.-F (2018). Glocken. In D. Morat & H. Ziemer (Eds.), *Handbuch Sound. Geschichte – Begriffe – Ansätze* (pp. 329–331). Metzler.

Missfelder, J.-F. (2016). Gesellschaft? Anwesend! Körper, Sinne und Medien in Rudolf Schlögls Früher Neuzeit. *Historische Anthropologie* 24, 131–134.

Pickering, H. & Rice, T. (2017). Noise as Sound "out of place": Investigating the Links Between Mary Douglas' Work on Dirt and Sound Studies Research. *Journal of Sonic Studies* 14. https://www.researchcatalogue.net/view/374514/374515/0/0. Date of Access: 24.01.2024.

Rancière, J. (2010). *Dissensus. On Politics and Aesthetics.* Continuum.

Rancière, J. (2004). *The Politics of Aesthetics. The Distribution of the Sensible.* Continuum.

Rudolph, H. (2013). Mit lautem Schalle. Zur Akustik als Medium der Herrschaftsrepräsentation bei Herrschereinzügen am Beginn der Neuzeit. In M. Schramm (Ed.), *Symbole, Zeremonielle, Rituale. Wirken und Wirkung von Militärmusik bei staatlicher Repräsentanz und hoheitlichen Anlässen* (pp. 19–48). Militärmusik der Bundeswehr.

Schiel, J., Schürch, I. & Steinbrecher, A. (2017). Von Sklaven, Pferden und Hunden: Trialog über den Nutzen aktueller Agency-Debatten für die Sozialgeschichte. *Schweizerisches Jahrbuch für Wirtschafts- und Sozialgeschichte* 32, 17–48.

Schlögl, R. (2019). Public Sphere in the Making in Early Modern Europe. *Annali dell'Istituto storico Italo-Germanico in Trento* 45(2), 23–40.

Schlögl, R. (2014). *Anwesende und Abwesende. Grundriss einer Gesellschaftsgeschichte der Frühen Neuzeit*. Konstanz University Press.

Schlögl, R. (2009). Power and Politics in the Early Modern European City. Elections and Decision Making. In R. Schlögl (Ed.), *Urban Elections and Decision- Making in Early Modern Europe, 1500–1800* (pp. 2–28). Cambridge Scholars Publishing.

Schulze, H. (2018). *The Sonic Persona. An Anthropology of Sound*. Bloomsbury Academic.

Schulze, H. (2016). Resistance and Resonance. A Political Anthropology of Sound. *The Senses and Society* 11, 68–81.

Shaw, D. G. (2013). The Torturer's Horse: Agency and Animals in History. *History and Theory* 52, 146–167.

Sterne, J. (2003). *The Audible Past. Cultural Origins of Sound Reproduction*. Duke University Press.

Thompson, E. P. (1958). Agency and Choice. Reply to my Critics. *The New Reasoner* 5, 89–106.

Thompson, M. (2017). *Beyond Unwanted Sound. Noise, Affect, and Aesthetic Moralism*. Bloomsbury Academic.

van der Linden, D. (2019). The Sound of Memory. Acoustic Conflict and the Legacy of the French Wars of Religion in Seventeenth-Century Montpellier. *Early Modern French Studies* 41, 7–20.

Part II
Ottoman Court Culture

Music Theory Sources in Ottoman Urban Culture and the Court Space Between the 14th and 15th Centuries

Using the Science of Music for Providing a Cultural Authority*

Cenk Güray

Introduction: Music and Cosmos

Regarding the 14th- and 15th-century Ottoman world, it can be strongly confirmed that music functioned as a way of perceiving the cosmos. Moreover, this function served as an effective tool for transmitting principles on which both madrasa education and the belief systems of various religious orders were based. During this period, a respectable number of texts were written on music theory. A great majority of these texts can be classified under the heading *edvâr*, meaning "cycles" or "circles". In fact, this term addresses a symbolic representation of the cosmos and cosmic principles, implicitly or explicitly, by means of music theory components like scales, tetrachords, pentachords, musical intervals, melodic motives, etc. – an approach that can be seen as the main methodological foundation of these texts. Based on these texts and a number of other contemporaneous written sources, such as legendary narratives sharing a common symbolic background unifying the cosmos with music, it can be inferred that in the Ottoman urban culture of the 14th and 15th centuries, a philosophy emanating from a cosmos-oriented view related esoteric concepts to a scientific methodology. This philosophy also underscored the main reasons for the ongoing contradictions and cracks in medieval Anatolia between the madrasa culture, corresponding to the universities of the Western world, and the esoteric belief systems of the Sufi orders.

The scientific heritage remaining in medieval Islam from the ancient Greek period consisted in the four mathematical sciences – the Aristotelian Quadrivium of arithmetic, geometry, astronomy, and music. At the madrasas, these were among the main areas of research. Since the ancient Greek period, music science or music theory had played a cen-

---

* I wish to express my sincere gratitude to Dr Ferhat Çaylı for his invaluable support in this paper.

tral role in the Quadrivium. It functioned to reflect the parallelism of music and cosmic harmony based on mathematical principles. Essentially, the school of Meşşai philosophy can be identified as the main means that carried the cosmos-music duality to the works of medieval Islam theorists like Farabi (872–950) and İbn-i Sina (980–1037). The effect of this philosophy can also be strongly seen in 13th- and 15th-century Anatolia through texts on music theory by Safiyüddin Urmevi (1216–1294), Abdülkadir Meragi (d. 1435), and Kutbeddin Şirazi (1236–1311). The followers of this school in Anatolia were called *ilim erbabı* (science masters) by the 15th-century theorist Ladikli Mehmed Çelebi. These masters were generally gathered around two important social environments: the madrasa, normally in urban settings, and the palace. It should be remembered that the political and social cracks that appeared in Anatolia during the 14th and 15th centuries opened the way for important cultural changes, changes that can be traced through the theoretical sources. Among the main evidence for these cracks was the transfer of the esoteric symbolism of music from the palace to the strengthening Dervish lodges, implying that a diversification of power took place. This diversification demonstrates how the sound of power was used to enhance cultural authority in medieval Anatolia.

The Role of Music Theory in Madrasa Education

It is known that music theory was a prominent part of educational and philosophical movements in the madrasa tradition in Anatolia between the 14th and 15th centuries. Music theory was also closely connected to the study of astronomy. Nasiruddin Tusi (1201–1274) and Safiyüddin Urmevi seem to be the two main Anatolian sources in which the link between astronomy and music can be found. The effects of this link can be followed in the works of Kutbeddin Şirazi. Indeed, it was most probably Şirazi who carried the Systematist School – so-called due to its strong connection to ancient Greek music theory based on the main musical scale called the greater perfect system – to Anatolia. This school was later followed by 15th-century theorists like Fetullah Şirvani (1417–1486) and others. Şirazi and Şirvani are both known to have been madrasa teachers and experts in this music-astronomy duality. It is possible to trace the content and function of music education in the madrasa tradition through their curricula.

The Function of Music Theory in the Madrasa Tradition

Music, or music theory in particular, as included in madrasa curricula followed the Aristotelian division of sciences called Quadrivium (İzgi, 2019, p. 409). The Quadrivium was also the basis of the Meşşai philosophical school of medieval Islam that placed the four mathematical sciences at the centre of their scientific thought, directly inspired by Aristotle. According to the rationalist, sensualist, and analytical concepts of the Meşşai school (Tomar et al., 2019, p. 208), these four sciences were the main agents enabling cooperation between human beings and the cosmos (Güray, 2017, p. 53). Music – being both a sensualist and rationalist media thanks to the audial and mathematical relations on which it depends – lay at the centre of this logic (Güray, 2017, p. 30). Farabi, İbn-i Sina, and Safiyüddin Urmevi can be considered to be among the important music theorists who followed the rules of the Meşşai school, which concentrated on the mathematical/audial/acoustic system behind music, for the most part excluding esoteric or mystical symbolism (Güray, 2017, pp. 52–64). The effects of this school were strongly seen in the madrasa tradition of the medieval Ottoman era (İzgi, 2019, pp. 127–130), but traces of two other sometimes contradicting schools can also be noted (İzgi, 2019, pp. 126, 412). The first of these represented an orthodox type of Islamic thought, which lead to a strong madrasa tradition in basic Islamic sciences like *kalam*[1] and *hadith*.[2] The second represented a heterodox type of Islamic philosophy that walked arm in arm with popular Islamic orders of the period such as the Mevlevi and Ahi sects. The formation and focus of these schools were closely connected to various cultural hegemonies and the social powers associated with them. Their unification opened a path to different preferences in scientific thought that had interesting implications regarding how music theory was addressed.

The Main Schools of Music Theory in Madrasa Education, the Palace, and Religious Orders: The Ways Authority Cooperated with Music

The schools of music theory in medieval Anatolia were classified several ways. The classification of Ladikli Mehmed Çelebi during the second half of the 15th century was the main motivation for most of these classification efforts. Çelebi classified his contemporary theorists under two divisions, namely "masters of science" (*ilim erbabı*) and "masters of practice" (*iş erbabı*) (Güray, 2017, p. 65). The theorists classified under the "master of science" category had a tendency to situate music theory primarily in a mathematical context, whereas the category "masters of practice" included theorists who were more engaged in the esoteric/mystical side of music theory and music practice, usually alongside mathematical considerations. In fact, this division was based on a consistent logical background

---

1 The science concentrating on the main principles of Islam, mainly based on verses of the Qur'an (Yavuz, 2022, pp. 196–203).

2 The science concentrating on the determination, transmission, and perception of the words, behaviour and thoughts of Prophet Muhammed (Kandemir, 1997, pp. 27–64).

that had arisen from the cultural and social life of the period. This background can be supported with a brief content analysis of theory manuscripts produced in the 14th and 15th centuries in Anatolia, in which traces of three different schools interacting with the "two divisions" put forward by Çelebi can be detected.

The Effects of the Herat[3]-Samarkand School: The Timurid Renaissance and the Iranian concept of "Sacred Geography"

During the Ottoman period, first signs of ongoing "official" interactions between Anatolia and Iran-Azerbaijan appeared during the reigns of Murad II and Mehmed II (the Conqueror), an effect of the Timurid Renaissance in Herat during the 15th century (Abbasoğlu, 2015, pp. 82–85) and later, of Safavid culture in Tebriz during the 16th century. The main representatives of Herat music tradition were the famous composer Abdülkadir Meragi and his descendants (İnalcık, 2011, pp. 47–56). Meragi and the followers of this tradition had a considerable effect on the medieval Ottoman madrasa tradition, which developed a specific system for transmitting music theory. Recep Uslu (2021a) has identified this tradition as part of a separate division that he calls the Middle Asian Systematist School (p. 106).

Abdülkadir Meragi

The famous theorist and composer Abdülkadir Meragi influenced Anatolian music culture during the 15th century with regard to both performance and theory. This influence continued with his son and grandson. At the Ottoman Palace all three were appreciated as musicians and composers during the reigns of Sultan Murad II, Mehmed II, Bayezid II, and Süleyman I (Süleyman the Magnificent). Taking his theoretical base from Safiyüddin Urmevi, Meragi developed his musical theories based on mathematics. Although the Timurid tradition followed a very conservative approach toward Islamic life, the esoteric ideas of the Iranian concept of "sacred geography" are not found in the writings of Meragi. He dedicated his *Makasıd'ül Elhan* (The Purposes of the Melodies) to Sultan Murad II in 1421. His son Abdülaziz (1405?–1485?), who worked for many years as a musician and teacher at the Ottoman Palace, dedicated his music theory volume *Nekavetü'l Edvâr* (The Exclusiveness of the Cycle) to Mehmed II. This text followed the theoretical approach of Abdülkadir Meragi with minor changes. The grandson of Meragi, Mahmud (Abdülkadirzâde Derviş Ûdî), was also a famous,

---

3   This school, an effect of the Timurid Renaissance, is presented with this name by Toomajnia (2017, p. 419).

respected musician at the Ottoman Palace towards the end of the 15th and the beginning of the 16th centuries, during the reigns of Bayezid II and Süleyman I. He wrote a text called *Makâsıdü'l Edvâr* (The Purposes of the Cycle), which unifies music theory with composition and performance practice. He dedicated the volume to Bayezid II (Bardakçı, 1986, p. 43).

Fethullah Şirvani

Fethullah Şirvani was one of the scholars from the Timurid Palace who travelled to and lived in Anatolia during the reigns of Murad II and Mehmed II. He carried the ideas of the Samarkand-Khorasan[4] way of "scientific thought" to Anatolia and the Ottoman Palace. He was taught at the madrasa of Uluğ Bey[5] in Samarkand (Akdoğan, 2009, pp. 23–24). In his text *Mecelletun Fi'l-Musika* (The Manuscript on Wisdom about Music), he lists as references the works of İbn-i Sina, Safiyüddin Urmevi, Nicomachus (60–120), Nasiruddin Tusi, and Ebu Abdullah Muhammed b. Ahmed b. Yusuf el-Harizmi (780–850). Through these references, it can be inferred that Şirvani represented the common ground between the Meşşai school and the Samarkand-Khorasan school. He dedicated his text to Mehmed II (Akdoğan, 2009, p. 43). He taught at Kastamonu Madrasa for a long time, specialising in mathematics, astronomy, logic, and *kalam*. Şirvani can be identified as having had a mathematics-based approach to music theory; he did not engage with the mystical side of music theory.

Benai (Kemalüddîn Şîr Alî-yi Herevî) (d. 1512)

As a very important representative of the Herat Palace and Herat-Samarkand school, the theoretical approach of Benai (Kemalüddîn Şîr Alî-yi Herevî) shows great similarities to the approaches of Abdülkadir Meragi and Alişah Bin Hacı Büke (second half of the 15th century). His text on music theory, *Risâle-i Mûsîkî* (The Manuscript of Music), written in 1483, concentrates on the *makam* (mode) and *avaze*[6] structures from a systematic-mathematical perspective. He writes about melodic structures based on scales composed on a *tabaka* (layer)/*devir* (cycle) methodology, unifying pieces in fourths and fifths into a certain hierarchical formula (Köprülü, 2016, pp. 1144–1151). The influence of this manuscript

---

4   Şirvani is listed as in important member of the astronomy- and mathematics-based Samarkand school by Fazlıoğlu (2003, p. 2).

5   Uluğ Bey (1394–1449), grandson of Timur, son of Şahruh, Timurid ruler, mathematician, astronomer. During his reign he strengthened the status of Samarkand as a centre of science and arts by establishing several institutions, including a very important madrasa (Unat, 2012, pp. 127–129).

6   In music theory manuscripts of the 15th century, these are secondary melodic structures usually defined as unifying two *makam* structures and corresponding to the seven planets.

is reflected in several later texts written in Anatolia, most probably through the madrasa connection carried from Herat to Anatolia by Benai's contemporaries.

Alişah Bin Hacı Büke

Alişah Bin Hacı Büke is another theorist of the 15th century who was known to have worked and been educated under the patronage and guidance of the Timurid ruler Hüseyin Baykara (1438–1507) and the philosopher, scientist, and poet Ali Şir Nevai (1441–1501) (Çakır, 1999, p. 3). He was also influenced to some extent by Kutbeddin Şirazi and Abdülkadir Meragi (Çakır, 1999, pp. 4–5). Like the other members of this school, such as Abdülkadir Meragi and Fethullah Şirvani, he concentrated on the mathematically verifiable side of music theory, components such as frequencies, intervals of consonance and dissonance, musical scales, and rhythmic patterns (Çakır, 1999, pp. 8–9). The mystical side of music theory regarding cosmic and natural symbolism did not represent a major part of his studies.

Mehemmed b. Sufi Seyyid Ahmed

Towards the end of the 15th century, Mehemmed b. Sufi Seyyid Ahmed was a madrasa instructor at Sahn-ı Seman Madrasa,[7] which was established by Fatih Sultan Mehmed. There is a possibility that Mehemmed b. Sufi Seyyid Ahmed was a follower of the Herat-Samarkand school, since in his short text on music theory (Uslu, 2007, pp. 99–104) his approach strongly follows the mathematics-based approach of the Meşşai school, Safiyüddin Urmevi, and Abdülkadir Meragi. His musical approach can be interpreted as similar to Şems-i Rumi of Tebriz, who wrote a manuscript containing the lyrics of compositions from the era of Mehmed II (Fatih) (Uslu, 2007, pp. 97–99).

Molla Câmi (Şirvani)

Molla Câmi (Şirvani) was born in Cam-Khorasan in the early 15th century (b. 1414). After being educated at Nizamiye Madrasa in Herat, he taught there in the following years. He was also educated in both mathematical and Islamic sciences at Uluğ Bey Madrasa in Samarkand. Molla Câmi (Şirvani) can be identified as a follower of the Meşşai tradition and the

---

7   A complex of advanced-level madrasas constructed during the reign of Mehmed II specialized in both metaphysical and physical-mathematical sciences. Based on many sources, the famous astronomer and mathematician Ali Kuşçu (1403–1474) from Samarkand was an important instructor and advisor at this madrasa complex (Unan, 2008, pp. 532–534). He can be identified as one of the main points of connection between the Timurid and Ottoman madrasa traditions.

Nakşıbendi sect. He also supported the İşrakiyye (Illuminationism) school of philosophy and exchanged letters with Bayezid II. These reflect the admiration Bayezid held for Câmi due to his strong scientific background (Kolukırık, 2013, pp. 139–140). In Câmi's music theoretical text *Risâle-i Mûsikî* (The Manuscript of Music), he demonstrates his knowledge of scales, intervals, the 12 *makam*s, 6 *avaze*s, and 24 *şube*s.[8] He was influenced primarily by İbn-i Sina of the Meşşai school and the followers of the so-called Systematist School, such as Safiyüddin Urmevi and Abdülkadir Meragi (Kolukırık, 2013, pp. 140–145). A specific major influence came from Meragi. Câmi discusses rhythmic structures, as well as, to some extent, the effects of *makam* structures on the nature of human beings (Kolukırık, 2013, p. 145). Câmi can be considered a follower of the mathematical theory school and a strong member of the Herat-Samarkand school. His works were influential in the Anatolian region.

Madrasa Theorists: The Influence on the Meşşai Tradition of the Esoteric Schools of Anatolia and the Iranian concept of "Sacred Geography"

In medieval Ottoman Anatolia, the balance between the mathematical/rational and the mystical/symbolic sides of music theory was sustained through the influence of esoteric schools. In fact, it was works by theorists in these schools that resulted in the compromise or consensus between the strong Meşşai tradition in Ottoman madrasas and Sufism-based philosophies such as İşrakiyye, as well as the esoterism of the Iranian "sacred geography" centred in the city of Tebriz.[9]

Kutbeddin Şirazi

Kutbeddin Şirazi was born in 1236 in Shiraz. He followed the schools of Nasirüddin Tusi in astronomy, İbn-i Sina in medicine, İbnü'l Arabi (1165–1240) and Sadreddin Konevi (1209–1274) in philosophy, and Safiyüddin Urmevi in music. In addition, as a follower of the İşrakiyye-based Suhreverdi order, he was a specialist in illuminationism. He de-

---

8   In music theory texts of the 15th century, melodic structures are classified into three categories according to their melodic structures and cosmic orientation, namely, as *makam*(s), *avaze*(s), and *şube*(s). The *makam*s were the primary and most popular melodic structures in the music of that century; there are twelve *makam*s corresponding to the twelve months and twelve horoscopes. The mostly descending secondary melodic structures, usually described as having evolved from the unification of two *makam*s, are called as *avaze*s, these corresponding to the seven planets. Finally, the *şube*s represent minor melodic modules that can be unified with other melodic lines to create larger melodic scales. They correspond to the four main elements – water, fire, air, soil – which are believed to form the main substance of all creatures (Güray, 2017, pp. 83–84).

9   Baharlu refers to Tebriz School regarding its specific miniature painting style (2021, p. 16).

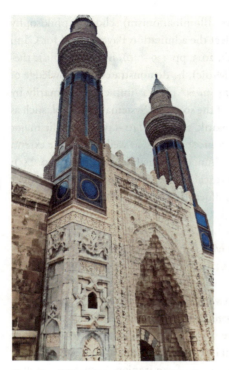

Fig. 1: Sivas-Gökmedrese (photographed by the author on 22 June 2023).

veloped a new theory involving the concept of "light"-symbolizing wisdom, believed to be the heavenly substance through which human beings were created and thus, the main constructive source unifying the creator, God, with those created, human beings. With his teachings unifying the philosophies of İbn-i Sina, Suhreverdi, and İbn'ül Arabi, Şirazi can be considered one of the most important scientific personalities in Anatolian life of the 13th and 14th centuries. It is possible that his prominent position in philosophy influenced the official direction of the Seljuk government regarding cosmic perception through science. Since Şirazi worked as a judge (*kadı*) in Malatya and Sivas, and was also a madrasa teacher at the Gök madrasa in Sivas (Fig. 1), he can be considered a representative, as both a lawyer and a scientist, of the official approach of the Seljuk government.

Under the philosophical influence of the three important philosophers İbn-i Sina, Suhreverdi, and İbn'ül Arabi, Şirazi's approach to music theory also reflected how they used music to develop their own philosophical rhetoric and ways of perceiving the cosmos through science (Şerbetçi, 2002, pp. 487–489). Şirazi's book *Dürretü't-tac* (The Pearl in the Crown) includes an important chapter on music theory and is the main source reflecting his views on the subject. The text contains five sections. The first three follow the mathematical-based approach of the Systematist School in a way very similar to the writings of Safiyüddin Urmevi (Wright, 1978, p. 24). But the last two chapters of the manuscript are unique and can be considered to represent original ideas of the author. Here, Şirazi's approach, while methodologically similar to his precursors, includes the *makam*s of his own period, as well as developments in systems of sound (Wright, 1978, p. 24).

Kadızâde Tirevi

Kadızâde Tirevi was another important actor in the science of 15th-century Ottoman Anatolia. Because he was the son of the judge (*kadı*) of Kastamonu, he was known by the nickname "Kadızâde". Tirevi is reported to have worked as a scientist during the mid-15[th]century during the reigns of Murad II and Mehmed II. As a madrasa teacher, Tirevi specialized in mathematics, first working at the Tire (İzmir) madrasa, after which he was appointed as a teacher in one of the *Sahn-ı Seman* madrasas in İstanbul during the reign of Mehmed II (Uygun, 1990, p. 15). Tirevi was twice appointed as the "judge" of Bursa, the second time during the reign of Bayezid II. In one source, he is reported to have been educated at the Samarkand Uluğ Bey madrasa. Regarding the madrasa tradition of his time, Tirevi was also known as an expert on the text *el-Mevâkıf* (The Important Issues of Kalam) – a work by Adudüddin el-Îcî (d. 1335) of Shiraz that was later commented on by Cürcânî (d. 1413), one of Tirevi's teachers. Generally speaking, Tirevi can be classified as a strong representative of both the Meşşai school of science and the Khorasan-Tebriz madrasa tradition. In Tirevi's text on music theory named *Risâle-i Mûsikî* (The Manuscript of Music), he refers directly to Farabi and İbn-i Sina, as well as to Kemaleddin Buhari, about whom we have limited knowledge. Tirevi also mentions that he read the text by Sayrafi of Tebriz called *Hülasatü'l Efkar* (The Essence of the Ideas), which is a transcription of Urmevi's *Kitâbü'l Edvâr* (The Book of Cycles). Tirevi's text mainly contains a mathematically based viewpoint of music theory, this supported by a comparatively short section regarding the mystical power of music in the human soul, as related to the theory of the four main elements believed to constitute the essence of every being in the cosmos.

Ahmedoğlu Şükrullah

Ahmedoğlu Şükrullah lived during the early-mid 15th century during the reigns of Mehmed I, Murad II, and Fatih Sultan Mehmed. His text on music theory consists primarily of a transcription of and commentary on Safiyüddin Urmevi's *Kitâbü'l Edvâr* (The Book of Cycles). Based on his background and his works, he seems to have been influenced by the mystic philosophers of Basra and Iran, such as İhvan-ı Safa and Şeyh Hasen-ı Kazeruni (Bardakçı, 2008, p. 28). Ahmedoğlu presented his manuscript to Murad II and was appointed for different missions by this sultan, including the post of official messenger of the Ottoman Palace in Edirne. Although how he transmitted music theory was strongly affected by the Meşşai school of science, as well as by Safiyüddin Urmevi, he was also philosophically close to Neo-Platonist, hermetic,[10] and İşrakiyye-based thoughts, most probably aligning with the mystical outlook of Sultan Murad II.

---

10 A philosophical approach searching for the secrets and essence of the universe through sciences such as mathematics, astronomy and alchemy whose roots were dedicated to the mythological Hermes Trismegistos (Prophet İdris in Islamic thought). The hermetic view sees the essence of the universe in the human being and thus puts the human soul at the centre of the cosmos (Kılıç, 1998, pp. 228–233).

Ladikli Mehmed Çelebi

Based on several records, Ladikli Mehmed Çelebi was active as a scientist during the mid- to end of the 15th century. He is reported to have worked on many mathematical-based sciences at madrasas near Amasya-Ladik, where he is thought to have lived. His approach to music theory was mostly mathematically based, following the Meşşai school, as well as the works of Safiyüddin Urmevi, Fethullah Şirvani, and Abdülkadir Meragi. He gave very little emphasis to the symbolic side of music. His text, *Risâletü'l Fethiyye* (The Manuscript of the Conquest),[11] contains a musical identification of melodic structures called *devir*s based on the consonant and dissonant intervals, the musical *tabaka* structures evolved through these intervals, the musical scales developed from such *tabaka*s, the mathematical verification behind this logic, and rhythmic structures (Tekin, 1999, pp. 247–250). He classified the *devir* structures into three divisions, namely *makam*s (twelve), *avaze*s (six), and *şube*s (twenty-four), without indicating a cosmic-symbolic relation regarding these divisions with the celestial bodies (Tekin, 1999, pp. 157–161). Ladikli Mehmed Çelebi was long a close companion of Bayezid II, starting with the period when the prince was a governor of Amasya. Considering the influences reflected in Çelebi's works, it can be presumed that he had an extensive madrasa education (Tekin, 1999, pp. 32–40).

The Mystic Khorasan-Anatolian School: Music-Theoretical Symbolic Theories in the Dervish Lodges and Poet Circles

The period from the 13th to 15th centuries witnessed the development of specific mystic dervish orders, which based their belief systems on philosophical texts such as the *Vahdet-i vücud* and *Vahdet-i mevcud*,[12] primarily the Khorasan-based Sufi schools such as Mevlevi or Bayramiyye, but also the Abdal troops[13] (Güray et al., 2020, pp. 33, 46, 50). It is evident that for the followers of these sects, the symbolic power of music was turned into a belief-transmission methodology. Thus some followers/dervishes of these sects – who were probably engaged in madrasa education as well – wrote texts on music theory that empha-

---

11 Presumed to have been written in honour of the conquest of Akkerman City of Bogdan by Bayezid II.

12 These two philosophical texts dominated medieval Islamic belief systems. The earlier one, *Vahdet-i Mevcud* (The Unity of Beings), represents a perception of God whose presence can be sensed as scattered – sometimes physically – all through the universe. The other, *Vahdet-i Vücud* (The Unity of Eternal Being), represents the obligation to attain the concepts of "being" and "eternity" only to God, whose symbolic body (*vücud*) can only be sensed by attempting to perceive the cosmos (Güray, 2018, p. 40).

13 A special dervish tribe of Islamic heterodoxy that used music and ritual dance as a prominent means of cultural transmission. This tribe is believed to have brought the seeds of the Alevi-Bektashi belief system from Khorasan to Anatolia (Güray, 2018, p. 25).

size the esoteric side of music. Most probably, the aim was to legitimatize music being used in the official rituals of these sects.

Hasan bin Ali

A text on music theory recently examined by Recep Uslu called *Mârifet-i Musiki Edvâr-ı Faryabi* (The Ingenuity of Music – The Book of Cycles of Faryabi), written near the end of the 14th century, is an interesting example of theoretical viewpoints from the esoteric/symbolic side of music. The author, Hasan bin Ali, discusses and refers to works by Safiyüddin and Meragi. But in his text, we see no signs of the mathematical-based approach of these earlier scholars to music theory other than in his classification of *makam* structures as 12 *makam*s, 6 *avaze*s and 48 *şube*s, which resembles Meragi's approach (Uslu, 2021b, p. 25). The author, most probably a *Mevlevi* dervish from Karaman, uses the symbolic side of music as a means of expression and emphasizes the practical descriptions of *makam*s, probably for the sake of "religious-based transmission" (Uslu, 2021b, pp. 125–133).

Hızır Bin Abdullah

Hızır Bin Abdullah was the main theorist of the Bursa Palace during the reign of Sultan Murad II (early to mid-15th century) and dedicated his *Kitâbü'l Edvâr* (The Book of Cycles) to him. His approach to music theory primarily covers practical definitions of *makam*s embedded in a world of symbolic expressions. His rhetoric is centred around a strong cosmic perception of the universe as it relates to music, with the celestial bodies linked to musical structures, specifically, linking the twelve *makam*s to the twelve horoscopes, the seven *avaze*s to the seven planets, and the four *şube*s to the four elements (Çelik, 2001, pp. 218–223). His way of life and musical approach coincided closely with the mystical/esoteric outlook of the Ottoman Palace during the reign of Murad II, which was strongly affected by the thoughts of many mystical dervish sects, including the Bayramiyye sect of Hacı Bayram Veli (1352–1430). These sects based their perception of God and the universe primarily on the "theory of cycles", which placed a cosmic cycle, presented through musical symbolism, at the centre of the interaction between God and human beings (İnalcık, 2020, p. 171; Güray et al., 2020, p. 46).

Yusuf El Kırşehri

Yusuf El Kırşehri, who lived during the late 14th and early 15th centuries, is known to have been a Mevlevi dervish who wrote an important text on music theory called *Risâle-i Mûsikî* (The Manuscript of Music). This text concentrates on practical descriptions of theoretical elements and *makam* structures, combined with a strong rhetoric about mystic symbolism addressing the esoteric function of music. The text constructs a relationship between cosmic harmony and the human soul, a typical characteristic of the Mevlevi belief system (Sezikli, 2014, p. 13). In fact, this text – whose concepts resemble those of the *Marifet-i Musiki* (The Ingenuity of Music) by Hasan bin Ali (Uslu, 2021b, p. 26) – can be identified as a milestone work. It details a mystical/esoteric approach to music theory that aims to utilize the mystic power of music as a tool for belief transmission. The text's *makam* classification is based on a system of "twelve *makam*s, seven *avaze*s, and four *şube*s", thus establishing the main framework for later Anatolian-based classifications of these structures (Sezikli, 2014, p. 13).

Bedr-i Dilşad

It is possible that Bedr-i Dilşad, which is thought to have been a nickname, has been confused with another contemporary philosopher named Mahmut Şirvani. Bedr-i Dilşad lived in the early to mid-15th century in Anatolia (Ceyhan, 1997, pp. 23–31). His work on music theory, called *Muradnâme* (The Book in Honor of Murad) – it was dedicated to Murad II – is a translation of a didactic *mesnevi* called *Kabusnâme* (The Book of Advice), which was written in 1082 by Emir Unsurü'l-Maali Keykavus for the education of his son (Ceyhan, 1997, p. 43). Scanning through the text, written in verses, and keeping in mind Bedr-i Dilşad's competence as a translator, it can be deduced that he worked in many different scientific areas, primarily in the Islamic sciences. But due to the text's references to Farabi, which are successfully reflected in the translated text (Ceyhan, 1997, p. 149), it can be sensed that he also had a background in the natural sciences. These pieces of information suggest that Bedr-i Dilşad may well have been a madrasa graduate. Since Bedr-i Dilşad found the Persian manuscript worth translating, even dedicating it to Sultan Murad II, we can assume that he shared its main scientific and cultural attitudes. The musical part of the text is written in a literary style that touches on both theoretical details and the practical side of music. The symbolic/mystical side of music is transmitted along with details about music theory; the theoretical approach has no mathematical background. The concentration is mainly on the practical sides of music theory. The classification of the *makam* structures is again based on cosmic symbolism, with the twelve *makam*s corresponding to the twelve horoscopes, the seven *avaze*s, to the seven planets, and the four *şube*s, to the four main elements (Ceyhan, 1997, p. 150).

Seydi

The 15th-century author Seydi wrote a text on music theory, possibly[14] under the patronage of Şeyh Mahbub (Arısoy, 1988, pp. 4–5). In its approach to music theory, the text, mainly written in verses, also follows cosmic and esoteric symbolism, again matching the *makam*, *avaze*, and *şube* structures to the horoscopes, planets, and four main elements (Arısoy, 1988, pp. 20–21). The text possibly had the function of transmitting religious philosophy through musical symbolism.

Conclusion: Texts on Music Theory and Music as a Means for Sustaining Cultural Power

As the above discussion shows, the 14th- and 15th-century Ottoman world was rich in texts on music theory. These texts were produced either in Anatolia, whether within the Ottoman Palace itself, in madrasas, or in dervish lodges, or they were received from representatives from neighbouring realms after being dedicated to Ottoman rulers. Many of these texts were, in fact, tools for sustaining authority. The first type – called here the Herat-Samarkand school – was a natural continuation of the Herat-Timurid influence on the Ottoman Palace and of the cultural interaction between these two Turkish dynasties. The second type was an outcome of the strong Ottoman madrasa tradition, reflected in the unification of the Meşşai school of science and mystical movements transmitted to Anatolia from Iran. This madrasa tradition was directly linked to the cultural authority of the Ottoman rulers. It aimed to construct a balance between the official sciences of Islamic Orthodoxy and the neighbouring Sufi-based traditions. It also established a control mechanism for radical religious movements. It should be remembered that music, whether performance, composition, or theory, was a strong mechanism that allowed the Ottoman rulers to sustain cultural power from two directions, namely, the arts and the sciences. This tradition that developed naturally in the cultural environment of late medieval Anatolia and was a specific combination of music science with esoteric belief systems, resulting in strong symbolic rhetoric for musical transmission through theory. This signalled the beginning of the transformation from the earlier Meşşai-based madrasa tradition to a more mystical perception-based compromise between the madrasas and the religious orders. This transformation resulted in a more esoteric way of approaching science as well as in a deeply expressive form of music and poetry. Moreover, this transformation enabled the followers

---

14   It cannot be clearly ascertained through the dedicatory notes, which address Şeyh Mahbub as the "owner" of the book, whether he was the author or the sponsor of the text.

of the mystic Khorasan-Anatolian school to enhance the power of the musical esoterism that had until then belonged to the palace and madrasa, and to carry this "power" to the Dervish lodges. The identification of the "belief system" through "musical esoterism" later turned out to be the main issue, showing the contradiction between the Islamic heterodoxy, especially that solidified by the Alevi and Bektashi orders, with the orthodoxy represented by the Ottoman authority.

If you wish to get to know yourself,
Look for the essence deep in the cosmos.
(Hacı Bayram Veli)

Bibliography

Printed Sources and Source Editions

Akdoğan, B. (2009). *Fethullah Şirvânî ve Mûsikî Risâlesi*. Bilge Ajans.

Arısoy, M. (1988). *Seydî'nin El-Matlâ Adlı Eseri Üzerine Bir Çalışma* [Master's thesis, Marmara Üniversitesi].

Bardakçı, M. (1986). *Maragalı Abdülkadir*. Pan Yayıncılık.

Bardakçı, M. (2008). *Ahmedoğlu Şükrullah: Şükrullah'ın Risâlesi ve 15. Yüzyıl Şark Musikisi Nazariyatı*. Pan Yayıncılık.

Çakır, A. (1999). *Alişah B. Hacı Büke'nin (?–1500) Mukaddimetü'l Usul Adlı Eseri* [Doctoral dissertation, Marmara Üniversitesi].

Ceyhan, A. (1997). *Bedr-i Dilşad'ın Muradnamesi*. Milli Eğitim Bakanlığı Yayınları.

Çelik, B. B. (2001). *Hızır Bin Abdullah'ın Kitabü'l Edvâr'ı ve Makamların İncelenmesi* [Doctoral dissertation, Marmara Üniversitesi].

Köprülü, G. (2016). Benai ve Musiki Risalesinde Makam Kavramı. *Rast Müzikoloji Dergisi* 4(1), 1142–1152.

Sezikli, U. (2014). *Risale-i Musiki: Kırşehirli Yusuf bin Nizameddin,* ed. by M. Kalpaklı, O. M. Öztürk & C. Güray. T. C. Kültür ve Turizm Bakanlığı.

Tekin, H. (1999). *Ladikli Mehmet Çelebi ve er-Risaletü`l Fethiyye'si* [Doctoral dissertation, Niğde Üniversitesi].

Uslu, R. (2021b). *Marifet-i Musiki Edvârı-1385*. Akademisyen Kitabevi.

Uslu, R. (2007). *Fatih Sultan Mehmed Döneminde Musiki: Şems-i Rumi'nin Mecmua-i Güfte'si*. İstanbul Fetih Cemiyeti Yayınları.

Uygun, M. N. (1990). *Kadızâde Tirevî ve Musikî Risâlesi* [Master's thesis, Marmara Üniversitesi].

Scholarly Literature

Abbasoğlu, Z. Y. (2015). *15. yy Herat Müzik Okulu ve Benâî'nin Risâle-i Mûsikî'si* [Doctoral dissertation, Marmara Üniversitesi].

Baharlu, I. (2021). Safevîler Döneminde Sema (Semah) (Kronikler, Seyahatnâmeler Ve Minyatürlerde). *Türk Kültürü ve Hacı Bektaş Veli Araştırma Dergisi* 97, 11–28.

Fazlıoğlu, İ. (2001). Osmanlı Felsefe Biliminin Arkaplanı: Semerkand Matematik-Astronomi Okulu. *Divân İlmî Araştırmalar Dergisi* 14(2003/1), 1–66.

Güray, C. (2017). *Bin Yılın Mirası: Makamı Var Eden Döngü Edvar Geleneği*. Pan Yayıncılık.

Güray, C. (2018). Devirsel İbadet Modelleri Olarak Semah-Semâ Uygulamalarının Tarihsel Kökenleri. *Türk Kültürü ve Hacı Bektaş Veli Araştırma Dergisi* 87, 23–48.

Güray, C., & Tekin Arıcı, E. (2020). Conceiving the Medieval Ottoman Music Culture Through Legendary Narratives. *Türk Kültürü ve Hacı Bektaş Veli Araştırma Dergisi* 96, 33–54.

İnalcık, H. (2011). *Has Bağçede Ayş u Tarab: Nedimler, Şairler, Mutripler*. İş Bankası Kültür Yayınları.

İnalcık, H. (2020). 2. Murad. In *TDV İslam Ansiklopedisi*, vol. 31 (pp. 164–172). TDV İslâm Araştırmaları Merkezi.

İzgi, C. (2019). *Osmanlı Medereselerinde İlim: Riyazi ve Tabii İlimler*. Küre Yayınları.

Kandemir, M.Y. (1997). Hadis. In *TDV İslam Ansiklopedisi*, vol. 15 (pp. 27–64). TDV İslâm Araştırmaları Merkezi.

Kılıç, M.E. (1998). Hermes. In *TDV İslam Ansiklopedisi*, vol. 17 (pp. 228–233). TDV İslâm Araştırmaları Merkezi.

Kolukırık, K. (2013). Molla Câmi ve Musiki Risalesi. *Bozok Üniversitesi İlahiyat Fakültesi Dergisi* 2013(4), 137–147.

Şerbetçi, A. (2002). Kutbüddin-i Şirazi. In *TDV İslam Ansiklopedisi*, vol. 26 (pp. 487–489). TDV İslâm Araştırmaları Merkezi.

Tomar, C., Şahin, H., Bayrakdar, M., & Küçükkaşçı, M. S. (2019). *İslam Tarihi ve Medeniyeti II*. Anadolu Üniversitesi Yayınları.

Toomajnia, J. (2017). Türkmen Ekolü ve Herat Ekolünün Biçimsel Karşılaştırması. *Uluslararası Sosyal Araştırmalar Dergisi-The Journal of International Social Research* 10(51), 419–432.

Unan, F. (2002). Sahn-ı Seman. In *TDV İslam Ansiklopedisi*, vol. 35 (pp. 532–534). TDV İslâm Araştırmaları Merkezi.

Unat, Y. (2012). Uluğ Bey. In *TDV İslam Ansiklopedisi*, vol. 42 (pp. 127–129). TDV İslâm Araştırmaları Merkezi.

Uslu, R. (2008). er-Risâletü'l-Fethiyye. In *TDV İslam Ansiklopedisi*, vol. 35 (pp. 126–127). TDV İslâm Araştırmaları Merkezi.

Uslu, R. (2021a). Makam Tablosu: Selçuklu Zamanı Anadolu ve Komşu Coğrafyasında Sistemcilerden Yeni Sistemcilere. In M. S. Tokaç, & C. Güray (Eds.), *Anadolu ve Komşu Coğrafyalarda Makam Müziği Atlası* (pp. 71–125). AKM Yayınları.

Wright, O. (1978). *The Modal System of Arab and Persian Music A.D. 1250–1300*. Oxford University Press.

Yavuz, Y. Ş. (2022). Kelâm. In *TDV İslam Ansiklopedisi*, vol. 25 (pp. 196–203). TDV İslâm Araştırmaları Merkezi.

Sensing the Sultan's Power
The Sound of the *Mehter* and other Sensorial Elements in the 1582 Festival[*]

A. Tül Demirbaş

It is impossible to explain and express all strangeness exhibited in this festivity, which is beautiful in every way.
(Peçevî, 1992, p. 65)

Introduction

During their long reign, the Ottoman sultans organized many events to celebrate important occasions. These included ceremonies and processions that were part of the court routine (such as *bayram* and *surre* processions), weddings, circumcision ceremonies, celebrations of military victories, and welcoming processions for diplomats and ambassadors.[1] Among them, considered unrivalled in Ottoman history due to its splendour, wealth, and duration, was the festival organized in 1582 by Sultan Murad III (r. 1574–1595) for his son Prince Mehmed's circumcision ceremony at the ancient Hippodrome (*Atmeydanı*) of Istanbul.

The 1582 festival is also one of the best documented celebrations in early Ottoman history. The identified archival sources include accounts of chroniclers who observed the festival or conveyed it from earlier narratives, odes spruced up with the sultan's embellishments, accounts of European observers and miniatures. With regard to the motivation and function of these sources, it is possible to make a distinction between two basic types of text. The first are the accounts prepared by Ottomans, mostly with the aim of gaining the sultan's favour. The second are the accounts of foreigners, with their main objective to

---

[*] I would like to thank Abdulmennan Mehmet Altıntaş for his help and guidance in reading the Ottoman sources, Joanna Helms for proofreading the chapter's first draft, Matthias Niggli for reading this paper at various stages, his suggestions and his help regarding the German sources, and Cristina Urchueguía for her detailed reading and comments that helped me to explore the subject more deeply.

[1] For a detailed account of various examples of Ottoman festivities, see And, 2020, pp. 21–53.

record or report on the history, traditions, social life, and cultural aspects of the Ottoman Empire as they observed them during their stay. In this regard, a brief overview describing the multinational guests at the festival and the multilingual sources of the case study will be provided in the following.[2]

Among all the Ottoman descriptions, *sûrnâme*s (imperial festival books) are the most thorough. Three festival books, written by Ferâhî, İntizâmî, and Mustafa Âlî, report detailed information about the 1582 festival.[3] They describe the preparation process, invitees, attendees, gifts, banquets and the programme of the shows and performances. Among these accounts, İntizâmî's book has become the primary source for the study of the festival due to its detailed narrative and miniatures that provide a visual depiction of the festival. There are also sources that include the festival as part of a chronological narrative in history books. For example, a description of the circumcision festival is found in the second volume of *Şehinşahnâme* (1592) prepared by Seyyid Lokmân, also illustrated with miniatures. Other sources that focus on the festival are Mustafa Âlî's *Künhü'l-ahbâr* (1598) and another contemporaneous chronicle by Mustafa Selânikî called *Târih-i Selânikî* (1563–1600). The 17th-century writers Mehmed Hemdemi Çelebi Solakzâde and İbrahim Peçevî continued the tradition of making the festival the subject of their narratives, describing by using accounts of their predecessors. In addition to the above-mentioned sources, there are poems and odes depicting the celebrations (such as the so-called *sûriyye* by Derviş Paşa, Nev'î, Ahmed Paşa, Ulvî, Mustafa Âlî and Bâli Çelebi).[4]

Furthermore, written descriptions still exist from foreign travellers, merchants, envoys, and guests. These significantly shaped the image of the sultan and Ottomans outside the Ottoman lands. *Descriptio Ludorum Variorumq[ue] & Spectaculorum* (1582) by George Leb-

---

2   Source criticism and comparisons between these sources are important for understanding the background of the festival. However, to keep this chapter concise, I have not undertaken a detailed or analytical discussion regarding the scope and focus of the various archival sources mentioned here. That can be found in my Ph.D. dissertation (Demirbaş, 2024). See also Kaya Şahin's comprehensive article on the narratives and historical sources dealing with the 1582 festival (2019, pp. 43–67).

3   Transliterated versions of these sources have been published by various scholars. For İntizâmî's *Sûrnâme-i Hümâyûn*, see Arslan, 2009; Procházka-Eisl, 1995; and Boyraz, 1994; for the historical background of this source, see Atasoy, 1997. For Ferâhî's account, see Özdemir, 2016. For Mustafa Âlî's *Câmi'u'l-Buhûr Der-Mecâlis-i Sûr*, see Öztekin, 1996 and Arslan, 2008. Unlike the other *sûrnâme*s, Mustafa Âlî's account does not follow the chronological order of the festival but has a thematic structuring. Although there is no information in his book that he made use of any other sources when writing, he did not describe the festival as an eyewitness. In fact, his detailed account of the events shows his competence in accessing sources (Fleischer, 1986, pp. 106–107; Öztekin, 1996, pp. 11–12). Recently, another *sûrnâme* written by a poet named Kadîmî has been identified by Türkan Alvan (2020). It consists mainly of eulogies and odes to the Sultan; only some parts are related to the festival of 1582.

4   These sources can be found in Toska, 1999, pp. 293–358; Arslan, 2011; Ergun, 1936, p. 321.

elski from the Polish delegation, and the Duke of Anjou's secretary Jean Palerne's *Peregrinations du S. Iean Palerne* (1606) were written as personal testimonies. The report of the representative of the Holy Roman Empire Nicholas von Haunolth, *Particular Verzeichnuss mit was Cerimonien Geprang und Pracht des Fest der Beschneidung des jetzt regierenden Türkischen Keisers Sultan Murath* (1590), is the most detailed Western account of the festival. In addition, a report today in the Modena State Archive, which has been published as a facsimile and translation by Nevin Özkan (2004), and a German text written by an anonymous person in 1582 and published under the title *Fugger Zeitungen* detail the circumcision festival as well. Finally, Reinhold Lubenau, Michel Baudier and Michael Manger are further chroniclers whose narrations are referenced with respect to the 1582 festival.

By examining eye- and ear-witness accounts retrieved from these various sources, this chapter examines the festival's sensorial elements in order to assess the extent they contributed to the overall effect and their purpose. To begin, the historical and political motivation for the festival will be described, taking into consideration the needs of Sultan Murad's politics, both domestic and international. Sultan Murad's personality as a ruler and reflections on his other qualities will also form an integral part of the first section. The next section examines the sensorial aspects of the festival, with a particular focus on sound. In this context, several questions are addressed. For example, which sounds were characteristic of the general atmosphere? What was their role and how did they contribute to the purpose of the festival? In the final section, the role of the *mehter*, the military music band, will be scrutinized and contextualized. First, the historical background of *mehter* music and its connection with the sultan will be addressed. Then, by referring to the aforementioned sources, the importance of their performance as an sonic element of the festival will be analysed.

The Background of the Imperial Festival

Political and Economic Context

In conventional historiography, the first half of the 16th century and the reign of Sultan Süleyman I (r. 1520–1566) is considered the "golden age" of the Ottoman Empire. The oft-repeated assertion that "the Ottoman Empire was at its strongest" at this time is frequently followed by another general assumption proclaiming that "the decline and collapse of the empire" started soon thereafter.[5] The basis of this historical periodization is a

---

5   The periodization of the 19th-century orientalist historians Joseph von Hammer-Purgstall and Mouradgea d'Ohsson are examples of this tendency.

comparison of the Ottoman Empire with its own idealized periods (before and after), as well as with some leading Western states at the time, such as France and Spain. A main argument for the theory of "decline" is the evaluation of Ottoman military successes in the West. From the 14th century onward, the Ottomans created an empire from a small principality, and subsequently expanded their lands. In their period of "decline", the wars were longer than the ones in the 15th century and the Ottomans confronted major powers from the East and West. The war against the Safavids lasted for twelve years (1578–1590), and directly thereafter, the longest war between the Ottomans and the Habsburg Empire took place, the Thirteen Years' War or the Long Hungarian War (1593–1606).

In addition, the thesis of decline assumes a loss of order in many Ottoman institutions, the state, and society. Historians referring to 16th-century sources[6] use this internal Ottoman "degradation" as a further explanation for the empire's subsequent collapse (İnalcık, 2003, pp. 46–57; 1998, pp. 15–28; Lewis, 1962).[7] Furthermore, the rise in the influence of the janissaries with their social and economic empowerment and accompanying revolts have also been discussed. Adding to that, harem women and eunuchs have been among the factors focused on by researchers (Faroqhi, 2012, p. 91).

However, from the 1980s onwards, an "anti-decline" historical narrative began to emerge that refuted this long-standing argument repeated by historians of the Ottoman Empire.[8] Scholars such as Cemal Kafadar, Donald Quataert, Rifaat Ali Abou-El-Haj, and Baki Tezcan have pointed out that some of the factors interpreted as signs of decline are unconvincing. For example, janissaries had taken up commercial activities in addition to their military-administrative duties already in earlier periods (Kafadar, 2019, pp. 29–37; Quataert, 2010, p. 199). And while the Ottomans' military power may have weakened, it was still sufficiently mighty to regain territory lost to the Venetians and Austrians, and to continue to fight the Persians and the Russians (Grant, 1999, pp. 179–201). Furthermore, the sultans' sharing of power could also reflect a period of changing ruling elites, social mobility, and the exchange of wealth. It could even be as early sign of democratization, rather than a sign of "collapse" (Abou-El-Haj, 1991; Tezcan, 2012).

Hence, the 16th century is perhaps the most debated period of the Ottoman Empire. It was a period not static enough to be fixed into a certain mould, but rather, its military,

---

6   The most commonly encountered sources are letters of advice (*nasihatnâme*), which became widespread in this period, written to the sultans, aiming to guide and give advice by sharing what was observed in the social, and religious spheres.

7   The Ottoman bureaucrat and chronicler Mustafa Âlî, as one example, associated political failure with the deterioration of high culture and the bureaucratic structure (Fleischer, 1986, pp. 214–231).

8   Dana Sajdi examines the historical background of this theory in detail and provides the academic literature on the subject, together with the counter-arguments that have been offered (2007, pp. 1–40). For another important and comprehensive study dealing with this issue, see Kafadar, 1997–1998, pp. 30–75.

cultural, and social changes were quite fluid. Furthermore, economic concerns that had already taken hold in the middle of the century increased during the reign of Murad III. A problem was rapid population growth in the villages and cities. Relative to this new population, there was insufficient grain production in many parts of Ottoman lands, one reason for the decrease in the rural population that can be seen at the end of the century (Faroqhi, 2016, pp. 466–471; Barkan, 1957, pp. 23–26; Fleet, 2016, p. 49).[9]

A phase of high inflation was the result of this unbalanced economic situation. In his comprehensive history *Künhü'l-ahbâr* (1598) Mustafa Âlî links the decline in the prestige of the dynasty and the weakening of state authority to the fall in the value of money during the reign of Murad III and the accompanying economic problems. The reduction of the silver content in coins by state officials led to a devaluation of the currency, which was followed by a cut in salaries at the new official exchange rate set by the sultan. The economic crisis eventually led to the janissary revolts of 1589, known as Beylerbeyi incident[10] (Fleischer, 1986, p. 297).

The Perception of a Sultan: Murad III

The sultan was rarely seen outside or even inside the palace. This practice was a part of the dynastic law instated during the reign of Mehmed II to regulate the ceremonial rules of the Ottoman court. According to these regulations, it was acceptable for the sultan to hide from the public to protect his greatness from the eyes of the people. Mustafa Âlî also states that according to this law, the sultan avoided visiting fortifications or meeting the people (Öztekin, 1996, p. 62).

Although it had been quite common in Ottoman history for the sultan to distance himself from his subjects, this behaviour was exacerbated in the case of Sultan Murad. He was particularly reluctant to appear in public. During his reign, from his accession to the throne until his death, Murad lived a very secluded life. Furthermore, he did not personally join his troops on the battlefield. He ruled the conflicts and the empire from the palace, charging his viziers to lead the armies (Çelebi, 2008, p. 311; Peksevgen, 2009, p. 401). This situation led to criticism and gossip about his power, and Ottoman chroniclers of the period particularly stressed this issue in their books. The sultan's avoidance of the battlefield, "unlike his predecessors", was a reason for disappointment about him. He was thought to be an inert and weak ruler, not a powerful sultan. Mustafa Âlî describes the "mass corruption" that began with Murad's accession to the throne and attributes it not only to economic problems, but also to the sultan's incompetence as a ruler (Fleischer,

---

9   On these food shortages in an Italian source, see Dursteler, 2018, p. 53.
10 This incident is considered to be the beginning or the first example of the janissary revolts, called the *Istanbul rebellions*.

1986, pp. 300–301). He argues that the sultan's neglect of state affairs and his failure to manage them wisely was the cause of the "decline".

German theologian Salomon Schweigger, in his travel book on Istanbul in the late 1570s, writes that the alleged reason for the sultan's reclusion was related to his epilepsy. Schweigger also states that the sultan's sexual power was affected by the disease, suggesting that he was not fond of sexuality "like the sultans before him" (1995, p. 144). It was expected of the sultan that he be "the shadow of God", the caliph of the Muslims, and the ruler of the empire. Accordingly, the sultan's health – mentally and physically – was an important parameter in assessing his power. Added to this was his sexual performance and competence. Sultan Murad's masculinity was a common topic, as can be seen not only in the example of Schweigger, but also in texts by other chroniclers mentioned below.

İbrahim Peçevî also refers to this matter in his chronicle (1641). According to him, it became a problem that for a long time the sultan was only with the mother of his son, Safiye Sultan, and then became impotent in his relations with other women, even if he wanted to have them. The sultan's mother, Nurbanu Sultan, believed that this situation had been triggered by "black magic" and that Murad's sexual appetite would be restored after the spell was broken by her efforts (1992, pp. 2–3).[11] However, narratives from later years continue to discuss his negative characteristics. Hans Jacob Breuning, who visited Istanbul in 1579, described Murad in his travelogue as a "sickly looking" man, and stated that even though he had to be careful because of his "fainting disease", he could not restrain his sexual activity (Breuning, 2012, p. 101). Another source, written by a Venetian diplomat, confirms the rumour about his epilepsy. In 1590, Lorenzo Bernardo's *relazione* (report) to Doge Pasquale Cicogna and the Venetian Senate gives information about the sultan's character, sexual life, and daily lifestyle, and states that he suffered from epilepsy and sometimes from earaches. It also states that the sultan was not a courageous man (Dursteler, 2018, pp. 59–60). In fact, he was lacking qualities such as bravery and generosity that make a "true prince" respectable.

Joseph v. Hammer-Purgstall does not mention this epilepsy problem in his extensive writings, but he, too, includes the sultan's abilities and characteristics, calling him "weak and delusional" (1840, p. 591). This perception of Sultan Murad by the people at the time as a rather weak and sick ruler is something that should be emphasized. Various sources suggest that the sultan had a neurotic personality. In his report, Bernardo described him as someone who could not be trusted (Dursteler, 2018, p. 60). Özgen Felek provides an analysis and psychogram of Sultan Murad based on his talismanic shirts and the dream letters he sent to his spiritual master. We learn from these letters that Murad described the sultanate

---

11   According to İbrahim Peçevî's account, Nurbanu Sultan believed that Murad had been bewitched by Safiye Sultan and her supporters, and the concubines who were close to Safiye were tortured to detect the spell. Nurbanu Sultan also presented new beautiful women to Murad to break the spell.

Sensing the Sultan's Power

and worldly duties as "an unbearable burden".[12] He suffered from anxiety and restlessness, as well as from the fact that he was not entirely mentally stable. These letters are a written expression of his fears, concerns, and disturbances (Felek, 2017, pp. 659–662).[13]

From these narratives discussing his poor health, short temper, and his tendency to make wrong decisions because of his many fears, we see that not only courtiers and Ottoman writers were aware of the sultan's weaknesses, but also foreigners. Under these circumstances, a grand and public celebration was an obvious means to prove the sultan's power, called into question by the aforementioned health problems, rumours about his manhood and masculinity,[14] and his refusal to run military campaigns. Thus, Sultan Murad ordered a splendid *sûr-ı hümâyun* (imperial festival) for the occasion of his son's circumcision ceremony, with celebrations that lasted over fifty days. These celebrations presented a powerful and sensorial festival to representatives from the various parts of the Ottoman lands, invited rulers and ambassadors, as well as the inhabitants of the city of Istanbul itself. The festival became the subject of many written accounts at the time as well as in later periods.

Creating a Powerful and Sensorial Stage

The preparations for the festival started one year in advance and began by examining records of the two circumcision celebrations held during the reign of Süleyman I. The sultan appointed his most trusted statesmen to organize and implement the festival. Invitation letters were sent with special envoys to government officials, administrators, and bureaucrats in Rumelia and Anatolia, all foreign heads of state of the period, as well as other rulers (Arslan, 2009, pp. 119–120; Haunolth, 1590, pp. 468–469).

Festivals are spatial and temporal events. The choice of venue – large squares, interiors of palaces or mansions, streets, on or near water, gardens – creates sensorial and emotional experiences shaped by temporality as well as by the spatiality itself. This important role of the spatial dimension of a festival was particularly the case for the 1582 circumcision festival. The celebrations took place in one of the most important social and political squares

---

12   In these letters, he also expressed his disapproval of being the sultan and complained about the burdensome nature of this task (Felek, 2012, pp. 35–36).

13   Felek notes the interest of many Ottoman sultans in "miracles" and gives information about the special preparation of such talismanic shirts for protection, strength, and encouragement. She also examines the function of such shirts in the case of Sultan Murad, considering the possibility that they served as a means of encouragement for him to go to the battlefield or as protection from his epilepsy, as mentioned above.

14   An important contribution on this matter is Felek's study on gender codes, which analyses the sources describing the 1582 festival (2019, pp. 141–170).

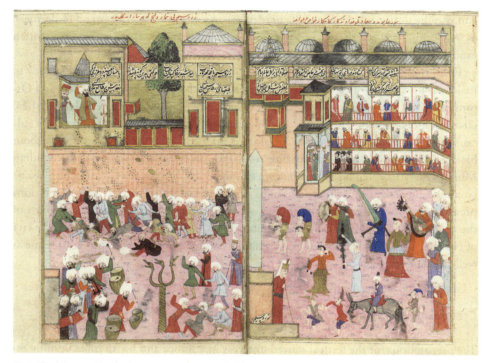

Fig. 1: The Sultan's golden scattering moment and the *mehter* at the 1582 festival.

of Istanbul from Byzantium times to the present day, the Hippodrome. In the 16th century, the Hippodrome was in the focus of attention of the city's visitors, and it featured in their narratives. At that time, this largest square of the city was used for "gaming" (sports, archery, wrestling) and was also the site of an open marketplace (Aktaş, 1996, p. 79; And, 2015, p. 55).[15]

The preparations for the 1582 festival area were extensive and differed from those for earlier festivals. Although in earlier festivities, architectural structures had been set up and advance arrangements were made, the scale of the measures undertaken for the 1582 festival were unrivalled: entire pavilions and galleries were constructed to host the guests of the festival, and even an amphitheatre was built (Stout, 1966, p. 55). The officials added an *exhedra* to the side of the İbrahim Pasha Palace facing the square to create a special vantage point for the sultan. A space for the prince and the women of the imperial harem was located near the sultan's pavilion. Thus, the sultan reinforced his power by placing himself

---

15   I would like to thank Şehsuvar Aktaş for sharing his dissertation with me.

and his family in a higher position in the festival area, isolated from the public. Ottoman and Christian dignitaries watched the festival from the three-story wooden lodge built next to the İbrahim Pasha Palace (see Fig. 1), from tents on the other side of the square (Selânikî, 1999, pp. 164–165; Stout, 1966, p. 59).

During the festival, tables were set up and covered with different dishes. A special protocol was followed by all the foreign guests, as well as the aghas, soldiers, hafiz, and courtiers attending the banquet. In addition, a huge feast was prepared for the common people, and gold and silver coins were scattered on trays (Öztekin, 1996, pp. 64–65, 254–256; Özdemir, 2016, pp. 172–173; Arslan, 2009, pp. 158–159, 327–328). The sultan also showed his benevolence by pardoning all prisoners and freeing them (Öztekin, 1996, pp. 260–262; Arslan, 2009, pp. 299–300). More than 10,000 people were circumcised at the festival, including the sons of state notables, the pages (*iç oğlanı*) of the palace, and poor children from the city. After the orphans were circumcised, the sultan gave them new, beautiful clothes and money (Arslan, 2009, pp. 472–475).[16] All of this reflected the sultan's ability to take care of his subjects and confirmed his superiority (Yelçe, 2021, p. 160; Karateke, 2005, p. 47). In addition to the celebrations held in Istanbul, the sultan ordered the organization of simultaneous celebrations in other cities in the Ottoman lands as befitted the power of the dynasty (BOA, A. {DVNSMHM.d.42/164-165).

The Hippodrome was the most important place in the city and thus it was the stage for a wide variety of performances. The impressive festivities described above relate nicely to the statement of Andrew J. Rotter that an "empire was many things" opening his work on the sensory history of the British in India and the United States in the Philippines. After briefly counting these "many things", he closes the paragraph by pointing out that "they were also in significant ways mediated by the senses, by perceptions of others formed through seeing, hearing, touching, smelling, and tasting" (Rotter, 2019, p. 1). The imperial festival of 1582 also contained these various sensorial elements. By stimulating the senses of smell, taste and touch, as well as the visual and auditory senses, it allowed all participants to experience the festive atmosphere.

While the celebration area was reshaped for this festival, other related architectural arrangements were made in the rest of the city. Sources state that the bay windows of certain buildings in narrow streets were demolished so that the gigantic *nahıls* could be moved to the square. These tree-shaped ornamental structures made of wax and decorated with precious stones and gold were a sign of power and wealth. In 1582, their size and abundance made them much more impressive than at earlier festivals (And, 2020, pp. 272–296; Nutku, 1981, pp. 24–28). Flower bouquets and three-dimensional garden models added

---

16 Hammer-Purgstall writes that many Christians from Greek, Albanian, and other nationalities converted to Islam and were also circumcised during the festival (1840, p. 520). For this information from eyewitnesses, see Palerne, 1991, p. 296, and Arslan, 2009, p. 401.

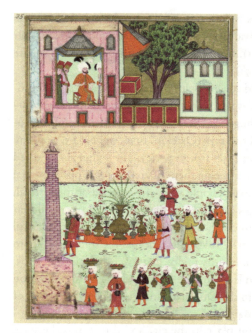

Fig. 2: Parade of spice-sellers at the 1582 festival.

visual and olfactory richness to the festival. In addition to the these, İntizâmî states that with the arrival of spice sellers, the fragrant scents of the festival site turned it into a garden of paradise (Arslan, 2009, p. 476) (see Fig. 2).

Another sensory dimension of the festival was lighting. Thousands of lanterns were hung on a large ring placed at the top of a pole erected in the middle of the square. They illuminated the entire square at night. Every night during the festival, not only was the square illuminated with torches, oil lamps, and lanterns, but also its surroundings and the city (Uran, 1942, p. 22; Öztekin, 1996, pp. 56–57). As described by Kadîmî, the lights on festival nights almost prevented the stars from appearing in the sky (Alvan, 2020, p. 65).[17]

Fireworks displays were another aspect of this sparkling environment. Their brightness, the sound they made in the night, and their splendid design made the celebrations very imposing and had a significant impact on the viewers. Such pyrotechnic explosions stimulated various senses: the auditory and visual but also the olfactory.

Finally, according to our current knowledge as provided by primary sources, the 1582 festival is the earliest example of an Ottoman artisan parade (Faroqhi, 2005, pp. 3, 19). The parade lasted twenty days and saw the passage of more than a hundred and fifty groups.[18] With their participation in the festivities, in the words of Stefano Yerasimos, "Atmeydanı became the essence of the vast empire" (2002, p. 36). They displayed their skills and amazed the audience with their massive moving wheeled workplaces (Bostanzâde, 2016, p. 78). They also represented the technological capacity of the Ottoman Empire, whose demonstration was an important part of political propaganda.

Sound – not only music, but all kinds of sounds, that appealed to hearing in each of its parameters (Smith, 2007, pp. 41–42) – had a great effect on the sensory experience in this atmosphere that spread throughout the city. The moving wheeled workplaces of the arti-

---

17   "Gice seyrinde şu deŋlü yandı mūm / Şu'lesinden gökde görünmez nücūm." All translations provided here and throughout this chapter are my own.
18   For an extensive study on Istanbul guilds, see Yi, 2004.

san guilds, shows with animals, war depictions, the prayers of imams, muezzins, religious groups in the parade, and of course the sound of the audience – applause, shouts, cheers, whispers, with all associated feelings, whether admiration, devotion, excitement, or fear – contributed to creating the sound of the festival. Among all these things, a particularly important sensorial experience came from the *mehter*, with its strong and direct connection to the sultan representing his power itself.

The Sultan's Music: The *Mehter*

The *mehter*, the military marching band, occupies a challenging place in Ottoman music history. Even though it was once regarded with interest and curiosity by Europeans[19] and has always been associated with the Ottoman Empire, knowledge about the music and performance of the *mehter* is relatively limited.[20] There is no exact information about the establishment of the *Mehterhâne* ("house of *mehter*"), a part of the Ottoman palace organization. The term is first encountered in texts from the 16th century. Historically, the name was also used to designate high-ranking servants and various classes of officials, with musicians forming only one part of this organization. Here, however, we focus only on the military music ensemble.

The *Mehterhâne* organization was divided into two sub-groups. The official ones – *mehterân-ı tabl ü alem-i hâssa* – were part of the *kapıkulu* system and in the service of the palace. These were professional musicians on state salaries, with their number varying in the 16th century from between two and three hundred. In addition to the official *mehter*, there were other *mehter* groups under the patronage of various people (such as the grand vizier, viziers, beylerbeys, janissary agha, etc.). These groups varied in number according to their sponsors' duties and ranks. Unofficial groups were called "artisan *mehters*" (*esnaf mehterleri*); their purpose was to supply public entertainment in the city.[21]

The official *mehter* carried the *tuğ*, the insignia of the sultan and sovereign, and accordingly, they represented the sovereignty and the dynasty. They had various functions, duties,

---

19 The word is translated from the Persian word *mihter*, meaning "the greatest". Walter Feldman (2012) expands this translation to "the greatest orchestra". It came to be known as "Janissary music" as a result of Christian Europeans experiencing janissary troops and their music during the wars (Jäger, 1996).

20 Today, the *mehter* is still used for important historical anniversaries, as well as folkloric and touristic events. However, most of the music they performed today was composed in the 20th century. Our knowledge about earlier *mehter* music is based on accounts of European observers. For selected research on this subject, see Haug, 2019; Wright, 2000; Tura, 2001.

21 Detailed information on *mehter* organization can be found in Sanal, 1964; Sanlıkol, 2011; Vural, 2012; Öztürk, 2019.

and uses. Their function in wars was of the utmost priority and going to the battlefield with the sultan or his appointee was meant both to encourage the army and to intimidate the enemy. The inseparability of the *mehter* and the sultan was visible in their performing at his accession ceremony and accompanying him on official trips. They played on victory celebrations, feasts, holidays, court festivals and, in addition, they performed communication and announcement functions. After the conquest of Constantinople, Mehmet II ordered the *nevbet*[22] to be played after prayers three times a day in Istanbul (Popescu-Judetz, 2007, pp. 63, 67–69). This indicates that the *mehter* not only represented military power, but also the religious and spiritual authority of the sultan, the caliph of Islam.[23]

Another example of the *mehter*'s display of might were ambassadorial processions. In 1591, a marching music band welcomed Friedrich von Kreckwitz and his entourage, who had been sent to Istanbul by Rudolf II to assume the embassy of the Holy Roman Empire. The performance was intended to be imposing and impressive, and yet the European witnesses experienced it slightly differently.[24] The pharmacist Friedrich Seidel, who was part of the delegation, described the music of the band accompanying them to their residence as noisy and unpleasant to the ear.[25] What is noteworthy here is that Seidel referred to the ensemble as "des Sultans Hoff Musica" (the sultan's court music) (1711, pp. 35–37). The validity of this nomenclature for the military music group will be examined below in the context of the 1582 festival.

Mehter Instruments: Masculine and Powerful

Records of the earliest examples of Turkish military music date back long before the term *mehter* was used. The *davul* or *tabl* (drum) and *kös* (large kettle drum), the most important instruments in the ceremony called *nevbet*, are mentioned in early texts together with the *tuğ*, the symbol of sovereignty. The *davul* is particularly significant here; historically, it was symbolically associated with the ruler (*Hakan*). Additionally, the *zurna* (shrill pipe) and the *boru* (or sometimes *nefir*) (a fretless brass instrument, similar to trumpet) were among

---

22 The word *nevbet* (or *nöbet*) is generally used in the meaning of "music performed by the *mehter* beating drums in front of the ruler".

23 Eugenia Popescu-Judetz describes the *mehter* as having been the voice of terror for non-Muslim communities (2007, p. 57).

24 An article by Edmund A. Bowles describes what Europeans who visited and observed the Ottoman lands wrote about the *mehter* and their instruments, as well as the impact of the music that reached Europe through wars and diplomatic visits (2006). For more on this topic, see also the chapters in this volume by Gamze İlaslan Koç on ambassadorial entrance ceremonies between the Ottomans and Habsburgs, and by Judith I. Haug on the 17th-century Europeans who wrote about Ottoman music.

25 "[…] dass einer sein eigen Wort nicht hören können / und für den übelklingenden Thon und Gethöne / die Ohren zustopfen müssen."

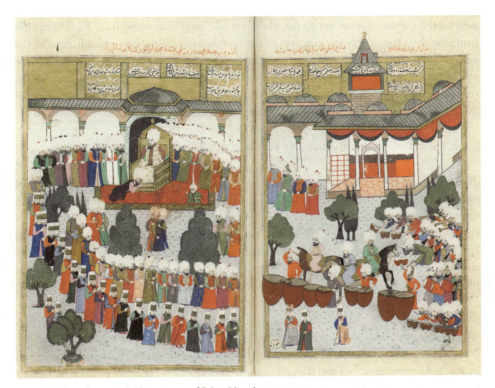

Fig. 3: *Mehter* performance in the presence of Sultan Murad.

the principal instruments. Other *mehter* percussion instruments were the *nakkâre* (small kettle drum), *zil* (cymbal), and *çevgân* (a crescent-shaped instrument with a long handle and rattles, bells or chains attached to it) (see Fig. 3).

In his book *Mevâidü'n-nefâis fî kavâidi'l-mecâlis* (1587), Mustafa Âlî describes various instruments according to their functions and effects, and categorizes them as "male" or "female" based on their use and performers (1978, pp. 84–85). Noteworthy are his descriptions of the instruments and the gender he ascribes to them. The music genre and its performers, who are identified with the ruler, are also arranged in a hierarchical order. He calls the *zurna* "the sultan of instruments", and the *nefir, nakkare, zinç [sanc]* and *nakrava*[26] the "sovereign's [*zurna*] high officials" (*hükümdarın erkânı*). When the *zurna* plays, the *davul* and all other instruments follow it; the effect of all other instruments disappears

---

26 A *nefir* is a wind instrument made of horn. The *nakkâre* are a pair of small drums made by stretching leather over a half-spherical copper body. The *zinc* or *sanc*, also sometimes referred to as *zil*, is a percussion instrument; it can be translated as cymbals. *Nakrava* may be another spelling of the percussion instrument known as *nağara*.

next to the *zurna*s. According to Âlî, these are all "male" instruments. Âlî's description confirms the Ottoman interpretation of the *mehter* as the sonorous embodiment of the sultan. They were inseparable from the sultanate, not only in sound but also visually due to their emblems. When the *mehter* players stood still, their playing position was in the shape of a crescent moon, the symbol of Islam and the Ottoman Empire. At the centre of this crescent were the drummers, with the others stationed behind and to the side of them.

Sonic Representation of the Sultan's Power at the 1582 Festival

To analyse the sensory atmosphere of a festival that took place over 440 years ago, one must focus on how the sources described it, "how it ma[de] full use of sensory imagery to create its effects" (Toner, 2014, p. 2). It is not surprising that the *mehter*, the symbol of the sovereign, played an important role in the sonic representation of power at the 1582 festival. We find information about the *mehter* primarily in documents regarding the festival expenses. In one such account, it is noted that 1,600 *akçe* were paid to the *mehter* for playing the *nevbet*. The same account also mentions the cost of 13 silver *tablbaz* (drums) (TSMA d.09715).

At the 1582 festival, the celebrations started with the entrance of the sultan to the festival area. The *mehter* was crucial for the grandiosity of the sultan's sonorous entrance (Özdemir, 2016, pp. 164–165). The sultan entered the Hippodrome on horseback, lavishly dressed and bejewelled, carrying swords and daggers, and, according to the narrative of Palerne, accompanied by musicians so that "the earth and sky resound with the noise they made" (Palerne, 1991, p. 283).[27] The grandees welcomed and escorted him to his lodge on foot as a part of the ritual and hierarchical order (Yelçe, 2014, p. 82). Before this entrance, a procession was held for the sultan's arrival from the imperial palace to the Hippodrome (see Fig. 4). It was an unusual situation for people to see the sultan, and for this reason, the sultan's procession moved among people filling the roads and shouting "Long live the sultan". In the words of İntizâmî, they "made the heavens ring with their applause". The sultan was also greeted with loud prayers (Arslan, 2009, p. 125). Palerne similarly described the euphoric atmosphere created by the sultan's arrival. People celebrated this exceptional moment by clapping their hands as a sign of endless blessings and joy (1991, p. 283). A similar ceremonial procession was organized for the prince to be circumcised. From the Old Palace[28] to the festival place, Prince Mehmed, dressed in clothes adorned with precious stones and

---

27   "[…] à l'arrivée desquels commencèrent incontinent à jouer les instruments avec tel bruit, que l'air & la terre en retentissoyent." I am grateful to Kate van Orden for her generous support in accessing this French source and my colleague Luc Vallat for his help in reading it.

28   After the conquest of Constantinople, Mehmed II built a palace in the Beyazıt district of today's Istanbul. This first palace subsequently became known as the Old Palace (*Eski Saray*).

carrying a sword and dagger adorned with jewels on his waist, radiated magnificence along the way, accompanied by the dignitaries of the state (Uran, 1942, pp. 24–25). Gigantic *nahıl*s accompanied this entrance (Fig. 5). The poet Nev'î wrote that the prince looked like a *nahıl,* resembling "a work of art created by God".[29] In addition, Âlî noted that while the prince was riding around the city on his horse like a moving sun, the *mehter* accompanied him thunderously and with harmonious sound.[30]

The processions of the sultan and the prince were considered noteworthy by both Ottoman and Western observers. In contrast, there is no mention of the *mehter* during the arrival of the sultanas (the sultan's female relatives). Their entrance is described as accompanied with many impressive forms made of sugar, along with performances of battles and a show by acrobats, but there is no mention of any military music. In an article analysing the 1582 festival as a display of manhood and masculinity, Felek draws attention to the public space being dominated by men (2019, p. 161). The circumcision celebrations were a stage for men, from the shows that were organized, to the spectators, to the miniatures depicting mostly male figures, to the narrators who recorded the event in history. In this respect, even if it is possible to question the presence of the *mehter* with sultanas, it is difficult to know whether this information would have been included in written or visual sources.

Fig. 4: The procession of the sultan at the 1582 festival.

There is an important connection between the loudness of the sound and the performance space. Various examples show that if a sonic element is so loud that it can be heard at a long distance, it is a symbol of power and political authority.[31] Comparing the ac-

---

29 "Gûyâ içinde hazret-i şehzâde bunların / Bir nahl idi ki yapmış onu sun'ı-girdigâr" (Olgun, 1937, p. 35). For the manuscript, see MFA D.342, fol. 110r.

30 "Yetişdi velvele-i kûs ü bang-ı tabl u nefîr / Şimâḫ-ı zümre-i kerrûba eyledi te'şîr / Bu zemzemeyle bu ġavġâyile o şâh-i cihân / Sitanbul içre güneş gibi eyledi seyrân" (Arslan, 2008, p. 402). For this reference in the manuscript, see Topkapı Palace Museum Archive (hereafter TSMA) B. 203, fols. 22v., 23r.

31 As an example of this, see also Corbin (1998), where bells are analysed as a symbol of sonic power in the French countryside.

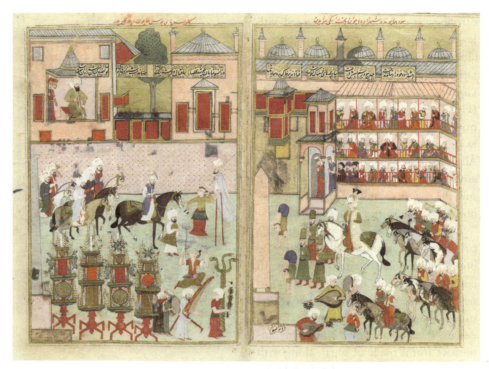

Fig. 5: The arrival of the prince at the 1582 festival. *Mehter* musicians on horses (right folio) and *nahıls* (left folio).

counts of observers, even from different cultural backgrounds and having different motivations, reveals that the *mehter* was a dominant element shaping the sonic atmosphere of the 1582 festival. Baudier described the arrival of the prince and the sultan, and the sonic intensity as follows:

> They were receiued with a double harmony: The first consisted of Hoboyes, Fifes, Drums, and Trumpets, with such a noyse as the Ayre and Earth ecchoed againe: The second, the acclamations of the people, who cried with a loud voice, Liue *Sultan Amurath*, and liue *Sultan Mahomet* his Sonne (1635, pp. 77–78).

As in Seidel's "Des Sultans Hoff Musica" example, in the sources this musical group is often associated with the sultan. In his account, İntizâmî used various literary names to characterize the greatness of the *mehter*. In different copies of his *Sûrnâme-i Hümâyûn*, it appears as *debdebe-i kûs-ı satveti tâs-ı asuman* ("splendour of irresistible power['s] drum") (Procházka-Eisl, 1995, p. 81; Arslan, 2009, p. 176).

Sensing the Sultan's Power

The *mehter* performed for all strata of society as an open-air music ensemble. Lubenau referred to the *mehter* as "Keisers musica" and noted that the band remained active even when they were not accompanying the sultan and his son. According to his narrative, they played all day long in a configuration of four big drums and eight small ones, along with ten trumpeters, of whom five played continuously, while the others alternated (1995, p. 55).

The musical band was in charge of informing the audience and gathered guests about the various phases of the festival. Mustafa Âlî explained that the community was made aware of the festival start by the announcement of the *kös* and *zurna*, and that they complimented the sound they heard. According to him, this music was "a gift that can touch the souls of the people" (Öztekin, 1996, p. 194).[32] *Tabl u nakâre-i şehen-şâh* ("Shahenshah's *tabl* and *nakâre*"), as İntizâmî calls it in another passage, also announced the scramble for food (*çanak yağması*).[33] Palerne and the aforementioned Italian report also note that the serving of food was announced with drums and trumpets (Palerne, 1991, p. 284; Özkan, 2004, p. 50).[34]

The last example of the "roaring" sound of the *mehter*[35] at the 1582 festival is the actual circumcision of Prince Mehmed, which took place on the 21st day of the celebrations. According to the sources examined for this study, this is the first example of the *mehter* taking part in the spectacle or performance taking place at night. The Italian report states that on the evening of the prince's circumcision, there was a great clamour, with countless fireworks, drums, trumpets and similar musical instruments, and that this continued all night long (Özkan, 2004, p. 54). Haunolth also noted that the great joy of the circumcision ceremony was celebrated with drums and pipes (*pfeiffen*), and many fireworks were set off on the same night to honour the occasion (1590, p. 510).

Conclusion

The imperial circumcision festival of 1582 was the longest, costliest, and most widely attended court celebration in the history of the Ottoman dynasty. It has been described as a "festival of the greatest". Circumcision was an important threshold in the life not only of a sultan's son, but of all men of the Islamic religion. One aspect contributing to a circumcision festival's particular importance was that it ensured the historical and cultural conti-

---

32   "Şūrnalar çalındı sūr-āsā / Oldı ol tuḥfe ḥalḳa rūh-efzā" (TSMA, B. 203, fol. 59v.).

33   This appears the same way in different copies of the book. For the Topkapı and Süleymaniye copies, see Arslan, pp. 192, 558 and Boyraz, 1994, p. 175; for the Vienna copy, see Procházka-Eisl, 1995, p. 115.

34   This report was also published in English; it is held in the records of the British State Archives (Butler, 1909, p. 178).

35   The expression "roaring" ("eine dröhnende Musik") is taken from the *Fugger Zeitungen* (Klarwill, 1923, p. 62).

nuity of a ritual which had been practiced and accepted since the distant past. As such, this ritual served the purpose of showing attachment to the glorious Ottoman heritage. This intent can also be observed in a sentence in the letter written on behalf of the sultan to the *defterdar* (provincial treasurer) of Damascus that "the celebrations that have been accepted since ancient times will be held as before" (BOA, A. {DVNSMHM.D.42/904). Moreover, let us emphasise again that this festival was organized during an economically and socially turbulent period. Accordingly, it was more than just a recurring ritual. The ritual together with the related celebration was a propaganda tool, a stage for a power show.

The festival was remarkable not only in its lavishness, but also in its purpose of symbolizing the sovereign's greatness. The extravagant celebrations were organized at a time that is not considered a strong or great period for the Ottoman empire, and by a sultan whose qualities as a ruler – who was supposed to be a strong, masculine, reliable, and powerful warrior – were questioned. Against this background, the festival had a broader meaning than a simple circumcision ceremony. It was the staging of the power and authority of Sultan Murad III. The preparation process, the festival programme from the beginning to end, the celebration site (the "stage"), the hierarchical order during the rituals, the banquets, guests, gifts, and the demonstrations all contributed to this large-scale show. Most importantly – and in conjunction with the above – it presented a diverse sensorial experience to the attendees.

Given the sultan's questioned character, it is interesting to see the various sensorial elements representing strength and masculinity at the festival of 1582. Although an accurate reproduction of a first-person experience of sound is not possible, we can nonetheless imagine the emotions and sensual experience evoked by the festival by reading how various eye-witnesses – Ottoman and foreigners alike – described it. There were many elements involved in the sensory atmosphere: lights covering the area, fragrant smells, the gigantic *nahıl*s symbolizing fertility and masculinity, generously distributed food, colourful clothing, musical, theatrical, and acrobatic performances, shows with exotic animals, massive decorations and structures, and finally, various kinds of mostly loud – what some would call "noisy" – sound. As this chapter has shown, sound, especially the sound of the *mehter*, played a crucial role in the 1582 festival in its sensory reception and the formation of emotions. *Mehterân* and their impressive performances have been associated with the ruler since the beginning of the Ottoman history. Sources emphasise the role of the *mehter* in creating the enthusiastic atmosphere during the 1582 festival, especially during the procession of the sultan and prince and their entrance into the historic Hippodrome. As the sultan's representative voice, the *mehter*'s loud and roaring presence can be understood as an extraordinarily important element to counteract the sultan's questioned governance and leadership abilities by people at the time.

Bibliography

Manuscripts

[İntizâmî] (1588). *Sûrnâme-i Hümâyûn*. Topkapı Palace Museum Archive, Istanbul. Hazine No. 1344.

BOA, A. {DVNSMHM.d.42/164-165. Judgment dated 1 Cemaziyelevvel 989/3 June 1581. Republic of Turkey Presidential State Archives – Ottoman Archives, Istanbul.

BOA, A. {DVNSMHM.D.42/904. Republic of Turkey Presidential State Archives – Ottoman Archives, Istanbul.

Mustafa Âlî (1585–1586). *Câmi'u'l-Buhûr Der-Mecâlis-i Sûr.* Topkapı Palace Museum Archive, Istanbul. Bağdat No. 203.

Nev'î (n.d.) *Nev'î Divânı*. National Library, Ankara. Microfilm Archive. MFA D.342.

Seyyid Lokman (1597). *Şehinşahnâme-i Murâd-ı Sâlis*, vol. 2. Topkapı Palace Museum Archive, Istanbul. Bağdat No. 200.

TSMA, d.09715. [Expenditures of the festival]. Topkapı Palace Museum Archive, Istanbul.

Printed Sources and Source Editions

Arslan, M. (2011). *Osmanlı Saray Düğünleri ve Şenlikleri – 8: Sûriyye Kasideleri ve Târihleri.* Sarayburnu Kitaplığı.

Arslan, M. (2009). *Osmanlı Saray Düğünleri ve Şenlikleri – 2: İntizâmî Sûrnâmesi (Sûrnâme-i Hümâyûn.* Sarayburnu Kitaplığı.

Arslan, M. (2008). *Osmanlı Saray Düğünleri ve Şenlikleri – 1: Manzûm Sûrnâmele*r, Sarayburnu Kitaplığı.

Baudier, M. (1635). *The history of the imperiall estate of the grand seigneurs their habitations, liues, titles … gouernment and tyranny.* transl. by E. Grimeston. https://www.proquest.com/books/history-imperiall-estate-grand-seigneurs-their/docview/2240941776/se-2. Date of Access: 25.01.2024.

Bostanzâde Yahya (2016). *Duru Tarih. Târih-i Sâf / Tuhfetü'l-Ahbab*, ed. by N. Sakaoğlu. Alfa.

Boyraz, Ş. (1994). *Surnâme-i Hümâyun'da Folklorik Unsurlar* [Master's thesis, Erciyes University].

Breuning, H. J. (2012). *Reise in den Orient*. Edition Winterwork.

Butler, A. J. (Ed.) (1909). Elizabeth: July 1582, 21–25. *Calendar of State Papers Foreign: Elizabeth*, vol. 16, *May–December 1582* (pp. 170–188), His Majesty's Stationery Office. https://www.british-history.ac.uk/cal-state-papers/foreign/vol16/pp170-188. Date of Access: 25.01.2024.

Dursteler, E. R. (2018). *In the Sultan's Realm: Two Venetian Ambassadorial Reports on the Early Modern Ottoman Empire*. CRRS.

Evliyâ Çelebi (2008). *Günümüz Türkçesiyle Evliyâ Çelebi Seyahatnâmesi: İstanbul*. Book 1, vol. 1, ed. by S. A. Kahraman & Y. Dağlı. YKY.

Hammer-Purgstall, J. von. (1840). *Geschichte des Osmanischen Reiches*, vol. 2. https://menadoc.bibliothek.uni-halle.de/ssg/content/titleinfo/1273161. Date of Access: 25.01.2024.

Haunolth, N. (1590). Particular Verzeichnuß / mit was Cerimonien / Gepräng unnd Pracht das Fest der Beschneidung deß jetzt regierenden Türckischen Keysers Sultan Murath / diß Namens deß dritten / u. Sohns/Sultan Mehemet gennant / welches vom andern Junii biß auff den 12. Julii deß 1582. Jahrs gewehret unnd continuiert hat / zu Constantinopel celebriert und gehalten worden. In J. Lewenklaw (Ed.), *Neuwe Chronica Türckischer Nation* (pp. 468–514). https://daten.digitale-sammlungen.de/0002/bsb00029261/images/index.html?id=00029261&groesser=&fip=xdsydeayaewqwwxdsydsdassdaseayaxdsydeaya&no=17&seite=482. Date of Access: 25.01.2024.

Klarwill, V. (Ed.) (1923). *Fugger-Zeitungen: ungeruckte Briefe an das Haus Fugger aus dem Jahren 1568–1605*. Rikola.

Lubenau, R. (1995). *Beschreibung der Reisen des Reinhold Lubenau*, vol. 2, ed. by W. Sahm. Institut für Geschichte der Arabisch-Islamischen Wissenschaften.

Mustafa Âlî (1978). *Görgü ve Toplum Kuralları Üzerinde Ziyâfet Sofraları (Mevâidü'n-nefâis fî kavâidi'l mecâlis)*, ed. by O. Ş. Gökyay. Tercüman.

Olgun, T. (1937). *Şâir Nev'î ve Sûriye Kasîdesi*. Aydınlık Basımevi.

Özdemir, M. (2016). *Ferâhî. Sûrnâme. Bir Özge Âlem. Osmanlı Pâyitahtında 1582 Şenliği*. Grafiker.

Öztekin, A. (1996). *Gelibolulu Mustafa 'Âlî. Câmi'u'l-Buhûr Der-Mecâlis-i Sûr*. Türk Tarih Kurumu.

Palerne, J. (1991). *D'Alexandrie à Istanbul. Pérégrinations dans l'Empire Ottoman 1582–1583*. Introduction and notes by Y. Bernard. Editions l'Harmattan.

Peçevî [İbrahim Efendi] (1992). *Peçevi Tarihi*, vol. 2, ed. by B. S. Baykal. Kültür Bakanlığı.

Procházka-Eisl, G. (1995). *Das Sûrnâme-i Hümâyûn. Die Wiener Handschrift in Transkription, mit Kommentar und Indices versehen*. Isis.

Seidel, F. (1711). *Denkwürdige Gesandtschaft an die Ottomannische Pforte*. https://www.digitale-sammlungen.de/de/view/bsb11098758?page=37. Date of Access: 25.01.2024.

Selânikî Mustafa Efendi (1999). *Tarih-i Selânikî*, vol. 1, ed. by M. İpşirli. Türk Tarih Kurumu.

Schweigger, S. (1995). *The Islamic World in Foreign Travel Accounts*, vol. 28: *Ein newe Reyssbeschreibung aus Teutschland nach Constantinopel und Jerusalem, durch Salomon Schweigger*, ed. by F. Sezgin. Institut für Geschichte der Arabisch-Islamischen Wissenschaften.

Toska, Z. (1999). Bir Armağan: Zübdetü'l-Eş'âr. In M. Kütükoğlu, G. Kut & E. Karabacak (Eds.), *Prof. Dr. Nihad M. Çetin'e Armağan* (pp. 293–358). İstanbul Üniversitesi Edebiyat Fakültesi.

Tura, Y. (2001). *Mûsikiyi Harflerle Tespit ve İcrâ İlminin Kitabı*. YKY.

Yerasimos, S. (2002). *Sultan Sofraları, 15. ve 16. Yüzyılda Osmanlı Saray Mutfağı*. YKY.

Wright, O. (2000). *Demetrius Cantemir: The Collection of Notations*, vol. 2: *Commentary*. Ashgate Publishing Company.

Scholarly Literature

Abou-El-Haj, R. (1991). *Formation of the Modern State: The Ottoman Empire Sixteenth to Eighteenth Centuries.* State University of New York Press.

Aktaş, Ş. (1996). *16. Yüzyılda Kentin Oyunu: Şenlik, İki Örnek: Avrupa'da Şarlken Dönemi Osmanlı'da 1582 Şenliği* [Doctoral dissertation, Ankara University].

Alvan, T. (2020). 1582 Tarihli Yeni Bir Surname Metni: Akşemseddin'in Torunu Kadîmî'nin Sûr-nâme'si. *Divan Edebiyatı Araştırmaları Dergisi* 25, 1–77.

And, M. (2020). *Kırk Gün Kırk Gece.* YKY.

And, M. (2015). *16. Yüzyılda İstanbul, Kent-Saray-Gündelik Yaşam.* YKY.

Atasoy, N. (1997). *1582, Sûrname-i Hümâyun, Düğün Kitabı.* Koçbank Yayınları.

Barkan, Ö. L. (1957). Essai sur les données statistiques des registres de recensement dans l'Empire ottoman aux XVe et XVIe siècles. *Journal of the Economic and Social History of the Orient* 1(1), 9–36.

Bowles, E. (2006). The Impact of Turkish Military Bands on European Court Festivals in the 17th and 18th Centuries. *Early Music* 34(4), 533–559.

Corbin, A. (1998). *Village Bells. The Culture of the Senses in the Nineteenth-Century French Countryside.* Columbia University Press.

Demirbaş, A. T. (2024). *Sonic Representations of Power: The Role and Perception of Sound in the 1582 Ottoman Imperial Festival* [Doctoral dissertation, University of Bern].

Ergun, S. N. (1936). *Türk Şairleri*, vol. 1. Suhulet Basımevi.

Faroqhi, S. N. (2016). Osmanlı Nüfusu. In S. Faroqhi & K. Fleet (Eds.), *Türkiye Tarihi, Bir Dünya Gücü Olarak Osmanlı İmparatorluğu 1453–1603*, vol. 2 (pp. 437–489), transl. by B. Üçpunar. Kitap.

Faroqhi, S. (2012). Post-Kolonyal Dönüm Öncesi ve Sonrasında İmparatorluklar: Osmanlılar. In D. Quataert & B. Tezcan (Eds.), *Hakim Paradigmaların Ötesinde* (pp. 83–104), transl. by A. Sever. Tan Kitabevi.

Faroqhi, S. (2005). Understanding Ottoman Guilds. In S. Faroqhi & R. Deguilhem (Eds.), *Crafts and Craftsmen of the Middle East* (pp. 3–40). Tauris.

Feldman, W. (2012). Mehter. In P. Bearmann, Th. Bianquis, C. E. Bosworth, E. van Donzel & W. P. Heinrichs (Eds.), *Encyclopaedia of Islam.* https://referenceworks.brillonline.com/entries/encyclopaedia-of-islam-2/*-SIM_5149. Date of Access: 25.01.2024.

Felek, Ö. (2019). Displaying Manhood and Masculinity at the Imperial Circumcision Festivity of 1582. *Journal of the Ottoman and Turkish Studies Association* 6(1), 141–170.

Felek, Ö. (2017). Fears, Hopes, and Dreams: The Talismanic Shirts of Murad III. *Arabica* 64, 647–672.

Felek, Ö. (2012). *Kitābü'l-Menāmāt, Sultan III. Murad'ın Rüya Mektupları.* Tarih Vakfı Yurt Yayınları.

Fleet, K. (2016). Osmanlılar, 1451–1603: Siyasi Bir Tarihe Giriş. In S. Faroqhi & K. Fleet (Eds.), *Türkiye Tarihi, Bir Dünya Gücü Olarak Osmanlı İmparatorluğu 1453–1603*, vol. 2 (pp. 47–76), transl. by B. Üçpunar. Kitap.

Fleischer, C. H. (1986). *Bureaucrat and Intellectual in the Ottoman Empire. The Historian Mustafa Âlî (1541–1600)*. Princeton University Press.

Grant, J. (1999). Rethinking the Ottoman "Decline": Military Technology Diffusion in the Ottoman Empire, Fifteenth to Eighteenth Centuries. *Journal of World History* 1(1), 179–201.

Haug, J. I. (2019). *Ottoman and European Music in ʿAlī Ufuḳī ʾs Compendium, MS Turc 292: Analysis, Interpretation, Cultural Context*. WWU Münster.

İnalcık, H. (2003). *Osmanlı İmparatorluğu Klâsik Çağ (1300–1600)*, transl. by R. Sezer. YKY.

İnalcık, H. (1998). *Essays in Ottoman History*. Eren Yayıncılık.

Jäger, R. M. (1996). Janitscharenmusik. In L. Lütteken (Ed.), *MGG Online*. https://www.mgg-online.com/mgg/stable/28607. Date of Access: 25.01.2024.

Kafadar, C. (2019). *Kim var imiş biz burada yoğ iken*. Metis.

Kafadar, C. (1997–1998). The Question of Ottoman Decline. *Harvard Middle East and Islamic Review* 4, 30–75.

Karateke, H. T. (2005). Legitimating the Ottoman Sultanate: A Framework for Historical Analysis. In H. T. Karateke & M. Reinkowski (Eds.), *Legitimatizing the Order: The Ottoman Rhetoric of State Power* (pp. 13–52). Brill.

Lewis, B. (1962). Ottoman Observers of Ottoman Decline. *Islamic Studies* 1, 71–87.

Nutku, Ö. (1981). Türk Şenliklerinin Güç ve Bolluk Simgesi: Nahıl. *Sanat Olayı* 1, 24–28.

Özkan, N. (2004). *Modena Devlet Arşivi'ndeki Osmanlı Devleti'ne İlişkin Belgeler (1485–1791)*. Kültür ve Turizm Bakanlığı.

Öztürk, O. M. (2010). Mehter Musikisi. In O. Elbaş (Ed.), *Mehter* (pp. 239–307). Grafiker Yayıncılık.

Peksevgen, Ş. (2009). Murad III. In G. Ágoston & B. Masters (Eds.), *Encyclopedia of The Ottoman Empire* (pp. 401–403). Facts On File, Inc.

Popescu-Judetz, E. (2007). *Türk Musiki Kültürünün Anlamları*, transl. by Bülent Aksoy. Pan Yayınevi.

Quataert, D. (2010). *Workers, Peasants and Economic Change in the Ottoman Empire, 1730–1914*. Gorgias Press.

Rotter, A. J. (2019). *Empires of the Senses: Bodily Encounters in Imperial India and the Philippines*. Oxford University Press.

Sajdi, D. (2007). Decline, its Discontents and Ottoman Cultural History: By Way of Introduction. In D. Sajdi (Ed.), *Ottoman Tulips, Ottoman Coffee. Leisure and Lifestyle in the Eighteenth Century* (pp. 1–40). Tauris.

Sanal, H. (1964). *Mehter Musikisi*. MEB.

Sanlıkol, M. A. (2011). *Çalıcı Mehterler*. YKY.

Smith, M. M. (2007). *Sensing the Past. Seeing, Hearing, Smelling, Tasting and Touching in History*. University of California Press.

Stout, R. E. (1966). *The Sûr-i Hümâyun of Murad III: A Study of Ottoman Pageantry and Entertainment* [Doctoral dissertation, Ohio State University].

Şahin, K. (2019). To Observe, To Record, To Depict: Memorializing the Circumcision of an Ottoman Prince, c. 1582–c. 1600. *History and Theory* 57, 43–67.

Tezcan, B. (2012). Bilim Üzerinden Siyaset: Erken Modern Osmanlı Bilimi Üzerine Düşünceler. In D. Quataert & B. Tezcan (Eds.), *Hakim Paradigmaların Ötesinde* (pp. 169–194), transl. by A. Sever. Tan Kitabevi.

Toner, J. (2014). Introduction: Sensing the Ancient Past. In J. Toner (Ed.), *A Cultural History of the Senses in Antiquity*, vol. 1 (pp. 1–22). Bloomsbury.

Uran, H. (1942). *Üçüncü Sultan Mehmedin Sünnet Düğünü*. Kâatçılık ve Matbaacılık Anonim Şirketi.

Vural, T. (2012). Osmanlı Dönemi Mehter Teşkilatı. *Zeitschrift für die Welt der Türken* 4(1), 315–330.

Yelçe, Z. (2021). Palace and City Ceremonials. In S. Hamadeh & Ç. Kafescioğlu (Eds.), *A Companion to Early Modern Istanbul* (pp. 143–167). Brill.

Yelçe, Z. (2014). Evaluating Three Imperial Festivals: 1524, 1530 and 1539. In S. Faroqhi & A. Öztürkmen (Eds.), *Celebration, Entertainment and Theatre in the Ottoman World* (pp. 71–109). Seagull Books.

Yi, E. (2004). *Guild Dynamics in Seventeenth-Century Istanbul*. Brill.

Illustration Credits

Fig. 1: Nakkaş Osman, *Şehinşahnâme-i Murâd-ı Sâlis*, vol. 2 (1597). Topkapı Palace Museum Archive, Istanbul. Bağdat No. 200, fols. 51r.–50v.

Fig. 2: Nakkaş Osman, *Sûrnâme-i Hümâyûn* (1583–1588). Topkapı Palace Museum Archive, Istanbul. Hazine No. 1344, fol. 35r.

Fig. 3: Nakkaş Osman, *Şehinşahnâme-i Murâd-ı Sâlis*, vol. 2 (1597). Topkapı Palace Museum Archive, Istanbul. Bağdat No. 200, fols. 160r.–159v.

Fig. 4: Nakkaş Osman, *Sûrnâme-i Hümâyûn* (1583–1588). Topkapı Palace Museum Archive, Istanbul. Hazine No. 1344, fol. 7v.

Fig. 5: Nakkaş Osman, *Şehinşahnâme-i Murâd-ı Sâlis*, vol. 2 (1597). Topkapı Palace Museum Archive, Istanbul. Bağdat No. 200, fols. 56r.–55v.

"... quando il Gran Signore vuole la musica"

17th-Century Europeans on Music and the Ottoman State

Judith I. Haug

The personal perceptions of participants and spectators of early modern ceremonies and rituals of power yield important insights into the physical and sensory components of these events that are distinct from factual descriptions (Stollberg-Rilinger, 2000, pp. 396–397, 404). The present contribution relies on an interconnected group of Europeans from the mid-17th century who shared experiences of certain important biographical and political events, such as their respective first arrivals in Constantinople, sultans' pageants, Ottoman and French state celebrations, as well as the negotiations and later renewal of the French-Ottoman capitulations in 1672–1673. Diplomats were invited to circumcisions or religious festivities (*bayrām*) and witnessed the famous train of the sultan when, for example, he moved the court to Adrianople.[1] Their descriptions of these occasions with regard to ceremonial and military music offer valuable information – albeit often in passing and from an outsider's view – about the soundscape of the Ottoman state, including military music, cannon salutes, and camel tack festooned with bells. They provide insights, on the one hand, into circumstances and occasions of music-making, and on the other hand – and more importantly – into the intellectual and/or emotional reactions of the foreign listeners, as well as their perception and interpretation of sound as an expression of power (cf. Labaree, 2020, pp. 402–403). Their accounts are complemented here by a description of the sultan's palace by the bicultural Polish-Ottoman court musician and interpreter ʿAlī Ufuḳī/Wojciech Bobowski (c. 1610–c. 1675),[2] who belonged to the same circle of people. In analysing selected passages referring to military music from his famous *Serai Enderum* (sic; MS London, British Library, Harley 3409; before 1665), special attention will be given to differences between its various translated versions. A main point is the transmission of information initially supplied by ʿAlī Ufuḳī and subsequently distorted in different ways by various people.

---

1   In keeping with the source material, historical place names are used here (Constantinople, Adrianople, and Smyrna, instead of İstanbul, Edirne, and İzmir).

2   Since ʿAlī Ufuḳī was known in Poland under his Polish first name Wojciech and not the Latinized version, Albert, it is preferable to use the former (Pawlina, forthcoming).

Ottoman ceremonial and military music, the *mehter-ḫāne* (Sanal, 1964; Sanlıkol, 2011, pp. 19–28, 41–58; Jäger, 2016; Feldman, 2021), is the most relevant aspect here, because military music is what Europeans were confronted with on a regular basis. Aksoy (2003, pp. 277–280; see also Labaree, 2020, pp. 406–407) has pointed out that Europeans were not exposed to the various kinds, genres, and stylistic categories of Ottoman-Turkish music to the same degree and that *mehter* music, along with the sophisticated music of the Mevlevī dervishes, was the most regularly observed and described type. Othering and demeaning value judgments are frequently encountered in this context,[3] which, in turn, fed into musical exoticism as "Turkish" or "janissary" music (see e.g., Pirker, 1990; Rice, 1999; Bowles, 2006; Parmentier, 2013).

Travel accounts and other texts written by Europeans about the Ottoman Empire have long been regarded crucial witnesses to help understand the perception of *other* music and music-making contexts, but also as sources for information on musical practices. This is clearly problematic for several reasons. Indeed, Ottoman sources on the topic exist, first and foremost the travelogue (*Seyāḥat-nāme*) by Evliyā Çelebi, a contemporary of ʿAlī Ufuḳī, and thus for a more complete picture, his writings should also be considered. Unfortunately, this would exceed the boundaries of the present contribution (see Öztürk, 2013; Sanlıkol, 2011, pp. 20–23, 41–46; Olley, 2023). It must be pointed out that knowledge of Ottoman sources that describe the sound of foreigners, especially in Constantinople, is still very limited. This is a significant area for future research.

Europeans Who Felt the Need to Write Something About the Music of the Country[4]

ʿAlī Ufuḳī/Wojciech Bobowski (Neudecker, 2005; Behar, 2005, pp. 17–52; Haug, 2019, pp. 39–85; Pawlina, forthcoming) forms a kind of centre for a circle from which the sources under consideration here have been selected.[5] In addition to his special source value as a European-born palace insider and a professional musician, he has been chosen as a starting point because his social and scholarly contacts are comparatively well understood. All of the French authors cited below either knew him or are likely to have known him. His description of Topkapı Palace forms the basis of the second section of the present

---

3   We cannot delve deeper into this important topic due to space constraints; see, e.g., Rice, 1999; Aksoy, 2003, pp. 271–284; Vural, 2012; Scharrer, 2019; Labaree, 2020, pp. 408–413 and passim.

4   This is how Aksoy (2003, p. 274) summarizes the diverse cast of Europeans who wrote on Ottoman-Turkish music ("[ü]lkenin musıkisi üstüne bir şeyler yazma ihtiyacı duyan Avrupalılar").

5   For a study of theatre performances at the French embassy, relying on the same set of sources, see Haug, 2023.

"... quando il Gran Signore vuole la musica"

chapter. His network of knowledge exchange can be reconstructed in a fairly reliable way. He was acquainted with Antoine Galland (1646–1715) (Omont, 1902/1, pp. 175–203; Abdel-Halim, 1964, pp. 11–43; Bauden, 2001; Gökçen, 2009, pp. 209–210), the secretary of the French ambassador Charles-François-Marie Olier, Marquis de Nointel (c. 1635–1685) (Vandal, 1900, esp. pp. 37–54; Michaud, 1979; Hitzel, 2010, pp. 281–285). Another intermittent member of the French embassy was the special envoy and interpreter chevalier Laurent d'Arvieux (1635–1702) (Bacqué-Grammont, Kuneralp, and Hitzel, 1991, pp. 23–24; Pârlea, 2015).[6] The ambassador also employed another interpreter, François, sieur de la Croix (*père*) (1622–1695) (Sebag, 1978, pp. 101–109; Dew, 2009, pp. 27–30). Two friends of the marquis's will also be cited, namely, the British embassy chaplain Dr John Covel (1638–1722) (Aksoy, 2003, pp. 71–72; Wilson, 2011, p. 8; Abbott, 1920, pp. 53–57, 368–372; Leedham-Green, 2004; Bent, 2010, pp. XXVI-XXXIII), and Italian traveller Cornelio Magni (1638–1692) (Vandal, 1900, p. 202; Meyer, 2009, p. 611). While the overall group of sources from the second half of the 17th century that could have been included in the study is considerably larger, it made sense to restrict it to authors who knew each other and witnessed the same events.

In a first step, we will look at three occasions when Ottoman state music was performed in different contexts and described by persons from the abovementioned circle, i.e., Antoine Galland, Laurent d'Arvieux, and François, sieur de la Croix. In their reports, a mix of factual descriptions, evaluations, and sensory or emotional responses can be observed. On 7 May 1672, Sultan Meḥmed IV left the capital for Adrianople, as he usually did in summer. This directly preceded the Marquis de Nointel's first trip to Thrace, where he hoped to renew the capitulations.

---

6   His travelogue was printed in 1735 (d'Arvieux, 1735, 6 vols.). This is, however, a heavily edited version; see Walsdorf, 2019, pp. 19–53.

Enfin, toutes les bandes finissoient par un concert de musique de cinq ou six hautbois, de quatre trompettes, de huict tambours, de tymbales et de cimbales dont l'harmonie en mesme temps guerrière et de resjouissance, avoit tout un autre air que je n'attendois dans ce pays, où je n'avois encore entendu rien de si charmant ny si bien concerté. [...] Tout cela estoit terminé par quinze tambours, autant de hautbois et autant de trompettes dont le son bruyant et retentissant faisoit une harmonie qui estoit toute de guerre. Mais ce qui faisoit tout trembler et frémir, c'estoit le tonnerre de quatre tymbales des plus grosses que j'aye jamais veues ny entendues dont quatre chameaux estoient chargés. Il n'y avoit personne qui, non seulement n'en fut estourdi, mais dont tout le corps et au dedans et au dehors ne fut emeu (Galland, 1881/1, pp. 132–133; cf. Gökçen 2009, pp. 215–216).

Ultimately, all the groups ended with a musical ensemble of five or six oboes [*zurnā*], four trumpets [*boru*], eight drums [*davul*], of timpani [*naḳḳare*] and cymbals [*zil*], whose both warlike and celebratory harmony had a whole different atmosphere which I did not expect in this country, where I had never heard anything so charming and so well in accord. [...] All of this ended with fifteen drums, as many oboes and as many trumpets whose noisy and booming sound created an entirely warlike harmony. But what made everything tremble and shake was the thunder of the four timpani, the largest I have ever seen or heard, with which four camels were loaded. There was nobody who was not only deafened but whose entire body was moved inside and out.[7]

Laurent d'Arvieux was also part of the delegation travelling to Adrianople in the summer of 1672. Hence, the following passage most probably describes the same event:

La marche de cette brillante jeunesse étoit fermée par quatre étendarts [...], qui étoient suivis de six Trompettes, six Haubois, deux Timballes qui donnoient le signal aux Trompettes de sonner de tems en tems, pendant que les autres instrumens joüoient continuellement (d'Arvieux, 1735/4, p. 534).

The march of this brilliant youth [the *içoğlan* palace pages] was closed by four standards [...], which were followed by six trumpets, six oboes, two timpani which gave the signal to the trumpets to play intermittently, whereas the other instruments played continuously.

---

7   All translations are the author's. The identification of the Ottoman instruments being referred to follows Gökçen, 2009, p. 210.

Cette marche étoit fermée par quinze Tambours, quinze Haubois, quinze Trompettes, trois paires de Timballes, & autant de Cimballes. Tous ces joüeurs d'Instrumens étoient parfaitement bien montés; excepté les Trompettes, tous les autres joüoient sans interruption, & formoient un concert également guerrier & melodieux. Le bagage parut ensuite : il avoit à la tête quatre chameaux qui portoient chacun un grosse paire de timballes d'airain de trois pieds de diametre, couvertes d'un cuir épais. Deux hommes assis dans des especes de paniers sur la croupe du chameau frappoient sur ces timballes, l'un avec deux baguettes, & l'autre avec une seule qu'il tenoit à deux mains comme une masse, ce qui faisoit un bruit si fort qu'on l'entendoit à une lieuë à la ronde. Soixante chameaux marchant deux à deux suivoient ces timballes étourdissantes [...] (d'Arvieux, 1735/4, p. 548).

This march was closed by fifteen drums, fifteen oboes, fifteen trumpets, three pairs of timpani and as many cymbals. All those instrumentalists were perfectly well mounted; except for the trumpets, all the others played without interruption and created a consonance both warlike and melodious. Afterwards, the baggage train came up: it was headed by four camels which each carried a large pair of bronze timpani of three feet in diameter, covered with thick leather. Two men seated in a kind of basket on the hindquarters of the camel beat those timpani, one with two sticks and the other with a single stick which he held with both hands like a sledgehammer, which produced a sound so loud it could be heard a mile around. Sixty camels marching two by two followed those deafening timpani (see also Bowles 2006, p. 538).

While the numbers of musicians are almost consistent (if Galland means "pairs of timpani" when he writes "timpani"), d'Arvieux's account contains a higher ratio of factual descriptions and fewer value judgments or emotional responses. He was a trained musician who had performed together with other Europeans in Smyrna (Pârlea, 2015); hence, his ear may have been more finely tuned to music and he found it easier to describe. In contrast, de la Croix mentioned the event quite briefly: "Un Concert d'Jnstruments [...] qui auoient quelque chose de plus guerrier que de charmant [...]" (a concert of instruments [...] which had something [about them] more warlike than charming) (de la Croix, 1670–1673, p. 348).

From September 12 to 14, 1672, the conquest of Kamianets-Podilskyi in today's Ukraine that had taken place ten days earlier was celebrated. This important victory of Grand Vizier Aḥmed Köprülü resulted in the incorporation of Podilia into the Ottoman Empire as the Eyalet-i Kamaniçe (Kołodziejczyk, 1992). On the evening of 12 September, "les tymbales qu'on entendit retentir dans le serrail et les décharges de canon qu'on y fit ensuite, confirmèrent que cette place si considérable estoit prise" (the timpani which were heard booming in the palace and the cannons fired afterwards confirmed that this very important town had been taken) (Galland, 1881/1, p. 208; cf. Gökçen, 2009, pp. 217–218). Cornelio Magni speaks of a "fonzione sontuosissima con sparo universale" (most glorious celebration with general shooting) (Magni, 1692, p. 35). Galland then proceeds to report revelry in the brightly illuminated streets, and people dancing and making music that did not meet his aesthetic standards ("concerts fort mal concertés"; Galland, 1881/1, pp. 210–212; cf. Gökçen, 2009, pp. 218–219). De la Croix describes the conquest of Kamianets-Podilskyi at length, adding many details to the picture, for example that the Ḳāʾim-maḳām (the governor of Constantinople) had ordered the foreign representatives to take part in the celebrations by illuminating their embassy buildings. The Seraglio cannons fired through the night and all foreign vessels moored in the city's port were ordered to join the general shooting, becoming part of the Ottoman soundscape of power and conquest (de la Croix, 1670–1673, pp. 414–417). This is a noteworthy instance of "performative Kommunikationsakte" (performative acts of communication) (Stollberg-Rilinger, 2004, p. 495) weaving together various levels of perception and performance, authority, rule, and submission. Regarding the question of sound and power as experienced by Antoine Galland, Laurent d'Arvieux, and the others, the fact that European representatives were ordered to join the celebration of the fall of a European town is certainly thought-provoking, but none of the sources comments on this beyond recording the succession of events.

Occasions for official or representative music performed by Europeans in Constantinople were mostly the entries of ambassadors and envoys. This often involved the question of whether foreign embassies were allowed to play music and fly their flags inside the city walls (Würflinger, 2020, p. 107; Jäger, 1998, pp. 145–175). The gun salute, a crucial element of politically employed sound, was used by both Ottomans and Europeans. As such, it was a shared sound of power opposed to the culturally distinct *mehter*. According to de la Croix, cannons decorated with the coats of arms of the rulers from which they had been taken were kept in the palace, trained on the entry of the port but fired only during celebrations ("Elles ne tirent qu'aux jours de festes de rejouissance publique, et deffendent l'Entrée du Port [...])" (de la Croix n.d., pp. 18–19). Another important issue in this context is the salute to Topkapı Palace expected from foreign representatives at the palace promontory. For instance, John Covel describes his arrival in Constantinople on 31 December 1670: "[...] we came to Anchor at the custome house on *Galata* side, having saluted the Seraglio as we past by with 11 guns". Also when returning from a journey, his ship "[s]aluted the Seraglio with 7 guns. Deo laus et gloria ex grato corde" (praise and glory to God from a grateful heart) (Bent, 1893/2010, pp. 144, 156). When the Marquis de Nointel took up his post in Constantinople and passed without shooting, it led to a diplomatic disturbance (de la Croix, 1670–1673, pp. 31–32; Vandal, 1900, pp. 52–55).[8] When d'Arvieux

---

8   On the topic of European-Ottoman diplomatic misunderstandings and gaffes, see Vogel, 2014.

arrived in 1672, his ship did not salute the Seraglio either. They did, however, greet Nointel with a gun salute when he boarded the ship (de la Croix, 1670–1673, p. 307). On the occasion of the birth of the Duc d'Anjou on 21 July 1672, various kinds of weaponry were discharged on the lawn of the Palais de France, French vessels in the port fired their guns, the ambassador's six liveried trumpeters played, and the *Te deum* was sung. Beforehand, however, Nointel had sent his interpreters to the Ḳā'im-maḳām to announce the festivities (Galland, 1881/1, pp. 172–175; de la Croix, 1670–1673, p. 39; d'Arvieux, 1735/4, p. 432; on the ambassador's trumpeters see Gökçen, 2009, pp. 219–220).

The renewal of the French capitulations at Adrianople in June 1673 was a crucial moment of Nointel's otherwise problematic tenure as ambassador. The Ottoman side acknowledged the event by sending the *mehter-ḫāne*. 'Alī Ufuḳī confirms that the *mehter* was customarily deployed to play for foreign ambassadors to celebrate important days (see below). This is the only time Galland uses the Ottoman-Turkish term.

Les méhtars ou joueurs d'instruments du Grand Seigneur et du Grand Visir vinrent régaler M. l'Ambassadeur de l'harmonie de leurs instruments, à cause du renouvellement des capitulations; mais leur harmonie, qui plaist si fort aux Turcs, n'est aucunement du goust des oreilles francoises (Galland, 1881/2, p. 97; cf. Gökçen, 2009, p. 222)

The *mehter* or instrumentalists of the Sultan and the Grand Vizier came to treat the Monsieur Ambassador to the harmony of their instruments on the occasion of the renewal of the capitulations; but their harmony, which the Turks like so very much, is not at all to the taste of French ears.

Compared with the passage cited above, Galland's contradictory emotional responses and his inconsistent value judgments are interesting. While he previously had found the sound of the *mehter* "charming and well concerted" and expressed his astonishment at the quality of the music-making, on an occasion of the *mehter* celebrating his own side, he concedes that it was "not at all to the taste of French ears". We are left to wonder what changed his mind and whether he himself was aware of this change.

Music and the State in *Serai Enderum*

The other source – or rather cluster of sources – under consideration here is a description of Topkapı Palace written in the 1660s by ʿAlī Ufuḳī/Wojciech Bobowski, a bi-cultural musician and interpreter. However, caution is advised: *Serai Enderum* should not be viewed as the realistic, reliable "emic" perspective against which all other descriptions must be tested. Such a source would have been Evliyā Çelebi, but this remains to be studied in detail. *Serai Enderum* was written with a specific audience in mind, and thus there are several issues that must be addressed, beginning with the context of its genesis. Around the time of its composition, ʿAlī Ufuḳī had the intention to return to Europe with the help of his British acquaintances (Neudecker, 2005). It remains unclear why this plan did not come to fruition (Haug, 2019, pp. 67–70). Pier Mattia Tommasino (2017, p. 44) connects *Serai Enderum* directly to this incident, interpreting the text as an attempt by the author to make himself interesting and credible for European readers who might help him relocate to Europe.

As far as the source situation allows us to conclude, the original text was composed by ʿAlī Ufuḳī before 1665. In addition to the well-known MS London, British Library, Harley 3409, which is dated 20 May 1665, Tommasino has identified two more witnesses in Italian libraries. One was copied from a "presentation copy" dated 22 September 1669 and dedicated to a Provençal family in Constantinople; the other one is also dated 20 May 1665 and hence copied from Harley 3409 (Tommasino, 2017, p. 42), or possibly the other way round. Another exemplar was in the possession of the Marquis de Nointel (Tommasino, 2017, pp. 42–44; Haug, 2019, pp. 144–145), as the English traveller George Wheler attests: "Le Marquis de Nointel a une description du Serrail écrite de sa [ʿAlī Ufuḳī's] main en Italien […]" (the Marquis Nointel has a description of the palace written by him [ʿAlī Ufuḳī] in Italian) (Wheler, 1679/1, p. 168). When John Covel returned to London from his post in Constantinople in 1677, he took a copy of the text with him and subsequently sold it to the collector Robert Harley (Haug, 2019, p. 83), i.e., it reached England some years after ʿAlī Ufuḳī's death and thus long after his attempt to relocate. Questions remain as to who wrote this copy of *Serai Enderum*, why it is so flawed, and whether the actual autograph still exists. The exemplar owned by the Marquis de Nointel is a strong candidate, since the ambassador must have known ʿAlī Ufuḳī, and Antoine Galland, who stated that it was "from his hand", would have been able to identify the writing. Unfortunately, the whereabouts of this manuscript are unknown.

The other copies identified by Tommasino could, regrettably, not be viewed to determine whether one of them is the autograph. Harley 3409 was clearly not written in ʿAlī Ufuḳī's rather distinctive hand, nor does it feature his characteristic spelling variants. Tommasino mentions "constant misuse of the etymological *h*", "absence of the anaphonesis", and "frequent mistakes in the morphological agreement" as typical deviations (2017, p. 45). When checking against the freely formulated Italian texts in his notation collection/commonplace book (Bobowski, 2020/1) (as opposed to texts copied from an extant source), only one instance of an absent anaphonesis could be identified (f. 2a/253a "nonciarlo"; f. 380a/222a/376a "gionsero" appears in a copied text; Bobowski, 2020/1, pp. 8, 367). While there are no instances of mistakes in the morphological agreement and misuse of the etymological *h*, ʿAlī Ufuḳī does have a number of spelling idiosyncrasies, for example, "sonar" instead of "suonare"; "batere" and "batuda" instead of "battere" and "battuta", and other cases of a single consonant instead of a double; and "pigla" for "piglia". He also uses the subjunctive ("credo che non consoni bene", 244a/90a; Bobowski, 2020/1, p. 130). In contrast to what Tommasino (2017, p. 42) supposes, it is highly probable that ʿAlī Ufuḳī did not learn Italian in Constantinople, but had acquired his knowledge of the language prior to his capture. Connections to Jesuits in his native Lviv make it possible that he had been educated by them, which would conveniently explain both the level of his Italian and his broad general knowledge (Hammer-Purgstall, 1830, p. 80; Babinger, 1936, pp. 156–157; Pawlina, forthcoming).

The English translation of the following passage about "musica di campagna" (field music), the *mehter-ḫāne*, imitates the rather breathless and not always very smooth style of the original, but I took the liberty of inserting punctuation and dividing long sentences into more intelligible portions. I have also given instrument names and other terms in standardized Ottoman-Turkish spelling.

Doppo il mezzo giorno uengano [sic] gli maestri musici di campagna, e iui fanno, come gli altri, gli loro istrumenti sono piffe; in turchesco Zurna, e Trombette; Boru sonano alla batuta di tamburo, Daul, o Niacchera piccola, Kadum o dumbelik et crotali zil, et iui ancora imparano a sonare gli tamburi di bronzo; che si portano sopra un Camello d'auanti il G.S. Questi tali sonatori alcuni habitano nelli appartamenti di fuori, e sono obbligati ogni mattina a una hora auanti il giorno a sonare il bon giorno, e a una hora e mezza di notte alla bona notte del G.S., nel lo scoprirsi la luna del loro Bairam, cosi ancora fanno mentre il G.S. fà qualche caualcata, con pompa uanno auguriare le bone feste. Alli Amb[asciatori] estranieri [replaces a deleted word] cosi ancora a tutti quelli che alla audienza publica hanno riceuto il fauore di un Kaftan, si con caricho di alcun officio allora uanno alle case sue e pigliano le mancie. Altri sono, che nel n.o di paggi, e habitano dentro, sonano nelle uigilie del loro Bairam, e quando si porta il menzionato tappeto o uero esce fuori del Seraglio alcun Paschia, ò, Beglerbeghi, ancora quando il G.S.re esce fuori a diporto suo con la barcha, insieme uanno doe piffe con una Niacchera per sonare mentre uogano gli suoi barcaroli che sono bostangi, ó giardinieri, e ogni uolta che uogano pigliano tre Zecchini per uno (MS Harley 3409, pp. 52–53).[9]

In the afternoon, the masters of the field music come and do the same as the others there [namely, give lessons in a room in the inner courtyard called *meşk-ḫāne*]. Their instruments are shawms (in Turkish *zurnā*) and trumpets (*boru*) which they play to the beat of drums (*davul*) or small nakers (*kudüm* or *dümbelek*) and cymbals (*zil*). And there they also learn to play the bronze timpani [*kös*], which are carried by a camel [walking] in front of the Sultan. Some of these musicians live in accommodations outside [of the palace] and have to play the morning salute every morning one hour before daylight and a night salute to the Sultan at one and a half hour of the night; also, when the moon first appears on *bayrām*, and likewise they do this when the Sultan rides out. They go in pomp to wish happy holidays to the foreign ambassadors and likewise to all those who have received the gift of a kaftan during public audience, when they are appointed to an office [and] go to their houses [outside the palace] and take the gratuity. There are others among the number of pages who live inside [the palace]; they play for the eve of their *bayrām*, and when the above-mentioned rug [a relic] is carried or when a *Pāşā* or *Beğlerbeği* [a high-ranking official] leaves the palace [service] and also when the Sultan goes out for a pleasure trip on the boat, together with him go two shawms and [a pair of?] nakers for playing while his oarsmen, who are *bōstāncı* or gardeners, row, and every time they row they receive three Zecchini each.

---

9   See also Magni, 1679, pp. 553–554; de la Croix n.d., pp. 143–144.

"... quando il Gran Signore vuole la musica"

In the chart below, the occasions when *mehter* played have been extracted from ʿAlī Ufuḳī's description, distinguishing between the musicians from "outside" and those living "inside". Some details are not entirely clear, since there is unfortunately not a great deal of information available (see also Sanlıkol, 2011, pp. 43–44; Jäger, 2016):

Occasion	Ensemble	Instruments
Every morning one hour before sunrise	Instrumentalists living outside	*zurnā, boru, davul, kudüm, zil* (*kös?*)
At 1 ½ hours of the night	Instrumentalists living outside	*zurnā, boru, davul, kudüm, zil* (*kös?*)
Sighting of the moon on the eve of *bayrām*	Instrumentalists living outside	*zurnā, boru, davul, kudüm, zil* (*kös?*)
Exits of the Sultan	Instrumentalists living outside	
Wishing foreign ambassadors happy holidays	Instrumentalists living outside	
Eve of *bayrām*	Music pages living inside the palace	
When the rug is carried	Music pages living inside the palace	
When a *Pāşā* or *Beğlerbeği* leaves palace service[10]	Music pages living inside the palace	
Sultan's pleasure trip on boat	?	2 *zurnā*, 1 [pair of] *kudüm*

Table 1: Occasions for *mehter* music.

The *mehter* was obviously heard frequently, forming a part of the daily routine and the yearly cycle in both the palace and town. Other occasions for field music inside the palace were feats of strength performed by the *balṭacı* guards in the palace during *bayrām* (Harley 3409, pp. 36–37; Girardin, 1666, pp. 123–124; de la Croix n.d., pp. 152–153). The leading of the Sultan's horses to their summer pasture was celebrated with a feast, and the procession was accompanied with "Tambours and Trompettes" (ibid., p. 302). On this occasion the *Peşrev*[11] "*Aṭ naḳlı*" ("Transporting the horses") notated by ʿAlī Ufuḳī would have been played (MS London, British Library, Sloane 3114, fol. 90a; Sanal, 1964, pp. 233–234, 260; Sanlıkol, 2011, p. 52).

---

10   This is described in more detail in MS Harley 3409, pp. 62–64.

11   In Ottoman classical music, *peşrev* is a complex, multi-sectional instrumental composition performed in various ceremonial, military, and entertainment contexts.

Distortions

The transmission of *Serai Enderum*'s various versions has not been explained satisfactorily, and many important facts are unknown. Going through the texts with a fine-toothed comb would yield many interesting insights, certainly about Ottoman state music and other aspects of palace life, but also about the mechanics of knowledge transmission. Such a comparative study remains a crucial area for future research. In connection with inadequate modern translations of 17th-century sources, İlhami Gökçen has pointed out: "It is another unfortunate circumstance that such falsehoods have entered Turkish music history, which has few written sources anyway" (Yazılı kaynakları zaten az olan Türk musiki tarihine böyle yanlışlıkların girmesi diğer talihsizlik olmaktadır) (Gökçen, 2009, p. 226). This is an ongoing problem in research based on these sources.

The excerpt below describing the training of palace musicians is relevant regarding both the topic at hand and the question of knowledge transfer. The versions taken into consideration here are the following, presented in chronological order:

- Manuscript Italian version, MS Harley 3409, dated 20 May 1665.
- Manuscript French version by Pierre de Girardin, MS Paris, Bibliothèque Nationale de France, NAF 4997, dated 10 November 1666.[12] In the Paris version of the source, the original "1666" has been overwritten as "1686" and is usually cited as such (Fisher and Fisher, 1985, p. 7; Tommasino, 2016, p. 43). Girardin arrived in Constantinople in 1685 as ambassador (Omont, 1902, p. 251), but he had already spent time there in the 1660s, learning Ottoman Turkish from none other than ʿAlī Ufuḳī (Haug, 2019, pp. 63, 68–69). Hence it is more likely that the translation was made during Girardin's first stay. The dating is corroborated by another copy of this text: MS Harvard, Houghton Library, Fr 103.
- Printed German translation from the Italian by Nicolaus Brenner. The translator's preface (p. [II]) is dated 6 March 1667, the text ends with the date 20 May 1665 (p. 144), the same as MS Harley 3409.
- Printed Italian version in Cornelio Magni's *Quanto di più curioso* (1679), dated 20 March 1670. Magni dates the letter in which he incorporated the *Serai Enderum* with 14 October 1672 (1679, pp. 602, 604).

This list is of course incomplete. It omits the other Italian MSS discovered by Tommasino, as well as the English version published by Sir Paul Rycaut in his *Present State of the Ottoman Empire* (1668) and (re-)translated into French (Rycaut, 1670) and Italian (Rycaut,

---

12 Edition Berthier, 1999; translated into Turkish as Yerasimos and Berthier, 2002. The French version also forms the basis of the abridged English translation Fisher and Fisher, 1985–1987.

Harley 3409 (1665)	NAF 4997 (Girardin)	Brenner 1667	Magni 1679
[48] Altro è Sanzèndebassi cio e capo, o maestro della musica, la qual[e] appresso gli Turchi e antica, e unica, quando il G.S.re uole la musica, lui e [?] di quella et l'accompagnia, resta con gli musici sin che finischa la musica, però non canta più, perche aspetta secondo luso, et suo grado ai cerca di esser promosso del Hasoda, al mio tempo fù un genoese rinegato. [...]	[157] Vn autre officier est le sazendeh Baschy ou maistre de la musique (laquelle chez les turcs se pratique [158] a l'ancienne maniere et est vniuoque, de sorte qu'ilz ne sçauent ce que c'est que des regles de cette science, et qu'ils ne pratiquent point notre methode pour les concerter). Sa fonction ne l'oblige qu'a acompagner les musiciens, lors que le grand Seigneur souhaitte de les entendre. Car cette dignité luy pouurant l'entrée et l'approchant fort du hhasodah il laisse jouer et chanter les autres sans estre obligé de tenir sa partie. Cette charge est ordinairement possedée par quelques estrangers renegats a cause qu'il s'entrouue assez souuent qui ont de l'experience, et peuuent donner des regles a cette musique qui de soy n'en admet aucune autre que l'éleuation ou diminution de la voix, de mesmes que ce que nous appellons le plainchant. [...]	[73] 19. Ein anderer heist *Sazende Basci*. Nemblich Maister ueber die Music/ welliche bey denen Tuercken alt/ aber nur einstimmig ist (so der Kayser selbige begehrt/ anordnet/ vnd biß sie vollendet/ [74] darbey verbleibet. Er aber vor seine Persohn/ vmb willen er vom selbigen *Caricho* oder Ambt in dem *Hasoda promoviret* zuwerden gewertig nicht mehr mitsinget. Zu meiner Zeit versahe dises Officium ein *renegirter* Genueser. [...]	[550] Sezendì Bascì vol dire mastro di capella, o musica numerosa frà turchi, & copiosa di voci: a tempo mio il maestro fù Genouese [...] rinegato:

Table 2: Comparison of four versions of *Serai Enderum*.

1673). However, Rycaut abridged the *Serai Enderum*, leaving out any passages that did not seem crucial to him, one of those passages unfortunately being the chapter on music in the palace.

The spelling of Ottoman-Turkish terms is a good indicator for the proximity of a text to the supposed original. First and foremost, it is not plausible that ʿAlī Ufuḳī, interpreter to the Ottoman state council, would have misspelled the name of the place he lived in for twenty years in the title of his work (Harley 3409: "Enderum" instead of "Enderun", with the "m" above the capital "U" like a ligature). This error was adopted by Nicolaus Brenner, the translator of the German version (1667), by Cornelio Magni ("Serrai Enderum", 1679, p. 502), and, most confusingly, by Girardin (1666, p. 8), who wrote "cette parole persienne Enderoum" next to a clumsy but correct rendering of the word in fully vocalized Arabic script ("enderūn"). The word Sāzende-başı ("head instrumentalist") is represented very differently in the sources under consideration, with transliterations of varying remoteness from the original Ottoman word. ʿAlī Ufuḳī used his own Polish-Italian-inspired romanization system and would most probably have Romanized the word as "sazende baßij" – a spelling adopted in none of the other versions.

Harley 3409, p. 38	Sanzèndebassi
Girardin 1666, p. 157	sazendeh Baschy
Brenner 1667, p. 73	Sazende Basci
Magni 1679, p. 550	Sezendì Bascì
de la Croix n.d., pp. 140–141	Sazende bachi

Evidently, various European native speakers have struggled with Ottoman-Turkish phonetics, especially "ı". Discounting that, an intriguing picture emerges in which the version of Harley 3409 is the least correct, introducing a spurious "n" and not representing the "ş", which would not have been difficult to transliterate into Italian ("sci", see Brenner and Magni).

One point that deserves further investigation is the musical knowledge of the person who copied and/or translated the original, or who copied and/or translated from a previous copy/translation. It appears the information originally given by ʿAlī Ufuḳī was not understood equally well by those who transmitted this information further. Most of his interlocutors were unfamiliar with Ottoman music. With the notable exception of John Covel (Haug, 2019, pp. 63–64), as far as we know they were uninterested in learning more. Some of the translated versions betray problems in grasping or evaluating any type of music-related information.

While it remains unclear whether Magni met ʿAlī Ufuḳī (whose date of death is unknown), he states that he had been assured the manuscript he was copying from was the

"... quando il Gran Signore vuole la musica"

original – or rather *an* original, since he presumed that ʿAlī Ufuḳī had produced multiple copies as a source of income (1679, p. 501). Magni stresses that he had transferred the text "without altering it in the least, just as it reached my hands" ("senza alterarla in minimo conto, tale, quale mi è giunta alle mani", ibid.). When comparing it with Harley 3409, however, this does not seem entirely credible. The passage "copiosa di voci" ("of multiple voices", i.e., polyphonic?) is factually wrong or at least erroneous, and absent from Harley 3409.[13] Magni may have worked with a different manuscript (such as the one dated 20 May 1655 identified by Tommasino?) and/or made alterations.

Brenner (1667, pp. [I–II]) describes in his preface how he used his time as a prisoner in the Yedikule fortress to translate the *Serai Enderum*. Unfortunately, he does not supply any information on how the original reached him and whether he knew ʿAlī Ufuḳī personally. The date of the Italian text in his hand is the same as Harley 3409, but the spelling of some musical terms is different, as for example "Muraba, Kiar, Xausch und Semai" (Brenner, 1667, p. 76) compared to the even less (!) correct "Muraba Kiar, Xauschsemai" (Harley 3409, p. 50). The most correct version, which also explains what is meant by the otherwise unfamiliar term "Xausch", is that of Girardin, who writes "Mourabbah, Kiar, Nasch et Semay" (1666, p. 168), i.e., the vocal genres of Murabbaʿ, Kār, Naḳṣ, and Semāʿī. It seems that at some point, an embellished capital "N" was misread as an "X", obviously by somebody without any knowledge of Ottoman music, and that this was subsequently copied by others equally uninformed. See also the more correctly spelled "Sazende Basci" mentioned above.

Regarding Girardin, the reader wonders where the many additions in his text originated. While completely European in outlook, they are not incorrect; it seems that the ambassador either had his own experiences with Ottoman music or had talked to a more knowledgeable person. As he states in the introduction, Girardin used various sources (1666, pp. 1–2), and indeed the text is more than just a French translation of the *Serai Enderum*. Another interesting feature is that he added Ottoman Turkish terms in Arabic script into the text or left spaces to fill in later. If Girardin wrote his description of the Ottoman Palace during his language lessons with ʿAlī Ufuḳī, it may mean that the latter was also the source of all the extra information (as well as the notation of two vocal pieces which were, alas, never inserted into the provided blank spaces). Comparing NAF 4997 with Girardin's journal (1685–1688), the handwriting does not seem identical at first glance, but the same characteristic embellished uppercase *P*s, *L*s, *C*s, and *Q*s can be found in both texts. Differences may be explained with the changed situations and types of record, the younger Girardin preparing a fair copy and the older Girardin writing quickly.

---

13   The labelling of Ottoman music as "ancient" and "monophonic" is a trope of European writing on the subject (Labaree, 2020, pp. 408–412).

While there are clear similarities to other versions, that of de la Croix does not seem to be a translation or direct transmission of the *Serai Enderum*. The exact relationship between de la Croix and ʿAlī Ufuḳī or his text has not yet been investigated in detail (another crucial area for future research). While de la Croix may well have been aware of the *Serai Enderum* descriptions, he most probably also relied on other sources, written or oral, as well as his own experience. The order of the material in his description is different from that in the *Serai Enderum*, and he introduces several details not found there. One example is his observation that the *santūr* (psaltery) was often used as the sole accompaniment to vocal performance (de la Croix n.d., p. 142). Confusingly, ʿAlī Ufuḳī, a *santūr* player himself, does not mention the instrument (Harley 3409, p. 51).

Concluding Remarks

With the present contribution, I hope to have shown two things: firstly, how carefully we must examine our sources, considering their writers with their personalities and agendas, the contexts of their genesis, and their intended audience, and secondly, how important sources with doubtful factual value are when it comes to matters of perception and sensory/emotional response. Do the European sources say more about the European perception of the Ottoman *other* than they do about the realities of Ottoman music (Labaree, 2020, pp. 402–404 and passim)? In many cases the answer is yes. And even if the answer is possibly no, this cannot be discerned from the distance of centuries. The case of ʿAlī Ufuḳī is different. Since he was both bi-cultural and bi-musical, locating his writings in the context of intercultural perception is difficult. Should the *Serai Enderum* be evaluated as a European source speaking from ʿAlī Ufuḳī's European identity to other Europeans in Constantinople and abroad?

Another aim of this study has been to show how necessary detailed work on the sources still is, despite the fact that most of them have been known and used for decades. In particular, an in-depth study elucidating the genesis of the *Serai Enderum*'s various versions is an important desideratum. It should be our goal to trace and understand processes of knowledge transfer and distortion and, using the tools of source criticism, arrive at a more accurate estimate of the reliability. Descriptions of state music coloured the perception of readers in Europe, if that was the intended readership. Journals are probably the most honest sources when it comes to questions of perception. The popular phrase "lost in translation" is frequently used in contexts such as the present one. But what if information was not simply lost in translation, but actively altered or discarded? More investigation of the sources is necessary to understand these mechanisms – especially in a case carrying so much (inter-/trans-)cultural context and baggage.

Bibliography

Manuscripts

[Bobowski, Wojciech/ʿAlī Ufuḳī]. [n.d.]. *Mecmūʿa-yı Sāz u Söz*. MS London, British Library, Sloane 3114.

[Bobowski, Wojciech/ʿAlī Ufuḳī]. [n.d.]. *Serai Enderum [...]*. MS London, British Library, Harley 3409.

[Girardin, P. de]. 1666. [Description du Sérail du Grand Seigneur, par M. de Girardin, ambassadeur de France à la Porte]. MS Paris, Bibliothèque Nationale de France, NAF 4997. https://gallica.bnf.fr/ark:/12148/btv1b10073802s. Date of Access: 21.04.2022.

[Girardin, P. de]. [n.d.]. *Mémoires sur les Turcs*. MS Harvard, Houghton Library, Fr 103.

[Girardin, P. de]. 1685–1688. *Journal de mon Ambassade à la Porte*, vol. 1. MS Paris, Bibliothèque Nationale de France, Fr. 7162. https://gallica.bnf.fr/ark:/12148/btv1b10509607j. Date of Access: 21.10.2020.

De la Croix, [F.]. [1670–1673]. *Mémoires de Delacroix, secrétaire de l'ambassade de Constantinople, contenants diverses relations [...]*. MS Paris, Bibliothèque Nationale de France, Fr. 6094. https://gallica.bnf.fr/ark:/12148/btv1b525052230

De la Croix, [F.]. [n.d.]. *Le Serrail des Empereurs Turcs [...]*. MS Paris, Bibliothèque Nationale de France, Fr. 6123. https://gallica.bnf.fr/ark:/12148/btv1b90605970. Date of Access: 09.03.2021.

Printed Sources and Source Editions

Bent, J. T. (Ed.). (2010). *Early Voyages and Travels in the Levant*. Hakluyt Society, 1893, reprint Cambridge University Press.

Berthier, A. (1999). *Topkapi: relation du sérail du Grand Seigneur*. Sindbad.

Bobowski, A./ʿAlī Ufuḳī. (2020). *Ottoman and European Music in ʿAlī Ufuḳī's Compendium, MS Turc 292: Analysis, Interpretation, Cultural Context*, ed. by J. I. Haug, vol. 1: *Edition*, vol. 2: *Critical Report*. readbox unipress.

Brenner, N. (1667). *Serai Enderum. Das ist: Jnwendige Beschaffenheit der Türckischen Kayserl: Residentz zu Constantinopoli [...]*. Johann Jacob Kürner.

D'Arvieux, L. (1735). *Memoires du Chevalier d'Arvieux, envoyé extraordinaire du Roy à la Porte [...]*, ed. by J.-B. Labat, 6 vols. Charles-Jean-Baptiste Delespine le Fils.

Fisher, C. G. & A. Fisher. (1985–1987). Topkapı Sarayı in the Mid-Seventeenth Century: Bobovi's Description. *Archivum Ottomanicum* 10, 5–81.

Galland, A. (1881). *Journal d'Antoine Galland pendant son séjour a Constantinople (1672–1673)*, ed. by C. Schefer, 2 vols. Ernest Leroux.

Magni, C. (1679). *Quanto Di più curioso, e vago hà potuto raccorre Cornelio Magni Nel primo biennio da esso consumato in viaggi, e dimore per la Turchia [...]*, vol. 1. Galeazzon Rosati:

https://books.google.com.tr/books?id=G9lw3NEXRjgC&hl=de&source=gbs_navlinks_s. Date of Access: 05.11.2020.

Rycaut, P. (1668). *The Present State of the Ottoman Empire [...]*. John Starkey and Henry Brome.

Rycaut, P. (1670). *Histoire de l'état present de l'Empire Ottoman [...]*, transl. by Monsieur Briot. Sebastien Mabre-Cramoisy.

Rycaut, P. (²1673). *Istoria dello stato presente dell'Impero Ottomano [...]*, transl. by C. Belli. Combi & La Noù: https://bdh-rd.bne.es/viewer.vm?id=0000037537&page=1. Date of Access: 24.02.2022.

Wheler, G. (1679). *Voyage de Dalmatie, de Grece, et du Levant*, vol. 1. Daniel Horthemels. https://gallica.bnf.fr/ark:/12148/bpt6k8727894v. Date of Access: 14.02.2022.

Yerasimos, S. & Berthier, A. (2002). *Topkapı Sarayı'nda yaşam. Albertus Bobovius ya da Santuri Ali Ufki Bey'in Anıları*, transl. by A. Berktay. Kitap Yayınevi.

Scholarly Literature

Abbott, G. F. (1920). *Under the Turk in Constantinople. A Record of Sir John Finch's Embassy 1674–1681*. Macmillan.

Abdel-Halim, M. (1964). *Antoine Galland : sa vie et son œuvre*. Nizet.

Aksoy, B. (²2003). *Avrupalı gezginlerin gözüyle Osmanlılarda musiki*. Pan Yayıncılık.

Babinger, F. (1936). Bobowski Wojciech z Bobowej. In Polska Akademia Nauk, Instytut Historii (Eds.), *Polski Słownik Biograficzny*, vol. 2 (pp. 156–157). Polska Akad. Umiejętności.

Bacqué-Grammont, J.-L., Kuneralp, S., & Hitzel, F. (1991). *Représentants permanents de la France en Turquie (1536–1991) et de la Turquie en France (1797–1991)*. ISIS.

Bauden, F. (2001). Nouveaux éclaircissements sur la vie et l'œuvre d'Antoine Galland (1646–1715). *Journal Asiatique* 289, 1–66.

Behar, C. (2005). *Musıkiden Müziğe. Osmanlı/Türk Müziği: Gelenek ve Modernlik*. Yapı Kredi Yayınları.

Bowles, E. A. (2006). The Impact of Turkish Military Bands on European Court Festivals in the 17th and 18th Centuries. *Early Music* 34, 533–559.

Dew, N. (2009). *Orientalism in Louis XIV's France*. Oxford University Press.

Feldman, W. (2021). Mehter. In K. Fleet, G. Krämer, D. Matringe, J. Nawas & E. Rowson, *Encyclopaedia of Islam, THREE*. http://dx.doi.org/10.1163/1573-3912_ei3_COM_36369. Date of Access: 09.01.2024.

Gökçen, İ. (2009). *Türk Musikisine Katkılar*. Ürün Yayınları.

Hammer-Purgstall, J. von. (1830). *Geschichte des osmanischen Reiches*, vol. 6. C. A. Hartleben.

Haug, J. I. (2019). *Ottoman and European Music in ʿAlī Ufuḳī's Compendium, MS Turc 292: Analysis, Interpretation, Cultural Context. Monograph*. readbox unipress.

Haug, J. I. (2023). "Representée avec beaucoup de succès": Theater and the French Embassy at Constantinople. In J. I. Haug & H. Walsdorf (Eds.), *Music and Mirrored Hybridities. Cultural Communities Converging in French, German, and Turkish Stage Productions (17th–20th Century) (pp. 195–200)*. Nomos.

Hitzel, F. (2010). Les ambassades occidentales à Constantinople et la diffusion d'une certaine image de l'Orient. *Comptes rendus des séances de l'Académie des Inscriptions et Belles-Lettres* 154, 277–92.

Jäger, R. M. (1998). *Europa und das Osmanische Reich in der Musik. Voraussetzungen und Ausprägungen gegenseitiger Rezeption und Assimilation des Fremden in der Musik bis zum Ende des 18. Jahrhunderts* [Unpublished Habilitation thesis, University of Münster].

Jäger, R. M. (2016). Janitscharenmusik. In L. Lütteken (Ed.), *MGG online*. https://www.mgg-online.com/article?id=mgg15525&version=1.0. Date of Access: 09.01.2024.

Kołodziejczyk, D. (1992). Ottoman Podillja: The *Eyalet* of Kam"janec', 1672–1699. *Harvard Ukrainian Studies* 16, 87–101.

Labaree, R. (2020). European Travelers on Music of the East: Religion, Musical Works, and the Otherness of the Ottomans. *Musical Quarterly* 102, 402–439.

Leedham-Green, E. (2004). Covel [Colvill], John. In *Oxford Dictionary of National Biography*. Oxford University Press. http://www.oxforddnb.com/view/article/6471. Date of Access: 09.01.2024.

Meyer, G. (2009). Le visage du colosse des Naxiens: Le témoignage des voyageurs qui firent escale à Délos au XVIIᵉ siècle. *Revue des Études Grecques* 122, 609–616.

Michaud, C. (1979). Raison d'État et conscience chrétienne. L'ambassade du marquis de Nointel auprès de la Porte Ottomane. *Revue des études sud-est européennes* 17, 257–267.

Neudecker, H. (2005). From Istanbul to London? Albertus Bobovius' Appeal to Isaac Basire. In A. Hamilton, M. H. van den Boogert & B. Westerweel (Eds.), *The Republic of Letters and the Levant* (pp. 173–196). Brill.

Olley, J. (2023). Evliya's Song: Listening to the Early Modern Ottoman Court. *Journal of the American Musicological Society* 76, 645–703.

Omont, H. (1902). *Missions archéologiques françaises en Orient aux XVIIᵉ et XVIIIᵉ siècles*, vol. 1. Imprimerie Nationale.

Öztürk, O. M. (2013). Evliya Çelebi Seyahatnamesi ve Mehter. In C. Yılmaz (Ed.), *Evliya Çelebi'nin dünyası* (pp. 191–198). Medam.

Pârlea, V. (2015). Images de soi et de l'autre en artiste à la croisée des regards dans les Mémoires du chevalier d'Arvieux. *Viatica [En ligne], L'Art des autres, 2015*, mis en ligne le 19/01/2021, https://revues-msh.uca.fr/viatica/index.php?id=463. Date of Access: 19.01.2021.

Parmentier, W. F. (2013). The *Mehter*: Cultural Perceptions and Interpretations of Turkish Drum and Bugle Music Throughout History. In M. Hüttler and H. E. Weidinger (Eds.), *Ottoman Empire and European Theater vol. I: The Age of Mozart and Selim III (1756–1808)* (pp. 287–305). Hollitzer.

Pawlina, A. (forthcoming). Life and Work of Wojciech Bobowski Revisited. Bobovius (Ali Ufkî) in Polish Source Material. *Rocznik Orientalistycny/Yearbook of Oriental Studies* 36.

Pirker, M. (1990). Pictorial Documents of the Music Bands of the Janissaries (Mehter) and the Austrian Military Music. *RIdIM/RCMI Newsletter* 15, 2–12.

Rice, E. (1999). Representations of Janissary Music (*Mehter*) as Musical Exoticism in Western Compositions, 1670–1824. *Journal of Musicological Research* 19(1), 41–88.

Sanal, H. (1964). *Mehter Musikisi. Bestekâr Mehterler, Mehter Havaları*. Millî Eğitim Basımevi.

Sanlıkol, M. A. (2011). *The Musician Mehters*. ISIS.

Scharrer, M. (2019). Zwischen Orient und Okzident: Musikerreisen abseits europäischer Wege, *Händel-Jahrbuch* 65, 185–203.

Sebag, P. (1978). Sur deux orientalists français du XVIIe siècle: F. Pétis de la Croix et le sieur de la Croix. *Revue de l'Occident musulman et de la Méditerranée* 25, 89–117.

Stollberg-Rilinger, B. (2000). Zeremoniell, Ritual, Symbol. Neue Forschungen zur symbolischen Kommunikation in Spätmittelalter und Früher Neuzeit. *Zeitschrift für Historische Forschung* 27, 389–405.

Stollberg-Rilinger, B. (2004). Symbolische Kommunikation in der Vormoderne. Begriffe – Thesen – Forschungsperspektiven. *Zeitschrift für Historische Forschung* 31, 490–527.

Tommasino, P. M. (2017). Travelling East, Writing in Italian. Literature of European Travel to the Ottoman Empire Written in Italian (16th and 17th Centuries). *Philological Encounters* 2, 28–51.

Vandal, A. (1900). *L'Odyssée d'un Ambassadeur. Les Voyages du Marquis de Nointel (1670–1680)*. Plon.

Vogel, C. (2014). The Art of Misunderstanding: French Ambassadors Translating Ottoman Court Ceremonial. In M. Sariyannis, G. Aksoy-Aivali, M. Demetriadou, Y. Spyropoulos, K. Stathi & Y. Vidras (Eds.), *New Trends in Ottoman Studies. Papers Presented at the 20th CIÉPO Symposium Rethymnon, 27 June – 1 July 2012*. University of Crete. https://anemi.lib.uoc.gr/metadata/7/8/e/metadata-1412743543-919456-15948.tkl. Date of Access: 09.01.2024.

Vural, T. (2012). Avrupalılara Göre Osmanlı Döneminde Askeri Müzik Geleneği. *Turkish Studies – International Periodical for the Languages, Literature and History of Turkish or Turkic* 7, 2569–2584.

Walsdorf, H. (2019). From Mishap to Mockery: Why and How *Le Bourgeois gentilhomme* was (Really) Born. In H. Walsdorf (Ed.), *Ritual Design for the Ballet Stage. Revisiting the Turkish Ceremony in Le Bourgeois Gentilhomme (1670)* (pp. 15–99). Frank und Timme.

Wilson, D. (2011). *List of British Consular Officials in the Ottoman Empire and its former Territories, from the Sixteenth Century to about 1860*. http://www.levantineheritage.com/pdf/List_of_British_Consular_Officials_Turkey(1581-1860)-D_Wilson.pdf. Date of Access: 09.01.2024.

Würflinger, C. (2020). Symbolic Communication in Habsburg-Ottoman Diplomatic Relations. The Grand Embassy of Johann Rudolf Schmid zum Schwarzenhorn (1650–51). *Legatio* 4, 95–122.

An Untold Battle of Music and Banners

Ambassadorial Entrance Ceremonies between the Ottoman and Habsburg Empires

Gamze İlaslan Koç

Backstage Negotiations

After wars were concluded with peace treaties, the Ottoman and Habsburg Empires exchanged ambassadors to reinforce their newly-established peace and "friendship" as defined in the respective treaties. Ambassadors virtually embodied their rulers, acting as an extension of their majestic images, which they carried to the host empires. Thus, homage or insult to the honour of an incoming diplomat denoted either the enhancement of the prestige of their ruler, or damage to that ruler's reputation. On one such occasion, the day before the exchange ceremony of the Ottoman and Habsburg ambassadors at the border in 1699, the Habsburg ambassador Graf von Öttingen instructed his translator to present his welcoming compliments to his counterpart, İbrahim Pasha. There was more than mere diplomatic courtesy in this greeting. The translator raised specific questions to the Ottoman ambassador and endeavoured to obtain written assurance regarding the organization of the coming ceremonial matters. Rather than a paraphrased report, he transcribed the entire dialogue verbatim (Türkei I 172-3, fols. 128r.–130r.; Türkei I 185-4, fols. 59r.–61r.). Since the details of the ceremony were of crucial importance, Öttingen did not wish to continue without clear assurance that his ambassadorial prestige would be respected.

His concerns were well-founded. According to the report from the Viennese archives, earlier, in 1665, the Ottoman ambassador to Vienna had verbally assured Walter Leslie, the Habsburg ambassador at the time, that his ceremonial entrances into Adrianople and Constantinople would be marked by trumpets, drums, and banners without any impediment. Yet despite these "sincerities" promised to Leslie, he was insulted in Adrianople by being forced to silence the music and roll up his banners. In response to Öttingen's request in 1699, the Ottoman ambassador affirmed that the "inconveniences" and "inequalities" at the time of Leslie's arrival were, to his knowledge, no longer to be expected. He justified the cancellation of the earlier promise as being due to transgressions of Leslie, whom he described as a "restless" and "stubborn" person. His accusations were directed not only toward Leslie, but also other "arrogant" diplomats to the Sublime Porte who had made similar demands. They, too, were faced with the "appropriate results" of their "overconfidence". But he asserted that the situation in Constantinople had changed and that the Ottomans had no objection to the new Habsburg ambassador's delegation flying a thousand banners and making as much noise as they wished. Yet he refused to provide a written confirmation, since this decision was not in his authority to make (Türkei I 172-3, fols. 128r.–v.).[1]

Ambassadorial entrance ceremonies to Vienna and Constantinople were complicated events and are challenging for historians to study. Printed materials such as newspapers, pamphlets, or copper engravings offer limited information, since they only reflect the final form of such ceremonies, not the complicated series of negotiations leading up them. Thus the document written by Öttingen's translator is quite unique. It shows the tense nature of the "backstage" bargaining process prior to the ceremonies, including the demands for musical representation. The visit to the Ottoman ambassador thirty-four years after the rebuke of the Habsburg ambassador Walter Leslie demonstrates how precedence established in earlier ceremonies was still remembered. Binding assurance in written form of ceremonial protocol was sought in order to strengthen the Habsburgs' hands in their struggle to gain equal footing with the Ottomans.

The so-called "acoustic", "aural", or "sonic turn" of the late 1960s received great attention both from musicologists and other social scientists, despite certain objections to calling it a "turn", rather than an extension or proliferation of existing sound studies (Braun, 2017, p. 89). The profound changes in the social sciences of the 1980s, a result of the overall impact of the rise of interdisciplinary studies, gave further impetus to studies of music and diplomacy and their intersection (Gienow-Hecht, 2015, p. 1). This growing body of scholarship has opened new avenues for reconceptualizing politics as an audible entity (Franklin, 2005, p. 7). These innovative approaches have introduced music and musical representations as novel historical topics of study. In contrast, earlier diplomatic history attributed leading agency and power only to state actors. "Sound diplomacy" enhanced diplomacy by considering both "social and cultural agents" as well as the socio-cultural environments where diplomatic scenes occurred (Gienow-Hecht, 2009, p. 5). Historians began to regard music as a medium for understanding power relations, hegemonic power, rivalries, and identity formation (Gienow-Hecht, 2015, p. 5).

Among the numerous functions of music with regard to power is its representation of sovereignty. Music has been shown to build relationships, promote prestige, transmit knowledge and ideas, and reflect self-representation and self-positioning. Underestimating

---

[1]   The quoted words are my translations from the original archival documents.

music and seeing it only from the perspective of aestheticism as an "artifice or an ornament in diplomatic practices" is misleading (Prévost-Thomas et al., 2018, p. 12). In addition to its uniting potential as an intermediator for communication and as a carrier of knowledge, music also divides. Music can promote both peace and violence (Mahiet et al., 2014, p. 5). Power is understood through the recognition and approval of others, and hence every musical representation (re)creates symbolic power (Fosler-Lussier, 2014, p. 273). Accordingly, analysing the musical performances at the Habsburg and Ottoman ambassadorial entrance ceremonies during the early modern period allows a reassessment of the power relations of the two sides and how these performances manifested the rivalry between them.

Playing and Displaying: Tracing Parity through Musical Representations and Peace Treaties

The Treaty of Zsitvatorok of 1606 is regarded a critical event that reshaped the relationship between the two empires, beginning a new era in which the oppressive military superiority of the Ottomans was replaced by bilateral relations in the form of parity (Strohmeyer, 2020, p. 973). The treaty brought about the recognition of titular equality between the sultan and emperor (whom the Ottomans had previously recognized only as "the king of Vienna"), the cessation of the Habsburgs' payment of a yearly tribute, and the obligation to send ambassadors bearing gifts to each other, in which reciprocity and equal standing of the empires came to the fore (Atçıl, 2021, p. 137).

In this chapter, this theoretical equality is re-examined by means of a micro-scale case study of one type of the empires' diplomatic ceremonial: musical performances during ambassadorial entrance ceremonies in the two imperial capitals. The study offers examples of how the two empires displayed their relationship to one another and portrayed their equality (or non-equality) through the medium of music. A detailed examination of the theory and practice of these ceremonial performances reveals a complicated reality beneath the outward appearance of equality. Indeed, the practice of diplomacy was often different than the abstract ideals presented in normative peace agreements.

Under the terms of the Treaty of Zsitvatorok of 1606, whose validity continued until the Treaty of Belgrade in 1740, the Ottoman and Habsburg courts appointed ambassadors to posts in each other's capitals. This formal exchange of ambassadors was also referred to explicitly in particular articles in various other treaties: in the sixteenth article of the Treaty of Carlowitz of 1699, the seventeenth article of the Treaty of Passarowitz of 1718, and the twentieth article of the Treaty of Belgrade of 1739 (Moser, 1740, pp. 65–66).

This chapter investigates whether the ambassadorial retinues of each side were able to engage in musical representation or not, based on case studies of ambassador exchanges following the peace treaties of 1627 (Szöny), 1665 (Vasvár), 1699 (Carlowitz), 1718 (Passarowitz), and 1739 (Belgrade). Coupled with the playing of music, another symbol of sovereignty was the display of unfurled banners. This was also a point of dispute between the two empires. Because of the interwoven nature of these two features, I have chosen to address them both.

Ambassadorial Entrance Ceremonies

The main chain of events of an ambassadorial journey consisted of each delegation having an audience with their own monarch, followed by a procession in their own respective capitals, the exchange of diplomats at the border, and an entrance ceremony into the capital of the host empire. After this, the incoming diplomat was received, respectively, by the Ottoman grand vizier or the president of the Habsburg Imperial War Council. Next came a welcome audience before the sultan or emperor, at which gifts were delivered. Despite the general tendency to see the welcome audience as the climax of such delegation visits, the principal ceremony was in fact the entrance ceremony because of its visibility and display of power in the public space. An entrance involved the active participation of the many high-ranking state officers who had organized the event, soldiers escorting the ambassadorial retinue, and onlookers from many different strata of the city's inhabitants. Indeed, entrance ceremonies provided the first official impression of a delegation in the public sphere. These spectacles mirrored the political relations between the parties and can be seen as a sort of "political barometer" (Teply, 1976, p. 71). How incoming diplomats were treated revealed current or planned foreign policies, either positive, with shows of exceptional favour and attention, or negative, with maltreatment and dishonour of the arriving party (Işıksel, 2019, p. 291; Karateke, 2007, p. 6). The ceremonies provided an opportunity to reveal the status or ranking between the host and the guest empire, as well as the hierarchy among other diplomatic agents present (Sowerby, 2021, p. 228; Hennings, 2021, pp. 55–56).

As the name implies, these ceremonies took place when ambassadors arrived at the opposing capital: Constantinople or Vienna. The Habsburg and Ottoman ceremonies shared some common characteristics. Upon their approach, the ambassadors lodged themselves in tents outside the city walls and notified the high-ranking diplomats of the host empire of their arrival. In return, they received a welcoming letter.[2] The parties arranged the exact date of the ceremony and negotiated their demands, ranging from the preparation of a protocol for their diplomatic residences, receipt of monetary allowances (*tayinat*), the or-

---

2   Habsburg diplomats arrived in Constantinople by land; the ceremonial procedure for seaborn diplomats was different. See Kütükoğlu, 1989, p. 215; Işıksel, 2019, p. 291.

der of the marching retinues, how they were to hold their muskets, to whether or not they could unfurl their banners and sound their music. This arduous bargaining process caused delays, since the parties did not always agree. The atmosphere of the ceremonial entries was tense, because any appeasement made by one of the parties might negatively affect their subsequent bargaining power. All were aware that each ceremony would become a precedent that could be used to determine the procedure of future ceremonies. On the day of the ceremony, the host empire sent high-ranking officers to welcome and accompany the incoming ambassador. Both empires presented a richly adorned horse from their imperial stables for the diplomat to ride during the ceremony, although the Ottomans made a point of only riding the Habsburg horse briefly before presenting an excuse to return it in favour of their own horses.[3] The marching route proceeded as a parade outside the city, beginning at Küçükçekmece (Ponte Piccolo) in Constantinople and Schwechat in Vienna, and concluding at the ambassador's diplomatic residence in the city of their new post.[4]

Between the empires, there were different practices in the processions. In the Ottoman Empire, the ceremony began in the early hours of the morning. In 1740, for instance, the Habsburg ambassador Corfiz Ulfeld noted that his entourage, accompanied by a specific Ottoman officer, moved from their tents in Florya Çiftliği toward Davudpaşa, where a banquet took place at around two o'clock in the morning (Türkei I 221-3, fol. 240r.). In Vienna, the entrance ceremonies began at around eleven o'clock. Perhaps the standard custom of the Ottomans of offering a banquet (*yemeklik*) before the parade led to this difference in starting times. It was a unique Ottoman custom to present flowers and fruits to the Habsburg ambassadors when they reached their lodgings at the end of the ceremony (Schönwetter, 1702, p. 72; Driesch, 1723, p. 158; Türkei I 221-3, fol. 244r.).[5] The Habsburgs emphasized their great admiration for the massive crowd of onlookers, as well as the sultan observing their solemn procession incognito (Driesch, 1723, p. 162; Niggl, 1701, p. 120), which reflected the high prestige they had received. The Habsburg delegates also informed the other European diplomats in Constantinople of their arrival. In return for this diplomatic courtesy, European representatives sent their officers and horses as a compliment, enlivening the ceremony and making it more comfortable for the incoming Habsburg diplomat. The Ottomans had no comparable reception with other diplomats in Vienna.[6]

---

3   For Kara Mehmed Pasha in 1665 and İbrahim Pasha in 1699: Schönwetter, 1702, p. 55; for Canibi Ali Pasha in 1740: OMeA ZA-Prot. 17, fol. 200r.

4   For the marching route from Schwechat to Leopoldstadt of the 1628 Ottoman embassy to Vienna, with details of street names, see Cevrioğlu, 2021b, pp. 91–93, 106. For the marching route in Istanbul of the Habsburg embassy in 1700, see C.HR.150/7475, and of 1740, MAD.d. 23771, p. 8.

5   The author of *Gründ- und Umständlicher Bericht Von Denen Römisch-Kayserlichen Wie auch Ottomannischen Groß-Bothschafften* is anonymous; hereafter this text will be referred to as Schönwetter, its publisher's name.

6   The news of the arrival had to be simultaneously sent to the other European diplomats in Constan-

1616, Freiherr Hermann von Czernin

In 1616, Freiherr Hermann von Czernin was the first Habsburg ambassador to enter Constantinople with drums, trumpets, and unfurled banners. The flying banners were decorated with images of the crucified Jesus and the imperial double-headed eagle (Wenner, 1622, pp. 46–47; Khevenhüller, 1723, p. 945; Strohmeyer, 2014, p. 491). This did not take place without controversy. Disagreement between the Ottomans and Habsburgs over one another's permission to use music and banners began with Czernin and continued thereafter.

The Ottoman sergeant-at-arms (*çavuşbaşı*) who welcomed Czernin and led the ceremony was discharged from his office immediately after the ceremony and condemned to death, although he was later forgiven through the intercession of Czernin (Wenner, 1622, p. 50). According to an old prophecy, if a flag of the cross flew in Constantinople, the Ottoman Empire would fall. The flags thus enraged the Muslims and the sultan himself (Hammer-Purgstall, 1829, p. 486). The banners and figures were the reason for the tumult and the dismissal of the sergeant-at-arms, but in this crisis no reference was made to the sounding of music. Like the entrance ceremony, the departure of the delegation required a procession. The departure parade was held on 20 July 1617, this time with flags rolled up but still accompanied by trumpets and drums; the deputy grand vizier still raised some objections (Wenner, 1622, p. 99).

This case shows that the two symbols of sovereignty – music and banners – had a hierarchy of importance. Here, more importance was attributed to the flags. Nonetheless, the music was also disputed, although Czernin convinced the Ottomans to allow it for his entrance and departure. Also the Habsburg delegation led by Mollard in 1618 was permitted to sound music but forced to roll up its banners. At his entrance to Constantinople in 1634, Johann Rudolf Puchhaimb was prohibited from both, as was Johann Schmid zum Schwarzenhorn in 1651 (Spuler, 1935, p. 180; Kolçak, 2023, p. 14, fn. 52).

1628, Recep Pasha and Hans Ludwig von Kuefstein

To renew the peace treaty of Zsitvatorok for the fourth time, Recep Pasha and Hans Ludwig von Kuefstein were exchanged as ambassadors in 1628. The ambassadorial entrance ceremony of the former into Vienna occurred on 21 October, and of the latter into Constantinople, on 25 November. Both planned to use banners and music as part of their ceremonial entrance. One day before the entrance of Recep Pasha, Habsburg authorities called on the citizens of Vienna to bring their own banners and muskets to accompany the Ottoman diplomat's procession.

---

tinople, since it would have otherwise caused trouble regarding precedence among them, as had occurred with the embassy of Öttingen in 1699 (Driesch, 1723, p. 154). For general information about this, see Sowerby, 2021, pp. 225–226.

The following day, the Viennese presented themselves in an orderly manner along the parade route (*Ordentliche Zeittungen* 1628, October 21; *Ordentliche Zeittungen* 1628, October 28). Archival documents and visual sources depicting the ceremony confirmed that Recep Pasha was accompanied by musicians who played military music at the ceremony. The Ottoman diplomat attempted to unfurl his banners, but was prohibited from doing so (For the engraving, see Anonymous, 1628; Burschel, 2007, p. 414; Jäger, 2011, p. 45; Cevrioğlu, 2021a, pp. 236–240).

The overall composition of the procession and the type and number of musical instruments can be determined from a copper engraving depicting the ceremony. The marching order is described in a historical account (Khevenhüller, 1726, pp. 277–278). It is clear that the Habsburgs intentionally structured the procession to diminish the visibility of the Ottomans. Hungarian soldiers escorting the Ottomans from the border occupied the first rows of the ceremonial procession. Some playing trumpets were on foot, while others played trumpets and drums on horseback. The Ottomans and their musicians were situated at the end of the parade. They were not left unaccompanied, but were interspersed with Habsburg military musicians playing trumpets and drums. According to the visual representation, the Habsburg musicians outnumbered the Ottoman ensemble by more than two to one.

The Habsburg ambassador Kuefstein knew that his counter-ambassador in Vienna had been allowed to play music during the entrance ceremony but prohibited from raising banners (Burschel, 2007, p. 414; Cevrioğlu, 2021a, pp. 241–242). Kuefstein expected equal treatment in Constantinople, but he received the news that the deputy grand vizier would neither permit him to unfurl his banners nor sound his music, despite earlier written assurances from the governor of Buda. Kuefstein's first reaction was to postpone the entrance ceremony, begin negotiations on the issue, and refer to the sultan. Still refused, Kuefstein found the situation unjust and unreasonable (Cevrioğlu, 2021a, pp. 242–244). The Sublime Porte informed him that the prohibition was not intended to belittle either the emperor or him, but was simply to maintain traditional Ottoman law (Khevenhüller, 1726, p. 269). In his ambassadorial report, Kuefstein suggested to the emperor that the issue of sounding music and flying banners either had to be resolved with the Ottomans upon the departure of the delegation, or the Habsburgs should keep their silence and not press their claims further (Cevrioğlu, 2021a, p. 294). Thus, despite theoretical parity in the post-Zsitvatorok period, inequality in ceremonial performances continued. The Habsburg embassy of 1628 was not allowed to sound music during its entrance ceremony, even though the Ottoman embassy had done so in Vienna (Teply, 1976, pp. 70–74, 118–119).

1665, Kara Mehmed Pasha and Walter Leslie

The next Ottoman–Habsburg war (1663–1664) was brought to an end by the Battle of St. Gotthard, a defeat for the Ottoman army. This led to the exchange of ambassadors

Kara Mehmed Pasha and Walter Leslie. The case of these two ambassadors exemplifies how both sides, in pressing for the use of music and banners, continually sought to outmanoeuvre one another, adopting various strategies to that effect.

When the Ottoman embassy reached Schwechat in Vienna, Kara Mehmed Pasha learned that the Habsburg emperor had forbidden them to play music or fly banners, and demanded that Habsburg court military musicians perform their music in front of the Ottoman ambassador (Yücel, 1996, pp. 300–301; Evliya Çelebi, 2003, pp. 88–89). The Ottomans objected to this staunchly. The Habsburg officers attempted to justify the measure by falsely claiming that in the protocol registries, there was no precedent of Ottoman musicians playing (Yücel, 1996, p. 300). According to the chronicle of Mühürdar Hasan Agha, the Ottomans responded that the military ensemble was a gift from the sultan who delegated them as ambassadors out of friendship; if they were forbidden to follow Ottoman protocol rules, how could their friendship be demonstrated? The Ottomans insisted on playing their music and raising their banners; otherwise, they would not agree to enter the city. The intensive and persistent counter efforts of the Habsburgs were unsuccessful. The entrance ceremony occurred on 8 June 1665, with the Habsburgs having given in to the Ottoman demand to play music and display their banners (Yücel, 1996, p. 301).[7]

Nevertheless, the Ottoman ambassador did not appreciate the participation of the military musicians of the "unbelievers" and their intrusion into his cortege (Evliya Çelebi, 2003, p. 88). On the day of the ceremony, Habsburg military musicians sounded their music just in front of the ambassador, while his ensemble played at the back; thus, both Habsburg and Ottoman military music was simultaneously played at the ceremony. Because the Habsburg military musicians occupied the first rows and outnumbered the Ottoman military band, Ralph Martin Jäger has referred to the entrance ceremony of Kara Mehmed Pasha as only a "partial victory" for the Ottomans (Jäger, 2011, p. 48).[8]

Evliya Çelebi reveals that the military ensemble of Kara Mehmed Pasha sounded its music not only at the entrance ceremony, but also at two banquets in Vienna: one in the garden of the emperor, the other in the garden of the emperor's mother (Evliya Çelebi, 2003, pp. 112–114). The predecessor of Kara Mehmed Pasha, namely Recep Pasha in 1628,

---

7 Determining the exact number of Ottoman and Viennese musicians is not easy. Numbers can be determined from the copper engraving at the Theatrum Europaeum (Meyer, 1672, pp. 1504–1508), archival documents in the Viennese archives, and notes by Evliya Çelebi (Jäger, 2011, p. 46), but these are not consistent with one another. Viennese sources make it clear that the total number of Viennese musicians outnumbered the janissary music ensemble, as had been the case for Recep Pasha in 1628. On the Ottoman musical instruments used in 1665, see: Jäger, 2011, p. 48; OMeA *ZA Prot. 2,* fol. 1184.

8 Though some scholars: (Aktan, 2019, p. 160) have stated that the Ottoman music played at the entrance ceremony of 1665 was the "first" music of this kind the Viennese had heard, this was not the case if considering the entrance of Kara Mehmed Pasha's predecessor Recep Pasha.

also had his music played on 2 January 1629 during the New Year celebrations at the Vienna court (Cevrioğlu, 2021a, p. 312). This shows the different attitudes of Habsburg authorities toward musical performances in the public streets of Vienna as opposed to those taking place in private imperial spaces. Controlling public spaces was far more significant for imperial charisma and power; only in private could the Ottomans play their music unhindered.

At the time Kara Mehmed took his mission to Vienna, the Ottoman sultan was in Adrianople. Thus, Walter Leslie held his ambassadorial procession and audience in that city instead of Constantinople. The date of his ambassadorial entrance ceremony (1 August 1665) was not arbitrarily chosen (Kolçak, 2012, p. 68), but was deliberately meant to fall on the anniversary of the Battle of St. Gotthard. As Leslie's retainer explained, the date marked "the glorious victory [...] when the arrogance of the Turks was humiliated [...], and they recognized what the unity of Christian potentates could do" (Tafferner, 1670, p. 74). Yet, at the Adrianople procession, neither the eight musicians with their silver trumpets nor the drummers with their silk banners stitched with the ambassadorial coat of arms were allowed to sound their music. Moreover, their banners remained rolled up. The Ottomans explained that it was customary to silence music and roll up flags in the presence of an Ottoman sultan (Tafferner, 1670, p. 75; Meyer, 1672, p. 1525). Leslie's retainers perceived this as manifesting the intolerance of the Ottomans and the indescribable arrogance of the Ottoman monarchs (Burbury, 1671, pp. 145–146; Tafferner, 1670, p. 77). Because the Ottomans justified this prohibition on the basis of the sultan's presence, a unique opportunity presented itself. Leslie requested permission from the grand vizier to leave Adrianople and enter Constantinople, where, in the sultan's absence, he could sound his trumpets and fly his banners unhindered. The grand vizier accepted this request and sent a letter to inform his deputy in Constantinople (Veltze, 1900, pp. 155–156). Leslie's departure procession from Adrianople on 26 August occurred with the "joyful" sounds of trumpets and flying banners (Meyer, 1672, p. 1531; Tafferner, 1670, p. 111). The entrance ceremony in Constantinople proceeded on 7 September and included, as promised, a music performance and the raising of banners. Tafferner described the ceremony as one of great splendour and honour, and emphasized that the joyful sounds of their trumpets and drums made it seem as if the city belonged to the Habsburgs. He imagined that Habsburg music gave the miserable hearts of Christian prisoners of war hope and rid them of their slavish sorrows. (Tafferner, 1670, pp. 116–118).

Thus Kara Mehmed Pasha was permitted to play music, but not without its ceremonial impact being blunted by the presence of Viennese musicians in his procession, and while Leslie could not have his music played in Adrianople, he was allowed to do so in Constantinople, albeit only because of the sultan's absence. The two empires were thus not operating on equal terms. Both sides struggled to fully implement their ceremonial ideals in the other's capital, while at the same time inhibiting their counterpart's ceremony in their own. Here as well, there was an imbalance: Leslie had to rely on the permission of the Ottoman authorities, whereas Kara Mehmed Pasha felt comfortable simply demanding that he have his way.

Musical Representation from a "Ritual of Unbelievers" to "Custom": 1700, İbrahim Pasha and Graf von Öttingen

The Treaty of Carlowitz was signed in 1699 in the aftermath of a series of Ottoman defeats. For the Ottomans, this had not only resulted in the loss of vast territories, but also losses in their reputation on the diplomatic front (Arı, 2004, p. 53). As a consequence, the Habsburg ambassadors became more self-assertive in their demands. A new phase began in the Ottoman Empire, that of transitioning from unilateral agreements to bilateral diplomacy. After the treaty's signing, the ambassadors İbrahim Pasha and Graf von Öttingen were dispatched to Vienna and Constantinople, respectively. When İbrahim Pasha arrived in Vienna, a Habsburg translator was sent to the ambassador to organize the ceremonial procession. This time, there were no references to music or banners among the bargaining points, which was already made when the ambassadors were at the border. Instead, the ambassador was warned to behave properly and show the Viennese officers appropriate courtesy. After Kara Mehmed Pasha's stay in 1665, the impression left behind had been his rude and offensive behaviour in his interactions with the Hofmarschall, for example, taking his boots off in the Hofmarschall's presence, not shaking hands with him, and not accompanying him out of the pasha's ambassadorial quarters. Moreover, the janissaries were ordered not to hold their muskets facing upward on their shoulders during the procession (OMeA ZA-Prot. 6, fols. 7r.–8r.; Türkei IV 13-3, fols. 1r.–2v.; Türkei I 173, 2–1, fol. 73r.).

The pasha made his official entrance into Vienna on 30 January 1700. He was accompanied by the mayor of Vienna, other high-ranking diplomats, and various commanders with their soldiers. Moreover, a large number of Viennese drummers and trumpeters were employed to accompany the entourage (Schönwetter, 1702, pp. 51–56; for images, see Fig. 1 and Felsecker, 1700).[9] The musical instruments played by the Ottoman military

---

9   In both the Viennese and Ottoman archival documents, the number of janissary band musicians is recorded as thirty (Türkei I 175-3, fols. 11r., 12v., 141r.; Uluskan, 2008, p. 256). The number of chamber musicians, the *Cammer Musicant*, are consistently recorded in the Viennese documents as five (Dervis Achmed, Chalil Cselebi, Dervis Ali, Mechmed Aga, and Sachin Cselebi [= Derviş Ahmed, Halil Çelebi, Derviş Ali, Mehmed Ağa, Şahin Çelebi]) (Türkei I 173-2-1, fols. 45v., 46r.; Türkei I 175-3, fols. 12r., 12v., 141v., 142r.). In contrast, in the Ottoman documents these musicians, referred to as *sazendegan*, are listed as numbering ten (Uluskan, 2008, pp. 256–257). Determining the exact number

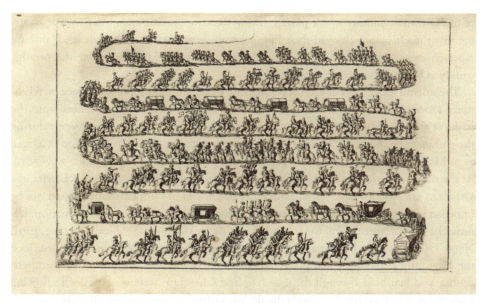

Fig. 1: Entrance ceremony of İbrahim Pasha to Vienna in 1700.

band during the ceremony are listed in the Viennese sources as shawms, small and large drums, trumpets, and cymbals (Türkei I 173-2-1, fol. 83r.; Schönwetter, 1702, p. 53).[10] The Habsburg accounts describe the Ottoman music as making a "very different and strange" sound (Schönwetter, 1702, p. 53; Lünig, 1719, p. 540). An earlier Habsburg retainer from the 16th century had similarly criticized Ottoman music as "noisy and discordant" (Demirbaş, 2021, p. 691). Indeed, the Habsburgs regularly expressed their negative impression

> of members in theses ambassadorial retinues is challenging for historians. For example, in one Viennese document, the number of members in the pasha's entourage during the exit from Adrianople is given as 672 and in the entrance to Vienna as 561 (HS B 222, fols. 44–45). Another Viennese archival record gives the number as 520 (Türkei I 173-2-1, fol. 46v.). Ottoman documents give the number of members in the entourage as 571 (Uluskan, 2008, p. 256). Thus, it has not been possible to determine the exact number of ceremonial musicians or of the members in the entire entourage.

10 The military musical instruments are mentioned in the Schönwetter account as follows: "Den Train die völlige Türckische Feld=Music, bestehend in Schallmeyen/Zimbeln/Trompeten/kleinen Paucken/ und gar grossen Trommeln/ so auf Pferden geführet und von beyden Seiten zugleich geschlagen wurden/ welche Music einen gar differenten und frembden Klang von sich gabe/ und ohne Aufhören continuirte." The Ottoman records generally do not specify the type of musical instruments used at particular diplomatic encounters, but a rare document about a banquet organized in Sadabad for the Habsburg ambassador in 1740 gives both the number of chamber musicians as well as the instruments: (*yevm-i mezburda ihzar olunan hanende* [singers] 13, *ney* [reed flute] 8, *tanbur* [long-necked lute] 4, *santur* [dulcimer] 2, *keman* [violin] 3, *sine-keman* [breast violin] 1, *düdük* [folk flute] 1, *nefir* [horn] 2, *çenk* [*çeng*/harp] 1, *miskal* [panpipe] 2) (MAD.d.23771, p. 16).

of the Ottoman military music played during these diplomatic encounters, while asserting that the Ottomans enjoyed their European music with great enchantment. Habsburg representatives and eyewitnesses were not eager to acknowledge the power and prestige conveyed by the Ottoman music.[11]

The solemn procession of Graf von Öttingen into Constantinople took place on 8 February 1700.[12] The Viennese court instructed him to obtain written assurances from the pasha at the border that he would be allowed to sound his music and fly banners during the entrance ceremony. This was to stress his parity with the Ottoman ambassador, as well as to hinder what had befallen his predecessor in 1665 (Türkei I 172-3, fols. 74r.–76v.). At the meeting at the border between the pasha and Öttingen's translator Lackowitz, the Ottoman ambassador gave verbal assurances that the Habsburg emissaries would not be impeded in Constantinople, but he refrained from providing a written confirmation. Ultimately, the entrance ceremony did include music and banners (Schönwetter, 1702, p. 71; Niggl, 1701, p. 119). In his dispatch to Vienna dated 23 February 1700, Öttingen described the ceremony as having taken place "with flying banners and the sounds of trumpets, drums, and hautboys through the gate [...] and Christians were watching with flowing tears and raising their hands towards the sky with happiness, as they were the first since the conquest of the city to have the luck to see freely flying Roman eagles and the holy image of Christ and Mary"[13] (Türkei I 173-2-2, fols. 172r.–172v.). After the Treaty of Carlowitz, the embassy of Öttingen was the first to have proper-sounding musical representation along with banners in the Ottoman capital, despite the sultan being present in the city. Nevertheless, the Ottomans sought diplomatic manoeuvres to lessen the effect of this and had Ottoman music played during the entrance ceremony as well. Just as the Viennese had sounded their own music during the entrance ceremonies of the Ottomans, Ottoman musicians accompanied the Habsburg musicians in the first rows of the entourage (Niggl, 1701, p. 118), with Öttingen and his entourage positioned at the end of the procession. Thus their physical location was encircled or trapped, mirroring the positions of the Ottoman procession into Vienna.

Silahdar, a contemporary Ottoman chronicler, described the Ottoman officers as attempting to disrupt the parade. The marching route of the Habsburg embassy was directed

---

11   Other musical activities of İbrahim Pasha included Ramadan celebrations and a visit to the opera. When he sounded his military music with "great tumult" during the celebrations of Ramadan in his diplomatic lodging in Vienna, the city inhabitants showed great interest. Moreover, he accepted an invitation of the emperor and went to an opera performance (HS B 222, fols. 51–53).

12   In the Viennese documents, his entourage is recorded as numbering 275, among them 23 musicians (Türkei I 175-3, fols. 4r.–5v.), whereas an Ottoman chronicler stated that his embassy comprised 150 people (Silahdar, 2018, p. 563).

13   Translation made by the author.

along a different path than usual, a path avoiding the centre of the city entirely. In addition to Öttingen refusing to silence his musicians and defending their right to play, he protested the orders to march outside the city centre (Silahdar, 2018, pp. 563–564). In the end, his entourage marched defiantly through the inner city (Türkei I 173-2-2, fol. 172v.; Silahdar, 2018, p. 562). The growing parity between the empires ultimately provided the Habsburgs with what they sought: an entrance ceremony for the ambassador with music and flying banners through the inner city. Although the Ottomans were unsuccessful, they sought to retain their imperial prestige by keeping the Habsburg music and banners under tight control. Öttingen's secretary noted that the Turks showed particular interest in the sound of the hautboys (Niggl, 1701, p. 119). But not all Ottoman onlookers shared this perspective: Silahdar, the Ottoman chronicler, was especially disturbed by the sounds of the Habsburg music, calling it a "ritual of the unbelievers" (*ayin-i batıl*) and regretting that it was performed openly in the capital. Moreover, Öttingen's insistence led the Ottoman chronicler to describe him as an "accursed pig" (Silahdar, 2018, p. 564).

1719, Dayezade İbrahim Pasha and Graf Damian Hugo von Virmond

With the Passarowitz treaty, the Habsburgs were granted undisputed possession of all of Hungary, resulting in an immense increase in the monarchy's financial resources and prestige, with a corresponding loss of Ottoman authority (Heppner et al., 2011, p. 54). The Ottoman ambassador Dayezade İbrahim Pasha made his entrance into Vienna on 14 August 1719. Musical representation and the unfurling of banners were now no longer a matter of conflict (Türkei I 185-4, fols. 102r.–103r.). As had become customary, Habsburg musicians played their trumpets and drums, and the Ottoman musicians positioned themselves at the end of the parade (Türkei IV 13-3, fols. 8r.–8v.). In contrast, the experiences of the Habsburg ambassador Graf Virmond in Constantinople during the corresponding ceremony represented the last attempt of the Ottomans to assert their dominance over the Habsburgs' musical representation. After this event, equality of practice was finally established (Fig. 2).

A few days before Virmond's entrance ceremony on 3 August 1719, the Ottoman court translator delivered a letter from the grand vizier granting the Habsburgs "permission" to sound their military music and fly their banners. This led to the Habsburg ambassador's annoyance and displeasure, about which he informed the Viennese court. In his view, this issue had already been settled. The notion that he needed "permission" to do what Ottoman ambassadors were already allowed to do in Vienna offended him (Türkei I 184-2, fols. 208r.–208v., Türkei I 185-2, fol. 16v.). His secretary Driesch also referred to Virmond's dissatisfaction (Driesch, 1723, pp. 157–158). Considering the arduous attempts of his predecessors to sound their music and unfurl banners, his irritation within the new diplomatic parity is understandable. Rather than needing to receive permission from the

Fig. 2: Entrance of Virmond in 1719.

grand vizier, he viewed it as his equal right and appropriate to the honour of himself and his emperor.

According to Driesch's account, the Ottoman court translator declared that during the entrance ceremonies of the British and Dutch envoys a year before, in 1718, both had been prohibited from sounding music or raising their banners, thus emphasizing how great an honour had been given to Virmond despite his not having requested it. According to the Ottoman protocol registers kept by the master of protocol (*teşrifatçıbaşı*) Selman Efendi, at the entrance ceremony to Constantinople of the newly-appointed English envoy on 5 May 1718, the envoy had asserted that it was British custom to unfurl their banners. Selman Efendi opposed them by pointing out that holding a procession with sounding trumpets and unfurled flags in the city where the sultan resided was against the law (*hilaf-ı kanun*). Despite the persistent objection of the British to this prohibition and insistence on flying their banners, the Ottomans succeeded in preventing the practice of an "unfounded concoction" (*zann-ı batıl*), as Selman Efendi phrased it (Sadaret Defterleri [A.} d.] 347, p. 20). The second example used to persuade Virmond was that of the Dutch envoy, who on 18 September 1718 returned to Constantinople from the treaty negotiations of Passarowitz. According to the Ottoman protocol registers, the Dutch envoy was also restrained from playing music and raising banners (Sadaret Defterleri [A.} d.] 347, p. 28). This evidence illustrates that the Ottomans continued to enforce their law forbidding incoming diplomats from manifesting their own symbols of sovereignty in the capital. Although envoys and ambassadors were ranked differently and thus it was logical that envoys did not receive the same treatment as ambassadors,[14] it is not surprising that the Ottoman court translator highlighted the privileged status of the Habsburg Empire, instead of referring to the "permission" offered in the grand vizier's letter.

Although Selman Efendi referred to the Western music and unfurled banners of the British and Dutch envoys in the protocol registries as "against the law" and an "unfounded concoction", with regard to the entrance ceremony of Virmond he simply noted that trumpets were played ("tranpetesin çalarak"). He makes no reference to Ottoman law, nor is there any mention of banners (Sadaret Defterleri [A.} d.] 347, p. 53). However, the Ottomans found a way to lessen Virmond's prestige: The Ottoman sergeant-at-arms did not accompany Virmond's entourage all the way to the ambassadorial lodging, but left them already in Eyüp (MAD.d.23771, p. 2). Virmond's report explains this deviation from established ceremonial rule as having been due to the excuse of the sergeant-at-arms that he was fasting for Ramadan and thus was tired (Türkei I 184-2, fols. 208v.–209r.). The chronicler Silahdar, who had called Öttingen's 1700 embassy a "ritual of unbelievers", did not change his mind and referred in the same way to the sounding of Habsburg music at Virmond's entrance ceremony in 1719 (Silahdar, 2018, p. 1105).

The dissatisfaction among the state authorities in Constantinople concerning the embassy's music and flags can also be seen in a report of the grand vizier to the sultan, in which the grand vizier calls the Habsburg ambassador thick-headed (*'gabî*), an insulting

---

14   There was also a hierarchy among the ambassadors; for instance, Hammer-Purgstall compares entrance ceremonies of the Habsburg and Russian ambassadors delegated after the treaty of Belgrade, while highlighting the pompous and more privileged status of the prior. Hammer-Purgstall bases his argument on the number of trumpeters of the Russian ambassador who were allowed to blow just a little, compared to those of the Habsburgs (Hammer-Purgstall, 1832, p. 31). Despite some scholars arguing that this Russian ambassador, Count Aleksandr Rumiantsev (Romançoff/Romanzoff/Rumjancevs) was prohibited from sounding his music in Constantinople in 1741 (Spuler, 1935, p. 181), Ottoman ceremonial registers confirm that they unfurled the banners and sounded their military music ("bu vech üzere bayrakları açub trompete ve tabl ve gayri sazlar çalarak"). Besides, apart from trumpeters who were given as two ("iki nefer trompete çalıcılar"), one drummer ("bir nefer tabl-zen"), there was also a standard-bearer on horseback ("atlı bir alfier" [alfiere]). For the abovementioned archival document, see D.TŞF. 2/4. Taken into account, the Russian ambassadors delegated after peace treaties demanded to be treated based on the example of Habsburg ambassadors in Istanbul, even an Ottoman ceremonial registers note that the entrance ceremony of Rumiantsev was designed based on the entrance ceremony of the Habsburg ambassador from 1740, so, it is not surprising that the Russians entered to Istanbul sounding their music ("sazların çalarak") (Çevik, 2018, p. 211). For an earlier version of such demands of a Russian diplomat from 1702 to be treated equal to the representatives of Habsburg rulers in Istanbul concerning the ceremonial matters, see Hennings, 2021, pp. 59, 63. The delegation of Rumiantsev's successor, Prince Repnin, also unfurled the banners and beat the drums in 1774 (Mansel, 1998, p. 204).

expression that should be interpreted as based on the grand vizier's inability to convince the ambassador. And yet, although the grand vizier refers to the ambassador with contempt, he also assures the sultan that the old customs had not been breached, despite the ambassador's ceremonial entrance featuring the playing of trumpets and the unfurling of three flags ("borusun çalmış ve üç bayrak açmış öyle geçmiş gitmiş"). The grand vizier framed the issue first by saying that the ceremony was conducted as it had been during the reign of Sultan Mustafa II, referring to the embassy of Öttingen in 1700. Secondly, in his report to the sultan the grand vizier quoted a sentence of Virmond: "I [the ambassador] had no opposition to the old customs" ("elçi dahi kadime muhalefetim yokdur demiş") (AE. SAMD.III 229/22040). The Ottoman statesmen did not appreciate Habsburg music and flags in the public space, but the ceremonial procession of the embassy after the Treaty of Passarowitz followed the "new" custom as had been established by Öttingen's embassy after the Treaty of Carlowitz.[15]

Although Virmond played music and unfurled his banners during his entrance ceremony, he refrained from doing so during the subsequent procession to meet the grand vizier and sultan. He was familiar with his predecessor's ambassadorial report and knew that there was no precedent for this. Still, he wished to do so, since he believed his banners and musicians should receive more "honour" from the grand vizier and "respect" from the sultan (Türkei I 184-2, fols. 210r.–210v.). He thus asked the Ottoman translator about the potential reaction of the Ottomans if he were to employ them, but the answer was not favourable. Virmond decided not to push the issue, citing the fact that Ottoman diplomats in Vienna had also not been allowed to fly their banners or sound their music when they met with the president of the Imperial War Council and the emperor.[16] What Virmond valued was equality; he was happy to leave his banners and music behind, as long as he knew doing so would not make him or his sovereign appear lower in status than the Ottomans.

15 Despite the conflict regarding prestige and symbolic power linked to Western-style music not being allowed in public spaces, both Virmond and his predecessor Öttingen had their musicians play at the banquets given by the grand viziers inside rooms of waterfront pavilions in Istanbul. An Ottoman archival document dating to 1700 states that Öttingen's singers sang vocal music ("elçinin hanendeleri dahi fasıl etmişlerdir") at a banquet (D.TŞF. 1/79); it was asserted by the embassy of Virmond that the idea to have the Habsburg musicians play at the banquet was originally on the request of the grand vizier, who wished to hear their music (Driesch, 1723, pp. 422–423).

16 According to John-Paul Ghobrial, Ottoman musicians accompanied foreign diplomats when they returned to their residences following audiences at the court. Although Ghobrial relies on a source from the second half of 18th century (Ignatius Mouradgea d'Ohsson's *Tableau général de l'Empire*), it is possible that this practice was also valid in the first half of the 18th century, the period under consideration here (Ghobrial, 2013, p. 73). At the banquet organized for Öttingen, he and his entourage were accompanied by the sound of kettle drums (*sade nağare [nakkare]*) (D.TŞF.1/79, 1/80) as they headed to the pavilion. This gives the impression that music played an important role not only in entrance ceremonies, but also in various ceremonial occasions, ranging from audiences to honorary banquets.

Fig. 3: Entrance of Canibi Ali Pasha in 1740.

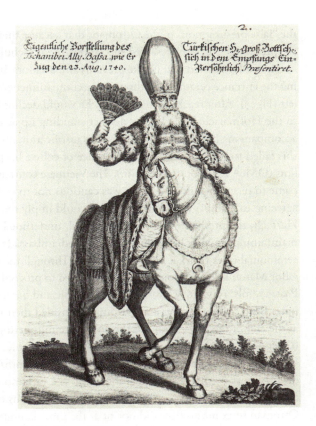

1740, Canibi Ali Pasha and Anton Corfiz Count Ulfeld

The Austria-Russia and Ottoman wars of 1736–1739 resulted in a triumph of the Ottomans, with territories ceded to the Habsburgs in 1718 returned to the Ottomans in the Treaty of Belgrade. Canibi Ali Pasha arrived in Vienna at the end of July 1740. As reflected in Viennese newspapers, his entrance ceremony, which was fully prepared to take place on 4 August, was suddenly cancelled because of his contracting a so-called "ailment". As will be shown, this was in reality an excuse to buy time for negotiating the ceremonial procedure. The ceremony finally took place only on 23 August (WD, Num. 60, p. 690; WD, Num. 63, p. 723; WD, Num. 67, p. 771). Contrary to earlier norms, the Ottoman ambassador insisted on receiving preferential treatment from the Viennese court and attempted to change the ceremonial procedure (OMeA, ZA-Prot. 17, fol. 149v.). While the parties sought to resolve this impasse, the Ottoman ambassador and his sizable cortege remained in their tents in Schwechat for almost a month. A Viennese source attributed the delay, as well as the "unnecessary attention" being devoted to the ceremonies by the ambassador, to the "false presumption" of the Ottomans that because they had acquired the upper hand in the preceding war, they deserved special treatment (Schumann, 1741, p. 190).

The pasha asserted that unlike previous ambassadors, he would ride his horse alone during the entrance ceremony without the accompaniment of Viennese officers to his right or left (Fig. 3). After reaching his lodging, he would decline to give welcoming compliments to the Hofmarschall, including neither standing up as the latter entered the room, nor accompanying him back to the stairs. His justification for this was ostensibly religious, but this failed to convince the Viennese, since of course his predecessors had also been Muslims (OMeA ZA Prot. 17, fol. 163r.). The Viennese court and the Ottoman pasha could not come to terms on this. The court was cautious not to violate existing ceremonial rules by agreeing to Canibi's demands, since this could imply the supremacy of the sultan. Joseph Harrach, the president of the War Council, underlined in his report the importance of maintaining equality between the exchanged ambassadors and following the established ceremonial rules (Türkei I 221-2, fol. 213v.). Through the mediation of the French ambassador Marquis de Mirepoix, they finally agreed to proceed with the ceremony (OMeA ZA-Prot. 17, fols. 158v.–163v., 181r.). Notably, music and banners did not play a role in this dispute. Both the Habsburgs and Ottomans sounded their music, with the latter positioned at the end of the procession. Of the entourage numbering 922 persons, 41 were musicians (OMeA ZA Prot. 17, fol. 197r.; Türkei I 221-2, fol. 134r.).

Canibi's counterpart, the Habsburg ambassador Corfiz Ulfeld, entered Constantinople on 11 August 1740. The British ambassador in Constantinople regarded the entrance ceremony a scandal because of its deviation from previous ceremonial rules. First of all, the Ottoman sergeant-at-arms did not sit at the same banquet table with the ambassador, although ambassadors normally ate in his company. The sergeant-at-arms also rode his horse to the right of Ulfeld, a position regarded as the place of honour in Ottoman customs; this disturbed the Habsburg ambassador because of status rivalries.[17] Finally, a typical entrance procession ended at the residence of the incoming diplomat; however, the sergeant-at-arms abruptly left Ulfeld and his entourage in Eyüp, before they had reached their destination.

---

17   The rivalry concerning riding a horse to the right at various ceremonial stages was not just a concern of Count von Ulfeld. One year later, in 1741, the Persian diplomat Hacı Han was also faced with the same treatment during his entrance ceremony, with the Ottoman officer riding to his right. This ultimately led the Persian delegate to protest by eating nothing but yoghurt at the banquet (*yemeklik*) in his honour (Hammer-Purgstall, 1832, pp. 24–25; Şemdanizade Fındıklılı Süleyman Efendi, 1976, pp. 102–103; Subhi Mehmed Efendi, 2007, pp. 672–674). According to an Ottoman ceremonial register with one page listing the entrance ceremonies of Venetian, Russian, Polish, British, and French diplomats from the 1670s to 1740, if the chief sergeant-at-arms were to ride his horse side-by-side with a diplomat, "tradition or custom" required the Ottoman to be on the right side, with the left side given to the foreign diplomat. This document shows that there were some cases in which the Ottoman sergeant-at-arms rode his horse in front of foreign delegates (D.TŞF.2/5).

An Untold Battle of Music and Banners   141

The Habsburgs were forced to continue the rest of the way unaccompanied (Türkei I 221-3, fols. 56r.–58r., 243v.).

None of these changes were decided on the day of the ceremony. The Ottoman court translator had visited Ulfeld prior to the procession and stated that since sounding music and unfurling the banners in the city was against Ottoman law, the procession was to proceed around the city rather than through it (Türkei I 221-3, fol. 236v.). Although Ulfeld opposed this ultimatum, a few days later, in a second visit, the translator made exhaustive efforts to convince him to roll up his banners and silence the music at the request of the grand vizier. The translator's pressure continued, but Ulfeld made no compromises, not even accepting the compromise of proceeding with banners but no music (Türkei I 221-3, fol. 237v.). In the end, he went through with his plans, using both banners and music. Thus, although the Ottomans made certain changes in ceremonial procedure to diminish the status of the Habsburgs, they could not or did not prevent the Habsburgs from this display of power. With regard to musical performance, the status of the Habsburg and Ottoman ambassadors was thus equal.

Conclusion

At the entrance ceremonies of 1700, 1719, and 1740, the Habsburg ambassadors were all able to sound their music and display unfurled banners. In negotiating with the Ottomans, they continually sought to preserve their image and their theoretical right of equality. For instance, they rejected the notion that they needed the "permission" of the grand viziers to do so. The Ottomans, in turn, created certain impediments for them, including changing the usual marching route and not accompanying the ambassadors the full distance to their residence. At the beginning of the 18th century, the Ottoman chronicler Silahdar described the European music and banners of both the 1700 and 1719 entrance ceremonies as a disturbing "ritual of unbelievers" (*ayin-i batıl*), which could be accepted only out of necessity (*bi'z-zaruri*) (Silahdar, 2018, p. 564). The master of ceremonies Selman Efendi described the practice as "against the law" and an "unfounded concoction". However, this perspective was not universal or static. Two decades later, in 1740, an Ottoman archival document about Ulfeld's entrance ceremony reveals a critical change. It refers to Ulfeld's three small banners overlaid with gold and the sound of their two trumpets not as a disturbance, but as a proper custom (*mutad*) (MAD.d.23771, p. 8). Although the Treaty of Belgrade was a victory for the Ottomans, they nonetheless did not manage to prevent the Habsburg ambassador from playing his music and displaying his banners after the treaty. Their victory was not such that they could dictate to the Habsburgs that they hide their symbols of sovereignty in the public sphere. Thus, by the time of Ulfeld's delegation in 1740, diplomatic parity in this respect was fully established. As has been argued by Güneş Işıksel, "as the sultan's supposed or real military superiority" began to diminish in the 17th century, the Ottomans redefined both the practices of diplomacy and their place in the world (Işıksel, 2019, p. 295). The transition from considering the Habsburgs as performing a "ritual of unbelievers" to their practice of music being seen as a "custom" shows us that the Ottomans had come to accept the Habsburgs as their equal in the musical representation at the entrance ceremonies to Constantinople and Vienna.

These examples show that the changes in the relationship between the two empires called for in normative peace treaties did not come into practice immediately. Rather than a sharp rupture, a more gradual transformation occurred, with new diplomatic ceremonial not being implemented all at once. Indeed, given its heavy reliance on precedent, it was not easy to change. Despite the Ottomans' loss of territory, they continued throughout this period to enjoy the right to sound their military music in Vienna. In contrast, the Habsburgs were not consistently allowed to do the same, despite their theoretical equality. The Ottomans still defined themselves as privileged and superior. As a result, musical representation became a point of rivalry and dispute throughout the 17th and the first half of the 18th centuries. The defeats of the Ottomans on the battlefields at the end of the 17th century gave impetus to Habsburg ambassadors in seeking equality in the organization of their entrance ceremonies and the right – not just the privilege – to play music and display their unfurled banners. The Ottomans came to accept this equality as well, seen in the conceptual transition from a "ritual of unbelievers" into "custom". From the perspective of the ceremonial deployment of music and banners, the 1699 Treaty of Carlowitz was more of a turning point than the 1606 Treaty of Zsitvatorok. It was only then that the Ottomans redefined their relationship with the Habsburgs as one of equality. As the Ottoman ambassador in 1699 told the Habsburg translator, referred to at the beginning of this chapter, the situation in Constantinople had changed.

Bibliography

Manuscripts

Haus-, Hof- und Staatsarchiv Vienna (HHStA)

Staatenabteilungen
   Türkei I, 172, 173,175, 184,185, 221
   Türkei IV 13

Oberhofmeisteramt (OMeA)
Zeremonialakten (ZA), Protokolle, vol. 2 (1660–1674); vol. 6 (1700–1709); vol. 17 (1739–1740)
Ältere Zeremonialakten (ÄZA), 19-38
Handschriftensammlungen
Blau (HS B) 222

Başbakanlık Osmanlı Arşivleri İstanbul (BOA)

Ali Emiri
III. Ahmed (A.E.SAMD.III), 229/22040
Bab-ı Defteri
Teşrifat Kalemi Evrakı, (D.TŞF.) 1/79, 1/80, 2/4, 2/5
Cevdet
Hariciye (C.HR.)150/7475
Sadaret Defterleri (A.} d.) 347
Maliyeden Müdevver Defterler (MAD.d.) 23771

Printed Sources and Source Editions

Anonymous. (1628). *Einzug des osmanischen Botschafters in Wien am 21. Oktober 1628*. (Inv. Nr. 199095). Wien Museum, https://sammlung.wienmuseum.at/objekt/368766/. Date of Access: 28.01.2024.

Anonymous. (1702). *Gründ- und Umständlicher Bericht Von Denen Römisch-Kayserlichen Wie auch Ottomannischen Groß-Bothschafften [...]*. Schönwetter.

Burbury, J. (1671). *A Relation of a Journey of the Right Honourable My Lord Henry Howard, from London to Vienna and thence to Constantinople [...]*. T. Collins and I. Ford.

Çevik, C. (2018). *Naili Abdullah Paşa Defter-i Teşrifat (Metin-Değerlendirme)* [Master's thesis, Beykent University].

Driesch, G. C. von den. (1723). *Historische Nachricht von der Röm. Kayserl. Groß=Botschafft nach Constantinopel [...]*. Peter Conrad.

Evliya Çelebi, D. M. Z. (2003). *Evliyâ Çelebi Seyahatnâmesi*, vol. 7, ed. by Y. Dağlı, S. A. Kahraman, & R. Dankoff. YKY.

Felsecker, A. J. (1700). *Einzug des osmanischen Botschafters Ibrahim Bassa in Wien am 30. Jänner 1700*. Wien Museum, https://sammlung.wienmuseum.at/objekt/370878/. Date of Access: 28.01.2024.

Hammer-Purgstall, J. von. (1829). *Geschichte des Osmanischen Reiches, Vierter Band: 1574–1623*. C. A. Hartleben.

Hammer-Purgstall, J. von. (1832). *Geschichte des Osmanischen Reiches, Achter Band: 1739–1774.* C. A. Hartleben.

Khevenhüller, F. C. (1723). *Annales Ferdinandei [...] von Anfang des 1608. biß zu End des 1617; 7/8.* M. G. Weidmann.

Khevenhüller, F. C. (1726). *Annales Ferdinandei [...] vom Anfange des 1628. bis zu Ende des 1631,* vol. 11. M. G. Weidmann.

Lünig, J. C. (1719). *Historisch- und Politischer Schau=Platz des Europäischen Hof- und Cantzley Ceremoniels,* vol. 1. Weidmann.

Meyer, M. (1672). *Theatrum Europaeum IX.* Merian.

Moser, J. J. (1740). *Der Belgradische Friedens-Schluß zwischen Ihro Kayserl. Majestät u. Der Ottomanischen Pforte [...].* Johann Felix Bielcken.

Neu-ankommender Currier Auß Wienn (Ordentliche Zeittungen) (21 October 1628, 28 October 1628).

Niggl, S. (1701). *Diarium, Oder: Außführliche curiose Reiß=Beschreibung / Von Wien nach Constantinopel und von dar wider zuruck in Teutschland/[...].* Georg Schlüter.

Schumann, G. (1741). *Die neue europäische Fama, welche den gegenwärtigen Zustand der vornehmsten Höfe entdecket.* Gleditsch.

Silahdar, F. M. A. (2018). *Nusretnâme İnceleme-Metin (1106–1133/1695–1721),* ed. by M. Topal. TÜBA.

Tafferner, P. (1670). *Der Röm. Kay. May. Leopoldi I. An Deß grossen Türcken Sultans Mehemet Cham Ottomanische Porten Anno 1665. Den 25. May abgeordnete Bottschafft [...].* Voigt.

Veltze, H. (1900). Die Hauptrelation des Kaiserlichen Residenten in Constantinopel Simon Reniger von Reningen 1649–1666. In *Mittheilungen des K. und K. Kriegs-, N.F., 12,* 57–169.

Wienerisches Diarium Num. 60 (27 Julii 1740); *WD, Num. 63* (6 Augusti 1740); *WD, Num. 67* (27 Augusti 1740).

Wenner, A. (1622). *Ein gantz new Reysebuch von Prag auß bis gen Constantinopel [...].* Halbmayer.

Yücel, A. S. (1996). *Mühürdar Hasan Ağa'nın Cevâhirü't-Tevârih'i* [Doctoral dissertation, Erciyes University].

Scholarly Literature

Aktan, B. (2019). Kara Mehmed Paşa'nın Viyana Elçiliği (1665). *Türklük Bilgisi Araştırmaları* 51, 147–176.

Arı, B. (2004). Early Ottoman diplomacy: Ad hoc period. In A. N. Yurdusev (Ed.), *Ottoman Diplomacy: Conventional or Unconventional? Ottoman Diplomacy* (pp. 36–65). Palgrave Macmillan.

Atçıl, Z. (2021). The Foundation of Peace-Oriented Foreign Policy in the Sixteenth-Century Ottoman Empire: Rüstem Pasha's Vision of Diplomacy. In T. A. Sowerby & C. Markiewicz (Eds.), *Diplomatic Cultures at the Ottoman Court, c. 1500–1630* (pp. 132–152). Routledge.

Braun, H.-J. (2017). An Acoustic Turn? Recent Developments and Future Perspectives of Sound Studies. *AVANT. Pismo Awangardy Filozoficzno-Naukowej* 1, 75–91.

Burschel, P. (2007). Der Sultan und das Hündchen: Zur politischen Ökonomie des Schenkens in interkultureller Perspektive. *Historische Anthropologie* 15(3), 408–421.

Cevrioğlu, M. H. (2021a). *Ottoman-Habsburg Interactions and the Ottoman Diplomacy during the First Half of the Seventeenth Century* [Doctoral dissertation, İzmir Katip Çelebi University].

Cevrioğlu, M. H. (2021b). Avusturya'da Osmanlı Diplomasisi: Büyükelçi Recep Ağa'nın Viyana Sefareti (1628–1629). *OTAM* 50, 81–111.

Demirbaş, A. T. (2021). Atmeydanı: The Stage of Sound and Power. *MSGSÜ Sosyal Bilimler Dergisi* 2(24), 681–699.

Fosler-Lussier, D. (2014). Afterword Music's Powers. In R. Ahrendt, M. Ferraguto, & D. Mahiet (Eds.), *Music and Diplomacy from the Early Modern Era to the Present* (pp. 267–275). Palgrave Macmillan.

Franklin, M. I. (2005). Introductory Improvisations on a Theme: Resounding International Relations. In M. I. Franklin (Ed.), *Resounding International Relations on Music, Culture, and Politics* (pp. 1–26). Palgrave Macmillan.

Gienow-Hecht, J. C. E. (2009). *Sound Diplomacy Music and Emotions in Transatlantic Relations, 1850–1920*. The University of Chicago Press.

Gienow-Hecht, J. C. E. (2015). Introduction: Sonic History, or Why Music Matters in International History. In J. C. E. Gienow-Hecht (Ed.), *Music and International History in the Twentieth Century* (pp. 1–30). Berghahn.

Ghobrial, J.-P. A. (2013). *The Whispers of Cities: Information Flows in Istanbul, London, and Paris in the Age of William Trumbull*. Oxford University Press.

Heppner, H., & Schanes, D. (2011). The Impact of the Treaty of Passarowitz on the Habsburg Monarchy. In C. Ingrao & J. Pesalj (Eds.), *The Peace of Passarowitz, 1718* (pp. 53–62). Purdue University Press.

Işıksel, G. (2019). Hierarchy and Friendship: Ottoman Practices of Diplomatic Culture and Communication (1290s–1600). *The Medieval History Journal* 22(2), 278–297.

Jäger, R. M. (2011). 1665 Yılında Viyana'da Kara Mehmet Paşa'nın Elçiliği Türk Temsilciliklerinde Mehteran Müziği ve Anlamı. In O. Elbaş, M. Kalpaklı, & O. M. Öztürk (Eds.), *Türkiye'de Müzik Kültürü Kongresi Bildirileri* (pp. 45–52). Atatürk Kültür Merkezi.

Hennings, J. (2021). Constantinople as a "Window on Europe": Peter the Great's Ambassador and Diplomatic Hierarchies at the Sultan's Court. In S. J. Karp, A. Alimento, E. Babaeva, V. J. Berelovič, P. R. Zaborov, & A. B. Kamenskij (Eds.), *Petr I i "okno v Evropu": = Pierre Ier et la "fenêtre sur l'Europe"* (pp. 54–73). Nauka.

Karateke, H. (Ed.). (2007). *An Ottoman Protocol Register Containing Ceremonies from 1736 to 1808: BEO Sadaret Defterleri 350 in the Prime Ministry Ottoman State Archives, Istanbul*. Ottoman Bank Archives and Research Centre.

Kolçak, Ö. (2012). Habsburg Elçisi Walter Leslie'nin Osmanlı Devlet Yapısına Dair Gözlemleri (1665). *Tarih Dergisi* 54, 55–89.

Kolçak, Ö. (2023). Habsburg Elçisi Walter Leslie'nin Osmanlı Ziyareti: Bir Tarihsel Anlatı İnşası (1665–1666). *Tarih Dergisi* 79, 1–38.

Kütükoğlu, M. (1989). 18. Yüzyılda Osmanlı Devletinde Fevkalâde Elçilerin Ağırlanması. *Türk Kültürü Araştırmaları* 27(1/2), 199–231.

Mahiet, D., Ferraguto, M. & Ahrendt, R. (2014). Introduction. In R. Ahrendt, M. Ferraguto & D. Mahiet (Eds.), *Music and Diplomacy from the Early Modern Era to the Present* (pp. 1–16). Palgrave Macmillan.

Mansel, P. (1998). *Constantinople City of the World's Desire 1453–1924*. St. Martin's Griffin.

Prévost-Thomas, C. & Ramel, F. (2018). Introduction: Understanding Musical Diplomacies-Movements on the "Scenes". In F. Ramel & C. Prévost-Thomas (Eds.), *International Relations, Music and Diplomacy Sounds and Voices on the International Stage* (pp. 1–19). Palgrave Macmillan.

Sowerby, T. A. (2021). Sociability and Ceremony Diplomats at the Porte c. 1550–1632. In T. A. Sowerby & C. Markiewicz (Eds.), *Diplomatic Cultures at the Ottoman Court, c. 1500–1630* (pp. 217–242). Routledge.

Spuler, B. (1935). Die Europäische Diplomatie in Konstantinopel bis zum Frieden von Belgrad (1739). II. *Jahrbücher für Kultur und Geschichte der Slaven* 11(2), 171–222.

Strohmeyer, A. (2014). The Theatrical Performance of Peace: Entries of Habsburg Grand Embassies in Constantinople (17th–19th Centuries). In M. Sariyannis, G. Aksoy-Aivali, M. Demetriadou, Y. Spyropoulos, K. Stathi, Y. Vidras, A. Anastasopoulos, & E. Kolovos (Eds.), *New Trends in Ottoman Studies Papers presented at the 20th CIEPO Symposium Rethymnon, 27 June–1 July 2012* (pp. 486–494). University of Crete-Department of History and Archaeology & Foundation for Research and Technology-Hellas-Institute for Mediterranean Studies.

Strohmeyer, A. (2020). Der Friede von Zsitvatorok 1606 und die Friedensschlüsse der 'Türkenkriege'. In V. Arnke, M. Rohrschneider, I. Schmidt-Voges, S. Westphal, & J. Whaley (Eds.), *Handbuch Frieden im Europa der Frühen Neuzeit / Handbook of Peace in Early Modern Europe* (pp. 969–984). De Gruyter and Oldenbourg.

Teply, K. (1976). *Die kaiserliche Großbotschaft an Sultan Murad IV. im Jahre 1628 des Freiherrn Hans Ludwig von Kuefsteins Fahrt zur Hohen Pforte*. A. Schendl.

Uluskan, M. (2008). Bir Osmanlı Elçisinin Yolculuk Hazırlığı: İbrahim Paşa'nın 1699 Avusturya Elçiliği. *Türklük Araştırmaları Dergisi* 20, 251–275.

Illustration Credits

Fig. 1: Anonymous. (1702). *Gründ- und Umständlicher Bericht Von Denen Römisch-Kayserlichen Wie auch Ottomannischen Groß-Bothschafften [...]*. Schönwetter. "Deß Türkischen Bottschaffters Einzug zu Wienn", p. 51.

Fig. 2: Driesch, G. C. von den. (1723). *Historische Nachricht von der Röm. Kayserl. Groß=Botschafft nach Constantinopel [...]*. Peter Conrad. "Einzug des Röm=Kaÿserlichen Groß=Botschaffters in Constantinopel", p. 159.

Fig. 3: Anonymous. Eigentliche Vorstellung des Türkischen He: Groß: Bottsch. / Tschanibei Ally Bassa wie Er sich in dem Empfangs Einzug den 23. Aug. 1740. persöhnlich præsentiret. Liechtenstein Princely Collections. https://www.liechtensteincollections.at/en/inv/GR03209. Date of Access: 28.01.2024.

Traces of Modern Ideas in the Music of the Ottoman Empire

Songül Karahasanoğlu & Suleyman Cabir Ataman

Introduction

Writing on music theory has a deep tradition in Islamic culture that can be traced back centuries. A vast amount of literature has been left behind. The Ottomans, as heirs to the Islamic civilization, also contributed to the literature in the field of music theory. Although continuing a tradition, writing on music theory in the Ottoman Empire had its own unique style. However, this style started to change during the process of modernization of the Ottoman Empire. The root cause of the change was not the music itself. The process of modernization started in the 18th century through efforts of the bureaucratic elite of the Ottoman empire, whose primary motivation was determining how to adopt or achieve the military technology used by the West (Mardin, 1991, p. 12). This process was begun by Mahmut I, Abdulhamit I and Selim III (Mardin, 1991, p. 13); nevertheless, the primary launch was undertaken by Mahmut II, who in 1839 declared the Tanzimat, a series of actions aimed at modernizing the Ottoman Empire (Mardin, 1991, pp. 13–16).

According to the *Dictionary of Sociology* by John Katsillis and Michael Armer, the concept of modernization, which – as the word suggests – can be defined as "the state of being modern", was based on the social, economic and political systems that emerged in the Western world between the 17th and 19th centuries. In the 19th and 20th centuries, it also took on the meaning of the process of these systems becoming widely applied in South America, Asia and Africa (Katsillis et al., 2003, p. 1883). On the other hand, Westernization (or Europeanization) can be defined as the process of adapting concepts such as industry, technology, politics, economy, life, law, norms, morality, perception, traditions, language, alphabet, religion, and philosophy to another culture (Thong, 2012). It is useful to emphasize the differences between these two concepts, because they are very prone to being confused. All in all, by looking at these definitions, we can make the following generalization for the expression modernization: Modernization is the adaptation and application of modernism in countries other than those where it was formed ontologically, while Westernization as a method of achieving modernization can be considered a subset of it.

Returning to our context, the footsteps of modernity in music could be heard before modernization began to be implemented in the Ottoman Empire by Mahmut I as a state policy. This period also corresponds to the *Lale Devri* (Tulip Era), which took place between 1718–1730. This era brought with it some changes, including the emergence of a new understanding in the areas of culture and art that had not previously existed in the East, including the emergence of a different meaning attributed to art. In this period, Europeans – known as "Franks" by 18th-century Ottomans – began to influence the cultural and artistic life of the Ottoman Empire, specifically in Istanbul. Members of the Ottoman elite were sent to Paris and were greatly influenced by French culture, bringing it back to Istanbul. Several movements that emerged in different areas of innovation during this period are worthy of mention (Özcan, 2003).

In short, an intellectual system from the West gradually became dominant in the Ottoman Empire. As a result, the tradition that the empire had inherited and carried on from the past gradually diminished, with this tradition turning into a entity quite different from it had been previously.

If we look at the origins of this transformation – this modernization – in the Ottoman Empire, it is difficult to conclude that these occurred organically. Rather it was a decision taken for various reasons by the bureaucratic elite controlling the state apparatus, such as ensuring the continuity of the state or maintaining a position of superiority. Cultural transformation was seen as one pillar for this. The main idea was that the cultural memory which depended on the classical past would be erased by transforming music. In effect, the Ottoman elite decided to suppress an auditory memory that was a legacy of the past. Initially, they undertook this at the court; the movement then spread to the rest of the society. Nevertheless, the music of the past was never completely forgotten, and it continues to be a sociogenetic element to the present day.

Since we cannot access sounds produced prior to the invention of sound recording technology, we can only rely on secondary sources to form a framework allowing us to imagine early soundscapes. Such sources can vary and can also be combinations of different sources. For instance, written music texts, instruments, musical scales, melodic patterns, and materials used in the construction of certain instruments, in connection with current living cultures, can help us imagine the sounds of the early modern era. However, deciding which sources to take into account is a fluid process, and no cross-cultural standards can be set. In this study, we have decided to use music theory as our basis in order to gain an understanding of the music of the Ottoman court along with its heritage and legacy.

The first reason to study sounds through music theory is that music theory, along with scholarly literature on it, stands at the intersection of science and art, since it is a scholarly process used to investigate an art. Moreover, we can add economics, politics, religion, and philosophy to these two fields. In this respect, music theory is extremely useful for understanding intellectual movements, since it has been affected by intellectual, artistic, and scientific transformations, epistemological paradigm changes, and mass preferences. In short, almost every aspect related to society, science, and art can be traced through the history of music theory. In this respect, this study shows that when examining the historical and social development of societies, work on the contents and history of music theory is not simply a fringe activity related to a specific branch of an art; it also reveals that this field contains traces of a full range of ideological, scientific, and artistic periodicities, and that it thus should be considered a mainstream scientific field.

Secondly, although there are instruments pictured on miniatures in illuminated manuscripts, especially in images of festivals, and although the instruments or their descendants illustrated in these miniatures are still known today, nevertheless, in the Islamic musical tradition, writing musical pieces is a new and modern idea that, with a few exceptions, doesn't go back further than the 17th century. Written musical pieces can enable us to draw a picture of a musical environment; however, having no information about their past is a great disadvantage. We therefore must search for a valid set of other resources, ideally, resources that are comparable for more than a couple of centuries.

Another reason for the choice of music theory to understand the sounds of the festivals at the Ottoman court is the relationship between music theory and authority. It is clear that music performance and writing music theory are completely different sets of activities. In other words, not everyone involved in music performance is, or was, also involved in writing music theory. Quite the contrary, historically music theory was an activity for an elite under the patronage of a monarch or a religious institution, or for educated persons of the period who were able to fund themselves for such artistic or scientific endeavours. This brings us to another important point, namely, the relationship between sound and power. One of the main areas of interest in Ottoman music theory has been to learn about the various types of music that were heard in the court. According to Halil İnalcık, the court was the highest authority in the Ottoman patrimonial state structure, where specialists in the sciences, arts, and crafts could gain prestige and money by marketing their skills. In this respect, the sultan, who was at the top of the palace as an institution, had a decisive influence on any branch of science, art, or craft he was interested in (İnalcık, 2011, pp. 5–21).

Summary of the Pre-Modern Era

In this section, we examine various music theorists in the Islamic period. However, a comprehensive history would go beyond the boundaries of our study here, so we will move towards the modern period by just touching on the major works of the most important figures.

The period between the 9th and 13th centuries or, more specifically, the period of the Umayyads and the Abbasids – referred to as "the Golden Age of Islam" by some historians (Arslan, 2013, p. 392) – was a period of time when the Islamic world saw its most sophisticated economic, scientific, and artistic achievements. In this period, knowledge from ancient Greece was acquired in the Islamic world through texts in Arabic. This allowed scholars of the period to continue certain debates on the contents of this knowledge, and to re-evaluate those parts they thought missing. The scientific subjects dealt with in that era were quite different than today. Thinkers continued to examine the relation between music and mathematics as had been passed down from ancient Greece, and serious reflections were also undertaken at the time on astronomy and/or astrology.

At this point, we must briefly examine the historicity of the concept of modernity. If we look at the development of modernity, it is related to the rediscovery of the idea of rationalism, which, along with capitalism, was one of the two pillars of ancient Greek influence in northwest Europe. In the period identified as the Golden Age of Islam, ancient Greek rationalism constituted an important part of Islamic thought and contained various elements that we consider modern still today.

The 9th-century thinker Al Kindi was one of his era's most important and influential figures. According to Fazlı Arslan, Al Kindi was the first person in the Islamic world who can be considered a philosopher (Arslan, 2015, pp. 47–50). According to various sources, the works written by Al Kindi included seven to ten texts on music, but only four have survived to the present day. Al Kindi can be considered a follower of Pythagoras, and he also led the theorists who succeeded him. In his works on music that are still extant, he focuses primarily on theoretical questions. Among other things, he refers to the concept of sound formation, and describes the sounds of the four-stringed oud played at that time (Tıraşçı, 2017, pp. 50–54).

Al Kindi's significance can be highlighted by two of his key accomplishments: First, he took part in the translation of ancient Greek texts into Classical Arabic; secondly, he was the first scholar known to have represented the relationship between music and astrology in Islamic literature. Moreover, he introduced such subjects as intervals and scales to the agendas of Muslim scientists of that period (Tıraşçı, 2017, p. 55), and he was the first to introduce the notion of a school of music in the Islamic civilization (Çoğulu, 2018, p. 34).

While Ahmet Hakkı Turabi states in his master's thesis on Al Kindi (1996, p. 67) that the nuances of Al Kindi's twelve half-tone system are exactly compatible with today's European system, Tolgahan Çoğulu has suggested that Al Kindi's system of half tones was different: a tone was divided unequally, with the parts corresponding to the *bakiye* and *kucuk mujhenneb* ranges within the generally accepted sound system of contemporary Turkish music (2018).

Following Al Kindi, Farabi (9th–10th century) was a key figure in the field of music theory. He was also referred to as *Ustad-ı Sani*, which literally means "the second master". The term "second" comes from the general attitude that he was the second great philosopher after Aristotle. In addition to music, he made eminent contributions to philosophy, astronomy, and mathematics. A look at Farabi's works on music reveals that he was active in both practice and theory. Farabi approached the subject from a quite practical angle, unlike the Pythagorean understanding in which numbers are at the fore. In Farabi's work, basic pitches are described within a Pythagorean understanding.

Instruments have an important place in Farabi's works. He provides detailed information about the pitch systems of instruments such as the Baghdad tanbur,[1] the Khorasan tanbur, and the oud. These instruments are significant since, according to Tura and Arslan, the Khorasan tanbur included the 17-pitch system that Safi al-Din and his school would later adopt (Tura, 1988, p. 173; Arslan, 2015, p. 64). This establishes an important connection between historical music practices and their counterparts today. The discussion of the Baghdad tanbur, on the other hand, refers to a pre-Islamic sound system, thus giving us some clues about the existence of other parallel sound systems (Arslan, 2015, p. 64).

The Ikhwan-i Safa, a group of scientists and philosophers who emerged in Basra[2] in the 10th century, was a "brotherhood" engaged in scientific and philosophical research, including mathematics, astronomy, and philosophy. They devoted one text to music (Uysal, 2000). Influenced by ancient Greek philosophy, they generally discuss music in the context of astrology and cosmic harmony.

Another important scholar of this period was undoubtedly Ibn Sina, or Avicenna as he is known in the West, who lived from 980 to 1037. He was a significant scholar who had an appreciable understanding of both Eastern and Western science. He wrote works on many different topics, including medicine, mathematics, philosophy, language, and religion. Ibn Sina was also interested in the science of music (Turabi, 2013, pp. III–IV) and made use of knowledge inherited from the ancient Greeks. Turabi states that Ibn Sina described music as one of the four branches of mathematics, along with geometry, arithmetic, and astronomy. However, when dealing with music theory, Ibn Sina emphasized that music should not only be considered according to Pythagorean ideas based on numbers and arithmetic, but also as a living auditory practice. On the other hand, he placed great importance on the pure elements of mathematical ratios (Turabi, 2013, pp. IX–X).

After a silence of almost two centuries due to social and political upheavals, the epoch-making works of Safi al-Din appearing in the 13th century made a substantial change in the focus of music theoretical writing. In Safi al-Din's examination of topics that had

---

1 Tanbur refers to a string instrument that might be the ancestor of the instrument called *baglama* and *tanbur* today.

2 Located in the south of modern-day Iraq.

been discussed by scholars before him, such as Al Kindi, Ibn Sina and Farabi, he refines their theories and points out the cosmological fallacies intertwined from ancient Greece until his time in the various sciences, including music. This understanding continued until the 15th century, when Abdulkadir Meragi wrote a commentary on Safi al-Din's work. The theorists of this period have been called *ilim erbabı*, or "masters of science".

The Modernization of the Ottoman Empire

In this section, we won't go into a detailed analysis or literature survey regarding the modernization of the Ottoman Empire. However, we do need to address its "why" and "how". As already mentioned above, there is a difference between modernization and Westernization. An important point that needs to be emphasized regarding modernization and Westernization is that modernization is the product of economic, cultural, and social transformations. In Western European societies, these transformations have developed gradually over time. However, for other societies that have become modernized – as for example Russia, Japan, or Turkey – modernization has been based on a transformation of the society through power. In other words, in the West, modernism has been the product of a centuries-long struggle against the power of the period, such as the Catholic Church. Over time, along with social and political transformations, modernism has created its own power practices with the restructuring of class orders and economic systems. In this process, modernism has redefined all social relations before it and drawn precise new boundaries for concepts such as religion, science, art, and crafts. Modernity as a tool for power is a product of its later stages. Nonetheless, if we look at modernizing societies, their modernization is often based on decisions taken by those in power, or by intellectual circles who have influence over those in power. We then see processes of societies being reorganized according to modern social and economic conditions and the restructuring of fields such as production, culture, and science according to modern paradigms. As such, the concept of modernity can be quite different between the place it emerged and the countries to which it later spreads.

The reason for emphasizing this small yet important distinction before examining the period of Turkey's Westernization is that the history of Turkey's relationship with the concept of modernity is a history of Westernization, not modernization.

The Concept of *Adwar* and the Tradition Behind It

Literally, the word *adwar* means "cycles" or "periods" (TDK, 2006); nevertheless, for about eight centuries the word was used in the sense of a "book of music theory". This started with Safi al-Din al-Urmawi (1216–1294), who was born in Urmia[3] and who wrote a revolutionary book called *Kitab-ul Adwar*, which literally means "book of cycles". The term *adwar* gained the meaning of "music theory book" following the publication of that work (Uygun, 2020, p. 98). To summarize, *Kitab-ul Adwar* addressed various acoustical matters, such as the creation of sound, proportions and intervals, the creation of scales by adding intervals to each other, and the emergence of octaves by articulating certain steps in musical scales. The term *devir* – or cycle – derives from a method of illustrating musical notes and pieces.

The most important feature distinguishing Safi al-Din al-Urmawi from other notable scholars such as Kindi, Farabi, or İbn-i Sina is that for them, the science of music was nothing more than either advocating or criticizing a particular theoretical debate that had been passed down from ancient Greece. However, Safi al-Din al-Urmawi introduced a new theoretical system and a practice that included more result-oriented elements. Until there is evidence to the contrary, it can be said that Safi al-Din al-Urmawi was the founder of the 17 unequal-tone system, which is, as the name indicates, based on dividing an octave into seventeen unequal tones. This system continued in the Islamic civilization and later in the Ottoman Empire; we can now consider it the most significant aspect of Islamic music theory and tradition.

Safi al-Din al-Urmawi was followed by Abdülkadir Meragi, a theorist who influenced almost all the theorists and music practitioners who came after him. He was born in the city of Maraga, which is in Iranian Azerbaijan today. There is a widespread belief that Abdülkadir Meragi, who lived in the 14th century, was the first person to use the term *maqam* for Safi al-Din's *devir* or "cycle". However, Arslan, in his 2015 study *Music in Islamic Civilization*, found that Shirazi had used the term *maqam* before Meragi (pp. 301–304).

Among the scholarly music theorists who lived in the 15th century, Fethullah Shirvani should be named. In the introduction to his text on music theory, Shirvani begins by saying that the science of music is mathematics for theorists (Akdoğan, 1996, p. 194), also stating that Pythagoras was one of the people who introduced music as a science (Akdoğan, 1996, p. 196). Here, it can also be observed that Shirvani benefited from the schools of both Ibn Sina and Farabi.

Ladikli Mehmet Çelebi was born in Anatolia and for this reason, he differs from the other music theorists. He is a harbinger of the fact that music theory gradually began to gain an Anatolian or Ottoman identity. Parallel to the school he followed, Çelebi bases his theory on a system of 17 pitches and 91 cycles. Unlike his predecessors, he also discusses intervals larger than fifths. However, unlike his predecessors, he increases the number of fifths from 12 to 13 (Çelik, 2001, p. 23).

---

3   In modern-day Iran.

The *Adwar* Tradition in the Ottoman Empire

After the 15th century, the *adwar* tradition entered yet another chapter. The school initiated by Safi al-Din al-Urmawi, which, in fact, also depended on a school started before his time, began to change. Instead of individual theoreticians, focus can be placed on the primary differences between the Safi al-Din al-Urmawi and his follower theorists.

Less Theory, More Practice

When we look at these early music theory schools, they present details that allow us to calculate with perfect precision, even centuries later, the intervals being discussed, and by extension, the pitches and sequences obtained from these intervals. This is thanks in part to the fact that the method they use in calculating intervals is based entirely on proportions, and thus the given measurements are not based on units. This allows their system to be perfectly adapted to any unit without error. In fact, the subject of calculating with ratios goes back much further than the Scholars, but this mathematical tradition, almost all of whose genera (quads) are still in use today, are the product of the Scholars School. However, theoreticians of these music theory schools did not see the need to make calculations that would have been considered advanced mathematics in that period. Essentially, they built their own musical understanding and ideas on an already established infrastructure.

A transformation in the naming of musical pitches also occurred. Although based on need, this transformation was much more than a simple reorganization of musical pitches for practical purposes. Designed in a well-organized way, these changes resulted in an irreversible change of the entire system as had been put forward in the past. The earlier theoretical framework had been based on a Persian numeral system, with pitches taking their names from ordinal numbers that were shifted when pitches with special names were inserted between them.

Pitches gained more importance due to the creation of the melodic modes called *maqams*. Unlike the case in earlier music theory schools, *maqams* were not generated as constant mathematical entities. Instead, they were created as "mobile" or "adjustable" entities with a close link to practice. Names of certain pitches are named after certain *maqamic* patterns.

Moreover, the language used for music theory works shifted from Persian or Arabic to Turkish. The impact of Persian remained for some time, but ultimately Turkish replaced them all.

In this period, celestial bodies and astrology also began to be related to music theory. In fact, the natural sciences began to be replaced by astrology, just as proof and explanation mechanisms and quantitative tools were replaced by metaphysics. It seems that analogy and metaphors began to be substitute systems in this period.

The Dissolution of the *Adwar Tradition*

The footsteps of modernity in theory can be traced back to a time even before modernization began to be implemented as an official policy in the Ottoman Empire. This period also corresponded to an extraordinary time in the history of the Ottoman Empire, the so-called "Tulip Period" (1718–1730). It was during this twelve-year timeframe that the reformation movements in the Ottoman Empire first emerged. This episode brought some changes in culture and art. In other words, it was also a time of the occurrence of an understanding that had not existed in the East previously, along with the rise of a distinctive meaning attributed to art. In this era, the Europeans began to take a place in the cultural and artistic life of the Ottoman Empire. There was evidence of modernization movements arising in several different areas during this period (Özcan, 2003).

If we look at the domain of art, we see an extraordinarily serious encouragement of it and, by extension, progress, especially in the field of literature. A number of poets produced nearly-limitless works in this period. Changes in this era were not limited to the fields of culture and the arts. It was also a time in which scientific developments from the West started to be introduced to the Ottoman Empire. At the same time, it was an age when countless numbers of mansion houses were built in Istanbul and some of them consisted of architectural works from Europe or new creations inspired by them. Simultaneously, the printing press also emerged in the country at about this time. There was serious progress in Istanbul's infrastructure, such as the construction of waterways or the repair of lighthouses and shipyards. Similarly, measures taken against some diseases and social projects – like the control of places such as coffeehouses, where the people consumed food and drink collectively – took place in this period (Özcan, 2003).

It is hard to claim that all the changes that emerged in the field of music and theory at this time originated from the Tulip Period. However, the dynamics that led to its emergence, the conditions that prepared the way for it, and the reflections of the intellectual transformation in the elite shaped both the theory and practice of this period. As a result, it is possible to position the Ottoman's relations with the West or the first Westernization movements in the Ottoman Empire further behind the official transformations such as the *Tanzimat*. In the late 17th and early 18th centuries, a process in which the influence of the West began to be felt indirectly in the field of theory evolved, and a new way of thinking coming from the West started to emerge.

Ali Ufki – or Albert/Wojciech Bobowski, wrote a book called *Haza Mecmua-i Saz-ı Söz*,[4] a collection of musical pieces in different forms with a modified Western notation system. Apparently, Ufki's work is the oldest known use of Western notation in Turkish music (Güray, 2012, p. 95). The content of the book suggests that it was started in 1650 and that the writing lasted for years (Cevher, 1995, p. 22). We also see that Nayi Osman Dede was another important figure of that time. He wrote two significant works in the field of music: *Rabt-ı Tabirat-ı Musiki*, and *Nota-i Türki* (Erguner, 1991, pp. 26–28). The former was written during the Tulip Period (Erguner, 1991, p. 50).

Additionally, another book was written during this period, which was impacted significantly by the impact of modernity. This book, written in a clear Turkish of that era, is called *Kitab-ı Ilm-ul Musiki Ala Vech-il Hurufat*, which can be translated as "The Book of the Science for Uncovering the Music by Letters". It is attributed to an Ottoman vassal prince of Moldavia known as Dimitrie Cantemir and written between 1691–1695 (Erguner, 1991, p. 49; Popescu-Judetz, 2000; 2014; Tura, 2001). However, this attribution has been challenged by some present-day scholars including, for example, Gökhan Yalçın. He claims that the book was not written by Cantemir and says that attribution to him is nothing but a misunderstanding or an unproven assertion that has been accepted for almost a century. He puts forward comparisons with related sources of that age, the attributed author's biography and also the language and the script used in the book (Yalçın, 2020, p. 79) in order to support his claim. Today, there is an increasing tendency among musicologists to accept this opinion.

Importantly, whether the book is ascribed either to Cantemir or someone else, it is still one of the most significant books that has ever been written about Turkish music theory. The main dispute that stands out in this book is the way the subjects in the work are handled. In the previous *adwar*s, the relationship between music and cosmology has less intensity in the new school than the old school. However, in this book, it is fair to say that this subject was taken a step further and that music theory was handled in a more focused way within its own system. Moreover, we see that the tradition of explaining music theory matters with numbers going back to ancient cosmological texts in traditional *adwar*s is not maintained in this book.

Yalçın Tura (2001) reveals the difference between Cantemir's (attributed) full and half pitch classification from the traditional classification. Full pitch refers to one of the main pitches of the scale of a specific *maqam* while half pitch refers to having less or no importance in the use of a certain *maqam*. Nevertheless, the understanding of full and half pitches is a concept that emerged with the Safi al-Din's school, because Kırşehri's *Adwar* talks about full and half pitches according to their position in the scale of a basic *rast maqam* (Doğrusöz, 2007, p. 160). However, the book addresses the existence of full and half

---

4   Which literally means "Collection of Instrumental and Vocal Works".

for all pitches, not just for one particular *maqam*. This issue is thus not only a matter of classification of pitches, but also an understanding of the classification of pitches around a main scale, which can be considered as a newly introduced idea. According to Tura, this classification comes from the logic of dividing an octave into 12 equal intervals, and further, into two main clusters like 7 main and 5 intermediate pitches (Tura, 2001, p. XXIX). A musical notation system based on Arabic letters was developed in the notation section, to which the second part of the book is devoted. Tura also suggests that the book's author was aware of Byzantine notation (2001, p. XXVIII).

Again, it can be claimed that a different approach was developed in terms of classification. In the book, the classification of *maqam*s was made for purely practical reasons and not according to cosmological analogies as had been the case in the *adwar* tradition. While this book classifies *maqam*s in the traditional four-part (*maqam, avaze, şube, terkib*) structure, only the category called *maqam* is classified in detail in seven different ways (Tura, 2001, pp. XXIX–XXX). According to Tura, this classification was valuable as the twelve *maqam*s that had been around since Safi al-Din al-Urmawi, and the classification in the form of *avaze, şube* and *terkib* (Tura, 2001, pp. XXIX–XXX) – whose numbers can be variable – were overturned and a new classification model was adopted.

At the end of the 18th century and the beginning of the 19th century, we meet Abdülbaki Nasır Dede. According to Tura, he did not follow the path of the traditional *adwar* writers (Tura, 2006, p. 15). In addition, Dede, who also developed a musical notation system based on the abjad system, published *Tahririye*, in which he scored many works with this notation system.

Conclusion

As mentioned above, due to the fact that we can't access the sounds produced before audio recording, we can only guess what these historic sonic landscapes were like. For our estimates to be relatively close to the reality of the time, clearly we must use all the resources at our disposal. For this study, we have chosen music theory as our primary resource to understand the sound of the pre-modern era at the Ottoman court. The primary reason for this is that music theory has long stood at the intersection of art and science. Furthermore, as an intellectual activity, music theory has long been related to power, since the scholars who produced music theory material enjoyed the patronage of either a court or a religious authority. Therefore, the music theory of any era contains clues about the surrounding power, politics, and intellectual trends.

If we consider the above discussion from a different perspective, one could say that the transformations in the Ottoman Empire cannot, in fact, be considered new in terms of musical history. When looking at the history of music theory, about which we have about ten centuries of knowledge to make an assessment, we can see that there have been successive periodic swings. These swings have essentially vacillated between two things: theory and practice. Of course, it would be a mistake to perceive this vacillation as a uniform sine wave. Summarizing the qualitative transformations in the history of music theory into a single sentence, we see two concepts following one another. With regard to which is stronger at what time – as in the dialectical understanding of "everything contains its opposite" – every period is essentially the product of an earlier process and the result of that process's internalization. Moreover, each process is influenced by the social, political, and economic atmosphere of the time period in question.

When we examine the history of music theory from Safi al-Din to the present day, we see two stages, each one responsible for the other. These stages are an extension and effect of historical and social conditions, leading to a constantly repeating plot of events. First, a theory is put forward and everything is handled with a systematic logic in a positive scientific format. Then the theory becomes simpler, or interest in the theory decreases, whereupon practice comes to the fore. Over time, the rules and constraints of the theory begin to be broken and practical elements are considered. This could be called theory revolution followed by practical revolution. Each practical cycle desires to return to the theoretical part of the theory-practice cycle and is fed by it. Each cycle focuses on a particular component, revealing those that are missing and the need for the next cycle. In the next cycle, the other component gains importance in order to eliminate the deficiency left in the previous cycle. This creates the subsequent need in the same way.

When we approach the modern era, we see several transformations taking place. For instance, instead of the number of *maqam*s being listed as 12, the existence of more *maqam*s is mentioned. Instead of esoteric elements being an ideology, with analogies of which fret corresponds to which zodiac sign and thus which fret is to be played in which order, the music itself comes into the foreground. Ideological concerns are pushed to the background and replaced with practical concerns. We can speak of a situation in which practice has taken the upper hand. Thus, entering the modern period, we see texts on music theory taking a different form.

Bibliography

Arslan, F. (2015). *İslam Medeniyetinde Musiki*. Beyan.
Akdoğan, B. (1996). *Fethullah Şirvânî ve Mecelletun fi'l-Mûsîka Adlı Eserinin XV*. Yüzyıl Türk Mûsikîsi Nazariyatındaki Yeri [Doctoral dissertation, Ankara Üniversitesi].

Cevher, H. (1995). *Ali Ufki Bey ve Haza Mecmu'a-i Saz u Söz* [Doctoral dissertation, Ege Üniversitesi].

Çelik, B. B. (2001). *Hızır bin Abdullah'ın Kitabu'l-Edvar'ı ve Makamların İncelenmesi* [Doctoral dissertation, Marmara Üniversitesi].

Çoğulu, T. (2018). El-Kindî'nin Ud Perde Değerlerinin Gitara Uygulanması ve Enis Gümüş'ün "El-Kindî" Eserinin Analizi. *Ahenk Müzikoloji Dergisi 3*, 32–43.

Doğrusöz, N. (2007). *Hariri Bin Muhammed'in Kırşehrî Edvarı Üzerine Bir İnceleme* [Doctoral dissertation, İstanbul Teknik Üniversitesi].

Erguner, S. (1991). *Kutb-i Nayi Osman Dede ve Rabt-ı Tabirat-ı Musiki* [Master's thesis, Marmara Üniversitesi].

Güray, C. (2012). *Bin Yılın Mirası Makamı Var Eden Döngü: Edvar Geleneği.* Pan Yayınları.

İnalcık, H. (2011). *Şair ve Patron.* Doğu Batı Yayınları.

Katsillis, J., & Armer, M. (2003). Modernization Theory. In E. F. Borgatta (Ed.), *Encyclopedia of Sociology 3* (pp. 1883–1888). Macmillan Reference USA.

Mardin, Ş., (1991). *Türk Modernleşmesi Makaleler IV.* İletişim Yayınları.

Özcan, A. (2003). Lale Devri. In A. Ağırakça, et al. (Ed.), *İslam Ansiklopedisi* (pp. 81–84). https://islamansiklopedisi.org.tr/lale-devri. Date of Access: 26.01.2024.

Popescu-Judetz, E. (2000). *Prens Dimitrie Cantemir*, transl. by S. Alimdar. Pan Yayınları.

TDK (2006). *Genel Türkçe Sözlük.* http://tdk.gov.tr. Date of Access: 26.01.2024.

Thong, T. (2012). 'To Raise the Savage to a Higher Level': The Westernization of Nagas and their Culture. *Modern Asian Studies 46*(4), 893–918.

Tıraşçı, M. (2017). *Türk Musikisi Nazariyatı Tarihi.* Kayıhan Yayınları.

Tura, Y. (1988). *Türk Musikisinin Mes'eleleri.* Pan Yayınları.

Tura, Y. (2001). *Kantemiroğlu Musikiyi Harflerle Tespit ve İcra İlminin Kitabı.* Yapı Kredi Yayınları.

Turabi, A. H. (1996). *El-Kindî'nin Musiki Risaleleri* [Master's thesis, Marmara Üniversitesi].

Turabi, A. H. (2013). *İbn-i Sina Musiki*, transl. by A. H. Turabi. Litera Yayıncılık.

Uysal, E. (2000). İhvan-ı Sava. In A. Ağırakça, et al. (Ed.), *İslam Ansiklopedisi*, vol. 22 (pp. 1–6). TDV.

Uygun, M. N. (2020). Kitâbü'l-edvâr. In A. Ağırakça, et al. (Ed.), *İslam Ansiklopedisi.* https://islamansiklopedisi.org.tr/kitabul-edvar. Date of Access: 26.01.2024.

Yalçın, G. (2013). Haşim Bey Mecmuasının Makam ve Tonalite Karşılaştırması Yönünden İncelenmesi. *International Periodical for The Languages, Literature and History of Turkish or Turkic 8*(6), 753–768.

Yalçın, G. (2020). *Kevseri Mecmuası.* Gece Kitaplığı.

The Discovery of Life's Pleasures in the Tulip Era

The Rise of City Life and a Worldly Perception in the Ottoman Empire

Ali Ergur

Introduction

The period between 1718 and 1730 can be thought of as a critical turn in Ottoman history. A period that ended the 17th century's destabilized political context, it also initiated a new process of social and political change. As a belittled and caricatured image of an imitated modern lifestyle, the Tulip Era (1718–1730) is generally presented in conservative Turkish historiography as a symbol of excessive adoration in Turkey of European culture. Accordingly, the imagery and discourse describing this specific period of Ottoman history are conceptualized as a set of imitative practices of an urban elite that aimed to transpose modern life into a social context that had neither the economic conditions nor the cultural values befitting such a superficial transformation. At least, this is the highly proliferated discourse, which became an clearly accepted *a priori* position among representatives of the ideology of Ottoman superiority, the connotation of Islamic power.

Naturally, the image of the Ottoman Empire, whether sublimed as an ideal or reduced to its Islamic holy war and conquest activity, has always tended to valorise the periods of political strength as an ideal political and cultural state, instead of considering history a dialectical process. Consequently, the dominant narrative of Ottoman history by conservative historians emphasizes the 16th century as the empire's ideal form, claiming that this century was the climax of Ottoman power, yet also marked the beginning of its decline. Since political power is the only criterion for such a perception of history, the period starting with the 17th century is not referred to as a source of pride in this conservative point of view. Nevertheless, contrary to the weakening of its political power, in the 17th century the Ottoman Empire entered a period of social change during which urban life emerged. Indeed, the conservative or linear conception of Ottoman history emphasizing the thesis of political decline has been largely criticized by some historians, especially from the 1980s onward (Sajdi, 2007).

The Tulip Era was the result of a politically destabilized yet culturally enriched social context. It was a period in search of relative peace and stability following military campaigns that had ended in defeats and territorial losses. Meanwhile, at the end of the 17th century, the Ottoman world had become a point of attraction for a number of European voyagers, as well as for permanent ambassadors who reported their observations about this period of change (Daş, 2017, pp. 171–172). From the first decades of the 18th century onward, the Ottoman state felt the need to explore other countries and cultures in order to understand what had gone wrong. These reciprocal contacts gave rise to a multitude of exchanges, helping the development of a relatively complex and accelerated life tempo, particularly in the big cities.

At the dawn of the 18th century, following the first observations made by Ottoman voyagers to Europe, and under the socio-psychological need to transition to a period of stability, a series of urbanistic movements began during the reign of Sultan Ahmed III. Most were orchestrated by the grand vizier (*Sadrazam*) Nevşehirli İbrahim Pasha. One of the most influential pioneering observations made by the first provisory ambassadors sent by the Sultan can be found in the travel diary and report of Yirmisekiz Mehmet Çelebi, who in 1720 wrote about the cultural and technical-material peculiarities he encountered in France (Rado, 2008). Although written in a general style of bravery, ideological exaggeration, and political propaganda, the diary of Yeniçeri Kâtibi Hasan, a soldier who had actively participated in the Prut Campaign of 1711, comprises some socio-economic observations in the undertones of his text (Yıldız, 2008). In these occasional reports, Ottoman pioneers who discovered the cultural landscape of changing Europe procured some clues for diagnosing the structural failures of the Ottoman state. Thus began a period of urban planning and construction (Tuna, 2013, p. 18) according to rational criteria and a cultural milieu that emerged with it (İnalcık, 2015b, p. 124). This was the Tulip Era, which in a sociological sense represented the tendency to adopt modern values, a result of the need to transform a long-lasting socio-political inertia. In the following, this specific and dominantly ill-perceived period of the Ottoman history will be analysed through an alternative sociological reading, whereby it will be possible to depict signs of modernization in values, mentalities, and psyches, as well as in material dimensions of social life. In short, we assert that the Tulip Era was the crystallization and the beginning of the modernization process in the Ottoman Empire. In addition to various other domains of everyday life, music and its social sphere occupy a particular place for understanding the interwoven structure of relations between urban actors, as well as for depicting the trend of social tendencies and change. Music, in our opinion, is the best and most direct symbolic matrix through which it is possible to follow the particularities of social change. Although we briefly mention transformations observed in the other arts, we take music as a soundscape of social structure and change, and thus place the emphasis on its particular character, which is easily infused into space and time. This chapter aims to reveal, albeit very compactly, the change in the structure and meaning of music at the beginning of the 18th century in the Ottoman cultural world. This period, essentially the short but historically dense interval called the Tulip Era, can be conceived as both the opening of the process of modernization and the end of the age of old-type, the *Ancien régime* empires and dynasties, such as the Ottoman, Habsburg and Burgundian. Although the period analysed in this chapter may seem, at first glance, to go beyond the historical framework of the present volume's topic, the Tulip Era is conceptualized as the outer historical marking of a period of a pre-modern series of political equilibria, and as becoming the scene of visible transformation toward a modern conception of life and politics. Music and its social world are the basic materials with which this historical bridge will be constructed.

Modern Tendencies in a Moving Urban Life

Although the 17th century was a period of political disorder, uncertainty concerning the sources of power, and a general tendency of decline in economic and organizational aspects in Ottoman social life (Özkaya, 1985, p. 245), it also presents a series of contradictions and oscillations. Even though a few reformist movements were launched and partially applied by some political elites, such as the Köprülü family, the unbalanced state of the budget remained more or less unchanged until the total dissolution of the Empire at the beginning of the 20th century (İnalcık, 2015a, pp. 17–28). The 17th-century Ottoman Empire seems to be a multi-faceted prism through which opposite forces and inconsistent images are refracted. Partial military successes were followed by important defeats, while political life underwent an unstable trajectory. Especially from the end of the century onward, a period of general decline escalated and gave rise to the first signs of territorial and political dismantling. Meanwhile, certain reformist ideas grew among the political elite, though they wouldn't become decisive enough until the 18th century, since they were pushed back by a block of resistance in the same circle of state elites. Niyazi Berkes, the renowned Turkish sociologist, has seen this polarization as a question of dissensus about the founding ideology of the Ottoman Empire: On the one hand, a group of elites felt the need to adapt the state to the changing world, through reforms giving rise to scientific inquiry, technological innovation, and thus social progress. On the other hand, a dominant group of conservatives insisted on remaining attached to the fundamental principles of the state: The order of the universe (*nizâm-ı âlem*), created by God, is the *raison d'être* for the state; if the latter remains conformed to His principles, its life will be endless (*devlet-i ebed-müdded*) (1978, p. 29). This basic conception favours the necessity of an unchanging structure in social life as well as in the political sphere. In addition to these two sides, the inevitable rise of Europe as a capitalist force, which triggered scientific methodology, innovation, and progress, had been added to the internal contradictions of the Ottoman world. In summary, at the end of the 17th century, the Ottoman Empire had arrived at the end of its political power. This was in fact a question of a clash of the modes of production: A declining social system based on agriculture and war was historically condemned to lose against another system animated by trade and discovery: the ethics of an unchanging world against the values of novelty, invention, and progress.

Nevertheless, in the same period, first tendencies for reforming military technology and then other institutions opened the Ottoman system, which had been, until then, quite closed to outer – and particularly the Christian – world, with a characteristically humiliating attitude. By this token, a relatively complex urban scene had emerged in the main cities, where commercial activities, links to European centres, and functional specializations increased. At the same time, successive wars, constant economic crises, and an unstable social environment created a general need for a peaceful social life. In this context, a series of urban planning movements arrived, as well as the rise of a new lifestyle that challenged a world conception based on religiously oriented sobriety and the unimportance of actual life, which elevated the significance of the afterlife. Although this was not an overall social change, the burgeoning of this new perception affected the different strata of society to various degrees. Music seemed to be the most comprehensive means for carrying the changing social tastes and expectations, as well as for representing a complete historical decorum of sensitivities. Indeed, artistic production and its aesthetic references began to change starting with the 18th century, reflecting thereby a more flexible urban life.

Wherever commercial activities increase and give rise to complex exchanges, the values according to which social logic is shaped are adjusted in terms of modernity. We won't pursue a discussion on the philosophical meanings of modernity here in the scope of a short chapter, but we should at least note that *modern* is not exclusively situated historically in the European experience. Instead, we should rethink the modern as a tendency of separation between the world of relations (intersubjective communicative actions) and the world of institutions (normative institutional structures) (Habermas, 1983, p. 70). Due to the progressive complexity of everyday life and commercial activities, social organization is realigned on a secular, class-based, rational, standardised, and worldly conception, supported by the rise of disentanglement processes in political, economic, legal, and symbolic institutions (Giddens, 1989, p. 183). These are tendencies which also encourage the emergence of an urban social life and the spatial reorganization fitting it. On a related note, we observe similar changes in the Ottoman context, though the economic circumstances were not the same. Among other characteristics of modernity, *worldliness* shows best the cultural milieu in which individuals discover their subjective reality in an objectified organization (Simmel, 1989, p. 282). It is also the sign of the relative abandoning of a fatalist and religious perception of the world, while replacing it with rationally conceived criteria and values. Moreover, the passage from the second half of the 16th to the beginning of the 18th centuries shaped a series of intellectual and scientific activities, though they remained very limited and "naive" (Emecen, 2018, p. 91). The rise of urban life on the eve of the 18th century seeded the premises of modern tendencies in the Ottoman world. Thus, the public space became the scene of individuality and worldliness, as well as that of power. Music of various forms spread out into the public space, with the sonic leading to the spectacular reconfiguration of the social.

Public Space, Individual Appearance, Worldly Pleasures

Despite cultural differences between the industrialising Europe of the 18th century and the pragmatically changing Ottoman society, the coming of modern tendencies caused similar social phenomena, such as the emergence of an urban public space. Indeed, the meticulously conceived urban planning projects realized during the Tulip Era fashioned a spatial but also symbolic delimitation of a new public space, though this short, exceptional period ended with a bloody riot (Unat, 2014, p. 52).[1]

Consequently, the physical reconstruction of the city – Istanbul in particular – implied the birth of a new matrix of signs, through which not only the relatively free-floating of the individual bodies was made possible, but also, and more importantly, new values associated with them proliferated into different circles of social life. Therefore, a worldly conception of life sparked among the higher and middle classes, in different forms and intensities. The progressive decline of the patrimonial power of sultans gave rise to the primacy of the bureaucratic forces and that of female figures in the Ottoman dynasty. The latter adopted and represented a worldly and hedonistic way of life that also functioned as a social model (Artan, 1992, p. 116).

Urban planning was not only conceived according to functional necessities of urban organization. Instead, the reshaping of the urban space was oriented significantly by aesthetic concerns. Yet this desire to make the urban space ordered and systematic, and yet also cos-

---

1   The Tulip Era ended on 28 September 1730 with a popular riot orchestrated by a group of rebel soldiers and shopkeepers as a reaction to the relatively rapid emergence of a European-oriented lifestyle of an elite minority, together with a rise in prices, which worsened the already precarious economic situation of the general population. The rebels demanded the execution of some of the leading figures of this first modernist era, and then the dethroning of Sultan Ahmed III. Most of the edifices built during the Tulip Era were destroyed; a number of central cultural individuals, such as the poet Nedîm, were killed. Although a brief period of terror and anarchy caused by the rebels reigned particularly in Istanbul, the state's armed forces, representing the new monarch Mahmud I, systematically killed all of the rebels and re-established a relative authority.

metic, crystallised into slowly growing modern sensibilities. This material transformation of urban space, even in limited areas, is akin to a rationally conditioned worldview.

As its projection into the world of intersubjective relations, rational thinking – or at least a slight inclination toward it – can release, as in the example of the Ottoman case at the beginning of the 18th century, a relative distancing from the values of traditional structures, which favour the idea of the individual as non-emancipated from the community, a religiously shaped perception of life, and therefore a precarious existence under the absolute will of God. Instead, with growing modern ambitions, the urban individual slowly became a relatively autonomous subject, negotiating life's meaning in his/her faith, and looking for ways of being in this actual world, which implied delivering him-/herself to life's pleasures. Consequently, the urban Ottoman subject presented him-/herself to the social space as a unity of experience of this-worldliness. In other words, the physical reconstruction of urban space inspired the idea of being a subjective expression and an actor of spontaneous encounters, and thus adventures, as it has been described by Georg Simmel (1989, p. 311). The sufficiently easy-living individual appeared in the Tulip Era in the newly-constructed and semantically redefined public space as a quasi-volatile unit of action. Public appearance, in addition to the traditionally traced paths of being, such as private spaces for women and a limited commercial or administrative sphere for men, was a kind of defeat of the long-lasting curtailment of individual expression. The immediate ground onto which the individual expression projected was the quest for life's pleasures. Poetry and music were two principal artistic domains through which a hedonistic life concept was represented.

Poetry, Music, Public Spectacles

The cultural spirit that animated the Tulip Era was most concretized in several artistic domains, together with a considerable amount of translation from Arabic or Persian classics (İnalcık, 2021, p. 308). This means that the Tulip Era was not a unidirectional Westernization initiative, but a pioneering programme of the Enlightenment. Traditional handicrafts were influenced somewhat by this urban movement. However, not all traditional handicrafts evolved at the same pace and with the same itinerary. For example, while miniature painting acquired a more dynamic character, the impetus for tile-making decreased visibly, despite the inconsistent efforts of Damat İbrahim Pasha, the leading political figure of the Tulip Era, for reanimating the art of tile-making (Uzunçarşılı, 1983, p. 557). It is possible to argue that the miniatures of the period were conceived by artists with shapes and drawings that were more colourful and moving. As the "final flair" of the art of the miniature, spectacles in public spaces, most accompanied by music, became more present in the imagination of artists (Kuban, 1986, p. 87). The miniature, with its caricature-like fine imaging, was invented by creative artists escaping the ban of anthropomorphic representations according to Islamic principles. The figures became more life-like, the scenes more realistically drawn in a style reflecting everyday interactions, the themes more oriented toward real-life themes and interactions, with an implicit tribute to life's pleasures. As has been observed in Enlightenment imagery, the return to nature was frequently chosen as the subject of miniatures of the 18th century. Vast landscapes with flora and fauna, scenes of hunting, aesthetically arranged gardens with happy-go-lucky individuals passing leisure time in the peaceful environment, accompanied by alcoholic beverages, fruit and various meals, were the topics preferred by the miniature artists of the 18th century. New techniques had been sought and invented as part of the innovative spirit. But the most important characteristic separating this period of miniature art from that of the previous centuries was the privileged place given to the individual, particularly in the paintings of Levnî (Kuban, 1986, p. 88).

As a well-rooted tradition, Dîvan literature, which was based solely on poetry, acquired a new scope in the Tulip Era, especially under the quill of the poet Nedîm, who concentrated exclusively on urban scenes, promenades, fantasies of pleasure, flirtation, carnal desires, implicit praise of homosexual encounters, ironically and allegorically described love, etc. Among the preferred urban buildings and neighbourhoods, Nedîm took hammams, gardens, promenade plains, fountains, taverns, boat trips, sumptuous houses, etc. as the stage for his frivolous narratives, which mixed reality and fantasy:

> I don't say the anguish caused by the hangman eye of this nymph-faced one,
> I don't say the scream of Nedîm caused by the sorrow of love,
> It is no obstacle to say his or her style and allure, but I cannot say his or her name,
> The one with rose cheeks, rosy gown, purple eye circles (Yesirgil, 1977, p. 89).

This is indeed the opposite of the Dîvan poetry of previous centuries, where we mostly find love in terms of the adoration of God's will. In early Dîvan poetry, even love for a human being is a metaphor for mystic experiences, while all descriptions of beauty implicitly indicate the virtue of an individual's life, which only has value if the person dedicates him-/herself to the love of God and a sober life consistent with it. The poetry of Nedîm can be considered the poetic landmark of the Tulip Era (Uzunçarşılı, 1983, p. 543).

Another artistic domain where meaningful changes occurred is music. Most of the authors who have analysed the modernization process of Turkish music defend the idea that these changes were ineffective because they were triggered by elitist top-to-bottom reform projects in the Ottoman period, as well as in the Republican era. The arguments of these authors (Tanrıkorur, 2003; Balkılıç 2009; Abacı, 2013; Öztürk, 2018; Ayas, 2020) are similar. They criticize the modernization process in music because they consider the European music imported into the Ottoman-Turkish milieu as simply an act of imitation. Nevertheless, this widely-accepted *a priori* argument has several problems. The most important discrepancy is the fact that this criticism takes the coming of European music to the Ottoman territory as the object of study, rather than analysing the transformations that can be observed in Turkish *makam* music itself. The latter entered a phase of a palpable process of change from the beginning of the 18th century onward. In addition to the technical transformations that Turkish *makam* music underwent, such as the preffered *makam*s being reduced and rhythmic cycles shortened, its social function and changed when it became part of public events, rather than a mystical experience among a close circle of friends. Through the 18th and 19th centuries, we observe a relative change in the nature of *makam*s used by composers, as well as a simplification in the structure of rhythmic cycles (*usul*). An important feature of this process of transformation is the progressive movement toward written music, a distinct sign of a modern attitude that aimed both to sum up and to classify the inventory of historical heritage and reconfigure it for future syntheses (Levendoğlu, 2004; Ergur & Aydın, 2006; Ayangil, 2008; Karakayalı, 2010; Ergur & Doğrusöz, 2015). On the other hand, music became the transporter of worldly feelings and actions into the public space. Again, it played the role of a spatial regulator of inter-class links by putting forward the *şarkı* (song) as nearly the sole form that was publicly appreciated and requested (Nardella, 2020, p. 6). This means that music became a vector for lyrics, which primarily reflected feelings and scenes associated with frivolity, love, and flirtatious sayings. Like the symbolic value of the poetry of Nedîm, Tanburî Mustafa Çavuş was a typical representative of a worldly attitude in music. Not only did his song lyrics convey a worldly perception of life, the musical structure of his songs are based on the concept of an urban popular "light music", music that is "easy-listening", a cultural product immediately meaningful and rapidly consumable. A typical and well-known example of the popular compositions of Tanburî Mustafa Çavuş is a highly joyful song entitled "Dök zülfünü meydâne gel" (Uncover your hair and come to the dance floor) in the *makam Hisar Bûselik*. This song's lyrics perfectly reflect the individual hedonistic conception of love, in contrast to transcendental divine love:

> Uncover your hair [in a cultural world where the hair is not publicly shown] and come to the dance floor [show yourself with courage and audacity],
> Drive your horse, come as sultans do [in a social stratification that did not allow every individual to ride a horse or travel in a wheeled cart]
> Take your def [a circular percussion instrument like a tambourine], come to the celebration//
> The mockingbird is yours; the rose garden is yours.
> Oh sweet love,
> I have been in love with you for a long time.
> My heart is full of expectation of your arrival, come please//

The Discovery of Life's Pleasures in the Tulip Era

You answered with your fame,
You burned my chest with your blazing fire,
Which is thirsty for you with its thousand lives// [...]

Starting with the Tulip Era, various important technical aspects of Turkish *makam* music changed, such as its sound system and rhythmic patterns, its being written down, changes of the instruments used, performative value, etc.

We can find examples of these changes in the new worldly conception of life and the emphasis on spectacles in the urban space, as for instance, the famous forty-day-long circumcision ceremony in 1720 for the sons of Sultan Ahmed III. Imperial events had already been celebrated publicly in past centuries, but for this circumcision event, not only were a series of public spectacles organized, but extravagance dominated the entire urban space and consciousness (And, 2020, p. 344). Music, dance, and poetry played a major role in such spectacles. Public festivities were not only social events and occasions for creating moments of frenzy, but also a means for control and reinforcing the sultan's reign, especially since his political power had been in decline from the 17th century onwards. In such public spectacles, music played a crucial role, given that it created an otherworldly force establishing social cohesion. But since music was more intrusive and efficient than the other arts, it was also a dependable means for political statements and ideological exposure. This included political movements emanating from the public space as well as from imperial power. Public performances of music thus had, by their very nature, a double-sided character: on the one hand, they shaped an ideological apparatus for the Ottoman throne, on the other, they created a context of public interaction. However, Ottoman public festivities functioned primarily as a conflict-absorbing ideological mechanism. Moreover, public festivities were used as a symbolic matrix through which imperial power could be reconfigured. This was done by including the larger urban space (Erdoğan İşkorkutan, 2017, p. 266) not only for a vast variety of social functions (mostly arts and crafts), but also for unusual spectacles with various types of appearances and representations. Public spectacles were also scenes of innovation and creativity, in addition to being a demonstration of social-economic actors. An example of an innovative scene was the appearance on the Golden Horn during the 1720 festivities of a submarine. In the shape of an alligator, it was one of the first submarines ever built in the world; it had also been used in a show during the circumcision "party". According to witnesses – it is mentioned by Raşit Metel in his *History of Turkish Submarines* in reference to *Sûrname* by Seyid Vehbi Hüseyin – the strange object surfaced from under the water, its mouth (hatch) was open, and belly dancers appeared from inside (1960, p. 1). While its appearance created a general feeling of fear, it also aroused the curiosity, delight, imagination, and pure amusement of the spectators. This is highly consistent with the underlying spirit of modern individualism: seeking life's pleasures and a global feeling of worldliness. Although spectacles at festivities were always the main feature of such events, in addition to confirming the roles of existing social actors and functions, at the beginning of the 18th century we observe a relative increase in extravagance and a search for unfamiliar, surprising, and challenging spectacles, as well as an appreciation for novel inventions. Compared to similar events in the 16th and 17th centuries, the festivities of 1720 can be considered the public affirmation of a new conception of the urban space, gathering not only everyday actors, but also the uncommon, odd, and even outlandish. Such a strong thirst for original and uncommon representations seems in line with the emergence of a modern conception of the world.

In this reformatting of the political and social spheres, music and soundscapes played a major and dominant role. This was not only due to their omnipresence, particularly during festivities. It was also due to their performing an *enwrapping function* at the intersection between political power, the public space, and the scene of representations, accomplished by juxtaposing urban material and immaterial diversity. Certainly, the spectacular character of imperial festivities was not only assured by music and sound; if we take into account the astonishingly colourful and animated character of such spectacles, other arts were also part of the urban space's redefinition. Yet, the music and soundscape of festival scenes were able to interlink, weave together, and orient both the ordinary (spectators) and extraordinary (players, parade actors) through their own ontologies, inevitably necessitating a constant diffusion through time and space. In contrast, other arts (particularly the visual ones) may be impressive in their moment, but they are less effective transversally. When we consider the sociological meaning of the Tulip Era, which saw the blossoming of a modern mentality through the rise of a worldly perception of life, a rationally conceived urban space, and, most importantly, an opening toward interactions with Western Europe, we can argue that the 1720 imperial festivities occupied a privileged place and formed a historical turning point.

Conclusion

The short historical period called the Tulip Era (1718–1730) marked the beginning of modern tendencies in the Ottoman social fabric. At the beginning of the 18th century, the general political decline was in dialectical opposition to an enriched cultural life. The Tulip Era was the first period in which signs of modern tendencies can be observed. It also marked the end of a period in which social life was characterized by a relatively closed worldview highly conditioned by religious principles. Significantly, the Tulip Era saw the introduction of urban planning and policies to reshape public spaces. The spatial reorganization of the city also prompted the appearance of the individual within a symbolic sphere, in a worldly conception of being, while at the same time, political power was reconfigured through the same public representations. As a consequence and as a sign of modern tendencies, as has been underlined by Simmel, women began to appear in the urban space as an attribute of worldly attitudes. Although covered according to social norms, the female body became asexualized and gender was no longer a matter of concern. This is another reason we see the Tulip Era as constituting the beginning of a modernization process. It was not just part of a series of top-to-bottom reformist movements, but it was also a sign of social changes projected onto its own cultural production. From a wider perspective, it is possible to perceive the entire Tulip Era as the moment a modern understanding of the world appeared in the Ottoman view. The imperial festivities of 1720 can be thought of as a kind of Weberian ideal of this first limited step of modernization, in the form of heightened extravagance and novelties. Although music had always been an inseparable part of such festivities and of the soundscape of public spaces, it acquired a new function in Ottoman urban society at the beginning of the 18th century. Music became more varied and eclectic, it began to envelop the public space due to its ubiquitous and multi-focal presence. This aspect of the music-sound matrix seems to have been enhanced by a rising popular culture, which included everyday interactions, once-banal values, and hedonistic individual attitudes favouring simplicity in an urban environment that was becoming ever more complex.

Bibliography

Abacı, T. (2013). *Gramofonlu Kahvehane, Memleketin Şarkısı Türküsü Üzerine Yazılar*. İkaros Yayınları.

And, M. (2020). *Kırk Gün Kırk Gece, Osmanlı Düğünleri, Şenlikleri, Geçit Alayları*. Yapı Kredi Yayınları.

Artan, T. (1992). Boğaziçi'nin Çehresini Değiştiren Soylu Kadınlar ve Sultanefendi Sarayları. *İstanbul Dergisi* 3, 109–118.

Ayangil, R. (2008). Western Notation in Turkish Music. *Journal of the Royal Asiatic Society* 18(4), 401–447.

Ayas, O. G. (2020). *Musiki İnkılabı'nın Sosyolojisi, Klasik Türk Müziği Geleneğinde Süreklilik ve Değişim*. İthaki Yayınları.

Balkılıç, Ö. (2009). *Cumhuriyet, Halk ve Müzik*. Tan Kitabevi Yayınları.

Berkes, N. (1978). *Türkiye'de Çağdaşlaşma*. Doğu-Batı Yayınları.

Daş, M. (Ed.) (2017). *İstanbul'da Fransız Elçiliği, Marki de Bonnac'ın Tarihi Hatırat ve Belgeleri*, transl. by A. Ş. Bizer. Türk Tarih Kurumu.

Emecen, F. M. (2018). Matruşka'nın Küçük Parçası: Nevşehirli Damat İbrahim Paşa Dönemi ve 'Lale Devri' Meselesi Üzerine Bir Değerlendirme. *Osmanlı Araştırmaları/The Journal of Ottoman Studies* 52, 79–98.

Erdoğan İşkorkutan, S. (2017). *The 1720 Imperial Festival in Istanbul: Festivity and Represenation in the Early Eighteenth-Century Ottoman Empire* [Doctoral dissertation, Boğaziçi University].

Ergur, A. & Aydın, Y. (2006). Pattern of Modernization as Indicators of a Changing Society, *Musicae Scientiae* Special Issue, 2005-2006, 89–108.

Ergur, A. & Doğrusöz, N. (2015). Resistance and Adoption Towards Written Music at the Crossroads of Modernity: Gradual Passage to Notation in Makam Music, *International Review of Aesthetics and Sociology of Music* 46(1), 145–174.

Giddens, A. (1989). *The Constitution of Society, Outline of the Theory of Structuration.* Polity Press.

Habermas, J. (1983). *The Theory of Communicative Action vol. 1: Reason and the Rationalization of Society.* Beacon Press.

İnalcık, H. (2015a). *Devlet-i 'Aliyye, Osmanlı İmparatorluğu Üzerine Araştırmalar-III, Köprülüler Devri.* İş Bankası Yayınları.

İnalcık, H. (2015b). *Devlet-i 'Aliyye, Osmanlı İmparatorluğu Üzerine Araştırmalar-IV, Âyânlar, Tanzimat, Meşrutiyet.* İş Bankası Yayınları.

İnalcık, H. (2021). *Has-bağçede 'ayş u tarab, Nedîmler Şâirler Mutrîbler.* İş Bankası Yayınları.

Karakayalı, N. (2010). Two Assemblages of Cultural Transmission: Musicians, Political Actors and Educational Techniques in the Ottoman Empire and Western Europe. *Journal of Historical Sociology* 23(3), 343–371.

Kuban, D. (1986). *Turkish Culture & Arts.* BBA.

Levendoğlu, O. (2004). XVIII. Yüzyıldan Bugüne Uzanan Makamlar ve Değişim Çizgileri. *Erciyes Üniversitesi Sosyal Bilimler Enstitüsü Dergisi* 17, 131–138.

Metel, R. (1960). *Türk Denizaltıcılık Tarihi.* Deniz Basımevi.

Nardella, F. (2020). The Late Ottoman *Şarkı* and the Interweaving of Registers: Towards an Ideology of Song. *Musicologist, International Journal of Musical Studies* 4(1), 1–33.

Özkaya, Y. (1985). *XVIII. Yüzyılda Osmanlı Kurumları ve Osmanlı Toplum Yaşantısı.* Kültür ve Turizm Bakanlığı.

Öztürk, O. M. (2018). How was the Traditional Makam Music Theory Westernized for the Sake of Modernization? *Rast Müzikoloji Dergisi* 6(1), 1769–1787.

Rado, Ş. (2008). *Paris'te Bir Osmanlı Sefiri, Yirmisekiz Mehmet Çelebi'nin Fransa Seyahatnamesi.* Türkiye İş Bankası Yayınları.

Sajdi, D. (2007). Decline and its Discontents and the Ottoman Cultural History: By Way of Introduction. In D. Sajdi (Ed.), *Ottoman Tulips, Ottoman Coffee, Leisure and Lifestyle in the Eighteenth Century* (pp. 1–40). Tauris Academic Studies.

Simmel, G. (1989). *Philosophie de la modernité, la femme, la ville, l'individualisme.* Payot.

Tanrıkorur, C. (2003). *Osmanlı Dönemi Türk Mûsikîsi.* Dergâh Yayınları.

Tuna, T. (2013). *Kıyı Köşe İstanbul.* E Yayınları.

Unat, F. R. (2014). *1730 Patrona İhtilâli Hakkında Bir Eser, Abdi Tarihi.* Türk Tarih Kurumu Yayınları.

Uzunçarşılı, İ. H. (1983). *Osmanlı Tarihi IV. Cilt, 2. Kısım, XVIII. Yüzyıl.* Türk Tarih Kurumu Basımevi.

Yesirgil, N. (1977). *Nedim, Hayatı Sanatı Şiirleri.* Varlık Yayınları.

Yıldız, H. (2008). *Prut Seferi'ni Beyanımdır, Yeniçeri Kâtibi Hasan.* Türkiye İş Bankası Yayınları.

Part III
Habsburg-Burgundian Court Culture

Une symphonie de faveurs

Les dons aux musiciens, entre communication politique et expression du pouvoir à la cour de Bourgogne (1404–1467)

Baptiste Rameau

"Étudier l'histoire de la musique et des musiciens au XVe siècle, c'est entrer dans le vif de la vie sociale" disait Jeanne Marix dans l'introduction de son ouvrage sur l'histoire de la musique et des musiciens à la cour de Bourgogne sous Philippe le Bon (Marix, 1972, p. 1). Si la question sociale est bien présente, la musique permet également de mieux comprendre la vie politique et notamment les pratiques de gouvernement au Moyen Âge.[1] Bien que cette dimension politique de l'art musical ait été démontrée par de nombreux travaux (Cullin, 2002; Clouzot et al., 2005), ces derniers se sont avant tout intéressés aux aspects théoriques, délaissant l'importance des liens qui unissaient le prince à ses musiciens. Ces relations, officielles et/ou personnelles, nous en apprennent pourtant beaucoup sur ces rapports complexes mêlant à la fois pratiques de gouvernement, fonctionnement des réseaux au sein de l'hôtel ducal et communication politique. Afin d'analyser au mieux ces dernières, nous avons décidé de nous concentrer sur le don qui, pour reprendre les mots d'Elodie Lecuppre-Desjardin, "se retrouve absolument à tous les niveaux de l'exercice du pouvoir" (Lecuppre-Desjardin, 2018, p. 138).

Comprendre et analyser ces liens supposent tout d'abord de définir, en préambule, ce que nous entendons ici par musicien. Nous avons décidé d'adopter une classification souple, nécessaire puisque le fonctionnel supplante, au Moyen Âge, l'instrumental pour reprendre les mots de Martine Clouzot (Clouzot, 2000); le terme renvoyant avant tout à "une activité et non un emploi" précise d'ailleurs David Fiala (2011, p. 167) et Rob. C. Wegman (2003, pp. 425–437). En conséquence, et pour retranscrire au mieux le regard porté par nos sources sur lesdits musiciens, nous distinguerons trois groupes dans notre étude: les ménestrels, les trompettes et les autres instrumentistes.

---

[1] Clouzot, 2007b, p. 137: "qu'elle soit présente à la cour dans les cérémoniels par la pratique instrumentale des ménestrels, ou qu'elle soit incarnée par le savoir théorique des clercs, la musique apparaît comme nécessaire au prince, de sa formation jusqu'au gouvernement, certes pour les divertissements qu'elle procure, mais surtout pour les vertus de mesure, de bonté, de justice qu'elle porte en elle depuis ses origines orphiques."

C'est donc aux interactions entre le prince et ses musiciens que nous nous intéressons dans cette communication. À travers cette dernière nous entendons proposer une ébauche de réflexion sur l'usage du don comme pratique de gouvernement au sein de la Grande Principauté de Bourgogne.

Les dons aux musiciens sous Jean sans Peur et Philippe le Bon: principales caractéristiques et évolutions

Sur la période 1404–1467, Jean sans Peur (1404–1419) a octroyé 27 gratifications nominatives; son fils, Philippe le Bon (1419–1467), a lui gratifié 182 fois ses musiciens.[2] La différence est donc très nette entre les deux principats. Comment l'expliquer? Si nous écartons d'emblée les considérations psychologisantes sur Jean sans Peur et son rapport à la musique,[3] les explications tiennent peut-être à une mobilisation accrue des musiciens dans la communication politique du duc de Bourgogne. Les gratifications sont en effet particulièrement nombreuses pendant les fêtes chrétiennes et les grands moments de la vie curiale comme les mariages ou les étrennes (Hirschbiegel, 2003, pp. 123–132); lesquelles témoignent, par l'entretien du plaisir, du rôle dévolu au prince comme relais vers l'harmonie dans la pensée aristotélicienne (Clouzot, 2007b, pp. 118–119; Guenée, 2002). Elles peuvent aussi traduire l'évolution des conceptions acoustiques et musicales que David Munrow et Martine Clouzot ont évoquées dans leurs travaux (Munrow, 1976; Clouzot, 2000, p. 618). Les dons ne viendraient donc pas seulement récompenser les "bons et aggreables services", comme l'énoncent les comptabilités, mais aussi souligner le rôle particulier des musiciens dans le dispositif communicationnel ducal. Nous le constatons par exemple au moment des étrennes où les musiciens sont, comme d'autres officiers,[4] récompensés pour avoir manifesté leur joie, crié et chanté "largesse" (Schnerb, 2005, p. 11).[5] Ces exemples démontrent donc, de manière préliminaire, la validité de notre hypothèse selon laquelle les gratifications ne visaient pas seulement à remercier le musicien pour son service mais bien à acter sa place au sein des gestes et de la communication propres à la société princière du XVe siècle (Althoff, 1996; 2002, p. 241). Analysons ces gratifications dans le détail.

---

2   Nous distinguons volontairement les gratifications nominatives de celles faites aux groupes, ces dernières ne permettant pas de savoir précisément qui profite de la largesse princière.

3   Vaughan, 2002, p. 233: "The assumption or assertion […] that under John the Fearless 'musical activities' were 'reduced to a minimum' is completely unfounded.".

4   ADN, B 2051, fol. 294v.: "Icelui seigneur leur en a fait [des étrennes] pour une fois departir entre eulx et les autres Roys d'armes, heraulx, poursuivans, trompettes et menestrelz de mondit seigneur pour leur estrine du premier jour de l'an oudit an IIIIcLXIII."

5   On retrouve cette situation dans un mandement relatif à un don lors du mariage d'Adolphe de Clèves où il est dit que le duc donne "pour leur crie et largesse" (ADN, B 2012, fol. 289r.).

	Trompettes	Ménestrels	Autres instru-mentistes	Total
Numéraire	9	10	0	19
Animaux	2	3	0	5
Objets d'orfèvrerie	0	2	0	2
Étoffes, fourrures et vêtements	1	0	0	1
Total	12	15	0	27

Tableau 1: Répartition des dons par type et destinataires sous Jean sans Peur.

	Trompettes	Ménestrels	Autres instru-mentistes	Total
Numéraire	89	62	23	174
Animaux	3	0	0	3
Objets d'orfèvrerie	2	3	0	5
Étoffes, fourrures et vêtements	0	0	0	0
Total	94	65	23	182

Tableau 2: Répartition des dons par type et destinataires sous Philippe le Bon.

Nous remarquerons tout d'abord un renversement des rapports entre les ménestrels et les trompettes. Alors que les premiers recevaient plus que les seconds sous Jean sans Peur, la tendance s'inverse et l'écart se creuse sous son successeur. Ajoutons à cette observation la présence de la catégorie "autres instrumentistes" qui s'explique par la place singulière occupée par Jean de Cordecil et Jean Ferrandes, arrivés avec Isabelle de Portugal (Sommé, 1995). Grâce aux travaux de Craig M. Wright et Jeanne Marix, nous pouvons retracer précisément le nom et les parcours des musiciens à la cour de Bourgogne (Wright, 1979; Marix, 1972). Prenons tout d'abord le cas des ménestrels. Sur la période retenue, c'est-à-dire 1404 à 1467, 18 personnages sont nommés dans le corpus (Marix, 1972, p. 186):

Plusieurs constats s'imposent. Premièrement, l'attachement de Philippe le Bon aux ménestrels de son père est assez important. Trois des huit ménestrels gratifiés par Jean sans Peur obtiennent des dons de son fils.[6] Le cas Jean Le Boulangier dit Pagot est singulier. Recruté en juin 1407 et gratifié cinq fois durant le principat de Jean sans Peur, il disparaît complètement sous le fils de ce dernier. Son décès explique peut-être sa disparition des archives bourguignonnes. Quant à Christophe d'Albourg, il réapparaît sous Philippe le Bon mais en tant que trompette. Qu'en est-il des plus gratifiés? Il s'agit, dans l'ordre d'importance, de Jean Karesme, Guillaume Caillet et Thibaud de Strasbourg. Le profil du premier,

---

6 Alphons et Jean Le Bonerre n'apparaissent qu'une fois. Quant à Claus le Tabourin, il est sans doute décédé au cours du principat de Jean sans Peur en raison de son ancien âge (ADCO, B 1543, fol. 109v.).

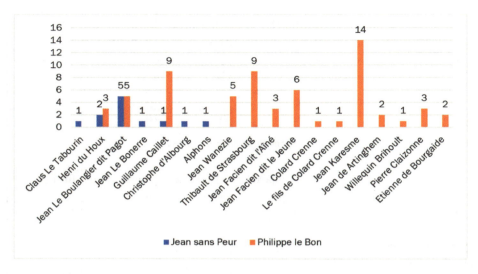

Graphique 1: Dons aux ménestrels du duc durant la période 1404–1467.

entré au service du duc en 1434, est intéressant car il est à la fois celui qui est le plus gratifié et celui sur lequel nous possédons le plus d'informations personnelles (Marix, 1972, p. 118). En outre, il est également retenu comme "roi des ménestrels", qualité qu'il récupère sans doute après le décès de Jean Facien dit l'Aîné, ancien roi des ménestrels de France puis de Bourgogne (Clouzot, 2010). Les deux autres personnages, Guillaume Caillet et Thibaud de Strasbourg sont tous les deux recrutés dès le principat de Jean sans Peur[7] bien que le second n'obtienne aucune gratification avant le principat de Philippe le Bon.

Parlons maintenant de la situation des trompettes. Vingt-huit individus nous sont connus pour la période (Marix, 1972, p. 187):

Plusieurs remarques méritent, là encore, d'être formulées. Premièrement, contrairement aux ménestrels, les trompettes recrutées par Philippe le Bon sont beaucoup plus nombreuses que sous son père (22 contre 6). Deuxièmement, l'attachement aux trompettes de Jean sans Peur est similaire en pourcentage au phénomène observé pour les ménestrels. Sur six personnages connus, deux entrent au service de son fils: Paulin Gambrin dit d'Alexandrie et Christophe d'Albourg. Quant à Antoine de Crapalique et François de Pouilles, ils connaissent des destins différents puisque le premier meurt avant juin 1418 et le second entre au service du duc de Milan (Wright, 1979, p. 47). Seuls les cas de Jean de Vedelay et Jean Moreau restent sans réponse même si la faiblesse des gratifications à leur égard semble

---

7   Guillaume Caillet serait entré au service de Jean sans Peur en même temps que Jean Wanezie, Jean Le Boulangier dit Pagot, Henri du Houx et Christophe d'Albourg (Wright, 1979, p. 46). Pour Thibaud de Strasbourg, nous renvoyons aux observations formulées dans Schnerb, 2005, p. 10.

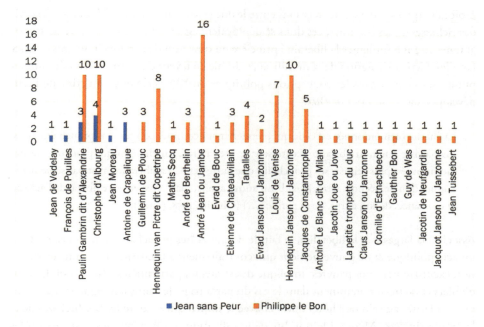

Graphique 2: Dons aux trompettes du duc durant la période 1404–1467.

indiquer qu'ils n'étaient pas intégrés à l'hôtel ducal. Revenons maintenant sur les personnages les plus gratifiés. Sur l'ensemble de la période, il s'agit, dans l'ordre d'importance, d'André Jean ou Jambe, Christophe d'Albourg et Paulin Gambrin dit d'Alexandrie. Que sait-on de ces individus? Peu de choses pour le premier. Quant aux deux autres, ils entrent au service de la Maison de Bourgogne sous Jean sans Peur (ADCO, B 1554, fol. 78r.; ADCO, B 1560, fol. 115v.) et sont qualifiés régulièrement comme "trompettes de guerre." Là encore, la fidélité à la Maison de Bourgogne semble déterminante pour obtenir des dons. Elle n'explique pourtant pas totalement l'intérêt particulier du prince pour certains de ses musiciens. D'autres attentions ducales, à l'image des dons pour les mariages ou les baptêmes, permettent de mieux apprécier certains liens qui unissaient le duc à ses officiers.

Mariage et compérage: pratiques curiales, liens personnels et communication politique

Parmi les nombreuses faveurs octroyées par le prince à ses officiers, ici musiciens, les gratifications pour les mariages et les baptêmes sont sans doute les plus révélatrices des logiques profondes qui façonnaient les relations entre le duc et ses commensaux. Mobilisant à la fois des richesses et des hommes, ces dons se déployaient également dans une sorte de scénographie visant à souligner la libéralité princière en direction de certains individus et leurs familles. Cette orientation de la munificence ducale en faveur d'hommes et/ou de familles puisait ses racines dans les conceptions politiques du XVe siècle que Christine de Pisan développe dans son *Livre de Paix*:

> La charité bien ordonnée est celle qui premièrement commence à ses plus prouchains amis, c'est-à-dire que non obstant charité soit de bien faire à un chascun qui pourroit, néantmoins où est plus tenus à ses prouchains que autre gent. [La libéralité n'est pas seulement] donner don de pécune, terre, joyaulx ou autres avoirs, mais aussi en estre liberal de l'aide de sa puissance, de son corps, de sa parole [...] (Charity, 1958, p. 148).

Associé à la largesse et la libéralité, le fait de donner à "ses prouchains amis" devient donc un acte politique et de gouvernement qui, contrairement à la charité chrétienne en direction exclusivement des pauvres, implique des stratégies particulières. Par la mobilisation d'objets et de tiers, notamment dans le cas du parrainage, les dons témoignent également des solidarités au sein de l'hôtel ducal et avec le milieu qui entoure les bénéficiaires de la largesse princière. Même si le nombre de gratifications en lien avec les mariages ou les baptêmes est assez faible pour les musiciens de Jean sans Peur et Philippe le Bon, et si leur portée politique est également à nuancer par rapport à d'autres personnages des réseaux bourguignons, ces dernières apparaissent cependant comme des exemples intéressants pour envisager la place desdits musiciens.

Prenons tout d'abord le cas des mariages. Sur l'ensemble de la période retenue, trois gratifications sont directement liées à des musiciens. Elles concernent, dans l'ordre chronologique, Thibaud de Strasbourg (ADCO, B 1622, fol. 111v.), André Jean ou Jambe (ADN, B 1933, fols. 89r., 89v.) et Paulin Gambrin dit d'Alexandrie (AGR, 46955, fol. 198r.). Si la variation des sommes octroyées est en soi intéressante,[8] les détails des mandements nous permettent de mieux apprécier la place qu'occupait chacun des trois musiciens au sein de l'hôtel ducal. Les expressions "pour et en faveur du mariage" et "en avancement de son mariage", employées pour le deuxième et le troisième musicien, renvoient à une pratique classique au sein des hôtels ducaux. L'objectif du prince n'était pas seulement d'aider aux dépenses, mais de rendre l'évènement plus fastueux afin de démontrer, par sa libéralité, la richesse de sa cour et les liens qu'il nouait avec certains officiers (Gonzalez, 2004, pp. 247–277). Le duc était-il présent? Difficile de le dire. Le mandement en faveur de Thibaud de

---

8   "100 fr. de 33 gros mon. de Flandre la pièce; 40 fr. de 32 gros mon. de Flandre le fr.; 60 l. de 40 gros mon. de Flandre la livre."

Strasbourg indique que la cérémonie fut faite "du sceau de mondit seigneur". Présent ou absent, le prince se fait ici marieur, une pratique qui visait non seulement à souligner le lien avec son officier mais également à étendre les réseaux bourguignons dans et hors de l'hôtel par le truchement du mariage. L'épouse joue ici un rôle central (Gonzalez, 1999). Relais indispensable pour l'autorité princière cherchant à étendre son influence, celle-ci est également "dépositaire de la mémoire de l'officier ducal" pour reprendre les mots d'Elizabeth Gonzalez dans son étude cité précédemment. C'est d'ailleurs le cas avec Marie Le Carlier, épouse de Paulin Gambrin dit d'Alexandrie et seule femme connue pour les musiciens étudiés. En lui octroyant 120 l. de 40 gros mon. de Flandre la livre en 1458, Philippe le Bon démontrait que les liens qui unissaient le duc et ses officiers s'affranchissaient de la mort (ledit musicien étant mort à cette date).[9] La fidélité dépassait donc les limites liées à la mortalité. À ces gratifications liées au mariage s'ajoutaient d'autres témoignages à l'image des dons lors des baptêmes.

Dans son étude sur le compérage à Florence durant la Renaissance, Christiane Klapisch-Zuber insiste sur le caractère politique du parrainage d'un enfant (Klapisch-Zuber, 1990, p. 123). Cette filiation spirituelle, différente du clientélisme, permettait au duc de renouveler sa relation avec son officier tout en réaffirmant qu'être "libéral de sa puissance" s'étendait aussi à sa famille. En d'autres termes, le duc offrait une protection non seulement à son officier mais également à sa descendance. Pour la période retenue, six gratifications nous sont connues. Elles concernent Jean Le Boulangier dit Pagot (ADCO, B 1558, fol. 91r.) et sa femme (ADCO, B 1558, fol. 118r.) ainsi qu'Henri du Houx pour le principat de Jean sans Peur (ADCO, B 1560, fol. 141v.). Sous Philipe le Bon, il s'agit de deux enfants d'André Jean ou Jambe (ADN, B 1945, fols. 112r., 112v.; ADN, B 1957, fol. 271v.) et un de Thibaud de Strasbourg (ADN, B 1933, fol. 129v.). Quels enseignements pouvons-nous tirer de ces gratifications?

Le premier concerne la forme du don. À l'exception de la première et de la dernière gratification mentionnée, toutes les autres prennent la forme d'un gobelet d'argent, qu'il soit doré ou émaillé. Cette pratique ne semble pas propre aux largesses en faveur des musiciens puisque les autres mentions de compérage mettent toutes en évidence des objets (hanaps, tasses, gobelets ou pots) liés à la table et notamment au fait de boire. Dans son étude de la parenté spirituelle en Europe, Agnès Fine a proposé une explication de ce type de cadeau par la symbolique. Selon elle, "gobelets ou couverts rappelaient métaphoriquement l'instrument [les cloches] qui, au baptême, avait transmis sa voix à l'enfant" (Fine, 1994, p. 76). Dans tous les cas, il s'agissait d'un objet ostentatoire que les parents pouvaient présenter à leurs convives, matérialisant ainsi, dans l'intimité de leur foyer, leur lien avec le prince

---

9   Cette dernière est mentionnée en 1458 comme bénéficiaire de 120 l. de 40 gros mon. de Flandre la livre "deue [...] a son dit fey mary" (ADN, B 2030, fol. 155v.). Sa femme touchait encore la pension de son défunt mari en 1462 (ADN, B 2045, fol. 125r.).

(Chattaway, 1999). Le deuxième enseignement concerne la forme même de l'action ducale (Brero, 2005). Philippe le Bon, comme son père avec l'enfant de Jean Le Boulangier dit Pagot, fait tenir deux des trois enfants en son nom. Cette transmission du nom matérialise un lien spirituel qui rapproche désormais les deux parties dans un ensemble "d'obligations de solidarité, de prestation et de contre-prestations" (Fine, 1994, p. 10). Pour le duc de Bourgogne, cette relation à l'égard d'un personnage de rang inférieur apparaît comme un investissement, une sorte "d'assurance-fidélité" pour reprendre les mots de Gonzalez (Gonzalez, 1999, p. 168). Elle pouvait être également une "option sur l'avenir" pour reprendre, là encore, les termes de l'autrice, le prince cherchant à faire de ses filleuls de futurs fidèles à sa cour. Dans les cas évoqués, seuls les enfants d'André Jean ou Jambe apparaissent dans les comptabilités bourguignonnes après leur baptême. Un mandement en date du 15 mars 1434 nous apprend que le duc octroya 20 fr. "pour la despense d'un jeune filz qu'il lui a fait apprendre son mestier et tenir avec lui, pour ce pour deux mois finiz le derrain jour de fevrier derrain passe" (ADN, B 1951, fol. 104r.). S'agit-il du premier enfant baptisé par Philippe le Bon? La proximité chronologique entre les deux mandements rend difficile d'établir formellement ce lien, mais il est tout à fait possible que les dates indiquées correspondent en réalité à des dons bien antérieurs. En acceptant l'idée selon laquelle les deux fils mentionnés sont une seule et même personne, ces deux actes témoigneraient de l'attention du parrain envers son filleul, lequel reprendrait en outre l'activité de son père en tant que trompette de guerre.[10]

Le second cas que nous souhaitons évoquer concerne une fille d'André Jean ou Jambe, laquelle reçoit, par un mandement en date du 24 avril 1444, 40 l. de 40 gros mon. de Flandre la livre "en contemplacion et avancement de son mariage" (ADN, B 1982, fols. 172r., 172v.). Promise à un certain Jean Le Mainuer, chirurgien de son état, la fille de la trompette du duc se voit aussi gratifiée "pour consideracion des services" de son père. Nous pouvons là encore nous poser la question de l'identité de cette enfant, peut-être celle que Philippe le Bon fit baptiser dans les années 1430. Là encore, la période chronologique entre les deux mandements ne permet pas de valider complètement cette hypothèse. S'il s'agit bien de la même personne, nous serions face à un deuxième exemple d'attachement du duc de Bourgogne envers ses filleuls. Cette fois, le prince serait directement lié à la promotion sociale de la famille d'André Jean ou Jambe. Par cet acte, il contribuerait à la fois à la dot de la future mariée, tout en réaffirmant, par cette gratification, la place très particulière occupée par André Jean ou Jambe dans les réseaux bourguignons.

La troisième et dernière remarque concerne la place des intermédiaires, ici incarnés par Jean Poissonnier, épicier du duc Jean sans Peur, Baudouin d'Oignies, écuyer et panetier

---

10   Un certain Antoine Jambe est nommé trompette de guerre en 1451 (Marix, 1972, p. 120; ADN, B 2008, fol. 88r.).

de Philippe le Bon et Charles comte de Charolais et fils dudit prince. Sur les six baptêmes recensés, trois sont donc marqués par la présence d'un intermédiaire. Si la présence de Jean Poissonnier et Baudouin d'Oignies s'explique peut-être par l'absence physique du duc de Bourgogne, ces derniers devenant des parrains par procuration (Gonzalez, 2004, p. 254), celle de Charles de Valois revêt une symbolique très différente. Âgé au moment du mandement de seulement trois ans, le comte de Charolais ne pouvait physiquement pas être celui qui tint le nouveau-né sur les fonts baptismaux. Pour autant, sa présence au moment de la cérémonie et sa mention comme acteur dans les comptabilités bourguignonnes manifestent la dimension très politique de l'évènement; Philippe le Bon souhaitant sans doute matérialiser ici l'idée de continuité ainsi que la relation très intense qui l'unissait à André Jean ou Jambe. Cette dernière s'était déjà illustrée avec Claux le Tabourin, ménestrel de Philippe le Hardi et survivant à son maître. Entré officiellement au service du premier duc Valois de Bourgogne en 1378, après son transfert de la cour de Flandre vers celle de Bourgogne (Wright, 1979, p. 24; ADCO, B 1452, fol. 24r.), le ménestrel, également joueur de tambourin, s'était vu gratifier des dons pour l'aider à "paier une maison qu'il a acheté à Paris" (ADCO, B 1463, fol. 131r.) et pour faciliter l'installation de son ménage dans la capitale (AN, B 4075, fol. 49v.). Jean sans Peur, soucieux de maintenir certains liens de fidélité constitués par son père, avait accordé à ce ménestrel désormais âgé 20 fr. "tant pour consideracion des bons services qu'il fist longuement à feu mondit seigneur comme pour lui et sa femme qui doresmais sont anciennes gens, mieux avoir leur substantation" (ADCO, B 1543, fol. 109v.). Ces deux exemples nous permettent d'insister sur certaines pratiques communes à plusieurs princes et qui témoignent, selon nous, de la vie d'une Maison princière indépendamment de la volonté personnelle du chef de cette dernière.

Dans les cas présentés, l'attention particulière des princes à leurs trompettes, qui plus est de guerre pour André Jean ou Jambe, illustre aussi et surtout, au-delà des aspects énoncés auparavant, la place prépondérante que ces instrumentistes occupaient au sein de la communication politique des ducs de Bourgogne.

Les ducs de Bourgogne et leurs trompettes

Au fil de notre propos, nous avons pu constater la place importante des trompettes dans l'entourage des ducs de Bourgogne et, en particulier, dans l'économie du don. Sur les gratifications recensées en faveur des trompettes, 65% concernent des individus qualifiés comme "trompettes de guerre". Martine Clouzot avait déjà dressé un constat identique en analysant l'iconographie princière (Clouzot, 2000, p. 620). Selon elle, l'exagération provoquée par le son de ces instruments, qui font d'ailleurs l'objet d'un renouvellement connu par un mandement en date du 28 août 1433 (ADN, 1951, fols. 93r.– 94v.), participait à la prise de possession sonore de la ville et de sa population. Elle traduisait, en somme, de manière symbolique, la domination de l'espace et des hommes ainsi que le retour à l'harmonie sociale imposée par la puissance ducale (Cartier, 1984, p. 161; Clouzot, 2000, p. 625). Les trompettes de guerre, distinguées des autres instrumentistes de haut (bombardes ou chalemies), occupaient donc une place centrale que l'on retrouve lors de certains grands évènements comme lors de la rencontre entre Philippe le Bon et Frédéric III, roi des Romains, à Besançon en 1442. Olivier de La Marche indique à ce propos que "les trompettes du duc de Bourgoingne ne sonnerent, depuis qu'il veit les enseignes du Roy des Rommains" (Beaune et al., 1883, p. 274). Nous pourrions également citer un don en faveur d'Antoine Le Blanc, dit de Milan, lequel reçut 10 fr. pour "alé de Chalon avec et la compaignie de monseigneur le Bastard de Saint Pol ou pais de Bourbonnaiz et ailleurs ou mondit seigneur l'envoit en armes" (ADN, B 1951, fols. 102v.–105r.). Ces instrumentistes représentaient donc à la fois la puissance du duc sur le champ de bataille et sa capacité à dominer l'espace en temps de paix. Bien que le principat de Philippe le Bon fasse, là encore, un peu d'ombre à celui de son père, l'intérêt du pouvoir pour les compétences des trompettes semble commencer dès Jean sans Peur en la personne d'Antoine de Crapalique.

D'abord membre de l'hôtel de Louis, duc de Guyenne et gendre du duc de Bourgogne, ce dernier reçoit deux gratifications (ADCO, B 1562, fol. 31v.) avant son entrée au sein de l'hôtel ducal en 1415 (Wright, 1979, pp. 48–49). Absent des pensions ou gages accordés aux musiciens, Antoine de Crapalique se voit néanmoins concéder les biens confisqués à Dijon d'un certain Gaspar de Lunier, originaire de Milan et partisan des Armagnacs (ADCO, 1 Mi art. 407, fol. 265r.). L'affaire ne semble pas si simple puisque le duc est obligé d'intervenir personnellement dans une lettre adressée à son épouse Marguerite de Bavière en date du 26 février 1418. Rappelant les "bons et aggreables services" de sa trompette, qu'il entend par ailleurs entretenir par la formule "esperons qui face ou temps avenir", Jean sans Peur demande à son épouse d'exécuter sa volonté en octroyant, sans avis du bailli de Dijon et des gens de ses comptes, les biens dudit Gaspar de Lunier pour un montant de 200 écus d'or. L'intervention ducale semble porter ses fruits puisque la trompette obtient, semble-t-il, les biens confisqués en mars 1418, comme en témoigne un récépissé dudit Antoine de Crapalique.

Si ce dernier ne profite pas longtemps de ses biens puisqu'il est tué dans une rixe contre Hennequin van Pictre,[11] l'acte princier est riche de sens. Il témoigne tout d'abord de la circulation importante des musiciens entre les hôtels princiers, pratique qui sous-entend par ailleurs une compétition accrue pour retenir les officiers. Il manifeste également la volonté du prince d'ancrer spatialement son officier dans ses possessions territoriales. Flo-

---

11 Jean sans Peur tente d'ailleurs d'obtenir la guérison de sa trompette suite à cette rixe par deux gratifications (ADCO, B 1594, fol. 138r.; ADCO, B 1594, fols. 138r., 138v.).

rence Berland a démontré l'importance de cette pratique pour Paris, cette dernière visant à consolider la présence bourguignonne au sein de l'espace parisien (Berland, 2011). Il s'agit, là encore, d'une des multiples manifestations du don comme outil de gouvernement et clé de lecture pour comprendre les relations complexes nouées entre le prince et ses officiers.

Si ces derniers incarnent la voix du duc, ils doivent aussi réaffirmer de par leur "estat" la puissance et la richesse de la cour bourguignonne. Plusieurs gratifications vont dans ce sens. Outre le don de 36 l. de 40 gros vieille mon. de Flandre la livre, octroyé à André Jean ou Jambe en 1433 pour "avoir et achetter quatre trompettes de guerre" (ADN, B 1951, fols. 93r.–94v.) (lequel témoigne sans doute du rôle singulier occupé par ce dernier), la majorité des gratifications qui nous intéresse concerne des dons en argent pour acheter un cheval ou directement sous la forme d'un animal. Si l'on écarte André Jean ou Jambe qui est le seul à recevoir des gratifications en numéraire pour acheter un cheval (ADN, B 1942, fols. 143r.–145r.; ADN, B 1972, fols. 193r., 193v.), les autres trompettes de guerre obtiennent tous des chevaux dont nous connaissons la robe, les détails ainsi que le prix. Christophe d'Albourg est ici le mieux doté avec trois chevaux,[12] Paulin Gambrin dit d'Alexandrie (ADN, B 1933, fols. 126v., 127r.) et Hennequin Janson, dit aussi Hennequin Janzonne (ADN, B 1945, fol. 162r.) en reçoivent respectivement un. Contrairement à d'autres aspects évoqués précédemment, les sources sont ici silencieuses sur les motivations ducales. Seul le don en faveur de Paulin Gambrin dit d'Alexandrie évoque une raison liée aux services rendus et à la fidélité de ce dernier au prince. Comment interpréter cette attention particulière des ducs de Bourgogne? Il existe bien des dons semblables pour d'autres individus comme Guillaume Caillet (ADCO, B 1558, fol. 108v.), Jean le Boulangier dit Pagot (ADCO, B 1560, fols. 124r., 124v.) ou encore Jean Wanezie (ADCO, B 1576, fol. 162r.) (ces derniers étant d'ailleurs régulièrement gratifiés par les princes), mais l'intérêt ducal pour "l'estat" de ses trompettes de guerre est manifeste. On le retrouve également dans un autre don, accordé à André Jean ou Jambe, au moment du siège de Belleville entre septembre et octobre 1434. Ce dernier reçoit alors 15 fr. "pour avoir et achetter une curasse pour lui armer et habillier" (ADN, B 1951, fols. 141r.–141v.).

Toutes ces gratifications témoignent bien du rôle particulier occupé par les trompettes de guerre, à la fois dans le domaine militaire mais aussi dans le dispositif visuel créé par Jean sans Peur et Philippe le Bon en temps de paix. Les miniatures étudiées par Martine Clouzot viennent confirmer cette quête de splendeur qui passe par l'octroi de chevaux à des individus censés précéder le prince lors de ses entrées solennelles, par exemple. Par la mobilisation de la vue et de l'ouïe, les trompettes imprimaient dans l'esprit du public la puissance du duc de Bourgogne. Grâce au cheval, animal noble et symbole de prestige pour la Maison de Bourgogne, les trompettes pouvaient en outre porter plus loin et plus

---

12   ADCO, B 1576, fols. 162r., 162v.; ADCO, B 1598, fol. 209v.; AGR, 46952, fol. 122v.

haut le son de leur instrument et ainsi glorifier plus encore le prince (Clouzot, 2007a, p. 169).

Conclusion

Si, comme le disait Jeanne Marix, l'étude de l'histoire de la musique et des musiciens permet bien de rentrer dans le "vif de l'histoire sociale", l'analyse des dons en faveur desdits individus ouvre, elle, la voie à une meilleure connaissance des rapports qui les unissaient au prince. Manifestation d'une munificence et d'une communication dont les musiciens apparaissent comme des rouages essentiels, les gratifications viennent également matérialiser les liens multiformes qui se nouent au sein de l'hôtel de Bourgogne.

L'analyse quantitative nous a permis de démontrer que l'augmentation numérique des dons allait de pair avec la part croissante des trompettes dans le cercle des musiciens gratifiés. Ce premier enseignement rejoint un second qui est lié à la multiplication des formes du don en faveur des officiers. Cette tendance ne semble pas propre à la cour de Bourgogne, Elizabeth Gonzalez ayant constaté des évolutions similaires dans l'hôtel d'Orléans (Gonzalez, 2004, pp. 247–277). Pour autant, les ducs de Bourgogne se distinguent par une attention plus importante à l'égard des musiciens, signe, peut-être, d'une place singulière de l'art musical à la fois comme pratique de gouvernement et rouage de la communication ducale.

Si l'intensification des dons en faveur des musiciens concerne également le reste de leur famille, traduisant ainsi une emprise plus forte du prince sur son officier, il ne faut pas pour autant y voir une simple relation de sujétion unilatérale et par définition inégalitaire. L'exemple d'André Jean ou Jambe, abondamment cité, est ici particulièrement éloquent. Grâce à ses compétences, identifiées par les nombreuses mentions de "bons et aggreables services", la trompette de guerre de Philippe le Bon a su s'élever socialement au sein de l'hôtel ducal, intégrant son fils comme musicien et mariant sa fille à un chirurgien. Cette ascension sociale, qui concerne donc le musicien et sa famille, démontre bien cette forme de réciprocité que le don, par essence souple et donc abondamment utilisé, permet d'apprécier (Martin, 2007). Le prince avait tout intérêt à manifester sa munificence, à la fois pour des raisons politiques, performatives et stratégiques.

Le fait que le personnage le plus présent dans notre propos soit une trompette de guerre n'est, là encore, pas dû au hasard. Comme l'a abondamment soulignée Clouzot, les trompettes de guerre occupent une place essentielle du fait de la spécialisation fonctionnelle de la musique au sein de la cour de Bourgogne (Clouzot, 2007a, p. 173). Arborant les couleurs du duc, elles caractérisent par leur pratique instrumentale un pouvoir qui entend imposer sa présence à tous. Le caractère assourdissant des trompettes qui soufflent vers le haut permet en effet au prince de rappeler symboliquement à tous que l'harmonie dont il est l'ordonnateur ne saurait être perturbée par un autre son que celui de ses instrumentistes. Plus que tout autre, les trompettes sont donc l'incarnation sonore du pouvoir qui domine l'espace et les hommes (Clouzot, 2000, p. 625). Nous retrouvons d'ailleurs cette symbolique chez Olivier de La Marche qui rappelle, dans ses *Mémoires,* comment les trompettes rythment également la vie du prince (Beaune et al., 1888, pp. 70–71). L'économie du don, par la place croissante des trompettes de guerre au sein des gratifications en faveur des musiciens, vient ici réaffirmer certaines hypothèses formulées par les spécialistes de cette question. Elle met enfin en exergue la vitalité des questions anthropologiques pour comprendre l'imbrication entre sphère publique et privée ou l'importance des échanges au sein des réseaux; éléments clés pour analyser le fonctionnement de l'État à la fin du Moyen Âge (Mattéoni, 2010, pp. 9–17; Gonzalez, 2004, p. 329).

Bibliographie

Manuscrits

Archives départementales de la Côté-d'Or (ADCO), Dijon

ADCO, B 1452.
ADCO, B 1463.
ADCO, B 1543.
ADCO, B 1554.
ADCO, B 1558.
ADCO, B 1560.

ADCO, B 1562.
ADCO, B 1576.
ADCO, B 1598.
ADCO, B 1622.
ADCO, 1 Mi art. 407.

Archives départementales du Nord (ADN), Lille

ADN, 1951.
ADN, B 1933.
ADN, B 1942.
ADN, B 1945.
ADN, B 1951.
ADN, B 1957.
ADN, B 1972
ADN, B 1982.
ADN, B 2008.

ADN, B 2012.
ADN, B 2030.
ADN, B 2045.
ADN, B 2051.

Archives générales du Royaume (AGR), Bruxelles

AGR, 46952.
AGR, 46955.

Archives nationales (AN), Paris

AN, B 4075.

Sources imprimées et éditions des sources

Beaune, H. & J. d'Arbaumont, Jules d' (Éds.) (1883). *Mémoires d'Olivier de La Marche, Maître d'hôtel et Capitaine des gardes de Charles le Téméraire*, vol. 1. Renouard.
Beaune, H. & J. d'Arbaumont, Jules d' (Éds.) (1888). *Mémoires d'Olivier de La Marche, Maître d'hôtel et Capitaine des gardes de Charles le Téméraire*, vol. 4. Renouard.
Charity, W. C. (Éd.) (1958). *The "Livre de la paix" of Christine de Pisan*. Mouton.

Études scientifiques

Althoff, G. (1996). Empörung, Tränen, Zerknirschung. "Emotionen" in der öffentlichen Kommunikation des Mittelalters. *Frühmittelalterliche Studien* 30, 60–79.
Althoff, G. (2002). Rituels et institutions. In J.-Cl. Schmitt & O. G. Oexle (Éds.), *Les tendances actuelles de l'histoire du Moyen Âge en France et en Allemagne* (pp. 265–268). Publications de la Sorbonne.
Berland, F. (2011). *La cour de Bourgogne à Paris (1363–1422)*, Atelier national de reproduction des thèses.
Brero, T. (2005). *Les baptêmes princiers. Le cérémonial dans les cours de Savoie et Bourgogne (XVᵉ–XVᵉ s.)*. Université de Lausanne.
Cartier, G. (1984). Musique et pouvoir à l'aube de la Renaissance: le métier du musicien à la cour des grands Ducs Valois de Bourgogne. *Renaissance and Reformation* 20(3), 157–175.
Chattaway, C. M. (1999). Looking a medieval gift horse in the mouth. The role of giving of gift objects in the definition and maintenance of the power networks of Philip the Bold. *Bijdragen en mededelingen betreffende de geschiedenis der Nederlanden* 114(1), 1–15.
Clouzot M. (2000). Le son et le pouvoir en Bourgogne au XVᵉ siècle. *Revue Historique* 302, 615–628.
Clouzot, M. (2007a). *Images de musiciens (1350–1500). Typologie, figurations et pratiques sociales*. Brepols.
Clouzot, M. (2007b). Musique, savoirs et pouvoir à la cour du prince aux XIVᵉ et XVᵉ siècles. In O. Cullin (Éd.), *La place de la musique dans la culture médiévale* (pp. 115–139). Brepols.

Clouzot, M. (2010). Roi des ménestrels, ménestrel du roi? Statuts, fonctions et modèles d'une "autre" royauté aux XIIIe, XIVe et XVe siècles. In T. Hiltmann (Éd.), *Les "autres" rois. Etudes sur la royauté* (pp. 24–43). Oldenbourg.

Clouzot, M. & Laloue, C. (Éds.) (2005). *Les représentations de la musique au Moyen Âge: actes du colloque des 2 et 3 avril 2004, Paris, Musée de la musique.* Cité de la musique.

Cullin, O. (2002). *Brève historie de la musique au Moyen Âge.* Fayard.

Fiala, D. (2011). La naissance du musicien professionnel au tournant du XVIe siècle. In F. Ferrand (Éd.), *Guide de la Musique de la Renaissance* (pp. 167–183). Fayard.

Fine, A. (1994). *Parrains, marraines. La parenté spirituelle en Europe.* Fayard.

Gonzalez, E. (1999). L'officier, sa femme et le duc. Place et rôle de la femme au sein d'un hôtel princier. In F. Autrand, C. Gauvard & J.-M. Moeglin (Éds.), *Saint-Denis et la royauté. Etudes offerts à Bernard Guenée* (pp. 157–168). Éditions de la Sorbonne.

Gonzalez, E. (2004). *Un prince en son hôtel. Les serviteurs des ducs d'Orléans au XVe siècle.* Éditions de la Sorbonne.

Guenée, B. (2002). *L'opinion publique à la fin du Moyen Âge d'après la "Chronique de Charles VI" du Religieux de Saint-Denis.* Perrin.

Guéry, A. (1984). Le roi dépensier. Le don, la contrainte et l'origine du système financier de la monarchie française d'Ancien Régime. *Annales* 39(6), 1241–1269.

Hirschbiegel, J. (2003). *Étrennes: Untersuchungen zum höfischen Geschenkverkehr im spätmittelalterlichen Frankreich der Zeit König Karls VI. (1380–1422).* Oldenbourg.

Klapisch-Zuber, Ch. (1990). *La maison et le nom. Stratégies et rituels dans l'Italie de la Renaissance.* Éd. de l'École des Hautes Études en Sciences Sociales.

Lecuppre-Desjardin, E. (2018). Largesse! De la magnanimité féodale à la stratégie gouvernementale dans les sociétés d'Ancien Régime. *Revue du MAUSS* 52(2), 132–148.

Marix, J. (1972). *Histoire de la musique et des musiciens de la cour de Bourgogne sous le règne de Philippe le Bon (1420–1467).* Réimpression de l'éd. de Heitz, 1939, Minkoff.

Martin, H. (2007). Compte rendu du livre d'Elisabeth Gonzalez, Un prince en son hôtel. Les serviteurs des ducs d'Orléans au XVe siècle. *Annales de Bretagne et des Pays de l'Ouest* 114(1), 215–217.

Mattéoni O. (2010). Introduction. In O. Mattéoni (Éd.), *Institutions et pouvoirs en France (XIVe–XVe siècle)* (pp. 9–17). Picard.

Munrow, D. (1976). *Instruments de musique du Moyen Âge et de la Renaissance.* Oxford University Press.

Schnerb, B. (2005). Musique, jeux et "apertises" à la cour de Jean sans Peur, duc de Bourgogne. In J.-M Cauchies (Éd.), *Poètes et musiciens dans l'espace bourguignon : les artistes et leurs mécènes* (pp. 7–21). Centre Européen d'études bourguignonnes.

Sommé, M. (1995). Les Portugais dans l'entourage de la duchesse de Bourgogne Isabelle de Portugal (1430–1471). *Revue du Nord* 310, 321–343.

Vaughan, R. (^{3}2002). *John the Fearless. The Growth of Burgundian Power.* The Boydell Press.

Wegman, R. C. (2005). Musical Offerings in the Renaissance. *Early Music* 33, 425–437.

Wright, C. M. (1979). *Music at the Court of Burgundy (1364–1419). A Documentary History.* Institute of Mediaeval Music.

Images sonores des rituels politiques dans les manuscrits enluminés des ducs Valois de Bourgogne Philippe le Bon et Charles le Téméraire (1419–1477)

Des musicalités pour "une bibliothèque monde"?

Martine Clouzot

Depuis les années 2000, l'historiographie de "la cour des ducs Valois de Bourgogne" a connu un fort renouvellement. La somme des travaux réunis en 2013 par Werner Paravicini, Torsten Hiltmann et Franck Viltart (Paravicini et al., 2013), marque notamment un tournant dans la critique historienne du "mythe bourguignon" (Paravicini, 2013; Schnerb, 2013), des "fastes et magnificences" de la cour et de leur influence sur celles des Habsbourg et des autres cours européennes et méditerranéennes. Dans ce contexte historiographique actualisé, le risque persiste toutefois de faire perdurer des stéréotypes sur "cette indélébile image de la *bourgondische pracht*" (Prevenier, 1992). Il l'est d'autant plus dès lors qu'il s'agit d'étudier certaines "représentations" des rituels et cérémoniels en musique dans les manuscrits précieux, car ceux-ci comptent parmi les contributeurs "propagandistes" de la communication politique des ducs, principalement de Philippe le Bon et Charles le Téméraire, et de la cour. Des travaux qui ont fait date en littérature, histoire des arts, archéologie et musicologie, peuvent, à l'insu de leurs auteurs, entraîner sur cette voie. C'est le cas de l'ouvrage collectif dirigé par Danielle Régnier-Bohler *Splendeurs de la cour de Bourgogne. Récits et chroniques* (Régnier-Bohler, 1996), tout comme les catalogues des magnifiques expositions sur les arts à la cour de Bourgogne (Laporte, 2004; Marti et al., 2008). Pourtant, ces réalisations collectives et internationales ont fait connaître des apports critiques fondamentaux, notamment en histoire sociale et économique. De même, depuis les années 2000, la Librairie ducale a bénéficié de travaux majeurs, tels ceux menés sous la direction de Bernard Bousmanne (Bousmanne et al., 2000–2015; Wijsman, 2010). Recensant le nombre important d'ouvrages bibliques, religieux et dévotionnels, ils ont montré combien les entrées des livres sous les principats de Philippe le Bon et Charles le Téméraire reflètent les idéaux politiques et les imaginaires mythiques pétris d'héroïsme à l'antique et d'idéaux chevaleresques au service de la magnificence ducale. Aussi, face à la composition de la

Librairie, il serait aisé de contempler, une fois encore, les enluminures "illuminant" les manuscrits et la musique qui y est figurée à des fins de glorification politique.

Cependant, au tournant du XXIe siècle, historiens, littéraires et historiens de l'art de la cour de Bourgogne n'ont pas manqué de rappeler la "face sombre de la splendeur" (Paravicini et al., 2009) en tenant compte de "l'envers du décor". Il est désormais possible d'aborder les livres ornés de la bibliothèque comme des objets résultant, tant par la commande que le don, des tensions et des ambivalences d'"une politique et une administration progressivement institutionnalisées et une culture de cour de plus en plus splendide", comme l'a récemment montré Klaus Oschema (Oschema, 2012, p. 40). Si l'évolution de la composition de la bibliothèque est révélatrice des projets contemporains de conquête de territoires et de croisade "orientale", l'analyse de ses ouvertures vers d'autres horizons mérite toutefois d'être frottée à la conception élaborée par Zrinka Stahuljak de "littérature connectée": la spécialiste de littérature médiévale la rapporte à l'idée de "bibliothèque monde" qui "fait réapparaître le lien entre la culture et la politique" (Stahuljak, 2020, p. 89).

Ces perspectives critiques et élargies invitent à analyser dans les enluminures des chroniques, romans et histoires de la Librairie ducale, les relations figurées entre le son musical, les instruments de musique et les rituels politiques que sont les banquets, les entrées solennelles et les batailles: quelles en sont les modalités figuratives? A quelles fins ces images font-elles voir et entendre des "musicalités" instrumentales du pouvoir? Quelles "représentations" politiques et "esthétiques", au sens ornemental et éthique du terme, les deux derniers Valois ont-ils voulu donner de leur puissance politique?

Une approche méthodologique: polysémie et agentivité des images de la musique

Par l'intermédiaire des livres enluminés, les images de la musique dans les cérémoniels de cour font voir et entendre le pouvoir des ducs, principalement de Philippe le Bon et, dans une moindre mesure, de Jean sans Peur et Charles le Téméraire. Philippe le Hardi, attaché à la cour royale à Paris, n'a pas vraiment développé de mécénat des livres, privilégiant plutôt le bâti architectural et ornemental, comme la Chartreuse de Champmol à Dijon ou le château de Germolles. Certaines des principales publications sur la Librairie ducale ayant déjà été mentionnées en introduction, le propos se veut d'abord méthodologique et historien, centré sur les "images de la musique instrumentale".

Le "fonctionnement" des images: discours polysémiques et "transtemporels"

Le corpus de manuscrits comprend en grande majorité les chroniques et les romans chevaleresques dont la matière narrative est située géographiquement et temporellement dans "l'Orient" impérial (la Grèce, Rome), en Méditerranée judéo-chrétienne (Jérusalem), le Saint Empire romain germanique des carolingiens et en Europe septentrionale (Flandres, îles anglo-saxonnes). Si ces livres précieux font partie de la représentation et de la communication politiques des ducs, leur entrée par commande ou don dans la bibliothèque, ainsi que leurs contenus et programmes thématiques autour de la chevalerie reflètent les dynamiques géopolitiques de la principauté et les visées idéologiques, royales puis impériales, des deux derniers ducs à l'échelle de l'Europe. Leurs formats impressionnants, ainsi que leurs usages ritualisés en font des objets sonores qui pourraient être qualifiés de "multimédia": la vocalité par la lecture à voix haute des récits épiques, associée à la visualité et la musicalité des images de la musique, fait entendre et voir le son d'un pouvoir idéalisé dans le cadre de rituels de cour. Ceux-ci concernent principalement les entrées et les banquets. Ces choix thématiques émanent des peintres et enlumineurs œuvrant au service de la cour, voire directement du duc Philippe le Bon.

C'est en historienne, et non en historienne de l'art ou en musicologue, que les questions de la figuration de la musique instrumentale dans des thématiques profanes et des cadres idéologiques et politiques sont abordées. Celles-ci sont situées à la croisée de l'anthropologie historique des images et d'une "histoire culturelle du social", selon la formule de Roger Chartier (Chartier, 1989; Ory, 2007). La méthode proposée ne s'inscrit pas dans ce que les archéomusicologues nomment "l'iconographie musicale". Leur approche est certes fort utile à la connaissance organologique, mais, de notre point de vue, elle resterait trop attachée au visible au détriment du visuel et du sonore. Elle restreindrait les champs de signification en grande partie car elle ne tiendrait pas assez compte de la nature particulière du support des images – le livre – et de son contexte social. En conséquence, les descriptions iconographiques restent parfois, nous semble-t-il, assez réductrices et littérales, trop attachées à ne voir dans les images que deux caricatures extrêmes: soit une "peinture du réel", soit une symbolique des instruments. C'est pourquoi la polysémie visuelle, articulée aux usages rituels des livres, paraît être un mode de fonctionnement consubstantiel aux images (Baschet et al., 1996; Baschet, 2008).

En effet, la réalité du figuré n'est qu'une apparence servant moins à représenter une "scène réaliste" qu'à évoquer des idéaux: à partir du "réalisme" figuratif, dans le cas par exemple d'un rituel comme un banquet ou une danse de cour, l'image énonce un ou plusieurs discours idéologiques et politiques "transtemporels" (Stahuljak, 2020, pp. 88–89) et spatiaux, combinant différents espaces, idées et périodes cumulés et imbriqués, mais rendus présents dans le temps du livre et le cadre fixe des miniatures. Ces modes de figuration articulant des "temporalités disjointes" produisent des musicalités faites de rythmes, de sonorités, de vocalités propres non pas à un ou des passés, mais au présent de l'époque contemporaine des images actualisé par les rituels et les pratiques du livre à la cour. Par ces qualités sensorielles, le son figuré contribue à rendre tangible un pouvoir en représentation.

Inséré dans ces montages d'"hétérochronies", de récits et d'imaginaires, le sonore participe à l'expression cumulée de la puissance politique (Stahuljak, 2020, p. 89).

A partir de ces modes de fonctionnement des images, on peut supposer qu'enlumineurs, commanditaires et "regardeurs" des enluminures se sont probablement délectés de leurs discours "pluriels", mêlant les anachronismes entre l'Antiquité et le XVᵉ siècle, les significations ambiguës et les paradoxes idéologiques qui en découlent. Il serait alors regrettable de réduire le caractère polysémique des miniatures à de simples scènes de genre, somme toute assez superficielles, du type "le banquet", "l'entrée solennelle", "la danse de cour", "le tournoi", "la bataille".

Sérialité, *agency* et communication sensorielle des images

La démarche globale consiste à partir du livre enluminé pour revenir à lui. Elle est fondée sur une analyse sérielle (Baschet, 1996) du corpus des manuscrits en fonction de critères focalisés d'abord sur le plus petit – les motifs instrumentaux – à ceux plus larges du milieu curial qui les a commandés, conçus avec les ateliers de copies et d'enluminures, choisis, reçus, offerts, utilisés, c'est-à-dire manipulés, contemplés, exposés, vocalisés, dans le cadre de cérémoniels de cour. A chacune de ces étapes, la communication sensorielle est à l'œuvre, garante de l'efficacité performative des images de la musique et donc de leur puissance politique.

La première série d'analyse du corpus prend comme critères de départ le visuel et le sonore, à savoir les instruments de musique figurés dans les images. La seconde qui lui est associée s'attache aux types de "joueurs d'instruments" et "ménestrels", tels qu'ils sont nommés dans les chroniques et les comptabilités ducales. La troisième inscrit ces motifs visibles de la musique dans la thématique générale des rituels que sont "les banquets", "les entrées solennelles", "les batailles". Enfin, elle leur donne sens dans la quatrième série: les types de manuscrits du corpus, c'est-à-dire les chroniques et les romans de chevalerie. Cette approche méthodologique par l'analyse sérielle permet de mieux saisir les raisons pour lesquelles les "concepteurs d'images" – dont Philippe le Bon ou Charles le Téméraire – et les enlumineurs ont associé la musique à l'image, le sonore au visuel, dans les représentations de certains rituels de cour. Elle contribue à mieux comprendre en quoi la musique a été pensée comme un élément performatif des images, capable d'exercer une *agency* (Gell, 1998) sur les "lecteurs" les "spectateurs", les "auditeurs", dans le contexte de la société qui les a produites.

En effet, en tant que *decor* et *ornatus*, aux sens rhétoriques et musicaux romains de "convenance", ces images fonctionnent comme des agents dynamiques d'une "culture de cour", dont les systèmes de représentation et d'action politique et esthétique consistent en des discours visuels et auditifs usant de codes, de modèles et de conventions passés et présents partagés par les élites curiales. Comme l'ont rappelé Thomas W. Gaethgens et Jean-Claude Schmitt (Schmitt et al., 2005), leurs finalités visent à modeler des comportements, notamment par l'imitation de faits passés, à exercer l'influence politique du pouvoir ducal *via* les réseaux sociaux et politiques, et à construire une *memoria* à partir du passé en vue du futur. Renouvelée aux XIVᵉ et XVᵉ siècles, cette communication "avant l'heure", pour reprendre Jean-Philippe Genêt (Genêt, 1997, p. 13), s'appuie sur des "formes-langages" organisées autour du son – la musique, la parole – et de l'image (verbale et visuelle) à l'adresse des cinq sens, dont la réceptivité cognitive et émotionnelle peut potentiellement se transformer en une puissance performative dans et par les rituels de cour.

Ainsi, en reprenant Daniel Arasse, les images trameraient leur "signification par des relations de surface, de proximité" (Arasse, 2006, p. 18), en configurant des motifs – les instruments –, des thématiques – les banquets, les entrées – dans des temporalités et des espaces éloignés, mais actualisés dans une société de cour qui en est friande. Ces processus visuels et sensoriels ne fonctionnent toutefois que dans et par les réseaux de clientèle et les sociabilités élitistes assurant la circulation des ouvrages par des dons, des prêts et des commandes aussi bien au sein des milieux curiaux, ecclésiastiques et urbains de la principauté, qu'à l'échelle des autres cours européennes. Ce sont les rituels et les cérémonies qui leur confèrent leur puissance visuelle, sonore et politique, les magnifiant dans le présent du XVᵉ siècle jusqu'à nos jours.

Une communication visuelle, musicale et aurale tournée vers "l'Orient"

L'un des intérêts des différentes sources bourguignonnes en matière de musique est leur grande cohésion qui appelle, de fait, des analyses critiques. Car le systématisme apparaît bien à l'œuvre dans les comptabilités, les livres enluminés, les récits chevaleresques et les mémoires. Schématiquement, ce que les concepteurs d'images ont choisi de faire figurer dans les manuscrits prestigieux, grand format, et les archives comptables semblent fonctionner "en réseau" et assurer une communication circulant du visuel au sonore et à l'oral/aural.

Des dépenses ducales pour *l'instrumentarium* et les ménestrels de l'Hôtel

Les manuscrits du corpus concernent principalement les chroniques, les histoires et les romans de chevalerie situés dans "la Terre d'Orient", la Romanité et la Lotharingie. Ils sont à intégrer dans les rêves de conquêtes religieuses et belliqueuses des ducs. Leurs miniatures et frontispices mettent en scène les principaux rituels curiaux de la représentation politique ducale. Certaines d'entre elles figurent ce qui est dénommé à l'époque l'ensemble des "bas"

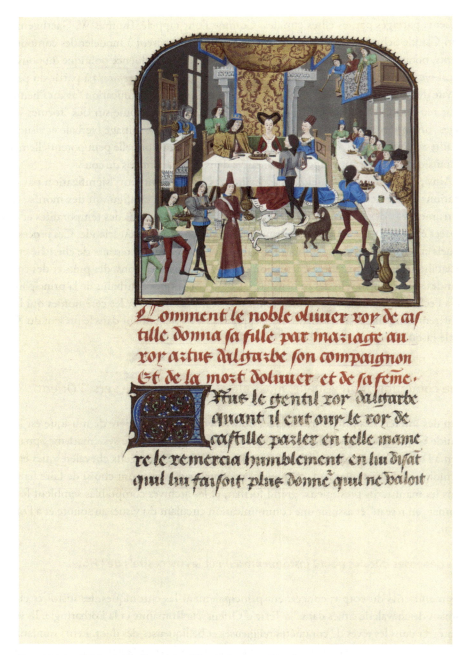

Fig. 1: *Histoire d'Olivier de Castille et Artus d'Algarbe,* Bruges, 1468–1480.

instruments. Celui-ci est constitué de cordes et de vents et caractérisés par des sonorités discrètes, telles les flûtes, le luth, la vièle à archet, la harpe. Ces instruments sont plus nombreux dans les livres de prières du duc où ils sont figurés entre les mains des anges et non des ménestrels. Dans les ouvrages profanes, la majorité des miniatures présentent les instruments de l'ensemble de "haut" qui est caractérisé par leur forte puissance sonore. Il regroupe les trompettes droites, les sacqueboutes, pour les embouchures; les chalemies et bombardes, les cornemuses pour les anches doubles; et les tambours pour les percussions.

L'attention portée par les enlumineurs à certains détails organologiques est remarquable, comme par exemple, une fontanelle, une pirouette et les clés visibles sur certaines bombardes. Les joueurs des "hauts" instruments sont presque toujours peints en trio, comme dans les miniatures dans l'*Histoire d'Olivier de Castille et Artus d'Algarbe* (voir Fig. 1) réalisées par l'atelier de Loyset Liédet pour Philippe le Bon, dans celles de la *Geste du noble roy Alexandre* (voir Fig. 2) composée par Jean Wauquelin à Mons, enluminée à Bruges puis donnée à Philippe le Bon, ainsi que dans les *Chroniques de Hainaut* de Jacques de Guise (Bruxelles, KBR, ms. 9244, fol. 73r.) également traduites par Wauquelin et enluminées par Guillaume Vrelant (Bousmanne, 1997). Les trios associent la trompette droite, la sacqueboute et la bombarde, ou deux trompettes et une chalemie, ou une trompette, une chalemie et une bombarde. Ces combinaisons instrumentales renforcent le volume sonore, rendant les images particulièrement "bruyantes". La convention iconographique répétée d'un manuscrit à l'autre, notamment par Liédet ou Vrelant, consiste à placer les musiciens dans une tribune surplombant la scène intérieure ou extérieure. Cette position apporte un éclat sonore supplémentaire aux instruments à vent.

Cependant, ces modes de représentation de la puissance des "hauts" instruments ne reposent pas que sur des conventions iconographiques. Ils correspondent à l'*instrumentarium* mentionné de façon récurrente dans les comptabilités de la Recette générale, et ce depuis le premier duc Valois Philippe le Hardi, ensuite sous son fils Jean sans Peur, et enfin exponentielle sous les deux derniers ducs. A l'Hôtel de Philippe le Bon, l'*instrumentarium* reste sensiblement identique en quantité que à celui de son grand-père, à savoir environ huit ménestrels de haut. Sous Charles le Téméraire, douze "trompettes de guerre" sont à son service. La prédominance des mentions de ces instruments par rapport à celles de "bas" est attestée par la documentation archivistique et littéraire (Marix, 1972; Wright, 1979; Clouzot, 2008; Fiala, 2013). Elle se lit notamment à travers les achats portant majoritairement sur les instruments à vent. Par exemple, Jean sans Peur fait acheter à Bruges, centre important de la facture instrumentale, cinq bombardes et chalemies qu'il donne à ses ménestriers en octobre 1413:

A Pierre de Prost, tourneur d'instrumens pour menestriers demourant à Bruges la somme de vint une livre dix solz de trente gros nouvelle monnoye de Flandres la livre avant dicte,

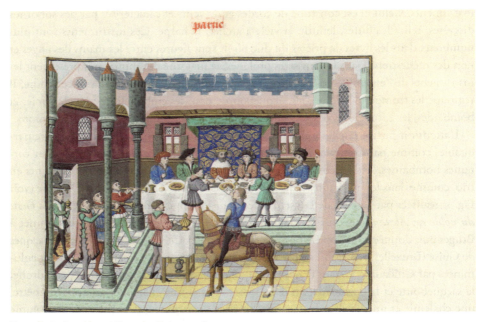

Fig. 2: *Geste du noble roy Alexandre, Bruges*, 1448–1450.

en quoy mondit seigneur estoit tenuz à lui pour la vendue et delivrance de cinq pieces d'instrumens, tant bombardes comme chalemies qu'il avoit bailliez et delivrez à ses menestriers ou mois d'octobre 1413, et lesquelz mondit seigneur avoit fait prendre et acheter de lui oudit pris. Comme plus a plain peut apparoir par les lettres de mon dit seigneur sur ce faictes et donnees en sa ville de Lille le XXe jour du dit mois d'octobre oudit an (Lille, Archives Départementales du Nord, B 1903, fol. 204).

Ce fabricant brugeois a également fourni Philippe le Bon en bombardes et chalemies.

A l'intérieur de l'ensemble de "haut" se dessine une hiérarchie établie, probablement, sur les qualités des joueurs, et peut-être sur des relations interpersonnelles entre ceux-ci et les ducs. En effet, une distinction au sein de l'ordonnancement de l'Hôtel est marquée par le titre de "roy des ménestrels". Elle se retrouve sous la plume du chroniqueur Olivier de la Marche à propos de la cour de Charles le Téméraire qui entretient six "haulz menestrelz qui sont gouvernés par un des menestriers qui est roy d'iceux" (Beaune et al., 1883, p. 71). Le "trompette des ménestrels", c'est-à-dire le chef des trios ou quatuors de "hauts" instruments à vent, est régulièrement mentionné dans les comptes de Philippe le Bon. Celui-ci a pour "trompette des ménestrels", Evrard Jansonne "retenu audit office" en 1422 jusqu'en 1440, "chef des ménestrels", Henri du Houlx, Jehan Wanezie, Guillaume

Fig. 3: *Fleur des Estoires de la Terre d'Orient*, par Hayton (Jean IV, archevêque de Sultanies, ordonnances de Timur Bey), 1300–1401.

Caillet, Thibaut de Strasbourg "ménétriers" (Paris, BnF, coll. De Bourgogne 23, fol. 2v.). A la mort de Charles VI, le duc réussit à retenir à sa cour les deux "roys des ménestrels" du roi de France, Jehan Facien et Antoine le Blanc, trompettistes (Marix, 1972, p. 115). D'autres "Roys des ménestrels" leur succèdent à la cour de Bourgogne. En 1431, Hennequin Jansonne est à son tour "trompette des ménestrels" jusqu'en 1445, auquel succède à ce titre Jacques Jansonne jusqu'en 1464, lui-même remplacé par un Jehan Jansonne.[1] Figurent également Jean Karesme "roy des ménestreulx" (Vander Straeten, 1972, p. 49), puis le plus célèbre Verdelet dont Martin le Franc, l'auteur du *Champion des Dames*, vante et chante la virtuosité: "Jamais on n'a compassé / N'en doulchaine, n'en flaiolet / Ce qu'ung nagueres trespassé / Faisoit, appelé Verdellet" (Paris, BnF, ms. Fr. 12476, fol. 98r.).

Ces quelques exemples de mentions comptables extraites des archives confirment, à partir du critère financier, la hiérarchie instrumentale de la cour que les enluminures mettent en scène dans des discours visuels et sonores. Ils dénotent le fonctionnement d'un système de communication au service de la puissance ducale.

---

[1] Lille, Archives Départementales du Nord, B 1969, fol. 111v.; B 1943, fol. 90v.; B 1942, fol. 1942, fol. 112v.; B 1982, fol. 45v.; B 2051, fol. 190v.; B 1991, fol. 42v.; Paravicini, 1984.

Images et médiatisation du banquet: "robes" et couleurs des ménestrels

Les figurations des trompettes, bombardes et chalemies animent les représentations des banquets, rituels diplomatiques souvent situés à la cour d'un roi ou romain, germanique ou "oriental". Dans nombre des manuscrits enluminés pour les ducs ou leur entourage, elles procèdent de conventions iconographiques, ainsi que d'une politique "médiatique" délibérée. Les vêtements des ménestrels en font partie, en raison de leurs "livrées" ou "robes", taillées sur un même modèle à la manière d'un uniforme. Dans la majorité des images, les enlumineurs représentent les ménestrels vêtus de magnifiques vêtements, comme dans les miniatures de la *Fleur des Estoires de la Terre d'Orient* offerte à Philippe le Hardi (voir Fig. 3) ou la *Geste de Renaut de* Montauban (Paris, BnF, ms. Fr. 764, fol. 214v.). Dans la première image, les quatre joueurs de trompette, de sacqueboute et de bombarde portent des bas de couleur rouge, verte et blanche; leurs robes aux manches dentelées sont longues et amples, aux tons violets, roses et bleus, d'intensité toutefois moindre à ceux des vêtements des figures royales de la miniature. La même diversité chromatique et vestimentaire se retrouve chez les trompettistes et joueurs de bombardes de deux autres images. Dans les manuscrits enluminés pour Philippe le Bon par Liédet, comme par exemple l'*Histoire d'Olivier de Castille et d'Artus d'Algarve* (Paris, BnF, ms. Fr. 12574, fol. 181v.) et l'*Histoire de Renaut de Montauban* (voir Fig. 4) les livrées les plus soignées au niveau du rendu des textiles et des couleurs sont celles des joueurs de "haut". Leurs robes sont bleues, rouges

Fig. 4: *Histoire de Renaut de Montauban*, 2ᵉ moitié du XVᵉ siècle.

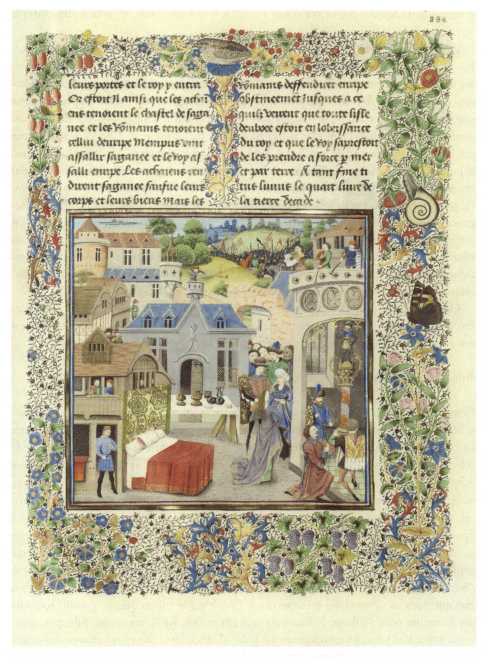

Fig. 5: *Fleur des Hystoires de Tite-Live* par Jean Mansel, avant 1467.

et vertes: la trilogie des couleurs s'ajoute à la trilogie instrumentale, le rythme chromatique scande celui des instruments.

De même dans un manuscrit de *La Fleur des Hystoires de Tite-Live* par Jean Mansel (voir Fig. 5), une miniature représente la réception solennelle dans un palais d'un couple royal. Au sommet de ce palais, trois ménestrels de cour soufflent dans leurs trompettes en direction du cortège royal. L'un d'eux joue de la sacqueboute, il est coiffé d'un chapeau et porte une livrée brodée et arbore le long de son bras gauche une longue manche de fourrure semblable à l'hermine. Dans une autre enluminure de l'*Histoire de Charles Martel* peinte par Liédet (Bruxelles, KBR, ms. 8, fol. 33v.), sur les trois ménestrels de "haut", c'est aussi le joueur de sacqueboute qui porte un chapeau, alors que les deux joueurs de bombardes restent tête nue. Enfin, dans une image de l'*Histoire du noble roy Alexandre* (Paris, BnF, ms. Fr. 9342, fol. 13r.), les trois joueurs de bombardes portent des robes dont la taille et l'élégance vont en décroissant: le premier musicien visible, joueur de chalemie, porte la plus longue et belle cape, tandis que le dernier est revêtu d'un simple surcot. Par ces vêtements relativement "standardisés", les images définissent ainsi avec justesse une fonction domestique au service de la personne ducale au sein de l'Hôtel et de la cour: les "ménestrels" exercent un "ministère", comme l'étymologie de leur nom l'indique.

On le voit, toute thématique du corpus indique une attention portée sur les livrées des musiciens du duc. Toutefois, des thèmes plus particuliers mettent en évidence d'autres traitements de faveur réservés aux ménestrels de "haut".

Entrées solennelles et batailles: rêves sonores de conquêtes "orientales"

Comme la thématique des banquets, celles des entrées solennelles et des batailles ont la particularité d'orner les chroniques et romans dont la matière narrative chevaleresque est située en "Orient". Les entrées solennelles s'organisent en partie autour des trompettistes de la cour ducale. Dans les images, ceux-ci sont presque toujours juchés sur un cheval, comme dans une miniature de l'*Avis pour faire le Passage de Guillaume Adam* (Bruxelles, KBR, ms. 9025, fol. 9r.) enluminée par Jean le Tavernier vers 1455 pour Philippe le Bon, ou bien dans une autre de la *Chronique* d'Enguerrand de Monstrelet (Paris, BnF, ms. Fr. 2679, fol. 413r.) figurant Philippe le Bon et sa suite à cheval. Un trompettiste à cheval, avec une trompette en forme de S habillée aux armes de Bourgogne, sonne aux côtés du duc faisant son entrée par la porte d'une ville, comme Philippe le Bon à Dijon dans le manuscrit de la *Fondation de l'Hôpital du Saint-Esprit* (voir Fig. 6). De même, dans les scènes de batailles, nombreuses par exemple dans les *Chronicques et conquestes de Charlemagne* enluminées en grisaille toujours par Tavernier pour Philippe le Bon vers 1458 (Bruxelles, KBR, ms. 9066, fols. 70r., 96r., 100r., 178r., 212r.), les ménestrels montent à cheval et soufflent dans leurs trompettes et sacqueboutes. Le contexte politique explique évidemment la présence et le recours aux chevaux.

Images sonores des rituels politiques dans les manuscrits enluminés

Fig. 6: *Fondation de l'Hôpital du Saint-Esprit de Dijon,* Couvent des Carmes, Peinture gouachée et or (style flamand), vers 1450–1460.

Les dépenses concernant les dons, comme l'a montré Baptiste Rameau,[2] indiquent en effet que les ducs offrent des chevaux à leurs trompettistes attitrés afin qu'ils puissent remplir leurs fonctions. Par exemple, les ordonnances de l'Hôtel de Philippe le Bon précisent qu'en 1426/1427 les "trompettes et ménétriers, chascun [reçurent] deux chevaulx a gaiges et un varlet a livree" (Lille, Archives Départementales du Nord, B 1925). Dans une société de cour, pour les élites chevaleresques, et dans le contexte de la Guerre de Cent ans, l'association de la trompette et du cheval ne repose pas seulement sur des aspects pratiques et circonstanciels, mais comprend aussi des buts politiques. En quelque sorte, la monture donne une valeur ajoutée aux instrumentistes, vis-à-vis des autres musiciens et de la population.

Le mémorialiste La Marche s'en fait le témoin en rapportant que

> Philippe le Bon avait douze trompettes de guerre, les meilleurs qu'il a sceu finer et sont iceulx trompettes gouvernez par l'ung d'eulx qui est leur chief [...].Et le chief des trompettes se doit tenir prest pour sçavoir quant on sonnera à cheval; et quant le prince le commande, les trompettes se départent et vont sonner a cheval; et si se mettent chascun en armes et en habillemens et se tire chascun dessoubz son chief et dessoubz sa cornette et les trompettes se tirent devers le prince comme la premiere fois [...] (Beaune et al., 1883, pp. 70–71).

En parallèle aux mémoires, des paiements dans les archives mentionnent la catégorie "trompettes de guerre". Sous Philippe le Bon, leur nombre s'élevait à six: Paulain d'Alexandrie resté cinquante ans au service de Philippe le Bon, Hennequin Coppetrippe, Guillemin de Plouc, Adrien de Bertelin, Antoine de Milan, Christophe d'Albourg déjà au service de Jean sans Peur, et Evrard de Bout (Vander Straeten, 1972, p. 47). Il eut ensuite dans les années 1452 Jacquot Jansonne, Laurent Vache, Antonin Jambe et André Jambe "deerste trompet van wapenen", qui restèrent au service de Charles le Téméraire (Vander Straeten, 1972, p. 49). Leur biographie est relativement connue, mais elle n'est pas notre objet (Marix, 1972, pp. 110–115).

La comparaison entre les enluminures, les chroniques et les comptabilités démontre ainsi que ces documents, bien qu'étant de nature différente, présentent une certaine cohésion "musicale" sur le plan des instruments de musique. La raison principale semble tenir à

---

2   Voir Rameau, *Les dons aux musiciens, entre communication politique et expression du pouvoir à la cour de Bourgogne (1404–1467)*, dans la présente publication, pp. 175–189, ainsi que sa thèse de doctorat d'histoire médiévale (en cours) sur *Le don dans la communication politique et symbolique des ducs Valois de Bourgogne: formes, pratiques et réseaux de fidélité (1404–1467)* en co-direction à l'Université de Bourgogne et à celle de Paris I-Panthéon Sorbonne (sous la direction de Martine Clouzot et Olivier Matteoni).

leur milieu social de commande, de don et d'usage: l'Hôtel et la cour des ducs. Ensemble, ils définissent et font entendre le son du pouvoir. Il faut alors reconstituer les raisons culturelles, mais aussi éthiques et esthétiques de ces choix sonores.

Les images des rituels en musique: un miroir des princes dans une "bibliothèque monde"

Les images "représentent" les cérémoniels auxquels la musique instrumentale contribue non seulement dans la figuration visuelle, mais aussi dans la "réalité" du *decorum* de la cour. C'est sans doute dans ce hiatus, ou au moyen des interactions entre rituel social et représentation figurée, que les discours idéologiques et leurs disjonctions temporelles – hétérochronies – sont les plus signifiants et les plus performatifs, notamment via la musique. En effet, les qualités intrinsèques de la *musica*, science du nombre et de l'harmonie, très liée à la rhétorique des arts oratoires romains et à la vocalité de l'Église médiévale, expliquent sans doute en partie la prévalence de ses figurations dans les précieux manuscrits de la Librairie ducale. Ses fondements platoniciens et aristotéliciens, cosmologiques, éthiques, esthétiques et politiques, la justifient. Ses figurations relèvent des "humanités" antiques prisées par les princes, leurs conseillers et clercs curiaux de haut rang. Avec les modèles auxquels elle est associée dans les miniatures, elle participe de l'image idéalisée du duc et de la cour.

Deux modèles culturels et politiques: le prince éduqué et conquérant

Ce n'est pas tant la "présence" des instruments dans les enluminures que l'"action" au sens d'agentivité de leur figuration dans le cadre d'une image et dans le dispositif ornemental et topographique d'un livre enluminé pour un prince, qui retient notre attention. Pour ce faire, il importe d'analyser la musique figurée au regard du prince et des modèles culturels antiques et bibliques convoqués dans les textes et les images. Toutefois, au-delà du recours convenu aux "anachronismes" historiques, il est intéressant d'observer les adaptations réalisées par les "gens de savoir" (Verger, 1997; 2002) au service d'une société de cour qui est tendue entre un passé mythique et une modernité présente, entre les cultures cléricales, urbaines et humanistes. Le travail du temps est à l'œuvre dans la narration visuelle et sonore des miniatures et des feuillets tournés, lus, chantés des livres, lors des rituels de cour. Associées à la musique, les "scènes de banquet", les "entrées", etc., transmettent principalement deux modèles complémentaires: dans une petite mesure, celui du prince éduqué et modéré; dans une large mesure, celui du prince chevalier chrétien et conquérant tourné vers la Méditerranée antique et "l'Orient" impérial et chrétien.

Comme leurs contemporains de la haute noblesse européenne, les ducs de Bourgogne, "princes de lys" issus de la dynastie royale des Valois, ont reçu une éducation morale et humaniste (Sterchi, 2005). Par l'intermédiaire des traités politiques appelés les "miroirs des princes", leurs maîtres, tels Baudouin de la Nieppe pour le jeune Jean – futur "sans Peur" –, ou Antoine Haneron *maistre d'escole et instructeur* (Sommé, 1998, p. 57) appelé à l'université de Louvain en 1441 par Philippe le Bon pour le comte Charles, leur ont enseigné les vertus aristotéliciennes et cicéroniennes de la dignité princière utiles au bien commun, reprises par la doctrine chrétienne (Lecuppre-Desjardin et al., 2010): la prudence, la force, la tempérance et la justice. Par la lecture – entre autres – de la *Politique* et de l'*Ethique à Nicomaque* d'Aristote et de Cicéron, ces dignitaires lettrés ont appris aux jeunes princes la modération nécessaire au gouvernement, à l'harmonie et la paix sociales dans leur principauté.

La *musica*, science numérique du *quadrivium* des arts libéraux, y contribue, en théorie, à travers les modèles antiques – Pythagore, les Muses – et bibliques – Tubalcaïn, le roi David –, célébrés dans les traités et la poésie allégorique de l'époque, tel le célèbre manuscrit du *Champion des dames* du prévôt de Lausanne Le Franc (Paris, BnF, ms. Fr. 12476, fol. 109v.; Charron, 2002) (voir Fig. 7). Dans la pratique, l'instruction des jeunes ducs incluait une initiation à la *musica* et au jeu instrumental, l'exemple le plus notable étant Charles le Téméraire jouant de la harpe (Marix, 1972, p. 19). La musique transposée dans les images rappelle les fondements gréco-latins des vertus de tempérance et de "joyeuseté". Les jeux et les "déduits" sont vertueux et dignes du prince dans la mesure où ils sont modérés et ordonnés avec raison. Figurés dans les images, ils rappellent à la société de cour qui les pratique que le prince en est le dispensateur, dépositaire de l'harmonie sociale.

Outre les auteurs de miroirs des princes, les chroniqueurs et les mémorialistes ont décrit les rituels que sont les tournois, les entrées et les festins. Concernant ceux-ci, le fameux "Banquet du Faisan" organisé par La Marche (La Marche, 1616, pp. 412–439; Caron et al., 1997; Cauchies 1994; 1998; Scharrer, 2014) apparaît comme un cas certes surdéterminé, mais représentatif, en écho aux manuscrits précieux, de "l'intermédialité" des supports et des modes de communication au service de la magnificence ducale. S'il a contribué à entretenir l'image des "fastes et splendeurs" de la cour de Bourgogne, sur le plan de la critique littéraire et historique, son organisation et ses contenus idéologiques et littéraires apportent plus d'éléments d'analyse sur les adaptations de modèles et de savoirs passés et présents nourrissant les imaginaires à des fins politiques et religieuses. La recherche des références culturelles et des modes d'expression des "entremets" du repas, par exemple, incite à dépasser le premier niveau de la "représentation" visible à la surface des images et des textes. Dans les "scènes de banquet", par exemple, les ménestrels sont toujours situés en relation triangulaire avec le prince et la cour, contribuant à la "représentation" ordonnée et harmonieuse de l'autorité: la puissance sonore se manifeste comme un des agents sensoriels de la puissance politique.

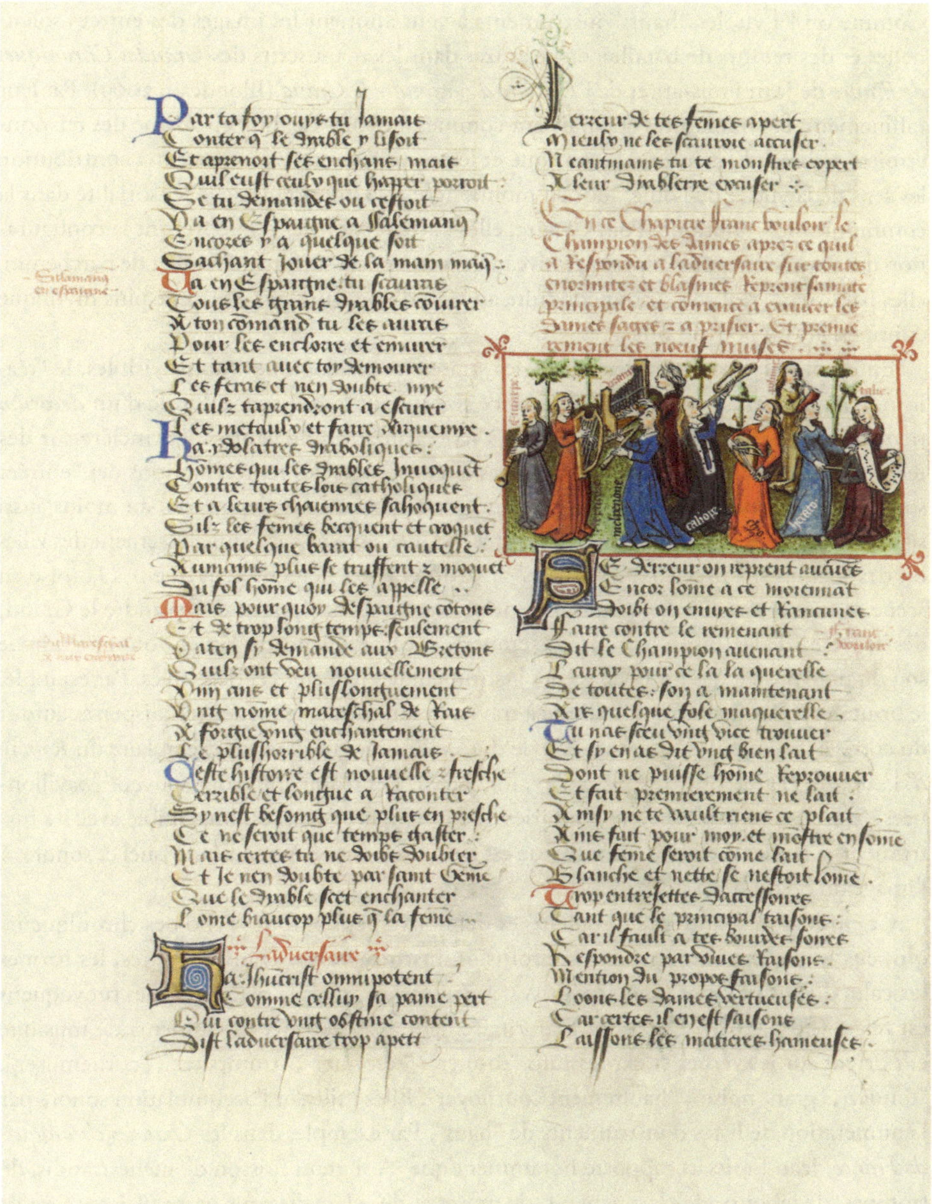

Fig. 7: *Le Champion des dames de Martin Le Franc*, 1440.

Comme on l'a vu, les "hauts" instruments à vent animent les images des entrées solennelles et des retours de bataille, entre autres dans les manuscrits des *Grandes Chroniques de France* de Jean Froissart et de l'*Histoire d'Alexandre le Grand* (Blondeau, 2009). Par leur raffinement, ces miniatures apparaissent comme une sorte de mise en abyme des relations étroites unissant la peinture, la musique et le pouvoir ducal. Elles mettent à contribution les sens de la vue et de l'ouïe, tout en montrant le rôle important de la sensorialité dans la communication politique. Pour ce faire, elles partent sur "réel" en reprenant la configuration des rituels de cour. Au premier niveau de lecture, à la surface du feuillet de parchemin, elles paraissent "réalistes", pour conduire au récit d'une autre histoire, celle plus mythique et impériale, du pouvoir ducal.

En effet, plus en profondeur, dans les strates "archéologique" moins visibles, le "réalisme" supposé n'est en effet qu'un artifice recouvrant la puissance ducale d'un *decorum* mythologique et idéalisé, indispensable à la légitimation de l'autorité princière sur des territoires discontinus et mouvants. En ces circonstances, les représentations des "entrées solennelles" au son des trompettes revêtent une importance égale, ou tout au moins aussi signifiante que les véritables "Joyeuses entrées". Que cela soit par l'embellissement des villes ou des manuscrits précieux, les "hauts" instruments participent activement à la mise en scène sonore et visuelle de la puissance princière. Situés à l'époque d'Alexandre le Grand, des Troyens, de la Toison d'or, ou des empereurs carolingiens, ces rituels font entendre le son du pouvoir par des mises en scènes instrumentales réfléchies et délibérées. Par exemple, le bruit des instruments est manifesté à travers la multitude de ménestrels dispersés autour du cortège d'Alexandre le Grand, *alias* le duc de Bourgogne dans un exemplaire du *Roman d'Alexandre* (Paris, BnF, ms. Fr. 22547, fol. 245v.). Les trompettes sont souvent "pavillonnées", c'est-à-dire habillées aux armoiries de Bourgogne, ce qui est impossible avec les instruments à cordes. Le blason héraldique est ainsi transformé en médium visuel et sonore, à l'image du cri du héraut d'armes.

Ces miniatures saturées de couleurs et de mouvement se font l'écho des chroniqueurs qui, eux aussi, mettent en mots la profusion instrumentale. Dans les textes, les formes lexicales du "bruit" sont assez répétitives et peu variées, mais le plaisir qu'elles provoquent est relaté (Fritz, 2011). Elles sont majoritairement associées aux instruments de musique et portent sur les verbes et expressions "sonner", "résonner", "trompeter", "cornemuser", "tonner", "grant noise", "haultement cournoyer". Elles utilisent l'accumulation sonore par l'énumération de listes d'instruments de "haut". Par exemple, dans les *Grandes chroniques de France*, Jean Froissart rapporte notamment que "A si grant fuisson de menestrandis, de trompes, de tabours, de claronchiaus, de muses et de calemelles que grant plaisance estoit à considérer et regarder" (Lettenhove, 1863, p. 244). Il en va de même dans les récits chevaleresques des tournois organisés avant et après les entrées. Dans le *Livre des faits du bon chevalier Messire Jacques de Lalaing*, Georges Chastellain décrit à grand renfort de trompettes la force de "Messire de Lalain joutant contre Monseigneur de Clèves à Bruxelles" en 1444: "[…] lors de tous costés encommencèrent à venir en démenant si grand bruit que par toute la ville on n'y eust oy Dieu tonner, des trompettes, clairons et ménestrels qui faisoient si grand mélodie que plaisir estoit de les oyr" (Lettenhove, 1866, p. 55). Les acclamations de la foule se font entendre: "Et lors de toutes parts trompette démenèrent grant noise pour rebaudir et esjouir la feste".

Le bruit "musical" est ainsi un moyen d'expression visuel et narratif d'un ordre social, celui de la cour, et de la représentation politique du prince. Il peut servir à confirmer trois points dans la lecture des images:

1. la place importante des "hauts" instruments dans l'ordonnancement domestique, et donc politique de la cour de Bourgogne, corroborée par les archives,
2. la permanence et la revivification des antiques modèles mythologiques, impériaux et chevaleresques à des fins de conquêtes territoriales et de légitimation politique,
3. l'association délibérée de la puissance sonore des "hauts" instruments, avec toute représentation du pouvoir principalement de Philippe le Bon et Charles le Téméraire.

Les livres enluminés de musique, miroirs du prince

Pour mieux saisir les réseaux de médias organisés par les ducs, leurs plus éminents conseillers, chevaliers, mémorialistes et "artistes", la méthode d'analyse des images demande de revenir au livre, à l'objet-livre enluminé pour le pouvoir. C'est une manière d'éviter de prendre les enluminures pour ce qu'elles ne sont pas, c'est-à-dire pour de simples "reflets" des pratiques musicales à la cour d'un prince du XVe siècle.

En effet, les images médiévales sont fondées sur des processus cognitifs et culturels bien plus complexes. L'association du son et du visuel dont elles usent résulte des méthodes oratoires gréco-latines appliquées aux pratiques vocales et mnémotechniques de l'enseignement, du discours et de la lecture. L'usage et la finalité de certaines méthodes oratoires consistent à transmettre des modes de comportements moraux au moyen d'images verbales et visuelles et de modèles exemplaires. Pour ce faire, les enlumineurs ont adapté les règles mnémotechniques de base héritées de l'Antiquité depuis Aristote, Quintilien et Cicéron, puis transmis aux médiévaux par les autorités que sont, entre autres, saint Augustin, Isidore de Séville, Boèce. Les bibliothèques humanistes des puissants de la principauté, qu'ils soient nobles chevaliers, prélats ecclésiastiques ou patriciens urbains, en témoignent par la présence des copies et des traductions des traités de rhétorique, de grammaire, de musique et des manuels d'éthique.

Les images procèdent par l'association et la répétition de motifs dans des thématiques bien identifiées, celles des cérémonies, produisant des codes visuels connus et partagés par les élites de cour. La combinaison systématique des instruments de "haut" avec la figure ducale dans le cadre des rituels des banquets et des entrées fait partie de ces processus cognitifs et sensoriels. Elle se comprend à diverses échelles, allant d'une enluminure à une bibliothèque. Dans la Librairie ducale, la plupart des chroniques, romans et histoires enluminés pour le duc s'ouvre sur un frontispice, c'est-à-dire sur une miniature peinte en pleine-page au tout début du livre: il met en scène soit le rituel de la remise du livre par l'auteur, comme dans les exemplaires successifs des *Chroniques de Hainaut*, soit le duc entouré de la généalogie mythique de la Maison de Bourgogne avec ses blasons héraldiques, comme dans *Le Champion des dames* de Le Franc. Fondée sur le procédé rhétorique antique de l'*ekphrasis*, cette page d'ouverture est appelée *Bildeinsatz* par les historiens de l'art et vise à exposer à la vue les sujets, événements et figures historiques exemplaires à se remémorer. Par l'intelligence et l'imagination, la mémoire est ainsi censée travailler, produire des images mentales et susciter des émotions grâce à la répétition et l'association (Carruthers, 2002).

En rapportant les images des "hauts" instruments aux livres enluminés pour les deux derniers ducs, il est manifeste que les miniatures associant le son des trompettes et des bombardes aux "banquets à la cour" et aux "entrées solennelles" constituent autant d'images à se remémorer par leur disposition dans les manuscrits et leur répétition d'un ouvrage à l'autre. Leur esthétique, recherchée et commandée par les codes et les goûts des ducs et de leurs entourages, devait exercer un pouvoir procurant probablement un plaisir personnel, mais aussi une satisfaction politique: le livre d'images, objet précieux de prestige, reproduit un ordre du monde passé et idéalisé où la musique allégorise la concorde et la puissance politique. Il se fait le "miroir du prince" et le "miroir du monde", dans la tradition antique et augustinienne du livre au Moyen Âge: il est décoré des ornements du discours selon les préceptes de Quintilien et Cicéron. D'un point de vue étymologique, le *decor* ou l'*ornatus* embellit le livre – ou tout autre objet ou monument – pour l'honorer comme il convient (*decet*) (Bonne, 1996, p. 218). D'après Isidore de Séville, *ornatus* est la traduction latine du grec *cosmos*, signifiant le monde, opposé au *chaos* et réunit les idées d'ordre, de monde et de beauté (Bonne, 1996, p. 238). La notion platonicienne d'ordre préside à l'idée d'harmonie, car elle est intrinsèquement fondée sur un contenu numérique et cosmologique analogue à la *musica*. Mais il faut aussi la saisir du point de vue de l'*actio* rhétorique, efficiente et performative: passant de l'esthétique à l'éthique, l'image de la musique, avec sa puissance sonore et ritualisée, agit sur les sens et fait agir, que cela soit par la remémoration, l'adhésion, l'imitation ou le rejet.

D'un côté, au moyen du livre orné, le prince bibliophile et lecteur peut idéalement apprendre la force, la tempérance et la prudence, entre autres grâce à l'harmonie de la musique, et peut-être transformer ses vices en vertus chevaleresques et chrétiennes. D'un autre côté, se faisant peindre en héros mythique, il peut perpétuer l'image éternelle de sa dignité et de sa puissance, rehaussées par l'éclat sonore des instruments de haut. Les idéaux figurés, entre autres avec les instruments de musique, prennent toutefois un sens et une puissance politique plus globale à l'échelle de la Librairie ducale.

Musicalités et temporalités pour une "bibliothèque monde"? : une question en guise de conclusion

Les livres enluminés sont à replacer dans le cadre de la Librairie ducale. Ornés (ou non) d'instruments de musique à forte puissance sonore, c'est dans cet espace, certes de bibliophilie et de culture, mais aussi de stratégie de communication qu'ils prennent leur sens et exercent leur influence performative. La thèse de Stahuljak présentant la Librairie ducale comme une "bibliothèque monde" faisant "réapparaître le lien entre la culture et la politique" (Stahuljak, 2020, p. 89) est d'autant plus convaincante qu'elle permet d'une part d'extraire les "images de la musique" de leur caricature figée de "représentations de la vie de cour": au-delà de la "splendeur", elle leur rend leur puissance d'*actio* rhétorique et mémorielle. D'autre part, le changement d'angle que propose la spécialiste de littérature médiévale apporte des éclairages critiques novateurs et stimulants. Il incite à ne pas considérer la Librairie de Bourgogne seulement comme une vitrine statique de la "puissance ducale", mais aussi comme une bibliothèque constitutive d'espaces géopolitiques imaginaires et historiques interconnectés entre l'Europe septentrionale, l'Europe centrale, la Méditerranée et "l'Orient". Tout en admettant une orientation propagandiste dans la bibliophilie ducale, le concept de "littérature connectée" qu'elle défend non seulement assume la "représentation" idéalisée de la cour que véhicule la Librairie, mais aussi aide à la dépasser plus largement. C'est ce que nous avons essayé de faire.

Comme dit précédemment, les copistes et enlumineurs œuvrant au service des deux derniers ducs, de leur cour et de leurs entourages, ont transposé au XVe siècle les cérémoniels des empereurs grecs et romains. Ils ont transformé les "entrées ducales" en entrées impériales, faisant voir et entendre autant les trompettistes de l'Hôtel ducal que ceux de l'empereur romain. De même, dans le manuscrit des *Faits et Conquestes d'Alexandre le Grand* (Paris, Musée du Petit-Palais, ms. 456, fols. 19v., 20v., 84v.–85r., 86r., 87r.) "la geste" est située en "Orient" combinée avec certains rituels chevaleresques: les images de banquets en musique prennent place dans la partie consacrée aux vœux vassaliques de fidélité amoureuse *versus* politique au projet de croisade "orientale", en l'occurrence à Constantinople. Les exemples sont nombreux tant le recours à l'anachronisme est un procédé commun à toute production narrative, musicale et visuelle.

L'usage culturel et social de l'anachronisme prend un relief plus politique quand il est rapporté à l'échelle de la bibliothèque. Sa composition, justement parce qu'elle est en constante évolution au gré des entrées et sorties d'ouvrages, lesquelles sont d'ordre bibliophiliques mais aussi politiques, ouvre sur des espaces et des temporalités impossibles, non réalistes eux aussi, car inscrits dans une géopolitique disjointe. C'est pour cette raison que Stahuljak la définit comme une "bibliothèque monde": elle "rassemble le monde dans sa matière première de manuscrits en parchemin qui sont la manifestation matérielle collective de la littérature, du récit devenu objet" (Stahuljak, 2020, p. 59). On peut ajouter les images dont la puissance esthétique est d'autant plus efficace qu'elle combine le visuel et le sonore. Si la bibliothèque est "une écriture du monde", elle est aussi une "musique du monde", celle idéalisée, rêvée, par le duc et la société de cour bourguignonne, dont l'une des principales caractéristiques visuelles et acoustique est de se vouloir "puissante" et de se représenter comme telle.

La Librairie ducale organise le monde, le sien, idéalement et mentalement, comme le font les images. Au-delà des enseignements historiques et éthiques du passé délivrés par les livres, l'idéalisation de cette "carte virtuelle" des imaginaires et des ambitions politiques ducales dessine un monde qui, certes est passé, mais est aussi en devenir. Elle allie par exemple avec Charles le Téméraire, les visées impériales bourguignonnes à la reconquête de la Lotharingie carolingienne. Le passé est appelé à "un devenir-monde" (Stahuljak, 2019): "le monde actuel est un monde en devenir". Or, les transferts temporels et les projections politiques sont actualisés notamment par les livres et les images auxquelles contribue la musique qu'elle soit spéculative ou pratique par les rituels de cour figurés et réels. Car la *musica*, "art du temps" depuis Pythagore, comme les "hauts" instruments figurés, procèdent de l'interconnexion entre les histoires et les espaces passés, présents et à venir.

Ainsi, si les rituels trouvent pour une bonne part des fondements et une légitimation dans les héritages antiques, "orientaux", méditerranéens, c'est leur combinaison dans le "montage" des images – et des mémoires – du XVᵉ siècle, autrement dit leur actualisation visuelle et cognitive, qui rendent la "musique" et les images puissantes. La force des deux est ainsi puisée dans le travail du temps, non pas linéaire, mais fait de temporalités – et de musicalités – imbriquées et en mouvement dans l'espace de la "représentation", du rituel de cour et de la "littérature connectée" de la Librairie ducale.

Bibliographie

Manuscrits

Bruxelles, KBR, ms. 8, *L'Histoire de Charles Martel*, vers 1470.
Bruxelles, KBR, ms. 9025, *L'Avis pour faire le Passage de Guillaume Adam*, XVᵉ siècle.
Bruxelles, KBR, ms. 9066, *Les Chronicques et conquestes de Charlemagne*, XVᵉ siècle.
Bruxelles, KBR, ms. 9244, *Chroniques de Hainaut* de Jacques de Guise, 1446.
Dijon, Archives Départementales de la Côte d'Or, AH, ms. A 04, *Fondation de l'Hôpital du*

Saint-Esprit de Dijon, Couvent des Carmes, Peinture gouachée et or (style flamand), vers 1450–60.

Lille, Archives Départementales du Nord, B 1903.

Lille, Archives Départementales du Nord, B 1925.

Lille, Archives Départementales du Nord, B 1942.

Lille, Archives Départementales du Nord, B 1943.

Lille, Archives Départementales du Nord, B 1969.

Lille, Archives Départementales du Nord, B 1982.

Lille, Archives Départementales du Nord, B 1991.

Lille, Archives Départementales du Nord, B 2051.

Paris, Arsenal, ms. 5073, *L'Histoire de Renaut de Montauban*, 2e moitié du XVe siècle.

Paris, Arsenal, ms. 5087, *La Fleur des Hystoires de Tite-Live* de Jean Mansel, avant 1467.

Paris, BnF, coll. de Bourgogne 23.

Paris, BnF, ms. Fr. 764, *La Geste de Renaut de Montauban*, 2e moitié du XVe siècle.

Paris, BnF, ms. Fr. 2679, *La Chronique de Monstrelet*, XVe siècle.

Paris, BnF, ms. Fr. 9342, *La Geste du noble roy Alexandre*, 1448–1450.

Paris, BnF, ms. Fr. 12201, *La Fleur des Estoires de la Terre d'Orient*, 2e moitié du XVe siècle.

Paris, BnF, ms. Fr. 12574, *L'Histoire d'Olivier de Castille et Artus d'Algarbe*, 1468–1480.

Paris, BnF, ms. Fr. 12476, *Le Champion des Dames* de Martin Le Franc, vers 1450.

Paris, BnF, ms. Fr. 22547, *Le Roman d'Alexandre*, milieu XVe siècle.

Paris, Musée du Petit-Palais, ms. 456, *Faits et Conquestes d'Alexandre le Grand*, Bruges, avant 1467.

Sources imprimées et éditions des sources

Beaune, H. & D'Arbaumont, J. (1883). *Mémoires d'Olivier de la Marche, maître d'hôtel et des gardes de Charles le Téméraire*, vol. 4. Renouard.

Beaune, H. & D'Arbaumont, J. (1894). *Mémoires d'Olivier de la Marche, maître d'hôtel et des gardes de Charles le Téméraire*, vol. 2. Renouard.

La Marche, O. (³1616). *Les mémoires de Messire Olivier de la Marche*. Antoine.

Lettenhove, K. de (1866). *Œuvres de Georges Chastellain*, vol. 8. Heussner.

Lettenhove, K. de (Éd.) (1883). *Œuvres de Froissart*, vol. 2. Devaux.

Paravicini, W. (1983). Die Hofordnungen Herzog Philipps des Guten von Burgund, II. Die verlorene Hofordnung von 1419/1421. Die Hofordnung von 1426/1427. *Francia* 11, 257–301.

Études scientifiques

Arasse, D. (2006). *Le Sujet dans le tableau*. Gallimard.

Baschet, J. & Schmitt, J.-C. (1996). Introduction. L'image-objet. L'image. Fonctions et usages des images dans l'Occident médiéval. In J.-C. Schmitt & J. Baschet (Éds.), *L'image. Fonctions et usages des images dans l'Occident médiéval* (pp. 7–57). Le Léopard d'Or.

Baschet, J. (2008). Introduction. L'image-objet. In J. Baschet (Éd.), *L'Iconographie médiévale* (pp. 25–64). Gallimard.

Baschet, J. (1996). Inventivité et sérialité des images médiévales. Pour une approche iconographique élargie. *Annales Histoire, Sciences Sociales* 1, 93–133.

Blondeau, C. (2009). *Un conquérant pour quatre ducs. Alexandre le Grand à la cour de Bourgogne*. CTHS.

Bonne, J.-Cl. (1996). Formes et fonctions de l'ornemental dans l'art médiéval (VIIe–XIIe siècles). Le modèle insulaire. In J.-C. Schmitt & J. Baschet (Éds.), *L'image. Fonctions et usages des images dans l'Occident médiéval* (pp. 207–249). Le Léopard d'Or.

Bousmanne, B. (1997). *"Item a Guillaume Wyeland aussi enlumineur". Willem Vrelant, un aspect de l'enluminure des Pays-Bas méridionaux sous le mécénat des ducs Philippe le Bon et Charles le Téméraire*. Brepols.

Bousmanne, B., Van Hemedryck, T. & Van Hoorebeeck, C. (2000–2015). *La Librairie des ducs de Bourgogne conservée à la Bibliothèque royale de Belgique*, 5 vol. Brepols.

Caron, M.-T. & Clauzel, D. (1997). *Le Banquet du Faisan. 1454. L'Occident face au défi de l'Empire ottoman*. Artois Presses universitaires.

Carruthers, M. (2002). *Machina Memorialis. Méditation, rhétorique et fabrication des images au Moyen Âge*. Gallimard.

Cauchies, J.-M. (1994). *Fêtes et cérémonies aux XIVe et XVIe siècles*. Publications du Centre européen des études bourguignonnes.

Cauchies, J.-M. (1998). *À la Cour de Bourgogne. Le Duc, son entourage, son train*. Brepols.

Charron, P. (2002). *Le Maître du Champion des dames. Un enlumineur du Nord de la France de la deuxième moitié du XVe siècle*. Brepols.

Chartier, R. (1989). Le monde comme représentation. *Annales ESC* 44(6), 1505–1520.

Clouzot, M. (2008). *Images des musiciens (1350–1500). Typologies, figurations et pratiques sociales*. Brepols.

Fiala, D. (2013). La cour de Bourgogne et l'histoire de la musique. In W. Paravicini, T. Hiltmann & F. Viltart (Éds.), *La cour de Bourgogne et l'Europe. Le rayonnement et les limites d'un modèle culturel* (pp. 377–402). Thorbecke.

Fritz, J.-M. (2011). *La Cloche et la Lyre. Pour une poétique médiévale du paysage sonore*. Droz.

Gell, A. (1998). *Art and Agency. An Anthropological Theory*. Clarendon Press.

Genêt, J.-P. (1997). Histoire et système de communication au Moyen Age. In J.-P. Genêt (Éd.), *L'Histoire et les nouveaux publics dans l'Europe médiévale (XIIIe–XVe siècles)* (pp. 11–29). Publications de la Sorbonne.

Hanno, W. (2010). *Luxury Bound. Ilustrated Manuscript Production and Noble and Princely Book Ownership in the Burgundian Netherlands (1400–1550)*. Brepols.

Laporte, S. (Éd.). (2004). *L'art à la cour de Bourgogne. Le mécénat de Philippe le Hardi et de Jean sans Peur (1364–1419). Catalogue de l'exposition organisée par le Musée des Beaux-Arts de Dijon et le Cleveland Museum of Art*. Éditions de la Réunion des Musées nationaux.

Lecuppre-Desjardin, E. & Van Bruaene A.-L. (2010). *De Bono Comuni. The Discourse and Practice of the Common Good in the European (13ᵗʰ–16ᵗʰ C.)*. Brepols.

Marix, J. (1972). *Histoire de la musique et des musiciens de la cour de Bourgogne sous le règne de Philippe le Bon (1420–1467)*. Réimpression de l'éd. de Heitz, 1939, Minkoff.

Marti, S.; Borchert, T.-H. & Keck G. (Éds.) (2008). *Karl der Kühne: (1433–1477); Kunst, Krieg und Hofkultur* [Katalog zur Ausstellung "Karl der Kühne (1433–1477)"; Historisches Museum Bern, 25. April–24. August 2008; Bruggemuseum & Groeningemuseum Brügge, 27. März–21. Juli 2009]. Belser.

Ory, P. (2007). *L'histoire culturelle*. Presses universitaires de France.

Oschema, K. (2021). Splendeurs et ambivalences. Images d'une cour entre tradition et innovation. In B. Maurice-Chabard, S. Jugie & J. Paviot (Éds.), *Miroir du Prince. 1425–1510* (pp. 36–42). Snoeck.

Paravicini, W. & Schnerb, Bertrand (2009). *La Face noire de la splendeur: crimes, trahisons et scandales à la cour de Bourgogne aux XIVᵉ et XVᵉ siècles*. Univ. Charles-de-Gaulle-Lille 3.

Paravicini, W., Hiltmann, T. & Viltart, F. (2013). *La cour de Bourgogne et l'Europe. Le rayonnement et les limites d'un modèle culturel*. Thorbecke.

Paravicini, W. (2013). Préface. La fin du mythe bourguignon? In W. Paravicini, T. Hiltmann & F. Viltart (Éds.), *La cour de Bourgogne et l'Europe. Le rayonnement et les limites d'un modèle culturel* (pp. 9–17). Thorbecke.

Prevenier W. (1992). *Le prince et le peuple. Images de la société du temps des ducs de Bourgogne, 1384–1530*. Fonds Mercator.

Régnier-Bohler, D. (1996). *Splendeurs de la cour de Bourgogne. Récits et chroniques*. Laffont-Bouquins.

Scharrer, M. (2014). Les animaux et la chanson courtoise des XVᵉ et XVIᵉ siècles. In M. Clouzot & C. Beck (Éds.), *Les oiseaux chanteurs. Sciences sociales et représentations dans les sociétés et le temps long* (pp. 121–134). EUD.

Schmitt, J.-C. & Gaethgens, T. (2005). *Hofkultur in Frankreich und Europa im Spätmittelalter. La culture de cour en France et en Europe à la fin du Moyen Age*. Akademie Verlag.

Schnerb, B. (2013). Richesse, historiographie, perception. Trois aspects d'une politique de prestige. In W. Paravicini, T. Hiltmann & F. Viltart (Éds.), *La cour de Bourgogne et l'Europe. Le rayonnement et les limites d'un modèle culturel* (pp. 55–61). Thorbecke.

Sommé, M. (1998). *Isabelle de Portugal, duchesse de Bourgogne. Une femme au pouvoir au XVᵉ siècle*. Presses Universitaires du Septentrion.

Stahuljak, Z. (2019). L'Empire des livres: imagination, matière d'Orient et archive du possible aux Pays-Bas bourguignons. *Tirant. Butlletí informatiu i bibliogràfic de literatura de cavalleries* 22, 195–206.

Stahuljak, Z. (2020). *Médiéval contemporain. Pour une littérature connectée. Essai*. Macula.

Sterchi, B. (2005). *Über den Umgang mit Lob und Tadel. Normative Adelsliteratur und politische Kommunikation im burgundischen Hofadel. 1430–1406*. Brepols.

Vander Straeten, E. (1972). *Les ménestrels aux Pays-Bas du XIIIᵉ au XVIIIᵉ siècle*. Minkoff.

Verger, J. (1997). *Les Gens de savoir en Europe à la fin du Moyen Age*. Presses univ. de France.

Verger, J. (2002). Culture universitaire, culture de cour à Paris au XIVe siècle. In W. Paravicini & J. Wettlaufer (Éds.), *Erziehung und Bildung bei Hofe* (pp. 167–176). Thorbecke.

Wijsman, H. (2010). *Luxury Bound. Illustrated Manuscript Production and Noble and Princely Book Ownership in the Burgundian Netherlands (1400–1550)*. Brepols.

Wright, C. (1979). *Music at the Court of Burgundy. 1364–1419. A Documentary History*. Institute of Mediaeval Music.

Illustration Credits

Fig. 1: Paris, Bibliothèque nationale de France, ms. Français 12574, fol. 181v., *Histoire d'Olivier de Castille et Artus d'Algarbe*, Bruges, 1468–1480, version digitale: https://gallica.bnf.fr/ark:/12148/btv1b8449031h. Date d'accès: 05.01.2024.

Fig. 2: Paris, Bibliothèque nationale de France, ms. Français 9342, fol. 13, *La geste ou histoire du noble roy Alixandre, roy de Macedonne*, Bruges, 1448–1450, version digitale: https://gallica.bnf.fr/ark:/12148/btv1b6000083z. Date d'accès: 05.01.2024.

Fig. 3: Paris, Bibliothèque nationale de France, ms. Français 12201, fol. 10v., *Fleur des Estoires de la Terre d'Orient, par Hayton* (Jean IV, archevêque de Sultanies, ordonnances de Timur Bey), 1300–1401, version digitale: https://gallica.bnf.fr/ark:/12148/btv1b8452199j. Date d'accès: 05.01.2024.

Fig. 4 : Paris, Bibliothèque de l'Arsenal, ms. 5073, fol. 117v., *Histoire de Renaut de Montauban*, 2e moitié du XVe siècle, version digitale: https ://portail.biblissima.fr/ark:/43093/mdata1d5e38866f1945ff521ad087bf8e8fad1c7590e0. Date d'accès: 05.01.2024.

Fig. 5: Paris, Bibliothèque de l'Arsenal, ms. 5087, fol. 394, *Fleur des Hystoires de Tite-Live* par Jean Mansel, avant 1467, version digitale: https://portail.biblissima.fr/ark:/43093/mdataabfa8107cb7e18571398a26ceac7b179a5d7e5cd. Date d'accès: 05.01.2024.

Fig. 6: Dijon, Archives Départementales de la Côte d'Or, AH, ms. A 04, Fondation de l'Hôpital du Saint-Esprit de Dijon, Couvent des Carmes, Peinture gouachée et or (style flamand), vers 1450–1460. Date d'accès: 05.01.2024.

Fig. 7: Paris, Bibliothèque nationale de France, ms. Français, 12476, fol. 109v. *Le Champion des dames de Martin Le Franc*, 1440, version digitale: https://gallica.bnf.fr/ark:/12148/btv1b525033083. Date d'accès: 05.01.2024.

Courts in Motion

Burgundian Court Sounds between Daily Life and Celebration*

Margret Scharrer

Introduction

The typical lifestyle of the high aristocracy in the Middle Ages and the early modern period was nomadic. Not only the nobility of France but also the highborn elites of other regions, like the emperor or the king of England and other princely families, were almost permanently on the move. The dukes of Burgundy, on whom I am going to focus, travelled between their towns, castles, abbeys, and *les pays de par deçà* and *par delà*, i.e., the territories of the Low Countries and the Burgundian lands. Strictly speaking, it wasn't only the dukes who commuted, but also the duchesses and the children they had together. All of them, including the duchess widow, if there was one, had their own comital households, places of residence assigned to them, and specific court ordinances (*Ordonnances de l'Hôtel*) (Paravicini, 2002a, p. 60; 2002b, p. 373). While the two dukes Philip the Bold and John the Fearless travelled mainly between Paris and the Burgundian lands,[1] their heirs, Philip the Good and Charles the Bold, much preferred the Low Countries and seldom came to the territories of their ancestors. In particular, they visited their palaces in the great Flemish and Brabantian cities of Bruges, Brussels, Lille, Ghent, and the country palace, Hesdin, in the Artois. Brussels, especially in the later years of Philip's reign, became the duke's favoured *hôtel* and accordingly, he undertook many fewer voyages (Paravicini, 1991, pp. 223–224, 230–244; Vaughan, 2002a, pp. 135–139; Lecuppre-Desjardin, 2004, pp. 30–40). This observation can also be confirmed for the duchesses Isabella and Margaret (Sommé, 1997; Vaughan, 2002b, pp. 158–159). In his early years, Charles the Bold developed a special love for Gorinchem (also Gorcum) in the province of Arkel (Paravichini, 1991, pp. 233–234). Under his reign, Brussels lost its primacy.[2]

---

*   I would like to express my gratitude to my husband Ulf Scharrer, who offered invaluable help in improving the English of this paper.

1   On the relationships between the dukes and Paris, see Paravicini & Schnerb, 2007.

2   It should be noted that the Burgundian dukes ruled over a continuously increasing territory with a wide network of residences. The Flemish cities and palaces were not available for the entire period

In this chapter, my focus will be on the travelling and sojourning dukes of Burgundy, especially Philip the Good and Charles the Bold, and the sounding "court body" that accompanied and represented them. This entourage was visible, but it also created an emblematic sounding space that to every ear conveyed the sense of power. My understanding of soundscape includes the social, political, and aesthetic aspects of courtly life, which I interpret as an encompassing space (Missfelder, 2012, p. 39). I will try to outline the way the court acted as a sounding vehicle, taking over and defining acoustically the space around it, creating and constructing "invisible realities" (Hölkeskamp, 2015, pp. 29–30). While I am aware that it was not only the courtly body which sonically shaped the surrounding landscape, it would be beyond the scope of this chapter to scrutinize the entirety of social, political, or natural sounds and their interactions. Accordingly, my focus will be on the acoustically acting "court body", which produced various soundscapes that radiated inwards and outwards and so conveyed specific messages.

The concept of the "court body" means the totality of all living beings belonging to the court, that travelled and stayed with it at certain locations, from the duke to the archer to the minstrel and trumpeter, along with animals.[3] This aligns well with an expanded understanding of sound in a broader sense, denoting the whole spectrum of audible acoustic phenomena, including technical noise, speech, musical expressions, and sonic statements of "fauna and flora", as well as silence (Beitsameter, 2018, pp. 89–90). With this in mind, I apply soundscape to the urban historical sound studies developed after the initial ground-breaking study by Raymond Murray Schafer, *The Tuning of the World* (1977).[4] As I see it, Schafer's concept of a sounding landscape was, in the first instance, taken up by urban musicological research, rather than court research.[5]

---

without restrictions. Sometimes ducal stays were obstructed by military conflicts and building activities (De Jonge, 2000; Maekelberg & De Jonge, 2018).

3   Author's note: The word "animals" in this chapter refers to "non-human animals", a term which, while more accurate, was rejected in the interest of readability and flow.

4   Although Schafer's study has been repeatedly criticised (Breitsameter, 2018, p. 93), his approach of soundscape still provides thought-provoking impulses. As a very good recent overview on music historical soundscape research, see Fabris, 2018. In contrast to historical musicology, the conceptual debates on soundscapes figure prominently in musicological anthropology.

5   Recently some interdisciplinary orientated scholars from related disciplines have been starting to apply Schafer's concept to the field of court studies. See e.g., Weißmann, 2021, the conference paper by Christopher Kreutchen "Soundscapes – Parameter frühneuzeitlicher Gartenraumkonzeption und Erlebniskultur" presented at the international conference "Licht und Klang in der europäischen Hofkultur Medien, Effekte, Symbolik" held in 2021 at Potsdam Castle Sanssouci; see https://sites. google.com/site/rudolstaedterak/bisherige-veranstaltungen. Date of Access: 29.01.2024. Soundscapes, also with a perspective on courts, is one of the fields pursued in current German medieval studies; see Clauss et al., 2020; Clauss & Mierke, 2022. For further research and respective research initiatives by Martin Clauss and Gesine Mierke, see the network funded by the German Research

The guiding questions of this chapter are: What constitutes a sounding court? What sounds and noises are characteristic of a court like that of Burgundy? What might have been the external effect? By this, I mean communicative and emotional processes that were consciously and unconsciously controlled by sounds and used in the sense of the ruler's execution of power. Furthermore, I follow up on Werner Paravicini's observation that everyday life and festive days at courts in the late Middle Ages started increasingly to overlap (1995, pp. 20–22) – an observation which corresponds in a way with Jörg Jochen Berns's argument suggesting that the ruler was never surrounded by "everyday acoustics" in the proper sense, since everywhere he sojourned, he was enfolded by a ceremonial and thus a "mobile sound cocoon" (2003, p. 544). I also ask what the typical inner sounds between everyday life and feast days were. And what do we know of everyday life, about which the sources convey much less information than they do about festive events? What kinds of sounds were typical or intended for in- and outside communication?

Within the scope of this chapter, I cannot cover this wide and complex field in its diversity and fullness. Therefore, I will explore the sounds of the travelling and incoming court only partially and provide some preliminary reflections. Thereafter, I shall outline the sojourning court with its inner and effusing sounds. This division allows me, to a certain extent, to follow Berns's typology of sound spaces. While the travelling and incoming court corresponds to the "mobile and variable acoustic space", the sojourning court conforms to the "immobile and non-variable" as well as to the "immobile and variable" acoustical spaces. In turn, these "arbitrary and artificial" sound spheres are surrounded by a "mundane and natural acoustical space" (2006, pp. 541–544).

Sounds of Travel

For major periods of time, the Burgundian rulers were *en route*. During the summer months in 1432, for instance, Duke Philip the Good travelled between Ghent, Antwerp, Malines, Brussels, Hesdin, Boulogne, Saint-Omer, Ypres, Courtrai, and Louvain (Van der Linden, 1940, pp. 101–103). Some three years later, in the winter of 1435, Philip and his consort Isabella[6] voyaged from Dijon to Arras. Their cortege comprised 72 carts, including: five for the duke's jewellery, four for his tapestries, one for his spices, one for the furniture of his chapel, one for his *trompettes et ménestrels* (trumpetists and minstrels), two for his artillery, five for his kitchen, three for his bread pantry, three for his wine pantry, and one for

---

Foundation "Lautsphären des Mittelalters": https://www.tu-chemnitz.de/phil/iesg/professuren/gdma/dfg-netzwerk.php. Date of Access: 29.01.2024. See also the contributions to this volume by Harriet Rudolph, Tobias Weißmann, and Moritz Kelber.

6   For more information on Isabella's travels and trains, see Sommé, 1997, pp. 41–42.

a giant tent. His wife Isabella's properties found their place in fifteen carts. The belongings of his baby son Charles rolled on the Burgundian roads in two carts. Each of these carts was drawn by five or six horses (Vaughan, 2002a, pp. 141–142; Lecuppre-Desjardin, 2004, pp. 26–27).

On travels like these, Philip, Isabella, and Charles were accompanied by their household, including servants, among them not only trumpet players and other instrumentalists (Marix, 1974, pp. 264–275) but also the chaplain-singers,[7] and at least until 1430, choirboys (Marix, 1974, pp. 61–62, 242–263; Strohm, 1993, p. 275). All of their possessions – professional and personal alike – were transported.[8] According to the oldest preserved *Ordonnances* of Philip the Good from 1426/27, five *trompectes de guerre* (military trumpeters) and six *menestriers* belonged to his household (Kruse & Paravicini, 2005, pp. 72–73). Moreover, there were certainly other "musicians",[9] but the court ordinance does not identify them explicitly. For the year 1426, the inventory of chaplain-singers and instrumentalists for the reign of Philip, compiled by Jeanne Marix from courtly invoices, indicates divergent amounts. Furthermore, it reveals that the number of musicians grew continuously (1974, pp. 265–275).[10] The rising ceremonial expenses also applied to the court music. Burgundy's dukes attached great importance to excellent court music, which is repeatedly documented by official chronicles.[11] Of course, they had a special interest in referring to the exclusivity of the Burgundian court music and telling its success story.

Also other sources attest to the musicians and singers accompanying the rulers in their "nomadic" lives. For example, Wilwolt of Schaumberg, who in the 1470s served Charles the Bold in military matters, relates that "sein cappellan, singer vnnd ander sülch leüth, die allweg, woe er hin zoch, den hoff volgen vnnd bey im sein musten, [...]" ([...] his chaplains, singers, and other people like them followed him and the court wherever he went, and had to be with him) (Ulmschneider, 2018, p. 104).[12] Numerous invoices testify

---

7   It still is to be firmly established whether the singers of the chapel travelled extensively or rather stayed in the churches where they held their benefices (Strohm, 1985, pp. 93–94). This can be done in the first instance by analysing the detailed numbers provided by the *écroes*.

8   On the professional equipment that was transported, see Marix, 1974, pp. 62–63.

9   Obviously there was an overlap in the domains of the minstrels and heralds. Hiltmann, 2011, pp. 27–29, 266. In addition, musicians could be concealed behind other offices that demanded musical competence. See Strohm, 1985, pp. 74–75. It should be stressed that music was a major educational factor at court (Scharrer, forthcoming).

10   David Fiala (forthcoming) is preparing a detailed prosopographic study on chaplain-singers and musicians under the reigns of Charles the Bold and Philip the Handsome. The database Prosopographia Burgundica initiated by Paravicini is also useful: http://burgundicae.heraudica.org/fmi/iwp/cgi?-db=Prosopographia%20Curiae%20Burgundicae&-loadframes. Date of Access: 29.01.2024.

11   See e.g., Buchon, 1827, p. 73; Beaune & D'Arbaumont, 1884, p. 89; Weller, 2000, pp. 57–58.

12   Source translations in this chapter are my own.

Courts in Motion

to payments for minstrels and other musicians whom the dukes encountered and whose services they engaged (Marix, 1974, pp. 58–77). Performances of the chapel are mentioned by accounts for many festive and everyday situations inside and outside of the duchy.[13] Indeed, the moving court also had permanent musical needs: fanfares for arrivals, departures, and other ceremonials, for daily spiritual matters, and for pleasure or against boredom. These musical needs contributed to the modification of the respective soundscape. They transferred messages. The "everyday acoustics" changed.

Although singers and instrumentalists were crucial to the sonic sphere of a court, many other things also contributed to the courtly soundscape. In the context of the processions, we make mention of the large number of people and animals that entered the city and travelled through the country in a great cavalcade. The ordinance of 1426/27 specifies 399 persons as members of the ducal household (Kruse & Paravicini, 2005, pp. 50–75). These people sometimes had servants themselves, and at least one and often more horses. For the trumpeters and minstrels, for instance, the ordinances and the *écroes* of the 1430s note: "deux chevaulx a gaiges et ung varlet a livree" (two horses with gage and one valet with board) (Kruse, 1996, p. 94; Kruse & Paravicini, 2005, p. 72).

It is difficult to determine how many people actually travelled across the country, though the arrangements may have varied depending on the situation and needs. Furthermore, the court ordinances are not complete, nor are the lists of the salaries of the individual court servants and offices. Paravicini estimates the number of people in the court household in April 1449 to have been more than a thousand, a figure he describes as "the same time too high and low".[14] In festive situations, on the other hand, the number of people and animals was significantly higher.[15] It can also be assumed that some métiers did not move, since they were confined to certain locations. This applies, for example, to the field of hunting. There is evidence that complete packs of hounds or birds of prey were not taken along (Niedermann, 1995, pp. 40–41). But it is probable that animals in menageries, like lions, dromedaries, apes, ostriches, and other extraordinary as well as local species, were also brought along on journeys. Certain studies reveal that the dukes and duchesses were fascinated by "exotic" animals and birds. Invoices document the keeping of various

---

13 See e.g., Dupont, 1760, pp. XVIII–XIX; Bertalot, 1911, p. 428; Marix, 1974, pp. 58–59, 67, 82; Vaughan, 2002b, p. 162.

14 Paravicini, 2002b, p. 373, with explanations of his estimates as well as the difficulty to reconstruct exact numbers. For a reconstruction of the court in November 1450 after the *gaiges-écroes*, see pp. 398–407. See furthermore, also with a discussion of the court of Charles the Bold, Paravicini, 2002a, p. 60.

15 Harm von Seggern calculated the number of people including the train of Margarete of York at her bridal procession in 1468 in Bruges as ca. 9250 persons. In total, he estimates that about 20000 people participated at her entry (2003, pp. 286–293, 437–458).

species of singing birds in aviaries.[16] "Exotic" as well as special rare animals or hunting birds like falcons were signs of power and played an important role in the staging of the aristocracy (Steinkrüger, 2013, pp. 153–156).[17] Their sonic expressions in festive and non-festive situations were essential for the courtly soundscape.

The number of people and horses and other animals could increase considerably if military actions were planned (see Fig. 1) or other special events were imminent, such as the meeting with the emperor and the imperial princes in Trier in 1473, or the coronation of Louis XI in Reims in 1461. In the context of the latter event, the chronicler Georges Chastellain reports that the Burgundians brought a great number of animals to be eaten. He mentions "400 sheep" and "80 fat horned animals" (Lettenhove, 1864, pp. 44–46; Hurlbut, 1990, pp. 269–272). Indeed, this was a special event, with Philip the Good actually in a state of competition with the high aristocracy. The situation was quite similar for his son Charles the Bold, who turned up outside the walls of Trier with a huge army. Regarding Charles, it should be stressed that he resided far less in his castles than in military camps for reasons of his militarily motivated expansionist politics.[18] Even though his train was much larger due to military actions and their associated military equipment, it also contained everything else that was normally transported between different castles, including all the utensils required for everyday life and festive situations. Of course, musicians were a part of these military moves as well. The chronicler Jean Molinet describes this vividly on the occasion of the siege of Neuss in 1474/75. During this period, Charles also invited guests to come to feasts in the military camp. Molinet reports that music was played daily at special times, which transformed the army camp into a paradise and made rough manners disappear (Buchon, 1827, p. 67).

We can imagine that princely corteges were very impressive for the public along the routes they travelled. The people and animals, as well as the equipment they carried, certainly created various kinds of noise. In addition, ducal processions were announced by

---

16 "Exotic" and domestic animals are documented in invoices. See, e.g., Laborde, 1849, pp. 7, 204, 216–218, 249, 372. For a study on birds, see Fouchecourt, 2014, and on menageries, Paravicini, 1991; Beck et al. 2001; Lombarde, 2014, pp. 192–193. Paravicini mentions bull and lion fights in Ghent (1991, p. 228).

17 Real and artificially created fantastic animals appeared at various types of festivals along with music. In addition to singing and the roaring of lions or stags, birds of different colours flew in festival halls. One banquet at which pheasant was served included a theatrical performance of a battue and a falconry accompanied by music. One chapter in a volume I am currently writing will be dedicated to musical staging with animals. Due to length constraints, here I do not discuss the complex situation regarding the sources on the Burgundian feasts of 1454 and 1468. See Herm, 2017, which provides a good overview.

18 The *écroes* demonstrate that the court gradually grew during the time of Charles the Bold. For examples, see Paravicini, 2002a, p. 60.

Fig. 1: The Return of the Duke of Burgundy to the Artois.

the *trompecte de guerre*, other *hauts instruments*, and probably also drummers (Clouzot, 2000). In addition, there were various kinds of sounding materials, such as little bells on saddle pads and other horse-gear, or on the aristocracy's clothing (Scharrer, 2022, pp. 93–103). Artillery shots were typical noises in the soundscape of incoming trains as well. It therefore comes as no great surprise that the Burgundian chronicler Chastellain describes aristocrats as "people of great noise" (Lettenhove, 1864, p. 46). Being exceedingly loud was a kind of "privilege" of the nobility and a descriptive topos in official reports. In fact, there were different grades, functions, and qualities of sounds, these corresponding to the status of the arriving person (Žak, 1979; Clouzot, 2000, pp. 618–619). For most of the public, seeing and hearing a duke and his cavalcade was undoubtedly an extraordinary event.

Some towns were visited by the dukes regularly and frequently. Certainly, the inhabitants of Bruges and Brussels were a bit more accustomed to their rulers. But the entrance of a ducal cavalcade was always a demanding and special event. With the physical presence of the ducal household, the appearance and the soundscape of a town or city altered considerably – accordingly, so did daily life. The arrival of the high nobility brought a "festive" lifestyle into a town. The "everyday acoustics" changed. Not only at the moment of entry, but also during a court's sojourn, its presence altered the sensual appearance of the environment completely. Sources repeatedly note that there were always great difficulties to accommodate the many people and animals. Information like this suggests that the soundscape changed extremely with the presence of a court.

It should also be stressed that Burgundy was an "international" magnet that attracted many people from other courts, such as, for example, diplomats or relatives. Aristocrats sent their children for education (Vaughan, 2002b, pp. 165–166; Lecuppre-Desjardin, 2004, p. 44). Courtiers came as visitors. The voyager Pero Tafur, who reached Brussels in the late 1430s, described court life under Philip as a series of festivities (Ross & Power, 1926, Chapter XXIII). And of course, the travelling diplomats, visitors, and princes did not come alone. Whether incognito or in their official capacities, these journeys always came with a great deal of ceremonial effort. This also involved a complex spectrum of sounds, and not only those produced by official trumpeters, minstrels, and drummers. We can imagine that the entire trains with all their beings created a complex sound sphere that jolted the inhabitants out of their daily routines. Also, after their entrance, the urban soundscape also changed significantly.

Sojourning Sounds

The sojourning court was audible in various ways. As Andrew Brown and Graeme Small have already underlined: "Even the sounds that came from the palace brought to mind the prince's immanence and majesty: at Ghent, the lions' cage was situated close by the entry of the *Prinsenhof*, its occupants there for passers-by to see and hear" (Brown & Small, 2007, p. 88). This makes it clear that we should differentiate between the direct sounds of the duke and his household, and the substituting sounds that could be heard even in his absence. Lions, which can be found on many dukes' coats of arms, played an important role in the ducal *repraesentatio maiestatis*. They were usually kept in stable cages, but sometimes they appeared at special feast occasions, like the ones in 1454 in Lille, or 1473 in Trier,[19] also implying that they were sometimes moved. Animals, either in one place or when being moved, were characteristic courtly sound markers. Their sounds were part

---

19 See e.g., Baader, 1864, p. 240; Beaune & D'Arbaumont, 1884, p. 354; Lafortune-Martel, 1984, pp. 88–93.

of both festive and non-festive situations and constituted a sign and symbol of power. At events like hunts, their sounds may have been the most significant.

However, the Burgundian court developed a particular preference for artificiality, in which the animate and the "phantastic" worlds interacted. The fascination of the dukes for automata imitating people and animals, producing artificial sounds, is tangible, especially in festivities and the "wonder castle and garden" of Hesdin. The sounds coming from such machines were of great variety: organs, clock mechanisms, bells, and perhaps those of hidden people. Descriptions of the mechanical objects at Hesdin castle say that they produced sounds of thunder and storms, and imitated the fall of rain (Marix, 1974, p. 131; Franke, 1997). In this way, the dukes demonstrated their knowledge of technology as well as their power over nature and its sounds.

Ducal rule was involved in all parts of courtly sound life. From getting up to going to bed, rituals structured the life of court society in a strict manner. These rituals mainly determined when the court was making noise and when it was silent. It is clear that the urban and rural worlds outside the court also had to be informed of its daily habits. When the duke was residing in the city, the local population heard the trumpeters' fanfares that awoke him so he could get on with the affairs of government. As the chronicler Olivier de La Marche reports:

> Le duc de Bourgoigne a douze trompettes de guerre, les meilleurs qu'il a sceu finer, [...]. Et le matin que le prince doit partir, ilz doivent tous ensemble venir faire une basture devant les fenestre du prince pour [le] resveiller à l'heur [...], et puis se partent eulx quatre et vont sonner à metre selle par les quatre parties de la ville [...], et au retour de chascun ilz doivent sonner ung mot à rentrer au logiz du prince [...].

> The Duke of Burgundy has twelve war trumpeters, the best he knew to obtain, [...]. And in the morning, when the prince wishes to leave, they shall all meet at his window and play a fanfare to awaken him in time [...], and after that they shall divide themselves into four to play it [= the fanfare] in the four parts of the city [...], and after each has returned, they shall sound a signal and enter the prince's palace (Beaune & D'Arbaumont, 1888, pp. 70–71).

Furthermore, the chronicler says, the *chief des trompettes* should always be prepared to call for riding away. In all outside actions, trumpeters were ordered near the duke. At the moment a suite or cortege, was complete, they had to blow a fanfare. Whether in the city, the field, or wherever the duke was, all entrances and exits were to be organized in this way. In principle, every part of the day's courtly-social structure was announced by signals that were either produced by trumpets or by bells (Paravicini, 1999, p. 338). These sounds did not just echo in the rooms of the ducal palace, they could also be perceived outside the court. La Marche relates that all steps of the duke outside of his *hôtel* were accompanied by signals. And even when he did not leave his palace, the established court ceremonial with its sounds ensured that his subjects heard him and were informed of his daily routine. Thus the presence of the duke could not be ignored. In this way he staged himself as ruler over the urban and rural spheres in everyday and festive rituals.

However, there was also a specific sonic inner life within the court itself. Every morning,[20] the duke and his entourage listened to a polyphonic mass[21] in the court chapel (see Fig. 2), or visited particular churches outside the court for mass or other religious celebrations.[22] In addition, Vespers and Compline were celebrated with music (Marix, 1974, p. 1; Strohm, 1993, pp. 275–281; Fiala, 2015, pp. 429–430).[23] It is quite certain that religious services were announced by bells, as were special parts of the liturgy.[24] It was therefore unmistakable when the duke was celebrating mass or canonical hours. However, the court clergy could also celebrate services at the court chapel if the duke was hearing the mass in another church or was completely absent from his palace.

Administrative sources give us an idea of the formation and staffing of the chapels of Philip the Good and of his successor. The number of members reported in the ordinances and the *écroes* are not exactly the same. This is not surprising because minstrels could be *en route* in diplomatic or other missions, and singers had their prebends in different churches in the duchy. On average, the chapel of Philip the Good comprised more than 20 people, consisting of 13 or 14 chaplains, 4 clerics, and 4 to 6 *sommeliers* (Marix, 1974, pp. 241–260; Fallows, 2011, pp. 30–32). At the beginning of the reign of Charles in 1469, the ordinances mention 13 chaplains, 6 clerics, 5 *sommeliers*, and 1 forager (Fallows, 2011, p. 64; Bessey et

---

20   According to various accounts of the reign of the third Burgundian Valois duke, this was not really "morning", since Philip probably attended mass until around noon or early afternoon. According to Richard Vaughan, Philip the Good actually received a dispensation from the pope to celebrate mass office in the afternoon (2002a, p. 128). The *Mémoriaux de Saint Aubert* note that in 1449 he held mass in Cambrai between 11 and 12 o'clock, before his meal (Dupont, 1760, pp. XVIII–XIX). This changed under Charles the Bold, when mass then took place at 8 o'clock in the summer, and 9 o'clock in the winter (Paravicini, 1999, pp. 337–338).

21   Only on Mondays did the chapel choir sing a Requiem in plainsong.

22   Various sources show that the dukes visited different sacred places during their stays in order to celebrate services there. See e.g., Strohm, 1985, pp. 95–96; Vaughan, 2002b, pp. 191–192.

23   See also the English translation of La Marche's description of the household: Brown & Small, 2007, pp. 94–95, 110–111. Krista de Jonge mentions that the palaces in Ghent, Bruges, and Lille comprised great chapel complexes including two chapels – a bigger and a smaller – and corresponding to them, two "private" oratories. One of the questions this brings: how was this complex used musically? It is probable that the *haulte messe* was celebrated in one of the chapels, while the *basse messe* took place in the oratories (De Jonge, 2000, pp. 131–134).

24   Andrew Brown mentions the bell tower of the chapel complex at the palace in Bruges (2011, p. 227).

Fig. 2: Philip the Good in/and his Chapel.

al., 2021, p. 67).²⁵ There was probably an extensive repertoire for Mass and Office, even though there are just a few manuscripts referring directly to sacred polyphony in the repertoire of the Burgundian court chapel. The musical plan did not only depend on the respective day of the week, but also on the liturgical calendar and special festivities of the court. Very likely there was a distinction between everyday life on the one hand and festivities on the other. Unfortunately, commissions of specific compositions for special occasions are also only rarely documented in the transmitted polyphonic music and other sources. Gilles Binchois's famous motet *Nove cantum melodie*, composed for the baptism of Antoine, the first son from Philip's third marriage in 1431, is one of the rare examples

---

25   The number of the chapel members increased as indicated by a note in the ordinances of 1474: "[…] quinze chappellains, deux demy chappellains, quarte clercs, six sommeliers et deux fouriers, […]." (Bessey et al., 2021, p. 219). In addition to the names of all the members, they also give the name of the organist (ibid., pp. 218–225). See Fiala (forthcoming).

still existing or attributable. However, it is not the only composition that reveals the high artistic capacity of the chapel and its members (Weller, 2000, pp. 61–63, 71–83). There must have been far more compositions for occasions such as baptisms. This is indicated by extremely rare surviving source documents, such as this one from the *Recette générale* of the year 1457: "Item pour avoir fait d'enluminure ung grand roll de parchemin d'un motet qui fu fait à la nativité de mademoiselle de Bourgiogne […]." (Item for the production of an illumination of a parchment scroll of a motet made for the birth of the mademoiselle of Burgundy […].) (Laborde, 1849, p. 467). This clearly means that a special motet was composed for the birth of Charles' daughter Mary. Like the composition, the scroll itself served representative purposes, as seen by the elaborate miniatures decorating the text.[26] Motets such as these suggest that in the inner life of the court, there were differences in the communicative and aesthetic sense between everyday and festive acoustic conditions. It remains to be explored the extent to which copies of such music were circulated, what music was performed outside the courtly sphere, and what the Burgundian dynasty saw as being communicated by such compositions.

It should also be pointed out that at the table, music was an important element (Marix, 1974, p. 1). Music was not only a diversion, but it had ceremonial purposes and also was used to regulate processes in the kitchens. In the different palaces there were various arrangements for the courtly needs. In Bruges and some other residences, for example, the dukes dined in a so-called *sallette*. In addition to this special dining hall, which was used for official dinners, the great hall served as a site for special festivities. For prominent festive events, like the 1468 marriage, a special wooden hall was constructed, including a gallery for the musicians. It is noteworthy that the *sallette* bordered directly on the great chapel and the corresponding oratory (Maekelberg & De Jonge, 2018, pp. 5–6, Fig. 6). Knowing this, we can assume that the chapel as a special musical space also played an active part in dining ceremonies. However, the situation changed in the 1450s with the renovations under Isabella of Portugal. Court accounts provide the information that the chapel was not accessible from the dining hall. Nonetheless, it seems that the great oratory and the *sallette* were connected (Maekelberg & De Jonge, 2018, pp. 9–10).

It is beyond a doubt that the sounds of "prayer" were common at the ducal table. Jehan le Robert reports regarding Philip's stay in Cambrai in 1449 that on one day the duke dined alone in the refectory. At the end of the dinner, Abbot Jehan was called up to "dire grace" (Dupont, 1760, pp. XX–XXI).[27] Unfortunately, the word *dire* does not explicitly set-

---

26   It can be assumed that this scroll was destined to be sent to other courts, or had the purpose of being shown at the Burgundy court itself. The scroll format had the advantage of the parchment not being folded. This was pointed out to me by Rob C. Wegman, with whom I exchanged ideas about scrolls. I plan to investigate the topic of music on 15th-century parchment scrolls in a future paper.

27   On the journey and this event, see also Vaughan, 2002a, pp. 129–130.

tle the question of whether the priest sang or spoke the grace. Much clearer in this point is Mathieu d'Escouchy, one of the chroniclers of the famous Feast of the Pheasant that took place in Lille in February 1454. He indicates that in the course of the first entremets: "[…] apprez icelle cloche cessée, commencèrent trois petis enfans d'eglise et ung teneur, une très doulce chanson: quelle elle fu, […] mais quant à moy, ce me sambla ung plaisant benedicite pour le commencement de soupper."[28] (After the bell had stopped ringing, three little church singers and a tenor began to sing a very sweet chanson: according to its shape […] and as far as I was concerned, it seemed to me a well-pleasing Benediction for the beginning of the supper.) (Beaucourt, 1863, p. 142).

Generally speaking, prayers were an important element at the table in the 15th century (and before). *Les contenances de la table* highlight table conventions and show very well that speaking the *Bénédicité* and the *Grâces* were similar to the washing of hands, and attests to tasting dishes being a common practice (Glixelli, 1921). There is musical evidence of practices like this, including some ritual knives with musical notation containing polyphonic settings. The most famous specimens date to the 16th century. However, such knives probably also existed in the second half of the 15th century (Bouvet, 2003; Dennis, 2010, p. 168). The Grace and Benediction were integral elements of table ceremonies in everyday life; according to evidence from Escouchy, they were also recited at feasts. Children were often asked to sing or speak the *Benedictio mensae*, as attested in *Les contenances de la table* (Fuchs, 1993, pp. 13–20). We learn from Escouchy that in the case of the Feast of the Pheasant, three young boys and one tenor also sang the "plaisant benedicite" in the form of a chanson. I wonder whether this musical form represents a common variant of Burgundian table ceremonial. What kind of repertory, besides the chanson, was scheduled in the 15th century? Could there have been psalm compositions, executed in a responsorial manner and performed by specialized musicians as well as by courtiers? The same questions can be asked regarding the Grace. It is quite probable that there was a reception of the liturgic repertory – also sung by aristocrats. This assumption is based, on one hand, on the interconnections between mass and aristocratic table rituals in general (Völkel, 2006), and on the other hand, on examples of ceremonial events that are known to have taken place in early modern times. Indeed, other sonic parts of mass rituals also found their way into table ceremonies of the high nobility, such as bell ringing, which is mentioned in the above Escouchy quotation. But we should consider that special silent moments were also introduced from the liturgy into table rituals (Völkel, 2006, pp. 87–89, 96).

As already mentioned, in addition to the ducal chapel singers, trumpeters, and musicians of the *haute* and *bas* minstrels, the accounts repeatedly note payments for musicians

---

28 La Marche mentions only "trois petitz enffans et une teneur chanterent une très douce chanson" (Beaune & D'Arbaumont, 1884, p. 356).

from other courts or towns of the duchy and from elsewhere, musicians who played for the duke or members of his family. This practice was not only characteristic of special festivity situations, but also of everyday life. Aristocratic guests came with their musicians to Burgundy. Furthermore, instrumentalists and singers of various towns and cities where the court paused or resided turned up to perform. In periods of feasts as well as in daily life, the sound of the Burgundian court and at other courts was "international" (Marix, 1974; Strohm, 1985, pp. 77–78; Fiala, 2002). This diversity resulted from the "internationality" of the court society itself. This leads to another typical characteristic: multilingualism. The Burgundian state was intrinsically multilingual, and through marital connections and various alliances and diplomatic connections, other languages and musical styles also accrued. In addition to French and Dutch dialects, languages represented at court included Portuguese, English, Italian, German, and Latin. The various musical styles resulting from international courtly connections were thus complemented by multilingualism.

This brings us to the matter of persons speaking and the relationship of this to the organization of the courtly soundscape. Different questions in this regard come up: Who was allowed to speak and when? Did the appearance of the duke cause silence? What literary texts were spoken and how were they performed? Were there moments of disorganized noise? Examining these issues is beyond the scope of this chapter and must be addressed by other specialists.[29]

The latter subject also raises the question of the sounds and music of the individual members of the court. Though the ceremonial regulated communal life, the individual courtiers had their own lives, developing musical initiatives, which in turn may have had an effect on the court. Here, I would like to mention the House of Cleves, which was famous for its rich musical tradition (Pietschmann & Rozenski, 2010), and Louis de Gruuthuse, who served Philip as his cup-bearer. From the library of the latter, the famous *Gruuthuse Songbook* has survived. It contains 147 Middle Dutch songs for single voice, most with stroke notation. Even if Gruuthuse was only given this manuscript and didn't purchase it himself, it shows his interest in Dutch music. At the same time, the manuscript demonstrates the "internationality" of Bruges and its orientation towards French, German and Flemish lyric and song cultures. The repertory alludes to the wide horizon of the purchasers and the climate at Bruges, because the manuscript itself experienced a reception in different social milieus.[30] It allows, among other things, the consideration that in the aristocratic sphere, not only a specific courtly repertoire circulated. This consideration is supported by the fact that the appearance of the songbook is not very prestigious. Therefore,

---

29 On this, see, e.g., Paravicini, 1999, pp. 338–339.

30 See e.g., Oosterman, 2005, pp. 39–46; Strijbosch, 2012. For more information and access to the digitalized manuscript, see: https://www.kb.nl/ontdekken-bewonderen/topstukken/gruuthusehandschrift. Date of Access: 29.01.2024.

the owner might have been more interested in the repertoire than in the artificial character of the manuscript.

Conclusion

It should have become clear that both travelling and resident courts produced distinct acoustic signals. The dukes and their ducal households made themselves heard: They moved loudly through the countryside, taking possession of cities and palaces with their sounds and imposing their acoustic daily routines not only on their own households, but also on the general population and the surroundings. On both a large and small scale, they consciously and unconsciously decided when noise or silence was to prevail, including how many people and animals were allowed to produce sounds or noises. With their sounding behaviour inside and outside the court, they created "invisible realities" of power and communicated specific messages.

The courtly soundscape was characterized not only by loudness penetrating outwards, but also by exclusivity and artistic power. Highly specialized musicians and singers from different countries performed at the daily and festive rituals, probably producing music in different national styles. Different languages were spoken, sung, and heard. The artificial sounds of automata were heard in the gardens and halls of palaces, sounds that were clearly reserved above all for the courtly elite. Only in the sacred spheres of towns which had a "semi-private" character (Weller, 2000, p. 58), specialized singers could be heard. In the outside world, though, fanfares resounded, as well as signals and noise along with the sounds of people and animals.

The volume level became considerably higher in festive situations because of the larger numbers of people, musicians, and animals. The urban space was jolted by shots of the artillery, and both sacred and civic bells rang. Descriptions of entry ceremonies say that artificial music was played. However, we should assume that even on these occasions, most of the people would not be able to listen to the artificiality, but would rather catch only some sort of indistinct noise. The court explicitly separated itself from the outside world, creating and living in its own "sound cocoon". In fact, the latter did not have a static character but a hybrid one which permitted the exchange of melodies, tunes, and words. But how this worked must remain the topic of another study.

Bibliography

Printed Sources and Source Editions

Beaucourt, G. du Fresne de (Ed.) (1863). *Chronique de Mathieu d'Escouchy*, vol. 2. Renouard. https://books.google.de/books?id=3E8YnfAzVEgC&printsec=frontcover&hl=de&-source=gbs_ge_summary_r&cad=0#v=onepage&q&f=fals2. Date of Access: 29.01.2024.

Beaune, H. & D'Arbaumont, J. (Ed.) (1884). *Mémoires d'Olivier de La Marche, Maître d'hotel et Capitaine des gardes de Charles le Téméraire,* vol. 2. Renouard. https://archive.org/details/mmoiresdolivie02lamauoft/page/354/mode/2up?view=theater. Date of Access: 29.01.2024.

Beaune, H. & D'Arbaumont, J. (Ed.) (1888). *Mémoires d'Olivier de La Marche, Maître d'hotel et Capitaine des gardes de Charles le Téméraire*, vol. 4. Renouard. https://archive.org/details/mmoiresdolivie04lamauoft. Date of Access: 29.01.2024.

Bertalot, L. (Ed.) (1911). Ein neuer Bericht über die Zusammenkunft Friedrichs III. und Karls des Kühnen zu Trier 1473. *Westdeutsche Zeitschrift für Geschichte und Kunst* 30, 419–430.

Bessey, V., Dünnebeil, S. & Paravicini, W. (Eds.) (2021). *Die Hofordnungen der Herzöge von Burgund*, vol. 2: *Die Hofordnungen Herzog Karls des Kühnen 1467–1477*. Peter Lang.

Buchon, J.-A. C. (Ed.) (1827). *Chroniques de Jean Molinet*, vol. 1. Verdière. https://gallica.bnf.fr/ark:/12148/bpt6k112092t.texteImage. Date of Access: 29.01.2024.

Dupont [Gradué en Théologie & C. R. de l'Abbaye de S. Aubert] (ca. 1760). *Histoire ecclesiastique et civile de la ville de Cambrai et du Cambresis*, vol. 2. Berthoud. https://www.digitale-sammlungen.de/de/view/bsb10273167?page=,1. Date of Access: 29.01.2024.

Kruse, H. & Paravicini, W. (Eds.) (2005). *Die Hofordnungen der Herzöge von Burgund*, vol. 1: *Herzog Philipp der Gute 1407–1467*. Thorbecke. https://perspectivia.net/receive/ploneimport_mods_00010705. Date of Access: 29.01.2024.

Laborde, L. (Ed.) (1849). *Les ducs de Bourgogne. Études sur les lettres, les arts et l'industrie pendant le XVᵉ siècle et plus particulièrement dans les Pays-Bas et le duché de Bourgogne*, vol. 2/1. Plon. http://mdz-nbn-resolving.de/urn:nbn:de:bvb:12-bsb10426829-2. Date of Access: 29.01.2024.

Lettenhove, K. de (Ed.) (1864). *Chastellain, Georges: Chronique, 1461–1464*. Heussner.

Ross, D. E. & Power, E. (Ed.) (1926). *Pero Tafur: Travels and Adventures (1435–1439)*. Harper & Brothers. http://depts.washington.edu/silkroad/texts/tafur.html#ch23. Date of Access: 29.01.2024.

Ulmschneider, H. (Ed.) (2018). *Ludwig von Eyb der Jüngere. Geschichten und Taten Wilwolts von Schaumberg*. Waxmann.

Scholarly Literature

Baader, J. (1864). Die Zusammenkunft Kaiser Friedrich's III. mit Herzog Karl dem Kühnen von Burgund zu Trier im Jahr 1473. *Anzeiger für Kunde der deutschen Vorzeit* NF 11, 202–207,

233–242. https://archive.org/details/anzeigerfurkunde11germ/page/n177/mode/2up. Date of Access: 29.01.2024.

Beck, C., Beck, P. & Duceppe-Lamarre, F. (2001). Les parcs et jardins des ducs de Bourgogne au XIVᵉ siècle. Réalités et représentations. In A. Renoux (Ed.), *"Aux marches du Palais". Qu'est-ce qu'un palais médiéval? Données historiques et archéologiques. Actes du VIIᵉ Congrès international d'Archéologie Médiévale* (pp. 97–111). Publications du LHAM. https://www.persee.fr/issue/acsam_0000-0000_2001_act_7_1. Date of Access: 29.01.2024.

Berns, J. J. (2006). Instrumenteller Klang und herrscherliche Hallräume in der Frühen Neuzeit. Zur akustischen Setzung fürstlicher *potestas*-Ansprüche in zeremoniellem Rahmen. In H. Schramm, L. Schwarte & J. Lazardzig (Eds.), *Instrumente in Kunst und Wissenschaft: Zur Architektonik kultureller Grenzen im 17. Jahrhundert*, vol. 2 (pp. 527–555). De Gruyter. https://doi.org/10.1515/9783110199949. Date of Access: 29.01.2024.

Bouvet, S. (2003). Les couteaux de bénédicité conservés au musée national de la Renaissance. *Musique, images, instruments* 5, 138–147.

Breitsameter, S. (2018). Soundscape. In D. Morat & H. Ziemer (Eds.), *Handbuch Sound. Geschichte – Begriffe – Ansätze* (pp. 89–95). Metzler.

Brown, A. (2011). *Civic Ceremony and Religion in Medieval Bruges c. 1300–1520*. Cambridge University Press.

Brown, A. & Small, G. (2007). *Court and Civic Society in the Burgundian Low Countries c. 1420–1530*. Manchester University Press.

Clauss, M.; Mierke, G. & Krüger, A. (2020). *Lautsphären des Mittelalters. Akustische Perspektiven zwischen Lärm und Stille*. Böhlau.

Clauss, M. & Mierke, G. (2022). *Akustische Dimensionen des Mittelalters. Methoden, Begriffe, Perspektiven*. Heidelberg University Publishing.

Clouzot, M. (2000). Le son et le pouvoir en Bourgogne au XVᵉ siècle. *Revue historique* 302, 615–628. https://www.jstor.org/stable/40956716#metadata_info_tab_contents. Date of Access: 29.01.2024.

De Jonge, K. (2000). Bourgondische residenties in het graafschap Vlaanderen. Rijsel, Brugge en Gent ten tijde van Filips de Goede. *Handelingen der Maatschappij voor Geschiedenis en Oudheidkunde te Gent* 54(1), 93–134. https://doi.org/10.21825/hmgog.v54i1.364. Date of Access: 29.01.2024.

Dennis F. (2010). Scattered Knives and Dismembered Song: Cutlery, Music and the Rituals of Dining. *Renaissance Studies* 24(1), 156–184. https://onlinelibrary.wiley.com/doi/10.1111/j.1477-4658.2009.00634.x. Date of Access: 29.01.2024.

Fabris, D. (2018). Urban Musicologies. In T. Knighton & A. Mazuela-Anguita (Eds.), *Hearing the City in Early Modern Europe* (pp. 53–68). Brepols.

Fallows, D. (2011). Specific Information on the Ensembles for Composed Polyphony, 1400–1474. In K. Kreitner (Ed.), *Renaissance Music* (pp. 27–78). Ashgate.

Fiala, D. (2002). Les musiciens étrangers de la cour de Bourgogne à la fin du XVᵉ siècle. *Revue du Nord* 84 (345/346), 367–387. https://www.cairn.info/revue-du-nord-2002-2-page-367.htm. Date of Access: 29.01.2024.

Fiala, D. (2015). Music and Musicians at the Burgundian Court in the Fifteenth Century. In A. M. Busse Berger & J. Rodin (Eds.), *The Cambridge History of Fifteenth-Century Music* (pp. 427–445). Cambridge University Press. https://www.cambridge.org/core/books/the-cambridge-history-of-fifteenth-century-music/892677394D-07D14739766752508C10BC. Date of Access: 29.01.2024.

Fiala, D. (forthcoming). *Le mécénat musical des ducs de Bourgogne et des princes de la maison de Habsbourg (1467–1506)*. Brepols.

Fouchecourt, A. (2014). Les oiseaux de cage à l'hôtel des ducs Valois de Bourgogne, Philippe le Hardi et Jean sans Peur (1364–1419). In M. Clouzot & C. Beck (Eds.), *Les oiseaux chanteurs: sciences, pratiques sociales et représentations dans les sociétés et le temps long* (pp. 225–231). Éditions Universitaires de Dijon.

Franke, B. (1997). Gesellschaftsspiele mit Automaten – "Merveilles" in Hesdin. *Marburger Jahrbuch für Kunstwissenschaft* 24, 135–158. https://doi.org/10.2307/1348690. Date of Access: 29.01.2024.

Fuchs, G. (1993). Das Tischlied als Tischgebet und Beitrag zur häuslichen Liturgie. *Jahrbuch für Volkskunde* 16, 7–28.

Glixelli, S. (1921). Les contenances de la table. *Romania* 47, 1–40. https://www.jstor.org/stable/45044406. Date of Access: 29.01.2024.

Herm, M. (2017). *Festberichte. Studien zu Form, Funktion und Rezeption von Festschrifttum des 15. Jahrhunderts aus Burgund und dem Reich* [Doctoral dissertation, University of Freiburg]. https://freidok.uni-freiburg.de/data/13145. Date of Access: 29.01.2024.

Hiltmann, T. (2011). *Spätmittelalterliche Heroldskompendien Referenzen adeliger Wissenskultur in Zeiten gesellschaftlichen Wandels (Frankreich und Burgund, 15. Jahrhundert)*. Oldenbourg. https://www.degruyter.com/document/doi/10.1524/9783486851526/html. Date of Access: 29.01.2024.

Hölkeskamp, K.-J. (2015). "Performativ turn" meets "spatial turn". Prozessionen und andere Rituale in der neuen Forschung. In B. Boschung, K.-J. Hölkeskamp & C. Sode (Eds.), *Raum und Performanz. Rituale in Residenzen von der Antike bis 1815* (pp. 15–74). Steiner.

Hurlbut, J. D. (1990). *Ceremonial Entries in Burgundy: Philip the Good and Charles the Bold (1419–1477)*. Ann Arbor.

Kruse, H. (1996). *Hof, Amt und Gagen: die täglichen Gagenlisten des burgundischen Hofes (1430–1467) und der erste Hofstaat Karls des Kühnen (1456)*. Bouvier. https://perspectivia.net//publikationen/phs/kruse_hof. Date of Access: 29.01.2024.

Lafortune-Martel, A. (1984). *Fête noble en Bourgogne au XVᵉ siècle. Le banquet du Faisan (1454): Aspects politiques, sociaux et culturels*. Bellarmin.

Lecuppre-Desjardin, E. (2004). *La ville des cérémonies. Essai sur la communication politique dans les anciens Pays-Bas bourguignons*. Brepols.

Lombarde, P. (2014). Le parc et les jardins. In V. Heymans (Ed.), *Le Palais du Coudenberg à Bruxelles. Du château medieval au site archéologique* (pp. 191–215). Mardaga.

Marix, J. (1974). *Histoire de la musique et des musiciens de la cour de Bourgogne sous le règne de Philippe le Bon (1420–1467)*. Koerner [Reprint of the first Edition, Heitz & Co. 1939].

Maekelberg, S. & De Jonge, K. (2018). The Prince's Court at Bruges: A Reconstruction of the Lost Residence of the Dukes of Burgundy. *Architectural Histories* 6(1), 1–14. https://doi.org/10.5334/ah.227. Date of Access: 29.01.2024.

Missfelder, J.-F. (2012). Period Ear. Perspektiven einer Klanggeschichte der Neuzeit. *Geschichte und Gesellschaft* 38, 21–47. https://zeithistorische-forschungen.de/reprint/3995?language=en. Date of Access: 29.01.2024.

Niedermann, C. (1995). *Das Jagdwesen am Hofe Herzog Philipps des Guten von Burgund*. Archives et Bibliothèques de Belgique.

Oosterman, J. (2005). Arnheimer Lieder als rätselhaftes Bindeglied in der Literatur um 1400. In B. E. H. Schmuhl & U. Omonsky (Eds.), *Musikalische Aufführungspraxis in internationalen Dialogen des 16. Jahrhunderts*, vol. 1: *Niederländisches und deutsches weltliches Lied zwischen 1480 und 1640* (pp. 37–51). Wißner-Verlag.

Paravicini, W. (1991). Die Residenzen der Herzöge von Burgund, 1363–1477. In H. Patze (Ed.), *Vorträge und Forschungen: Fürstliche Residenzen im spätmittelalterlichen Europa* (pp. 207–263). Thorbecke. https://journals.ub.uni-heidelberg.de/index.php/vuf/article/view/15904/9770. Date of Access: 29.01.2024.

Paravicini, W. (1995). Alltag bei Hofe (Introduction). In W. Paravicini (Ed.), *Alltag bei Hofe. 3. Symposium der Residenzen-Kommission der Akademie der Wissenschaften in Göttingen, Ansbach, 28. Februar bis 1. März 1992* (pp. 9–31). Thorbecke.

Paravicini, W. (1999). Ordre et règle. Charles le Téméraire en ses ordonnances de l'hôtel. *Comptes rendus des séances de l'Académie des Inscriptions et Belles-Lettres* 143, 311–359. https://www.persee.fr/doc/crai_0065-0536_1999_num_143_1_15992. Date of Access: 29.01.2024.

Paravicini, W. (2002a). "Ordonnances de l'Hôtel" und "Escroes des gaiges". Wege zu einer prosopographischen Erforschung des burgundischen Staats im fünfzehnten Jahrhundert. In K. Krüger, H. Kruse & A. Ranft (Eds.), *Werner Paravicini. Menschen am Hof der Herzöge von Burgund. Gesammelte Aufsätze* (pp. 41–63). Thorbecke.

Paravicini, W. (2002b). Soziale Schichtung und soziale Mobilität am Hof der Herzöge von Burgund. In K. Krüger, H. Kruse & A. Ranft (Eds.), *Werner Paravicini. Menschen am Hof der Herzöge von Burgund. Gesammelte Aufsätze* (pp. 371–426). Thorbecke.

Paravicini, W. & Schnerb, B. (Eds.) (2007). *Paris, capitale des ducs de Bourgogne*. Thorbecke. http://www.prosopographia-burgundica.org/index.php?action=parcourir&ouvrage=35. Date of Access: 29.01.2024.

Pietschmann, K. & Rozenski, S. (2010). Singing the Self: The Autobiography of the Fifteenth-Century German Singer and Composer Johannes von Soest. *Early Music History: Studies in Medieval and Early Modern Music* 29, 119–159. https://www.jstor.org/stable/40800910. Date of Access: 29.01.2024.

Schafer, R. M. (1977). *The Tuning of the World*. Knopf.

Scharrer, M. (forthcoming). Höfische Räume im Ritual gestalten: Burgunds Eliten als Tänzer, Musiker, Sänger und Sprecher. In M. Clauss, C. Jaser & G. Mierke (Eds.), *Medialisierung des Ephemeren*. Dimensionen des Akustischen in Texten, Bildern, Artefakten des Mittelalters. Böhlau.

Scharrer, M. (2022). Klangliche Inszenierungen. Burgunds Herzöge als Klangkörper. *Das Mittelalter* 27(1), 91–109. https://heiup.uni-heidelberg.de/journals/index.php/mial/article/view/24543/18447. Date of Access: 29.01.2024.

Seggern, H. von (2003). *Herrschermedien im Spätmittelalter: Studien zur Informationsübermittlung im burgundischen Staat unter Karl dem Kühnen*. Thorbecke.

Sommé, M. (1997). Vie itinérante et résidences d'Isabelle de Portugal, duchesse de Bourgogne (1430–1471). *Revue du Nord* 79(319), 7–43. https://www.persee.fr/doc/rnord_0035-2624_1997_num_79_319_5204. Date of Access: 29.01.2024.

Steinkrüger, J.-E. (2013). Thematisierte Welten. Über Darstellungspraxen in Zoologischen Gärten und Vergnügungsparks. Unpublished transcript.

Strijbosch, C. (2012). Review: F. Willaert (Ed.) (2010), Het Gruuthuse-handschrift in woord en klank. Nieuwe inzichten, nieuwe vragen. Koninklijke Acad. voor Nederlandse Taal- en Letterkunde. *Zeitschrift für deutsches Altertum und deutsche Literatur* 141(2), 248–252. https://www.jstor.org/stable/41698884. Date of Access: 29.01.2024.

Strohm, R. (1985). *Music in Late Medieval Bruges*. Oxford University Press.

Strohm, R. (1993). *The Rise of European Music, 1380–1500*. Cambridge University Press.

Van der Linden, H. (1940). *Itinéraires de Philippe le Bon, Duc de Bourgogne (1419–1467) et de Charles, Comte de Charolais (1433–1467)*. Palais des Academies.

Vaughan, R. (2002a). *Philip the Good. The Apogee of Burgundy*. Boydell Press.

Vaughan, R. (2002b). *Charles the Bold. The Last Valois Duke of Burgundy*. Boydell Press.

Völkel, M. (2006). Der Tisch des Herrn. Das gemeinsame Zeichensystem von Liturgie und Tafelzeremoniell in der Frühen Neuzeit. In P.-M. Hahn & U. Schütte (Eds.), *Zeichen und Raum. Ausstattung und höfisches Zeremoniell in den deutschen Schlössern der Frühen Neuzeit* (pp. 83–102). Deutscher Kunstverlag.

Weißmann, T. C. (2021). *Kunst, Klang, Musik: Die Festkultur der europäischen Mächte im barocken Rom*. Hirmer.

Weller, P. (2000). "Nove cantum melodie", the Burgundian Court, and Binchoi's Early Career. In A. Kirkman & D. Slavin (Eds.), *Binchois Studies* (pp. 49–83). Oxford University Press.

Žak, S. (1979). *Musik als "Ehr und Zier" im mittelalterlichen Reich. Studien zur Musik im höfischen Leben, Recht und Zeremoniell*. Pfäffgen.

Illustration Credits

Fig. 1: The Return of the Duke of Burgundy [Philip the Bold] in the Artois. Jean Froissart, *Chroniques*, vol. 2, British Library, Royal MS 18 E I, fol. 12r.

Fig. 2: Philip the Good in/and his Chapel. *Traité sur l'oraison dominical*, ca. 1457, Brussels, Koninklijke Bibliotheek van Belgie MS 9092, fol. 9r.

Marian Devotion as an Expression of Power

Aspects of Repertoire at the Court of Margaret of Austria with a Special Regard to Her "Court Composer" Pierre de la Rue

Daniel Tiemeyer

This chapter highlights a specific aspect of female rulership in the early modern era by connecting the widespread Marian devotion of around 1500 with the use of music as a means of staging political as well as representative power. Margaret of Austria was not only an important patroness of the arts, she was also a distinguished ruler who paid a great deal of attention to public appearances and receiving her subjects. She served as a regent of the Habsburg-Burgundian Low Countries from 1507 until 1515, when Charles V came of age and took over power, and again from 1517 until her death in 1530.[1] During these periods, she led the entrusted provinces to a time of economic prosperity and political stability (Blockmans & Prevenier, 1999, pp. 206–234). In addition to the official portraits[2] she conveyed to the public, Margaret presented herself both as a confidante of the Queen of Heaven and as a worldly, caring *mediatrix* for her people who advocated their pleas and desires.

An introduction to the veneration of the Virgin Mary in around 1500 will be given here, as well as insights into Margaret's personal education and the strategies she pursued to publicly exhibit her own Marian devotion. Pierre de La Rue was the main composer of the *Grande chapelle* and provided a significant amount of liturgical music that served to underline the serenity and devotion of Margaret and the Habsburg dynasty. Therefore, this chapter will place a special emphasis on La Rue's Marian masses, analysing their liturgical and material diversity, as well as their heterogenous compositional structures.

The Virgin Mary

The primary devotional aspect of Mary lies in her motherhood of Jesus Christ, which gives her a prominent position as the intermediary between the faithful on the one hand and God on the other. Her function as a *mediatrix* is essential,[3] because she is seen as listening

---

1   For biographical and historical details, see Tamussino, 1995; Winker, 1966 and Soisson, 2002.

2   The best-known series of these official portraits were painted by Bernard van Orley.

3   On the *mediatrix* topos, cf. Wiesenfeldt, 2008.

to the sorrows, wishes, and worries of believers and making sure to put in a good word for them in heaven. Therefore, she plays an essential role in the salvation of the individual praying to her: This relationship of trust builds the core of the Marian devotion.

In order to worship the mother of God, a large number of holy feasts and liturgy were created through the centuries. Pivotal for the stipulation of a fixed number of Marian ceremonies[4] was the pontificate of Sixtus IV (1469–1484) (Strohm, 2005, p. 322). In around 1500 this comprised six major feasts, these derived in part from the Bible – especially the Gospel of St. Luke – and from apocryphal narrations. The first group of feast days consists of the Annunciation of the Archangel Gabriel, Mary's Visit to her cousin Elisabeth, and her Purification in the Temple. The second group consists of Mary's own birth, the feast of the Immaculate Conception and, as a final stage, her apotheosis, her Assumption into heaven. These six main feast days are joined by numerous smaller ones that vary greatly by region. A considerable number of daily prayers result in the omnipresent devotion of the Virgin, most prominently, the *Ave Maria* stemming from the angelic greeting in the Gospel of Luke. Moreover, the daily cycle of the Hours is closed with the singing of the *Magnificat*, the praise of Mary, at the end of the Vesper. Within the liturgical week, Saturday is devoted to her (Harper, 1991, p. 134). During the annual cycle, four major Marian antiphons are sung in a regularly changing pattern, first introduced in the 13th century by the Franciscan order (Harper, 1991, p. 132): *Alma redemptoris mater* (from Advent to Purification), *Ave regina caelorum* (from Lent to Easter), *Regina caeli* (from Easter to Pentecost) and finally, the *Salve regina*, which is sung until the cycle starts anew in Advent. The worship of Mary therefore structured both the cycle of the holy year and the daily service and, as such, was an integral part of daily life in around 1500.

In addition to the liturgical celebrations, further aspects of worship were developed to highlight Marian devotion.[5] These include the consecration of churches and cathedrals to the Virgin, such as Notre-Dame de Paris or Onze-Lieve-Vrouwekerk in Antwerp, as well as pilgrimages to shrines and other places dedicated to her. Another important point was the founding of lay brotherhoods, monasteries, and orders devoted to Mary. These institutions were financed primarily by wealthy patrons, from kings to merchants, who paid for Mary's daily worship to redeem themselves and assist their paths to salvation. The donors also offered precious gifts to these Marian institutions, such as altarpieces, paintings, and further adornments. Marian devotion thus promoted a patronage of the arts that led to a wide-spread iconography and commissioning of paintings, book miniatures, and statues. A further result was the growth of a manifold literature consisting of Marian legends, mir-

---

4   A helpful summary of the Marian feasts is given in Rothenberg, 2011, pp. 13–23, and in Jounel, 1987, pp. 130–149. Thorough background information is provided in the relevant articles of *Marienlexikon* of Bäumer, Remigis/Scheffczyk, 1988–1994.

5   For more on the topic of different aspects of Marian devotion, cf. Wiesenfeldt, 2012, pp. 74–95.

acles, stories, and tales from the life of Mary. In sponsoring the authoring and publication of such works, patrons again showed their reverence to the Mother of God so that she might listen more closely to their pleas in her function as the *mediatrix*.

Margaret of Austria – Education and Marian Devotion

The art historian Dagmar Eichberger has estimated that Margaret of Austria owned over twenty portraits of Mary, which were displayed all over her city-palace (Eichberger, 2002, p. 213), the Court of Savoy in Mechelen.[6] Therefore, the regent was surrounded by the Mother of Christ, ever able to seek her counsel in a private ambience. In that period, this was a typical facet of Marian devotion, also reflected in the devotional habits of other female regents and rulers.

This is not surprising, since Margaret happened to grow up in the vicinity of the most powerful and ambitious women of her time. In 1483, when barely three years old, she was sent to the royal court of France to marry the dauphin, later King Charles VIII, and was raised to become the Queen of France. Anne de France, daughter of King Louis XI and regent of the kingdom, was thus Margaret's first reference person or "mother figure" (Cluzel, 2002). Her concept of education can be reconstructed with the *Enseignements* she wrote for her own daughter Suzanne from 1503 to 1505. These "instructions" painstakingly explain how a woman has to behave in society and especially at the royal court. It is a moral guideline epitomizing the state of the art of proper female demeanour and composure. Typically, Anne makes many allusions to God, and, more importantly at the end of the book, to the Virgin Mary herself, advising her daughter to be devoted not only to God, but "aussi à la doulce vierge Marie, en luy priant que, de sa grâce, vueille estre vostre advocate vers son cher filz"[7] (Chazaud, 1874, pp. 126). The Marian devotion of Anne is prominently depicted in the triptych of the cathedral of Moulins, which shows both Anne and her husband in a praying position on both sides of the crowned Virgin with the child. Anne de France and Pierre de Beaujeau are portrayed with their name-saints and Anne is accompanied by her daughter Suzanne, thus representing the magnificence of the Dukes of Bourbon.

Another important female figure in the early life of Margaret was Queen Isabella of Castille, arguably the most prominent woman of her time (Liss, 2004). In court propaganda, Isabella is frequently compared to and identified with the Virgin Mary herself

---

6   Eichberger examines Margaret of Austria and her Marian devotion from the insightful perspective of an art historian (2002, pp. 206–228).

7   "But also, to the sweet Virgin Mary, by praying to her that, through her grace, she may be the advocate to her dear son." This and further translations by the author.

(Weissberger, 2008, p. XVI), especially after she gave birth to her son Juan, who was presented as the new saviour of the dynasty and eventually married Margaret in 1497. From Isabella, too, Margaret received a thorough education not only in culture and behaviour, but also in politics, diplomacy, and administration.

Finally, the dowager duchess and widow of Charles the Bold, Margaret of York, must be mentioned.[8] Margaret's grandmother established herself in Mechelen and supported her stepdaughter Mary against the French aggressions after the death of Charles in the battle of Nancy on January 5th, 1477. She basically raised both Philip the Handsome and Margaret of Austria, at least during the time the latter was residing in the Low Countries from 1493 to 1497, and again from 1500 until 1501. It was Margaret of York who completed Margaret of Austria's political, social and religious education. She commissioned portraits and miniatures that depict her together with saints, if not together with the Virgin Mary, thus displaying her faith and the high moral standards that were expected from female regents.

Margaret as Regent and Promoter of Marian Devotion

When Margaret of Austria took over the regency of the Habsburg-Burgundian Low Countries she was well prepared for the task and immediately started working on her public image. After the death of her third husband, Philibert II of Savoy, she refused further marriages, which was ultimately accepted by her father. Thus, just like her grandmother, she chose the status of a widow, which secured her a considerable amount of political independence.[9] In the following, this chapter will examine the basis of Margaret's Marian devotion and offer examples of how she publicly displayed her veneration of the Virgin by patronizing the arts, especially music.

The visual self-representation of Margaret's Marian devotion can be traced in three images portraying her together with the Virgin Mary. The first example is a diptych, executed by the Master of 1499 and dating to around 1501–1505 (Eichberger, 2002, pp. 208–213). In comparison to the above-mentioned triptych in the cathedral of Moulins, here Margaret is depicted alone. She is positioned on the right side, kneeling and praying to Mary in a lavishly decorated room that is furnished with a burning hearth and a carpet bearing Margaret's coat of arms. Margaret's clothing includes a black habit, indicating that her husband Philibert II was still alive, and a magnificent yellow-golden gown. Margaret is praying to

---

8   For further details, see Weightman, 1989 and Eichberger, 2005.

9   Barbara Welzel points out these "advantages" of widowhood: "No longer wives, daughters or candidates for marriage, widows were for the first time in their lives in the position of assuming roles which they could personally define. Their dowries ensured them economic security, and as widows they enjoyed a high degree of prestige" (2005, p. 103).

the Virgin with the child, and the intimacy of the scene is underlined by a benevolent gesture of the infant Jesus towards her. Mary herself is positioned on a throne and crowned by two flying angels hovering above her.

The second example stems from the beginning of Margaret's famous *Chansonnier* (B-Brus MS 228), which commences with the Marian motet *Ave sanctissima Maria* by Pierre de la Rue. An image showing the regent in reverence to the Virgin is found on the opening page of the manuscript. The miniaturist seemingly took over the colour code of the above diptych by depicting Margaret in the initial of the contra-tenor voice in another golden dress. This time, however, she wears the white habit of a widow, which she donned through her entire life after the untimely death of Philibert II. She is placed beneath a red baldachin which emphasizes her noble descent and is kneeling, similarly to the diptych, in front of an open prayerbook. Furthermore, the initial of the bassus voice carries an image with her coat of arms, which is embellished with four marguerites. Finally, Margaret is positioned on the same axis as the holy couple, mother and child, which is set within the superius initial on the verso side. Her direct appeal is expressed through her prayer *memento mei*. Another subtle means of showing the intimate interaction between the two groups is the use of the inverted colours of gold and blue, which are used for the gloriole and the gown of Mary and Margaret's dress and the cloth of the prie-dieu, respectively.

A third example that shows the sphere of complacency and intimacy of Margaret's Marian devotion is found on a full page in the Sforza book of hours (GB-Lbl Add. Ms. 34294, fol. 61r.). Here, Margaret is not depicted as a devotee or confidante of the Virgin Mary, but is directly interacting with her as part of the Holy Story. Quoting the traditional posture and positioning outside an open city gate, Margaret is depicted as Elisabeth, Mary's older cousin, and thus part of the *Visitatio*. Her facial physiognomy makes the identification unquestionable.

These are but three of many examples that carefully stage the visual self-representation of Margaret in the holy orbit of the Virgin Mary. It must be stressed that these pieces of art were exhibited primarily in private or semi-private spaces, reserved only for the personal use or the immediate social surroundings of the governess of the Low Countries. To emphasize her Marian devotion in a more public space, she made use of the sonic display of vocal polyphony, an asset for which her court was especially renowned.

Margaret's Patronage of Marian Music and La Rue's Contribution

When Margaret took over power in the provinces of the Low Countries and set up her court in Mechelen, she inherited the famous *Grande chapelle*[10] and thus the resources to pursue

---

10 An excellent overview of this ensemble is given in Meconi, 2003, pp. 53–92 and Picker, 1965, pp. 9–31.

her own "Marian mission": the exhibition of her deep devotion to the Virgin through music (Wiesenfeldt, 2012, pp. 107–117). This was a specific aspect of her character. Indeed, it can be argued that this promotion of Marian music was a unique feature of Margaret's Marian devotion and distinguishes her from other contemporary female rulers like Anne de Bretagne.

Together with the ensemble of the *Grande chapelle*, Margaret also inherited the Alamire-workshop.[11] Not only did it operate to provide music at the court, but it also collected and compiled music imported from other places. In these manuscripts, La Rue is by far the most represented composer, followed by Josquin and other colleagues who worked for the Habsburg-Burgundian or the royal French court. Assuming that the music copied into these manuscripts was also sung, one can draw a compilation of the (Marian) repertoire that was used at the court of Margaret. The iconography is meticulously created and conveys both political and religious messages. Naturally, the depiction of the Virgin with the Child and thus the ostentatious exhibition of Marian devotion is visually and ideologically embedded in these manuscripts. Thus, these codices not only transport the contemporary musical repertoire of the court of Margaret, but also serve as a part of the construction of her public image.

With the "court composer" Pierre de la Rue, Margaret had a productive musical expert at her disposal. He remained in the service of the Habsburg dynasty throughout his career from around 1493 until his retirement in 1516.[12] The epitaph on his tomb remembers him as a devout man; it is therefore likely that he also shared the devotional agenda of his patroness. The sheer number of La Rue's Marian compositions in relation to those by other colleagues such as Josquin is staggering. Of thirty masses, altogether thirteen were created on Marian topoi. In addition to this, he composed one of the first – if not the first – complete cycles of *Magnificat* settings. Seven of its eight toni are transmitted in various sources; only the *Magnificat tertii toni* is missing, though it is mentioned in a later inventory from the court of Philipp II of Spain.[13] Furthermore, he composed six settings of the *Salve regina* that was very popular in the Low Countries and was used during the regional *lof* or *Salve* services, as well as numerous Marian motets.

After an examination of the origin of the Marian material, I will investigate on the basis of examples the means with which La Rue integrated Marian melodies and templates into his masses. This analysis will necessarily lead to a heterogeneous and diverse picture, since La Rue makes use of such chants in a very complex and varied way. Oftentimes he sim-

---

11   Invaluable for researching the repertoire of these manuscripts is still the catalogue Kellman, 1999.

12   Details about La Rue's final years are provided in Meconi, 2003, pp. 43–49.

13   See Meconi, 2003, pp. 322–323, where the inventories of the libraries of Mary of Hungary and Philipp II of Spain are listed: "Y mas otro libro […] ques de los ochos tonos, de Pedro De la Rue, en que ay Magnificas y otras obras" (There are also eight books with the eight toni from Pierre de la Rue that contain Magnificat and other pieces).

ply quotes the beginning of the plainchant and develops a free continuation of his *cantus firmus*. But there are other instances where he follows the melodic outline of the pre-existing material closely. The main motives of the chant are frequently integrated into strong cadences or text-based intersections, thus becoming audible in these specific moments. Another approach is the loosening of the hierarchy of the *cantus firmus* in favour of a set of imitations in all voices, which still derive their melodic structure from the original chant. There are also examples that show no apparent use of pre-existing material – at least that we know of – and thus offer the possibility that La Rue created this material by himself. The high quality of the Marian masses demonstrates not only the composer's skill, but also reflects on the public image of Margaret as a patron and supporter of the cult of Mary. Therefore, the analysis of their contrapuntal shape and the material that La Rue utilized for their composition refers directly to Margaret's self-image as a faithful Marian devotee.

Scrutinizing the compositional techniques applied by La Rue to his masses shows not only his proficiency as a musician, but also his all-encompassing approach to the devotion of Mary. This is not only mirrored by the spiritual championship of his patron Margaret, but also in his deep faith as is documented on his epitaph. There, he is not only mentioned as "nobile cui nomen musica sacra dedit", but also "assiduus superi cultor Christique minister, castus et a Veneris crimine mundus erat".[14]

La Rue's Marian Masses

The next section compiles La Rue's Marian compositions and provides an overview of their structural shape and compositional techniques. Following the alphabetical order of the edition of the Corpus Mensurabilis Musicae (CMM), La Rue's Marian masses include the following compositions:[15]

Missa Assumpta est Maria (4v) – cantus firmus
Missa Ave Maria (4v; Credo 5v) – cantus firmus
Missa Ave Sanctissima Maria (6v, 6 ex 3 canon) – canonic
Missa Conceptio tua (5v) – cantus firmus

---

14 The epitaph has been destroyed, but the inscription has been transmitted through several copies that are given in Meconi, 2003, p. 51: Her translation of the cited lines reads as follows: Pierre de la Rue "to whom sacred music gave a noble name" and "tireless worshipper of God and minister of Christ, he was pure and free from the crime of Venus." The latter obviously is referring to La Rue's life of sexual abstinence and deep devotion.

15 Another useful table, providing the CMM dating of the compositions, can be found in Wiesenfeldt, 2010, p. 146.

Missa Cum jucunditate (4v; Credo 5v) – ostinato technique
Missa de Beata Virgine (4v) – ordinarium based
Missa de Septem doloribus (5v) – seven-note motto, cantus firmus and quotation
Missa Inviolata (4v) – partially paraphrased and segmented cantus firmus
Missa Ista est speciosa (5v) – cantus firmus
Missa O gloriosa domina / Margaretha (4v) – freely composed (?)
Missa Sancta Dei genitrix (4v) – ostinato and full voice imitation
Missa Sub tuum praesidium (4v) – paraphrased cantus firmus, initial mottos

According to the Heidelberg chapel inventory, La Rue wrote at least one additional Marian mass, the four-voice *Missa Mediatrix nostra*, which refers to one of the quintessential liturgical and devotional functions of Mary. Unfortunately, its paper manuscript did not survive to the present day (Lambrecht, 1987, p. 215).[16] Further links to the Virgin Mary can be found in the *Missa de Sancta Anna*, a mass dedicated to Mary's mother, and the *Missa de Virginibus*, which is devoted to the feast of the virgins.

Liturgical and Melodic Material

In a first step, the original Marian material will be investigated. In general, La Rue's masses are based on *cantus firmus* drawn mainly from antiphons. For example, the *Missa Assumpta est Maria* is based on the antiphon sung on the second Vespers of the feast of the Ascension on 15 August, and the *Missa Ave Maria* is derived from the famous antiphon of the Annunciation. Following this are the *Missa Conceptio tua* and *Cum jucunditate*, which are both connected to the feast of the Nativity. The first borrows its melodic shape from the Magnificat antiphon *Maternitas tua*, while the second is modelled and dominated by an ostinato consisting of the first six notes of the fifth antiphon of the second Vespers of the feast. More antiphons are used in the two masses related to the *Commune Virginem*, the chant for the Vespers in *Missa Ista est speciosa*,[17] and the text of *Missa de Virginibus*, although the melody has not been identified. The next three masses are connected to the honorary feast of the Beata Maria Virginem (BMV). The *Missa Sub tuum praesidium* is not only one of the oldest prayers in Christianity, it also borrows its melodic outline from the antiphon for the BMV. Second, the *Missa Inviolata* is based on a sequence in the Festis BMV, and the *Missa O gloriosa domina* takes its text, but not the melody, from the

---

16 The first volume of this ambitious study consists of an edition of the inventory. It lists La Rue's mass in the third part on fol. 90r., together with other masses by La Rue, de Orto, Josquin, and Obrecht. The choir book is described there as "etlich messe in Jn papir ein gestochen vnd Jn Conpert gewick-helt" (roughly: there are some masses written on paper and bundled in vellum).

17 This chant is no longer used, but can be found in the *Antiphonale Pataviense* of 1519 on fol. 273r. (Schlager, 1985).

Marian hymn *O gloriosa domina, excelsa supra sidera*. One of La Rue's most innovative compositions is his *Missa de Beata Virgine*, based on the fitting chant-melodies for each of the ordinary sections. This setting initiated a dynamic tradition of BMV-masses, most notably followed by Josquin. The next mass is one of the most mysterious and intricate of all of La Rue's compositions, the *Missa de Septem doloribus*, which served as a liturgical backbone for the newly founded cult of the Seven Sorrows and equipped the feast with its own polyphony. This mass has been subject to a great number of recent studies.[18] Despite all efforts, however, none has been able to identify the melodic origin of the chants used. It therefore seems likely that La Rue invented the melodic material himself. Not only is this his longest mass, it is also based on a seven-tone motto that might bear reference to the symbolism of the feast of the Seven Sorrows the mass was written for. The final two masses are different in design since they are not based on *cantus firmus* melodies. The *Missa Sancta Dei genitrix* is built on an ostinato in the tenor that also spreads to the other voices. Finally, the *Missa Ave Santissima Maria* – doubtlessly dedicated to the feast of the Annunciation – represents a parody mass of La Rue's eponymous motet and features an intricate 6 ex 3 canon throughout the piece.

Compositional Techniques Featured in La Rue's Marian Masses

Having provided the liturgical, material, and melodic framework of La Rue's Marian masses, in the following their contrapuntal features will be analysed. Full melodies as well as short motives derived from the original chant create an additional layer of meaning that is activated through the action of singing – and reading – by the chapel members, and by listening by the participants of the divine service. When the melodies of the chants are audible, they provide the service and the faithful with an intrinsic, semiotic support that emphasizes the intensity of the devotional rite. La Rue uses and intertwines these well-known melodies within the set of the ordinarium in such a heterogeneous way that Christiane Wiesenfeldt has fittingly labelled his approach as "encyclopaedical". She concludes that "La Rues umfängliches, marianisch beinahe enzyklopädisch anmutendes Repertoire an Marienmessen [...] nicht von Margarete von Österreichs Repräsentationswillen und -gestik als diplomatische *mediatrix* zu trennen sind"[19] (2012, p. 116). This claim will be investigated by analysing a representative selection of La Rue's Marian masses.

---

18   For the aforementioned sources, see Snow, 2010; Thelen & McDonald, 2016, and Wiesenfeldt, 2024 (forthcoming).

19   "La Rue's rich and with regard to Marian compositions almost encyclopaedic repertoire of Marian masses is inseparable from Margaret's concept of her self-representation as diplomatic mediatrix."

La Rue's *Missa de Beata Virgine* utilizes the principle of an ordinary mass, with the composer selecting the proper chant for each of the five sections: Kyrie IX, Gloria IX, Credo IV, Sanctus IX and Agnus Dei XVII [examples 1–5]. These melodies, which represent the most important contrapuntal factors, are prominently placed in the tenor, but also appear in the other voices. The layout of the voiced texture, however, appears in many varieties that can be demonstrated in the Kyrie. Initially, all voices are shaped in a rather homo-rhythmic way, thus the chant is only discernible through its melodic outline. Secondly, the Christe features a pre-imitation set, with the initium of the chant melody taken over by the tenor in measure 16. Finally, the Kyrie II features a rigid *cantus firmus* structure, with the melody in the tenor progressing in long note values and accompanied by a free-flowing setting of the outer voices.

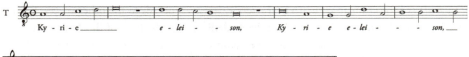

Note example 1a & 1b: Kyrie IX

Note example 2a & 2b: Gloria IX

Note example 3a & 3b: Credo IV

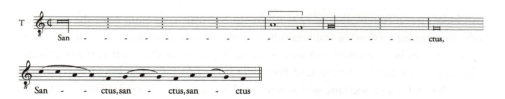

Note example 4a & 4b: Sanctus IX

Note example 5a & 5b: Agnus Dei XVII

The Gloria is intertwined with the tropus *Spiritus et alme*, which produces an additional referential layer of Marian devotion in the mass.[20] It starts with an imitation based on the Gloria IX melody through all four voices (bb. 1–4). La Rue utilizes almost the entire chant, selecting the fitting melodies to the correct wording and combining this with the above-mentioned trope. The dominance of the tenor is completely abandoned in the first part, substituted by an elaborate imitation-progress that also features highly flexible voice combinations (from duos to three and full voices). Within this flexible texture, the trope is interpolated in the upper voice duo (bb. 42–47 and 51–57) and at the end of the first part in the superius only. This last element is of high interest because it finalizes this section with the strong acclamation of Mary with the trope *ad Marie gloriam*. This line is sung in all four voices and set in a very broad and sonorous manner (bb. 73–78). After this caesura, the *Qui sedes* commences with a double imitation of the chant in tenor and superius (bb. 79–83) and is further embellished with interjections of the trope in the upper and lower voice duo (bb. 92–105). The short *Amen*-melisma is presented in the superius and finalizes the Gloria (bb. 116–121).

The beginning of the Credo features a kind of acoustic illusion, since it seems to be shaped as a proportion canon, but this only applies for the length of the first note determining the entry of the imitations. Generally, this Credo is structured as an imitation setting prominently displaying the chant melody meandering through all four voices. Therefore, the Sanctus forms a great contrast to the two previous movements, because it

---

20   The classic study on this trope is still Schmid, 1988.

exhibits a clear hierarchical *cantus firmus* structure in which the tenor bears the main melody, surrounded by flowing imitations in the other voices. Unusual for La Rue, the *Pleni sunt* is also set in four voices and quotes the main pitches of the chant at the beginning. The same is true for the three-voiced *Benedictus*.[21] The *Missa de Beata Virgine* also provides two different Osanna sections, which is unusual for La Rue in general.[22] The latter bears a similarly rigid *cantus firmus* set as the Sanctus, thus forming a cyclic conclusion. One final detail can be observed in the Agnus Dei. Whereas the Agnus I shares a *cantus firmus* layout that imitates the initial motive of the chant in all four voices before the tenor takes over the contrapuntal basis, the Agnus II features a *cantus firmus* with a new melody that does not stem from the Agnus XVII. On the contrary, it can be suggested that the tenor follows the initial motive of a *Benedicamus domino* melody[23] twice, with a variant at the repetition, thus referring to the chant that traditionally closes the mass service.

The *Missa Assumpta est Maria* is dominated by the *cantus firmus* technique, the chant melody being firmly attached to the tenor. Instead of using the mixolydian mode on G, La Rue transposes it to C, thus creating one of his typical compositional features, a relatively low tessitura[24] (example 6). In order to form a cyclic connectivity, all movements of the mass except the Credo begin with a motto four bars in length. The chant is very prominently put in long note values in the tenor, never adopted by any other voice, which is uncharacteristic of La Rue's style. Melodic freedom or flexibility is rarely achieved, but it is found in the first part of the Gloria after the initial and before the final statement of the chant (bb. 10–43 and bb. 81–127). Surprisingly, the beginning of the Credo does not refer to the chant at all, but commences with two lengthy juxtapositions of duos (superius–contra, bb. 1–12, and bb. 20–23; tenor–bassus, bb. 12–20, and bb. 24–24) before a cadence is formed and the chant finally appears in the tenor in measure 32. After the *Qui cum Patre et Filio* section (bb. 112–116), the chant is suspended altogether until the end. La Rue's Ascension mass thus features a classic role model of the *cantus firmus* technique, focussing on both the hierarchical preponderance of the tenor and the use of a motto at the beginning

---

21 Only very rarely did La Rue incorporate the initial motive or fragments of the choral in these two intermediate movements.

22 Another exception is the *Missa de Septem doloribus*, which will be discussed below.

23 Cf. the melody given in *Liber Usualis*, 1964, p. 63. Transposed to F, the initial five pitches are virtually the same. As a matter of fact, although difficult to prove, this nonetheless suggests a possible influence on the shape of the final *cantus firmus* (bb. 21–38).

24 The melody can be found in the *Liber Usualis*, 1964, p. 1605. The author is generally well aware of the problems of using modern editions of chant to describe and localize melodic material for polyphony that was composed roughly 450 years ago. But an investigation has shown that the melodic features especially of Marian chants proved extremely stable, with but a few minor variations in melodic shapes between the *cantus firmus* of the polyphonic masses and the modern edition of the plainchant.

Marian Devotion as an Expression of Power

Note example 6a & 6b: *Missa Assumpta est Maria*

of nearly every movement. The differences and small variations in between, let alone the unique shape of the Credo, clearly demonstrate the flexibility with which La Rue could operate within the confined form of this compositional technique.

A different approach is found in the *Missa Ave Maria*, another example of *cantus firmus* structure, but this time, La Rue involves more voices than just the tenor to interact with the melody of the antiphon[25] (example 7). Instead of the chant being rigidly highlighted in the tenor voice, at the beginning of the Kyrie all the surrounding voices state the chant's melody in a three-voice imitation set (contra–superius–bassus) before the tenor commences in bar 10. After the initial imitation, the tenor takes over and shapes the rest of the Kyrie. A similar technique is applied in the Gloria, which begins with a lengthy duo of the upper voices before the tenor takes over in bar 10 (and the bassus follows the imitation in b. 12). The rest of the first section is melodically free, the *cantus firmus* reappearing only at the *Qui tollis* (bb. 68), which follows the same concept of chant presentation. Unique is the expansion of the Credo, which increases the number of voices to five and makes use of a rigid *cantus firmus* technique with long note values in the tenor interspersed with free-imitative sections. The beginning is featured with two lengthy bicinia that imitate the chant melody in upper and lower duos before the tenor primus provides a prolonged version of the chant from measure 29 onwards. The *Crucifixus* is again formed with an imitation set at the beginning, followed by the *cantus firmus* in long note values (bb. 90–110). The Sanctus, Osanna, and Agnus Dei follow the same model described above: pre-imitation of the chant motive, followed by the *cantus firmus* in the tenor voice.

---

25 The melody can be found in *Liber Usualis*, 1964, p. 1679, in the Dorian mode. La Rue transposes the chant from D to A. He also substitutes the audible cue of the rising fifth following the characteristic initium with a third (with dotted rhythm) and a whole-tone step (cf. bb. 3, 5, 10 and 12/13).

Note example 7a & 7b: *Missa Ave Maria*

Marian Devotion as an Expression of Power

The five-voiced *Missa Conceptio tua* is also a *cantus firmus* mass based on the Magnificat antiphon *Maternitas tua*.[26] The main melody is generally pre-imitated by the other voices until the tenor primus enters. This central voice dominates the structure in the Kyrie, Credo and Sanctus/Osanna. The whole melody is fully quoted throughout the Credo, which also shares long *cantus firmus* free sections with the Gloria. The Agnus Dei, by contrast, is of special importance since it is composed in a very different manner. To begin, the complete Agnus I is provided with a canon between tenor primus and secundus (*fuga in dyathessaron*) (DJu MS 5,[27] fol. 23v.). The Agnus II then changes the texture of the *cantus firmus* altogether by presenting the melody in the superius instead of in the tenor primus.[28] Thus, the chant, progressing in the note values of breves and longae, crowns the five-voice set with its melodic appearance in the highest register, concluding the mass with an acoustic climax.

The *Missa Ave sanctissima Maria* is one of the most palpable displays of La Rue's compositional craftsmanship, since it features a thorough canonic *tour de force* with 6 ex 3 voices. The contrapuntal technique clearly seems to be the focus of attention, with allusions to the motet of the same name that occur at the beginning and end of each movement and, as the centrepiece, in the Credo. It is genuinely one of La Rue's most complex masses, finding predecessors only in Ockeghem's *Missa prolationem* or Josquin's *Missa ad fugam*. Nevertheless, it also offers a twofold allusion to the virgin Mary, first by underlining the revered greetings to her in the title and in a self-referential hint to La Rue's own motet, *Ave sanctissima Maria*, and second, by the interpolation of an external melody in the Agnus II, where from bars 36 to 56, La Rue quotes the Marian prayer *O dulcis amica Dei, rosa vernans atque decora* in canon in the two upper voices. He thus opens an additional layer of Marian devotional poetry, interwoven with a slightly erotic demeanour.[29]

A different technique is applied in the *Missa Cum jucunditate*, which prominently features the use of a chant-derived ostinato that is consistently repeated in the tenor (examples 8a & 8b).[30] What is more, the six-note motive is ubiquitously present throughout the

---

26   The melody can be found in *Antiphonale Monasticum*, 1934, p. 1085, and in Kreider, 1974, p. 25.

27   This manuscript is dedicated to Frederick III, Elector of Saxony, and was most likely produced in the second half of the 16th century; cf. Kellman, 1999, p. 95.

28   This is also highlighted optically in the source D-Ju MS 5, where the superius is not only accompanied by the text of the Magnificat antiphon in red ink, but the initial of the voice features a singing face, thus clearly indicating the chant melody's appearance (D-Ju MS 5, fol. 24v., in the top left corner).

29   Despite the fact that the text can be tracked within the motet *O dulcis amica Dei* from Johannis Prioris in the St. Gallen manuscript CH-SGS MS 462, fol. 1r., there is no apparent congruency between the shape of the melodies to be found.

30   Without over interpreting numerical symbolism, if one counts all the repetitions of the melody in the tenor voice, the ostinato-motive and the full quotation of the chant in the Credo included, they add up to the surprisingly round number of one hundred repeats (16 in Kyrie, 28 in Gloria, 25 in Credo, 12 in Sanctus and 19 in Agnus Dei).

Note examples 8a & 8b: *Missa Cum jucunditate*

Note example 9: *Missa Cum jucunditate, Credo*

mass, being frequently pre-imitated in the other voices. The whole mass is thus dominated by a short motive consisting of a pendulum of a minor third and a following upper cambiata. La Rue adds significant changes to its texture by introducing a fifth voice in the Credo (example 9) and by quoting the full chant for the first time at the metaphorical lines *et ascendit in caelum* (Credo, bb. 89–117). The choral is repeated again at *unum baptisma* (bb. 145–164), and initiates the final *Amen*-melisma by splitting off and sequencing the initial motive. Another compositional feature worth mentioning occurs in the Sanctus, where the ostinato in the tenor is transformed into a descending sequence chain. The motive is sung five times while stepwise descending from d^1 to g (bb. 2–25). All these sequences are contrasted by different melodic material in the other voices. A last aspect is the formation of the final section of the mass itself. La Rue extracts the quintessential interval

Marian Devotion as an Expression of Power

of the swinging third and repeats it in a stepwise rising manner in superius and bassus (bb. 64–75).

One of La Rue's best researched masses is the *Missa de Septem doloribus*. Nonetheless, the provenance of its melodic material still lies in obscurity. Connected to the newly established Marian feast in the Low Countries and frequently transmitted in the Alamire codices, it is La Rue's only mass to which an entire manuscriptis dedicated: B-Br MS 215–216, which contains two masses for the Seven Sorrows (La Rue's mass and an anonymous one), Pipelare's motet *Memorare mater Christi*, and Josquin's *Stabat mater*, as well as plainchant material that apparently was newly composed to bolster the musical-liturgic foundation of the feast. This choir book was commissioned and owned by Margaret's important finance officer Charles de Clerc, as indicated by the depiction of his coat of arms.[31] It is the composer's longest, most lavishly executed mass setting. It is furnished with various *cantus firmi* whose texts are highlighted in red ink in the tenor primus. They are found through the whole mass, thus creating another referential layer of text in addition to the liturgy of the mass. All five sections commence with a mysterious, usually seven-note motive consisting of thirds and holding the highly diverse sections together (examples 10 and 11).[32] This "motto" appears alternatingly in the low and the high voice duos, and is divided in the Agnus between the contra and tenor secundus. The mass is also known for the famous interpolation of a quote of Josquin: In the second Osanna, La Rue inserts the prayer *O mater Dei, memento mei* in the tenor primus that stems directly from the last line of Josquin's famous motet *Ave Maria* (Sanctus, bb. 171–182) (example 12). This reference not only pays homage to an esteemed colleague, but also enhances the emphasis on the devotion of the Virgin Mary.

This investigation of both the origin of the material and its compositional application showcases the stylistic diversity and variety applied by La Rue to his group of Marian masses. A further step will examine the conveyance of Margaret's Marian agenda through the intentional dissemination of precious court manuscripts.

A Special Case of Transmission. *Missa O gloriosa domina/Margaretha* – The First Mass Composed for a Female Ruler?

Striking images depicting Marian devotion are found the miniatures in the precious choir books of the Alamire sources. The recipients of these valuable codices where carefully selected and included mostly members of the Habsburg family, but also the high aristocracy

---

31 See B-BR MS 215–216, fol. 2r., in the initial of the contra-tenor; cf. also Kellman, 1999, p. 67.

32 The seven notes of this emblematic motive might refer to the seven sorrows. It can be visually and audibly best perceived at the beginning of the Credo.

Note example 10: *Missa de Septem doloribus, Credo*

Note example 11: *Missa de Septem doloribus, Sanctus*

Note example 12: *Missa de Septem doloribus,*

of Europe. The books themselves were probably only rarely displayed, and only to distinguished visitors, diplomats, or family members. Nonetheless, the miniatures created a "semi-public space" through their rich image programmes, in which social status, claims to rulership, and religious devotion were deliberately communicated to the beholder.

La Rue's mass *O gloriosa domina/Margaretha* might be the first composition that was dedicated to a female ruler.[33] The title of the Marian mass directly addresses Margaret herself, but the transmission of the composition poses some intricate problems. First, it must be stated that in its transmission, *O gloriosa domina* was chronologically the first title used for the mass.[34] The four surviving sources of the mass display the seemingly interchangeable titles of *domina* and *Margaretha*, thus putting Margaret at the highest level of the hierarchy. She is referred to both by name and social function (*domina*), and thus linked to the devotional service of a Marian mass. Despite all efforts to locate the melody of the hymn in earlier sources, La Rue's original material has not been found.[35] Therefore, one

---

33 Andrea Ammendola argues that despite the reference in the title, there is no compositional connection to Margaret and therefore excludes the mass from the group of masses dedicated to rulers: "Da […] die Widmungsträgerin nicht Teil der Komposition ist, zählen diese Werke [additionally mentioned are Champion's *Missa Ducis Saxoniae* and Gombert's *Missa A la Incoronation*, D.T.] nicht zum engeren Kreis der Herrschermessen" (2013, p. 251).

34 Ammendola, 2010, p. 74, and Meconi, 2003, p. 130.

35 The hymn's melodic development in the tenor of La Rue's mass is vague at best, since it only follows

Marian Devotion as an Expression of Power

must argue that the composition is devoid of any *cantus firmus* framework mirroring La Rue's creative approach to his other Marian masses.[36] When we look at the four main sources transmitting the mass within the corpus of the Alamire scriptorium, we can add some further thoughts about the question of whether it represents a Marian programme or is dedicated to Margaret as La Rue's patroness and regent. Jozef Robijns has rightfully suggested that the mass may not necessarily be dedicated to a worldly ruler at all, but be addressing the namesake saint instead (1954, p. 89).[37] That Saint Margaret was revered by Margaret of Austria is illustrated by precious items in her personal collection: She owned a carefully crafted initial "M" carved from boxwood featuring depictions of several key moments in the life of the saint.[38] In addition, the possessions of the regent included "various images of the saint, for example in paintings, on liturgical textiles and on jewellery" (Eichberger, 2005, p. 180). Thus, the saint was very important at the court of Mechelen and so it is likely that the mass was composed for her feast day, July 20. Nonetheless, the personal attachment to Margaret becomes plain in the manuscript V-CVbav MS Capp. Sist 36, a gift for the music-loving Pope Leo X (Giovanni de Medici). The mass is transmitted on fols. 50v.–65r. and bears the name of the composer in capital letters as well as the title in red ink in the tenor: "O gloriosa margaretha cristum pro nobis exora". Moreover, the initial of the contra-tenor (fol. 51r.) bears the crest of Margaret of Austria: a lavishly decorated rhombus on a bright green basis with the coat of arms of the duchy of Savoy on the left and the combined heraldry of Habsburg-Burgundy on the right. Since this manuscript is devoid of any other iconography pointing towards Saint Margaret, the work's identification with the ruler Margaret of Austria becomes more likely. Meconi also hints at this possibility by stating that the mass could have been either performed on the patron's feast day, "or at any time that the chapel wished to pay special homage to their acting ruler" (Meconi, 2003, p. 130). But the Vatican source is the only transmission in which we can clearly distinguish this political context. D-Ju MS 5, which intriguingly shows the same template[39] as the above-mentioned source, exchanges the coat of arms with another

---

the course of a descending movement followed by an ascending one, this evening out and leading to a cadence.

36 The possibility of the use of solmisation leads to no result either; the corresponding pitches of Mar-ga-re-tha (la – la – re – la) are not found in the composition, also not as part of the quart-pendulum shaping the outline of the main melody.

37 He also refers to La Rue's masses for the saints Antonius, Hiob, and Anna, giving one to consider, "dat we dit werk niet aantreffen in de prachtige codices uit Brussel of Mechelen, welke op last van Margaretha von Oostenrijk werden uitgevoerd" (that we do not find this work in the magnificent codices of Brussels and Mechelen, which were prepared at the behest of Margaret of Austria).

38 An image of the initial can be seen in the catalogue of Eichberger, 2005, p. 181.

39 The Kyrie initial consists of the same template with another colouring. Also, the style of the grotesques and the fact that the bassus initial provides two faces, is virtually identical.

grotesque, thus eliminating any political reading. In accordance with this, the text, given in all four voices in red ink, provides the variant *O gloriosa domina*, expanding the tenor with the hymn-text *supra excelsa sidera*. Most frustrating for any further search for a political meaning or aspects of self-representation of Margaret is the Spanish source from the Montserrat monastery E-MO MS 773. The manuscript is heavily mutilated, virtually all iconography has been cut out, making a contextualized political reading impossible. Only the vast chunks of missing parchment offer the possibility that the choir book contained a huge intentionally encrypted display of a distinct message. Whether it featured a depiction of the namesake patron saint or of Margaret herself in combination with the Virgin Mary or, again, her coat of arms is impossible to guess. The title of the mass reads "O gloriosa margareta cr[istu]m p[ro] nobis exora", thus following the version of the Vatican source. The last codex, conserved in I-Sub 248, was compiled at a later date and is on paper. It contains no iconography at all, transmitting only the music. It provides the title ascription in red ink "Missa O gloriosa d[omi]na sup[ra] excessa sidera. Rue", thus following the version of the Jena manuscript (D-Ju MS 5). The later print *Missae tredecim quatuor vocum a praestantiss. Artificib. Compositiae* from Nürnberg (1539) does not lead us any further either: The title of La Rue's mass is only given with the two words *O gloriosa*, thus completely eliminating any possible intentional ascription to Margaret (Otto, 1539).[40]

Conclusion

The Marian devotion of Margaret of Austria was a typical phenomenon of the time she lived in. It served both as an expression of her strong private desire for personal devotion and as a means of public representation and self-portrayal. In her political function, Margaret equalled the most vital functional aspect of Mary by serving as an advocate, an intermediary between the population and the emperor. Just as Mary was seen as taking the pleas of the devout to her son in heaven, Margaret took care of the problems and demands of her subjects by negotiating with either her father Maximilian I or her nephew Charles V. Politically, the public display of Marian devotion served Margaret to legitimate her regency. Indeed, she is thus depicted as one of the most important members of the Habsburg family. Thus Margaret herself, who remained childless, was transformed in the public imagination into a devout, pious, and responsible mother of her people, a worldly *mediatrix* of the population of the Habsburg-Burgundian Low Countries. A vital part in this conveyed self-image was the commission of Marian music, a practice that distin-

---

40 This intricate anthology of older masses from around 1500 contains works by Obrecht, Josquin, Brumel, Isaac, and La Rue, including the latter's *Missae Cum jucunditate*, *O gloriosa* and *De S. Antonio*.

guished Margaret of Austria from other female rulers and regents of her time. Within her musical patronage no one stands out like Pierre de la Rue with regard to compositional output. His masses transmitted in the Alamire codices, including the lavish execution and iconographical embellishment of these choir books, highlight this productive cooperation between the patron and her protégé in a most refined manner of self-representation.

Bibliography

Manuscripts

GB-Lbl Add. MS. 34294. London, British Library, *Sforza Book of Hours*, ca. 1486–1520.
B-Br MS 215–216. Brussels, Bibliothèque royale de Belgique, ca. 1512–1526.
B-Br MS 228. Brussels, Bibliothèque royale de belgique, ca. 1516–1523.
CH-SGS MS 462. St. Gallen, Stiftsbibliothek, ca. 1510–1520.
D-Ju MS 5. Jena, Thüringer Universitäts- und Landesbibliothek, ca. 1512–1521.
E-MO MS 773. Montserrat, Biblioteca del Monestir, ca. 1508–1516.
V-CV bav MS Capp. Sist 36. Vatikan, Biblioteca Apostolica Caticana, ca. 1513–1521.

Printed Sources and Source Editions

Antiphonale Monasticum (1934). Desclée.
Schlager, K. (Ed.) (1985). *Antiphonale Pataviense* (Wien 1519). Faksimile. Bärenreiter.
Chazaud, M. A. (1874). *Les enseigements d'Anne de France à sa fille Susanne de Bourbon*. C. Desrosiers.
Liber Usualis (1964). Desclée & Socii.
Otto, J. (1539). *Missae Tredecim Quatuor Vocum A Praestantiss: Artificib: Compositae*. H. Formschneider (D-Ju, Bibliotheca Electoralis, Konvolut Sign. 4 Mus.6c).

Scholarly Literature

Ammendola, A. (2013). *Polyphone Herrschermessen (1500–1650). Kontext und Symbolizität*. V&R Unipress.
Ammendola, A. (2010). Zwischen musikalischer Tradition und Widmung: Polyphone Herrschermessen für Angehörige des Hauses Habsburg. In J. Heidrich (Ed.), *TroJa 8. Trossinger Jahrbuch für Renaissancemusik (2008/2009): Die Habsburger und die Niederlande. Musik und Politik um 1500* (pp. 71–88). Bärenreiter.
Bäumer, R. & Scheffczykn, L. (1988–1994). *Marienlexikon*, vol. 1–6. EOS-Verlag.

Blockmans, W. & Prevenier, W. (1999). *The Promised Lands: The Low Countries under Burgundian Rule, 1369–1530*, ed. by E. Peters, transl. by L. Fackelmans. University of Pennsylvania Press.

Cluzel, J. (2002). *Anne de France. Fille de Louis XI, duchesse de Bourbon*. Fayard.

Eichberger, D. (2005). *Women of Distinction. Margaret of York & Margaret of Austria*. Brepols Publishers.

Eichberger, D. (2002). *Leben mit Kunst. Wirken durch Kunst: Sammelwesen und Hofkunst unter Margarete von Österreich, Regentin der Niederlande*. Brepols Publishers.

Harper, J. (1991). *The Forms and Orders of Western Liturgy from the Tenth to the Eighteenth Century: A Historical Introduction and Guide for Students and Musicians*. Clarendon Press.

Jounel, P. (1987). The Veneration of Mary. In A. G. Martimort (Ed.), *The Church at Prayer: Introduction to the Liturgy* (pp. 130–156). Liturgical Press.

Kellman, H. (Ed.) (1999). *The Treasury of Petrus Alamire. Music and Art in Flemish Court Manuscripts 1500–1535*. Ludion Editions.

Kreider, J. E. (1974). *The Masses for Five and Six Voices by Pierre de la Rue* [Doctoral dissertation, Indiana University].

Lambrecht, J. (1987). *Das "Heidelberger Kapellinventar" von 1544 (Codex Pal. Germ. 318). Edition und Kommentar*, vol 1. Heidelberg Bibliotheksschriften.

Liss, P. K. (2004). *Isabel the Queen: Life and Times*. University of Pennsylvania Press.

Meconi, H. (2003). *Pierre de la Rue and Musical Life at the Habsburg-Burgundian Court*. Oxford University Press.

Picker, M. (1965). *The Chanson albums of Marguerite of Austria*. University of California Press.

Robijns, J. (1954). *Pierre de la Rue (circa 1460–1518). Een bio-bibliographische Studie*. Universiteit te Leuven.

Rothenberg, D. J. (2011). *The Flower of Paradise. Marian Devotion and Secular Song in Medieval and Renaissance Music*. Oxford University Press.

Schmid, B. (1988). *Der Gloria-Tropus Spiritus et alme bis zur Mitte des 15. Jahrhunderts*. Hans Schneider.

Snow, E. (2010). *The Lady of Sorrows. Music, Devotion, and Politics in the Burgundian-Habsburg Netherlands* [Doctoral dissertation, Princeton University].

Soisson, J.-P. (2002). *Marguerite – Princesse du Bourgogne*. Grasset & Fasquelle.

Strohm, R. (2005). *The Rise of European Music, 1380–1500*. Cambridge University Press.

Tamussino, U. (1995). *Margarete von Österreich. Diplomatin der Renaissance*. Verlag Styria.

Thelen, E. & McDonald, G. (2016). The feast of the Seven Sorrows of the Virgin. Piety, politics and plainchant at the Burgundian-Habsburg court. *Early Music History* 35, 261–307.

Weightman, C. (1989). *Margaret of York: Duchess of Burgundy 1446–1503*. Sutton.

Weissberger, B. F. (2008). Introduction. Questioning the Queen, Now and Then. In B. F. Weissberger (Ed.), *Queen Isabel I of Castile. Power, Patronage, Persona* (pp. XI–XXIV). Tamesis Books.

Welzel, B. (2005). Widowhood: Margaret of York and Margaret of Austria. In. B. Eichberger (Ed.), *Women of Distinction* (p. 103–113). Brepols Publishers.

Wiesenfeldt, C. (2024, forthcoming). Composing Compassion. Pierre de La Rue's "Missa de Septem Doloribus". In D. Burn, H. Meconi & C. Wiesenfeldt (Eds.), *Pierre de la Rue and Music at the Habsburg-Burgundian Court*. Brepols Publishers.

Wiesenfeldt, C. (2012). *Majestas Mariae. Studien zu marianischen Choralordinarien des 16. Jahrhunderts*. Franz Steiner Verlag.

Wiesenfeldt, C. (2010). "Mediatrix nostra" – "Unsere Vermittlerin". Marianische Topoi in Pierre de la Rues Messen für Margarete von Österreich. In J. Heidrich (Ed.), *TroJa 8. Trossinger Jahrbuch für Renaissancemusik (2008/2009): Die Habsburger und die Niederlande. Musik und Politik um 1500* (pp. 143–160). Bärenreiter.

Wiesenfeldt, C. (2008). "Majestas Mariae" als musikgeschichtliches Phänomen? Einflüsse der Marienverehrung auf die Messe des 16. Jahrhunderts. *Archiv Für Musikwissenschaft* 65(2), 103–120.

Winker, E. (1966). *Margarete von Österreich. Grande Dame der Renaissance*. Verlag Georg D. W. Callwey.

The Soundscape of the Imperial Diet in the Age of Emperor Maximilian I*

Moritz Kelber

Imperial Diets as a Subject for Musicology

The image of pre-modern music is strongly influenced by the idea of topographically defined spaces. This also applies to research on early modern soundscapes in the field of musicology. When investigating the sound of late medieval Bruges or the soundscapes in Counter-Reformation Bavaria, we assume that the topographical space is a central aspect for creating meaning (Strohm, 1990; Fisher, 2004). The author of this text is by no means an exception, since his dissertation was on the music at the Augsburg Imperial Diets (or *Reichstage*) of the 16th century. Restricting the viewpoint to Augsburg seemed a sensible means for limiting the research subject. However, when looking at the ephemeral sound of the *Reichstag* in the 16th century, it becomes clear that topographical spaces are by no means the only categories for mapping soundscapes of the past.

A 16th-century Imperial Diet was a state of emergency, sometimes lasting months, during which the tectonics of courtly and urban life changed fundamentally, and with it, also the tectonics of musical life (Aulinger, 1980; Kohler, 1987). Generally speaking, Imperial Diets were gatherings of all the estates of the Holy Roman Empire (Moraw, 1980) at which the emperor (or king), the electors, princes and counts, cardinals, bishops, abbots, and the envoys of the imperial cities discussed important political questions like taxation or the wars against France or the Ottoman Empire. Before the 17th century, when the *Immerwährende Reichstag* met in Regensburg (Meixner, 2008), meetings were held in various cities of the Empire, for example in Nuremberg, Regensburg, or Speyer. The princes travelled to an Imperial Diet accompanied by numerous servants, among them secretaries, artists, and often musicians (Aulinger, 1987). There are no exact numbers of how many singers and instrumentalists visited an average *Reichstag*. Judging from the extant sources, however, it is possible to assume that it was a considerable number. The higher the rank of

---

* This paper is based on the author's dissertation, which was published in German: Kelber, 2018.

a dignitary was inside the imperial hierarchy, the bigger was his musical entourage. This can be illustrated by records from the Bavarian court about the preparations for the Diet in 1594. When Duke Wilhelm V decided to cancel his trip to Regensburg and sent his son instead, the court sent only half of the initially planned number of musicians (Kelber, forthcoming). Meetings of the imperial estates shaped the politics of the Holy Roman Empire as early as the Middle Ages. The term *Reichstag* was first used in connection with the Diet in 1495 in Worms and thus was not established until the reign of Maximilian I (Moraw, 1995). Under his leadership, around 13 Diets were held in various cities. Augsburg and the city of Worms, where Maximilian's first Imperial Diet as Roman king was held in 1495, stand out as particularly frequent meeting places of this period (Kelber, 2018, p. 31).

In various fields and disciplines, recent scholarship has outlined that sound and music must be considered important tools for creating meaning in the context of political events (Missfelder, 2012; Morat, 2010; Leopold, 2011; Voigt, 2008). Thus, this chapter is concerned with more than charting the soundscape of the Imperial Diet under Emperor Maximilian I, since it is probably self-evident that the Imperial Diet is a prime example of a "Soundscape of Power" (Heidrich, 2010). The main goal is to examine the structural interweaving of various elements of this soundscape and to reveal mechanisms of how power was represented and possibly also exercised through sound. To this end, four vital elements of the *Reichstag* will be discussed. In a first step, imperial entries – a practice that is generally assigned to the sphere of ceremonial – will be juxtaposed with dance, which many scholars tend to place in the realm of a political event's festive framework (Kelber, 2018, pp. 15–16). After that, the sound design of enfeoffment ceremonies shall be examined together with that of the many tournaments held during the Imperial Diets of the first two decades of the 16th century. The aim is to draw a picture of the *Reichstag* as a complex soundscape of power, shaped by topographical locations as well as by ephemeral mechanisms determined by traditions and rituals.

Entries and Dance

The entries of an emperor, king, or an important prince were ceremonial highlights of every Imperial Diet (Johanek & Lampen, 2009). Due to the presence and active participation of numerous imperial princes, these processions were particularly glamorous in the context of a *Reichstag* (Aulinger, 1980, pp. 193–199). The entry ceremony, which was also called *Adventus*, united various traditions, each of which had its own "dimension of meaning" (Rudolph, 2011, p. 80). Ideas of processions in Greek and Roman antiquity mingled with the image of the biblical entry of Christ into Jerusalem. Furthermore, the processions of newly elected popes in Rome were an important model for many local entry practices (Kantorowicz, 1944).

Late medieval and early modern entries were resounding events. Gun salutes, the ringing of bells, the playing of trumpeters and minstrels, and the singing of the clergy were natural components of these elaborate celebrations (Kelber, 2018, pp. 84–100). Dieter Mertens speaks of the "obligatory noise" without which no prince could appear anywhere in a suitable manner (Mertens, 1998, p. 47). The historian thus emphasizes the sheer loudness of these events. In the case of the entry of an emperor or a king, the ritual meant nothing less than his assumption of power, and the sound of bells and trumpets served, among other things, to legitimize this legal act. However, the splendour of sound was by no means limited to volume during entry ceremonies. Minstrels and singers sounded music on roadsides during the processions, which often lasted several hours. Music was not a mere accompaniment; it served "to structure time" as well as "to elaborate content" (Bölling, 2009, p. 248). Entries in the context of an Imperial Diet involved many different groups of people. In addition to the secular and ecclesiastical dignitaries and their entourages, the official representatives of the hosting city were involved. Several thousand people marched in long processions through narrow streets. Not only the Empire but also the host city "presented itself as a community" (Schweers, 2009, p. 39). This sprawling self-portrayal has led the historian Gerrit Jasper Schenk to characterize imperial entries as a form of theatre (Schenk, 2003, p. 40).

Around 1500, we discover a great variety of festive and ceremonial cultures throughout Europe. Fuelled by the popularity of Francesco Petrarca's *Trionfi*, in Italy there was a quite elaborate culture for glamorous processions as early as the 15th century (Cummings, 1992). While the traditions in Rome, the *joyeuses entrées* in the Netherlands, or the magnificent *entrées solennelles* in France have already been studied with regard to music (Tammen, 2008; Chartrou, 1928; Fenlon, 2004), this aspect has been largely neglected so far for the ceremonial of the Holy Roman Empire (Bölling, 2009). The reason for this deficit is presumably not only a lack of scholarly interest or the absence of sources. It is probably also due to the rather sober appearance of the Empire's ceremonial – especially in contrast to other regions of the continent. Typical elements of the *joyeuses entrées* such as fireworks or *tableaux vivants* are only documented towards the middle of the 16th century. Thus, scholars hoping for reports of imperial processions that approach the splendour of festivals in other parts of Europe are likely to be disappointed. However, the lack of "artistic" splendour certainly does not mean that the imperial ceremonial was not characterized by a remarkable richness of acoustic expressions.

Entries in the age of Maximilian were usually divided into two main parts. During the first secular part of the procession the emperor was welcomed outside the city by princes and local dignitaries and then led into the town in a large procession. This part was acoustically shaped by the playing of the emperor's trumpeters and those of the imperial princes, as well as gun salutes, bell ringing, and the cheering of the people at the roadside. The second (ecclesiastical) section of the ceremonial, in which the dignitary was led to the main church for a concluding service by the urban clergy, was additionally accompanied by the singing of liturgical music, for which each diocese had its own regime. The trumpeters of the imperial princes were distributed throughout the procession, while the imperial court music, which always provided the largest number of musicians, usually rode in close proximity to their lord (Kelber, 2018, pp. 84–100).

> Item am 25. tag aprilis, was am sontag acht tag nach oster, gen der nacht umb siben, reit ein der römisch kaiser Friedrich. Man rit im entgegen bis für sant Servaci, dann er kam von Saltzpurg her, […]. [A]lso het man ain kostlichen weiten himel [Baldachin] gemacht, darinn das reich gemalt, mit vergulten standen. Den himel trugen ob dem kaiser vier von räten, […]. [A]m ersten raiten vil grafen, ritter und edel, darnach 14 trummeter, die pliesen; darnach des kaisers sun, hertzog Maximilian, […] (Hegel, 1892, pp. 237–238).

> Item: on 25 April, which was a Sunday eight days after Easter, at about seven o'clock in the evening, the Roman emperor Frederick rode in. One rode to meet him in front of St. Servatius, because he came from the direction of Salzburg. […] For this occasion, a beautiful canopy was made with golden carrying rods, in which the imperial eagle was worked in. This canopy was carried above the emperor by four members of the city council. […] First rode many counts, knights, and nobles, behind them 14 trumpeters playing their instruments. Then [came] the emperor's son, Duke Maximilian, […].[1]

This description of the entry of Emperor Frederick III and his son Maximilian into Augsburg in the context of a *Hoftag* gathering in 1473 already shows the pattern that would characterize the chronicles of the Imperial Diets for decades to come, not only in Augsburg but throughout the Empire. The Augsburg patrician Hektor Mülich here describes 14 trumpeters riding directly in front of Archduke Maximilian. The mention of the number and the direct proximity of the musicians to their employer can even be found in texts that are otherwise rather sparse with descriptions of acoustic impressions. Although a ruler's procession was certainly a soundscape co-created by numerous actors, the emphasis on the acoustic dominance of the emperor in many contemporary accounts is quite clear. After all, the emperor took possession of the Reichstag's venue for the duration of the event, a process I have called "klangliche Inbesitznahme" or "acoustic appropriation" (Kelber, 2018, p. 209). It seems, however, to be less about the actual volume of the performance and more

---

1   Unless indicated otherwise, the translations in this chapter are by the author.

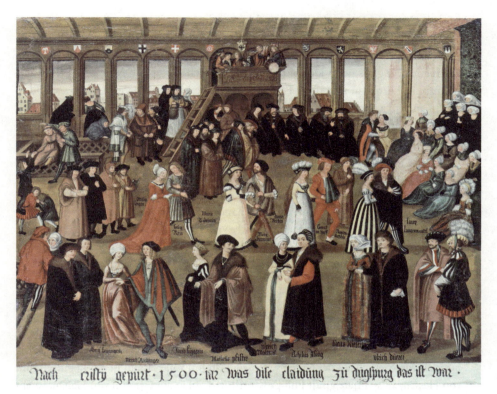

Fig. 1: Anonymous, *Augsburger Tanzbild*, c. 1500.

about a symbolic (numerical) superiority, for the playing of the trumpeters and the drumming of the timpanists must have been rather difficult to hear amid the roar of the salutes and the ringing of bells.

The courtly life of the late Middle Ages and the early modern period was shaped by banquets and balls. Maximilian and his court celebrated frequently and lavishly. Furthermore, these festivities were also extensively documented in the emperor's representational writings (Fink, 1992). Augsburg was one of his favourite cities and one may assume that he knew the local dance hall very well. One important documentation of the local dancing culture is the so-called *Augsburger Tanzbild* from the time around 1500 (Fig. 1). It shows citizens at some form of processional dance. The dancers, whose names are explicitly given in the picture, can almost all be situated in the Augsburg upper class (Kelber, 2019). The composition of the society framing the dance is less clear-cut. Some scholars think they can identify Bianca Maria Sforza, Maximilian's wife, and her entourage on the tribune at the right edge of the picture (Habich, 1911). Indeed, the queen was present in Augsburg in

1500 for the Imperial Diet, which makes this assumption at least plausible. For the topic at hand, however, the picture is more significant as a document of the symbolic importance of dancing in the time of Maximilian. Although it only hints at actual contemporary dance practices, it gives us an idea of the processional character of a *basse danse*, the dominant dance in Europe at that time. Festivals like that embodied the idea of "to see and to be seen" – and, to a certain extent, the idea of "to hear and to be heard".

Physical distance played an important role in all pre-modern festive cultures. In courtly life, a person's rank was expressed by their distance from the highest-ranking personality (Kelber, 2018, p. 125): The closer a duke, bishop, or patrician rode to an emperor during a procession, the higher was his position in the hierarchy of the Empire (Schenk, 2003, p. 306; Rudolph, 2011, p. 105). Dancing was one of the most intense forms of physical proximity in public, indeed, the touching of hands could establish a special form of connection between political actors. A particularly vivid example of the focus on order and hierarchy can be found in Andreas Zayner's chronicle of the Imperial Diet of Cologne in 1505. He describes a magnificent banquet at the meeting of the estates, which was immediately followed by a ball.

> Item zu dem banket sind ob 1000 essen geben und ganz zierlich zugericht und sein gesessen bey zway stunden. Und and kgl. Mt. tafel ist gesessen die H[erzo]gin. von Lunenburg an ir B[ischo]f von Trier K[ur]f[ürst], darnach ain G[rä]fin von Waldeck, an sie H[erzo]g Fridrich von Sachsen, zu der linken seiten ain G[rä]fin von Nassau, ist ain L[and]g[rä]fin von Hessen, an sy Pf[alz]g[ra]f Philips K[ur]f[ürst], an in ain G[rä]fin von Hanau, ist ain M[ark]g[rä]fin von Baden, an sy M[ark]g[raf] Joachim K[ur]f[ürst] etc. Dargegen uber M[ark]g[ra]f Fridrich, H[erzö]g[e] von Brauensweig, Wirtenberg, Hessen, und alwegen ain frau zwischen in.
>
> Den ersten tanz hat ir k[öni]gl[ich] M[ajes]t[ät] mit der H[erzo]gin von Lunenburg, den andern der B[ischo]f von Trier mit der von Nassau, den dritten tanz M[ark]g[ra]f. Joachim mit der G[rä]fin. von Hanau, den vierden H[erzo]g. Fridrich von Sachsen, und hat solche banket gewert drey or gen tag (Heil, 2008, p. 1202).

> Item: about 1,000 meals were served at the banquet and were arranged very nicely, and they sat for two hours. And at the king's table sat the Duchess of Lüneburg, next to her the Bishop and Elector of Trier; then a Countess of Waldeck, next to her Duke Frederick of Saxony; on the left side a Countess of Nassau, who is a Landgravine of Hesse, next to her Elector Philip (of the Palatinate); next to him a Countess of Hanau, who is a Margravine of Baden, next to her, Elector Joachim (of Brandenburg), etc. Opposite, Margrave Friedrich, the Dukes of Brunswick, Württemberg, Hesse, and always a woman between them.
>
> The first dance was danced by the king with the Duchess of Lüneburg, the second by the

Bishop of Trier with the [Countess] of Nassau, the third by Margrave Joachim with the Countess of Hanau, the fourth by Duke Friedrich of Saxony. And the banquet lasted until five o'clock in the morning.

Detailed lists of dance couples and their order that can be found throughout the chronicles of the 16th century. This may seem obsessive at first glance, however, these lists underline the ceremonial character of courtly dancing. Since mixed-sex dancing enjoyed great popularity in late medieval and early modern Europe, dancing – unlike many other court rituals and ceremonies – required the involvement of women. Female courtiers thus became part of courtly representation and political action. Reports of dance festivities are often the only evidence of the presence of women in the context of important political events (Kelber, 2018, pp. 124–131). As can be seen from the cited chronicle from 1505, in which the women, unlike the men, are only mentioned by their title but not by name, the court ladies and burgesses were by no means self-determining actors on the stage of the dance hall. They were, on the contrary, mere instruments of political influence (McManus, 2002, p. 55). An anecdote from the Reichstag in 1518 seems instructive in this context: In a letter to his city council, a Regensburg envoy complains that it was easier (for a man) to get a hearing at the imperial court if he had pretty daughters than through diplomatic efforts (Gemeiner, 1824, p. 330, fn. 641).

The idea of *acoustic appropriation* (klangliche Inbesitznahme) can help to understand early modern dance culture. In 1504, Maximilian was again in Augsburg for a meeting that sought to settle the Bavarian succession dispute. This so-called *Schiedstag* (a meeting dealing with the resolution of a specific conflict) was marked by exuberant festivities. On 31 January 1504, it was not Maximilian himself but Duchess Kunigunde of Austria, Maximilian's sister and the wife of Bavarian Duke Albrecht IV, who had invited the guests to the city's dance hall. Numerous dignitaries present at the *Schiedstag* had accepted her invitation.

> Item am Dornstag jn der nacht hatt er ain kostlich momerei gehapt, daby ist sein schwester die hertzogin und jr tochtern drei und etliche fürsten und vil vom adel gewesen uff dem tantzhuss, da ist m. h. king komen wol mit 70 personen bj den 40 spilleuten all in puren kleiden geklait und sunst by 30 person auch in purn clait geklait, darunder send 6 junckfrowen und frowen burgerin gewessen und haben ain buren tantz gehabt, darnach haben sie die puren claiden abgethon und ist der king selb jn gulden stuck geclait gewesen und die sechs frowen ouch in rot karmesin atlas mit gulden stuck verbrent kostlich geklait und haben uff welsch getantz und luten geschlagen und ander saitenspiel gesungen [...] (Klüpfel, 1846, p. 498).

Item: on Thursday night, he held a magnificent mummery. His sister the duchess, and three of her daughters and several princes and many of the nobility were in the dance hall. The king came with about 70 people, 40 of whom were minstrels, all dressed in peasant clothes, and the other 30 were also dressed in peasant clothes – including 6 young women and burgesses – who danced a peasant dance. They then took off their peasant dresses. The king himself wore a golden brocade and the six women were splendidly dressed in crimson atlas, which was also interwoven with golden brocade, and they danced in Italian, played the lute, and sang to other stringed instruments.

Maximilian, who apparently was quite eager to celebrate, arrived somewhat late. Nevertheless, he made a roaring entrance, for he was accompanied by around 70 people. If the chronicle of the envoy of the city of Ulm is correct, he entourage included a total of 40 minstrels, all dressed as peasants. The peasant dance that followed was probably quite frivolous by courtly standards – all legitimized by the masquerade (Schnitzer, 1999, pp. 186–189). For a brief moment, the rigid corset of courtly etiquette was stripped away, only to be underlined all the more clearly a short time later. Beneath their peasant clothing, Maximilian and his companions wore a most splendid wardrobe. The number of 40 minstrels mentioned by the Ulm chronicler may reflect a sound impression rather than an exact number. Nevertheless, the king's appearance at his sister's party must be described as noisy. Indeed, on that evening, he took acoustic control of the Augsburg dance house. To grasp the political dimension of Maximilian's entrance, the concept of acoustic appropriation becomes helpful. Acoustic dominance of a space was important not only during processions, but also during dance festivals. Thus, the intentional design of a soundscape was one of the key instruments in the toolbox of symbolic communication.[2]

Enfeoffments and Tournaments

Another main pillar of the imperial ceremonial was the festive bestowal of a fief by the emperor or king (Kelber, 2018, pp. 107–114). These enfeoffments, which were frequently framed by lavish festivities, were the highlights of many Imperial Diets. During the reign of Maximilian, numerous acts of investiture took place in the open air (these are referred to as flag-enfeoffments). At these, the emperor presented himself to the imperial public as the undisputed sovereign. A splendid and expensive ceremony also promised glory and attention to the recipient of a fief. There is extensive evidence of the sound design of enfeoffments in the late Middle Ages from both textual and pictorial sources (Kelber, 2018,

---

2   For the concept of "symbolic communication", see Stollberg-Rilinger, 2008.

p. 112). However, descriptions of enfeoffments in the age of Maximilian hardly mention more than the presence of musicians. A chronicle of the 1505 Imperial Diet in Cologne is a good example of the lack of detailed descriptions from that period. It merely documents the trumpeters' participation.

> An dem tag umb drey or nach mittag ist kgl. Mt. auf das tantzhaus komen, mit im all. Ff. mit pfaffen, und turnierten ganz zierlich. Haben sich die Kff., nemlich [...], all in irn abit anton und sind zu dem stal [= Stuhl], der mit guldin tuchen bedeckt gewesen gangen. Hat sich kgl. Mt. auch anton, ain ksl. cron aufgehapt und im die Kff. all entgegen. Damit die trumater aufplasen, hat Mgf. Fridrich kgl. Mt. das zepter und swert vorgetragen, also hat sich kgl. Mt. niedergesetzt und die Kff. neben ir Mt., und die andern Ff. des Reichs sind nachainander gestanden und die kgl. Mt. den nachfolgendenden Ff. gelihen (Heil, 2008, p. 120).
>
> That day at three o'clock in the afternoon the king came to the dance hall, together with all the ecclesiastical and secular princes, who held a beautiful tournament. Then the electors put on their robes and went to the throne, which was covered with golden cloths. The king also put on [his robe] – he was wearing an imperial crown – and the electors all went to meet him. When the trumpeters blew, Margrave Frederick [of Brandenburg] carried his sceptre and sword ahead of the king. So, the king sat down [on the throne] and the electors sat next to their majesty, and the other princes of the Empire stood one behind the other and the king conferred the fief on the following princes.

From the second half of the 16th century, however, there are more elaborate reports of enfeoffments – at a time in which enfeoffments in the open air had already become an exception (Kelber, 2018, pp. 341–352). These allow some conclusions about the acoustic design of the rituals in the *aetas Maximilianea*. Figure 2 shows a woodcut from 1566 depicting a feudal ceremony at the Imperial Diet of Augsburg (Steinberg, 1934). The illustration was created as an addition to one of the extensive printed reports documenting the event (Francolin, 1566a). Enfeoffments had become a media event in the course of the century (Rudolph, 2011, pp. 308–324). They were documented extensively in books that list the participants and describe every chapter of the ritual.[3] The printed image shows the Weinmarkt, the square between the Fugger palaces, and the now-demolished Tanzhaus as it probably appeared in Maximilian I's time.

---

3   For the 1566 enfeoffments, see Francolin, 1566 and 1567; Mameranus, 1566.

Fig. 2: *Enfeoffment at the Weinmarkt in Augsburg.*

A closer look at the picture and in the extant chronicles reveals that the imperial trumpeters were placed on the huge wooden throne that was built for the enfeoffments which took place during the Diet. This display of the court musicians on a balcony directly above the emperor is of great symbolic power and reminds us of ephemeral festive architecture in other parts of Europe. However, during an enfeoffment, an emperor's highly decorated throne – unlike other ephemeral festive structures – was not only important for a few minutes during an entry procession, but was the absolute centre of attention for several hours. First and foremost, the presence of the trumpeters in the immediate vicinity of the emperor was the sounding representation of secular and military power. As mentioned elsewhere, this special positioning of the imperial court musicians as an "audible crown" – because of its almost altar-like appearance – had a sacral component, underlining as well the sovereign's God-given power as a ruler (Kelber, 2018, p. 348). A prince who received a fief – in our 1566 example, the Saxon Elector August – had to take care to have an appropriate acoustic representation as well. For the Augsburg celebrations, the acoustic counterpart to the imperial court music was formed by no fewer than 25 mounted trumpeters, recruited from both the Elector's retinue and other imperial princes (Kelber, 2018, p. 349).

Enfeoffments were complicated ceremonies in which an elector or duke, accompanied by his entourage, circled an emperor's throne several times on horseback. The ritual was probably intended to resemble a military manoeuvre, with the trumpeters' signals playing an important coordinating role in the narrow streets of a city, filled with large numbers of people. From the almost protocol-like reports of 1566, it becomes clear that every part of the ceremony was accompanied by at least one signal or fanfare. For the citizens present, the acoustic interplay between the two parties must have been a special experience: The playing of the court trumpeters was here no longer just an abstract symbol of secular power, but a very concrete means of military communication that preceded the galloping of armed knights in the middle of the city. It certainly also had a warning function. In his German chronicle, the herald Nicolaus Mameranus implies an acoustic rivalry between the two groups of trumpeters with phrases such as "gegeneinander geblasen" ("blowing against each other") (Mameranus, 1566, fol. R4r.), which he only resolves at the end where he writes: "Es haben auch die Kay. und Churf. Trommeter, in sollichem abzug, wie gebreüchlich, uberlaut und herrlich geblasen." ("The imperial and electoral trumpeters have, as is customary, blown excessively and magnificently in this departure") (Mameranus, 1566, fol. S2v.). Here an additional layer of meaning becomes apparent: The joint music-making of the two groups at the end of the enfeoffment represented something like a happy end. It was the symbol of the unity of the Empire and could be understood as the material embodiment of the state itself.

There was hardly a big Imperial Diet during the reign of Emperor Maximilian that took place without tournaments. The princes of the Empire and the enthusiastic tournament fighter Maximilian competed against each other in various types of contests (Fink, 1992; Breiding, 2012). Tournaments were already accompanied by music in the Middle Ages. The surviving textual and pictorial sources – although the state of research is more than sparse – show a broad spectrum of tournament music, ranging from the playing of courtly trumpeters and army timpanists, to typical alta-ensembles and field music with flutes and drums. Sometimes the competitions were framed by scenic episodes, chants (so-called *Devisen*), and the playing of all kinds of minstrels. It was quite common for the combatants to appear in so-called "tournois à theme", that is, dressed as historical figures. The theme of the tournament also influenced the musical design (Lindell, 1990).

One of the more frequently discussed tournaments in the history of the Imperial Diets under Maximilian was the duel between the Roman king and Claude de Vaudrey in 1495 (Cuspinian, 1540, p. 729). It was documented in a woodcut depiction in Maximilian's semi-fictional autobiography *Freydal* in the early 16th century.[4] From a mid-16th-century description written by Johann Jakob Fugger and published in the 17th century by Sigmund von Birken, the acoustic structuring of the tournament becomes very clear.

> Am neunten tag/ kamen beyde Helden/ wolgerüst und neben der Lanze mit einem langen Küris-Schwerd bewehret/ in die Schranken. Keiner redte kein wort mit dem andern/ und als die Trompeter zum dritten mal aufbliesen/ legten sie beyderseits ein/ und traffen wol auf einander/ doch daß die Lanzen an den Hernischen abglitschten. […] Endlich begunte K. Maximilian mit einem Stoß/ ihme zum herzen zuraumen: da dann der fremde Ritter sich erhabe/ und zusagte/ daß er an des Uberwinders Hof sich gefangen stellen wollte. Also ward wieder aufgeblasen/ und K. mit jedermans frohlocken in sein Einlager begleitet (Fugger & Birken, 1668, pp. 1376–1377).

> On the ninth day, both heroes came into the barriers well-armed and carrying a long sword in addition to the lance. Neither spoke a word to the other. And when the trumpeters blew their trumpets for the third time, they put in on both sides and hit each other, but in such a way that the lances slipped off the armour. […] Finally, King Maximilian began to strike him in the heart with a blow: but then the foreign knight rose up and promised that he would surrender to the victor's court. So, the trumpets were blown again, and the king was escorted to his camp amid the cheers of all.

The staggered signals of the trumpeters – the actual fight did not begin until the third call – drew the public's attention to the beginning and end of the tournament of Worms.

---

4 See, Maximilian I, *Freydal*, Vienna, Kunsthistorisches Museum (KHM), Kunstkammer, Inv.-Nr. KK 5073, table 39. https://www.metmuseum.org/art/collection/search/748481. Date of Access: 27.01. 2024.

But they also had a legal function, since after all they indicated to the fighters the beginning and end of this utterly dangerous sporting contest. To a certain extent, they marked and legitimized the space in which one was allowed to inflict violence on one's opponent.

The symbolic languages of tournaments and enfeoffments were remarkably close to each other. The celebrations both served primarily as a display of military power, and the complex choreographies could have hardly worked without coordination through sound signals. However, sound was not only a means to structure the schedule of these events. In both enfeoffments and tournaments, elements of military practices were transferred visually and acoustically into the centre of a city, offering the audience the opportunity to immerse themselves into a world known to many only from legends and stories. Imperial Diets offered both tournaments and enfeoffments to a particularly large public. In a society where the legitimacy of power was based primarily on personal testimony, the physical presence of a large number of people during such events was of particular importance (Stollberg-Rilinger, 2008, p. 64).

The question of exactly what music was played as part of ceremonies and rituals in the period around 1500 remains largely unresolved. For the first half of the 16th century, there is hardly any evidence from the German-speaking world providing detailed information about the fanfares and the signals of the time. In recent years, Silke Wenzel has been able to reconstruct a few melodies from the second half of the 16th and the 17th century, which probably also allow conclusions to be drawn about what the playing of court trumpeters might have sounded like at the time of Emperor Maximilian (Wenzel, 2012; 2018).

*

An Imperial Diet is arguably a prime example of a *soundscape of power*. However, it is not a soundscape in a traditional sense. The acoustic space of the *Reichstag* was necessarily ephemeral. It manifested itself at different times in different places. Although its acoustic manifestation was influenced by the geographical conditions at the respective venue, the decisive factor for the sonic shape of the *Reichstag* was the imperial ceremonial and transregional festive cultures. The contrasting analysis of the soundscapes of the Imperial Diet in this paper shows that entries, dances, enfeoffments, and tournaments shared a sounding symbolic grammar that structured these ceremonies and festivities, reflected and embodied hierarchies, and even served as an instrument for waging conflicts.

Bibliography

Printed Sources and Source Editions

Cuspinian, J. (1540). *De Caesaribus atque Imperatoribus Romanis opus*. Kraft Müller. VD16 C 6477. https://mdz-nbn-resolving.de/urn:nbn:de:bvb:12-bsb10143255-2. Date of Access: 27. 01.2024.

Francolin, J. (1566). *Kurtzer Bericht, Welcher gestalt von der Römischen Keyserlichen Mayestat, Kayser Maximilian, dis Namens dem andern, Der Churfürst Augustus von Sachssen, etc. unser gnedigster Herr, Seiner Chruf. G. Reichs Lehen und Regalien, auff den itzigen irer Key. May. ersten Reichstag, ahier zu Augspurg, den 23. des Monats Aprilis offentlich unterm Himel empfangen*. s. n. VD16 ZV 6025. https://mdz-nbn-resolving.de/urn:nbn:de:bvb:12-bsb11207496-4. Date of Access: 27.01.2024.

Francolin, J. (1566). *Warhafftige Beschreibung. Wellicher massen vonn der Roemi. Kay. May. Unnserm Allergnedigsten Herrn der Hochwürdigst Fürst und Herr Herr Goerg Administrator des Hochmaisterthumms in Preüssen Maister Teütschs Ordens in Teütschen und Welschen Lannden auff disem Jrer May. Ersten zu Augspurg gehaltenem Reichstag den 9. May. Anno etc. 66. Die Lehen offentlich under dem Himmel empfangen hat*. Hans Zimmermann. VD16 ZV 6026. https://mdz-nbn-resolving.de/urn:nbn:de:bvb:12-bsb10200722-6. Date of Access: 27.01.2024.

Francolin, J. (ca. 1567). *Vera descriptio quomodo Sa. Cae. majestas Maximilianus secundus etc. In suis primis comitijs. Augustae habitis. Illustrissimo Duci Saxoniae Augusto etc. Investituram sui Electoratus & Dominiorum nonnullorum concesserit. Die 23. April. An: 1566*. Philipp Ulhart. VD16 F 2214. https://mdz-nbn-resolving.de/urn:nbn:de:bvb:12-bsb00022727-8. Date of Access: 27.01.2024.

Fugger, J. J. & Birken, S. von (1668). *Spiegel der Ehren des Höchstlöblichsten Kayser- und Königlichen Erzhauses Oesterreich*. Endter. VD17 23:231732Y. https://mdz-nbn-resolving.de/urn:nbn:de:bvb:12-bsb10864524-4. Date of Access: 27.01.2024.

Gemeiner, C. T. (1824). *Der Regensburgischen Chroniken vierter und letzter Band. Stadt Regensburgische Jahrbücher vom Jahre 1497 bis zum Jahre 1525*. Montag- und Weißische Buchhandlung. https://mdz-nbn-resolving.de/urn:nbn:de:bvb:12-bsb10721901-5. Date of Access: 27.01.2024.

Hegel, K. von (Ed.) (1892). *Die Chroniken der schwäbischen Städte*, vol. 3. Die Chroniken der deutschen Städte vom 14. bis ins 16. Jahrhundert, vol. 22. Augsburg. F. A. Perthes.

Heil, D. (Ed.) (2008). *Deutsche Reichstagsakten unter Maximilian I. Der Reichstag zu Köln 1505. Deutsche Reichstagsakten, Mittlere Reihe*, vol. 8. Vandenhoeck & Ruprecht.

Mameranus, [N.]. [1566]. *Kurtze un[d] eigentliche verzeychnus, Augsburg*. Franck. VD16 M 443. https://mdz-nbn-resolving.de/urn:nbn:de:bvb:12-bsb10987831-0. Date of Access: 27.01.2024.

Klüpfel, K. (1846). *Urkunden zur Geschichte des Schwäbischen Bundes (1488–1533)*, vol. 1. Literarischer Verein Stuttgart. https://mdz-nbn-resolving.de/urn:nbn:de:bvb:12-bsb11440015-5. Date of Access: 27.01.2024.

Scholarly Literature

Aulinger, R. (1980). *Das Bild des Reichstages im 16. Jahrhundert. Beiträge zu einer typologischen Analyse schriftlicher und bildlicher Quellen*. Vandenhoeck & Ruprecht.

Aulinger, R. (1987). Reichsstädtischer Alltag und obrigkeitliche Disziplinierung. Zur Analyse der Reichstagsordnungen im 16. Jahrhundert. In A. Kohler & H. Lutz (Eds.), *Alltag im 16. Jahrhundert. Studien zu Lebensformen in mitteleuropäischen Städten* (pp. 258–290). Verlag für Geschichte und Politik.

Bölling, J. (2009). Musicae utilitatis. Zur Bedeutung der Musik im Adventus-Zeremoniell der Vormoderne. In P. Johanek & A. Lampen (Eds.), *Adventus. Studien zum herrscherlichen Einzug in die Stadt* (pp. 229–266). Böhlau.

Chartrou, J. (1928). *Les entrées solennelles et triomphales à la Renaissance, 1484–1551*. Les Presses Universitaires de France.

Cummings, A. M. (1992). *The Politicized Muse. Music for Medici Festivals, 1512–1537*. Princeton University Press.

Breiding, D. (2012). Rennen, Stechen und Turnier zur Zeit Maximilians I. In Kreisstadt St. Wendel & Stiftung Dr. Walter Bruch (Eds.), *'Vor Halbtausend Jahren …'. Festschrift zur Erinnerung an den Besuch des Kaisers Maximilian I. in St. Wendel* (pp. 54–84). Stiftung Dr. Walter Bruch.

Fenlon, I. (2004). Music and Festival. In R. Mulryne, H. Watanabe-O'Kelly & M. Schewring (Eds.), *Europa Triumphans. Court and Civic Festivals in Early Modern Europe* (pp. 47–55). Ashgate.

Fink, M. (1992). Turnier- und Tanzveranstaltungen am Hofe Kaiser Maximilians I. In W. Salmen (Ed.), *Musik und Tanz zur Zeit Kaiser Maximilians* I. (pp. 37–45). Edition Helbling.

Fisher, A. J. (2004). *Music and Religious Identity in Counter-Reformation Augsburg, 1580–1630*. Ashgate.

Habich, G. (1911). Der Augsburger Geschlechtertanz von 1522. Mit einer Doppeltafel in Lichtdruck und neun Textabbildungen. *Jahrbuch der Preußischen Kunstsammlungen* 32, 213–235.

Heidrich, J. (Ed.) (2010). *Die Habsburger und die Niederlande. Musik und Politik um 1500*. Bärenreiter.

Johanek, P. & Lampen, A. (Eds.) (2009). *Adventus. Studien zum herrscherlichen Einzug in die Stadt*. Böhlau.

Kantorowicz, E. (1944). The 'King's Advent'. And The Enigmatic Panels in the Doors of Santa Sabina. *The Art Bulletin* 26, 207–231.

Kelber, M. (2018). *Die Musik bei den Augsburger Reichstagen im 16. Jahrhundert*. Allitera.

Kelber, M. (2019). Augsburger Tanzbild. In H. Lange-Kracht (Ed.), *Ausstellungskatalog Kaiser Maximilian I. (1459–1519). Kaiser, Ritter, Bürger zu Augsburg* (Maximilianmuseum Augsburg, 15.06.–15.09.2019) (p. 248). Schnell & Steiner.

Kelber, M. (forthcoming). Rudolphine Prague and its Relations to Austrian and German Courts. In E. Honisch & C. Leitmeir (Eds.), *Brill Companion. Rudolphine Prague*.

Kohler, A. (1987). Wohnen und Essen auf den Reichstagen des 16. Jahrhunderts. In A. Kohler & H. Lutz (Eds.), *Alltag im 16. Jahrhundert. Studien zu Lebensformen in mitteleuropäischen Städten* (pp. 222–257). Vertrag für Geschichte und Politik.

Leopold, S. (2011). Der politische Ton. Musik in der öffentlichen Repräsentation. In M. Kintzinger & B. Schneidmüller (Eds.), *Politische Öffentlichkeit im Spätmittelalter* (pp. 21–39). Thorbecke.

Lindell, R. (1990). The Wedding of Archduke Charles and Maria of Bavaria in 1571. *Early Music* 18, 253–269.

McManus, C. (2002). *Women on the Renaissance Stage. Anna of Denmark and Female Masquing in the Stuart Court (1590–1619)*. Manchester University Press.

Meixner, C. (2008). *Musiktheater in Regensburg im Zeitalter des Immerwährenden Reichstages*. Studio Verlag.

Mertens, D. (1998). 'Uß notdurften der hl. christenheit, reichs und sonderlich deutscher nation'. Der Freiburger Reichstag in der Geschichte der Hof- und Reichstage des späten Mittelalters. In H. Schadek (Ed.), *Der Kaiser in seiner Stadt. Maximilian I. und der Reichstag zu Freiburg 1498* (pp. 30–54). Kore Edition.

Missfelder, J.-F. (2012). Period Ear. Perspektiven einer Klanggeschichte der Neuzeit. *Geschichte und Gesellschaft* 38, 21–47.

Morat, D. (2010). Sound Studies – Sound Histories. Zur Frage nach dem Klang in der Geschichtswissenschaft und der Geschichte in der Klangwissenschaft. *Kunsttexte.de/Auditive Perspektiven* 4. https://doi.org/10.18452/6846. Date of Access: 27.01.2024.

Moraw, P. (1980). Versuch über die Entstehung des Reichstags. In H. Weber (Ed.), *Politische Ordnung und soziale Kräfte im Alten Reich* (pp. 1–36). Franz Steiner.

Moraw, P. (1995). Der Reichstag zu Worms von 1495. In Landesarchivverwaltung Rheinland-Pfalz (Ed.), *1495. Kaiser, Reich, Reformen: Der Reichstag zu Worms* (pp. 25–37). Landesarchivverwaltung Rheinland-Pfalz & Landeshauptarchiv Koblenz.

Rudolph, H. (2011). *Das Reich als Ereignis. Formen und Funktionen der Herrschaftsinszenierung bei Kaisereinzügen (1558–1618)*. Böhlau.

Schenk, G. J. (2003). *Zeremoniell und Politik. Herrschereinzüge im spätmittelalterlichen Reich*. Böhlau.

Schnitzer, C. (1999). *Höfische Maskeraden. Funktion und Ausstattung von Verkleidungsdivertissements an deutschen Höfen der Frühen Neuzeit*. De Gruyter.

Schweers, R. (2009). Die Bedeutung des Raumes für das Scheitern oder Gelingen des Adventus. In P. Johanek & A. Lampen (Eds.), *Adventus. Studien zum herrscherlichen Einzug in die Stadt* (pp. 37–55). Böhlau.

Steinberg, S. H. (1934). Zwei Bilder von der Belehnung des Kurfürsten August von Sachsen (1566). *Bulletin of the International Comitee of Historical Sciences* 6(4), 259–268.

Stollberg-Rilinger, B. (2008). *Des Kaisers alte Kleider. Verfassungsgeschichte und Symbolsprache des alten Reiches*. C. H. Beck.

Strohm, R. (1990). *Music in Late Medieval Bruges*. Clarendon Press.

Tammen, B. (2008). Musique et danse pour un jeune prince. La joyeuse entrée de l'archiduc Charles à Bruges en 1515. *Musique, images, instruments* 10, 18–49.

Voigt, B. (2008). *Memoria, Macht, Musik. Eine politische Ökonomie der Musik in vormodernen Gesellschaften*. Bärenreiter.

Wenzel, S. (2018). *Lieder, Lärmen, 'L'homme armé'. Musik und Krieg 1460–1600*. Von Bockel.

Wenzel, S. (2012). Das musikalische Befehlssystem von Pfeife und Trommel in der Frühen Neuzeit. Herrschaft in Form scheinbarer Selbstbestimmung. In P. Moormann, A. Riethmüller & R. Wolf (Eds.), *Paradestück Militärmusik. Beiträge zum Wandel staatlicher Repräsentation durch Musik* (pp. 277–298). transcript.

Illustration Credits

Fig. 1: Anonymous, *Augsburger Tanzbild*, c. 1500, oil on canvas, 95.5×119 cm, Augsburg, Maximilianmuseum, Inv.-Nr. 3821.

Fig. 2: *Enfeoffment at the Weinmarkt in Augsburg*, woodcut, 1566, Universitätsbibliothek Salzburg, Druckgraphiken, G 67 III.

Part IV
Expanding the Scope: Rituals and Sounds Across Borders

Ad sonum campanæ et tubæ

Power-Reflecting Sonic Elements of Early Modern Republic of Dubrovnik (1358–1667)

Tin Cugelj

As an early modern haven on the eastern Adriatic coast, the Republic of Dubrovnik (Ragusa) was both an exception in the geographical space and a fine example of a European city-state. Its well-tuned class society and internal aristocratic government, cleverly obtained and expended finances, and remarkable external politics contributed to creating a relatively peaceful, prosperous, and content community, and, eventually, one of the most developed early modern cities of historical Croatian lands. The Republic's long-lasting political and economic stability guaranteed the development of cultural and musical life, which was incorporated in the activity of the civic musicians – a professional corpus of instrumentalists at the Republic's disposal – whose activity was only a layer of Dubrovnik's acoustically abundant daily life. There, the citizens murmured, clamoured, and yelled in the streets, squares, and at the market; city criers announced new proclamations made by the government; music was played in the streets, in numerous taverns, private houses, and in churches; the bells tolled throughout the day during the greater sacred and secular festivities, enriching the festive soundscape of processions and theatre plays.

While most sonic elements of the broad urban sound profile were an inevitable part of the city's auditory environment, other human-made or human-influenced sounds bore both explicit and concealed qualities. In that context, *every* sound inherently offered a piece of information: they communicated the context of the citizens' surroundings, notified of urban events, warned about potential dangers. Although most of the sounds were a consequence of intentional action, their essence was unintentional. However, a series of sounds were used throughout the city with an explicit intention: to communicate time, bells rang in specific intervals; a signal on the city crier's trumpet announced a new proclamation; people were called to Mass by the sound of the church bells. Previous research has already established that in many communities, sounds bore intrinsic power-reflecting qualities, thus forming the acoustic system that "worked in subtle ways to shape individual and collective identities, and to reinforce patterns of authority", further establishing "a hierarchy of authority, which determined who could make what sort of noise and when" (Garrioch, 2003). In that context – bearing in mind that what we consciously hear, and

Fig. 1: Dubrovnik, anonymous author, ca. 17th century (Institute of Art History Dubrovnik).

the way we interpret it, is historically and culturally determined (Smith, 1999) – sounds need to be understood individually within the different cultural semiotic system(s) to understand how they influenced and shaped identities of communities and individuals within.

Using a selection of archival and narrative sources, this paper will isolate sonic elements of the Ragusan auditory environment that bore the power-reflecting quality and investigate their usage and meaning to show how political dominance was communicated internally and externally in the preservation of the Republic's image. Additionally, it will show how some sounds had an intrinsic and inconspicuous role in preserving the societal structure, which guaranteed internal stability and consequentially provided the Republic with a solid base on which it built its external politics. Lastly, understanding the Ragusan sonic environment undoubtedly deepens our understanding of the Republic's daily functioning and the complex relationship between the government and society, thus pointing towards novel research directions that are yet to be pursued.

Ceremonial Exits, Installations and Funerals: Reflections of Secular Power

Since the beginning of the Republic, the role of the rector embodied a secular power image, despite being more of a personification of the state than an actual position of power (Lonza, 2009). The rector's month-long mandate effectively disenabled tactical political moves, while the real protagonists of politics were the Senate (*Consilium Rogatorum*) and the two councils (*Consilium Minor, Consilium Maior*). The image and importance of the secular power were nevertheless still closely tied to the rector's role and have been reflected daily through his ceremonial exits. His every movement outside the palace was regulated, and he was forbidden to exit without eight to ten courtiers closest to him by status (Luccari, 1605, pp. 159–160; Šoljić et al., 2002, pp. 90–91; Lonza, 2009, pp. 52, 54). Dressed entirely in the official garments of the palace, they walked in front to create a more powerful appearance (Appendini, 1802/2016, p. 215; Lonza, 2009, pp. 49–50), musically accompanied by the civic musicians' short musical patterns.[1] This almost everyday ritual appearance was striking both visually and aurally for all observers: the courtiers, dressed in red with black belts, accompanied the rector dressed in a long, richly wrinkled toga made out of silk damask, thus visually standing out in the Ragusan streets paved with bright white stone (Lonza, 2009, pp. 57–70). The musical performances of the ensemble,[2] whether elaborate or not, had the potential to immediately grasp citizens' attention and lead their ears and eyes towards the abstract concept of the Republic suddenly materializing in the street. As observed by Lonza (2009, pp. 51–52), it moreover "provided an invitation to anybody who wanted to join the daily procession, kept the movement of it steady, and, by indicating the beginning and the end of the ritual, provided a clear temporal and functional frame". As indicated by Lambert Courtoys the Younger – one of the *maestri di cappella* – the main purpose of the ensemble's existence was "to ornament the illustrious and excellent republic" (*Acta Consilium Rogatorum* 87, fol. 155r., as cited in Demović, 1981, p. 260). In

---

1 The musical repertoire played for this occasion from the 13th to the 17th centuries is somewhat dubious. When it comes to the later periods, the ensemble of the civic musicians was substituted by *Banda del principe* and consisted of wind players; there is some proof about "marcie che si usano à sonare avanti sua ecc. il signor Rettore" [marches that are usually played before his excellency sir Rector] (Lonza, 2009, p. 50, fn. 117). In 1605, Lukarević described that "when the rector exits the palace, he is followed by twenty-four members of the Minor Council" and "*una copia di musica*, and all civic secretaries and officials of the palace, all dressed in red" (Luccari, 1605, p. 160).

2 The prevalence of *alta* instruments in the ensemble of the Rector's Chapel indicates that no other option for the smaller Rector's band would be viable during the 15th, 16th, and mid-17th centuries. For the tables of musicians, see appendix in Cugelj, 2019, pp. 37–43. In the 18th century, a group of wind players, oboists and bassoonists, have fulfilled the role (Lonza, 2009, p. 50). Interestingly, Philippe du Fresne-Canaye mentions that the rector is accompanied by a group of bagpipes (*cornemuses*) (du Fresne-Canaye, 1897, p. 15).

that way, the ensemble became the sonic personification of the Republic, while the musicians glorified it by embellishing the rector's presence, thus provoking strong feelings of belonging and reminding the observers of their communal identity. Without the auditory element, the procession could easily have passed unnoticed in the crowd surrounding the rector, which the government wanted to avoid: an ordinance of the Senate from 1552 narrates that the Rector was to be accompanied by the whole Minor council "to preserve his reputation and greatness", and with it, that one of the Republic (*Acta Consilium rogatorum* 51, fol. 23r.).

The rector was the main actor at another two events that hosted powerful sound elements: the installation and the funeral. The monthly installation of the new rector included a threefold ritual celebration centred around oath-taking that expressed both the submissiveness of the people to the current suzerain and his official public recognition in front of laity and clergy (Šoljić et al., 2002, pp. 82–83, 124–125; Lonza, 2009, pp. 77–83). During the installation, a small procession was needed: the rector and his entourage processed from the city hall to the cathedral and back, during which a special bell continuously tolled (Cerimoniale II, ff. 186v.–187r., as cited in Lonza, 2009, pp. 81, 449).[3] The sound was not only the accentuation of the significant event or announcement of the rector's procession but a tool for creating an acoustic unity, as nobody in the city could have escaped the imposing sound of the bell. The second oath, set in the cathedral, included the performance of *laudes regiæ* that the two selected priests were obliged to sing from the pergola (Šoljić et al., 2002, pp. 82–83).[4] The singing itself, originating in the Byzantine times of the Republic, was to recognize the newly instituted leader and accession to the top of the governmental pyramid, despite its limited and short mandate. As the ritual changed throughout the centuries, Lonza (2009, p. 80) observed, it lost the symbolism tied to the rector's loyalty to the people and became just another element of the administrative installation, a symbol of accepting the concept of the abstract state. As the tradition of singing *laude* was never abandoned, it stood for a long-lasting, embedded tradition of acknowledging power, first meant for the overpowered Byzantine kings, and now fitting for a rector, a political figure without actual power, while still retaining its original function and symbolic meaning.

While the installation of the rector and other officials reflected power actively with the inclusion of sound, a ceremony of opposite character was accompanied with overtones of

---

3   On the special bell, see DAD, *Detta*, vol. 17, fol. 56v., as cited in Kralj-Brassard, 2014, p. 138.

4   The *laudes* were first mentioned in the year 1000, then again in an agreement with the Byzantine emperors in the 12th century in which Ragusans obliged themselves to sing *laudes* three times a year for the king in the cathedral, and finally even written down in the statute. Concurrently with changing patrons and governing rule, the names in the *laudes* changed, while the basic responsorial form and tradition stayed practically unchanged until the fall of the Republic in 1808. For more on the singing of *laude* in the feast of Saint Blaise in 1588, see Cugelj, 2020, pp. 246–247.

grief, condolences, and silence (cf. Lonza, 2009, pp. 90–116). To reflect power during the funerals, the government manipulated the sound space imposing and removing silence. The funeral was announced by the bell of the Major Council at midnight a day before and did not stop ringing until the casket was in the grave, marking the end of the funeral (Crijević, 1603/2001, p. 310; Luccari, 1605, p. 160; Cerimoniale I, fol. 84r., as cited in Lonza, 2009, p. 450). While the imprecise wording enables different interpretations regarding the continuity of bell tolling, it nevertheless captured the potent sign of power: the interruption of the inhabitants' sleep was an expression of the government's control over their daily rhythm, which is further supported by the official cessation of any city activity until the new rector was installed. Thus, all administrative offices, shops, and workshops were closed (Cerimoniale I, fol. 87v., as cited in Lonza, 2009, pp. 452, 94), eliminating many sounds resulting from human activity. The city was silenced as grief and sorrow were forced upon the community collectively. This was appropriately accompanied by the modification of the city gates' drums, covered with black cloths (Luccari, 1605, p. 160), resulting in a dampened, muffled, imperfect and unclear sound – a strong symbol of a leaderless government. In addition, if the rector's death struck during the carnival time, all celebrations – the masquerades, dances, games, plays, and preparations for the generally festive time of the year – were appropriately cancelled (Lonza, 2009, p. 94), thus further imposing the appropriate collective grief.[5]

Seven Hundred Cannons: External Sonic Reflections of Political Power

All aural expressions of power presented to this point had been inward-oriented: their goal was to establish and maintain the authority and to keep any destabilization of the internal societal structure at bay. On the other hand, the image of a peaceful, stable Republic was a crucial element of the diplomatic strategy, as the Republic's geographic position unavoidably made it a part of most East-West itineraries and trading routes, in which it played an important role by connecting continental and maritime trade. Additionally, as the eastmost Catholic trading country with a great diplomatic relationship with the Ottoman Empire, Dubrovnik had a privileged trading position in moving goods between the Catholic and Ottoman worlds (cf. Appendini, 2016, pp. 203–205, 233–254; Tadić, 1939). Indeed, its positive image was primarily preserved through precisely developed diplomatic behaviour (welcome committees, council presentations, gifting, meal hosting, and city

---

5   Similar sound suppression is seen only in the death in the rank higher than the rector – the king. Diversis reports that "when they confidently confirm the death of their lord, the Hungarian king, the Ragusans dress in sorrowful clothes, while the sound of brass and winds is forbidden until the new king is chosen, e.g. for at least two months." (Diversis, 1440/2004, pp. 112, 133, 187–188).

Fig. 2: Bay of Kotor with Dubrovnik (Camocio, 1572).

touring) (Razzi, 1595, pp. 63, 81; Diversis, 2004, pp. 114–115; Appendini, 2016, pp. 218–219; Lonza, 2009, pp. 203–221), but a constituent part of it was the active use of cannons.

The multi-layered nature of the latter sound event should be observed from various perspectives. As a part of the diplomatic ritual, cannons had dual symbolism masked under the veil of courtesy and civilized behaviour: the military power of the Republic was measured in the number of cannons,[6] while the guests' social rank was expressed by the number of the cannon shots (Razzi, 1595, pp. 64, 94; Tadić, 1939, p. 260; Lonza, 2009, p. 186). Semantically, it is difficult to detach the sound event from its intrinsic (and primary) military connotation. Nonetheless, early modern communities had a way of giving priority to different meanings through experience: not only that the news of upcoming extraordinary events such as the visit of a dignitary would have been circulated in the community beforehand – and thus provided a necessary context for appropriate sonic discrimination – but the irregular rhythm of the cannon shots would have warned the community that a sudden military action was underway, while the regularity and distinctively controlled sound event gave way to the other, diplomatic meaning, that was equally easily recognized

---

6   Çelebi (2011, p. 207) observed that "the mighty city" had "700 canons".

by the guests, considering their clear contextualization of the sound event.[7] Lastly, the third layer – containing the power-reflecting quality associated with the cannon shots – manifested both internally and externally: it provided the community with information about the visitors' importance and the level of political importance the government was attributing to it, while concurrently showing the visiting party the high level of diplomatic courtesy, demonstrating "civilized behaviour" and military power of the peaceful Republic.

Bells and Trumpet-Messengers as an Expression of Power

When looking at any early modern urban landscape, it is easy to notice the round and square towers dictating the vertical rhythm as the tallest landmarks of the landscape. While the gigantic clocks offered visual temporal references, the most obvious information the bells offered were both aural and visual references of time and space. As Schafer (1993, pp. 55–56) observed, "the association of clocks and church bells was by no means fortuitous; for Christianity, it provided the rectilinear idea of the concept of time as progress" as "in the seventh century it was decreed in a bull of Pope Sabinianus that the monastery bells should be rung seven times each day, punctuating the canonical hours".

Thus, according to their early societal integration, it is not accidental that almost every official document of the Republic, including the statute, starts or includes the phrase *ad sonum campane*. What seems merely like a persistent part of the notarial formula reflects the actual practice and written testimony of the inseparable sound of the auditory environment,[8] as Dubrovnik's size enabled any bell toll to be heard everywhere by everyone. The three major church-bells of the cathedral, Franciscan and Dominican monasteries, dominated the urban auditory environment in the south, east, and the west, while being complemented with a series of smaller bells of appropriately smaller churches, such as the church of Saint James Pipunar with its single bell, Saint Nicholas, Saint Roch, or Our Lady of Carmel with their triple bells (Diversis, 1440/2004, pp. 47–53, 140–148; Marinković, 2017). The lavish tolling sound left the Ottoman traveller Evliya Çelebi highly affected during his Dubrovnik visit: surprised by the vast number of bells, he described how

---

7   Events are described in Tadić, 1939, p. 260, and Lonza, 2009, pp. 186–189. Çelebi (2011, pp. 210–211) described the result of how well the communities were informed about their arrival, saying how "all the infidels came out to greet us, and as we could hardly move because of the crowds, we were able to take note of the marketplace".

8   As presented through this paper, the bells have been already mentioned in several cases: the bells were used as a fire alarm, to mark time, to call to mass, during the installation of the new rector as a ritual tool of unification of the soundscape, to mark the closing of the city gates, and accompanied the funeral of the Rector.

"there are myriads of bells, large and small, hanging on every house and every church", and, dazzled by the ringing, he depicted how on Sunday and "any one of their inauspicious holidays, from the sound you would think the Antichrist had appeared" (Çelebi, 1967, p. 422; Çelebi, 2011, p. 207). As he reports, the pealing was most exciting during Easter (*Sarı Saltık*), the feasts of Saint George (*Hıdırellez*), Saint Nicholas, Saint Demetrius of Sermium (*Kasum*), and Saint Michael the Archangel (Çelebi, 1967, p. 422; Çelebi, 2011, p. 402). Strategically placed on the eastern end of the main street *Placa*, the city clock tower with a huge bell provided, as mentioned, both spatial and temporal information. While the bell towers and clockworks of Bruges and Spanish towns (see Strohm, 1985, p. 3; Marín, 2002, p. 58) both had bells with a separate name and unique significance to which a certain tone and message could be associated – thus creating a sound-signal – we do not know if Ragusan towers rang similarly. However, we can assume the presence of a signalling pattern concerning the distinction made between the daily bells and those marking death, as we have seen in the case of the rector's funeral.

Another set of distinctively named bells with a purely governmental purpose (Nedeljković, 1984, p. 207) was located in the city hall (*campanile del rezimento*). Although the primary data does not uncover details of their construction, the idea of government centralization present throughout the period (cf. Diversis, 1440/2004, pp. 54–55, 149–150) enables conclusions about their position that needed to pervade the dual role: to summon the councillors and to inform the rest of the city. Thus, the atrium of the Rector's palace was a perfectly suitable place to install the bells, as the good projection in and out of the complex of the palace would have been guaranteed by its position and shape.[9] The triple bell signalled the meetings of the councils, each in a specific way: the Minor Council gathered after the third chime of the small bell, the Major Council after the third sound of the big bell, and the Senate on a single sound of the middle bell (Diversis, 1440/2004, pp. 65–66, 157). Contrary to what was previously established, that "in every town, the biggest bells (those whose sound carried furthest) were the most powerful and prestigious" (Garrioch, 2003, p. 16), it seems that in Dubrovnik, the government bells were used according to their carrying quality (corresponding to summoning capability) rather than the usual power-related symbolism.[10] Instead of representing the most politically influential council – the *Consilium rogatorum,* the Senate – the biggest bell's dominating sound was used to summon the most numerous, yet politically least influential council, gathering

---

9   The currently installed bell gable in the atrium is a subtle hint where the previous bells might have stood, provided the Rector's palace was rebuilt in the spirit of the often praised Ragusan traditionality after the 1667 earthquake.

10 For more on the political importance of governmental bodies in the Republic (Lonza, 2009, pp. 85–89).

PALACE OF THE ANCIENT DOGES AT RAGUSA.

Fig. 3: Interior of the Rector's palace with a single bell-gable (Ainsworth, 1866).

all nobles aged 18 and older (Diversis, 1440/2004, p. 66),[11] thus disassociating from the "biggest-greatest" correlation. Nevertheless, as a significant number of Ragusans has been involved in the councils, there is no doubt that the community learned to distinguish the government bells' different sounds, and through direct association with the ongoing work in the government and assigning those who responded to the bell with equal political importance, indirectly responded to the hierarchy of power imposed by the government that initially associated meaning to individual bells. In that way, the government directly maintained the consciousness of the social and political structures that were an essential element guaranteeing the existence and well-being of the Republic.

Another embodiment of a sonic practice can be found in the documents of the Republic. *Ad sonum tubicte* was an actual practice of sounding the trumpet by a messenger just before communicating the ordered proclamation. From the first known employment of a trumpet-messenger, the activity can be traced deep into the mid-17th century with more than 40 trumpeters throughout the period (cf. Reformationes 1, 17 and 1, 25, as cited in

---

11   From 1455, that was raised to 20. For the ordinance, see See chapter 459 in Branislav M. Nedeljković, ed., Liber viridis (Beograd: Srpska akademija nauka i umetnosti, 1984), 402.

Demović, 1981, pp. 204, 277–281). The sound event embodied a clear intent of gathering and captivating the audience in the first place[12] but also reflected the usual practice of the government's intrusion into the population's auditory environment. To hear the proclamation, they would require some level of silence that was induced by sounding the trumpet: as Garrioch (2003, p. 18) stated, "the ability to *produce* (or induce) silence as a mark of respect was a privilege of authority," thus the fact that the messenger was a governmental officer entitled him to *produce* silence as a result of respect for authority.

Imposed Silence as a Reflection of Ecclesiastical Influence

The internal stability of the Republic depended significantly on the harmonious relationship between the government and the population but equally on a stable, undoubted religious preference, or, as Razzi (1595, p. 61) cleverly said, "kingdoms are most often lost when the faith is gone." To maintain religious homogeneity, the sacred leaders primarily had to preserve a good relationship with the government,[13] but also with the laity, upon which the unity depended. Preconditioned by the supreme, almost universal requirements from the Holy See, the predispositions for religious homogeneity were easily met: the secular republic was synchronized with the rhythm of the densely filled liturgical calendar; several divine cults coexisted; and most importantly, certain saints became a long-integrated part of Ragusan identity, eventually making the Catholicism *itself* a part of it. Aided by the government's long-lasting and unquestionable inclination towards traditionalism, not much was needed to sustain good piety – only smaller "sonic reminders of faith" were necessary. These were entrusted to the familiar sound of bells: daily pealing summoned inhabitants to Mass and provided a temporal reference for personal devotion, while on Sundays and feast days – by being sounded longer and more intensely – they invoked the importance of the day and Catholic values that were ingeniously embodied in saintly figures.[14] Nevertheless, despite the stable religious state, the religious authorities were still aware of the importance, power, and benefits of greater festivities and saintly celebrations. Hence, they

---

12 As Garrioch noted, "all these cries were ignored unless some keyword, note, or half-heard phrase suggested their relevance", thus a trumpet sound greatly increases the chances of the message being successfully passed to the population (Garrioch, 2003, p. 8).

13 Understandably, the relationship between the government and the Ragusan church was complex. Most problems arose from the imbalance of the ideals of sacred and secular leadership that was one of elementary issues during the centuries of the Republic, which was constantly worked on. An example can be seen in Lonza, 2009, pp. 133–151.

14 As previously picturesquely described by Evliya Çelebi. We find similarities throughout Catholic Europe: in Jaca, for example, the pealing of the bells would announce all twenty-one main feast days, and all Sundays (Marín, 2002, p. 54).

utilized the two biggest cults – Saint Blaise[15] and Corpus Christi[16] – to boost the religious homogeneity throughout the year, providing the Ragusan government with a platform to reinforce its image and power.

On the other hand, the domination of the temporal remained in the clerical domain. During Christmas and Easter, as the liturgical ceremonial was prioritized, the governmental one became dampened – it was deemed inappropriate to interfere with the sacred, so the secular government did not cross that boundary (Lonza, 2009, p. 335). While one would expect that the sacred power was reflected most extrovertedly during the two most important Catholic feasts, neither Christmas nor Easter celebrations seem to have been explicitly used in that way. Sources are silent about the sound and music during the Christmas day Mass – the peak moment of the cycle. On the other hand, despite the fact that the secular ceremonial did not actively interfere with the sacred one, the statute still obliged the clergy to incorporate and sing the *laudes regiae* during the biggest Catholic feasts (Šoljić et al., 2002, pp. 84–85; Lonza, 2009, p. 336), which reflected the high level of the intertwining of sacred and secular. Additionally, on 27 December after the Vespers, the civic musicians played in front of the church of Saint Blaise to gratify the patron for the past feast (Lonza, 2009, p. 336). The civic musicians were used in the same manner as during the ceremonial exits: by expressing thanks to the patron while being the aural representation of the government, they symbolized the Republic itself gratifying the patron, concurrently evoking collective piety, empathy, and gratitude among the witnesses.

The Easter cycle started with a short pre-Lent period: a week from Fat Thursday was filled with carnival festivities, abruptly ceasing with Ash Wednesday, when a series of bans on secular activities were put into effect to stimulate the period of penance, good deed-making, restraint and fasting. The bans prohibited not only masks, pageantry, and plays but also dancing, music-making, and working, thus suppressing the secular noise and imposing silence (Solovjev, 1936, p. 58; Lonza, 2009, pp. 338–346). As seen during the nighttime, the tactic of imposing silence using government ordinances was an effective

---

15   While the political and cultural aspects of the feast of Saint Blaise have been most thoroughly inspected by Lonza (2009, pp. 357–386; 2017, pp. 19–39), the author of this chapter has recently analysed its liturgical musical elements in Cugelj (2020).

16   The most comprehensive cultural and historical analysis of the feast and the procession of Corpus Christi in Dubrovnik has been done by Lonza (2009, pp. 269–293), while some of the aspects have also been mentioned in Kunčević (2020, pp. 95–99), and Janeković-Römer (2015, pp. 432–438). Furthermore, comprehensive comparative studies of the feast have been done by Rubin (1991), and Walters, Corrigan, and Ricketts (2006), while valuable insights for the feast in Venice have been provided by Selfridge-Field (1975), Muir (1981), Glixon (2003), and Fenlon (2006, 2018). The feast and its aspects in Spain and Barcelona have been thoroughly inspected by Very (1962) and Kreitner (1995), Mateos Royo (1998), Nelson (2000), Borgerding (2006), while the feast in Bruges has been observed by Strohm (1985).

tool in demonstrating secular power, while the latter use in prohibiting secular sounds during the greatest of Catholic festivities shows that they were a powerful sacred tool as well. Perhaps, if we follow the symbolism of the civic musicians as an aural representation of the Republic itself, then by demanding silence from the ensemble, the sacred leadership elegantly silenced, in effect, the secular Republic, thus imposing its political power. Finally, the last imposition of silence is seen on Maundy Thursday, when the bells were tied to prevent them from ringing, and the organ door was closed as the visual symbol of silence (Lonza, 2009, pp. 347–350). As Garrioch (2003, p. 13) observed, the whole Eastertide – drenched in silence that was a powerful reminder of Christ's suffering and death – must have been "eerie and discomforting for people accustomed to the almost incessant tolling of the bells." Hence, the end of the Republic-wide imposed silence on Easter morning with singing *laudes* must have been both a symbolic and literal sign of relief: the physical discomfort of the imposed silence and piety was finally ceased as Christ is resurrected. Finally, the *laudes* symbolized the focal return to the secular from the sacred, marking both the end of the Easter festivities and once more imposing the status of the secular government, which was interwoven with the sacred, yet predominant.

Processions as a Reaffirmation of Dual Power: Saint Blaise and Corpus Christi

As shown, both sacred and secular authorities displayed power by imposing silence during events. However, their greatest exhibition of power occurred in the liturgically most solemn, politically vital, and sonically most lavish events of the year – not separate but deeply intertwined. Not surprisingly, the most important feasts were also the most represented in the narrative and other sources: celebrating the saintly cult of Saint Blaise and the feast of Corpus Christi, which included lavish processions in many elements similar to those in Venice, Florence, and Barcelona.[17]

The most important aspect of creating a communal identity was the formation of a saintly cult: choosing the patron, acquiring the relics, determining individual churches' benefactors, and introducing celebrations tied to feast days articulated an image of a city or state, its traditions and roots (Lonza, 2009, p. 235). In Dubrovnik, the cult was formed around the miracle of Blaise of Sebaste, 4th-century physician and bishop of Sebaste,[18]

---

17   In Venice, the ducal processions present many similar elements to the two Dubrovnik processions mentioned here (Friedrichs, 1995, p. 182; Kisby, 2006, pp. 28–44).

18   According to Razzi, in 871, the Venetians tried to seize Dubrovnik and incorporate it into their territory under the disguise of going to the East. Not aware of the Venetian threat, Ragusans welcomed them generously. The Venetian plan would unwind without difficulty if Saint Blaise had not

which was celebrated between the Christmas cycle and the Lent season, reaching the peak of the saint's *triduum* on 3 February. Combined with the independent rise of the Ragusan state, Saint Blaise became its ever-present patron and was diligently built into the civic identity, symbolizing an amalgam of medieval Christian values and political humanist ideology (Janeković Römer, 1999, p. 374; Lonza, 2017, p. 19; Cugelj, 2020, p. 225). Accompanying the Republic's mid-14th century independence and an effort in the creation of civic identity, the feast of translation and *adventus* of the saint's hand was introduced on 5 July, while – for the exact reason of maintaining the identity – the cult infiltrated the feast of Forty Martyrs (9 March), which was celebrated in Saint Blaise's sign from the early 15th century (Solovjev, 1936, p. 103; Diversis, 1440/2004, pp. 95, 177; Lonza, 2009, pp. 251–252, 383–386).

The sonically rich environment during the *triduum* of Saint Blaise included the ever-present aural presentation of the state – the civic musicians – playing antiphonally with the personification of the military state – drummers of the ceremonial troops – thus symbolizing the harmonious relationship between the two (Lonza, 2009, p. 362). The ecclesiastical power and harmony were expressed during the solemn first vespers in the cathedral, where all Dominicans and Franciscans of the Republic (and not only the city) joined in the chant performance during which the sheer number of the friars represented the strength of the ecclesiastical Republic. The cathedral and the titular church of Saint Blaise were both filled with sound: the parallel services occurring within them were physically connected with the solemn procession carrying relics, during which the sacred power was clearly expressed through the sonic predominance both in the physical and sonic urban territory of Dubrovnik. The church doors were left open to ease the procession, which – considering the proximity of two churches – enabled the expansion of the liturgical space from the spatial limits of the churches to the wider urban centre, while the sonorous singing of *Te deum laudamus* expanded the sonic territory to the limits of the city walls and possibly even echoing outside them, thus creating an *ad hoc* acoustic (comm)unity that demonstrated the glorious harmony of sacred and secular power, and – symbolically – the strength of the unified Republic.

The night silence of the main feast day was broken at dawn with loud drumming and the sonorous cannon *salve* (Appendini, 1802/2016, pp. 207–209; Lonza, 2009, p. 364), that "echoed everywhere around on the shore and nearby hills and valleys" (Razzi, 1595, p. 139). Contrary to the dual symbolism of greeting foreign officials, these had a different meaning: announcing the importance of the festivity, they were used to express gratitude and respect

---

appeared to a devout priest Stojko and warned him about the Venetians' true intent (Cugelj, 2020, p. 225). For more on this event as described by Serafino Razzi and how it developed into a yearly celebration, see Cugelj, 2020, pp. 225–226 and chapter '*Sv. Vlaho: parac, slava, čast i dika*' (St. Blaise: Protector, Glory, Honor and Pride) in Lonza, 2009, pp. 357–386.

(to the patron saint), and by overwhelming the aural space of the whole Republic, the sonic event became a tool in creating (and maintaining the previously established) unified acoustic community that would materialize in the city for the grand procession later that day. The lavishly celebrated and densely organized civic ritual[19] was interwoven with visual and auditory elements of power that culminated at the central part of the festivity – the solemn Mass and procession on the saint's day – that integrated all layers of Ragusan society: from three councils, through government officials, clergy, to the people, it implied the harmonious unity of the Ragusan community. As the government strictly regulated the order of the procession, it highlighted the solid interior political power and concurrently implied a sense of order, especially when foreign guests were invited to take part in the procession (Diversis, 1440/2004, p. 93; Lonza, 2009, pp. 200, 370).

The latter practice was a part of the annual *Corpus Christi* procession,[20] which, as Friedrichs (1995, p. 69) noted, contained "political messages [that] sometimes got embedded in the observances" of many European cities. While the ecclesiastical focus during the feast of Saint Blaise was on elaborate liturgy, Corpus Christi focused on the procession (Diversis, 1440/2004, pp. 96, 178). Despite the slight changes in the ceremonial, the processions were similar in political gestures, social order, and visual and sonic elements of power, thus corroborating their established intention (cf. Diversis, 1440/2004, pp. 96–98, 178–179). However, the grandiosity, importance, and expression of ecclesiastical power during Corpus Christi can be noticed in the much greater sonic space it covered. Unlike the Saint Blaise procession, which was limited to the cathedral and the urban space of the saint's church, the Corpus Christi procession started at the cathedral and went through *Ulica od crevljara* (today *od puča*), reaching Onofri's fountain and returning to the cathedral through *Placa* (today *Stradun*) (Diversis, 1440/2004, pp. 94, 96–97, 176, 178). The expanded physical area corresponded to equally greater sonic space, whose goals were equal to any civic procession of the Republic: to unify the Ragusan community and to imply and strengthen social, religious, and political order that played such a significant role in the preservation of internal and external stability of the Republic.

Conclusion

The vivid soundscape of the early modern republic of Dubrovnik hosted sounds that were a part of a usual acoustic experience in any early modern European city-state such as Flor-

---

19 For a complete assessment of visual and ritual elements and expression of power, see Lonza, 2009, pp. 357–383.

20 For example, in 1532, French envoy Antoine de Rincon took part in the Corpus Christi procession (Tadić, 1939, p. 228).

ence or Venice, yet the scale of the sound palette was proportional to the physical size of the urban space. However, the concealed acoustic system with the semiotic system unique to the community made the difference. Thus, sounds accompanying the events with the rector in the spotlight (ceremonial installation and deinstallation, funeral) or symbolizing government (trumpet-messengers) in all cases produced an acoustic unity signifying the harmonious Republic concurrently bearing the message of the government's oversight over the community through the manipulation of sound and silence. The governmental councils were sonically manifested by the *campanile del rezimento*, whose chimes – corresponding to carrying quality and summoning capability rather than the usual power-related symbolism (biggest-greatest) – were differently associated than in other European city-states. The internal reflection of political power was complemented with the system of externally-oriented elements common to other European countries (the cannon *salve*) through which the government showed the embraced international diplomatic behaviour and communicated the importance of the incoming party to the citizens.

Although Catholicism was an inseparable part of the Ragusan identity, the sacred power was exerted daily through the sounds of church bells and during the events of the densely filled liturgical calendar. Both secular and sacred authorities used the feasts of Saint Blaise and Corpus Christi to reinforce their image and power, yet during the temporal, the sacred overtook the secular by manipulating sound and silence. Lastly, the saintly cult of Saint Blaise and processions tied to it presented the deep intertwining of the secular and ecclesiastical state, joining all the elements of exerting power present in the Republic to create the inseparable acoustic community that demonstrated the glorious harmony and strength of the unified Republic.

Finally, while the direct efficiency of the described power-reflecting sonic elements of the Ragusan auditory environment is questionable due to the lack of direct primary references, their nature showed that they had been an inseparable layer of general expressions of power throughout the centuries, thus contributing to the internal and external conservation of stability. The narratives of authors throughout the history of the Republic – ranging from Diversis (1440), Razzi (1595), Crijević Tuberon (1603), and Luccari (1605) to Appendini (1802) – challenge the long-lasting political and social perseverance of the Republic, whose harmonious integrity would be non-existent without highly-effective methods of achieving and pertaining political, social, and religious stability.

Bibliography

Archival Sources

State Archive in Dubrovnik, *Acta Consilium rogatorum* 3.51, fols. 23r.–24v.

Printed Sources and Source Editions

Appendini, F. M. (2016). *Povijesno-kritičke bilješke o starinama, povijesti i književnosti Dubrovčana*, transl. by A. Šoljić. Matica hrvatska–Ogranak Dubrovnik.

Camocio, G. F. (1572). *Isole famose, porti, fortezze, e terre maritime*. Alla libraria del segno di S. Marco.

Çelebi, E. (1967). *Putopis, Odlomci o jugoslavenskim zemljama*, transl. by H. Šabanović. Svjetlost.

Çelebi, E. (2011). *An Ottoman Traveller: Selections from the Book of Travels of Evliya Çelebi*, ed. by R. Dankoff, transl. by S. Kim. Eland.

Crijević Tuberon, L. (2001). *Commentarii de temporibus suis*, transl. by V. Rezar. Hrvatski institut za povijest.

Janeković Römer, Z. (Ed.). *Filip de Diversis: Opis slavnoga grada Dubrovnika*. Dom i svijet.

du Fresne-Canaye, P. (1897). *Le voyage du Levant (1573)*, ed. by H. Hauser. E. Leroux.

Luccari, G. (1605). *Copioso Ristretto degli Annali di Rausa*. Antonio Leonardi.

Nedeljković, B. M. (Ed.). (1984). *Liber viridis*. Srpska akademija nauka i umetnosti.

Razzi, S. (1595). *La storia di Raugia: Scritta nuouamente in tre libri / da F. Serafino Razzi …* Vincentio Busdraghi.

Šoljić, A., Šundrica, Z., & Veselić, I. (Eds.) (2002). *Statut grada Dubrovnika: Sastavljen godine 1272*. Državni arhiv.

Solovjev, A. (1936). *Liber omnium reformationum civitatis Ragusii*. Srpska kraljevska akademija.

Scholarly Literature

Borgerding, T. (2006). Imagining the Sacred Body: Choirboys, Their Voices, and Corpus Christi in Early Modern Seville. In S. Boynton & R.-M. Kok (Eds.), *Musical Childhoods and the Cultures of Youth* (pp. 25–48). Wesleyan University Press.

Cugelj, T. (2019). *De Trombonis: Trombone and Trombonists in Renaissance Croatia* [Master's thesis Fachhochschule Nordwestschweiz, Musik-Akademie Basel, Schola Cantorum Basiliensis].

Cugelj, T. (2020). Serafino Razzi's Storia Di Raugia, or, How Renaissance Dubrovnik (might Not Have?) Heard Polyphony in February 1588: Towards a Liturgical Reconstruction of the Feast of Saint Blaise. *Arti Musices* 51(2), 221–265.

Demović, M. (1981). *Glazba i glazbenici u dubrovačkoj republici. Od početka XI. do polovine XVII. stoljeća.* Jugoslavenska akademija znanosti i umjetnosti.

Fenlon, I. (2006). Magnificence as Civic Image: Music and Ceremonial Space in Early Modern Venice. In F. Kisby (Ed.), *Music and Musicians in Renaissance Cities and Towns* (pp. 28–37). Cambridge University Press.

Fenlon, I. (2018). Music, Ritual, and Festival: The Ceremonial Life of Venice. In K. Schiltz (Ed.), *A Companion to Music in Sixteenth-Century Venice* (pp. 125–148). Brill.

Friedrichs, C. R. (1995). *The Early Modern City, 1450–1750.* Longman.

Garrioch, D. (2003). Sounds of the City: The Soundscape of Early Modern European Towns. *Urban History* 30(1), 5–25.

Glixon, J. (2018). Music at Parish, Monastic, and Nunnery Churches and at Confraternities. In K. Schiltz (Ed.), *A Companion to Music in Sixteenth-Century Venice* (pp. 45–78). Brill.

Janeković Römer, Z. (1999). *Okvir slobode: Dubrovačka vlastela između srednjovjekovlja i humanizma.* HAZU–Zavod za povijesne znanosti u Dubrovniku.

Janeković Römer, Z. (2015). *The Frame of Freedom: The Nobilitz of Dubrovnik between the Middle Ages and Humanism.* HAZU–Zavod za povijesne znanosti u Dubrovniku.

Kisby, F. (2006). *Music and Musicians in Renaissance Cities and Towns.* Cambridge University Press.

Kralj-Brassard, R. (2014). Detta presvijetlog i preuzvišenog gospodina kneza: Troškovi Dvora u Dubrovniku od 16. do 19. stoljeća. *Anali Zavoda za povijesne znanosti Hrvatske akademije znanosti i umjetnosti u Dubrovniku* 52(1), 131–160.

Kreitner, K. (1995). Music in the Corpus Christi Procession of Fifteenth-Century Barcelona. *Early Music History* 14, 153–204.

Kunčević, L. (2020). *Vrijeme harmonije. O razlozima društvene i političke stabilnosti Dubrovačke republike.* HAZU–Zavod za povijesne znanosti u Dubrovniku.

Lonza, N. (2009). *Kazalište vlasti: Ceremonijal i državni blagdani dubrovačke republike u 17. i 18. stoljeću.* HAZU–Zavod za povijesne zananosti u Dubrovniku.

Lonza, N. (2017). Sveti Vlaho, božanski zaštitnik Dubrovnika. In K. Horvat-Levaj (Ed.), *Zborna crkva sv. Vlaha u Dubrovniku* (pp. 19–39). Dubrovačka biskupija, Zborna crkva sv. Vlaha.

Marín, M. Á. (2002). Sound and Urban Life in a Small Spanish Town during the Ancien Régime. *Urban History* 29(1), 48–59.

Marinković, A. (2017). O gradnji, funkciji i rušenju krstionice-zvonika dubrovačke romaničke katedrale. *Ars Adriatica* 7, 83–98.

Muir, E. (1981). *Civic Ritual in Renaissance Venice.* Princeton University Press.

Nelson, B. (2000). Ritual and Ceremony in the Spanish Royal Chapel, c. 1559–c. 1561. *Early Music History* 19, 105–200.

Royo, J. A. M. (1998). All the Town is a Stage: Civic Ceremonies and Religious Festivities in Spain during the Golden Age. *Urban History* 26(2), 165–189.

Rubin, M. (1991). *Corpus Christi: The Eucharist in Late Medieval Culture.* Cambridge University Press.

Schafer, R. M. (1993). *The Soundscape: Our Sonic Environment and the Tuning of the World*. Destiny Books.

Selfridge-Field, E. (1975). *Venetian Instrumental Music from Gabrieli to Vivaldi*. Blackwell.

Smith, B. R. (1999). *The Acoustic World of Early Modern England: Attending to the O-Factor*. University of Chicago Press.

Strohm, R. (1985). *Music in Late Medieval Bruges*. Clarendon Press.

Tadić, J. (1939). *Promet putnika u starom Dubrovniku*. Turistički savez u Dubrovniku.

Very, G. F. (1962). *The Spanish Corpus Christi Procession: A Literary and Folkloric Study*. Tipografia Moderna.

Walters, B. R., Corrigan, V. J., & Ricketts, P. T. (2006). *The Feast of Corpus Christi*. Pennsylvania State University Press.

Illustration Credits

Fig. 1: Anonymous, *Veduta of Dubrovnik before the earthquake of 1667*, ca. 17th century, Društvo prijatelja dubrovačke starine [Society of Friends of Dubrovnik Antiquities], no inventory number, no digitized version accessible. A copy is kept in the Franciscan monastery of Friars Minor, Dubrovnik. Source: Institute of Art History Dubrovnik.

Fig. 2: Giovanni Francesco Camocio, *Bay of Kotor with Dubrovnik*, 1572, from *Isole famose, porti, fortezze...*, Venice, 1574, plate 19, New York Public Library, Schwarzman Rare Books Collection, *KB 1572, digitized version: https://digitalcollections.nypl.org/items/6863f050-f304-0135-9f5b-051ae5389df3. Date of Access: 27.01.2024.

Fig. 3: William Francis Ainsworth, *Palace of the ancient doges at Ragusa*, 1866, from *All round the world: An illustrated record of voyages*, digitized version: https://babel.hathitrust.org/cgi/pt?id=wu.89073047383&seq=9. Date of Access: 27.01.2024.

Durch Klang zur Harmonie

Koreanische Hofmusik
der Joseon-Dynastie zur Zeit von König Sejong*

Jieun Kim**

Einleitung

Die Musik des koreanischen Hofes hängt eng mit dem konfuzianischen Konzept der Joseon-Dynastie (1392–1910) zusammen. Obwohl sich die heutige koreanische Gesellschaft vom Konfuzianismus entfernt hat, wird die Hofmusik noch immer regelmäßig auf staatlicher Ebene aufgeführt, um das kulturelle Erbe zu erhalten und sie an die nächsten Generationen weiterzugeben. Traditionell verfügt die koreanische Hofmusik über eine große Besetzung. Die Aufführung gestaltet sich als eine Symbiose aus Instrumentalmusik, Gesang und Tanz. Seit Mitte des 20. Jahrhunderts, d.h. nach der japanischen Kolonialzeit (1910–1945) und dem Koreakrieg (1950–1953), wird jedoch zumeist in reduzierten Besetzungen musiziert. Diese sind rein instrumental, da die zugehörigen Texte der Stücke nicht mehr erhalten sind bzw. das heutige Publikum den ursprünglichen Text – chinesische Schriftzeichen (*Hanmun* 한문) oder altes Koreanisch (*Yet Hangeul* 옛 한글) – nicht mehr versteht.

Die Wurzeln der traditionellen koreanischen Musik wie der dazugehörigen Hofmusik besitzen eine über 1000 Jahre alte Geschichte, die vor allem ins Nachbarland China ver-

---

* Anmerkungen zu Übersetzung, Umschrift und koreanischen Namen: Die Übersetzungen der koreanischen Texte ins Deutsche wurden von der Verfasserin angefertigt. Für die Transkription aus dem Koreanischen wurde die *Revised Romanization of Korean* (2000) verwendet. Koreanische Personennamen im Text wurden in der Reihenfolge Vorname-Familienname geschrieben, auch wenn im Koreanischen die umgekehrte Reihenfolge (Familienname-Vorname; ohne Leerzeichen) verwendet wird. Ergänzungen der Verfasserin bei Zitaten wurden in eckigen Klammern hinzugefügt. Eigennamen, einschließlich Personennamen, Institutionen und Orte wurden in normaler Schrift angezeigt, während koreanische Termini, Musikinstrumente und Buchtitel in Kursivschrift gesetzt wurden. Koreanische Termini sowie Werktitel werden nur bei erstmaliger Nennung in folgender Reihenfolge dargestellt: *Transkription* Koreanisch (ggf. chinesische Schriftzeichen; deutsche Übersetzung) oder deutsche Übersetzung (*Transkription* Koreanisch; ggf. chinesische Schriftzeichen). Das koreanische Zitat wird in der Reihenfolge "deutscher Übersetzung" und "Koreanisch" angezeigt.

** An dieser Stelle möchte ich mich bei Margret Scharrer bedanken. Ihre wertvollen Kommentare und umfangreiche Bearbeitung haben diesen Artikel entscheidend geprägt.

weisen. Die traditionelle Musik wandelte sich jedoch über diesen langen Zeitraum sehr stark und nahm mehr und mehr einen koreanischen Charakter an. Die Zeit Sejongs – eines Königs der Joseon-Dynastie – gilt in der koreanischen Musikgeschichtsschreibung als Beginn einer eigenständigen koreanischen Hofmusik, denn in dieser Zeit wurde erstmals am Hof versucht, die aus China importierte Hofmusik im Stil der zeitgenössischen und landesspezifischen Kultur zu überarbeiten.

Wie aber hängt nun die koreanische Hofmusik mit dem konfuzianischen Konzept zusammen? In welchen Gattungen wurde musiziert und worin bestehen ihre musikalischen Merkmale? Ziel des Aufsatzes ist es, westlichen Lesern einen ersten verständlichen Über- und Einblick über die koreanische Hofmusik der Zeit von König Sejong zu geben.[1] Der erste Teil vermittelt deshalb einführendes Grundwissen. Anschließend stehen König Sejong und seine Musikpolitik im Mittelpunkt. Der dritte Teil wendet sich einem konkreten Musikbeispiel zu: dem *Yeominrak* im *Bonnaeui*, Sejongs Vertonung der ersten *Hangeul*-Literatur. Im Fazit fasse ich die Bedeutung von Sejong für die koreanische Musikgeschichte zusammen.

Meine Untersuchungen basieren vor allem auf Primärquellen. Zentral ist dabei die Sammlung der Annalen der Joseon-Dynastie in Korea (*Joseonwangjo Sillok* 조선왕조실록; 朝鮮王朝實錄),[2] die erste *Hangeul*-Literatur *Yongbieocheonga* 용비어천가 (龍飛御天歌) sowie Notenbücher und Choreographien dieser Zeit.

---

1 Siehe dazu vor allem folgende Literatur: Kim, 2021; Moon, 2013; Sheen, 2016; H.-J. Song, 2012, 2014; J. Song, 2020.

2 *Joseonwangjo Sillok* sind die jährlichen Aufzeichnungen der Joseon-Dynastie in Korea, die von 1392 bis 1865 aufbewahrt wurden. Der Begriff *Sillok* bedeutet "Wahre Aufzeichnungen von Ereignissen, die tatsächlich stattgefunden haben, so wie sie waren". Die *Joseonwangjo Sillok* umfassen 1.893 Bände und sind der 151. Nationalschatz Koreas sowie im UNESCO-Register "Memory of the World" aufgeführt. Die *Joseonwangjo Sillok* sind tägliche Aufzeichnungen, die die gesamte Geschichte und Kultur der Joseon-Dynastie abdecken, einschließlich Politik, Militär, sozialen Institutionen, Gesetzen, Wirtschaft, Industrie, Transport, Kommunikation, traditioneller Kunst, Handwerk und Religion, geordnet nach den aufeinanderfolgenden Königen. Die *Sillok* wurden zusammengestellt, wenn der Nachfolgekönig die Zusammenstellung der Annalen des ehemaligen Königs anordnete. Die Materialien für die Zusammenstellung der *Sillok* wurden nach folgendem Schema veranlasst: *Sacho* (史草, Entwurf historischer Aufzeichnungen vom Verantwortlichen für die Erstellung der Annalen), *Sijeonggi* (時政記, Aufzeichnung zu den wichtigen Regierungsangelegenheiten vom Verantwortlichen für die Erstellung der Historie), *Seungjeongwon Ilgi* (承政院日記, ein vom königlichen Sekretär geschriebenes Tagebuch), Uijeongbu-Registrierung (議政府謄錄, Protokoll des höchsten Entscheidungsorgans), *Bibyunsadeungnok* (備邊司謄錄, Aufzeichnungen über das Zivil- und Konföderationsabkommen) und *Ilseongnok* (日省錄, Tägliche Aufzeichnungen des königlichen Hofes und wichtiger Beamter) usw. Darunter war *Sacho* eine der wichtigsten Grundmaterialien für *Sillok*. *Sacho*: Die Authentizität der *Joseonwangjo Sillok* hängt mit dem Herstellungsprozess der *Sacho* zusammen, wie folgt: Die *Sacho* wurde von acht *Sagwan* (Verantwortlichen für die Geschichtsschreibung) verfasst, bestehend aus zwei *Bonggyo* (奉教), zwei *Daegyo* (待教) und vier *Censor* (檢閱). Diese

Grundwissen zur koreanischen Hofmusik

Ursprung und Grundgedanke

Die Geschichte der eigenständigen Hofmusik Koreas begann mit der Joseon-Dynastie, die für über 500 Jahre als pro-konfuzianisches Herrschergeschlecht regierte. In der Joseon-Dynastie glaubte man, Politik beruhe auf *Ye* 예 (禮), der Moral, sowie *Ak* 악 (樂), der Musik. Diese Anschauung wurde unter dem Begriff *Yeak* 예악 (禮樂) zusammengefasst (*Sejong Sillok*, 1430b). Das heißt, ihr politisches Ideal basierte auf dem Gleichgewicht von *Ye* und *Ak*. *Ye* bedeutete in diesem Zusammenhang: Funktion zur Ordnung (Moral) und *Ak*: die Funktion zur Harmonie. *Ye* und *Ak* besaßen jeweils noch eine zweite Bedeutung: *Ye* bezeichnete Zeremonien und *Ak* eine darstellende Form der Kunst. Entsprechend wurden Rituale und Zeremonien nicht nur instrumental, sondern auch vom Tanz und Gesang der koreanischen Hofkünstler:innen begleitet. Die Joseon-Könige verließen ihren Palast nicht oft, ergab sich aber die Gelegenheit zu einem Ausflug, wurden sie stets von prächtiger Musik begleitet. Die Hofmusiker:innen, die als Teil der königlichen Prozession mitmarschierten, spielten für gewöhnlich auf Blas- und Schlaginstrumenten, da diese zu Fuß leicht mitzuführen waren. Bei solchen Prozessionen wurde nicht getanzt und gesungen, es erklangen lediglich Instrumente (H.-J. Song, 2014).

Wie aber standen nun Moral, Musik und Politik miteinander in Zusammenhang? Konfuzianischen Lehren zufolge entwickelt sich die Moral aus der Erfassung und Anerkennung von Unterschieden. In dieser Akzeptanz von Unterschieden sah man das Fundament für Respekt. In der Moral bzw. der Einhaltung von Umgangsformen und Höflichkeiten verstand man dieser Philosophie zufolge nichts anderes als einen Ausdruck von Respekt. Musik dagegen, so meinte man, entstehe durch Gefühle und habe die Macht, unterschiedliche Vorstellungen zusammenzubringen (Cho, 2007; J. Song, 2020).

Verantwortlichen nahmen immer an allen staatsbezogenen Sitzungen teil und führten detaillierte Mitschriften über den Inhalt der vom König und den Beamten besprochenen Staatsangelegenheiten. Niemand durfte *Sacho* lesen, und die *Sagwans* durften jeweils mit niemandem über den Inhalt diskutieren. Idealiter sollte kein König befugt sein, Inhalte zu löschen oder zu bearbeiten. Derjenige, der der Außenwelt Informationen über den Inhalt der Annalen zukommen ließ, wurde bestraft. Die gedruckten *Sillok* unterlagen strengster Kontrolle. Siehe dazu: Kang, 2016; H. Kim, 2008; NIKH, o.J.

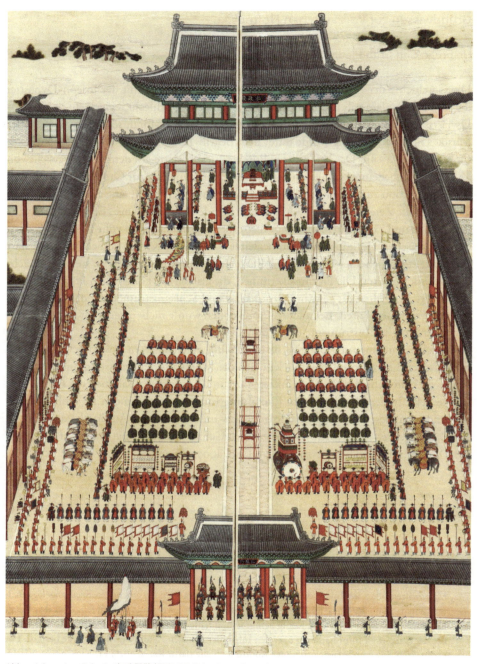

Abb. 1: *Injeongjeonjinhado* (仁政殿陳賀圖) [Bildliche Darstellung der Festlichkeiten zum 60. Geburtstag von Königin Sunwon und zum 41. Geburtstag von Königin Shinjeong].

Durch Klang zur Harmonie

Gattungen der koreanischen Hofmusik

Jedes Werk der Hofmusik aus der Joseon-Dynastie ist auf zwei Ebenen zu kategorisieren. Zum einen kann sie nach den fünf Arten von nationalen Ritualen oder Zeremonien eingeteilt werden.[3] Diese sind bekannt als *Orye* (오례; 五禮; fünf Rituale): *Gilrye* (Rituale für Ahnenriten; 길례; 吉禮), *Hyungrye* (Beerdigungen; 흉례; 凶禮), *Binrye* (빈례; 賓禮; Zeremonien im Zusammenhang mit der Diplomatie), *Gunrye* (군례; 軍禮; militärische Zeremonien) und *Garye* (가례; 嘉禮; fröhliche Anlässe wie Geburtstage oder Hochzeiten in der königlichen Familie, siehe Abb. 1). Zum anderen wird sie nach ihrer Herkunft in *Aak* und *Dangak*, chinesisch, sowie *Hyangak*, koreanisch, eingeteilt. *Aak* (아악; 雅樂) stammt aus dem 9. Jahr von König Yejong (1116) der Goryeo-Dynastie. Der Gesandte Jiksung An (安稷崇) brachte neue Musikinstrumente und Noten mit, die als ein Geschenk von Huizong (徽宗, 1082–1135) aus der Song-Dynastie (960–1279) gelten. Der Begriff *Dangak* (당악; 唐樂) beschreibt wörtlich die Musik der Tang-Dynastie (China, 617/18–907). Er bezieht sich auf Musik, die während der vereinten Shilla (676–935) und der Goryeo-Dynastie aus China importiert wurde. Dagegen handelt es sich bei *Hyangak* (향악; 鄕樂) um die in Korea von Koreanern seit der Shilla-Dynastie entwickelte Hofmusik (J. Kim, 2015, S. 41; Song, 2015, S. 7–9, 22).

Musikalische Merkmale

Die Hofmusikpraxis verlangt ausschließlich ein koreanisches Instrumentarium.[4] Sie ist einstimmig und verwendet Fünf- oder Sechstonskalen, die mit *Es* oder *C* als Grundton beginnen; es gibt keine Harmonik. In manchen Fällen ist ein Schlagzeug für das rhythmische Element verantwortlich. Ein Schlaginstrument *Bak* 박 in Form eines offenen Fächers dient dazu, Anfang und Ende eines Musikstücks zu signalisieren. Eventuelle zeitliche Verzögerungen in der Wiedergabe und Dauer einer Note zwischen verschiedenen Instrumenten werden als "natürlich" angesehen. Der Text wird meistens in chinesischen Schriftzeichen geschrieben, da chinesische Schriftzeichen während der Joseon-Dynastie in den Ahnenriten und in den meisten Schriftstücken (insbesondere während der frühen Joseon-Dy-

---

3 *Orye* 오례 ist eines der fünf staatlichen Rituale und leitet sich aus dem alten chinesischen Buch *Jurye* 周禮 ab. *Orye* wurde während der Goryeo-Dynastie in die koreanischen Königshöfe aufgenommen.

4 In diesem Zusammenhang beziehen sich die koreanischen Instrumente auf die Instrumente für traditionelle Musik, die während der Goryeo-Dynastie aus China importiert oder während der Joseon-Dynastie hergestellt wurden. Die traditionelle Klassifizierung von koreanischen Musikinstrumenten wird nach der Herkunft des Instruments in *Aakgi* (Instrumente für *Aak*), *Dangakgi* (Instrumente für *Dangak*) und *Hyangakgi* (Instrumente für *Hyangak*) oder nach dem Material des Instruments in acht Typen eingeteilt: Metall, Stein, Saite, Bambus, Flaschenkürbis, Erde, Leder, Holz.

nastie) gängig waren. Nicht nur in der Hofmusik der Joseon-Dynastie, sondern in der koreanischen Hofmusik überhaupt, werden weder die Namen der Komponisten noch die der Dichter überliefert. In der Joseon-Dynastie gab es Berufe wie Hofmusiker, Musikforscher und Straßenmusiker, aber nicht die Bezeichnung des Komponisten.[5] Im Gegensatz zu aktuellen koreanischen Musiktraditionen, in denen die Autorschaft von Liedtexten und Kompositionen oft ausdrücklich genannt wird, ist diese für die koreanische Hofmusik irrelevant. Dafür gibt es verschiedene Erklärungsansätze: Erstens spiegelt sie möglicherweise die kollektive Natur der Kompositionen und Inszenierungen wider, bei denen der Fokus weniger auf individuellen Schöpfern liegt, sondern vielmehr auf der Harmonie und dem Gesamtereignis. Zweitens können die Gründe dafür am königlichen Hof selbst und den höfischen Etiketten vermutet werden. Unsere heutige Auffassung von Autorschaft kann zudem nicht auf frühere Epochen und schon gar nicht auf die der Joseon-Dynastie übertragen werden.

Verschiedene offizielle höfische Überlieferungen berichten darüber, dass einige Könige wie Sejong (4. König), Sejo (7. König) und Yeonsangun (10. König) über eine musikalische Begabung verfügten (Ha, 2012). Die meisten Hofmusiken entstanden sehr wahrscheinlich als Gemeinschaftsproduktionen der verschiedenen Hofmusiker:innen.[6]

König Sejong und seine Musikpolitik

Sejongs "Vermächtnis"

Sejong der Große (*Sejongdaewang* 세종대왕; 世宗大王, 15.05.1397–08.04.1450, siehe Abb. 2) war der 4. König der Joseon-Dynastie. Er ist bekannt als ein herausragender Förderer der Wissenschaften. Während seiner 32-jährigen Regierungszeit (1418–1450) entstanden große Teile des koreanischen Kulturerbes. Er gründete das königliche Forschungsinstitut *Jiphyeonjeon* 집현전 (集賢殿; Versammlungshalle der Weisen), um Wissenschaftler in verschiedenen Disziplinen auszubilden. Die Studieninhalte bestanden vor allem darin, das politische System des alten China zu vermitteln, sowie Bücher über Geschichte, Literatur, Philosophie, Musik, Medizin, Astronomie, Landwirtschaft, Geografie, den Konfuzianismus u.a. Themen zu verfassen. Infolgedessen wurden während der Regierungszeit von Sejong über 80 wissenschaftliche Bücher in verschiedenen Forschungsbereichen geschrieben. Sejong selbst galt als ein bewanderter Linguist, Literat und Musiker. Darüber hinaus zeigte er großes Interesse an den Naturwissenschaften und ließ Astronomen und Erfinder wie

---

5 In Korea gab es ab Beginn des 20. Jahrhunderts professionelle Komponist:innen, d.h. erst nach der Verbreitung westlicher Musik und Kultur durch westliche Missionare Ende des 19. Jahrhunderts.

6 Das Originalquellenmaterial zur Hofmusik der Joseon-Dynastie befindet sich in den *Joseonwangjo Sillok* (Annalen der Joseon-Dynastie): http://sillok.history.go.kr/. Datum des Zugriffs: 10.01.2024.

Durch Klang zur Harmonie

Abb. 2: *Sejongdaewang* [Foto, Statue von König Sejong auf dem Gwanghwamun-Platz in Seoul].

Yeong-sil Jang 장영실 ausbilden (Kim, 2008). Die Erfindung des koreanischen Schriftsystems *Hangeul* ist eine der wichtigsten Errungenschaften Sejongs. Er nannte die neu erfundene Buchstabenschrift *Hunminjeongeum* 훈민정음 (*Sejong Sillok*, 1443).[7] Bevor er *Hunminjeongum* im Jahr 1446 öffentlich bekanntmachte, ließ er *Jiphyunjeon*-Wissenschaftler eine Dichtung in *Hangeul* schreiben, um die Praktikabilität der neuen Schriftzeichen zu testen (*Sejong Sillok*, 1445a). Infolgedessen wurde 1445 das epische Gedicht *Yongbieocheonga* 용비어천가 geschrieben und 1447 veröffentlicht.[8] *Yongbieocheonga* ist das erste literarische Werk auf Koreanisch, das vor der Veröffentlichung im *Hunminjeongeum* geschrieben wurde. Die *Hangeul*-Schriftzeichen und das neue Schriftsystem wurden mit dem Buch *Hunminjeongeum* (1446) eingeführt. Zweck und Prinzipien erläuterten die *Jiphyunjeon*-Gelehrten darin in chinesischen Schriftzeichen *Hanmun*.

Sejongs musikalische Errungenschaften

Die koreanische Hofmusik und ihre Aufführungspraxis waren unter Sejong von besonderem königlichem Interesse. Während seiner Regierungszeit wurden die Geschichte und die Grundlagen von *Yeak* im Sinne der konfuzianischen Politik intensiv erforscht. Gemäß ihren Idealen erfolgten schließlich die Bewahrungs- und Ausbesserungsarbeiten an den Instrumenten. Ihrem Einfluss unterlagen Besetzung, Melodie, Satzlänge und Aufführungsverfahren. Auch Dekorationen und Kostümen kamen bei herrscherlichen Zeremonien eine besondere Bedeutung zu.

Eine der wesentlichen Ideen Sejongs für die Hofmusik bestand darin, dass er anordnete, die von China überlieferten Hofmusiken (*Aak* und *Dangak*) in den koreanischen Stil zu transferieren. Zu Beginn der Joseon-Dynastie wurden die Ahnenriten noch von

---

7   *Hunminjeongeum* heißt die "richtige Stimme, um das Volk zu lehren". *Hangeul*, das heutzutage die koreanische Sprache bezeichnet, bedeutet "die einzige Schrift" und wurde erstmals Anfang der 1910er Jahre von koreanischen Sprachwissenschaftler:innen wie Sikyung Joo 주시경 verwendet.
8   *Yongbieocheonga* bestand aus insgesamt zehn Bänden und wurde König Sejong am 5. April 1445 (in seinem 27. Regierungsjahr) von Je Kwon, Jeong Inji und Ji An gewidmet.

chinesischer Musik begleitet. Sejong war jedoch der Auffassung, dass sich die koreanischen Könige, welche zu Lebzeiten koreanische Musik gehört hatten, nach dem Tod wohl kaum an der chinesischen Musik erfreuen würden. Deshalb versuchte er die rituelle Ahnenmusik einer Erneuerung zu unterziehen (*Sejong Sillok*, 1425b). Seinem Vorhaben, "neue Musik" für Rituale zu schaffen, widmete er sich nach der Schaffung der koreanische Schrift *Hunminjeongeum*. Laut den Annalen von König Sejong, *Sejong Sillok*, forderte dieser in seinem 27. Regierungsjahr (1445) das königliche Sekretariat *Seungjeongwon* (承政院) auf, für eine "gute (neue) Musik" zu sorgen:

> Unser Land [Joseon] liegt am Rande des Fernen Ostens, also ist die Musik nicht die gleiche wie in China. Einstmals wurde uns in der Tang-Dynastie ein Musikinstrument geschenkt. Generationen vergingen, danach brach die Musik zusammen. […] Um das *Yongbi*-Gedicht [*Yongbieocheonga*] nun für die Blas- und Saiteninstrumente einrichten zu können, versuchen die *Changgabi* [Weibliche Künstlerinnen, die singen und tanzen], es auf die *Dangak* [Musik der Tang-Dynastie] abzustimmen, […]. Es wäre auch gut, die Worte des Heimatlandes mit der Melodie der Musik der Tang-Dynastie in Einklang zu bringen, ihre Form und ihren Klang zu lernen und es zukünftigen Generationen zu ermöglichen, sie zu sehen und zu hören (*Sejong Sillok*, 1445b).

> 우리 나라는 멀리 동쪽 변방에 있어 음악이 중국과 같지 않다. 옛적에 당(唐) 나라에서 악기(樂器)를 하사하였는데, 그 뒤에 세대가 멀어서 음악이 무너졌다. […] 이제 용비시(龍飛詩)를 관현(管絃)에 입히고자 하여 창가비로 하여금 당악(唐樂)에 맞추려 하니, […] 본국의 음악[音]을 당률(唐律)에 합하게 하여 그 모양과 소리를 익혀서 후인이 보고 듣게 함도 좋을 것이다.

Die Ausführungen von Sejong vermitteln die Idee zu einer neuen Hofmusik als eine Kombination von chinesischer Musik mit koreanischer Poesie. Obwohl Sejong seiner Auffassung Ausdruck verlieh, dass sich die Musik von *Joseon* von der chinesischen unterscheiden sollte, wählte er dennoch einen Kompromiss aus beidem, der neugeschriebene koreanische Texte *Yongbieocheonga* mit chinesischer Musik (bzw. Musik im chinesischen Stil) vereinte. Doch scheint dieses Resultat von königlicher Seite noch immer hinterfragt worden zu sein, denn einige Jahre später komponierte Sejong selbst Musik für *Yongbieocheonga*, wie es in den Quellen heißt. In seinem 31. Regierungsjahr ließ er die *Gisaengs* (Künstlerinnen) und Musiker seine Komposition nach dem Text des *Yongbieocheonga* spielen und sagte: "Jetzt gebe ich euch neue Musik, genießt diese nach Herzenslust." (*Sejong Sillok*, 1449a) [이제 그대들에게 신악(新樂)을 내리니 마땅히 마음껏 즐기라.] Bemerkenswert ist, dass in diesem Zusammenhang von "neuer Musik" (*Sinak* 신악 新樂) die Rede ist. Dass Sejong selbst diese neue Musik komponierte, geht aus den höfischen Annalen (*Sejong Sillok*) hervor, die am Tag nach der Aufführung aufgezeichnet wurden. In einem Eintrag vom 11. Dezember in seinem 31. Regierungsjahr (1449) heißt es beispielsweise:

Der König war sehr bewandert in der Musik. Alle Rhythmen der neuen Musikstücke wurden von ihm gesetzt. Er machte Musikstücke an einem Abend, als er sich in den Rhythmus fand, während er mit einem Stock den Takt klopfte (*Sejong Sillok*, 1449b).

임금은 음률을 깊이 깨닫고 계셨다. 신악(新樂)의 절주(節奏)는 모두 임금이 제정하였는데, 막대기를 짚고 땅을 치는 것으로 음절을 삼아 하루저녁에 제정하였다.

Sejong soll, wie die Quellen mitteilen, für seine neue Musik sogar die Instrumente entwickelt und hergestellt haben. Zahlreiche offizielle historische Dokumente, darunter die *Sillok*, teilen mit, er habe über ein hervorragendes Gehör verfügt und Musik eigenständig komponiert. Ein bekannter Nachweis, der von seinen besonderen Hörfähigkeiten kündet, findet sich im *Sejong Sillok*. Dort ist zudem die Reden von seiner Entdeckung des L-förmigen Klangsteins *Pyungyeong*:

Chinesische *Gyeong* [Klangsteine] harmonieren nicht wirklich, aber die jetzt hergestellten Hartsteine scheinen richtig zu sein. Es ist schon eine gute Sache, einen soliden Stein zu haben. Der nun zu hörende Klang ist sehr klar und schön. […] Aber was ist der Grund dafür, dass der Klang der ersten (der neunten Note) etwas hoch ist? (*Sejong Sillok*, 1433)

중국의 경(磬)은 과연 화하고 합하지 아니하며, 지금 만든 경(磬)이 옳게 된 것 같다. 경석(磬石)을 얻는 것이 이미 하나의 다행인데, 지금 소리를 들으니 또 한 매우 맑고 아름다우며, […] 다만 이칙(夷則) 1매(枚)가 그 소리가 약간 높은 것은 무엇 때문인가.

Sejong scheint sich des Öfteren mit Yeon Park (1378–1458), einem Hofmusiker und Musiktheoretiker, über die Verordnung und Überarbeitung der Hofmusik ausgetauscht zu haben. Den *Sejong Sillok* zufolge beauftragte er diesen in seinem 7. Regierungsjahr, verschiedene Musikbücher sowie eine Instrumental- und Notationskunde zu verfassen und die Melodien von *Hyangak*, *Dangak* und *Aak* gründlich zu prüfen und aufzuschreiben (*Sejong Sillok*, 1425a). Offensichtlich ging es Sejong u.a. um die genaue Unterscheidung der Ritualmusiken in traditionelle chinesische Musik, wie sie vor allem in Zeremonien für die Vorfahren erklang, und koreanische Musik, die für alle anderen Bereiche relevant war. Überliefert wird, dass Park dem König mehrmals über den Fortgang der Forschungen zur Ritualmusik *Aak* berichtete. Als Ergebnis seiner Bemühungen konnte er im 12. Regierungsjahr das Buch *Aakbo* (Noten für *Aak*) vorlegen. Im Auftrag des Königs entstanden zudem das *Minyo* sowie zahlreiche weitere Kompositionen, Musikabschriften, Choreographien und eine Enzyklopädie der Musikinstrumente (*Sejong Sillok*, 1430).

Verwirklichung politischer Ideale durch Musik

Richtige Staatsführung im Königreich Joseon stand für korrekte Umgangsformen, die moralisches Leben und Musik verbanden und miteinbezogen. Angenommen wurde, dass Musik den Menschen Harmonie bringe und das Gleichgewicht zwischen der Menschheit und dem Universum wiederherstelle (H.-J. Song, 2012; J. Song, 2015).

Sejongs Ansichten wurzelten in der Philosophie seiner Vorgänger. Demnach bedeutet *Yeak* (*Ye* und *Ak*) die Grundlage der Politik. Allerdings begann sich während seiner Regierung eine etwas andere Vorstellung von Musik zu etablieren (H.-J. Song, 2014): Nach königlicher Auffassung hatten *Yeak* (*Ye* und *Ak*), repräsentativ für die Symbiose von Ordnung und Harmonie, im Gleichgewicht zu sein. Das Gleichgewicht sollte in Kultur, Tradition und Musik inner- und außerhalb des Hofes den idealen Zustand darstellen. In diesem Zusammenhang nahm *Ye* eine wesentliche Rolle ein. Ideelles Ziel des Denksystems war es jedoch, die Lebensumstände der Menschen zu verbessern, sie für *Ak* zu sensibilisieren, sie generell für Musik empfindsam zu machen und diese richtig erlernen zu lassen. Sejong vertrat die Ansicht, dass *Ye* bereits gut umgesetzt und integriert war, während es aber an Interesse und Praxis von *Ak* noch mangele. Mit anderen Worten, das Problem des Ungleichgewichts zwischen *Ye* und *Ak* war das Hauptmotiv, das schließlich zur Reform des Musiksystems während der Sejong-Zeit führte.

Eines der grundsätzlichen Probleme bestand darin, dass in der "alten" Auffassung von *Yeak* nur *Aak* als richtige Musik galt, während alle anderen Formen auf Ablehnung stießen. Noch in der Sejong-Zeit wurde *Aak* als ein wichtiger Bestandteil der *Yeak*-Symbiose angesehen, trotzdem gab es einige Kritik, dieser gemäß *Aak* einer grundsätzlichen Reform bedurfte. Die Ansicht, dass *Hyangak* ganz und gar abzulehnen sei, stellte die königliche Politik jedoch weiterhin in Frage, und so teilte Sejong seinen Untertanen bezüglich des *Jongmyo*-Rituals mit:

> Unser Land ist ursprünglich an *Hyangak* gewöhnt. [...] Wie wäre es, wenn wir die Musik [den *Hyangak*] verwenden würden, die unsere Vorfahren im Alltag [ihrer Lebzeit] hörten? (*Sejong Sillok*, 1425b)

> 우리 나라는 본디 향악(鄕樂)에 익숙한데 [···] 조상 어른들의 평시에 들으시던 음악을 쓰는 것이 어떨지.

Sejongs Idee verweist auf die wichtige Rolle, die *Hyangak* im ursprünglichen *Yeak*-Verständnis zukam. Ferner heißt es, dass "*Aak* originär kein koreanischer, sondern ein chinesischer Klang ist" [아악(雅樂)은 본시 우리 나라의 성음이 아니고 실은 중국의 성음인데] (*Sejong Sillok*, 1430a) und "es nicht angebracht ist, alle *Hyangak* [= koreanische Musik] zu verwerfen, um chinesische Musik [= *Aak*] zu benutzen" [중국의 풍류를 쓰고자 하여 향악(鄕樂)을 다 버리는 것은 단연코 불가하다]. (*Sejong Sillok*, 1431).

Trotz dieser Auffassung konnte sich *Hyangak* aufgrund des Widerstands verschiedener Untertanen nicht in den Ahnenriten etablieren (*Sejong Sillok*, 1428). Der König versuchte allerdings das zuvor erwähnte, neu komponierte Werk in *Aak*, d.h. in der Gattung der *Jeryeak*, der Hofmusik für Ahnenzeremonien, aufzunehmen. Laut des Testaments von *Sejong Sillok* aus dem Jahr 1449 wurde versucht, bei *Jongmyojerye*, der Ahnenzeremonie zur Verehrung der verstorbenen Könige und Königinnen der Joseon-Dynastie, neu geschaffene Musikstücke wie *Bongnaeeui* und *Yeominrakman* und *Chihwapyung* aufzuführen. Der König teilte dem *Seungjeongwon* diesbezüglich mit:

Obwohl *Sinak* [neue Musik] nicht in *Aak* verwendet werden darf, kann sie nicht abgeschafft werden, weil sie die Verdienste der Vorfahren des Monarchen widerspiegelt. Wenn *Euijeongbu* [Verwaltungsregierung] und *Kwanseubdogam* [das für Musik zuständige Regierungsamt] dies gemeinsam beobachten und sagen, ob es gut oder schlecht ist, werde ich für Gewinn und Verlust verantwortlich sein (*Sejong Sillok*, 1449b).

이제 신악(新樂)이 비록 아악(雅樂)에 쓰이지는 못하지만, 그러나, 조종(祖宗)의 공덕을 형용하였으니 폐할 수 없는 것이다. 의정부와 관습 도감(慣習都監)에서 함께 이를 관찰하여 그 가부를 말하면, 내가 마땅히 손익(損益)하겠다.

Demnach wollte er seine Musik den Ahnenzeremonien beim "konfuzianischen Schrein" einbringen, sodass sie nun *Aak* (in diesem Zusammenhang bedeutet *Aak* Musik für Ahnenzeremonien) zugehörig sein würde. Letztendlich konnte sich Sejong mit seinen Vorhaben nicht durchsetzen, da er an verschiedenen lokalen Institutionen und Gewalten scheiterte. Es blieb also bei der alten Art von *Aak*, wie sie seit der Goryeo-Dynastie praktiziert wurde.

Das *Yeominrak* aus dem *Bongnaeui* (1447)

Zu Anfang der Joseon-Dynastie initiierte Sejong verschiedene Musikprojekte, um in seinem Königreich eine harmonische Ordnung herzustellen. Dafür schuf er mehrere Musikstücke, unter denen sich nicht nur zeremonielle Musik für seine Vorfahren, sondern auch spezielle Musik für seine Untertanen befanden. Zu diesen gehört das Stück *Yeominrak*. Es wird im *Bonnaeui* überliefert und entstand wohl während seines 29. Regierungsjahres (1447), ein Jahr nach der Erfindung von *Hangeul*.

Besetzung und Intention

Die Quellen teilen mit, dass Sejong selbst die Texte vertonte (*Sejong Sillok*, 1449b). Er fügte diesen auch Tänze hinzu, um eine darstellende Hofkunst namens *Bongnaeui* zu schaffen. Diese Art der Staatsmusik verband Hofmusik (Instrumentalmusik mit Gesang) und Hoftanz auf der Basis der ersten *Hangeul*-Literatur. Die Sammlung beinhaltet Kompositionen wie *Yeominrak*, was etwa bedeutet "die Musik, die man zusammen mit dem Volk genießt". Enthalten ist außerdem *Chihwapyung*, das die Entschlossenheit des Königs besingt, mit Wohlwollen zu regieren. Der im letzten Satz stehende Begriff *Chipunghyung* bedeutet: alles in bester Ordnung für die Untergebenen. Wie aus dem Titel hervorgeht, erfolgte dies im Sinne einer Regierung, die Frieden und Wohlstand idealisierte.

Textherkunft

Unter Sejong entstand zudem eines der bedeutenden staatlichen Literaturwerke, geschrieben im neuen Alphabet: *Yongbieocheonga*, was so viel wie "Die Lieder der gen himmelstürmenden und herrschenden Drachen" bedeutet. Die Dichtung besteht aus 125 koreanischen Gedichten und der entsprechenden klassischen chinesischen Poesie. Jedes Kapitel ist mit einem ausführlichen Kommentar versehen.

Die Texte für das *Yeominrak* stammen aus den Kapiteln 1, 2, 3 und 4 sowie 125 des *Yongbieocheonga*. Kapitel 1 und 125 stellen den Anfangs- bzw. Schlussteil der Dichtung dar und haben unregelmäßige Reime, während die mittleren Teile 2, 3, 4 eine regelmäßige Reimstruktur aufweisen.

Der erste Teil des *Yeominrak* beschreibt die Gründung der Joseon-Dynastie und wünscht dem Land für viele Generationen Frieden und Wohlstand. Im zweiten Teil heißt es, dass, gleich einem tief im Boden verwurzelten Baum, den der Wind nicht umzustürzen vermag, der zahlreiche Blüten und Früchte trägt, auch das Königreich Joseon mit starken Wurzeln lange bestehen bleiben und zahlreiche Blütezeiten erleben werde. Teil drei stellt die Anfänge der Könige der Zhou-Dynastie den Begründern von Joseon gegenüber. Teil vier beschreibt die Geschichte der Könige von Zhou bzw. der Gründer von Joseon, die ihre Hauptstädte aufgrund der Invasion ihrer jeweiligen Feinde verlegen mussten. Der letzte und fünfte Teil umfasst drei Zeilen. In der ersten Zeile wird auf die Zeit verwiesen, in der die Hauptstadt des Landes gegründet wurde. Dem Land wird zudem viel Glück gewünscht. Die zweite Zeile bittet den zukünftigen König, den Himmel zu respektieren und

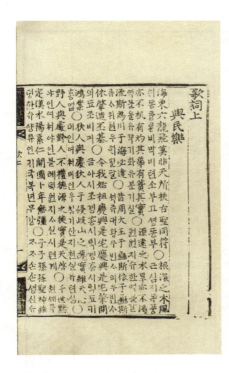

Abb. 3: *Yeominrak*.

sich gut um seine Untertanen zu kümmern. Die dritte Zeile fordert den zukünftigen König auf, die Erfolge und Opfer seiner Vorfahren zu ehren.

Form und Stil

Das *Bongnaeui* beinhaltet einem Ausruf, der den Beginn und das Ende der Aufführung ankündigt, ein Vor- und Nachspiel, das beim Ein- und Auszug von Musikern und Tänzern erklingt, und drei weitere große Sätze in der Mitte. Insgesamt besteht es aus sieben Teilen: *Jeoninja, Jinguho, Yeominrak, Chihwapyung, Chuipunghyung, Huinja* und *Toeguho*. Unter ihnen entsprechen *Jeoninja* und *Huinja* dem Vor- und Nachspiel. *Jinguho* und *Toeguho* sind die jeweilig nachfolgenden Rufe. Während das *Yeominrak* auf chinesischen Texten beruht, sind *Yongbieocheonga. Chihwapyung* und *Chuipunghyung* auf koreanische Texte vertont (Vgl. Tab.). *Bonnaeeui* stellt eine Aufführungskunst dar, in der sich Musik, Gesang und Tanz verflechten und in ihren Kunstformen ergänzen.

Titel	Beschreibung	Text	Instrumente
Jeoninja	Eingangsmusik		
Jinguho	Ankündigung Beginn		
Yeominrak	Satz 1	chin. Text	*Dangak + Hyangak*
Chihwapyung	Satz 2	kor. Text	*Hyangak*
Chipunghyung	Satz 3	kor. Text	*Hyangak*
Husinja	Ausgangsmusik		
Teoguho	Ankündigung Ende		

Tabelle: Aufbau der *Bongnaeeui*

Wie bereits erwähnt entstand der Text des *Yongbieocheonga* hauptsächlich in *Hangeul*. Hinzu kamen chinesische Poesie sowie ausführliche Kommentare zu den verschiedenen Texten. Die Sprache der Poesie wurde auch auf den Musikstil übertragen. Der erste Satz

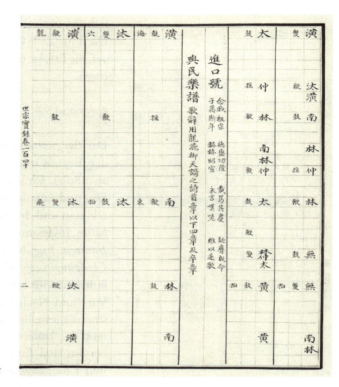

Abb. 4: Anfangsteil *Yeominrak* von Joseon aus dem *Sejong Sillok*

Yeominrak aus dem *Bonnaeui*, basierend auf einem chinesischen Text aus dem *Yongbieocheonga*, enthält eine Musik im chinesischen Stil (*Dangak*). Die Musik im zweiten und dritten Satz (*Chihwapyung* und *Chipunghyung*) wurde im koreanischen Stil (*Hyangak*) komponiert. Während *Dangak* eine sechsstufige Tonleiter mit dem Grundton *C* verwendet, basiert *Hyangak* auf einer fünfstufigen Tonleiter mit dem Grundton *Es*.

Laut Sukhie Moon kann *Yeominrak* aufgrund der folgenden musikalischen Merkmale als eine Musik im *Hyangak*-Stil betrachtet werden: Erstens besteht *Yeominrak* aus den Tönen *Hwang, Tae, Jung, Im, Nam* und *Mu*, welche den westlichen Tönen *Es, F, As, B, C* und *Des* entsprechen.[9] Hier fungiert der letzte Ton *Mu* (*Des*) wie ein kurzer Nebenton. Mit Ausnahme von dem Nebenton *Des* entsprechen die restlichen Töne (*Es, F, As, B, C*) der *Pyungjo* genannten Tonleiter des *Hyangak*-Genres. Auch die Länge und Tonhöhe der ausgehaltenen Noten, die das Ende einer Phrase bilden, folgen dem *Hyangak*-Stil (Moon, 2013).

Der erste Satz, *Yeominrak*, basiert auf chinesischen Schriftzeichen. Allerdings wurden

---

9   *Hwang, Dae Tae, Hyup, Go, Jung, Yu, Im I, Nam Mu,* und *Eung* können als Notennamen in *Hyangak* jeweils mit *Es, E, F, Ges, G, As, A, B, H, C,* und *Dis* verglichen werden. Dieselben Notennamen wie oben entsprechen *C, Cis, D, Dis, E, F, Fis, G, Gis, A, Ais, H* in *Aak* und *Dangak*.

nicht nur chinesische Instrumente für *Dangak*, sondern auch koreanische Instrumente für *Hyangak* besetzt. Der auf koreanische Texte komponierte 2. und 3. Satz, *Chihwapyung* und *Chipunghyung*, integrierte ausschließlich koreanische Instrumente für *Hyangak*.

Noten und Aufführungspraxis

Das *Bongnaeui* (siehe Abb. 4) kam als eine Art "Marsch" in den königlichen Zeremonien der Joseon-Dynastie zur Aufführung. Die Musik wurde in *Jeongganbo*-Notation (das traditionelle koreanische Notationssystem) aufgeschrieben, die während der Herrschaft von Sejong entwickelt wurde und bis heute überliefert ist. *Jeonggan* 정간 (井間) heißt "Vierecke", während *Bo* 보 (譜) "Noten" bedeutet. Die *Jeongganbo*-Notation wird von oben nach unten und von rechts nach links gelesen (siehe Abb. 3). Die Tonhöhe wird in der ersten Spalte von rechts als Notenname notiert, der Schlag der Schlaginstrumente hingegen in der zweiten Spalte von rechts.

In der *Jeongganbo* kann man den Rhythmus anhand der Vierecke zählen. Es gibt verschiedene Ansichten, welcher westliche Notenwert einem Viereck entspricht, bzw. für wie viele Sekunden er gespielt werden soll. Die Transkription der obigen *Jeongganbo* in westlicher Notation lautet wie folgt:

Notenbeispiel: Übertragung des Anfangsteils des *Yeominrak*.

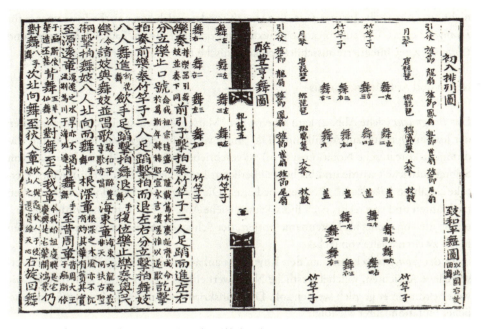

Abb. 5: Tänzerformationen des *Bongnaeeui* aus dem *Akhakgwebeom*.

Die Musikenzyklopädie *Akhakgwebeom* der Sejong-Zeit überliefert zudem die Choreographie von *Bongnaeeui*, in der die Anordnung und Bewegung der Tänzer:innen ausführlich erklärt wird. In *Jeoninja* und *Huinja* treten Tänzerinnen ein bzw. aus, und in den Hauptteilen *Yeominrak*, *Chihwapyung* und *Chuipunghyung* werden verschiedene Tanzstile in den jeweiligen Sätzen aufgeführt.

Der Tanz *Bongnaeui* wird heutzutage am *Hangeul*-Tag in Korea gespielt, um die Verkündigung von *Hangeul* durch Sejong zu feiern. Auch bei Zeremonien für den Ahnenschrein der königlichen Familie zu Ehren des königlichen Hofes und für die zivilen und militärischen Behörden wird er aufgeführt.

Fazit

Nach dem Konzept von *Yeak* sollten die Moral für Ordnung und die Musik zwischen unterschiedlichen Geschlechtern, Wertvorstellungen und Kulturen für Harmonie sorgen. Musik spielte eine wichtige Rolle in der Staatsauffassung und Philosophie der Joseon-Dynastie. Sie erklang nicht nur zum Vergnügen der Menschen, sondern verfolgte auch das Ideal, ihre Herzen zum Guten zu bewegen und dadurch eine ideale Gesellschaft zu kreieren.

Um diesen Prozess zu unterstützen, soll Sejong selbst zum Pinsel gegriffen und das Stück *Yeominrak* komponiert haben. Damit gedachte er sich selbst und andere stets daran zu erinnern, dass er mit seinen Untertanen eng verbunden war. Er soll aber nicht nur komponiert und Musikinstrumente erfunden haben, man schreibt ihm auch die Erfindung des koreanischen Notensystems *Jeongganbo* zu. In diesem erfolgte die Niederschrift bzw. Transkription sämtlicher Hofmusik. Seit Anfang des 20. Jahrhunderts, d.h. mit der Rezeption westlicher Musik und deren Notenschrift, veranlasste das National Gugak Center die in *Jeongganbo* notierte Musik in die westliche Notenschrift zu übertragen. In welchem Tempo die Noten heute gespielt werden, ist nicht nur ein wichtiger Diskussionspunkt in der westlichen Übertragung, sondern auch in der historisch informierten Aufführungspraxis Koreas. In den höfischen Aufzeichnungen der Joseon-Dynastie wird nur erwähnt, dass (Jahr für Jahr) die Hofmusik immer schneller gespielt wurde. Wie schnell sie aber genau gewesen sein könnte, ist noch immer fraglich. Die meisten koreanischen Hofmusiken werden von Koreanern als "zu langsam" bewertet (An, 2011). Das Tempo der damaligen Zeit zu finden und dieses entsprechend der aktuellen Musikkultur neu zu interpretieren, gehört zu den Aufgaben der aktuellen Forschung.

Sejongs Versuch, chinesische und koreanische Musik zu verbinden, bedarf noch weiterer Forschungen. In der Praxis dürfte es ein komplexer und zugleich komplizierter Vorgang gewesen sein, koreanische und chinesische Instrumente zusammenzubringen. Sejongs Bestreben, "reine" koreanische Musik, *Hyangak*, als Ahnenmusik für seine Vorfahren zu schaffen – obwohl die koreanische Musik nicht aufgeführt wurde – hat unter dem Gesichtspunkt der *Hyo* 효 (孝 "Respekt vor den Eltern") im Konfuzianismus eine immense Bedeutung. Das große Engagement Sejongs für die Musik verdeutlicht, welch wichtige und komplexe Rolle ihr im staatlichen, herrscherlichen und rituellen Verständnis zukam. Bemerkenswert ist, dass dieser König ihr besonders verbunden war und gedachte, ihr eine ganz besondere Gestalt zu geben. Offensichtlich strebte er an, sich damit in die Geschichte seiner Dynastie auf besondere Weise einzuschreiben.

Bibliographie

Handschriften

National Institute of Korean History. *Sejong Sillok* [Wahre Aufzeichnungen von Sejong; 세종실록; 世宗實錄] der *Joseonwangjo Sillok* [Annalen der Joseon-Dynastie 조선왕조실록; 朝鮮王朝實錄]. http://sillok.history.go.kr/. Datum des Zugriffs: 10.01.2024.
Aak yeonjuui tadangham deunge daehae uinonhada (1430a, 11. September). *Sejong Sillok* (Bd. 49). http://sillok.history.go.kr/id/kda_11209011_001. Datum des Zugriffs: 10.01.2024.

Agseoleul chanjibhage hago, aggiwa agbobeob-eul sseoseo chaeg-eul mandeuldolog yejo-eseo hada (1425a, 24. Juli). *Sejong Sillok* (Bd. 27). http://sillok.history.go.kr/id/kda_10702024_003. Datum des Zugriffs: 10.01.2024.

Dangsangaggwa danghaageul ilsie hamkke yeonjuhaneun ilhyangag yeonju munje deungeul san-guihage hada (1425b, 15. Oktober). *Sejong Sillok* (Bd. 30). http://sillok.history.go.kr/id/kda_10710015_005. Datum des Zugriffs: 10.01.2024.

Gimjongseoga yeoageul pyehal geoseul aloeda (1430b, 28. Juli). *Sejong Sillok* (Bd. 49). http://sillok.history.go.kr/id/kda_11207028_002. Datum des Zugriffs: 10.01.2024.

Gwonje jeonginji anji deung-i 《*yongbieocheonga*》 *10gwoneul ollida* (1445a, 5. April). *Sejong Sillok* (Bd. 108). http://sillok.history.go.kr/id/kda_12704005_003. Datum des Zugriffs: 10.01.2024.

Hunminjeongeumeul changjehada (1443, 30. Dezember). *Sejong Sillok* (Bd. 102). http://sillok.history.go.kr/id/kda_12512030_002. Datum des Zugriffs: 10.01.2024.

Imgeumi geunjeongjeoneseo hoelyeyeoneul bepuleossneunde, cheoeumeulo aageul sayonghada (1433, 1. Januar). *Sejong Sillok* (Bd. 59). http://sillok.history.go.kr/id/kda_11501001_003. Datum des Zugriffs: 10.01.2024.

Joheun eumageul mandeul geoseul seungjeongwone jeonjihada (1445b, 13. September). *Sejong Sillok* (Bd. 109). http://sillok.history.go.kr/id/kda_12709013_002. Datum des Zugriffs: 10.01.2024.

Jongchin munmu 2pum isang deungui gwanwonege sayeonhada (1449a, 10. Dezember). *Sejong Sillok* (Bd. 126). http://sillok.history.go.kr/id/kda_13112010_001. Datum des Zugriffs: 10.01.2024.

Sasinhoelyee sayonghal eumage daehae nonuihada (1431, 2. August). *Sejong Sillok* (Bd. 53). http://sillok.history.go.kr/id/kda_11308002_001. Datum des Zugriffs: 10.01.2024.

Sinakui jonpye yeobuleul uijeongbuwa gwanseub dogameseo nonuihage hada (1449b, 11. Dezember). *Sejong Sillok* (Bd. 126). http://sillok.history.go.kr/id/kda_13112011_001. Datum des Zugriffs: 10.01.2024.

Veritable Records of the Joseon Dynasty. (o. J.). National Institute of Korean History. http://sillok.history.go.kr/intro/english.do. Datum des Zugriffs: 10.01.2024.

Wondangwa sajigui pungunloeujeusaseonnong deungui jesae hyangageul sseuji moshage hada (1428, 4. Januar). *Sejong Sillok* (Bd. 39). http://sillok.history.go.kr/id/kda_11001004_013. Datum des Zugriffs: 10.01.2024.

Sekundärliteratur

An, D. (2011). *Jeongjo chiseeorok*. Purme.

Cho, N. (2007). A Study on the Music (樂) in Confucianism. *Journal of Eastern Philosophy* 49, 83–116. https://doi.org/10.17299/tsep..49.200702.83. Datum des Zugriffs: 10.01.2024.

Ha, J. (2012). Gajang eumagjeog jaeneungi ttwieonassdeon wangeun nugu? *Offizieller Blog des National Gugak Center.* https://blog.naver.com/gugak1951/20170752389. Datum des Zugriffs: 10.01.2024.

Kang, M. (2016). The Reassessment of the Common Views of the Studies on Sillok (實錄). *Kyujanggak* 49, 247–278. https://doi.org/10.22943/kyujg.2016..49.006. Datum des Zugriffs: 10.01.2024.

Kim, H. (2008). Phases of Document and Record in Joseon Period: Reappraisal on Sacho and Sijeonggi. 古文書研究 32, 43–65. https://doi.org/10.21027/manusc.2008.32..002. Datum des Zugriffs: 10.01.2024.

Kim, J. (2015). Sacrificial Rituals and Music. In H. Kim (Hrsg.), *Ritual Music of the Korean Court* (S. 29–72). National Gugak Center. https://www.gugak.go.kr/site/program/board/basicboard/view?menuid=001003002005&pagesize=10&boardtypeid=24&boardid=17829&lang=ko. Datum des Zugriffs: 10.01.2024.

Kim, S. (2008). An Example of an Imaginative Approach toward Documentary Literature – Centered in the Related Records of Jang Young-Sil. *Dongyang Studies in Korean Classics* 27, 5–38.

Kim, S. (2021). Music Practice and Theory of King Sejong and Sejo along with the Prefaces of Each Sillok Akbo. *JANGSEOGAK* 46, 259–289. https://doi.org/10.25024/jsg.2021.46..259. Datum des Zugriffs: 10.01.2024.

Moon, S. (2013). The Musical Composition of Bongnaeui in the Annals of King Sejong. *The Research of Performance Art and Culture* 27, 285–320. https://doi.org/10.35150/korear.2013..27.010. Datum des Zugriffs: 10.01.2024.

Sheen, D. (2016). A Reconsideration on the Theory of Gochwi – Ak (鼓吹樂) related to the New Music in The Music of Sejong's Annals. *Studies in Korean Music* 60, 125–144.

Song, B. (1998). Sejongdaewangui eumag eobjeoge daehan yeogsajeog jaejomyeong-21segileul apdugo-. *Journal of Sejong-Studies* 12·13, 29–61.

Song, H.-J. (2012). The Purpose and Method of Exploiting Music in Politics during the Reign of King Sejong. *The Eastern Art* 20, 187–220.

Song, H.-J. (2014). Recognition of Lie-Yue (禮樂) Thinking and Reorganization of National Ritual Music in Reign of King Sejong. *The Journal of Korean Studies* 51, 111–142. https://doi.org/10.17790/kors.2014..51.111. Datum des Zugriffs: 10.01.2024.

Song, J. (2015). Introduction. In H. Kim (Hrsg.), *Ritual Music of the Korean Court*, 7–28. National Gugak Center. https://www.gugak.go.kr/site/program/board/basicboard/view?menuid=001003002005&pagesize=10&boardtypeid=24&boardid=17829&lang=ko. Datum des Zugriffs: 10.01.2024.

Song, J. (2020). Musical Realization of Sejongsillog-agbo Bonglaeui. *The Chin-Tan Society* 135, 383–402.

Abbildungsnachweise

Abb. 1: Uigwe-Amt der Joseon. (1848). *Injeongjeonjinhado* 〈인정전진하도(仁政殿陳賀圖)〉 [Malerei auf Seide, 1 und 2 Bilder in: 무신년진찬도병(戊申年進饌圖屛), Paravent insgesamt 8 Bilder, jeweils 141.5 x 49.5 cm]. National Museum of Korea, Seoul, Korea, Nr. 13243.

https://www.museum.go.kr/site/main/relic/search/view?relicId=731. Datum des Zugriffs: 10.01.2024.

Abb. 2: Kim, H.S. (2014). *Sejongdaewang* [Foto, Statue von König Sejong auf dem Gwanghwa-mun-Platz in Seoul]. Dari Photo Art.

Abb. 3: *Yeominrak*. (Joseon). *Akjanggasa* [A collection of music pieces of late Goryeo to early Joseon; 樂章歌詞], o. S., Academy of Korean Studies (4-6774). http://encykorea.aks.ac.kr/Contents/Item/E0036342#modal. Datum des Zugriffs: 10.01.2024.

Abb. 4: *Yeominrak*. (Joseon). *Sejong Sillok* (Bd. 140). http://sillok.history.go.kr/id/kda_11001004_013. Datum des Zugriffs: 10.01.2024.

Abb. 5: *Bongnaeeui*. (Joseon). *Akhakgwebeom*, 1988, Seoul National Gugak Center, S. 127, National Gugak Center.

Notenbeispiel: *Yeominrak*. (2017). *Hangukeumak Nr. 36*. Eunhapub, 7, National Gugak Center.

The Soundscape of the Popes
Music, Sound and Communication Strategies
of Early Modern Papacy

Tobias C. Weißmann

After Pope Julius II passing away three weeks earlier, people in Rome and far beyond had been waiting impatiently to learn who would be his successor as the head of the Catholic Church. On the morning of 13 March 1513, the time finally came: The windows that had been walled up at the beginning of the conclave were thrown open and Cardinal Alessandro Farnese spoke with a raised voice to the people gathered below, proclaiming, "I announce to you with great joy, we have a pope: the most eminent and most reverend Lord Giuliano de' Medici [...], who has taken the name Leo X".[1] "After these words had been announced," the Florentine doctor Giovanni Giacomo Penni writes in his account of the election and coronation of his compatriot, "for two hours there was heard much clamour and noise of mortars and other artillery in Hadrian's Castle [Castel Sant'Angelo] and the Apostolic Palace, as well as the playing of various instruments and the ringing of bells, and the people were shouting 'VIVAT LEO' and 'PALLE, PALLE', that it seemed as if the heavens were resounding and thundering."[2]

It may come as no surprise that the election of Leo X, who was to become one of the great patrons of music and the visual arts of the Italian Renaissance, was announced with such an extensive sound choreography. The election of Christ's vicar on earth was an event of the utmost importance, not only for the universalist Papal Church, but also for the social and political fabric at the papal court and in the Vatican State: After all, the pontiff was both the spiritual head of Catholic Christendom and the temporal ruler of the city of Rome and the Papal State, which was one of the larger territorial states of the Italian pen-

---

1   "Et la mattina seguente, ad hore XIV, rotta la finestra del conclave, quale era murata, forno per el. r. Alessandro Farnesio, diaco, cardinale de S. Eustachio, tal parole con alta et intelligibile voce publicate: 'Gaudium magnum nuntio vobis, papam habemus, reverendissimum dominum Joannem de Medicis, diaconum cardinalem Sanctae Mariae in Domenica, qui vocatur Leo decimus.'" (Penni, 1513, s.p.).

2   "Finite de publicare le dicte parole, fu sentito per spatio de doi hore, nel Castello Adriano, et il Palazzo Apostolico, tanto strepito, et romore de bombarde, at altre artiglierie, et suoni di varij instrumenti, et Campane, e voce di Populo gridare VIVA LEONE, et PALLE, PALLE, che parea proprio il Cielo tonitruasse, o fulminasse." (Penni, 1513, s.p.; see Cummings, 1992, pp. 11–14).

insula in the early modern period (Pastor, 1925–1933; Prodi, 1987; Signorotto & Visceglia, 1998; 2002; Büchel & Reinhard, 2003). As the papacy was an elective monarchy whose sovereign was always a celibate cleric elected by the cardinals from their circle, dynastic continuity was systematically prevented. Rather, the entire leadership changed with a new pope, since a newly elected pontiff often belonged to a faction opposed to his predecessor, which is why he entrusted his own confidants with positions of power. This more or less regular change of the ruling elite ensured a highly competitive social climate at the court and in the city, which was reflected in an incomparable cultural flowering of music and the visual arts by means of extensive patronage.

Since the Papal States, unlike hereditary monarchies, remained without a head during the period of *sede vacante*, between the death of a pontiff and the election and enthronement of his successor, this was a time of great uncertainty and, not infrequently, social and political unrest in the city. While the rituals were, in any case, of great significance at the papal court (Visceglia & Brice, 1997; Visceglia, 2002; DeSilva, 2022), the ceremonies surrounding the election and investiture of a new pontiff were of particularly outstanding importance due to this power vacuum and the need to legitimize the new pope (Fagiolo, 1997; Boiteux, 2002; Wassilowsky, 2010).

This paper investigates the constituent rituals of the papacy, the election and coronation of a pontiff, and the taking possession of the Lateran, the so-called *possesso*, and asks what function music and sonic manifestations fulfilled for the announcement and legitimization of a new pope. These were highly complex, ceremonially determined events, and an in-depth treatment could fill entire books. Thus, the focus here is on those acts that were performed in the urban space before the eyes and ears of the general population. As will be argued, within the multimedia interplay of the rituals, music and sound pursued a dual communication strategy which aimed to demonstrate symbolically the legitimacy of the pontiff and the social hierarchies at the papal court and to make the power of the papacy and the Catholic Church tangible to the senses. The study can build on rich research on musical culture at the papal court,[3] on the significance of music for papal ceremonies[4] and on festival culture in early modern Rome,[5] while methodically connecting to studies on symbolic communication[6] and on sound as an instrument of urban communication and courtly representation in the pre-modern era.[7]

---

3   For music at the papal court see Starr, 1987; Janz 1994; Reynolds, 1995; Sherr, 1998; Pietschmann, 2007; 2012; Rostirolla, 2017; Weißmann, 2024.

4   For these studies, see Schimmelpfennig, 1994; Žak, 1994; Bölling, 2006; Wald-Fuhrmann, 2012.

5   For festivals in early modern Rome, see Fagiolo dell'Arco et al., 1977–1978; 1997; Fagiolo, 1997; Weißmann, 2021.

6   For symbolic communication in early modern Europe, see Stollberg-Rilinger, 2004; 2010; 2013.

7   For these studies, see Žak, 1979; Berns, 2006; Atkinson, 2016; for recent research, cf. the work of

The Soundscape of the Popes

The basis of this study, whose temporal focus extends from the late 15th to the end of the 17th century, is the comparative evaluation of different types of sources: the *Caeremoniale Romanum* of 1488, diaries of various papal masters of ceremonies, hand-written and printed accounts such as eyewitness accounts and festival books, as well as etchings and engravings. These offer different information and must be critically examined according to their genre characteristics.

The Election and Proclamation of a New Pope

Due to the importance of the election of the pope, the *Caeremoniale Romanum* devotes its first chapter, *De electione Romani pontificis*, to the ceremonies taking place between the death of a pontiff and the enthronement of his successor (Dykmans, 1980, pp. 27–52). This fundamental work, written by the papal master of ceremonies Agostino Patrizi Piccolomini with the support of his predestined successor Johannes Burckard and completed in 1488, is a comprehensive set of rules for all papal ceremonies. It was to remain largely valid until the second half of the 20th century. According to Patrizi, after a nine-day *novena* for the deceased pontiff, the papal election began with a Mass *de Spiritu Sancto* in St. Peter's Basilica before the cardinals moved into conclave, while the papal chapel sang the hymn *Veni creator spiritus*, which was intended to ensure the Holy Spirit's assistance for a successful election.[8]

While in the 16th century, the conclave had taken place in the rather small Pauline Chapel, with the conclave reform of Gregory XV in 1621/1622, it was transferred to the Sistine Chapel, where the pope was no longer elected by the homage of a two-thirds majority of the cardinals (*per adorationem*), but by the casting of ballots (*scrutinium*) – a secret election that each cardinal had to make exclusively according to his conscience in the face of Michelangelo's fresco of the *Last Judgement* (Wassilowsky, 2010).

As is well known, the conclave, which could last several days, weeks or even months, took place *in camera*, i.e., behind closed doors, and thus to the exclusion of "the public". In order to satisfy the enormous interest in Rome and the rest of the world, from the end of the 16th century onwards, etchings and engravings were produced showing the floor plan of the Vatican Palace, surrounded by small images depicting the central

---

the research project "The Sound of Power. Sound as an Intermedial Category of Courtly Festive Rituals in an Intercultural Perspectives in the 15th–17th Centuries", as well as the contributions in this volume.

8   "Crucem precedunt familiares cardinalium laici, et immediate cantores cantantes hymnum *Veni creator Spiritus. Quamvis hodie hoc non sit in usu de cantoribus et cantus.*" (Dykmans, 1980, p. 36, l. 24 – p. 37, l. 3, cf. Bölling, 2006, p. 197).

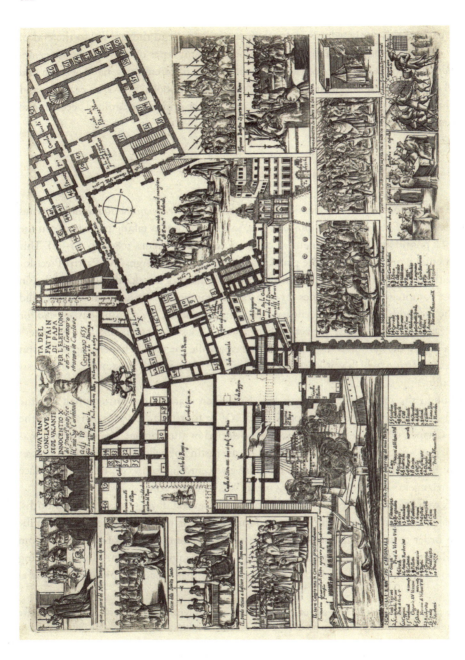

Fig. 1: Floor plan of the Vatican Palace and ceremonies of the *sede vacante* after the death of Innocent X in 1655, etching by an unknown artist.

The Soundscape of the Popes

moments of the ceremonies during the *sede vacante* and the election (Fig. 1). After the election, the walls in all the openings of the Apostolic Palace, which had been erected to guarantee the autonomy of the process, were taken down, and the Cardinal Superior announced the joyful news to the impatiently waiting population – as described above for the election of Leo X – through a window in the sacristy with the famous words: "Annuntio vobis gaudium magnum, papam habemus" ("I announce to you with great joy, we have a pope").[9] While Patrizi leaves it at this terse statement, Burckard reports in his diary that the election of Innocent VIII on 29 August 1484 was followed by manifold sonic manifestations: Upon the verbal announcement, the people cheered, while the bells of St. Peter's Basilica and the Apostolic Palace rang "cum magna potentia" and the palace guards fired salutes continuously and "in triumphum".[10]

In the course of the 17th century, the public announcement was finally made from the Benediction Loggia of the façade, completed in 1612, of the new building of St. Peter's Basilica. The *Compitissima Relazione* by an unknown author of the election of Alexander VIII on 6 October 1689 gives a comprehensive account of the sonic reaction to the announcement made by Cardinal Francesco Maidalchini, accompanied by the master of ceremonies, Candido Cassina, in the Benediction Loggia through a large window opening to the crowd gathered in St. Peter's Square:

> At this point the people, who had already gathered since 23:30, filled with unimaginable joy and contentment, began to shout from all parts of the Piazza, "Vivat Pope ALEXANDER VIII", "Vivat the new Pontiff", "Vivat the House of Ottoboni", and repeating these similar voices several times, obliged the nearby echoes, and more than those of the marvellous temple of St Peter to respond with the same. The universal jubilation doubled, however, and spread with amazement to each one in a moment throughout the city, when the usual cannonade at Castel Sant'Angelo was joined by the applause of the citizens and the festive rumbling of the artillery of the muskets, the trumpets and the drums of the soldiers squadded in that great square of St. Peter's, and the bells of all the churches of Rome.[11]

---

9   "Interim vero prior diaconorum, aperta sacrarii fenestrella, qua populus expectans videri potest, crucem profert alta voce clamitans: Annuntio vobis gaudium magnum, papam habemus." (Dykmans, 1980, p. 49, l. 13–15).

10 "His dictis, omnibus populus acclamavit, campane palatii et basilice s. Petri cum magna potentia pulsate sunt, et scoppetterii custodie palatii in triumphum sine intermission scoppettos oneratos emiserunt [...]." (Thuasne, 1883, p. 63).

11 "All'hora il Popolo essendo già vicino il tocco delle 23 hora, e meza, ripieno d'allegrezza e contento immaginabile, incominciò da tutte le parti della Piazza a gridare Viva Papa ALESSANDRO VIII. Viva il nuovo Pontefice, Viva Casa Ottoboni, e replicando queste voci simili più volte, obligò gl'Echi vicini, e più di quelli del maraviglioso Tempio di San Pietro à rispondergli con le medesime. Raddoppiandosi però il giubilo universale si sparse con maraviglia d'ogn'uno in un momento per tutta

This sound choreography of popular acclamation, the playing of drums and trumpets, musket shots in St. Peter's Square, cannonades from Castel Sant'Angelo, and the ringing of the bells of all the churches of Rome had become the norm for all papal elections of the early modern period, as countless reports in normative and descriptive sources attest.

Following the announcement, the newly-clothed pontiff was carried into St. Peter's on the *sedia gestatoria*, for which, according to Patrizi, the full peal of bells and other "signs of joy" ("signa letitie") were heard.[12] During the entrance into the cathedral, as later sources report, the papal singers sang the antiphon *Ecce sacerdos magnus*.[13] The fact that this venerable moment did not always go off without a hitch is evidenced by another account of the aforementioned election of Alexander VIII:

> Our Lord could not pass, nor those who accompanied him, among the numerous crowds of people who, in order to see him at close quarters, sought to approach him. Wherever he passed, a repeated Vivat resounded, which prohibited the hearing of the sweet chant of the Pontiff's Chapel.[14]

When the pope had arrived at the high altar, the prior of the cardinal bishops intoned the solemn *Te deum laudamus*, which was then continued by the papal singers.[15] This Ambrosian hymn, in which the praise of God and of the sovereign came together, was an integral part of the coronations of emperors and kings (Žak, 1982) and was often made known outside the church with sonic elements (Weißmann, 2021, pp. 131–132, 142–

---

     la Città, quando dato il solito Cenno à Castel Sant'Angelo s'unì à gl'applausi de' Cittadini il festivo rimbombo dell'Artiglierie de' Moschetti, delle Trombe, e Tamburri delle Soldatesche squadronate in quella gran Piazza di San Pietro, e delle Campane di tutte le Chiese di Roma." (Compitissima Relazione, 1689, s.p.).

12   "Dum hec agentur, porte conclavis omnes aperiuntur, repagula muriqui ostiorum et fenestrarum deiciuntur, pulsantur campane, et signa letitie omnis generis eduntur. Pontifex novus, precedente cruce et cardinalibus, ad ecclesiam sancti Petri descendit […]." (Dykmans, 1980, p. 50, l. 16–18).

13   "Si prese ciò fatto la Croce, e precedendo i Musici di Cappella, cantando l'Antifona *Ecce Sacerdos magnus &c.* fù Sua Beatitudine in Sedia Pontificale portato in San Pietro […]." (Compitissima Relazione, s.p). Cf. Bölling, 2006, pp. 199–200.

14   "Non poteva passare Nostro Signore, nè chi l'accompagnava, trà la numerosa folla di Gente, che per vederlo da vicino, à lui procurava accostarsi. Risuonava da per tutto, ov'egli passave, un replicato Viva, che toglieva all'udito il dolce contento della Ponteficia Cappella." (Sincero Racconto, s.p).

15   "Arrivato pure N.S. all'Altare Maggiore di quella Patriarcale, sopra quello fù posto à sedere; & il Signor Card. [Antonio] Bichi più antico Vescovo Card. trà quei ivi si trovarono, intuonò l'Hinno *Te deum laudamus*; che fù seguitato da Musici." Sincero Racconto, s.p. Already Patrizi mentions the *Te deum laudamus*: "Tum surgens, a cardinalibus super altare ad sedendum constituitur cum mitra, et prior episcoporum genuflexus incipit: *Te deum laudamus*, quem hymnum cantores prosequuntur." (Dykmans, 1980, p. 50, l. 21–23).

143). The climax of the canonizations in St. Peter's Basilica, for example, was choreographed sonically between the interior and exterior spaces, as Bartolomeo Lupardi reports of the canonization of Francis de Sales by Alexander VII on 19 April 1665:

> His Holiness then laid down his mitre and intoned the beginning of the hymn (*Te deum laudamus*), and his voice was answered in an instant by various festive voices and sounds of many drummers and trumpets, applauding on earth to the accidental glory, which at that moment was raised to the Saint in heaven, followed by the noise of the firing of the bombs and mortals in St. Peter's Square and Castel Sant'Angelo, and hearing at once the air and hearts filled with universal jubilation, the devout sound of all the companies of the churches of Rome.[16]

At the conclusion of the first function at St. Peter's after the papal election, the pontiff gave the solemn blessing to the people before being carried to his chambers. To celebrate this extraordinary event, further cannonades resounded from Castel Sant'Angelo on this and the following two evenings, while cardinals, aristocrats and ambassadors illuminated their palaces with wax candles and the people lit up the night with countless bonfires as a sign of joy.[17] On the election of Gregory XV on 9 February 1621, the papal master of ceremonies Paolo Alaleone de Branca reports in his diary: "In the Castel Sant'Angelo the bombardments were discharged as usual, and by the most illustrious Lords Cardinals and by the envoys of the princes the usual lights and fires were made."[18] Such illuminations, with which the organizers demonstrated their loyalty to the pope or another monarch and which were often coupled with the drummers and trumpeters continually playing, were a core element of festival culture in early modern Europe (Weißmann, 2021, pp. 172–174).

---

16 "Indi deposta da sua Santità la mitra intuonò il principio dell'Hinno (*Te deum laudamus*) & alla di lui voce risposero in un'instante varie, e festeggianti voci, e suoni di molti Tamburri, e Trombe, che applaudevano in Terra alla Gloria accidentale, che in quel punto s'accrebbe al Santo nel Cielo, seguendo appresso lo strepito dello sparo delle Bombarde, e de' Mortaletti nella piazza di San Pietro, e nel Castel Sant'Angelo, e udendosi in un'subito riempir l'aria, & i cuori di giubilo universale, il devoto suono di tutte le Campane delle Chiese di Roma." (Lupardi, 1665, p. 6).

17 "L'istessa sera, e l'altre due seguenti sparò di nuovo il Castello, e si fecero per tutta la Città fuochi, e luminarij grandissimi, adornandosi ogni fenestra di lumi, e quelle de' Signori Cardinali, de' Prencipi, e degl'Ambasciadori di numerose Torcie di Cera bianca, che duravano acceso fino alle trè hore della notte, buttandosi il rimanente al Popolo in segno d'allegrezza." (Compitissima Relazione, 1689, s.p).

18 "In Arce Sancti Angeli fuerunt exoneratae bombardae de more, et ab Illustrissimis Dominis Cardinalibus et Oratoribus principum ac aliis de sero fuerunt facta luminaria solita et foci." (Wassilowsky et al., 2007, p. 102).

The Coronation of a Pope

Due to the extensive preparations, the coronation of a pope did not take place until several weeks after his election. This rite, which was highly significant for the consolidation of papal power, always began with a solemn mass in St. Peter's Basilica, during which the *Gloria*, the *Laudes regiae*, special responsories, *Adventus* chants and a solemn *Te deum laudamus* were sung (Schimmelpfennig, 1974; Bölling, 2006, pp. 197–200). After the final blessing, the pontiff was carried on the *sedia gestatoria* into the portico of the basilica, while the Cappella Sistina sang the antiphon *Corona aurea*, which referred to the papal tiara.[19] The actual coronation was performed in front of the cathedral façade on a specially erected platform and thus in front of the eyes of the people gathered in St. Peter's Square (Dykmans, 1980, pp. 75–76). After the prior of the cardinal bishops had intoned the *Pater noster* and various antiphons and responsories followed, he crowned the pontiff with the papal crown, the tiara, whereupon the clergy surrounding him as well as the people acclaimed *Kyrie eleison*.[20] Finally, the pope blessed the people, accompanied by an indulgence, the extent of which was read out in both Latin and Italian. As with the announcement of the election, an extensive sound choreography took place at the conclusion of the coronation, as reported, for example, by Alaleone de Branca on the coronation of Urban VIII on 29 September 1623: "And he gave a solemn blessing to the people and granted a plenary indulgence [...] and immediately many bombardments were discharged in the Castel Sant'Angelo by the Swiss Guard. The trumpeters and timpanists from Switzerland resounded."[21]

---

19 Paolo Alaleone de Branca mentions the chant at the coronation of Urban VIII on 29 September 1623: "In lodia sedit in sede gestatoria supra locum accomodatum tabulis, et videbatur ab omnibus, qui fuernt in Platea Sancti Petri, et tunc Cantores Cappellae Apostolicae cantarunt antiphonam 'Corona Aurea' et caetera." (Wassilowsky et al., 2007, p. 375, l. 131–134). According to Burckard, the papal singers responded immediately to the coronation with *Corona aurea*; cf. Dykmans, 1980, p. 75, App. to l. 20; cf. Bölling, 2006, p. 198.

20 "Et cum omnes prelati convenerint, et populus ex basilica in plateam exierit, diaconus a sinistris deponit mitram consuetam e capite pontificis, et diaconus a dextris thyaram, quod regnum appellant, triplici corona ornatum, pontificis capiti imponit, populo acclamante *Kyrieleison* [sic]. Et diaconus a dextris latine, a sinistris vero vulgariter, publicant plenarias indulgentias." (Dykmans, 1980, p. 75, l. 19–p. 76, l. 4); cf. Schimmelpfennig, 1974, pp. 214–219.

21 "et dedit solemnem benedictionem populo et concessit indulgentiam plenariam [...] et statim in Arce Sancti Angeli fuerunt exoneratae multae bombardae et in Platea Sancti Petri à militibus Helvetiis. Tubicines sonarunt et timpanistae Helvetii." (Wassilowsky et al., 2007, p. 376).

The Cavalcade through the City and the Possession of the Lateran

In the 15th century, the solemn occupation of the Lateran immediately followed the coronation, but from the election of Julius II in 1503 onwards, the so-called *possesso* took place a few weeks later.[22] This ceremony always began with a pompous *cavalcata*, with which the pope, accompanied by numerous representatives of the Curia, the city, the Roman nobility, and foreign powers, marched from St. Peter's to the Basilica of St. John Lateran. From the second half of the Cinquecento, the *iter*, which always began at St. Peter's, led first through the Borgo district, passed Castel Sant'Angelo to cross the Tiber via the Ponte Sant'Angelo, then climbed the Capitoline Hill, walked the full length of the Roman Forum, passed the Colosseum, to end in the Lateran Basilica, the pope's episcopal seat. By passing the city's most important places and monuments, the cavalcade referred to the model of ancient Roman triumphal processions: First the *exitus* from the Vatican, second the *ascensus* to the Capitoline Hill, where the pope was honoured by the city government of the Popolo Romano, third the *triumphus* on the Forum Romanum, where the pope received the homage of the Jewish community, which was interpreted as the triumph of the New over the Old Testament, and fourth the *introitus* into the Lateran Basilica, where the pope received a silver and a golden key as symbols of his temporal and spiritual power (Fosi, 2002, p. 36).

While the buildings along the way were decorated with textiles and sometimes even with ephemeral works of art, temporary triumphal arches were erected on behalf of the city administration or nobles at various symbolic sites, such as the Capitoline Square and the Roman Forum, which glorified the pope with their iconographical programmes featuring virtues, allegorical and biblical figures, as well as scenes from the life of the new pontiff.

Prints such as the etching by Louis Rouhier of the cavalcade of Clement IX on 3 July 1667 (Fig. 2), which were produced from the end of the 16th century onwards on the occasion of the *possessi* and distributed throughout Europe, show the *corteo* in a highly typified form, moving in serpentine lines along the most iconic sites. The offices and functions of the various individual participants and groups are indicated by the inscriptions, since the order of the procession, conceived by the papal masters of ceremonies, manifested the hierarchy of the papal court.[23] Thus, the development of the order of procession in the course of the 16th century was an indicator of the changing relationship between the pontiff and the city: At the end of the century, when pontifical power was consolidated in Rome, the representatives of the city were marginalized and the old baronial families relegated to a secondary role (Fosi, 2002, p. 34). The *possesso* represented and imposed pontifical sover-

---

22 See Cancellieri, 1802; Fosi, 2002; Emich, 2005; DeSilva et al., 2020.

23 For the order of the procession in the *Caeremoniale Romanum*, cf. Dykmans, 1980, pp. 76–81.

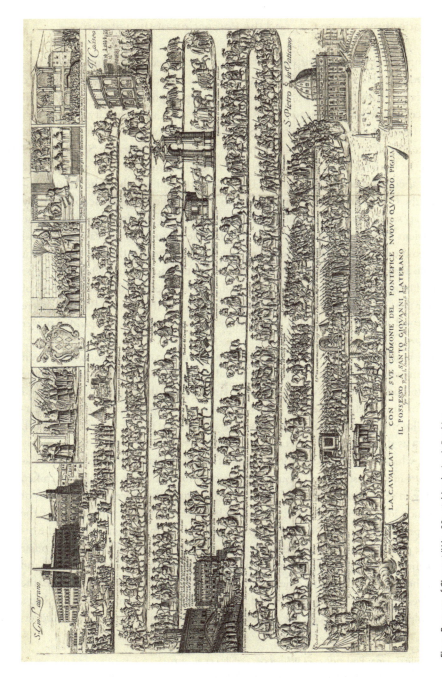

Fig. 2: *Possesso of Clement IX in 1667*, etching by Louis Rouhier.

The Soundscape of the Popes

eignty on the Roman people and, even more importantly, to the foreign powers, whose representatives participated in the cavalcade in a privileged position.

Although they did not sing during the procession, the papal singers took part in the procession to the Lateran (Bölling, 2006, pp. 129–130). As Patrizi writes, they rode on horses and dressed in the *superpelliceum*, which distinguished them as part of the papal chapel and thus as the pope's clerical vanguard.[24] At Leo X's *possesso* on 19 November 1513, the Venetian Marino Sanudo observed "about 25 Singers of the Pope, [dressed] with their coats and on horseback."[25] The Cappella Pontificia was thus only visually present at the *cavalcata*.

In their stead, instrumental music and sonic manifestations played an important role in this performative ceremony. At various points in the *corteo*, drummers, trumpeters and piffari (pipers), in the 15th century a veritable *alta ensemble*, played, not only announcing the procession audibly from afar, but also fulfilling important representative functions. Since antiquity, trumpets served as emblems of power for emperors and other potentates; from the 12th century onwards, they were also used as sounding insignia by municipal dignitaries in northern Italy – as well as in Rome (Žak, 1979, pp. 51–66, 108–120). After the popes had gained city rule in the early 15th century, they also quartered trumpeters – together with the papal troops – in Castel Sant'Angelo, which then served as the papal fortress (Žak, 1994, pp. 185–188). Together with drummers, cornetists, trombonists, and piffari, they were later called *musici* or *piffari di Castello* and played at papal ceremonies in the urban space, as well as at festivities in the papal palaces (Rostirolla, 1986, pp. 174–175).

Under Clement VII, a balcony was erected for the palace trumpeters above the *custodia*, which led to St. Peter's Square and from where trumpeters blew before papal blessings or certain announcements (Redig de Campos, 1967, p. 122; Žak, 1994, p. 189). Drummers and piffari became part of the processions in Rome at the latest under Cesare Borgia, the dreaded *condottiere* and son of Alexander VI, who valued their military sound just as much as his father's successor Julius II, who is also remembered for his military campaigns (Žak, 1994, pp. 189–190; Bölling, 2009, pp. 237–238). Since antiquity, drums, trumpets, and other wind instruments had been used in the military as a means of coordinating and disciplining troops, and also as a tool of psychological warfare. The papal master of ceremonies, Paris de Grassis, refers to those instruments several times in his *Tractatus de equitatione pape per urbem in solemnitate non pontificali*. In the seventh chapter, *De agendis per Castellanum Sancti Angeli*, for example, he explicitly writes that although cardinals also had the right to be honoured acoustically in front of their title church by drummers, trumpeters, and piffari, this homage was paid to the pontiff as soon as he was present (Dykmans, 1985, pp. 386–393, 455–456; Bölling, 2009, p. 236).

---

24   "Cantores deinde equitant cum superpelliciis" (Dykmans, 1980, p. 79, l. 1–2). Cf. also Bölling, 2006, pp. 129–130.

25   "Cantori dil Papa zercha 25, con le cotte et bene a cavallo" (Sanuto, 1886, col. 84).

Fig. 3a: Mounted trumpeters and drummers of the Capitol at the *possesso* of Gregory XV in 1621, detail of an engraving by an unknown artist.

In addition to the papal musicians, the municipal musicians, the so-called *musici del Popolo romano* or *del Campidoglio*, also played at the *possesso* (Cametti, 1925). The tasks of the city's musicians, also known as *musici dei Conservatori*, which in the 17th century included five to six trombonists and two to four cornetists, ranged from playing at audiences and meals of the conservators to mass celebrations in Roman churches and the papal *possesso* (Cametti, 1925, pp. 106, 115–117). In written accounts and prints, the drummers and trumpeters are virtually omnipresent, although the textual and pictorial sources often give different and contradictory information about their number and position within the processional order. The engraving by an unknown artist of the *possesso* of Gregory XV on 9 May 1621 shows on the left panel in the third row, five mounted trumpeters, who are identified as "5 Trombete de Cavalleggieri" and bear the papal coat of arms on the pennants of their instruments (Fig. 3a). Immediately below, the artist has depicted some drummers, who are labelled "14 tamburi del Campidoglio". On the right panel, in the third row, "4 trombete del pop[opolo] Ro[mano]" march through an ephemeral triumphal arch (Fig. 3b), while in the middle of the lowest row another mounted musician can be seen, described as "trombeta della retro guardia". Alaleone

Fig. 3b: Mounted trumpeters of the *popolo romano* passing an ephemeral triumphal arch at the *possesso* of Gregory XV in 1621, detail of an engraving by an unknown artist.

de Branca, on the other hand, reports in his diary of said *possesso* only that drummers and mounted trumpeters of the *Popolo Romano* preceded the Roman senators.[26]

In times of mourning, trumpets were not used in processions, as evidenced by the statutes of Castel Sant'Angelo (Rostirolla, 1986, pp. 189–190, no. 30, 35). At the entry of Leo X after his return from Florence in 1516, as Paris De Grassis writes in his diary, trumpet fan-

---

26 "Tympanistae Populi Romani et tubicines equitum levis armaturae in medio equitationis incedentes, Capitaneus militum Helvetiorum post Senatores Populi Romani [...]." (Wassilowsky et al., 2007, p. 168, l. 184–186).

Fig. 4: Muted trumpets, silent muskets and cannons at the funeral procession for the death of Clement IX in 1669, detail of an engraving by Giovanni Battista Falda.

fares and other displays of splendour were decidedly dispensed with, as the cavalcade fell during Lent. When a pope died, the usual sonic manifestations were inverted (Delicati, 1884, pp. 29–30; Žak, 1994, p. 191). During the solemn funeral procession in which the papal body was transferred from the Quirinal Palace to St. Peter's, where it was laid out for the people to pay homage, the trumpets fell silent or were blown softly and mournfully with mutes. An engraving by Giovanni Battista Falda of the funeral procession for the death of Clement IX on 9 December 1669 shows two mounted trumpeters ("Trombe Sordine") at the beginning of the procession, while in the row that can be seen behind the papal corpse, soldiers carry mute cannons and shouldered muskets, none of which are used (Fig. 4). Instead of loud salute shots and cannonades from Castel Sant'Angelo, the symbols of the papal worldly power remained silent as a sign of mourning. During the *possesso*, the drummers and trumpeters functioned as the sounding insignia of the Pope as secular ruler, their playing being less concerned with aesthetic artifice than with volume and acoustic-symbolic presence (Wald-Fuhrmann, 2012, p. 151).

While these "mobile" musicians accompanied the entire procession, the pope was occasionally offered musical performances as he passed certain festival apparatuses, which, like the ephemeral works of art themselves, were donated by aristocrats, church congregations, religious orders, or the city administration as a sign of their deference to the new pontiff. For the *possesso* of Leo X on 11 April 1513, for example, Marino Sanudo reports in his diary

Fig. 5: Cannonade from Castel Sant'Angelo at the *possesso* of Clement IX in 1667, detail of an etching by Louis Rouhier.

of a triumphal arch in front of the Zecca with integrated rooms for musicians, "where verses were sung",[27] and in another triumphal arch at the Banchi, there were hollow rooms "in which were certain fellows who recited good verses, and one who threw money, but little."[28] A good century later, Agostino Mascardi noted for the *possesso* of Urban VIII on 19 November 1623: "At the roots of the Capitol were a number of choirs of musicians, whose concert of voices and instruments represented the harmony of virtues and effects in Urban's well-disciplined soul."[29] It seems as if the singers were supposed to animate the ten larger-than-life stucco figures erected at the entrance to the Capitoline Hill, which also represented the virtues of the pontiff. Of Innocent X's *possesso* on 23 November 1644, Antonio Gerardi again reports that on passing the ephemeral triumphal arch erected by the Duke of Parma on the Roman Forum: "His Holiness was greeted with a musical concert of trumpets, and then with a numerous salvo of mortars."[30]

27 "Questo era un archo bellissimo che piava tute doe strade, et lì erano vacui, dove furon cantati versi." (Sanuto, 1886, col. 86); cf. Cummings, 1992, p. 50.
28 "Questo archo haveva alcuni vacui conzati al proposito, in li quali erano certi garzoni che rezitavano versi boni, et uno che butava danari, ma pochi." (Sanuto, 1886, col. 85).
29 "Alle radici del Campidoglio erano alcuni chori di musici, che nel concerto delle voci, e degli strumenti rappresentavano l'armonìa delle virtù, e degli affetti, nell'animo ben disciplinato d'Urbano." (Mascardi, 1624, p. 22).
30 "fu Sua Santità salutata con un concerto musicale di Trombe, e poi con una numerosa salva di mortaletti." (Gerardi, 1644, s.p.).

The greatest sound volume of the cavalcade was produced by the cannonades fired from Castel Sant'Angelo and other places. Of Gregory XV's *possesso* on 9 May 1621, for example, Alaleone de Branca reports: "Bombardments were discharged in St. Peter's Square, in Castel Sant'Angelo, at the Capitoline Hill, and in St. John's Square in the Lateran after a public and solemn blessing was given."[31] In the prints, this military sound is usually visualized by clouds of smoke emanating from Castel Sant'Angelo (Fig. 5).

Alessandro Macchia offers a comprehensive impression of the soundscape of a papal *corteo* in his account of the *possesso* of Leo XI on 17 April 1605:

> And so great was the noise of the incredible people, who were in the streets from St. Peter's to St. John Lateran, that between the shouting "vivat LEO XI" & the salutes made by the soldiers of the Popolo Romano, from the Castel Sant'Angelo, from the Capitoline Hill, & other private places through which [the procession] passed, that one could scarcely make out the words of the other, & this was increased also by the ringing of the bells, which in all churches rang, and trumpets & drums, which also accompanied the cavalcade.[32]

When the Pope finally arrived at the Lateran, the archpriest and the clergy of the patriarchal church marched to meet him, preceded by a canopy and a small bell called a *tintinnabulum*, accompanied by the full ringing of the basilica's bells and salutes of the papal guard (Fig. 6). According to Patrizi, this certainly smallest sound producer of the *possesso* symbolized the Real Presence of Christ in the Blessed Sacrament, which was carried along in a monstrance on a white horse and distinguished with a canopy.[33]

Arriving at the portico of the basilica, the pontiff took his seat on a marble throne, threw three handfuls of coins among the people, who, according to Patrizi, then had to acclaim that Saint Peter himself had elected the pope.[34] The pontiff then entered his episcopal church

---

31 "Fuerunt exoneratae bombardae in Platea Sancti Petri, in Arce Sancti Angeli, in Capitolio et in Platea Sancti Ioannis Lateranensis post datam | benedictionem publicam et solemnem." (Wassilowsky et al., 2007, p. 167, l. 37–39).

32 "Et era cosi grande il rumore dell'incredibile popolo, che da S. Pietro fino à S. Giovanni Laterano era per le strade, che tra il gridare viva LEONE XI. & le salve che li furno fatte dalli soldati del Popolo Romano, dal Castello S. Angelo, dal Campidoglio, & altri private luoghi per dove passò, che appena s'intendeva il parlare l'un dall'altro, & questo veniva accresciuto anche dal suon delle Campane, che per tutte queste Chiese sonavano, e trombe, & tamburi, che accompagnavano anche eglino la Cavalcata." (Macchia, 1605, s.p).

33 "Et post eos ducitur per familiarem sacriste, rubeo etiam indutum, et baculum in sinistra habentem, equus albus mansuetus, ornatus ut illi duodecim, portans sacramentum, habens ad collum tintinnabulum bene <sonans>. Et supra portatur baldachinum cum armis pape et sacramenti per cives Romanos, qui inter se mutantur tredecim vicibus, ut unaqueque regio habeat suam partem." (Dykmans, 1980, p. 78, l. 14–18); cf. Bölling, 2006, p. 130.

34 Dykmans, 1980, p. 82. For medieval precursors of this rite, cf. Schimmelpfennig, 1974, pp. 240–243.

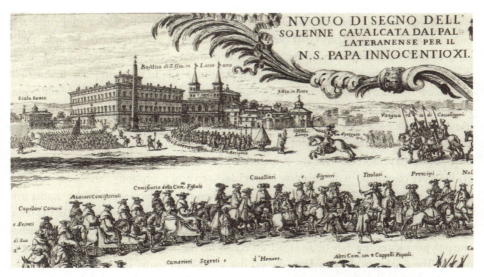

Fig. 6: Arrival at the Lateran Basilica with salute shots and *tintinnabulum* at the *possesso* of Innocent XI in 1676, detail of an engraving by Giovanni Battista Falda.

to the sound of the *Te deum laudamus* to bless the people at the high altar, after which he moved to the Lateran Palace to take possession of it. While Patrizi prescribed that the pope, seated on a porphyry throne in front of the portal of the Chapel of St. Sylvester, first received the *ferula* and the keys of the basilica and the palace, and then, on a second throne, a belt of red silk and a purple purse with allegorically significant objects, in later times the pope had already been presented with the symbolic keys in the portico of the basilica – and thus before the eyes of the people.[35] With the possession of the Lateran, the rites of passage of the papacy were completed and the power of the new pontiff was consolidated.

Signs and Emotions: The Dual Communication Strategy of Papal Rituals

The constitutive rituals of the early modern papacy were complex multimedia ceremonies that communicated with the population and the international "public" through an interplay of performative, visual, and sonic elements. In this multimedia context, music and other sounds fulfilled important functions: The liturgical and legal texts spoken and sung in the course of the ceremonies in the interior and the portico of St. Peter's and St. John Lateran's

---

35 For the *possesso* of Gregory XV on 9 May 1621, Alaleone de Branca reports: "Absoluta oratione idem Illustrissimus Dominus Cardinalis Archipresbyter praesentavit Papae duas claves, quarum una erat aurata, alia vero argentata […]." (Wassilowsky et al., 2007, p. 164, l. 27–29).

Basilicas were not only essential components of the ceremonies, but constituted them. It was only through their articulation that the election, coronation, and investiture became legally valid. In the case of the chants, it was less a matter of the aesthetic quality of the performance than of the right words being articulated at the right moment, in the right place, by the right people, combined with appropriate actions and gestures (Žak, 1994, p. 176; Wald-Fuhrmann, 2012, pp. 145–146). Since they were of the highest liturgical or legal importance, the normative texts of the papal masters of ceremonies strictly regulated the wording and the performers (Bölling, 2006). The majority of the chants were probably sung as Gregorian chant, the time-honoured unison chant of the church. Which of the chants performed by the Cappella Sistina were *choraliter*, in *falsobordone* or in elaborate vocal polyphony cannot be said with certainty, since the sources provide no information on this. In fact, some of the chants performed by papal singers were probably in unison to ensure the comprehensibility of the texts, although in the course of the 16th and especially in the 17th century, an increase in more elaborate polyphonic texture may be assumed, especially for the *Te deum laudamus* (Bölling, 2006, p. 253). The singing of the papal singers was not suitable for festive occasions in front of the general public due to their limited acoustic range, but also due to its artificiality, which was only accessible to an elite circle (Wald-Fuhrmann, 2012, p. 152).

While these acts of ceremonial speaking and singing were valid and effective in and of themselves or by being performed in front of a select group of people, the proclamation of the election of the pope, the actual act of coronation, and the cavalcade of the *possesso*, on the other hand, were directed at as large an audience as possible, using long-distance instruments such as drums, trumpets, and other wind instruments, as well as extra-musical sound generators. Far more than the visual aspects of the rituals, the loud sonic elements were able to draw attention to the events over greater distances, thus creating "publicity". In the societies of the early modern period, which were largely based on personal interaction and communication, deliberately controlled noise was the most important means of establishing officiality and legitimacy in legal life (Žak, 1979, pp. 8–9). While the sound radius of drums and trumpets was limited to squares and neighbourhoods, salutes, cannonades, and the general ringing of bells could be heard throughout the city. The extensive sound choreographies united all of Rome into a single sound space and ensured the officiality of these constituent ceremonies of the papacy.

In interaction with the visual media of the rituals in urban space, music and other sounds pursued a dual communication strategy: to articulate symbolically conveyed messages and to manipulate the people affectively-emotionally (Weißmann, 2021, pp. 213–222). At first, as the normative texts of the papal masters of ceremonies state, not only the full ringing of bells, but also drums, trumpets, musket shots, and cannonades functioned as "signs of joy"[36]

---

36   "signa letitie" (Dykmans, 1980, p. 50, l. 18).

The Soundscape of the Popes

that were supposed to articulate the joy of Catholic Christianity over the election and coronation of a pontiff. At the same time, these instruments of war, reinterpreted as instruments of joy, served as proof of the sovereign power and military potency of the popes as secular rulers of the Papal States. After all, deafening noise was considered an essential element of courtly representation, which placed the prince, who had such noise-generating means at his disposal, close to mythological deities or the Christian God in the sense of ruler iconography (Žak, 1979, pp. 12, 16–17).

In addition to symbolic communication, music and sonic manifestations aimed to stir the emotions of the people. As a systematic evaluation of numerous written accounts of festivals and ceremonies in 17th-century Rome suggests, these were essentially aimed at evoking three main affects (Weißmann, 2021, pp. 218–222). While the most frequently mentioned one, joy (*allegrezza, allegria, ilarità* etc.), is primarily associated with musical performances and the playing of drums and trumpets, the second may at first seem surprising: horror (*horrore* or *orrore*). One can easily imagine how the deafening noise of the mortars, cannonades, or fireworks, which exceeded the everyday experience of contemporaries and could only be compared to acts of war and elemental forces, directly affected those present. An indication of their affective potential can be found, for example, in the report of a cavalcade organized by Alexander VI in honour of a Ferrarese legation on 23 December 1501, during which the horses refused to cross the Bridge of Angels because of the ear-splitting gun shots.[37] The third affect, which became increasingly important in the festive context in the course of the 16th century and was to become the central affect in the 17th century, is amazement (*meraviglia*) (Weißmann, 2021, pp. 221–222). While early modern art theory, since Giorgio Vasari's *Vite*, has understood *meraviglia* as the evocation of the recipient's admiration as a reaction to a work of art, contemporary accounts use *meraviglia* to refer to both the "amazing" effect of various festival elements or moments, and the ideal-typical and intended reception by the audience in the sense of admiration.

With their strategy of sensorial overwhelming, music and other sounds thus corresponded to the demands of the ceremonial science established in the 17th century, which propagated multisensory stimulation to manipulate the population and thus followed the topos of the sensuality and lack of rationality of the lower classes that had been common since ancient times.[38] The evocation of joy was intended to win the Roman people over to the pontiff and his goals, while the evocations of horror and amazement aimed to generate reverence for the new head of the Catholic Church and the Vatican State.

---

37 "fu trato tante bombarde che non se podeva odir e li cavalli erano spaventati, che non voleva intrar sopra el ponte, ma pur passano e arivono al palazzo dil papa." Report by Zuan Batista Scabalino from December 1501, cited in: Thuasne, 1885, p. 177.

38 See Berns et al., 1995, therein especially Gestrich, 1995; Rahn, 1995.

The approval of the people was demonstrated by shouts of *vivat*, which also fulfilled a legal function after the announcement of the election and the coronation of the pontiff. Finally, since antiquity, the acclamation, i.e., a crowd shouting *una voce*, was a central element of ruler legitimation and could not be missing at any election or coronation of a sovereign (Kantorowicz, 1958, pp. 125–128). Already medieval reports of coronation ceremonies emphasize the loudness and unanimity of the acclamations, as they expressed divine elections (Žak, 1979, p. 11). In early modern ceremonial literature, the intensity and volume of the jubilation was explained as an indicator of the people's approval or even "love", which is why accounts of festivities often describe the people's expressions of joy in panegyric exaggeration (Weißmann, 2021, pp. 134–135). The shouting of the people was thus not simply an appealing accessory, but an indispensable, if only conditionally controllable, component of the sound spectrum of papal rituals.

The entity of sounds, ranging from the spoken and sung liturgical and legal texts and the elaborate polyphonic chants of the Cappella Pontificia, to the acclamation of the people, the playing of drums and trumpets, and the ringing of bells to mortar shots and cannonades, can be understood as a soundscape that interfered with the bustling urban acoustic environment of early modern Rome.[39] Like other cities, the capital of the Papal States had a specific sound spectrum formed by the totality of everyday sounds (Kendrick, 2002; Garrioch, 2003; Atkinson, 2016). The musical and sonic elements of the papal rituals overlapped this urban soundscape for the duration of the events and only unfolded their meaning and impact through their difference from the everyday sonic environment.[40]

Within the grand rituals of the papacy, music and sound thus fulfilled a variety of functions. They drew attention to special moments within the ceremonies over great spatial distances and thus created "publicity". Even more than the visual elements, they were able to evoke emotions, to delight, to frighten, and to amaze the people through their immediate physical presence, thus creating reverence for the monarch among the population. The great sound choreographies that transformed the whole city into a vast sound space united all participants in an emotional community for the duration of the event. Through a differentiated use of sound, early modern papal ceremonies aimed both to demonstrate social hierarchies at the papal court, and to make the power of the papacy and the Roman Catholic Church tangible to the senses.

---

39 Soundscape was introduced as a term and concept by the Canadian composer and sound researcher R. Murray Schafer (1994).

40 For the soundscape of the festival culture of the European powers in 17th and 18th century Rome, cf. Weißmann, 2021, pp. 124–135.

Bibliography

Printed Sources and Source Editions

Compitissima Relazione delle Cerimonie fatte dentro, e fuori del Conclave nell'Elezzione del Sommo Pontefice Alessandro Ottavo seguita li 6 Ottobre 1689 [...]. (1689). Paolo Moneta.

Delicati, P. & Armellini, M. (Eds.) (1884). *Il diario di Leone X di Paride de Grassi*. Maestro delle Cerimonie Pontificie. Dai volumi manoscritti degli Archivi Vaticani della S. Sede. Tipografia della Pace di F. Cuggiani.

Dykmans, M. (Ed.) (1980–1982). *L'oeuvre de Patrizi Piccolomini ou le Cérémonial papal de la première Renaissance*. 2 vols. Biblioteca Apostolica Vaticana.

Gerardi, A. (1644). *Trionfal Possesso della Santità di Nostro Signore Innocentio X alla Sacrosanta Basilica Lateranense seguito il dì 23 Novembre 1644* [...]. Lodovico Grignani.

Lupardi, B. (1665). *Relatione delle Cerimonie, et apparato della Basilica di S. Pietro nella Canonizatione del glorioso Santo Francesco di Sales Vescovo di Genova fatta dalla Santità di N. S. Alessandro VII il di XIX Aprile MDCLXV* [...]. Giacomo Dragondelli.

Macchia, A. (1605). *Relatione del Viaggio fatto dalla S.D.N.S. PP. Leone XI nel pigliare il Possesso a San Giovanni Laterano* [...]. Guglielmo Facciotto.

Mascardi, A. (1624). *Le Pompe di Campidoglio per la S.tà di N.S. Urbano VIII. quando pigliò il possesso* [...]. Bartolomeo Zannetti.

Penni, G. G. (1513). *Cronicha delle magnifiche et honorate pompe fatte in Roma per la Creatione & incoronatione di Papa Leone X. Pont. Opt.* Marcello Silber.

Sanuto, M. (1879–1903). *I Diarii*. 59 vols. Fratelli Visentini Tipografi Editori.

Thuasne, L. (Ed.) (1883–1885). *Johannis Burchardi Diarium sive rerum urbanarum commentarii (1483–1506)*. 3 vols. Ernest Leroux.

Wassilowsky G. & Wolf, H. (2007). *Päpstliches Zeremoniell in der Frühen Neuzeit. Das Diarium des Zeremonienmeisters Paolo Alaleone de Branca während des Pontifikats Gregors XV. (1621–1623)*. Rhema.

Scholarly Literature

Atkinson, N. (2016). *The Noisy Renaissance. Sound, Architecture, and Florentine Urban Life*. Penn State University Press.

Berns, J. J. (2006). Herrscherliche Klangkunst und höfische Hallräume. Zur zeremoniellen Funktion akustischer Zeichen. In P.-M. Hahn & U. Schütte (Eds.), *Zeichen und Raum. Ausstattung und höfisches Zeremoniell in den deutschen Schlössern der Frühen Neuzeit* (pp. 49–64). Deutscher Kunstverlag.

Berns, J. J. & Rahn, T. (Eds.) (1995). *Zeremoniell als höfische Ästhetik in Spätmittelalter und Früher Neuzeit*. Niemeyer.

Boiteux, M. (2002). La vacance du siège pontifical. De la mort et des funérailles à l'investiture du pape: les rites de l'époque moderne. In J. P. Paiva (Ed.), *Religious Ceremonials and Images. Power and Social Meaning (1400–1750)* (pp. 103–141). Palimage Ed.

Bölling, J. (2009). Musicae utilitas. Zur Bedeutung der Musik im Adventus-Zeremoniell der Vormoderne. In P. Johanek & A. Lampen (Eds.), *Adventus. Studien zum herrscherlichen Einzug in die Stadt* (pp. 229–266). Böhlau.

Bölling, J. (2006). *Das Papstzeremoniell der Renaissance. Texte, Musik, Performanz.* Peter Lang.

Büchel, D. & Reinhard, V. (Eds.) (2003). *Modell Rom? Der Kirchenstaat und Italien in der Frühen Neuzeit.* Böhlau.

Cametti, A. (1925). I musici di Campidoglio ossia 'il concerto di trombone e cornetti del senato e inclito popolo romano' (1524–1818). *Archivio della R. Società Romana di Storia Patria* 48, 95–135.

Cancellieri, F. (1802). *Storia de' solenni Possessi de' Sommi Pontefici detti anticamente Processi o Processioni dopo la loro Coronazione dalla Basilica Vaticana alla Lateranense [...].* Luigi Lazzarini.

Cummings, A. M. (1992). *The Politicized Muse. Music for Medici Festivals, 1512–1537.* Princeton University Press.

DeSilva, J. M. (2022). *The Office of Ceremonies and Advancement in Curial Rome, 1466–1528.* Brill.

DeSilva, J. M. & Rihouet, P. (2020). *Eternal Ephemera. The Papal Possesso and Its Legacies in Early Modern Rome.* Iter Press.

Dykmans, M. (1985). Paris de Grassi. *Ephemerides Liturgicae* 99, 383–417.

Emich, B. (2005). Besitz ergreifen von der Kirche. Normen und Normkonflikte beim Zeremoniell des päpstlichen Possesso. In G. Wassilowsky & H. Wolf (Eds.), *Werte und Symbole im frühneuzeitlichen Rom* (pp. 83–99). Rhema.

Fagiolo, M. (1997). L'Effimero di Stato. Dal Conclave al Possesso. In M. Fagiolo (Ed.), *La Festa a Roma dal Rinascimento al 1870*, vol. 2 (pp. 8–25). Allemandi.

Fagiolo, M. (1997). *La festa barocca. Il Settecento e l'Ottocento.* Edizioni De Luca.

Fagiolo dell'Arco, M. & Carandini, S. (1977–1978). *L'Effimero barocco. Strutture della festa nella Roma del '600.* 2 vols. Bulzoni.

Fagiolo dell'Arco, M. & Carandini, S. (1997). *La festa barocca.* Edizioni De Luca.

Fosi, I. (2002). Court and City in the Ceremony of the Possesso in the Sixteenth Century. In G. Signorotto & M. A. Visceglia (Eds.), *Court and Politics in Papal Rome, 1492–1700* (pp. 31–52). Cambridge University Press.

Garrioch, D. (2003). Sounds of the City. The Soundscape of Early Modern European Towns, *Urban History* 30(1), 5–25.

Gestrich, A. (1995). Höfisches Zeremoniell und sinnliches Volk. Die Rechtfertigung des Hofzeremoniells im 17. und 18. Jahrhundert. In J. J. Berns & T. Rahn (Eds.), *Zeremoniell als höfische Ästhetik in Spätmittelalter und Früher Neuzeit* (pp. 57–73). Niemeyer.

Janz, B. (Ed.) (1994). *Studien zur Geschichte der päpstlichen Kapelle.* Biblioteca Apostolica Vaticana.

Kantorowicz, E. (1958). *Laudes regiae. A Study in Liturgical Acclamations and Mediaeval Ruler Worship.* University of California Press.

Kendrick, R. L. (2002). *The Sounds of Milan, 1585–1650*. Oxford University Press.

Pastor, L. von (1925–1933). *Geschichte der Päpste seit dem Ausgang des Mittelalters*. 16 vols. Herder.

Pietschmann, K. (Ed.) (2012). *Papsttum und Kirchenmusik vom Mittelalter bis zu Benedikt XVI. Positionen – Entwicklungen – Kontexte*. Bärenreiter.

Pietschmann, K. (2007). *Kirchenmusik zwischen Tradition und Reform. Die päpstliche Kapelle und ihr Repertoire unter Papst Paul III. 1534–1549*. Biblioteca Apostolica Vaticana.

Prodi, P. (1987). *The Papal Prince. One Body and Two Souls: The Papal Monarchy in Early Modern Europe*. Cambridge University Press.

Rahn, T. (1995). Psychologie des Zeremoniells. Affekttheorie und -pragmatik in der Zeremoniellwissenschaft des 18. Jahrhunderts. In J. J. Berns & T. Rahn (Eds.), *Zeremoniell als höfische Ästhetik in Spätmittelalter und Früher Neuzeit* (pp. 74–98). Niemeyer.

Redig de Campos, Deoclecio (1967). *I palazzi vaticani*. Cappell.

Reynolds, C. (1995). *Papal Patronage and the Music of St. Peter's 1380–1513*. University of California Press.

Rostirolla, G. (2017). *La Cappella Giulia 1513–2013. Cinque secoli di musica sacra in San Pietro*. 2 vols. Bärenreiter.

Rostirolla, G. (1986). Strumentisti e costruttori di strumenti nella Roma dei papi. Materiali per una storia della musica strumentale a Roma durante i secoli XV–XVII. In L- F. Tagliavini & J. H. Van der Meer (Eds.), *Restauro, conservazione e recupero di antichi strumenti musicali* (pp. 171–226). Olschki.

Schafer, R. M. (1994). *The Soundscape. Our Sonic Environment and the Tuning of the World*. Destiny.

Schimmelpfennig, B. (1994). Die Funktion der Cappella Sistina im Zeremoniell der Renaissancepäpste. In B. Janz (Ed.), *Studien zur Geschichte der päpstlichen Kapelle* (pp. 123–174). Biblioteca Apostolica Vaticana.

Schimmelpfennig, B. (1974). Die Krönung des Papstes im Mittelalter dargestellt am Beispiel der Krönung Pius' II. (3.9.1458). In *Quellen und Forschungen aus italienischen Archiven und Bibliotheken* 54, 192–270.

Signorotto, G. & Visceglia, M. A. (2002). *Court and Politics in Papal Rome, 1492–1700*. Cambridge University Press.

Signorotto, G. & Visceglia, M. A. (Eds.) (1998). *La corte di Roma tra Cinque e Seicento. 'Teatro' della politica europea*. Bulzoni.

Sherr, R. (Ed.) (1998). *Papal Music and Musicians in Late Medieval and Renaissance Rome*. Oxford University Press.

Starr, P. F. (1987). *Music and Music Patronage at the Papal Court 1447–1464*. UMI.

Stollberg-Rilinger, B. (2013). *Rituale*. Campus.

Stollberg-Rilinger, B. (Ed.) (2010). *Die Bildlichkeit symbolischer Akte*. Rhema.

Stollberg-Rilinger, B. (2004). Symbolische Kommunikation in der Vormoderne. Begriffe – Thesen – Forschungsperspektiven. In *Zeitschrift für Historische Forschung* 31, 489–527.

Visceglia, M. A. (2002). *La città rituale. Roma e le sue cerimonie in età moderna*. Viella.

Visceglia, M. A. & Brice, C. (Eds.) (1997). *Cérémonial et rituel à Rome (XVIᵉ–XIXᵉ siècle)*. École française de Rome.

Wald-Fuhrmann, M. (2012). Mit Pauken und Trompeten. Strategien und Dokumentation des zeremoniellen Einsatzes von Musik am Papsthof des ausgehenden 15. Jahrhunderts. In K. Pietschmann (Ed.), *Musikalische Performanz und päpstliche Repräsentation in der Renaissance* (pp. 139–154). Bärenreiter.

Wassilowsky, G. (2010). *Die Konklavereform Gregors XV. (1621/22). Wertekonflikte, symbolische Inszenierung und Verfahrenswandel im posttridentinischen Papsttum*. Hiersemann.

Weißmann, T. C. (2021). *Kunst, Klang, Musik. Die Festkultur der europäischen Mächte im barocken Rom*. Hirmer.

Weißmann, T. C. (2024). Space, Sight, and Music in the Sistine Chapel. In J. Berger (Ed.), *Listening in the Past. Sound, Space, and the Aesthetics of the Sublime* (pp. 161–185). Lever Press.

Žak, S. (1994). Cappella – castello – camera. Gesang und Instrumentalmusik an der Kurie. In B. Janz (Ed.), *Studien zur Geschichte der päpstlichen Kapelle* (pp. 175–223). Biblioteca Apostolica Vaticana.

Žak, S. (1982). Das Te Deum als Huldigungsgesang. *Historisches Jahrbuch* 102, 1–32.

Illustration Credits

Fig. 1: Floor plan of the Vatican Palace and ceremonies of the *sede vacante* after the death of Innocent X in 1655, etching by an unknown artist, 230 x 346 mm. Amsterdam, Rijksmuseum, RP-P-OB-38.851.

Fig. 2: *Possesso* of Clement IX 1667, etching by Louis Rouhier, 374 x 518 mm. Los Angeles, Getty Research Institute, P850003 (bx.1*,f.9).

Fig. 3a: Mounted trumpeters and drummers of the Capitol at the *possesso* of Gregory XV in 1621, detail of an engraving by an unknown artist (left panel), 264 x 437 mm. Amsterdam, Rijksmuseum, RP-P-OB-38.849.

Fig. 3b: Mounted trumpeters of the *popolo romano* passing an ephemeral triumphal arch at the *possesso* of Gregory XV in 1621, detail of an engraving by an unknown artist (right panel), 264 x 438 mm. Amsterdam, Rijksmuseum, RP-P-OB-38.850.

Fig. 4: Muted trumpets, silent muskets and cannons at the funeral procession for the death of Clement IX in 1669, detail of an engraving by Giovanni Battista Falda, 232 x 342 mm. Amsterdam, Rijksmuseum, RP-P-OB-36.031.

Fig. 5: Cannonade from Castel Sant'Angelo at the *possesso* of Clement IX in 1667, detail of an etching by Louis Rouhier, 374 x 518 mm. Los Angeles, Getty Research Institute, P850003 (bx.1*, f.9).

Fig. 6: Arrival at the Lateran Basilica with salute shots and *tintinnabulum* at the *possesso* of Innocent XI in 1676, detail of an engraving by Giovanni Battista Falda, 322 x 467 mm. Amsterdam, Rijksmuseum, RP-P-OB-36.026.

The Power of Silence
What Came Before and After Morales' Music in Mexico City in 1559?*

Grayson Wagstaff

Studies of urban soundscapes in late medieval and early modern Europe have proliferated in the last several decades, with scholars presenting innovative discussions of sonic life in various regions, research that delineates a rich culture of noise and the hubbub of life, as well as many kinds of music including both the written "academic" traditions and improvised music of various kinds. In musicology, one of the seminal scholars in this trend was Reinhard Strohm, with his pathbreaking study of the urban soundscape of medieval Bruges (Strohm, 1985). Another important leader in these efforts has been musicologist Tim Carter, a specialist in early modern Italy (Carter, 2000; 2002).[1] In addition to pointing out what a limited segment of music practices musicologists had traditionally sought to analyse, scholars in various disciplines have demonstrated that these earlier soundscapes were quite textured with a complex co-existence of sounds – some used as signals, such as bells that kept time or announced various events, as did cannons and other weaponry – along with the noise of civic and sacred life, business, and recreation. As we now acknowledge, cultural artifacts such as music manuscripts and prints that were traditionally the focus of studies of chant and polyphony at courts, cathedrals, and wealthy monasteries provide only limited evidence. Written polyphony in particular was a rare echelon of life, the purview before 1600 of highly trained experts, including children, whose performances often were done for a very small "audience". Awareness of our myopic focus in the past requires us to place such elite music in a broader context, although the records for such discussion vary greatly from time to time and place to place.

Even though scholars now admit that life was many-clangored in all parts of Europe, we currently know less about the sound worlds of certain regions. For some cities in Spain and Portugal, we have a more nuanced understanding of the complexity of sounds intermingling in early modern locales (Knighton, 2018; Mazuela-Anguita, 2018; Ros-Fábregas,

---

* Thanks to these several colleagues who either read a draft or made suggestions for this research: William John Summers, María Luisa Marina Vilar Payá, Jesús A. Ramos-Kitrell, Linda A. Curcio-Nagy, Omar Morales Abril, Drew Edward Davies, and Joseph Santo.

1 Carter refined some issues in Carter, 2018, pp. 25–52.

2009). Some research on later periods has examined issues likely similar to 16th-century practice (Carreras, 2018). Re-creating the musical life and other sounds of urban Spain, especially those shaping religious experiences, was a goal of clerics and civic leaders in the early colonies in Latin America. What evidence is there for the soundscape of the early colonial New World cities?[2] Despite Geoffrey Baker's much lauded success in researching Colonial Quito, the web of musical activity and noise in many Latin American colonies before 1650 has not been the subject of in-depth soundscape studies, a situation reflecting a lack of evidence for some cities (Baker, 2008; Wagstaff, 2010). Mexico City remains one of those urban spaces before 1650 about which much remains to be discovered or at least hypothetically re-created. Although I will not attempt in this chapter to present such a comprehensive study of Mexico City, the Viceregal capital of New Spain in the Habsburg Empire, I will ask some leading questions and offer hypotheses that may provide starting points for work contextualizing one of the seminal ceremonies in early Colonial Mexico.[3]

After the institution of Viceregal governance was introduced, with its associated court and interplay of Catholic liturgy at civic events, much of Spanish Habsburg court ceremony ca. 1530 began to be reflected in various events in New Spain. For some ceremonies, this required the creation of an "event planning" network coordinating many skilled artists, crafts people, musicians, and other experts. Among the most complex events were death rituals – which had become a defining aspect of Spanish Habsburg ceremony – that would be used after 1550 by Viceregal authorities as a symbol of power. As with many events, these death rituals featured Catholic ceremonies as proof of monarchic and courtly piety; because of this, Church culture and ritual give much of the frame, although certainly not all, for how sound and ceremony were presented in the city, with urban spaces used as a dramatic stage.[4] In such royal/imperial/viceregal events, music was only one of the arts displayed and hearing only one of the senses manipulated in these multimedia productions, an apt theatrical term (Wagstaff, 2002a). Such ceremonies included examples of most of the elite courtly arts disciplines practiced in 16th-century Spain with, perhaps, dance alone omitted, although highly choreographed movements were included. For the series of commemorations called *exequias* or *honras funebres* mounted in November 1559 in memory of the Emperor Charles V, who had died in 1558, various arts media were certainly meticulously planned.[5]

---

2   Bermúdez (2001), who examined the Tierra Firme coastal region of Columbia, Venezuela, and Panama, has authored one of the seminal studies of New World cities before 1650.

3   Here, I use the terms *Colonial Mexico* and *Colonial New Spain* as is common in various disciplines in English-language research.

4   Schwaller (2011) contextualizes Catholic mission activities in New Spain as techniques gained from the Reconquest in Spain of Muslim-controlled areas. See also Nader, 2000, pp. 11–47.

5   Stevenson (1952) provided a seminal discussion of this event.

If we base our hypothesis on later practices, Charles' death would have been announced when the *cedula*, the official decree, arrived from Madrid: there seems to have been a standard practice in the Latin American colonies that this announcement was made along with the playing of what was called an "untuned", perhaps muted, drum (Baker, 2008, pp. 33–34). The sound of the drum, draped in black cloth, added to the funereal aesthetic symbolized by black garb worn by the *pregonerio* or town crier. A similar drum, used as a signal to gather attention, may also have been used in the processions discussed below, providing coordination for the choreography of those participating in the ritual; it was likely again "clothed" with black draping to represent death. Baker found that the inclusion of the drum in announcements was typical in some colonial cities of South America during the 17th century, but certain public announcements also included the use of "discordant trumpets", as was the case at Cusco in 1645 during the announcement of the death of Elizabeth (wife of Philip IV), who had died the previous year (Baker, 2008, pp. 33–34). Would instruments have been used in other aspects of the ceremonies in Mexico City? In 1543, *ministriles*, identified as native peoples, were paid by the Cathedral for an event not related to *honras* (Actas de Cabildo, 1543/06/01). In the 1590s, *trompetas* were specifically mentioned in Mexico City Cathedral records, again not specified as a death ritual (Actas de Cabildo, 1591/06/07). In Spain in the early 16th century, it was noted that both drums and "muted" trumpets were played when Isabella's body was moved in cortege through Cordoba in Andalusia toward her resting place, the Capilla Real in Granada (Martín Barba, 2008, p. 36). This Iberian document, however, raises the cautionary tale that use of instruments was curtailed soon after by authorities when Isabella's body reached Granada, meaning that practices varied, even in nearby cities where we could assume they were similar. Likewise, cities in the Spanish Americas likely had distinct traditions contrary to what could be thought typical.[6]

Bells would have been tolled, again if we base our assumptions on later practice, to announce the death of the emperor. Such church bells, *campana*, are mentioned in the cathedral *actas* as early as 1539, with the specific warning that the bells were to be used only at specified times to announce liturgical services (Actas de Cabildo, 1539/08/14). The tolling of bells was obviously a delicate issue: In the notice, the sacristan was being severely criticized for ringing them at unapproved times, which seemingly had caused havoc in the streets. This marking of time, both clock time and the ritual time of the daily Office services, was crucial in civic life and Church culture. Which other churches in Mexico City in 1559 had larger bells that could have communicated across distances in the city?[7] The Fran-

---

6 Zapata Castillo (2017) based her discussion of the announcement in Mexico City on 17th-century practice in Chile.

7 Molina Álvarez (2007) gives a sense of the interplay of sounds from different institutions. However, much of the evidence postdates 1600.

ciscan Church of San José, where the *honras* were presented, was a larger complex in 1559 than was the Cathedral itself and likely had significant and varied bells. The Franciscans, as did other religious orders, installed bells in the 16th century as a way of communicating with native peoples, to control time, and to organize the liturgical day (Dutcher Mann, 2013). What soundscape did this create? If one stood on the Zocalo, the main plaza of Mexico City, in front of the Cathedral then under construction in 1559, what polyphony of bells from different churches did one hear?

There is little evidence for the preparation of the complex ceremonies; the Cathedral's governing chapter specified that boys from a nearby school would participate, requiring vestments to be made:

> …para las honras de nuestro Emperador – que está en gloria – se hiciesen doce sobrepellices para los muchachos del colegio de San Juan, que se pongan aquel día para ayudar a misa […] Y también, sacase el tafetán negro que fuese menester para hacer una túnica y tunicela; y lo demás que fuere con los señores de cabildo (Actas de Cabildo, 1559/11/07).

> …for the *honras* of our Emperor – who is in heaven – twelve *sobrepellices* [vestments] should be made for the boys of the colegio of St. John, so they will be ready that day to assist at Mass […] And also, black taffeta as may be needed should be made available to make a tunic [vestment for the subdeacon] and dalmatic [vestment for the deacon]; and the rest to be done by the members of the chapter.[8]

Obviously, the expense and acquisition of black taffeta was of greater immediate concern than was training the boys. They almost certainly would have sung chant, adding their voices to the presentation in which many peoples of the colony participated, either as "performers" or in building and decorating the many ephemeral structures. These boys likely included sons of native leaders who were systematically brought into the Church to maintain the social order of the pre-Columbian hierarchy.[9] Such assisting at Mass, with all the ritualized movements into and out of the church and around the alter during the service, required a great deal of knowledge. These movements also would have created their own rhythm of noise, with footfalls, clanking of liturgical accessories such as the censor and other metal objects, and other accidental, unplanned sounds. This incidental noise, like that of the footsteps in the procession, would have melded with planned music. The advanced state of education, including music, for indigenous children must be empha-

---

8   Translated by the author. Thank you to Joseph Santo for advice on the terms used for specific vestments.

9   Curcio-Nagy describes this as a system in which "Christian religion came through a native filter, namely the indigenous elite" (2000, pp. 155–156).

Fig. 1: Francisco Cervantes de Salazar: Túmulo Imperial de la Gran Ciudad de Mexico, title page.

sized, despite the brutality ongoing in New Spain. The level of music making described in the *honras* discussed below is significant, given that this region had come under Spanish control only with the brutal defeat in 1523 of Mexicas of Tenochtitlan by Cortez, his soldiers from Spain, and their indigenous allies, various peoples who fought against the "Aztec" military rulers.[10] That the era was brutal should not be lost in the discussion below. Indeed, this period was extraordinary for the rapidity with which European music was transferred to New Spain and for the brilliance repeatedly noted regarding native peoples learning a foreign music, all of which occurred during enormous suffering and destruction of native cultures among the many ethnic groups in New Spain. Understanding any aspect of music in 16th-century New Spain is complicated by many factors, not least the Spanish

---

10   The esteemed historian Elliott (2021) recently underscored that the word *Aztec*, although used in English-language scholarship across disciplines as a catch-all term, distorts understanding of different ethnic groups. This includes those such as the people of Tlaxcala, near Mexico City, who were Nahuatl speaking and ethnically Mexicas, as were the rulers of México-Tenochtitlan who brutally governed central Mexico. The Tlaxcalans, or Tlaxcaltecs, were *not* reigned by Tenochtitlan and, like several other groups, joined with Cortez's forces against the Mexicas.

filter through which much evidence is transmitted (Davies, 2021). For us, the complexity of understanding these *honras* from the perspective of indigenous peoples is greatly complicated by the presence of many different cultures with their own languages and religious and cultural traditions, as well as their differing relationships to the rulers of Tenochtitlan and later to the Spanish Viceregal authorities (Elliott, 2021). Because of this fundamental issue, I will avoid using the word *Aztec* as a catch-all term for the indigenous peoples of New Spain.

Despite the lack of further evidence, leaders of Viceregal New Spain, I contend, considered the success of these events proof that Mexico City was a world capital, a leading city in the Habsburg realm (Ellsworth Hamann, 2010). A Spanish-born chronicler of the ceremonies presents the city not only as mature in its Catholic faith and ritual, but also worthy as an *urban* centre that participated in Imperial ritual symbolizing the continuity of Habsburg power.[11]

Scholars now take for granted the essentially urban nature of the colonial enterprise in Latin America (Baker, 2011). Indeed, Mexico City in 1559 had not only a nascent cathedral and many other churches, including those of Franciscans and other religious orders, but also its own recently founded university, the Real y Pontificia Universidad de México. This created a network of expertise in music as well as bells and other sounds and rituals, complexity that is crucial to understanding the sonic experience of 1559. The network of urban spaces, lauded for its obviously advanced urban planning, provided an optimal setting for processions. The decision was made to begin the *honras* procession outside the Viceregal palace, adjacent to the cathedral, and move through the streets to the Church of San José. This allowed for a larger church to be used, incidentally one associated with *los naturales* or indigenous peoples, and for a grander procession. Various media had to be considered for the ceremony; in 1559, the cathedral itself had no completed space with a ceiling high enough for an appropriate catafalque.

What specific evidence for sounds that does exist from Mexico 1559 relates to sacred liturgical music. Written polyphonic music, such as that by Andalusian Cristóbal de Morales, whose works were sung at the 1559 *exequias*, was a primary symbol of both the idealized "pure" Catholicism of Spain and Habsburg political stability (Olton, 2010). This music, as did all the architectural and visual art tributes as well as the chronicle of the event, demonstrated that Viceregal Mexico had a mature lettered elite, scholars of various fields in the sciences and humanities as well as musicians and artists who could present a commemoration of the mythical Emperor bearing comparison to such events in Spain.[12] And

---

11   On Viceregal governance and culture in New Spain, see González, 2021, pp. 215–236; the balance of power among church institutions is examined in the same volume in Rubial García, 2021, pp. 137–162. Also, Ramos-Kittrell discusses the later period (2021, pp. 424–439).

12   About the lettered elite, Baker emphasizes the centrality of urban life in the Colonial Americas and

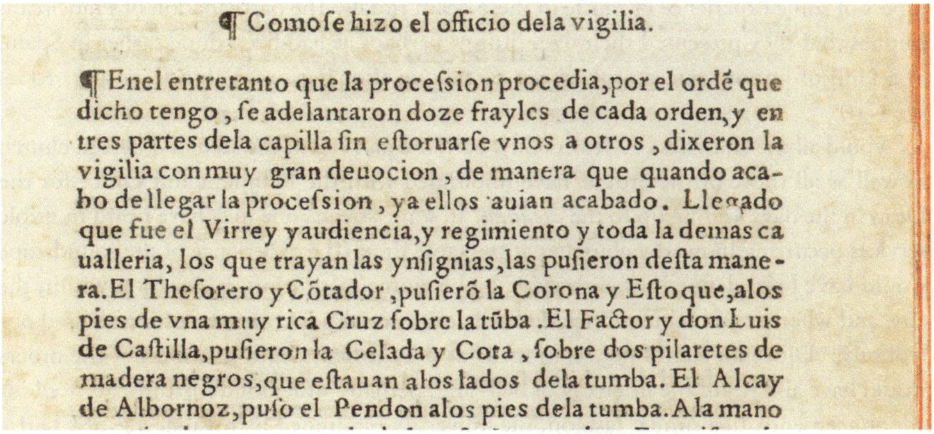

The Power of Silence 349

> ¶ Como se hizo el officio dela vigilia.
>
> ¶ Enel entretanto que la procession procedia, por el ordé que dicho tengo, se adelantaron doze frayles de cada orden, y en tres partes dela capilla sin estoruarse vnos a otros, dixeron la vigilia con muy gran deuocion, de manera que quando acabo de llegar la procession, ya ellos auian acabado. Llegado que fue el Virrey y audiencia, y regimiento y toda la demas caualleria, los que trayan las ynsignias, las pusieron desta manera. El Thesorero y Cõtador, pusierõ la Corona y Estoque, alos pies de vna muy rica Cruz sobre la tũba. El Factor y don Luis de Castilla, pusieron la Celada y Cota, sobre dos pilaretes de madera negros, que estauan alos lados dela tumba. El Alcay de Albornoz, puso el Pendon alos pies dela tumba. A la mano

Fig. 2: Francisco Cervantes de Salazar: Túmulo Imperial de la Gran Ciudad de Mexico, fol. 25r.

yet, the written polyphony carefully described by the chronicler was but a small slice of the sounds, including music, that one heard during such commemorations. Monophonic music remained the basic sound of services. Some chants were memorized from written exemplars, while other genres in the services were recited in a semi-improvised system of "tones" matching certain texts such as Psalms with surrounding melodies. Chant in New Spain, which reflected local pre-Tridentine traditions from Andalusia/Castille differing from melodies in Rome, would have been the basic sound in day-to-day presentations of the Office and Mass (Wagstaff, 2011). This liturgical monophonic practice was itself a kind of soundscape into which polyphony was added. Copies of polyphonic works, specifically those by Morales, were likely sent from Spain for the event in question, which would have altered the interplay of music compared to day-to-day services.[13] That the chronicler did not mention extended chants in various services implies he assumed one would have known the typical sounds encountered. His silence on this pervasive aspect allows us to suggest that awareness of many sounds was assumed among educated readers of the chronicle, especially those in Madrid advising Charles' son King Philip II. Cervantes, I propose, assumed such educated advisers intuited the elite urban sounds of Mexico City to resemble those of cities in Spain, particularly Seville and Toledo, which had influenced such death rituals.

The music in the featured services of the Office and Requiem sung by Cathedral musical "forces" may be the best-documented sound of the event, but again it was only one

---

the idealized city with "harmony" as a goal of civic life (2011, pp. 1–20).

13 Polyphonic works by Spaniard Juan Vásquez were also likely included but are not specified in the chronicle.

aspect of sonic experience of music in these death rituals. The participation of Franciscans implies that they presented their own liturgy, perhaps as had been done earlier in Spain, as a kind of honour guard around the catafalque after its completion (Kreitner, 2004, pp. 1–11).

Would all the churches of Mexico City, both the parishes of the secular diocesan church as well as all those of the orders, have resounded with the Requiem and Office for the Dead in the days leading up to the *exequias*? In some streets, one may have heard multiple services occurring in nearby churches at the same time. The experience of the soundscape would have been defined for each cleric by his home institution, its location within the city, and whether each church included only chant or also had written or improvised polyphony.[14] Diocesan clerics not "stationed" at the Cathedral and members of the orders would have also heard the interplay of bells and, perhaps, other loud instruments used for announcements. In a similar fashion, the university – founded by royal decree of Charles in 1551 – likely had its own liturgical services. Some professors were clerics, and there is evidence from Spain, specifically Salamanca on which Mexico City's university was based, for death rituals among academics with distinct ceremonial traditions (Wagstaff, 2011).

Much of the planning for the *honras* as well as how it was reported was shaped by earlier ceremonies in Spain and Catholic traditions important in Iberian life. Although the interplay of various arts media was meticulously crafted, music was a central aspect of the tradition, with *exequias* during the epoch of the Catholic monarchs providing models (Knighton, 2005, pp. 93–97). For Mexico City, many details are known about the music in one portion of the ceremonies because it was described by Cervantes de Salazar, professor of rhetoric at the university, thus a leading member of the lettered elite. A priest since 1554, he was later made a Canon of the Cathedral (Cervantes, 1560). Although his status as Canon was not official in 1559, I would proffer that he should be considered a member of the city's ecclesiastical hierarchy.[15]

In addition to knowledge of music, Cervantes was also aware of liturgy and ceremonial in death rituals and had likely participated in such *honras* in Spain.[16] Sadly, he gives no

---

14 Comparatively little is known about music among the religious orders, including Franciscans, in early New Spain. Their practices may have had a mixture of more complex written polyphony with simple formulaic practices as in later Franciscan missions in Alta California. The participation of female religious orders is not mentioned.

15 Francisco Cervantes de Salazar, a humanistic author and scholar, was born ca. 1515 in Toledo. After study at the University of Salamanca and later work in the circle of Charles V, he moved to New Spain around 1550. There he became in 1553 the first professor of rhetoric at the new university and was ordained a priest in 1554. See Real Academia de la Historia, available at: https://dbe.rah.es/biografias/11971/francisco-cervantes-de-salazar. Date of Access: 27.01.2024.

16 During a sojourn in Osuna, Spain, Cervantes (1560) likely met the music theorist Juan Bermudo and perhaps also Morales. See Stevenson, 1952, pp. 87–88.

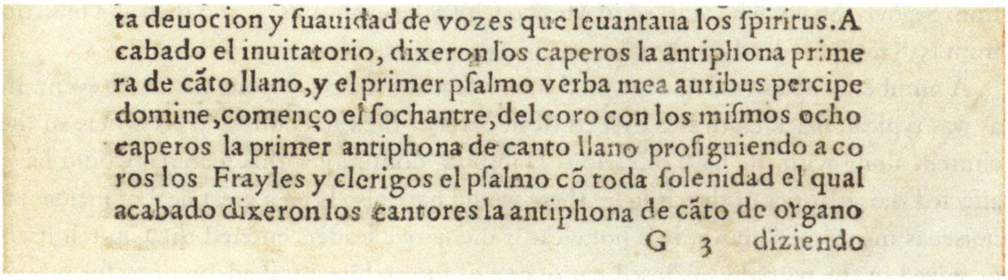

The Power of Silence

ta deuocion y suauidad de vozes que leuantaua los spiritus. A
cabado el inuitatorio, dixeron los caperos la antiphona prime
ra de cãto llano, y el primer psalmo verba mea auribus percipe
domine, començo el sochantre, del coro con los mismos ocho
caperos la primer antiphona de canto llano prosiguiendo a co
ros los Frayles y clerigos el psalmo cõ toda solenidad el qual
acabado dixeron los cantores la antiphona de cãto de organo

G   3   diziendo

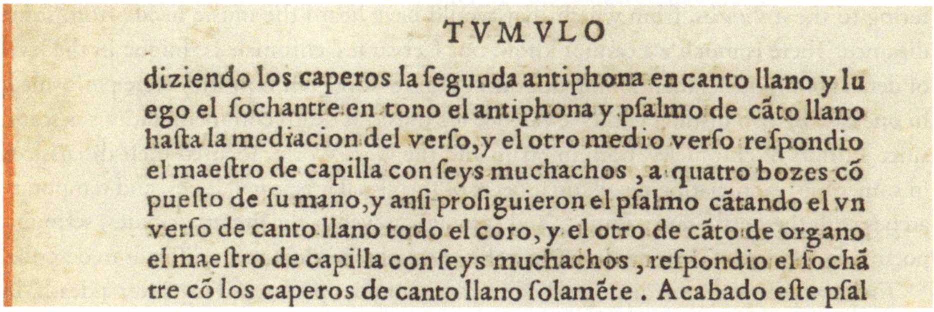

TVMVLO

diziendo los caperos la segunda antiphona en canto llano y lu
ego el sochantre en tono el antiphona y psalmo de cãto llano
hasta la mediacion del verso, y el otro medio verso respondio
el maestro de capilla con seys muchachos , a quatro bozes cõ
puesto de su mano, y ansi prosiguieron el psalmo cãtando el vn
verso de canto llano todo el coro, y el otro de cãto de organo
el maestro de capilla con seys muchachos , respondio el sochã
tre cõ los caperos de canto llano solaméte . Acabado este psal

Fig. 3a & 3b: Francisco Cervantes de Salazar: Túmulo Imperial de la Gran Ciudad de Mexico, fols. 25r. and 25v.

information whatsoever on sounds except the music performed during the two featured liturgies, Matins and Mass. It is possible that he did not attend the other events, which did not have the "see and be seen" aspect of the two main services, or that he assumed that everyone knew there would be other liturgies, likely sung in chant, which did not merit reference.

For a document that provides much information about music in the above two services, Cervantes' chronicle implies that until one crucial moment, Mexico City was largely – what I might even label *mystically* – silent. Then when all of the Viceregal society was gathered, including the native leaders who had participated in the procession, music – intensely Spanish in genre and style – began to be sung.[17] This highly tradition-bound music, which was closely associated with Charles V and later Habsburg monarchs, heightened the religious experience of ceremonies defining Catholicism in Spain in its ritualized commemoration of death (Eire, 1995). In addition to works by the Spaniard Morales, pieces composed in Mexico City were performed. Cervantes specifically mentions music "compuesto de su mano", composed by his own hand, by the chapel master Lázaro del Álamo

---

17 Cervantes makes no reference to an organ or other instruments being used. At the funeral of Philip II in San Jerónimo in Madrid in 1598, Morales' invitatory was sung by four soloists (Ruiz Jiménez, 2015).

from Segovia, Spain, who worked in Mexico City as a singer in 1554, and then as a maestro from 1556 until his death in 1570.[18]

A number of acoustical issues would have affected listeners' experience of the event. If, as was typical, black cloth was draped from parts of the catafalque and elsewhere in the church, along with the flags of various Habsburg dominions, this material would have affected the acoustics of the church. There would have also been a great deal of incidental noise, as mentioned above. It is not clear if the native leaders entered the Church itself or stayed in the partially enclosed patio, one of the architectural adaptations for ministering to the *naturales*, from which they would have heard the music inside from some distance. There is much we cannot know, but Cervantes' chronicle is unique in the level of detail about music, mentioning not only specific works but how they were performed, in one case by two distinct choirs. Evidence for music at death commemorations is scant, since authors of chronicles, both in Spain and the New World, focused their discussion, in sometimes excruciating detail, on aspects of the visual arts, catafalques, and temporary arches with their elaborate paintings and carvings, as well as the literary tributes, sermons, poems, and epitaphs. As today, music was for most observers far more difficult to describe.

These *exequias* must be distinguished from ceremonies performed just after a death. In Spain, when a monarch, royal family member, or ecclesiastical leader died, there was a period of mourning with liturgical presentations typically about nine days long. This period featured a kind of "lying in state" similar to modern practices with luminaries,[19] as well as the Requiem Mass and Office for the Dead. In contrast, *honras*, with these same services as well as other kinds of masses, were presented well after the burial. This time lapse allowed a catafalque to be built as well as other preparations of the visual, literary, and musical elements to be made; in the later Middle Ages, *honras* began to be presented as commemorations not necessarily in the city where the person had died (Ruiz, 2012, pp. 309–310). In Spain, by the 1530s, these rituals had become multi-day "performances" with elaborations of Matins and processions with polyphonic music. The polyphony that proliferated quickly after 1500 can be interpreted as a sonic representation of the idealized "pure" Catholicism of Spain, as well as of the good death taught in the Church's *Ars moriendi* tradition (Sanmartín Bastida, 2006; Eire, 1995, pp. 24–34). By 1550, composers in Spain had developed a polyphonic repertory for Matins and death processions, as well as for the Requiem, with all genres closely based on the melodies and performance practices of chant (Wagstaff, 2004). Music for death rituals encoded pedagogical and theological aims, since propaganda as the Church in Spain was seeking to portray itself as free of Jewish and later Moslem influences,

---

18 In 1568, Archbishop Montúfar praised the quality of Alamo's *motetes, villancicos y chanzonetas*.

19 Music in royal funerary rituals in and near Barcelona was well documented after the death of Juan II of Aragón in January 1479; Kreitner (2004) interpreted the 1479 event as seminal for development of sacred music in Spain.

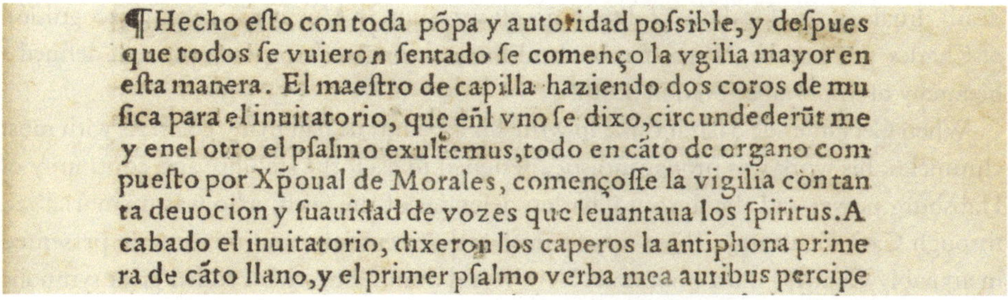

The Power of Silence

> ¶ Hecho esto con toda pōpa y autoridad possible, y despues
> que todos se vuieron sentado se començo la vgilia mayor en
> esta manera. El maestro de capilla haziendo dos coros de mu
> sica para el inuitatorio, que enl vno se dixo,circundederūt me
> y enel otro el psalmo exultemus,todo en cāto de organo com
> puesto por Xꝓoual de Morales, començosse la vigilia còn tan
> ta deuocion y suauidad de vozes que leuantaua los spiritus.A
> cabado el inuitatorio, dixeron los caperos la antiphona prime
> ra de cāto llano,y el primer psalmo verba mea auribus percipe

Fig. 4: Francisco Cervantes de Salazar: Túmulo Imperial de la Gran Ciudad de Mexico, fol. 25r.

while continuing to struggle with the presence of converts and their cultural traditions.[20] Much about evangelization in New Spain reflected techniques of the Reconquest in Spain. Thus, because of their close association with the sacrament of extreme unction, these services of the Liturgy for the Dead would have been powerful symbols in New Spain, namely, recognition of a new sacred passage from life to death (Lara, 2008, pp. 144–149).

Given Cervantes' background and his obvious goal to document elite Spanish culture, his approach should not surprise us, one in which sound represented power on that day in November 1559 when New Spain mounted its best documented Habsburg *honras*. That power was announced by music of the Spanish composer Morales. His *Circumdederunt me*, an invitatory for Matins, is believed to be the first European polyphonic work cited by name in a description of a New World event.

This highly effective setting, with its presentation of the melody and structure of chant, is shaped both by Spain's medieval liturgies, which differed from Roman tradition, and by a somewhat grander sound that Morales perhaps created for earlier *honras* in Spain (Wagstaff, 2002b). This antiphon alternated with his more austere four-voice setting of the Psalm, *Venite exsultemus*, in a lengthy opening complex, some 15 minutes of music, all of which Cervantes reports was sung in polyphony. The music had such "devocion y sauvidad" that it lifted "the spirits" according to his chronicle (Cervantes, 1560, fol. 25r.). Morales was uniquely fitting as a sonic symbol of Spanish Habsburg power and New World aspiration. Born in or near Seville, the gateway to New World colonization, Morales – after establishing himself in Spain – worked for a decade in Papal employ in Rome, and, afterward, in Toledo, the seat of ecclesiastical power in Spain. He would be closely associated with the Emperor, composing the motet *Jubilate Deo* in honour of the meeting of Charles V with Pope Paul III and Francis I in 1538, and meeting Charles on several occasions, creating speculation that Morales sought a job. *Circumdederunt* would not have been sung in

---

20 Beginning in the later 15th century, numerous bishops in Spain alluded in Synodal Constitutions to "foreign" music in death rituals, as well as mentioning genres associated with Jewish and Moslem traditions.

death rituals except for those of dignitaries. It was sung in Mexico, in part, as recognition of Charles' good death (Wagstaff, 2002b). Morale's work is *about* power, since it defined a hierarchy of importance even in death.

When Cervantes de Salazar came to write his account, he had many goals. As with most chronicles, his work was propagandistic, designed to exalt the stability and continuity of Habsburg power and the devout Charles, defender of the faith, who was memorialized through Catholic liturgy. These *very* Spanish style ceremonies and music were presented in arguably Charles's most important New World dominion, which added great symbolic meaning (Zapata Castillo, 2017, pp. 129–135). Cervantes perhaps wanted to present Mexico City to other New World cities as the leading capital, but he knew his most important audience was in Madrid, the court advisors.[21] This required him to present the participation of indigenous peoples in a very particular manner. To be perceived as Christian in 1559 by clerics and the few other educated Spaniards in New Spain meant, in a sense, acting European. Before 1550, clerics in Mexico were primarily members of religious orders, although there was a growing number of secular clergy. Whatever one's level of understanding of Christian dogma, one demonstrated faith by participating in sacred – meaning European – ceremonies. For Habsburg court rituals transplanted to Mexico, to be Christian, one had to act, or be in the process of learning how to act, like a Spaniard, by participating in ceremonies of the somewhat ascetic Catholicism promoted by Isabella and Ferdinand and enshrined in court, subsequently Viceregal, ceremony. Such rituals reflected a mix of Spanish, Burgundian, and pan-European practices defining Habsburg court ceremonial, traditions evolving in the mid-16th century that included a unique mix of music (Robledo Estaire, 2000, pp. 3–21).

Historian Carlos Eire states that medieval Catholicism made sense of life (and here, also death), helped communication, and "imposed order" (Eire, 2016, pp. 20–21). The description of native peoples' behaviour obviously reflected this new order. Cervantes includes references to the decorum shown by indigenous people bringing Spaniards to tears, who obviously interpreted this decorum as submissive acceptance of the dignity and symbolism of the tributes to Charles.[22] Processions for the *exequias* in which native peoples participated were far more inclusive than were other Viceregal events, and have been interpreted as the ultimate representation of the Colonial body politic, from its "head" to its "feet" in terms from that era (Caneque, 2004, pp. 131–132). That these processions in *honras* were a "perfect microcosm of Colonial Mexican society" highlights the profound symbolism of the essential rituals of Spanish Catholicism, kingship, and Viceregal authority (Caneque,

---

21 Bermúdez mentions the *exequias* for Charles in Santa Fe, Colombia, as having been an event with singers, but he does not discuss what music might have been included (2001, p. 179).

22 The one identified reaction to the *honras* by an indigenous person was a drawing of the catafalque (Olton, 2010, pp. 10–26).

The Power of Silence
355

2004, pp. 131–132). The presence of native peoples in such rituals signified Habsburg stability, just as did paintings on the catafalque of pre-Columbian kings offering tribute to Charles (Olton, 2010, pp. 17–23).

What was the nature of the silence preceding the music that represented Spanish monarchal, cultural, and religious domination? Was this quiet thought necessary by Cervantes for the impact of music he then describes? In his mind, were the other sounds and music simply not worthy of mention? Was his presentation of events shaped in part by a desire to demonstrate that native peoples had acquired the etiquette and bearing of Spanish ceremony? What of other sounds? Were there stops or stations during the procession with responsories, chant or polyphony, as typically done at these events? Were instruments included in the procession? Did any indigenous people sing laments in their native language in memory of Charles? Such non-Latin laments would likely have been harshly judged by authorities, as had other music at funereal ceremonies that was prohibited by bishops in Spain in synodal constitutions beginning around 1500. Much about the approach of teaching native peoples in Mexico grew out of techniques developed during the Reconquest in Spain. Strictures governing behaviour and non-clerical music at death rituals were likely enforced in New Spain. Of course, Cervantes, highlighting the very Spanish nature of the events, probably would not have mentioned indigenous music if he had heard it. His propagandistic approach was much influenced by Church culture, especially that of the cathedral, defining what was proper and respectable. Native leaders, like the Viceroy and other Spaniards present, were expected to model Spanish Catholic etiquette, just as Charles's life and death were portrayed as pedagogically instructive. This again highlights the limitations of evidence, all of which comes to us from a very prejudiced lettered elite, educated in Spain.

Cervantes implies that much of the ritual, especially the processions, was very quiet. Did learning to act Spanish mean being quiet? There is some later evidence from the colonial Americas: Baker has discussed an account by Don Alonso Carrio de la Vandera, whose 1773 *El lazarillo de ciegos caminates* states that Corpus Christi processions in Cuzco featured "a solemnity and a *silence* [emphasis mine] in which only holy praise is heard"; Baker interprets this as quiet required for the "serious" part of the event, with its "Hispanic" music and liturgy (Baker, 2008, pp. 35–36). At least one 16th-century ecclesiastic in Spain discussed this issue: Martín de Azpilcueta Navarro, in his *Discurso del silencio que se deve guardar en los Diuinos Oficios, principalmente en el Coro*, published posthumously in 1588. It emphasizes the silence required of those in liturgical services "in the choir" (Azpilcueta Navarro, 1588). He derides those who talk out of place as *rustico*, again emphasizing the assumed urbane quality of educated elites in Catholic liturgy. With the strong connections between Mexico City and Salamanca, such concerns over etiquette and "learning how to act" were likely assumed by Cervantes and the organizers of the *honras*.

Some sounds associated with death rituals were sensitive issues to elites, especially clerics: weeping and other "cries" at funerals were frequently condemned by bishops as excessive and unnecessarily distracting (Wagstaff, 2002a). Such expressions of grief were grouped together with "foreign" practices, including musical laments, and frowned upon perhaps because such actions were associated with paid mourners, poor people who served as a kind of civic demonstration of respect for the deceased. These sounds were also thought to bring with them the taint of non-Christian practices, in Spain associated with Jews and Moslems (Wagstaff, 2002a). When Cervantes describes that native people "sobbed" and that their bearing brought Spaniards to tears, the author is venturing into a problematic topic. The calm acceptance of death taught in *Ars moriendi* tracts emphasized the hope of heavenly reward and not the sadness of grief of those left behind. Perhaps Cervantes risks this sensitive topic just to emphasize the impact of the native peoples' dignity.

The evidence as well as lack of evidence for sounds other than the elite music from Spain or based on Spanish tradition tells us, of course, much more about Cervantes – his goals, education, and prejudices, as well as the genre of medieval or early modern royal chronicle – than about his experience in 1559 in Mexico City, what happened and was heard by participants, rapt observers, or even those paying little attention. As it is today, Mexico City was no doubt a noisy place in the mid-16th century, one in which rituals, sounds, and all of life collided in unexpected, complex, beautiful, and bombastic ways. The interplay of many kinds of noise, some planned as signals, as well as the ambient sounds of movement and talk, created a complex sonic texture that provided a backdrop for music. Assumptions from Spain help us to suggest aspects of a hypothetical soundscape, as do later references from the Spanish Americas. Silence was seemingly conceptualized by the lettered elite as the proper canvas on which elite liturgical music in sacred liturgy was to be presented. What emerges, other than the likely complexity of what was heard, with the different assumptions made by Cervantes and his small cadre of educated Iberians, as opposed to those of indigenous peoples, is the limitations of what we as music scholars emphasized in the past. This leaves us with many questions. Perhaps by asking them, I will prompt more investigation, research that may lead to a better understanding of this extraordinary event.

Bibliography

Manuscripts

Archivo del Cabildo, Catedral Metropolitano de México
Actas de Cabildo, 1539/08/14. MUSICAT: MEX 79000029.

Actas de Cabildo, 1543/06/01. MUSICAT: MEX 79000062.
Actas de Cabildo, 1559/11/07. MUSICAT: MEX 79000126.
Actas de Cabildo, 1591/06/07. MUSICAT: MEX 79000471.

Printed Sources

Azpilcueta, M. de (1588). *Discurso del Silencio que se Deue Guardar en los Diuinos Oficios, Principalmente en el Coro*. Pedro Lasso.

Cervantes de Salazar, F. (1560). *Túmulo Imperial de la Gran Ciudad de Mexico*. Antonio de Espinosa.

Scholarly Literature

Baker, G. (2008). *Imposing Harmony: Music and Society in Colonial Cuzco*. Duke University Press.

Baker, G. (2011). The Resounding City. In G. Baker & T. Knighton (Eds.), *Music and Urban Society in Colonial Latin America* (pp. 1–20). Cambridge University Press.

Bermúdez, E. (2001). Urban Musical Life in the European Colonies: Examples from Spanish America, 1530–1650. In F. Kisby (Ed.), *Music and Musicians in Renaissance Cities and Towns* (pp. 167–180). Cambridge University Press.

Caneque, A. (2004). *The King's Living Image: The Culture and Politics of Viceregal Power in Colonial Mexico*. Routledge.

Carreras, J. J. (2018). Topography, Sound, and Music in Eighteenth-century Madrid. In T. Knighton & A. Mazuela-Anguita (Eds.), *Hearing the City in Early Modern Europe* (pp. 85–100). Brepols.

Carter, T. (2000). Urban Musicology. *Early Music* 28(2), 313.

Carter, T. (2002). The Sound of Silence: Models for an Urban Musicology. *Urban History* 29(1), 8–18.

Carter, T. (2018). Listening to Music in Early Modern Italy: Some Problems for the Urban Musicologist. In T. Knighton & A. Mazuela-Anguita (Eds.), *Hearing the City in Early Modern Europe* (pp. 25–52). Brepols.

Curcio-Nagy, L. A. (2000). Faith and Morals in Colonial Mexico. In M. C. Meyer & W. H. Beezley (Eds.), *The Oxford History of Mexico* (pp. 151–183). Oxford University Press.

Davies, D. E. (2021). Colonialism and Music in Habsburg New Spain. In A. H. Weaver (Ed.), *A Companion to Music at the Habsburg Courts in the Sixteenth and Seventeenth Centuries* (pp. 439–464). Brill.

Eire, C. M. N. (1995). *From Madrid to Purgatory: The Art and Craft of Dying in Sixteenth-Century Spain*. Cambridge University Press.

Eire, C. M. N. (2016). *Reformations: The Early Modern World, 1450–1650*. Yale University Press.

Elliott, J. H. (2021). Mastering the Glyphs: New Histories of the Conquest of Mexico Look to

Nahuatl-language Sources for a Fresh Perspective on Aztec Society. *The New York Review of Books* 2, 31–33.

González, I. E. (2021). Permanence and Change in Mexico City's Viceregal Court, 1535–1821. In J. F. López (Ed.), *A Companion to Viceregal Mexico City, 1519–1821* (pp. 215–236). Brill.

Hamann, B. E. (2017). An Artificial Mind in Mexico City (Autumn 1559). *Grey Room* 67(1), 6–43.

Knighton, T. (2005). A Meeting of Chapels: Toledo, 1502. In J. J. Carreras & B. García García (Eds.), *The Royal Chapel in the Time of the Habsburg: Music and Ceremony in Early Modern European Court* (pp. 88–102), transl. by Yolanda Acker. Boydell Press.

Knighton, T. (2018). Orality and Aurality: Contexts for the Unwritten Musics of Sixteenth-Century Barcelona. In T. Knighton & A. Mazuela-Anguita (Eds.), *Hearing the City in Early Modern Europe* (pp. 295–308). Brepols.

Kreitner, K. (2004). *The Church Music of Fifteenth-Century Spain*. Boydell Press.

Lara, J. (2008). *Christian Texts for Aztecs: Art and Liturgy in Colonial Mexico*. University of Notre Dame Press.

Mann, K. D. (2021). Defining Time and Space: Franciscans and Bells in Northern New Spain. In T. M. Cohen, J. T. Harrison & D. R. Galindo (Eds.), *The Franciscans in Colonial Mexico* (pp. 259–286). University of Oklahoma Press.

Martín Barba, J. J. (2016). Guayas, Lutos, y Exequias en el Itinerario Del Cortejo Fúnebre de Fernando El Católico. *De Medio Aevo* 9(1), 23–60.

Mazuela-Anguita, A. (2018). Soundworlds and Spatial Strategies of the Social Elite: The Contribution of the Requesens Noblewomen to the Soundscape of Sixteenth-century Barcelona through the Palau de la Comtessa, In T. Knighton & A. Mazuela-Anguita (Eds.), *Hearing the City in Early Modern Europe* (pp. 197–218). Brepols.

Molina Álvarez, D. (2007). *Campanas de México*. Impresiones Gama.

Nader, H. (2000). The Spain that Encountered Mexico. In M. C. Meyer & W. H. Beezley (Eds.), *The Oxford History of Mexico* (pp. 11–47). Oxford University Press.

Olton, E. (2010). To Shepherd the Empire: The Catafalque of Charles V in Mexico City. In J. Beusterien & C. Cortez (Eds.), *Hispanic Issues On Line,* vol. 7 (pp. 10–26).

Ramos-Kittrell, J. A. (2021). Music and Literature in New Spain: The Politics of Buen Gusto in 18th-Century Mexico City. In J. F. López (Ed.), *A Companion to Viceregal Mexico City, 1519–1821* (pp. 242–439). Brill.

Robledo Estaire, L. (2000). La Estructuración de las Casas Reales: Felipe II Como Punto de Encuentro y Punto de Partida. In R. Estaire, T. Knighton, C. Bordas Ibáñez & J. J. Carreras (Eds.), *Aspectos de la Cultura Musical en la Corte de Felipe II* (pp. 3–21). Fundación Caja Madrid.

Ros-Fábregas, E. (2009). Urban Music in Renaissance Spain. *Early Music* 37(3), 355–416.

Rubial García, A. (2021). City of Friars, City of Archbishops: The Church in Mexico City in the Age of the Hapsburgs, In J. F. López (Ed.), *A Companion to Viceregal Mexico City, 1519–1821* (pp. 137–162). Brill.

Ruiz, T. F. (2012). *A King Travels: Festive Traditions in Late Medieval and Early Modern Spain*. Princeton University Press.

The Power of Silence 359

Ruiz Jiménez, J. (2020). Funeral Rites of the King Philip II in the Convent of San Jerónimo in Madrid. *Paisajes Sonoros Históricos*: http://historicalsoundscapes.com/evento/1127/madrid/en. Date of Access: 27.01.2024.

Sanmartín Bastida, R. (2006). *El Arte de Morir: la Puesta en Escena de la Muerte en un Tratado del Siglo XV.* Iberoamericana.

Schwaller, J. (2011). *The History of the Catholic Church in Latin America: From Conquest to Revolution and Beyond.* New York University Press.

Stevenson, R.M. (1952). *Music in Mexico: A Historical Survey.* Crowell.

Wagstaff, G. (2002a). Processions for the Dead, the Senses, and Ritual Identity in Colonial Mexico. In L. P. Austern (Ed.), *Music, Sensation, and Sensuality* (pp. 167–180). Psychology Press.

Wagstaff, G. (2002b). Cristóbal de Morales' Circumdederunt me, An Alternate Invitatory for Matins for the Dead, and Music for Charles V. In D. Crawford (Ed.), *Encomium Musicae: Essays in Memory of Robert J. Snow* (pp. 27–45). Pendragon Press.

Wagstaff, G. (2004). Morales's Officium, Chant traditions, and Performing 16th-century Music. *Early Music* 32(2), 225–243.

Wagstaff, G. (2010). Review of Imposing Harmony: Music and Society in Colonial Cuzco, by G. Baker. *Journal of the American Musicological Society* 63(3), 652–658.

Wagstaff, G. (2011). The Big Sombrero, Dead Professors, and Chant Sources: Aspects of Salamantine Tradition. In K. E. Nelson (Ed.), *Cathedral, City, and Cloister: Essays on Manuscripts, Music and Art in Old and New Worlds Ontario* (pp. 135–156). The Institute of Mediaeval Music.

Zapata Castillo, M. Á. (2017). *Música, Muerte y Ceremonial: La articulación del poder a través de la música en el ritual funerario de los Austrias en España y Nueva España* [Doctoral dissertation, Universidad Autónoma de Madrid].

Illustration Credits

Fig. 1: Cervantes de Salazar, Francisco: *Túmulo Imperial de la Gran Ciudad de Mexico* (Mexico City: Espinosa, 1560). Title page. RB 106408. The Huntington Library, San Marino, California.

Fig. 2: Cervantes de Salazar, Francisco: *Túmulo Imperial de la Gran Ciudad de Mexico* (Mexico City: Espinosa, 1560). fol. 25r. RB 106408. The Huntington Library, San Marino, California.

Fig. 3a & 3b: Cervantes de Salazar, Francisco: *Túmulo Imperial de la Gran Ciudad de Mexico* (Mexico City: Espinosa, 1560). fols. 25r. and 25v. RB 106408. The Huntington Library, San Marino, California.

Fig. 4: Cervantes de Salazar, Francisco: *Túmulo Imperial de la Gran Ciudad de Mexico* (Mexico City: Espinosa, 1560). fol. 25r. RB 106408. The Huntington Library, San Marino, California.

Commanding Sounds and Sights

A Case Study of State Processional Music in Late Ming China (1572–1644)

Joseph S. C. Lam

Introduction

Since 2012, China has implemented the national policy of "Chinese Culture Goes Global" (*wenhua zou chuqu*), a policy promoting general and scholarly interests in historical and traditional China, and stimulating the publication of many precious sources on historical Chinese music and performing arts. Examinations of these sources have led to a number of practical and theoretical questions. What and how do preserved words and images tell us about sounds and sights that vanished centuries ago? What does a historical and musical understanding of the past signify for the present? A prime example of such questioning of China's musical past is recent scholarship on Chinese state processions and processional music (Ren, 2014; Zeng, 2015). Among the numerous historical and musical sources that have been examined is a pair of two gigantic and thematically interrelated scroll-paintings (*changjuan*). Drawn on two long rolls of silk, they present panoramic yet detailed views of late Ming (1572–1644) state processional music, challenging viewers to decipher their multi-media performance and cultural-historical significance.

Superficially, what the scroll-paintings reveal is clear: a Ming dynasty (1368–1644) emperor and his entourage travelling back and forth between the Forbidden City in Beijing and the Ming Tombs in the capital's northern suburbs. As depicted, the emperor is young but commanding; his state processions are grand spectacles performed by hundreds, if not thousands, of court officials, soldiers, and musicians who play drums, gongs, and wind instruments, making loud, rhythmic, and repetitive sounds that project imperial authority and power.

The scroll-paintings present the travelling emperor as a commanding young man, whose imperial and physical body is tightly shielded by his imperial guards and fully enveloped by his processional music. The scroll-paintings do not show any commoners witnessing the imperial parades or listening to the state processional music performed, even though their presence as active or passive audience is historically documented. By not showing the commoners, the scroll-paintings visually suggest that they were a powerless audience, who silently kowtowed to the depicted emperor, whose presence was more heard than seen. However, it clearly commanded obedience from the commoners in the audience. They knew that any challenge or resistance to the emperor and his processional music would be considered an offense punishable by death. That brutal forces substantiate imperial authority and power is common knowledge in authoritarian cultures and societies, Chinese or not.

To probe the scroll-paintings as a historical and visual source of Chinese music, to analyse its visual representation of late Ming state processional music performance and discourse, and to explore issues of music as a form and tool of hard or soft power, this chapter unfolds in six parts. The first, which is this introduction, presents the topic of Chinese state processional music in its historical and contemporary contexts. The second part introduces elements that either constitute the scroll-paintings' visual content, or frame its interpretation. These elements include but are not limited to the physical attributes of the scroll-paintings, their provenance, the Ming and court tradition of painting, state procession and state processional music, its musical instruments, and traditional theories and practices. The third part interprets cultural and historical meanings of the depicted state processions with reference to Emperor Shenzong's biography (1563–1620; r. 1572–1620). The fourth part describes the visual content of the scroll-paintings in question, listing the types of musical instruments depicted and underscoring the ways the scroll-paintings project music performance, listening, and interpretive practices in late Ming China. The fifth part theorizes on the scroll-paintings' strategic representation of state processions as spectacles that performatively and ritually manifest the depicted ruler's emperorship and manhood. The sixth part concludes this chapter, aligning observations about late Ming state processions and processional music with international theories about music as a performance and discourse of cultural-social-imperial-nationalistic agendas.

Chinese Scroll-Paintings as Historical and Musical Sources

The two scroll-paintings in question are currently held in the Palace Museum in Taipei, Taiwan, and can be readily viewed online (National Palace Museum, N.D.) and through facsimiles (National Palace Museum, 1980s-1; and National Palace Museum, 1980s-2). The first painting, which is now known as the *Chujing tu* (Imperial procession departing from the Forbidden City), measures 92.1 cm by 2,600.3 cm.[1] When it is unrolled and viewed from right to left, the scroll-painting presents a Ming emperor and his entourage departing the Forbidden City for the mausoleums of imperial ancestors in the Tianshoushan

---

[1] See the animation film based on these paintings: https://theme.npm.edu.tw/exh105/npm_anime/ DepartureReturn/ch/index.html. Date of Access: 28.01.2024.

(Heavenly Longevity Mountains) area, a northwestern suburb of present-day Beijing. As cultural, historical, and tourist sites, the mausoleums are now collectively called the Ming Tombs (Paludan, 1981). The second painting, namely, the *Rubi tu* (Imperial procession returning to the Forbidden City) measures 92.1 cm by 3,003.6 cm. When it is unrolled and viewed from the left to the right, it shows a Ming emperor's procession returning to the Forbidden City from Xishan (the Western Mountains), travelling on river and on land. For discussion convenience in this chapter, the *Chujing tu* will be specifically called the *Departure* and the *Rubi tu*, the *Return*; collectively, they will be addressed as the *Scrolls*.

Little about the *Scrolls'* provenance is known, except that in 1747, they entered the Qing dynasty (1644–1911) collection of imperial portraits housed inside the Nanxun dian (Palace of Southern Fragrance), a stand-alone building located on the western side of the outer court (*waichao*) in the Forbidden City. Since then, the *Scrolls* have been studied by court officials and art connoisseurs, who have argued about the identity of the emperor depicted in the *Departure* and the *Return* (Na & Kohler, 1970). Based on historical information about Ming emperors, and based on what the *Scrolls* visually communicate, three Ming emperors could qualify as the depicted ruler: by name, they are Yingzong (1424–1464; r. 1435–1449 and 1457–1464), Shizong (1507–1566; r. 1521–1566), and Shenzong. Identification of the emperor depicted in the *Scrolls* is critical for deciphering their visual narrative. Unless his identity can be ascertained, the visual data provided by the scroll-paintings cannot be meaningfully interpreted in the contexts of Ming biography, culture, and history. A consensus about the emperor's identity was reached in 2004, when Zhu Hong, a Taiwanese historian, published a definitive study. By aligning architectural, geographical, and historical data about Beijing and the Forbidden City with visual information presented in the *Scrolls*, he surmised that the emperor depicted was Shenzong and that the visit represented took place in March, 1583 (Zhu, 2004).

Zhu's verdict is predicated on the Chinese tradition of producing and viewing scroll-paintings as visual documents that accurately preserve/represent historical events and personages (Fong, 2003). Drawn on long rolls of silk cloth, scroll-paintings tell stories with flowing and linear sequences of scenes, each a visual tableau that highlights particularized agents and their actions and messages. Imperial China has produced many visually detailed and historically informative scroll-paintings. An example noted for its revealing information on Chinese court processions is the *Dajia lubutu* (Imperial procession, a scroll-painting; 1053) from the Northern Song (960–1127), which measures 51.4 cm by 1,481 cm. Visually, it reports Emperor Renzong's (1010–1063; r. 1022–1063) state processions to the suburban altar where he offered grand sacrifices to Heaven, the main deity, and its companions, the emperor's defied imperial ancestors (Ebrey, 1999).

Like the *Dajia lubutu*, the *Departure* and the *Return* belong to a distinctive group of large scale Chinese court documentary paintings. Most are products of court painting academies (*huayuan*) and court painter-officials, who not only painted as needed or as requested by their superiors, but who also managed the circulation and preservation of collected court paintings. Court and documentary scroll-paintings were produced to serve specific goals. Stylistically, they tend to showcase verisimilar visuals more than painterly imaginations.

Given their grand scale, realism, and painterly perspectives and structure, the *Scrolls* can hardly be accidental products. In all likelihood, they were ordered by Shenzong or someone high up in his court, people who wanted to preserve historical memories of the emperor's parades, and project realistic understandings, or satirical comments, on his being an able, dutiful, and filial young sovereign. In other words, the *Scrolls* were purposefully created for interested or targeted viewers, who would have had cultural-historical knowledge and the artistic skills to readily grasp and meaningfully negotiate the scroll-paintings' explicit and implicit messages.

For the reasons outlined above, the *Scrolls* were probably produced by a team of court painters working under one or multiple artistic directors. Arguably, they either had personal experience of Shenzong's 1583 parades or had substantive knowledge about late Ming state processions. Otherwise, they could not have accurately and vividly depicted the emperor, his large entourage and their costumes, carriages, horses, musical instruments, and ritual paraphernalia.

With panoramic perspectives and realistic details, the *Scrolls* visually describe Shenzong's 1583 visit to the imperial mausoleums, highlighting his potent emperorship and manhood. Technically known as *yeling* (emperors' honouring of imperial ancestors by visiting and offering sacrifices at the latter's mausoleums), Shenzong's visit was an occasional but required state ritual. In historical China, legitimate and effective rulers presented themselves as filial sons. Thus, in addition to the regular performance of state sacrifices to Heaven, Earth, and other supernatural forces and dynastic founders, Chinese emperors would occasionally honour their ancestors by visiting and performing sacrificial rituals at the latter's mausoleums. Ideologically and politically, the ritual visits and performances signified the Chinese and Confucian way of living hierarchically and obediently – when filial sons ritually respect parental and state authorities, they demonstrably perform their socially and politically assigned roles. Chinese emperors travelled to their ancestors' mausoleums with large entourages, generating large-scale multi-media and moving spectacles that effectively and ritually conveyed a wealth of imperial messages to their voluntary and involuntary witnesses. For convenience in the discussions in this chapter, Shenzong's *yeling* exercise in the spring of 1583 will be called the *visit*; his militarily, musically, and ritually choreographed state processions from the Forbidden City to and back from the mausoleums, the *parades*.

Historical China discussed state processions under the rubric of *lubu*, a term that literally refers to court carriages and chariots featured in imperial parades. Discursively, the term is used as a synonym for state processions; all were meticulously performed according to culturally-historically established court conventions, and by hundreds if not thousands of court staff and military guards. As such, *lubu* spectacles display, or are constituted, by a wealth of elocutionary and symbolic features, all of which were theoretically and practically negotiated before they were activated, so that they would accurately manifest and project the traditional and/or occasional meanings of state processions that travelling emperors wanted to advance. As public spectacles, state processions elicited critical and diverse reactions from both courtiers and commoners. While they could hardly challenge parades and their imperial messages *in situ*, their reaction to and interpretations of emperors could be manipulated into political forces that could help build up or topple imperial authorities and powers.

Sonically, the music Shenzong's parades played has vanished and is for the time being not verifiably knowable. However, many traces of its sounds and performance practices are still known, and have been heuristically discussed under the rubric of *guchui*. Literally, the term means music played with drums and wind musical instruments, but it is often used as a historical nomenclature for Chinese court/state processional music. When performed by a multitude of court musicians and with a large number of graduated drums, gongs, flutes, shawms, and other musical instruments, *guchui* made loud and rhythmic sounds that late Ming elite and commoners would comprehensively understand but could not, indeed, were not allowed to duplicate in their daily and expressive lives. As much as they may have wanted to emulate their rulers' processional music, which was an effective sonic declaration of identities, authorities, and privileges, they could only play much reduced versions of imperial *guchui*.

Collectively, processional and/or presentational music of Ming elite and commoners is known as *chuida* (celebratory and/or processional music played with a variety of wind and percussion musical instruments) or *luogu* (processional and/or theatrical music played mostly with drums and gongs). Late Ming *guchui*, *chuida*, and *luogu* have substantive overlaps in their aesthetics, composition, performance, and listening practices, a musicological understanding suggested by preserved historical sources. Some genres of late Ming *chuida* and *luogu* processional music are clearly forerunners of several types of traditional processional and/or instrumental music that are still performed today (Yuan, 1987) – in addition to verbally recorded links in musicians' biographies and transmitted composition titles, the genres use similar musical instruments and performance practices. Judging from what and how contemporary performances of traditional processional music sound like,[2] and assuming their being musical echoes of what was played and heard in late Ming China, Shen-

---

2   The Zhou Family Band: A Chinese Wedding and Funeral Band in Europe, 2017: https://www.youtube.com/watch?v=OxwERrXo6RM. Date of Access: 28.01.2024.

zong's *guchui* can be historically heard as music that was loud, rhythmic, and repetitive. And this is what the *Scrolls* vividly project with their detailed visual depiction of musical instruments and their playing by Shenzong's musician-soldiers.

As documented, the people of the late Ming period understood that instrumental and processional music had a long history in China. Allegedly, Han dynasty (202 BCE to 220 CE) Chinese soldiers learned tunes and performance techniques of wind and percussion musical instruments from non-Han peoples living in Western China, as well as in Central and Western Asia. Soon after that, processional music became a standard feature of Chinese court and military exercises. For example, upon successful completion of military campaigns, Ming armies sang victory songs (*kaige*) with wind and percussion accompaniments (Zhang, 1975). Ming commoners would also perform loud, rhythmic, and percussive music at local and ritual activities, such as those celebrating the mid-autumn and New Year festivals, and those requesting supernatural grace during times of solar and lunar eclipses (*jiuri fagu*), droughts, and other life-threatening crises.

By late Ming China, powerful officials and wealthy commoners had learned from imperial parades that processional music could performatively and sonically project people's social-political identities and agendas. Thus, the rich and powerful in late Ming China hired full bands of musicians to play processional music while escorting their trips across town, thus telling people who they were or aspired to be, and showcasing human and material resources that they prodigiously controlled. As described in historical texts and as embodied by excavated examples of Ming dynasty stoneware dolls of musicians playing in funeral bands, the elite's processions were long, with their *chuida* and *luogu* music loud, rhythmic, and repetitive. Such sonic attributes of the music were often noted by late Ming authors. For example, Zhang Dai (1597–1684), a celebrated Ming essayist, wrote that at local festivals, people played wind and drum music so loudly that its sounds rocked the earth and flipped the sky (*dongdi fantian*) (Zhang, 2014).

As loud, rhythmic, and repetitive music, wind and percussion music could be readily played by all kinds of professionals and amateurs. The Ming court hired multi-talented performers who were artistically and socially interrelated. Recent scholarship has demonstrated that as an official institution, the late Ming court painting academy operated pragmatically (Sung, 2013). It counted the professional male painters it hired as members of the Brocade Guards (*jinyiwei*), a palace army whose primary mission was to serve the emperors' intelligence, personal, and security needs. Some members of the Brocade Guards, however, also doubled as *guchui* instrumentalists. In other words, in the late Ming court, there were men who functioned as Brocade Guards-cum-musicians-cum-painters. It is most likely that some of these multi-talented men participated in Shenzong's parades of 1583. Their personal experiences are one reason why the *Scrolls* have such panoramic and detailed representations of Shenzong's parades.

Commanding Sounds and Sights

Fig. 1: "Shenzong as a young emperor"; from the *Departure*.

Their loyalty to Shenzong and knowledge about his imperial and physical being are arguably among the reasons why they painted Shenzong, their sovereign, as an able, commanding, intelligent, pleasure-seeking, and martial young man, although they may have also merely been following orders to depict Shenzong positively. In the *Departure*, he is depicted as a young ruler wearing elaborate armour, holding a whip in his right hand and a set of arrows and bow in his left. He rides a majestic black horse with a wide decorated saddle, and his torso is turned to show his assertive manner: staring not only at his parade audience, but also anyone examining the *Scrolls*. He is surrounded by soldier-musicians (Fig. 1). In the *Return*, he is presented as an imposing but relaxed man. Enjoying music and delicacies, he takes a boat ride to return to the Forbidden City. As depicted, he physically dwarfs the imperial guards and eunuchs performing music and other chores on his imperial barge and on those floating by it (Fig. 2).

Viewed casually, the musical and visual representation of Shenzong's parades is a more-or-less accurate report of what happened; viewed critically, the visualization in the *Scrolls* is unmistakably creative and discursive. In relative and quantitative terms, the *Scrolls* showcase the soldier-musicians' male bodies and their vigorous playing of wind and percussion musical instruments. With such visuals, the *Scrolls* painterly project the travelling Shenzong as a commanding and capable emperor.

Fig. 2: "Shenzong returns to the Forbidden City"; from the *Return*.

Shenzong's Visit to the Imperial Mausoleums

The projection is unmistakable when the emperor's 1583 visit is analysed in its biographical, cultural, geographical, and historical contexts. The visit was a political and ritual necessity, but it was also a potentially risky undertaking. It made the emperor travel outside the Forbidden City and exposed him to potential dangers. While he could have skipped the visit, to perform his imperial and filial duties responsibly, Shenzong had to rule not only with edicts, but also acts representing his being a courageous and filial son.

To visit the mausoleums, Shenzong had to travel over a substantial distance, passing through mountains and over rivers. By contemporary standards, the distance he physically travelled is hardly long – the geographical distance between the Forbidden City and the Tianshoushan mausoleums is only about thirty miles. In Ming China, however, that distance was experienced as extensive, one that Shenzong and his large entourages could only pass through with pomp and precautions. As described in the *Mingshi* (Ming history) (Zhang, 1975, fascicle 60, pp. 1475–1477), it took Shenzong and his entourage one and a half days to complete each of the back and forth trips between the Forbidden City and the mausoleums. Each trip was punctuated by the emperor's staying overnight at an outlying palace, where he could rest and where he could hold an audience with local officials and commoners.

To ensure the trip's success and to guard against potential dangers as well as expected or unexpected criticism, Shenzong's visit could only take place after the court had made extensive ritual preparations and security contingencies. The court could not afford to underprepare. The Tianshoushan and Xishan areas where the mausoleums are located were close to the northern border of the empire and thus were open to attacks by the empire's ethnic and political rivals living in the grasslands just beyond the Great Wall. Any ritual or operative missteps that might occur during a visit could be construed by the court's rivals as negative omens for the empire.

During his long reign of forty-eight years, Shenzong took four trips to the mausoleums (Lin, 1996). In March 1580, he made his first visit to the mausoleums. Despite being ritually simplified, it demonstrated that he was a filial son and a dutiful emperor. In 1583, Shenzong visited the mausoleums in both the spring and the autumn. The spring visit is the one documented in the *Scrolls*. The primary reason for making these trips was to offer state sacrifices to Ming imperial ancestors. A second reason was Shenzong's search for sites where his own mausoleum could be built. Emulating the acts of his celebrated and worthy predecessors, Shenzong wanted to monumentalize his imperial being and achievements by building his own mausoleum. It would ideologically and physically demonstrate his personal control of the court and by extension, the Ming empire. In the autumn of 1584, Shenzong took his fourth and last visit to the mausoleums, honouring his ancestors and confirming his decision to build his mausoleum in the Tianshoushan area. There he rested until his mausoleum was excavated in 1956. Three years later, it was opened to the public as an underground Ming palace/museum, a permanent monument to Shenzong's emperorship and personhood.[3]

Shenzong ascended to the Ming throne in 1572 as a ten-year-old child (Huang, 1981; Lin, 1996). In 1578, he married and became an adult. Nevertheless, until 1582, he ruled under the control of Zhang Juzheng (1525–1582), a strict teacher and an authoritarian regent. From 1580 through 1584, Shenzong repeatedly visited the imperial mausoleums to politically and ritually declare to his court that he had become a mature and capable emperor. This declaration was unmistakable because it was backed by Sheonzong's bodily and personal actions. As a matter of fact, Shenzong's first visit impressed Zhang Juzheng so much that the latter promptly submitted his resignation letter and offered to immediately return control of the Ming court to his imperial protégé. Implementing court protocol, Zhang's resignation request was declined and he was asked to continue his service as a regent.

In June 1582, Zhang died and Shenzong took full control of the courts while filially following directives from his birth mother, the Empress Dowager Cisheng (1545–1614).

---

3   To read about the museum, see Anonymous, 2015: http://www.china.org.cn/english/features/museums/129077.htm. Date of Access: 28.01.2024.

In August 1582, Imperial Consort Wang gave birth to Shenzong's first son. In the spring of 1583, a political movement to dismantle Zhang Juzheng's personal and political legacy was launched. Promptly, the movement snowballed into an extensive purge that exposed Zhang's hypocrisy – he had indulged in expensive comforts while making the young Shenzong live sparingly. Bombarded by the accusations, Shenzong became distraught. To vent his anger, Shenzong took vindictive measures against his former mentor. In August of 1583, he stripped Zhang of an honorary title that he had bestowed on the official. In April 1584, the young emperor confiscated the deceased official's estate, causing Zhang's family members and followers great suffering. In 1585, Shenzong customized and performed a sacrificial request for rain, demonstrating his understanding and use of rituals and spectacles to exercise his imperial authority and power.

In 1586, Shenzong's favourite consort, Lady Zheng (d. 1620), gave birth to his third son, an event that necessitated the timely appointment of an heir apparent. By tradition and by moral dictate, Shenzong should have appointed his first son born four years earlier. However, because of his love for Lady Zheng and other personal reasons, he procrastinated, triggering political developments that soon paralyzed his court, dividing it into supporters and critics. Incessantly, they fought against one another, using the succession issue as an excuse to manipulate the emperor and advance their own political agendas. Fifteen years later, in October 1601, Shenzong finally designated his first son as the crown prince.

Because of the succession issue, Shenzong and his officials were often at odds with one another. Aggressive and righteous officials, such as Hai Rui (1514–1587), for example, harshly criticized the emperor, characterizing his love for Lady Zheng as sexual indulgence, his drinking and craving for money as excessive gluttony, and his treatment of court officials as unwise vengeance. To passively but not ineffectively fight with these officials, Shenzong stopped holding morning audiences with them from the summer of 1589 on, rendering court operations chaotic and unproductive. Shenzong, however, never stopped being a commanding and strong-willed emperor. During the decade of the 1590s, he played active roles in directing battles with Mongolians operating in Ningxia (1592), the Japanese who invaded Korea (1592–1593 and 1597–1598), and a group of ethnic minority people who lived in Guizhou (1599–1600).

As historian Ray Huang has reported, Shenzong was an enigmatic emperor; his imperial actions pushed Ming China into a course of decline and subsequent collapse (Huang, 1981) – in Chinese political chronology, the empire collapsed in 1644. There is no denying that Shenzong's indulgent acts shaped Ming history and reception of his emperorship and manhood. He probably missed many opportunities to reinvigorate late Ming China. For example, had he paid more attention to the Western knowledge and technology, including music, that Matteo Ricci (1552–1610) and other Jesuits introduced to his court, late Ming China might not necessarily have collapsed in the way it did. And had Shenzong critically

Commanding Sounds and Sights

engaged with Western music, he might have found new sounds and rhythms to express his emperorship and personal being.

Musicians and Musical Instruments in Shenzong's Parades

How musical was Shenzong? How and why did he have *guchui* played to announce his commanding and travelling emperorship and manhood? Some answers can be found by scrutinizing the panoramic yet detailed representation of Shenzong's parades in the *Departure* and the *Return*. Structurally and thematically speaking, the *Departure*, which unfolds from right to left, is divided into three developmental parts. The first part presents the rear of a state procession leaving the Forbidden City – the emperor's entourage is being sent off by court officials standing outside the palace, bidding farewell to their ruler. The second part, the bulk of the painting, shows the emperor and his entourage travelling towards the mausoleums in a series of processional formations. The third part shows the vanguard of the parade, namely the officials and soldiers who are approaching the mausoleums, where they would make various preparations for the emperor's sacrificial activities.

The *Return* is similarly panoramic. Unrolling from left to right, it is structurally and thematically divided into five parts. The first part shows the mausoleums and their mountainous surroundings, where troops of soldiers march in military formations and groups of palace staff gallop between their duties. The second part shows the imperial armada: a series of nineteen barges of different sizes, the largest transporting the emperor. The third part presents imperial guards in various formations, marching on land and ahead of and/or by the side of the imperial barges. The fourth part depicts imperial ladies' grand carriages and palanquins – Shenzong's imperial mother and consorts were politically required to participate in his *yeling* exercises. The fifth part shows the vanguard of the parade, with soldiers and officials marching over a bridge leading directly to the western entrance of the capital city and on to the Forbidden City.

Collectively and visually, the *Scrolls* project Shenzong's parades as spectacles performed by a multitude of soldiers, eunuchs, and palace staff, whose identities and roles were practically and symbolically defined by how they travelled, the clothes or armour they wore, the horses they rode, and the banners and weapons they carried. Revealingly, the *Scrolls* present the parades as male activities – imperial ladies who travelled with the emperor are hidden inside grand carriages. And except the eunuchs, all the male participants of the parades are depicted as handsome men with masculine bodies and virile comportment. Proudly and professionally, they fulfil their military, musical, and ritual duties, a performance that favourably reflects on Shenzong's court.

Fig. 3: "An imperial *guchui* band in Shenzong's parades"; from the *Departure*.

Significantly, the depicted soldier-musicians are also the guards travelling close to the emperor. Judging from how they hold or play musical instruments, they are making loud, rhythmic, and repetitive sounds, sounds that constitute a complex and multivalent soundscape moving with the travelling emperor. Viewed visually, the depicted soundscape is mute. Viewed with a historical knowledge of late Ming musical culture, the visually preserved soundscape is almost audible. This is particularly the case when viewers of the *Scrolls* compare the depicted soldier-musicians and their musical instruments to their contemporary counterparts in traditional wind and percussion music played and listened to in China today. Through comparative and musical interpretations, informed viewers can readily deduce what Shenzong's *guchui* sounded like.

The *Departure* features three bands of sixteen soldier-musicians each. All three play the same types and numbers of musical instruments, which are: four bronze horns (*tongjiao*), two small barrel drums (*yaogu*), two hand-held nippled, medium-sized gongs (*zhongluo*), two shawms (*suona*), two flutes (*chi*, or *hengdi*), two pairs of wooden clappers (*paiban*), one pair of small cymbals (*xiaobo*), and one small frame-held gong (*dianzi*) (Fig. 3). The first two bands travel immediately ahead of the emperor, clearing the way for his approach to the mausoleums; the third group follows right after him, creating a musical and secure rear for him.

Fig. 4: "Soldier-musicians playing *guchui* music on an imperial barge"; from the *Return*.

The *Return* presents eight groups of eunuch/soldier-musicians. Four groups travel on boats floating ahead of, next to, and after the emperor's barge. The first boat carries eleven musicians playing one small hand-held stringed hour-glass drum (*jiegu*), a pair of wooden clappers, two reed-pipes (*guanzi*), one mouth organ (*sheng*), one flute (*di*), one set of frame-held small gong-chimes (*yunluo*), one pair of cymbals, one frame-held large drum (*tanggu*), one frame-held large gong (*daluo*), and one handheld small gong (Fig. 4). The second boat carries ten musicians; they play one barrel drum, one hand-held stringed barrel drum, one pair of wooden clappers, one mouth organ, one pair of frame-held large gongs, one hand-held small gong, one large frame-held drum, one pair of small cymbals, and one reed-pipe. The third and fourth boats each carry four soldiers with horns resting on their shoulders. Six groups of soldier-musicians travel ahead of the imperial armada, galloping towards the Forbidden City, with the first group the one travelling close to the emperor's barge. With the exception of the second group, all of the groups feature horn-carrying and horse-riding soldier-musicians. The second group features ten soldier-musicians; they play two flutes, two pairs of wooden clappers, two hand-held medium-sized nippled *gong*s, one pair of small cymbals, one frame-held small gong, and two barrel drums (Fig. 5).

Except for the horn players, the soldier-musicians are depicted as if they are actually striking or blowing their instruments. For example, the small cymbal player in the second band in the *Departure* is depicted holding one of his arms higher than the other as if he has

Fig. 5: "Horse-riding *guchui* musicians"; from the *Return*.

just forcefully struck the cymbals and is now pulling them in different directions. Similarly, many of the musicians, such as those playing the small handheld gongs or wood clappers, are depicted as if they are paying attention to the rhythms their partners are playing – to make coordinated sounds, ensemble musicians have to hear and see what their colleagues are doing.

The *Scrolls* meticulously depict the musical instruments. In terms of organological shape and construction, all are represented realistically. They are either identical or similar to what late Ming commoners used to play in their own *chuida* and *luogu* music, a fact that many late Ming music sources confirm. For example, the *Sancai tuhui* [An illustrated encyclopaedia of earthly, heavenly, and human talents; 1607) describes the *yunluo* as a frame-held set of thirteen small bronze gong-chimes (Wang & Wang, 2011, fascicle 3, pp. 24a–40b). The verbal description fits what the *Scrolls* depict, except that the depicted instrument has only eleven constituent small gongs. The encyclopaedia says that to play the *yunluo*, a musician holds the long wooden stick attached to the base of the frame of the instrument with his left hand; his right hand holds a small mallet, which is used to strike the gongs to make melodies. *Yunluo* are still played today in a similar way.

With concise descriptions, the encyclopaedia and similar Ming historical sources tell a lot about how late Ming people played and listened to *guchui*, *chuida*, and *luogu* music as sonic indicators of personal and institutional identities and authorities. For example, the encyclopaedia explains that Ming people understood the small frame-held gong (*dianzi*) as deriving from what ancient night guards patrolling the streets had played to mark the passing of time and announce the security service they were providing. The encyclopaedia also declares that the flutes, horns, and shawms that late Ming commoners played in their processional music had morphed into quotidian tools with diverse ethnic, social, and political associations. For example, the large nippled single gong, which originated from southern ethnic China, was played and enjoyed not only for its deep and resonant sound, but also for its representation of non-Han peoples and cultures.

Commanding and Travelling Sounds and Sights of Shenzong's Parades

When blown or struck, the melody and percussion musical instruments depicted in the *Scrolls* and described above readily generated loud and forceful sounds, sounds that effectively projected human and natural powers. They were sounds that could be readily used to constitute imperial parades and state processional music. As *guchui*, such a processional music forcefully and sonically projected Shenzong's emperorship and manhood. When its sounds and visual representation are analysed in their historical, performative, musical, and visual contexts, the music is intelligible and unmistakable (Nelson, 1998/1999).

Chinese history has comprehensively documented state processions as being large scale spectacles that both affectively and intellectually projected imperial expressions with coordinated and culturally-historically established sounds, sights, bodily movements, and ritual paraphernalia. As performed, seen, and heard, parade expressions in different media affectively touched performers and audiences, and intellectually triggered their conventional and/or creative understandings of the spectacles they were witnessing.

As constituents of spectacles moving along specified routes and times, parade expressions in different media appealed to participants in dissimilar but complementary ways. For example, the sight of the Brocade Guards' handsome faces, virile comportment, and colourful and elaborate court costumes undoubtedly made late Ming commoners feel as if they were experiencing Ming court splendour and imperial masculinity. The parade sights, however, blurred as soon as they moved out of the spectators' direct and focused view.

Compared to parade sights, the sounds of a procession were semantically abstract or multivalent; such sounds, however, travelled great distances in physical space and lasted long in temporal time. Until they were no longer audible, parade sounds did not blur and their messages were not easily distorted. This was particularly true for the loud, rhythmic, and repetitive sounds made with metallic gongs, thundering drums, and shrill wind instruments. With such sounds, *guchui* communicated imperial messages to voluntary and involuntary audience/parade bystanders. They could not help but accept the sonic communications. This is because they could not prevent *guchui* sounds from hitting their eardrums when and where they voluntarily or non-voluntarily assembled to observe the passing of travelling emperors. There and then, the audience had to bear the sounds until the marching and playing musicians moved away. How this loud, rhythmic, and repetitive wind and drum music forced itself on its audience was unmistakable and could be characterized in the following terms. The louder and more rhythmic parade sounds were, the stronger the impression they made on hearing participants; the stronger the impressions parade sounds made, the longer their commanding sonorities and authoritarian meanings were remembered by the participants. As time passed, memories of the music faded, but all could be "refreshed" with notated, verbal, or visual representations. This is perhaps why the *Scrolls* highlight Shenzong's soldier-musicians and their playing of *guchui* musical instruments.

It is also why the absence of commoners in the *Scrolls* demands scrutiny. There is no definitive data on how late Ming commoners witnessed Shenzong's parades, which were large-scale occasional spectacles that stretched over expansive spans of space and time. In other words, they generated sights and sounds that could hardly have been ignored by commoners living between Beijing, the capital, and the Tianshoushan and Xishan areas. They had little choice but to voluntarily or involuntarily witness Shenzong's parades.

Such witnessing indexes two contrasting but equally revealing scenarios of *guchui* performance and reception. First, if commoners voluntarily witnessed the parades close-up, they would have participated as passive players, since they could only hear Shenzong's loud, rhythmic and repetitive sounds silently, thus demonstrating their submission to his authority and force. Second, if commoners were ordered to witness the parades, their compliance registered their submission to the emperor. In both scenarios, commoners could only see and hear what the court had its soldier-musicians play. They played to make Shenzong's emperorship and physical being audible in controlled ways. As a Son of Heaven, Shenzong could not be seen or heard by commoners as they wished. Only the privileged could have a face-to-face audience with the emperor. To make Shenzong's performance as a filial Son of Heaven audible and thus knowable to as many commoners as possible, the court invited or compelled commoners to voluntarily or involuntarily witness his parades. There and then, the commoners had to kowtow to the passing emperor, whose presence was readily knowable but hardly challengeable.

Commoners had no chance to encounter their ruler directly. They could only listen and submit. And the more they understood the music, the more they would have been overwhelmed by the ruler's authority and power, which involved unlimited access to all kinds of human and material resources. It is significant that the *Scrolls* minutely depict soldier-musicians and eunuch-musicians, the musical instruments they play, and the performance gestures they make. Through such visual details, the court painters of the *Scrolls* evoked the complexities of Shenzong's *guchui*, sonic nuances that reflect the ruler's complex emperorship and manhood. Any viewer of the *Scrolls* would see that the *Departure* and the *Return* feature different musical instruments, tools that could be used to generate contrasting and differing sonic timbres, dynamics, and textures. Painterly, the *Departure* features horse-riding soldier-musicians playing more percussion than melody musical instruments, while the *Return* displays eunuch-musicians travelling by boat and playing more melody-wind instruments. The percussion instruments they play are specialized. For example, the two frame-hung single gongs and barrel drums they play are quite a bit larger than those played by the horse-riding soldier-musicians.

The painterly depiction of musical instrumentation in Shenzong's parades is eloquent. Depicted are sounds with distinctive timbres, dynamics, and textures being used to project dissimilar or contrasting messages about the emperor. Shenzong's eunuch-musicians in the *Return* playing more melodious *guchui* music registers not only differences in parade times, sites, and processes, but also contrasting sides of Shenzong's manhood. By detailing the instrumentation of his "water music", for instance, the *Scrolls* evoke how he felt as he left the mausoleums by boat. Floating on the river towards the Forbidden City, Shenzong knew that he had fulfilled his political and ritual duties as a filial son/ruler. Satisfied with what he had pulled off, he could relax, enjoy an imperial feast of delicacies, and expose his genuine self as a young and pleasure-seeking emperor. As documented historically, Shenzong kept two operatic troupes in his palace; one for his empress dowager and one for his own entertainment needs (Liu, 1963, pp. 39–41).

Shenzong knew his music and its functions. Like his subjects, he subscribed to Confucian and traditional *yue* aesthetics and performance practices. *Yue*, a Chinese word usually translated into English as music, involves much more than the composition, performance, and appreciation of musical works defined by stylized, structured, and meaningful sounds. As theorized and practiced by historical and Confucian Chinese musicians and patrons, *yue*/music is, however, multi-media and discursive. Its expressive structures, styles, and meanings are generated and constituted not only by created sounds, but also by the times and sites when and where they are played by individual musicians for targeted audiences or patrons.

Traditional Chinese aesthetic theory declares that *yue*/music creates a genuine communication between sincere heart-minds of performers and audience. Ideologically and pragmatically, historical and imperial China claimed that *yue* was not only a multi-media performance art, but also a cultural-social-political performance and discourse (Cook, 1995; Lam, 2022). As expressed in the *Shi daxue* (Great Preface to the *Classics of Poetry*), people express their thoughts and emotions with words. When their words do not fully express what they feel and/or want to communicate, they sing – with or without musical instruments. When their words and singing do not fully reveal what they harbour in their hearts and minds, they dance, or make bodily gestures and movements. *Yue*/music is not composed or played to entertain people's eyes and ears; it is to be practiced as an indispensable tool of self-cultivation and governance. Together with ritual, penalties and policies, *yue*/music is a pillar of Chinese social and political living. And because *yue*/music is so expressive and functional, it should be handled with care. Ideologically speaking, only dynastic founders and meritorious rulers have the legitimate right to implement *yue*/music to serve their empires. One such form of *yue*/music available to Shenzong was, needless to say, the *guchui* that his Brocade Guards-cum-musicians-cum painters played and preserved in writings and paintings.

Concluding remarks

Viewing the biographically, historically, musically, and painterly informative *Scrolls*, 21th century Chinese have not only developed new understandings of historical Chinese processional *yue*/music, but have also found creative ways to reconstruct it for themselves and their global partners. As confirmed by enthusiastic concert reviews, loud, rhythmic, and repetitive Chinese wind and percussion music today has gained a niche in the global music market. It also has a place in international scholarship on music as a performance and discourse of imperial institutions and powers. As this chapter has reported, processional music is an integral part of large scale and multi-media spectacles that perform and negotiate social-political institutions and hierarchical roles and powers in human and expressive worlds. Such performances and negotiations are effective because their sounds, sights, and values are artistically, culturally, and historically interconnected.

As witnessed *in situ*, as visually represented in the *Scrolls*, and as heard through contemporary "reconstructions", late Ming Chinese state processional music was sonically different from its contemporaneous counterparts played in historical courts in Asia, Europe, and the Middle East. As sonic demonstrations of political and social power exercised by hierarchically organized institutions and personages, however, all genres of state processional music are theoretically and practically comparable in one way or another. All are creatively and deliberately performed, historically and socially sustained, and ideologically heard and interpreted (Rice, 2017).

Bibliography

Printed Sources and Source Editions

Anonymous. (1630s). *Taichang xukao* [Further records from the Court of State Sacrifices], fascicle 4, pp. 68–75. *Xiku quanshu* edition. Shanghai guji.

Liu, R. Y. (1963). *Ming gongshi* [History of Ming court activities and institutions]. Beijing guji.

Wang, Q. & Wang, S. Y. (Eds.) (2011). *Sancai tuhui* [An illustrated encyclopaedia of earthly, heavenly, and human talents]. Shanghai guji.

Zhang, T. Y. (Ed.) (1975). *Mingshi* (Ming History). Zhonghua shuju.

Scholarly Literature

Cook, S. (1995). "Yueji" – Record of Music: Introduction, Translation, Notes, and Commentary. *Asian Music* 26(2), 1–96.

Ebrey, P. (1999). Taking Out the Grand Carriage: Imperial Spectacle and the Visual Culture of Northern Song Kaifeng. *Asia Major, Third Series* 12(1), 33–65.

Fong, W. C. (2003). Why Chinese Painting is History. *The Art Bulletin* 85(2), 258–280.

Huang, R. (1981). *1587, A Year of No Significance: The Ming Dynasty in Decline*. Yale University Press.

Lam, J. S. C. (2022). *Kunqu, A Classical Opera of Twenty-First-Century China*. Hong Kong University Press.

Lin, J. S. (1996). *Wanli di* [A biography of Shenzong]. Jilin wenshi.

Na, C. L. & Kohler, W. (1970). *The Emperor's Procession: Two Scrolls of the Ming Dynasty*. National Palace Museum.

Nelson, S. E. (1998/1999). Picturing Listening: The Sight of Sound in Chinese Painting. *Archives of Asian Art* 51, 30–55.

Ren, F. B. (2014). *MingQing junli yu junzhong yongyue yanjiu* [Military ritual and music in Ming Qing China]. Zhongyang yinyue xuanyuan.

Paludan, A. (1981). *The Imperial Ming Tombs*. Yale University Press.

Rice, T. (2017). *Remodeling Ethnomusicology*. Oxford University Press.

Sung, H. M. (2013). Rediscovering Zhang Jin and the Ming Painting Academy. *Archives of Asian Art* 63(2), 179–187.

Yuan, J. F. (1987). *Minzu qiyue* [Chinese instrumental music]. Renmin yinyue.

Zhang, D. (2014). Huqiu zhongqiu ye [Mid-Autumn night at Tiger Hill]. *Tao'an mengyi* (pp. 144–146). Shanghai guji chubanshe.

Zhu, H. (2004). Mingren chujing rubi tu benshi zhi yanjiu [A study of the *Departure* and the *Return*]. *Gugong xueshu jikan* 22(1), 183–213.

Zeng, M. Y. (2015). Zhongguo lidai lubu guchuiyue bijiao yanjiu [A historical and comparative study of Chinese state processional music]. *Zhongguo yinyue* 2, 73–81.

Illustration Credits

Fig. 1: "Shenzong as a young emperor," illustration prepared by the author from the National Palace Museum, Taipei, *Mingren hua chujing tu* [Imperial procession departing from the Forbidden City, a scroll-painting by Ming painters] (1980s), a facsimile publication of Anonymous, *Mingren hua chujing tu*, Zhonghua 000054, the National Palace Museum, Taipei.

Fig. 2: "Shenzong returns to the Forbidden city," illustration prepared by the author from the National Palace Museum, Taipei, *Mingren hua rubi tu* [Imperial procession returning to the Forbidden City] (1980s), a facsimile publication of Anonymous, *Mingren hua rubi tu*, Zhonghua 000055, the National Palace Museum, Taipei.

Fig. 3: "An Imperial *guchui* band in Shenzong's parade," illustration prepared by the author from the National Palace Museum, Taipei, *Mingren hua chujing tu* [Imperial procession departing from the Forbidden City, a scroll-painting by Ming painters] (1980s), a facsimile publication of Anonymous, *Mingren hua chujing tu*, Zhonghua 000054, the National Palace Museum, Taipei.

Fig. 4: "Soldier-musicians playing *guchui* music on an imperial barge," illustration prepared by the author from the National Palace Museum, Taipei, *Mingren hua chujing tu* [Imperial procession departing from the Forbidden City, a scroll-painting by Ming painters] (1980s), a facsimile publication of Anonymous, *Mingren hua chujing tu*, Zhonghua 000054, the National Palace Museum, Taipei.

Fig. 5: "Horse-riding *guchui* musicians," illustration prepared by the author from the National Palace Museum, Taipei, *Mingren hua rubi tu* [Imperial procession returning to the Forbidden City] (1980s), a facsimile publication of Anonymous, *Mingren hua rubi tu*, Zhonghua 000055, the National Palace Museum, Taipei.

Setúbal Soundscapes

Performing Power in a Portuguese Urban Environment During the Early Modern Period

Ana Cláudia Silveira

The following contribution focuses on the urban soundscape of the port city of Setúbal, in Portugal, and is mainly based on archival sources and chronicles related to public events organized within this urban space in the transition from the Middle Ages to the early modern period. The intent is to highlight the important role of sounds and music, particularly for the affirmation, representation, and ritualization of political power.

Urban rituals have received an increasing amount of attention during the last decades in a number of disciplines, including architecture, religion, history, geography, and anthropology, and soundscape as an object of research has evolved considerably since Reinhard Strohm's seminal publication of 1985. Nonetheless, there is still a need to develop both fields of research in order to establish a better articulation between them.

Both historians and anthropologists have recently been examining the significance of public ceremonies, festivities, rituals, and spectacles as a way to transmit ideological concerns and to ensure political communication by its association to specific civic or political projects (Buescu, 2010, p. 37). The "theatricalization" of specific ideas and beliefs, offering allegories to enable the visualization of certain aspects, was a means to achieving such purposes. Thus, civic ceremonies had enormous relevance as a tool of social or urban promotion and were understood as a form of propaganda. Events such as the *adventus* or *joyeuses entrées*, weddings, tournaments, funerals, and processions were opportunities to celebrate and affirm political power (Tabri, 2004, pp. 89–94; Alves, 1986, p. 9; Coelho, 2010, pp. 144–165; Briggs, 2015, p. 38).

Each one of these events assembled relatives, neighbours, members of religious confraternities, and town governors or officials and were instrumental for improving a community's cohesion (Asenjo González, 2013, pp. 35–61). Therefore, they had both a social articulation function and a strong propagandistic character, as we will see.

The port of Setúbal offers an interesting contribution with respect to this matter, since several documented events of different natures occurred within this urban space during the above-mentioned time period. Relevant information about the sonorities associated with ceremonies is provided, related in particular to royal visits and entries into the town, meetings of the Chapter of the Military Order of Santiago and of the Military Order of Avis, visitations promoted by the officials of the Order of Santiago, important weddings, and religious festivities such as the celebration of Easter, Corpus Christi and the day of Saint James (São Tiago), some of them comprising processional ceremonies.

The Port of Setúbal: Urban Settlement in the Domains of the Military Order of Santiago

In the 13th century, Setúbal was integrated into the domains of the Military Order of Santiago, an institution holding both the secular and the ecclesiastical jurisdiction over this urban space and its surrounding territory. The geographical specificity of this space, a sea port that was able to control access to a wider territory, in conjunction with the high potential provided by the vast resources available in its territory and the trade flows it provided, justify the unique status of Setúbal within the network of commanderies of the Order of Santiago in Portugal. The territory was integrated into the *Mesa Mestral*, the Order's administrative government directly depending on the Master of the Order. This factor cannot be dissociated from Setúbal's economic and strategic relevance and its gradual affirmation as one of Portugal's main sea ports.

The consequences of the more generalized surge of development experienced in Europe from the 11th century and due to the exceptional conditions offered by the mouth of the Sado River, which favoured the development of fisheries and exploitation of salt marshes, enabled the participation of Setúbal in international trade networks from the 14th century. A dynamic urban centre was established that benefited from mercantile wealth, thus attracting a growing population seeking political status. The importance of Setúbal for the Order of Santiago was reflected in the receipt of important rental revenues, which became the main source of income of the *Mesa Mestral*, and in the establishment of important political and administrative structures in the city, such as the Palace of the Order, as well as buildings for tax collection and commercial warehousing, which were located next to the main quay on the town's riverside. The influence of the Order of Santiago was decisive in multiple ways, including the presence of a growing number of officers representing the institution, and the promotion of planned urban interventions modelling the physical evolution of the urban space and promoting its topographic organization (Silveira, 2021, pp. 827–844).

During the 15th century, the administration of the Order of Santiago was undertaken by members of the royal family. At the beginning of the 16th century, Jorge de Lencastre, illegitimate son of King John II (r. 1481–1495), was named Master of the Order of Santiago as well as Master of the Military Order of Avis. As a means of social and political affirmation, he started a project of rebuilding the Palace of the Order of Santiago in Setúbal, as is recorded in unpublished accounts of the institution. These documents allow us to reconstruct the spatial organization of the residence and the interior decoration of several rooms. They also provide information about the building materials and decorative elements, as well as the presence of luxury goods like a library, certain pieces of furniture, and other items, including an organ (Silveira, 2016, pp. 79–81). These references to a library and musical instruments give an indication of the social distinction, refinement, and cultural standards of the humanistic education Jorge de Lencastre had received from Cataldo Parísio Sículo, a former scholar from Bologna University who came to Portugal as his tutor (Knighton, 2017, pp. 99–100; Nelson, 2017, p. 206). By 1533, there was also an organ in Saint Julian Church, and organists and singers were employed by the Order of Santiago (ANTT, MCO, OS/CP, Livro 15, fol. 263; Idem, Livro 21, fols. 161v.–162v.; Idem, maço 6, nº 432; Idem, maço 7, nº 528).[1] This shows that the Master of Santiago was organizing musicians in a similar way to that being put into practice at the same time by the Portuguese royal house (Nelson, 2017, pp. 213–228). The Royal Chapel of the Portuguese kings was certainly influenced by the political and diplomatic connections they had established with other courts, connections that also influenced the circulation of musicians (Knighton, 2017, pp. 18–19), as shown by an analysis of the several regulatory documents and regiments describing procedures to adopt for this purpose. Moreover, the organization of the Royal Chapel was used as a model to be followed by the chapels organized by the noble houses,[2] including the chapel of Jorge de Lencastre, the Master of the Order of Santiago, and his successors. With regard to this, it is worth remembering that written sources about the religious practices of Portuguese military orders are scarce (Oliveira, 2010, pp. 26–27). Further research is needed on the religious life and spirituality of these institutions (Mattoso, 2011, p. 437), as this will be pivotal for understanding and contextualizing the musical performances and production that took place at their churches and convents.

At the time, the environment of Setúbal was changing, with various construction projects being undertaken by the Order of Santiago, the crown, and the local government. Churches were enlarged, new city gates were built and streets opened, and a new city hall and a monumental aqueduct were built. A modern plaza was laid out, bordered by the new city hall and the Palace of the Order of Santiago (later to become the Palace of the

---

1   Santa Maria Church had had an organ until 1510, but it was no longer in use (Santos, 1969, p. 133). See also Páez Ayala, 2015, pp. 53–54.

2   In 1299, the Royal Chapel was institutionalized in Portugal by King Dinis (r. 1279–1325) and was developed from that time by the following kings (Ferreira, 2008, pp. 46–86). From the reign of D. Duarte (r. 1433–1438), an Ordinance of the Royal Chapel is known that follows the model of the Royal Chapel of the king of Aragón, which inspired the organization of music ensembles in certain Portuguese noble houses (Ferreira, 2014, pp. 33–50; Porto, 2014, pp. 40–41).

Duque of Aveiro, the descendants of Jorge de Lencastre) next to the parish church of Saint Julian, one of the most important churches in the urban area. This plaza became a topographical centrepiece not only of commercial activity, but also of social and political ceremonial, a focal point in the urban space where the spectacle of power took place, where civic festivals were staged, and where ceremonial processions proclaiming the prestige of the represented institutions and of the city itself arrived (Silveira, 2019, pp. 31–34).

The Role of Sound in Religious and Civic Ceremonies

As in any other city, daily life in Setúbal was marked by many kinds of sounds. Among them were those related to the activity of town criers responsible for proclaiming official messages, sentences, or auctions of assets, as well as the announcements made by horns and trumpets, or by the various bells present in the urban environment.

However, special occasions justified the use of exceptional sounds or extraordinary levels of sound volume, either by incorporating music in ceremonies or by producing the loud noises commonly accepted as a symbol of power, legitimacy, and authority. By conferring greater solemnity to events, sound was a means of emphasizing announcements (Moreno Arana, 2018, pp. 243–244). It thus was a powerful means of communication due to the emotions it provoked and its ability to influence or direct individual and collective behaviour (Lecuppre-Desjardin, 2005, p. VII). By presenting a few examples of documented events that took place in Setúbal during this period, we will illustrate the importance of the city's soundscape, including how it reinforced ideological or political messages, amplifying the effect of the communication associated with these events.

Religious festivities were times of joy and solemnity to which music contributed. In Setúbal, Easter and Saint James Day (*São Tiago*), the 25th of July, were among the most important celebrations. Although there are no complete records of these feasts in Setúbal, it can be assumed that their organization was similar to the events in Alcácer do Sal, a nearby urban space also administered by the Order of Santiago and where Saint James Day was also celebrated. Preparations for these festivals required the streets along the processional route to be cleaned and decorated, and the church to be adorned. The beginning of the rituals was announced by the ringing of bells (ANTT, MCO, OS/CP, maço 7, nº 528). The festivities started with a solemn Vespers mass and continued with a morning procession, which progressed to the rhythm of bells. Large numbers of participants were usual, including common citizens, aldermen, clergy, and the knights of Santiago displaying their insignia. The day was also marked by the distribution of fruit and wine to the entire population, and by the organization of entertainment, including music and dancing. (Pereira, 1999, pp. 194–196). Also bullfights took place: Several contemporary documents describe bulls being run during such celebrations (ANTT, MCO, OS/CP, maço 3, n° 163, fol. 56; ANTT, MCO, OS/CP, maço 51, n.n., fol. 41).

These celebrations were similar to those for Corpus Christi,[3] which at that time was one of the most important events in Portuguese towns, as well as in other Christian countries. Corpus Christi was both a religious and civic festivity, whereby "the body of Christ functioned as a metaphor for the social body" (Burke, 1993, pp. 29–30), thus merging political and religious agendas (Cavi, 2015, p. 220). This explains why its organization required the involvement of a wide variety of institutions, not only religious institutions, but also municipal and aristocratic representatives. The Corpus Christi festivities started the night before the holiday proper, with some of the young men of the city singing and dancing through the streets (ANTT, Chancelaria de D. Afonso V, Livro 16, fol. 121r.; Idem, Livro 38, fol. 66r.). A later document describing the Corpus Christi procession is key to understanding its organization, since it gives detailed information about the hierarchical order to be followed and the elements that had to be integrated (BFDL, Códice 49, fols. 109v.–111r.). The high moment of the festival was the procession, which was announced by the sound of a trumpet, a common practice that is documented as having been done in several cities (Louro, 2010, pp. 65–66). While it is clear that the procession followed a specific itinerary, this unfortunately is not described in any surviving document. However, we can presume that the route included both the churches of Saint Mary and Saint Julian, which stood inside the town walls, and the Praça Nova do Sapal, the main square, which as mentioned above had been established during the first half of the 16th century when the new city hall was built. Usually, the chosen route was carefully prepared by the authorities, in order to highlight the urban environment's most emblematic and scenic spaces and buildings. These were often objects of recent transformations, such as renovated churches or recently opened streets and squares. This practice allowed the latest urban changes to be highlighted. These were also promoted by various urban institutions also involved in the organization of the religious festivities. The procession route thus became a ritualized performing space, contributing to reinforce the image and the power of the urban government (Smith, 2018, p. 231). It followed by streets that had been cleaned, as ordered by municipal regulations, and decorated with flowers and textiles in the windows. The procession included the organized participation of craftsmen carrying their standards, flags, and symbols, and was accompanied by dances, which reflected not only the ideal organization of society presented hierarchically, but also served as a symbol of urban identity (Escrivà-Llorca, 2018, pp. 107–108). Street theatre, special decorations such as flowers, games, music and dance, mystery plays and allegoric scenes commissioned by craftsmen

---

3   For Corpus Christi festivities in Portugal, see Gonçalves, 1996; Barros, 1993, pp. 117–136; Silva, 1993, pp. 195–212; Coelho, 2010, pp. 162–164; Louro, 2010, pp. 53–73.

were essential components not only of the parade, but also of the general festivities that took place in Setúbal and elsewhere.[4] During the procession, music had a liturgical and ceremonial role. There are references to dances performed by women during the parade, as well as to the presentation of theatrical scenes accompanied by music. Music was also part of the re-creation of exotic scenarios. On many occasions, this included the participation of the *mouriscos*, the Muslim minority, who were allowed to perform their own music and dances to symbolize their integration and submission to the Christian society (Knighton, 2017, p. 16; Oliveira, 2019, pp. 109–110).

The Corpus Christi procession was the model for other processions. In addition to its religious character, it also represented entertainment, a fun time and a break in daily life. It was also an important event for promoting the cohesion of the community and for drawing attention to the city government. Music contributed to signalling and embellishing the event, increasing its dignity and solemnity, and transmitting a sense of harmony. It created feelings of belonging and identity, key elements that helped civic authorities achieve their purpose (Curto, 2011, pp. 181–182). Furthermore, music enabled the immediate perception of institutional power (Grippaudo, 2018, p. 311). Indeed, religious and civic festivities were harnessed by "the emergent modern state as an instrument of rule" (Strong, 1984, p. 19).

Funerals were also occasions at which people were allowed to express feelings by singing and crying. In this case, special reference must be made to the Muslim minority who lived in Portuguese urban spaces even after the Inquisition was established. Although they were *conversos*, they maintained their traditional practices and participated actively in the funeral of the Master of Santiago in the mid-16th centuries, with women gathering outside the city walls to mourn and cry. Usually this was coordinated by one woman, who pronounced certain words that provoked weeping ("alevantava as palavras que provocava aos outros a choro"), pulling of their hair and scratching of their faces, this accompanied by dancing to the sound of bagpipes and horns, and by songs in Arabic related to Moorish chivalry. These rituals ended with a meal (*cuscuz*) offered to the participants, which was also accompanied by dances and singing (ANTT, Tribunal do Santo Ofício, Inquisição de Lisboa, processo nº 565; Barros, 2020). This was later remembered and used by the Inquisition to persecute some of the participants accused of heretic behaviour (Barros, 2020). The practices documented in Setúbal were, however, evidence of the respect that the Muslim community had for the Master of Santiago and a recognition of the healthy conviviality between the two religions in the mid-16th century.

Weddings were also important occasions. We have documents describing the wedding of the heir of the house of Aveiro in 1618 to Ana Dória, daughter of the Prince of Melfi,

---

4   In the case of Setúbal, a detailed description of this event has survived: BFDL, Códice 49, fols. 175v.–178r.

Setúbal Soundscapes

who came from Genoa to Setúbal by ship. This is documented in the testimony of João Baptista Lavanha, the king's chronicler, who was also the organizer of the event (BA, Ms. 51-IX-8, fols. 165r.–173v.).[5] When the galleys arrived in the Sado estuary, the military garrisons along the coast gave a signal and the moment was announced with trumpets and drums, as well as with artillery and harquebus salutes, including from docked ships carrying salt and fishing boats. The municipal government organized festivities that included music, dances, and bullfights.

The following day, the route of the Genoese galley entering Setúbal harbour was announced by the exchange of artillery fire between the ducal palace, the forts of Outão and São Filipe, and the various vessels escorting the galley, which also had musical instruments on board. The arrival in Setúbal took place to the sound of artillery, shawms, and trumpets, and was accompanied by dancing. In the streets, a large number of people, not only from the city, but also from nearby towns and even from Lisbon, greeted the princess with music. In the courtyard of the ducal palace, ten infantry companies gave artillery salutes as the hierarchically organized procession headed for the church of São Julião, where the wedding was then celebrated. When the ceremony was over and the newly-wed couple left the church, the ringing of bells and drums, shawms, and trumpets were heard once again, fulfilling their heraldic function (Strohm, 2018, p. 286). Such a special moment required an impressive level of sound to reinforce the importance of the event and the newcomers, mobilize the community to celebrate their arrival, and express the power of the city's rulers (Lecuppre-Desjardin, 2004, pp. 167–172). The description of this event highlights the luxury of the decorations of the ducal palace and the variety of the displays, including musicians, artillery, bonfires, and fireworks. It also describes the adornments worn by the ducal family and even the abundance and diversity of the opulent banquet served at the ducal palace. All of this signalled liberality, which was a means of enhancing reputation and, by extension, a demonstration of power (Lecuppre-Desjardin, 2004, p. 122; Nelson, 2017, pp. 201–202).

Since Setúbal was an important maritime port, the festivities were not only concentrated inside the town walls, they also took place on the river and at maritime sites near the town. This symbolically highlighted the city's source of economic prosperity and its civic identity. Similar receptions on the Tagus River had earlier been given to Eleanor of Austria, Queen of Portugal from 1518 to 1521 (Godinho, 2020, p. 93), and to Joanna of Habsburg, Princess of Portugal from 1552 to 1554, whose arrival by ship in Lisbon in 1552 to marry the heir of the Portuguese crown was accompanied by garlanded vessels, some with musicians playing on board, and announced by artillery fire (Alves, 1986, pp. 38–39; Buescu, 2017, pp. 157–163). The Tagus River was also the scene for Philip II's entry into Lisbon in 1581,

---

5   See also Caldas & Coutinho, 2019, pp. 116–117.

Fig. 1: The port of Setúbal in 1668 (Maria Baldi Pier).

when he arrived at the beginning of his reign as king of Portugal as Philip I (r. 1581–1598), which official accounts describe as being preceded by the sound of ruling artillery as if a war was destroying the city. The display of mock sea battles as well as water spectacles (*naumachia*) during ceremonial entries and festivals was recurrent in this period.[6] This included musicians on board the galleys performing on slide trumpets. Such events in Lisbon also included naval inventions that imitated fantastic and mythological sea creatures, a reminder of the city's legendary origin, as well as its status as the centre of the Portuguese empire and a global hub.[7]

Among these selected examples, we may also include the royal entry of Philip III into Setúbal on 1 October 1619. This was recorded by the king's chronicler João Baptista Lavanha (Lavanha, 1622, fols. 73v.–74v.; Carvalho, 1968, pp. 17–22),[8] who produced an illustrated commemorative report of the royal visit to the kingdom of Portugal. This publication, intended as a testimony of princely magnificence, is an example of a particular literary genre that emerged during this period (Strong, 1984, pp. 21–22; Alves, 1986, p. 11; Soromenho, 2000, pp. 23–33; Cardim, 2001, p. 107; Megiani, 2001, pp. 646–647; Godinho, 2020, pp. 59–60).

The ritual of a royal entry had been known in Portugal since earlier periods. Like religious processions, it included the cleaning and decorating of the main streets the royal parade would follow. Its entry through one of the city gates was marked by a salute ceremonial. The king was received by the municipal authorities, whereupon the alderman made a welcoming speech and gave the keys of the city to him. Then a procession was held within the urban walls until the arrival in one of the main churches. The procession was accompanied by music, dance, theatre performances, displays of ephemeral *apparati*, re-creation

---

6   This kind of event has been seen as a revival of a tradition of the Roman Empire (Strong, 1984, p. 42).

7   See Fernández-González, 2015, pp. 89–95, in which a citation of a contemporary poem is included: "Once his Majesty / had boarded his galley, / the thunder of artillery / performed a *horrisonous* salute; / the bellicose galleys / [were] in an ordered squadron: the royal [galley], as the lady / [and] patron, in their midst", and Resende, 2000, pp. 95–97. Also on this topic, see Soromenho, 2000, pp. 22–23.

8   About this voyage and, in particular, the royal entry into the city of Lisbon, see Soromenho, 2000, pp. 23–28.

of *tableaux vivants,* allegoric scenes and mystery plays, sometimes commissioned by the city council or by the city's craftsmen. The festivities often ended with bullfights, opulent meals, night lights, and firework displays (Alves, 1986, pp. 15–16; Gomes, 1995, pp. 318–319; Brochado, 2007, pp. 53–56). The latter associated the royal presence with light (Lecuppre-Desjardin, 2004, pp. 265–266).

The scale of these ceremonies and the symbols displayed were related to the political ambitions of the town where they took place, since the inclusion of a town in the royal itinerary highlighted the political importance of that community (Cardim, 2001, p. 109). They also reflected the political ambitions of the monarchy, as can be seen in developments during the reign of King Manuel I (r. 1495–1521), when the staging of his political power began to contain symbols of his overseas domains. Entry parades included exotic elements such as elephants, rhinos, and even a jaguar on the back of a Persian horse, visual expressions of the enormity of the Portuguese empire he had built. Thus, entry rituals were part of a system of political communication between the king and each visited city.

Entry rituals also represented political stabilization, as had developed parallel to the consolidation of monarchical power at the beginning of the 16th century. At that time, a *Regimento* was issued to the city of Lisbon containing the procedures and regulations to follow when receiving the king (*Livro dos Regimentos dos Vereadores e Oficiais da Câmara,* 2020, pp. 37–40; Alves, 1986, pp. 29–30; Brochado, 2007, pp. 56 –57; Buescu, 2010, p. 39; Coelho, 2010, pp. 165–166). While we don't know of such a document for Setúbal, nonetheless the above model was adapted and applied in many towns, with the procedures following a ritualized set of standardized steps that were used throughout the 16th century, reinforcing the strong socio-political dimension associated with a royal visit. Indeed, such visits were occasions for expressing royal authority (Alves, 1986, pp. 52–65; Megiani, 2008, pp. 138–149; Briggs, 2015, p. 38). Royal visits became increasingly sumptuous, inspired perhaps by the Flemish *joyeuses entrées* known due to the Habsburg house's rule during the reign of Carlos V.[9] They acquired a special political significance in Portugal during the period of the Iberian Union (1581–1640), when the Portuguese and Spanish crowns were united and the king was typically absent from Portuguese territory. Since royal visits were rare, they were designed to be remembered for a long time. For example, Philip II visited Portugal in 1581, but the next royal visit only took place in 1619, when King Philip III – who usually resided in Valladolid or Madrid (Williams, 2010, pp. 109–150) – visited his kingdom of Portugal for the first time. The memory of such visits had to be kept as long as possible, and thus the image of the monarch required special care (Brochado, 2007, p. 58).

---

9   About these ceremonies, see Cauchies, 1998, pp. 137–152; Blockmans, 1998, pp. 155–172; Lecuppre-Desjardin, 2004, pp. 138–154; Trélat, 2015, pp. 144–145.

During the visit of Philip III to Portugal between May and October of 1619, Setúbal was included among the towns receiving the king. The royal delegation arrived in Setúbal on 1 October 1619 and remained until 4 October (BNP, Lavanha, 1622, fols. 73v.–74v.). The delegation entered by one of the city gates, the Porta Nova (New Gate). Built toward the end of the 15th or beginning of the 16th century, it was one of the city's most representative gates. Here, the king was received by the city council and the ecclesiastical authorities in a salute ceremonial. Upon the arrival of the royal parade, the most senior member of the town administration gave a welcome speech in honour of the king and delivered the key to the town to him. The king entered the adorned city and a procession with music and dance led him to Saint Mary's Church, where he was received by the Prior of the Military Order of Santiago. After his prayer, the king went to the Palace of the Duque of Aveiro, which was located on the riverfront and had recently benefitted from architectural renovations. Although no reference is made to the organization of firework displays, as reported in other cities, we do know that during the night, the town was illuminated everywhere. On the next day, a fishing event was organized on the river in front of the palace. The same day, the king, who was also the Master of the Military Religious Orders of Avis, Christ and Santiago, chaired the Chapter of the Military Order of Avis, which took place in Saint Mary's Church, receiving all the knights, who, dressed in white habits, arrived in a procession.

To make the royal visit a performative ritual, a wide range of events were combined to create an astonishing and magnificent atmosphere. The visual component was important: ritual clothing, ephemeral triumphal arches, protocol and hierarchy, ornaments, garlands and tapestries, magnificent food and pastries, lights, bullfights and fishing events. But sound was also a crucial component, going beyond mere entertainment and pleasure. Sound contributed to the emotional atmosphere of the event, making it meaningful for the participants. Each sound manifestation was associated with a specific location in the urban space, such as the city gate, or the main square in front of the city hall (Lecuppre-Desjardin, 2004, pp. 171–172). Theatre performances, dance and music, proclamations and speeches, women crying, fires and torches: depending on the circumstances, each was used not only to express joy or sadness, but also to communicate precise deliberate messages. Sounds were used to represent power. Through a soundscape of trumpets and bells, chanted litanies, acclamations, music, speeches and sermons, and even artillery shots, crowds experienced an overwhelming ambience in which emotions arose through all the senses. The participation of all social groups at such events enabled a celebration of the city's unity in all of its diversity (Tabri, 2004, p. 121). Since this unity guaranteed stability, performing these rituals renewed the political legitimacy of the government (Lecuppre-Desjardin, 2004, pp. 138–139).

Conclusion

The above examples show that the presence of music in the urban environment of 16th-century Portugal – its growing importance for ecclesiastical and political institutions, as well as its being used as integral part of public ceremonies – made it one of the most relevant tools for the representation of power. Moreover, they highlight the character of public festivities as both religious and civic events, since such festivities were intended to present the ideal organization and order of society. The urban space assumed a privileged stage for this representation. Within this context, artistic expressions and manifestations included aspects related to the presence of members of religious minorities integrated into Portuguese society.

Music and sound were harnessed as an instrument of rule by the early modern state in more structured and intentional ways than in earlier periods (Strong, 1984, p. 19), thus making sound an important element of the social and political ceremonial. For the early modern state, music and sound were powerful instruments of communication. Provoking joyful feelings and reinforcing festive atmospheres, they contributed to the emotional involvement in events of every participant and thus of the community itself (Cardim, 2001, p. 113; Lecuppre-Desjardin, 2004, pp. 262–264). Providing an appropriate soundscape emphasized the prestige of the city's institutions, thus maximizing its performance of political power.

Bibliography

Manuscripts

Arquivo Nacional da Torre do Tombo (ANTT), Chancelaria de D. Afonso V, Livro 16, fol. 121r; Idem, Livro 38, fol. 66r.

ANTT, Mesa da Consciência e Ordens (MCO), Ordem de Santiago / Convento de Palmela (OS/CP), Livro 15, fol. 263 r.; Idem, Livro 21, fols. 161v.–162v.; Idem, maço 3, nº 163, fol. 56; Idem, maço 6, nº 432; Idem, maço 7, nº 528; Idem, maço 51, n.n., fol. 41).

ANTT, Tribunal do Santo Ofício, Inquisição de Lisboa, processo nº 565.

Biblioteca da Ajuda (BA), Ms. 51-IX-8, fols. 165r.–173v.

Biblioteca da Faculdade de Direito de Lisboa (BFDL), Códice 49 [Tombo da Capela de Santo Estêvão de Setubal].

Biblioteca Nacional de Portugal (BNP), Lavanha, J. B. (1622). *Viagem da Catholica Real Magestade del Rey D. Filipe II Nosso Senhor ao Reyno de Portugal.*

Scholarly Literature

Alves, A. M. (1986). *As Entradas Régias Portuguesas. Uma visão de conjunto*. Livros Horizonte.

Asenjo González, M. (2013). Fiestas y Celebraciones en las Ciudades Castellanas de la Baja Edad Media. *Edad Media. Revista de Historia* 14, 35–61.

Barros, A. (1993). A Procissão do Corpo de Deus nos Séculos XV e XVI: a Participação de uma Confraria. *Revista da Faculdade de Letras. História, II série, Porto* 10, 117–136.

Barros, M. F. L. de (2020). Cumprir Marrocos em Portugal: a comunidade mourisca de Setúbal no século XVI. In F. J. Mártinez (Ed.), *Entangled Peripheries. New Contributions to the History of Portugal and Morocco: Essays in Homage to Eva Maria von Kemnitz*. CIDEHUS. 10.4000/books.cidehus.12368. Date of Access: 28.01.2024.

Blockmans, W. (1998). Le Dialogue Imaginaire Entre Princes et Sujets: les Joyeuses Entrées en Brabant en 1494 et en 1496. In J.-M. Cauchies (Ed.), *À la cour de Bourgogne. Le duc, son entourage, son train* (pp. 155–172). Brepols.

Briggs, L. (2015). 'Concernant le service de leurs dictes Majestez et auctorité de leur justice'. Perceptions of Royal Power in the Entries of Charles IX and Catherine de Médicis (1564–1566). In J. R. Mulryne, M. Ines Aliverti & A. Maria Testaverde (Eds.), *Ceremonial Entries in Early Modern Europe. The Iconography of Power* (pp. 37–52). Ashgate.

Brochado, A. (2007). Poderes Concorrentes na Entrada Régia de 1581: Poder Representado e Poder Imaginado. *Cadernos do Arquivo Municipal de Lisboa* 9, 49–65: http://arquivomunicipal.cm-lisboa.pt/fotos/editor2/92.pdf. Date of Access: 28.01.2024.

Buescu, A. I. (2017). Entradas Régias em Portugal no Século XVI. Uma Revisita. In A. L. de Faria & I. Drumond Braga (Eds.), *Problematizar a História - Estudos de História Moderna em Homenagem a Maria do Rosário Themudo Barata* (pp. 143–163). Caleidoscópio.

Buescu, A. I. (2010). Festas Régias e Comunicação Política no Portugal Moderno (1521–1572). *Comunicação & Cultura* 10, 35–55.

Burke, P. (1993). Cities, Spaces and Rituals in the Early Modern World. In H. de Mare & A. Vos (Eds.), *Urban Rituals in Italy and the Netherlands. Historical Contrasts in the Use of Public Space, Architecture and the Urban Environment* (pp. 29–37). Van Gorcum.

Bussels, S. (2005). Jaunty Joys and Sinuous Sorrows: Rhetoric and Body Language in a Tableau Vivant of the Antwerp Entry of 1549. In E. Lecuppre-Desjardin & A.-L. Van Bruaene (Eds.), *Emotions in the Hearth of the City (14th–16th Century)* (pp. 257–269). Brepols.

Caldas, J. V. & Coutinho, M. J. P. (2019). Os Paços dos Duques de Aveiro em Setúbal. In A. Cunha Bento, I. Gato de Pinho & M. J. Pereira Coutinho (Eds.), *Património Arquitectónico Civil de Setúbal e Azeitão* (pp. 111–139). LASA - Liga dos Amigos de Setúbal e Azeitão / Estuário.

Cardim, P. (2001). Entradas Solenes: Rituais Comunitários e Festas Políticas, Portugal e Brasil, Séculos XVI e XVII. In I. Jancsó & I. Kantor (Eds.), *Festa: Cultura & Sociabilidade na América Portuguesa*, vol. 1 (pp. 97–124). Editora da Universidade de São Paulo / Fapesp / Imprensa Oficial.

Carvalho, J. C. A. (1968). *Acontecimentos, Lendas e Tradições da Região Setubalense*, vol. 2. Junta Distrital de Setúbal.

Cauchies, J.-M. (1998). La signification politique des entrées princières dans les Pays-Bas: Maximilien d'Autriche et Philippe Le Beau. In J.-M. Cauchies (Ed.), *À la cour de Bourgogne. Le duc, son entourage, son train* (pp. 137–152). Brepols.

Cavi, S. de (2015). Corpus Christi in Spanish Palermo: two Baroque *Apparati* by Giacomo Amato for the Duke of Uceda (Viceroy of Sicily, 1687–1696). In F. Checa Cremades & L. Fernández-González (Eds.), *Festival Culture in the World of the Spanish Habsbourgs* (pp. 219–241). Ashgate.

Coelho, M. H. da Cruz (2010). A Festa – a Convivialidade. In B. Vasconcelos e Sousa (Coord.), *A Idade Média,* vol. 2: J. Mattoso (Dir.): *História da Vida Privada em Portugal* (pp. 144–169). Círculo de Leitores.

Curto, D. R. (2011). *Cultura Política no Tempo dos Filipes (1580–1640).* Edições 70.

Escrivà-Llorca, F. (2018). The Procession of the Relics of São Roque (Lisbon, 1588): a Royal Entry? In T. Knighton & A. Mazuela-Anguita (Eds.), *Hearing the City in Early Modern Europe* (pp. 101–116). Brepols.

Fernández-González, L. (2015). Negotiating Terms: Philip I of Portugal and the Ceremonial Entry of 1581 into Lisbon. In F. Checa Cremades & L. Fernández-González (Eds.), *Festival Culture in the World of the Spanish Habsbourgs* (pp. 87–113). Ashgate.

Ferreira, M. P. (2014). Observações sobre o Regimento da Capela de D. Duarte. In C. Fernandes Barreira & M. Metelo de Seixas (Eds.), *D. Duarte e a Sua Época. Arte, Cultura, Poder e Espiritualidade* (pp. 33–50). Instituto de Estudos Medievais.

Ferreira, M. P. (2008). Panorama da Música em Portugal na Idade Média e no Renascimento (448–1578). In M. P. Ferreira (Ed.), *Antologia da Música em Portugal na Idade Média e no Renascimento,* vol. 1 (pp. 9–93). Arte das Musas / Centro de Estudos de Sociologia e Estética Musical.

Godinho, A. F. C. (2020). *A Invenção do Triunfo: Memória, Saberes e Sensibilidades nas Entradas Régias Portuguesas (Séculos XVI–XVII)* [Master's thesis, Universidade NOVA de Lisboa]: https://run.unl.pt/bitstream/10362/94627/4/Dissertacao_final_invencao_triunfo.pdf. Date of Access: 28.01.2024.

Gomes, R. C. (1995). *A Corte dos Reis de Portugal no Final da Idade Média.* Difel.

Gonçalves, I. (1996). As Festas do «Corpus Christi» do Porto na Segunda Metade do Século XV: a Participação do Concelho. In *Um Olhar sobre a Cidade Medieval* (pp. 153–176). Patrimonia Historica.

Grippaudo, I. (2018). Music, Religious Communities, and the Urban Dimension: Sound Experiences in Palermo in the Sixteenth and Seventeenth Centuries. In T. Knighton & A. Mazuela-Anguita (Eds.), *Hearing the City in Early Modern Europe* (pp. 309–326). Brepols.

Knighton, T. (2017). Instruments, Instrumental Music and Instrumentalists: Traditions and Transitions. In T. Knighton (Ed.), *Companion to Music in the Age of the Catholic Monarchs,* vol. 1 (pp. 97–144). Brill.

Knighton, T. (2017). Introduction. In T. Knighton (Ed.), *Companion to Music in the Age of the Catholic Monarchs,* vol. 1 (pp. 1–21). Brill.

Lecuppre-Desjardin, E. (2004). *La Ville des Ceremonies. Essai sur la Communication Politique dans les Anciens Pays-Bas Bourguignons.* Brepols.

Lecuppre-Desjardin, E. & Van Bruaene, A.-L. (Eds.) (2005). *Emotions in the Hearth of the City (14th–16th Century)*. Brepols.

Livro dos Regimentos dos Vereadores e Oficiais da Câmara (Livro Carmesim). Estudo Introdutório, transcrição paleográfica, sumários e índices (2020). Câmara Municipal de Lisboa.

Louro, J. P. R. (2010). *A Iconografia Musical da Custódia de Belém* [Master's thesis, Universidade NOVA de Lisboa]: https://run.unl.pt/bitstream/10362/4823/1/DISS.%20Mestrado%20A%20Iconografia%20Musical%20da%20Cust%C3%B3dia%20de%20Bel%C3%A9m.pdf. Date of Access: 28.01.2024.

Mattoso, J. (2010). A Vida Religiosa e Espiritual nas Ordens Militares. In I. C. Ferreira Fernandes (Ed.), *Ordens Militares e Religiosidade. Homenagem ao Professor José Mattoso* (pp. 11–21). Câmara Municipal de Palmela / Gabinete de Estudos sobre a Ordem de Santiago.

Megiani, A. P. T. (2008). Entre Arcos Triunfais e Fogos de Artifício: Práticas Efémeras e o Diálogo dos Poderes nas Visitas Régias dos Filipes a Lisboa (1581–1619). In J. Ferreira Furtado (Ed.), *Sons, Formas, Cores e Movimentos na Modernidade Atlântica: Europa, Américas e África* (pp. 137–160). Annablume / Fapemig.

Megiani, A. P. T. (2001). A Escrita da Festa: os Panfletos das Jornadas Filipinas a Lisboa de 1581 e 1619. In I. Jancsó & I. Kantor (Eds.), *Festa: Cultura & Sociabilidade na América Portuguesa*, vol. 1 (pp. 639–653). Editora da Universidade de São Paulo / Fapesp / Imprensa Oficial.

Moreno Arana, J. A. (2018). Música y Poder Municipal en Jerez de la Frontera. Siglos XVI–XVII. *Historia. Documentos. Instituciones* 45, 241–268.

Nelson, B. (2017). Music and Musicians at the Portuguese Royal Court and Chapel, c. 1470–c. 1500. In T. Knighton (Ed.), *Companion to Music in the Age of the Catholic Monarchs*, vol. 1 (pp. 205–241). Brill.

Oliveira, A. M. S. (2019). *Charamelas e Trombetas: em Torno da Música na Cronística Portuguesa dos Finais da Idade Média* [Master's thesis, Faculdade de Letras da Universidade do Porto]: https://repositorio-aberto.up.pt/bitstream/10216/123145/2/361108.pdf. Date of Access: 28.01.2024.

Oliveira, L. F. (2010). Para o Estudo da Religiosidade dos Freires: as Fontes e Alguns Problemas. In I. C. Ferreira Fernandes (Ed.), *Ordens Militares e Religiosidade. Homenagem ao Professor José Mattoso* (pp. 23–30). Câmara Municipal de Palmela / Gabinete de Estudos sobre a Ordem de Santiago.

Oliveira, L. F., Fonseca, L. A. da, Pimenta, M. C. & Costa, P. P. (2011). The Military Orders. In J. Mattoso (Ed.), *The Historiography of Medieval Portugal, c. 1950–2010* (pp. 425–439). Instituto de Estudos Medievais.

Páez Ayala, A. (2015). *La Orden de Santiago: Liturgia y Música (ss. XV–XVII)*. Junta de Andalucía.

Pereira, M. T. L. (1999). Feira e Festas em Alcácer nos Tempos Tardo-Medievais. In I. C. Ferreira Fernandes (Ed.), *Ordens Militares: Guerra, Religião, Poder e Cultura – Actas do III Encontro sobre Ordens Militares*, vol. 1 (pp. 193–200). Edições Colibri / Câmara Municipal de Palmela.

Porto, H. F. T. (2014). *Os Cantores na Administração nos Reinados de D. Manuel I e de D.*

João III, Lisboa [Master's thesis, Universidade NOVA de Lisboa]: https://run.unl.pt/bitstream/10362/13737/1/Porto.2014.pdf. Date of Access: 28.01.2024.

Resende, A. F. de (2000). Romance da Entrada del Rey Philippe o Primeiro em Portugal em Lisboa. In F. B. Alvarez (Ed.), *Portugal no tempo dos Filipes, Política, Cultura e Representações* (pp. 95–100). Edições Cosmos.

Santos, V. P. dos (Ed.) (1969). Visitações de Alvalade, Casével, Aljustrel e Setúbal (Ordem de Santiago): Arquivo Nacional da Torre do Tombo, vol. 7: R. Lino, L. Silveira, A. H. de Oliveira Marques (Eds.), *Documentos para a História da Arte em Portugal*. Fundação Calouste Gulbenkian.

Silva, M. J. V. B. M. da (1993). A Procissão na Cidade: Reflexões em Torno da Festa do Corpo de Deus na Idade Média Portuguesa. In M. J. F. Tavares (Ed.), *Jornadas Inter e Pluridisciplinares A Cidade* (pp. 195–212). Universidade Aberta.

Silveira, A. C. (2016). As Casas da Comenda Mestral de Setúbal. In L. F. Oliveira (Ed.), *Comendas Urbanas das Ordens Militares* (pp. 65–83). Edições Colibri.

Silveira, A. C. (2019). O Património da Família Vilalobos / Miranda Henriques em Setúbal na Transição do Século XV para o XVI. In A. C. Bento, I G. de Pinho & M. J. P. Coutinho (Eds.), *Património Arquitectónico Civil de Setúbal e Azeitão* (pp. 23–45). LASA - Liga dos Amigos de Setúbal e Azeitão / Estuário.

Silveira, A. C. (2021). Setúbal: um Núcleo Urbano Integrado na Mesa Mestral da Ordem de Santiago em Portugal no Final da Idade Média. In I. C. Ferreira Fernandes (Ed.), *Actas do VIII Encontro sobre Ordens Militares: Ordens Militares, Identidade e Mudança* (pp. 827–850). Câmara Municipal de Palmela.

Smith, B. (2018). Sounding Shakespeare's London: the Noisy Politics of Ceremonial Entries. In T. Knighton & A. Mazuela-Anguita (Eds.), *Hearing the City in Early Modern Europe* (pp. 229–239). Brepols.

Soromenho, M. (2000). Ingegnosi Ornamenti: Arquitecturas Efémeras em Lisboa no Tempo dos Primeiros Filipes. In J. Castel-Branco Pereira (Ed.), *Arte Efémera em Portugal* (pp. 21–49). Fundação Calouste Gulbenkian.

Strohm, R. (2018). On the Soundscape of Fifteenth-Century Vienna. In T. Knighton & A. Mazuela-Anguita (Eds.), *Hearing the City in Early Modern Europe* (pp. 279–294). Brepols.

Strohm R. (1993). *The Rise of European Music, 1380–1500*. Cambridge University Press.

Strohm, R. (1985). *Music in Late Medieval Bruges*. Clarendon Press.

Strong, R. (1984). *Art and Power. Renaissance Festivals, 1450–1650*. The Boydell Press.

Tabri, E. (2004). *Political Culture in the Early Northern Renaissance. The Court of Charles the Bold, duke of Burgundy (1467–1477)*. Mellen Press.

Trélat, P. (2015). Lo Recevè com Tanta Festa et Alegrezza, Che Non Si Potrebbe Scrivere: Vie de Cour et Société Urbaine à Nicosie (XIVe–XVe Siècles). In L. Courbon & D. Menjot (Eds.), *La Cour et la Ville dans l'Europe du Moyen Âge et des Temps Modernes* (pp. 131–147). Brepols.

Williams, P. (2010). *El Gran Valido. El Duque de Lerma, la Corte y el Gobierno de Felipe III, 1598–1621*. Junta de Castilla y León.

Illustration Credits

Fig. 1: Sanchez Rivero, A., Sanchez Rivero, A. M. de (Eds.) (1933). *Viaje de Cosme de Médicis por España y Portugal (1668–1669),* Lamina LI. Junta para Ampliación de Estudios y Investigaciones Científicas / Centro de Estudios Historicos.

The Sound of Victory

The Triumphant Entry of King Sigismund III Vasa into Vilnius in 1611

Aleksandra Pister

Introduction

On a hot 24 July 1611, Sigismund III Vasa, the Grand Duke of Lithuania and King of Poland, and his multitudinous entourage made a triumphant entry into Vilnius, the capital of the Grand Duchy of Lithuania (GDL).[1] The procession was to mark a special occasion. After an almost two-year siege of Smolensk (now belonging to the Russian Federation), the military of the Polish-Lithuanian Commonwealth (PLC) had managed to win back the town from Russia. The powerful elite of the PLC perceived this victory as reclaiming Smolensk, rather than a seizure of new territories. The town, which had been part of the GDL since 1395, had been occupied by the Muscovites in 1514, remaining under their rule for almost a century, until its liberation on 13 June 1611 (Filipczak-Kocur, 2009, p. 50).

During early modern Lithuanian history, several wars were fought against Russia. One of them was the war of 1609–1618 between the Polish-Lithuanian Commonwealth and Russia (also known as the Polish-Muscovite War), which was driven by Sigismund III Vasa's ambition to rule the Muscovy. At that time, Muscovy was being torn apart by internal political unrest and fights over the throne. The PLC took advantage of the situation and occupied Moscow. A group of Moscow's noblemen accepted Prince Władysław Vasa, a son of Sigismund III Vasa, as their new tsar. In 1613, however, Michael Romanov was elected tsar, with the PLC thus failing to realize its ambitions in Moscow. In 1618, the Truce of Deulino was signed, handing the lands of Smolensk to the GDL (Rickard, 2007).

Politics and power, and the music surrounding them, or their acoustic representation, have always been intertwined. This episode in early modern Lithuanian history was no

---

[1] This research project has been funded by the European Social Fund (project No 09.3.3-LMT-K-712-19-0066) under the grant agreement with the Research Council of Lithuania (LMTLT): https://www.if.vu.lt/mokslas/podoktoranturos-stazuotes#dr-aleksandra-pister-gainiene-muzika-viesuju-rysiu-ir-kulturos-diplomatijos-tarnyboje-lietuvos-didziosios-kunigaikstystes-valdovo-ir-didiku-dvaruose. Date of Access: 09.01.2024.

exception. The return of Sigismund III Vasa to Vilnius after his victory at Smolensk became a massive celebration of his triumph, accompanied by various sounds in the capital. The whole Smolensk war campaign, which had taken a few years, impacted not only on the lives of the king, his closest associates and family members, but also his court music ensemble.

This chapter focuses on the musical soundscape of Sigismund III Vasa's triumphant entry into Vilnius on 24 July 1611. It investigates the course of the celebration and the sonic elements therein: the musical and urban sounds, and the music played in the closed and open spaces of the capital of the Grand Duchy of Lithuania. The research aims to analyse, contextualize, and assess the pieces of music performed or conceivably performed during the event. This includes their genres and the potential identification of the composers based on the manuscript *Dies Triumphi in faustissimum reditum Sigismundi Tertii Poloniae et Sueciae Regis de Smolensco ab ipsius Majestate expugnato, Vilnae XXIV Iulii celebrata A. D. M.DC.XI.* (1611) and other historical and musical sources of that time. Additionally, this chapter attempts to describe the role of music in the celebrations and public relations effort surrounding the ritualistic proclamation of a given military victory. The research methodology includes descriptive, historical, contextual, and analytical approaches.

The Smolensk Campaign and the Relocation of the Royal Court to Vilnius

The ruling monarch of the PLC spent most of his time in the capital of Poland, Kraków, and from the late 16th century onwards, in Warsaw. The Lithuanian nobility wanted the sovereign to reside in Vilnius, the GDL capital. Despite this, members of the House of Vasa (except for Władysław IV Vasa) rarely visited Lithuania. However, when the siege of Smolensk started in 1609, Sigismund III Vasa, his second wife, Constance of Austria, the future heir to the throne, Prince Władysław, and the court moved to Vilnius to be closer to the territory to be conquered. The monarch himself travelled to Smolensk, but his court stayed in Vilnius from 1609 to 1611, until he returned following his victory (Ragauskienė, 2003, p. 366). The musical chapel was also transferred to Vilnius.

According to the written historical sources and sources of music that survive, the then Master of the Chapel (*maestro di cappella*), the Italian, Asprilio Pacelli, relocated to Vilnius (Patalas, 2021, p. 41). Naturally, when the chapel master moved to Lithuania, a significant number of the chapel musicians came along too. One of them, the Venetian Giovanni Valentini, had also worked for the king at the court as a first organist, teacher, and composer, serving for about ten years, from 1604/1605 to 1614 (Weaver, 2012, p. XIV; Steinheuer, 2020). Valentini reached the peak of his career a little later, while serving at the Habsburg court in Graz and for the Holy Roman Emperor Ferdinand II in Vienna, one of

Fig. 1: Sigismund III Vasa, King of Poland, Grand Duke of Lithuania, etc.

the most prestigious European court music ensembles of the period.[2] It is likely that this significant career leap had been influenced by the favour of Constance of Austria, the wife of Sigismund III Vasa and importantly, the sister of Emperor Ferdinand II.

The only evidence that Valentini worked in Vilnius is his collection of motets *Motecta IIII. V. & VI. vocum*, published in 1611 by the Angelo Gardano & Fratres printing house in Venice.[3] Valentini dedicated this publication to the GDL nobleman and famous military commander Jan Karol Chodkiewicz (ca. 1570–1621), signing the dedication letter on 10 March 1611, in Vilnius: "Datum Vilnae die 10. Mensis Martii Anno Domini. M D C X I. Illustrissimae Magnificentiae tuae Famulus obsequentissimus Ioannes Valentini."[4] And Chodkiewicz, a talented military commander, renowned for his significant victories in the wars against Sweden – especially for the victorious Battle of Kircholm (now Salaspils)

---

2   Valentini worked for the Archduke of Austria, later the Holy Roman Emperor, from 1614 until his death, occupied the top position of *maestro di cappella* from 1626, and was ennobled. See Federhofer & Saunders, 2001.
3   For more on this collection of motets by Valentini, see Pister, 2022, pp. 8–29.
4   See Valentini, 1611, dedicatory preface.

in 1605 – the great hetman (i.e., leader of the army) of Lithuania, elder of Samogitia, and later, the voivode (i.e., military governor) of Vilnius, was indeed personally charged with leading the military action in Smolensk (Ragauskienė, 2003, p. 367).

The victory in Smolensk was celebrated multiple times in various towns. The first celebration was held at the location of the historical event. Two weeks after the seizure of Smolensk, on 26 June, Sigismund III Vasa invited his soldiers to the Smolensk castle. After mass with a sermon that ended in a joyful *Te deum*, the celebration of the victory began: Drums and trumpets roared and salvos of cannons thundered. In his letter of 28 June, the Lithuanian Chancellor, Lew Sapieha, wrote to his wife that the sovereign honoured all senators and soldiers in the castle, everybody got drunk and "[…] His Highness the King himself was pleased" (Saviščevas, 2011, pp. 67–68). Later the victory was ceremoniously commemorated in Vilnius, Kraków, Warsaw, Poznań and even Rome (Filipczak-Kocur, 2009, p. 55).

Celebration in Vilnius

Following the victory in Smolensk, various publications were released in Vilnius (Kocur, 2009, pp. 50–59). Our knowledge of the programme for the celebration in Vilnius, its participants, and the soundscape comes from the laudatory manuscript *Dies Triumphi in faustissimum reditum Sigismundi Tertii Poloniae et Sueciae Regis de Smolensco ab ipsius Majestate expugnato, Vilnae XXIV Iulii celebrata A. D. M.DC.XI.*[5] This illuminated manuscript intended for the sovereign contains a meticulous description of the day-long ritual to celebrate the triumph, and a particularly rare annex – uncommon for such sources – of a few notated vocal compositions performed during the festivities.

The manuscript accurately describes the route of the procession taken by Sigismund III Vasa and his entourage and the stops in the city, where the monarch was congratulated through various art forms. At a broader level, the patterns followed by this triumphal entry were quite standard in 16th century Europe, and so it is interesting to see the same patterns still being followed at the beginning of the 17th century – including such elements as the entry into the city, archways on the route, the procession to the church, the singing of *Te deum*, etc.

That day, the ruler was first welcomed outside the city. At about ten o'clock in the morning, his closest family members and the most important people in the state came from Vilnius to meet him: his wife Constance of Austria, his sixteen-year-old son from his first marriage to Anne of Austria, Prince Władysław Vasa, and his sister Anna Vasa of Swe-

---

5   In writing this chapter, the modern edition of the manuscript was also used: Ulčinaitė & Saviščevas, 2011.

Fig. 2: The ceremonial procession route taken by Sigismund III Vasa on 24 July 1611, through Vilnius, capital of Lithuania, marked on a map by Johann Georg Maximilian von Fürstenhoff from ca. 1750.
1. Medininkai Gate (Gate of Dawn)
2. Uniate Church of the Holy Trinity
3. Orthodox Church of the Holy Spirit
4. Vilnius City Hall
5. Church of St. John
6. Church of St. Francis and Bernard (Bernardine's Church)
7. Castle Gates
8. Lower Castle of Vilnius

den, members of the Senate, the clergy and the nobility, and an escort of armed soldiers (Ulčinaitė & Saviščevas, 2011, p. 114).

The king entered the capital through the Medininkai Gate, now called the Gate of Dawn (the route of the procession is outlined in Fig. 2). He then passed houses of worship from different denominations: the Uniate Church of the Holy Trinity, the Orthodox Church of the Holy Spirit, and the Jesuit Saint John's Church. He marched past Vilnius city hall and on to the Bernardine Saint Francis and Saint Bernard Church (Bernardine's Church), where a solemn service was held.[6] Towards the evening, the king arrived at his residence in the capital, the lower castle of Vilnius, where the festivities continued until sunset.

The procession was magnificent. In addition to the members of the royal family joining the large entourage, more than a thousand people participated.[7] Moreover, an unrecorded number of people from different social strata congratulated the ruler as he stopped at several triumphal arches. There, visual arts, theatre, poetry, and music were on display or performed. The archways, erected for the occasion, bore emblems and epigrams; next to them, theatre pieces were staged, congratulatory speeches given, poetry recited, and chants sung. The victorious city witnessed "the blare of trumpets and the rumble of drums coming from all the sides".[8] The streets were filled with the clamour of citizens, and anyone passing by the temples heard the resounding church bells (Ulčinaitė & Saviščevas, 2011, pp. 142–143).

This description of a triumphant city at the beginning of the 17th century refers several times to various musical and urban sounds. Sources of this kind often lack specificity – the authors of the pieces performed, specific compositions, and their performers are not named, and the account is usually limited to general descriptions. In this case, we find that the celebration of the victory involved a multifaceted acoustic majesty. Some of the music was played in open spaces, i.e., while the ruler was moving through the city and when he stopped at the triumphal arches. As the ruler entered his residence, musicians sang, copper drums rolled, a plethora of trumpets blared from the upper and lower castle, and military cannons thundered (Ulčinaitė & Saviščevas, 2011, pp. 150–151). The open-space soundscape could be heard by a large and varied public – members of different estates, not only

---

6   This church was chosen because the Cathedral Basilica had been destroyed by fire in 1610, and also because the victory was achieved on 13 June, the day of the Saint Anthony of Padua, a friar of the Franciscan Order.

7   At the front of the procession, 300 Tatar horsemen, 100 lightly-armed Cossacks, 100 armoured Germans led by the Knight of Malta Bartholomew Nowodworski, 100 spear-armed soldiers and 300 marching royal infantrymen, 30 GDL noblemen of high rank joined by their large retinues, and the king's courtiers also took part in the procession. Behind the sovereign followed GDL chancellor Lew Sapieha and GDL marshal Krzysztof Moniwid Dorohostajski – both were senators and had participated in the Smolensk campaign (Ulčinaitė & Saviščevas, 2011, pp. 120–124). Other important public figures of the time are also listed (p. 133). The procession was joined by 400 citizens on horseback, surrounded by a few thousand pedestrians (p. 140).

8   "[…] undiquaque, nil nisi, clangor tubarum, nil nisi rebombo timpanorum personat." (Ulčinaitė & Saviščevas, 2011, p. 136).

The Sound of Victory 403

the highest nobility, but also nobles of the lower ranks, city dwellers, the poor, as well as members of all the different religious communities. Evidently, this triumphant entry was not only aimed as representation and honouring of the victor, but also at creating publicity for the event.

Part of the festivities took place in a closed space, where only a limited number of noblemen and the most important political figures in the state could be present.[9] At the penultimate stop, a service (perhaps Vespers) was performed at the Bernardine Church, and the hymn *Te deum* was solemnly and devoutly sung:

> May the living God himself, one and in trinity, bear eternal honour and grace, may he receive endless gratitude, when his Grace [the King] illuminated the city of Vilnius with his exultant entry and traversed it, before he arrived at the royal palace and castle, due to his piety and faith, he first crossed the threshold of the church and said his prayers to God, making all [people], overjoyed, fall on their knees before God by his example, inciting them all, united in their common desire, to sing in unison *Te Deum laudamus*.[10]

Although the manuscript mentions only this hymn, the court music ensemble residing in Vilnius at that time surely must have graced such a solemn service with their music. The singing of *Te deum* was usually the pinnacle of musical representation at great ceremonies, characteristically accompanied by the shooting of salvos and the ringing of church bells. In this instance, the bells of the Bernardine Church might have been used; also, the bells across the city could have resounded simultaneously. The manuscript specifically mentions that the big bells of the Uniate and Orthodox churches were rung.[11] Giovanni Valentini must have played as well, as a member of the chapel ensemble. It is highly probable that on this occasion some of his instrumental canzonas from *Canzoni a IIII, V, VI, VII et VIII voci*, a collection published in 1609 in Venice and dedicated to the ruler, were performed (Valentini, 1609). Specifically, polychoral *canzonas* would address the needs of musical representation for such a ceremony.

---

9 Among them, there were Greek Catholic priests, who congratulated the ruler with humility and reverence (Lat. "[...] a Clero Graeco, qui etiam eo diverterat, reverenter humiliterque salutatur") (Ulčinaitė & Saviščevas, 2011, p. 148).

10 "Quo nomine, ut ipsi laus Deo vivo, ipsi uni ac trino, gloria in sempiternum referatur, ipsi gratiae immortales persolvantur, simul atque Serenissimus ingressu suo felicissimo civitatem Vilnensem illustravit, eamque transivit, antequam ad Arcem et Regiam descendit, pro sua pietate & religione, inprimis limina Sacrae Aedis salutat, vota Deo persolvit, omnes inusitata praecordiorum laetitia exardescentes pronos in terram coram Deo exemplo suo prosternit, omnes Hymnum Te Deum Laudamus unanimi voce iunctisque alacritatis suspiriis occinere facit." (Ulčinaitė & Saviščevas, 2011, pp. 105–106, 148).

11 See fn. 14.

In this context, it is worth remembering the above-mentioned Pacelli, *maestro di cappella* of Sigismund III Vasa's musical chapel, and his setting of *Te deum*, which was published in 1608 as part of the collection *Sacrae cantiones* (in Venice, Angelo Gardano & Fratelli printing house). This collection of printed music was dedicated to Sigismund III Vasa. The *Te deum* for two choirs and an organ (CATB, CATB and *basso continuo*, i.e., the organ) used to be performed on various solemn occasions. It is very likely that the polychoral *Te deum* was performed on this occasion as well, since it was already part of the ensemble's repertoire. It is known that there was an organ in the Bernardine Church as early as the late 16th century (Janonienė, 2010, p. 157). Later, in 1614, a larger organ was built: It was said to be the biggest and most modern in the whole of the GDL. The organ was funded by the Lithuanian magnate and military commander Jan Karol Chodkiewicz, mentioned above, who had taken part in the Smolensk military campaign, and the castellan of Vilnius, Hieronim Chodkiewicz (Janonienė, 2010, p. 156).

There was a great deal of noise and tumult upon the arrival at the castle. Not only consisting of musical sounds, it was, however, an organized acoustic proceeding. Next to a luxurious arch built on the queen's order, trumpets blared, drums rolled, and musicians sang. The courtyard of the castle filled up with horses and men, military cannons blasted. Excitement took over, people all over the city fired guns into the air, and 400 of the king's infantrymen, shooting in the castle, caused a hail of projectiles (Ulčinaitė & Saviščevas, 2011, pp. 150–151). This soundscape of rejoicing Vilnius shook the walls of the castle and frightened people until sunset (Ulčinaitė & Saviščevas, 2011, pp. 150–152).

The record of this day of triumph gives a quite detailed description of the triumphal arches built in honour of the victor. Unfortunately, engravings of these arches are not included in the records. But the source describes their appearance, listing the symbols, epigrams, and other inscriptions found on the arches (for example, the virtues of the ruler that led to the victory are enumerated), as well as some of the recited verses (Ulčinaitė & Saviščevas, 2011, pp. 154–305).

Uniate singing in honour of the sovereign

From a musical point of view, two pieces whose musical notation is bound at the end of the manuscript are especially valuable.[12] These are two sacred works that were sung by the Greek Catholics of Vilnius (who accepted the Orthodox union with the Roman Catholic Church and were subsequently called Uniates) to congratulate the ruler as he passed by the

---

12   Pieces in the original manuscript fols. 80r.–82r.; Pister, 2011 (facsimiles with transcriptions into modern notation, transcribed by Aleksandra Pister).

Fig. 3: Modulatum a Graecis, cum Sancta Romana Ecclesia unitis, dum Sacra Regia Maiestas triumphans transiret. *Hospodij, śiloiu twoieiu wozweseli sie Car,* fol. 80r.

Church of the Holy Trinity. The music notation indicates: "Sung by Greeks, united with the Holy Roman Church, when His Most Sacred Majesty the triumphant King went past" (see Fig. 3).

Uniates, or Greek Catholics, appeared in the PLC at the end of the 16th century, when part of the GDL Orthodox Church accepted the primacy of the Pope, but continued to practice their own rites (Kirkienė, 2017, p. 38). A union agreement between the Orthodox and Catholic Churches of the PLC – the Union of Brest – was concluded at an ecclesiastical meeting (synod) in Brest in 1596, and was later confirmed by Sigismund III Vasa's edict of 15 December 1596. An independent metropolitanate, the Metropolitanate of Kyiv, separate from Moscow, was established, consisting of the GDL and Polish Orthodox dioceses. It was independently managed by the Metropolitan of Kyiv, who was nominated by the sovereign and appointed by the Pope. This way, the Orthodox Christians of the GDL were divided into the supporters (Uniates) and the opponents (Disuniates, "Schismatics") of the union. Gradually, the Uniates of Vilnius became the largest Uniate community within the GDL. In the 17th century, when the Metropolitanate of Kyiv was annexed by Moscow, the Metropolitan of Kyiv moved his residence to Vilnius.[13]

The PLC Orthodox Christians separating from the Patriarchate of Constantinople became a political and denominational victory for Sigismund III Vasa. Being a radically Catholic ruler, he hoped to establish Catholicism as the only official denomination in the country. The king fervently supported the idea of the union, promising Uniate bishops equal rights with Catholic bishops and seats in the senate of the state. During the celebrations of the reclamation of Smolensk in Vilnius, such a welcome by the Uniates of the capital was a public expression of their loyalty to the sovereign. Surprisingly, the ruler was also congratulated by the Orthodox branch, which he did not recognize. This congratulatory moment is depicted as follows:

His Sacred Royal Highness proceeds and goes past an immense building devoted to the Holy Trinity of the Greeks, united with the Roman Church, and an Orthodox shrine on the opposite side of the street nearby. One and then the other, following the Greek rite, ring the large bells (their sound and melody is particularly enjoyed by the Greeks), slightly calming the rumble of timpani and the blare of trumpets. When His Majesty stops here briefly, the voices of dancing and singing worshippers observing the Greek rite resound, both sufficiently resonant and pleasant to the listeners' ears.[14]

---

13   For more about the Uniates in Lithuania, see Adadurov et al., 2017.

14   "Progreditur Sacra Regia Maiestas, transit prope Graecorum cum Romana Ecclesia unitorum Sanctissimae Trinitati sacram amplissimamque Aedem, parte ex una, ex altera vero, non longe a Schismaticorum templo. Utrique more Graeco campanas maiores, pulsant, earumque resonanti concentu ac melodia, qua Graeci vel maxime delectatur, timpanorum strepitum clangoremque tubarum nonnihil tranquillant. Subsistente hic aliquantisper Sacra Regia Maiestate, voces psallentium canentiumque more Graeco exoriuntur & satis canorae ac non insuaves, auribus adstantium hauriuntur." (Ulčinaitė & Saviščevas, 2011, pp. 143–144).

The Sound of Victory

The manuscript contains two anonymous psalm settings, *Hospodij, śiloiu twoieiu wozweseli sie Car* (The King shall rejoice in thy strength, O Lord) and *Se nine blahosłowi hospoda* (Behold, bless ye the Lord). In the margins next to the music notation, Latin psalm equivalents are indicated with the full verses of psalms written out in respective places. The first psalm is *Domine in virtute tua laetabitur Rex* (Psalm 20), and the second is *Ecce nunc benedicite Dominum* (Psalm 133). Nevertheless, singers must have performed in Old Church Slavonic, because trying to sing the melodies in Latin reveals that in some parts, certain words run out of melody notes, making it necessary to divide longer rhythmic values into shorter ones, with many words acquiring thereby incorrect emphasis.[15]

Alongside the music, these two specific psalm texts were chosen deliberately. Presumably the purpose of the notation is not only to show that there *was* singing, but also to highlight *what* was sung in this context. *Hospodij, śiloiu twoieiu wozweseli sie Car*, is a thanksgiving for the success and victory God had blessed upon the King. This text expresses glory and honour, and gives confidence in future success. *Se nine blahosłowi hospoda*, a psalm used *inter alia* for solemnities, says to praise God and mentions God's blessing, which in this context may be associated with Sigismund III Vasa. Both psalms suit the triumphant occasion perfectly.

Psalm 20 (21)

Old Church Slavonic	Latin	English
Hospodij, śiloiu twoieiu wozweseli sie Car,	Domine, in virtute tua laetabitur Rex,	The King shall rejoice in thy strength, O Lord:
y o spaseny twoiem wozraduie sie zelo,	Et super salutare tuum exsultabit vehementer.	exceeding glad shall he be of thy salvation.
Zelaniie serla [sic – serca] ieho dal iesi iemu, y chotenie ustnu ieho niesy lisil,	Desiderium cordis ejus tribuisti ei, et voluntate labiorum ejus non fraudasti eum.	Thou hast given him his heart's desire: and hast not denied him the request of his lips.
iako predwaril śi ieho błahoslowenyiem błahostynnym, położil iesi na hlawie ieho wenec od kameny czesnaho.	Quoniam praevenisti eum in benedictionibus dulcedinis; Posuisti in capite ejus coronam de lapide pretioso.	For thou shalt prevent him with the blessings of goodness: and shalt set a crown of pure gold upon his head.
żiwota prośyl iest w tebe y dal iesi iemu dolkotu [sic – dolhotu]	Vitam petiit a te, et tribuisti ei longitudinem dierum,	He asked life of thee, and thou gavest him a long life:

---

15   For more about the structure of the pieces, see Pister, 2011, pp. 86–89.

dnei, wo wieki weka, y wo weki [sic – wieki] weka.	in saeculum, et in saeculum saeculi.	even for ever and ever.

Psalm 133 (134)

Se nine blahosłowi hospoda wsij rabi hospodni Stoiaszcze wo chrame ho [sic] hospodini [sic – hospodni] wo dworech domu Boha naszeho w noszczech wozdezite ruki. Waszu [sic – Waszy] wo swetaia błohosłowite hospoda, Błohosłowit ten hospod od Syona Sotworywy nebo zemlu [sic – nebo y zemlu].	Ecce nunc benedicite Dominum, omnes servi Domini: qui statis in domo Domini, in atriis domus Dei nostri. In noctibus extollite manus vestras in sancta, et benedicite Dominum. Benedicat te Dominus ex Sion, qui fecit cælum et terram.	Behold, bless ye the Lord, all ye servants of the Lord, which by night stand in the house of the Lord. Lift up your hands in the sanctuary, and bless the Lord. The Lord that made heaven and earth bless thee out of Zion.

After a deeper examination of the music, it becomes clear that its function in the manuscript is symbolic rather than practical. Only fragments of these polyphonic works is notated here: *Hospodij, śiloiu twoieiu wozweseli sie Car*, starts with an *Altus* C-clef on the first stave and on the second stave continues as a *Cantus* part until the end, while *Se nine blahosłowi hospoda,* contains a complete *Altus* part.

A reconstruction (performance) of these musical fragments is hindered by the lack of a mensuration sign next to the clef, obscuring the meter. Besides, there are notation inaccuracies.[16] Based on note grouping, rests, the nature of added dots (only dots of addition,

---

16 In the first piece *Hospodij, śiloiu twoieiu wozweseli sie Car*, above the line "y chotenie ustnu ieho niesy lisil" (fol. 81r.), there should probably be two *brevis* rests notated on the first stave, and *semibrevis* and *minima* rests in the same place on the fourth stave, because the word *błahostynnym* is found earlier (on the third stave) under this particular rest combination; the same word when sung the second time should last the same amount of time. Some notation inaccuracies can also be found in the second piece *Se nine blahosłowi hospoda*. The first stave (fol. 81v., Fig. 3) probably lacks a dot next to the first *semibrevis* note C, since the rhythmic combination of a dotted *semibrevis* and a *minima* is encountered a few more times in the chant. Whereas the dot between the two *semibrevis* G notes on the first stave (*Hospoda*) looks like a dot of division (*punctus divisionis*), but dots of division are not used in binary mensural notation, so it is probably unnecessary here. The second stave contains *brevis* and *semibrevis* rests; this notation is likely inaccurate, because at three other places in the piece we find the combination of *brevis* and *minima* rests. Besides, the following phrase on the third stave (fol. 81v., Fig. 3) sounds more coherent stylistically when it is started with a *semibrevis* rest (an incomplete measure) than sung starting on the downbeat, leading to more syncopation.

punctus additionis, are found here) and other notation elements, it might be suspected that the rhythmic values of *brevis* and *semibrevis* are divisible into two parts in both psalms. Hence, the meter would be *tempus imperfectum prolatio minor* (C). This gives the impression that the aim was more to record the specific texts sung by Uniates on the occasion of the triumph, than to notate the pieces in a way that would allow somebody to perform them following the notation.

However, the polyphonic structure can be identified in the melody line and rests in the notation, under which further text is written (see Fig. 3 and 4). The latter text was sung by another voice(s) in alternation. Also, based on the soprano and alto C-clefs used in the parts and the typical cadential formulas characteristic for polyphony of that period, it is possible to assume that these pieces may have been sung by at least four voices – *Cantus*, *Altus*, *Tenor*, and *Bassus*. Perhaps they could have been psalm motets?

These Uniate psalms demonstrate the interface of Eastern and Western culture in music. They are notated in the Western, white mensural notation, which was not used to notate Orthodox sacred music. The Old Church Slavonic text is transliterated in Latin characters with Polish graphemes (for example, the sound *sh* is written as *sz*, and *tch* as *cz*).[17] Actually, writing an Old Church Slavonic text in Latin characters was quite common during this period, especially among the communities in the PLC of Western cultural orientation. Whenever the text is written in Latin characters, it is always based on Polish orthography, which was regional, i.e., used not only by the ethnic Poles in the territory of Poland, but also by Lithuanians, Ruthenians, and others.

The manuscript ends with laudatory verses of Schismatics, i.e., the PLC Orthodox Christians (Disunites), "recited by the youth on stage" (see Fig. 5). This means that congratulations from an unrecognized religious community were accepted by the ruler and were important, too, since this showed their loyalty to the sovereign in the presence of a war against a country that shared their same religion – Russia.

Short poems were created specifically for this occasion: *Salve, Magnorum Rex* (Hail to the King, born of the seed of the great Kings), *Te Mosci exitio servarunt fata* (The fate protects thee, dooming the Muscovite to perish), *Non plus depulso quondam gavisa tyrano est* ([It] did not rejoice more when it overthrew the tyrant). They contain verses glorifying the sovereign and also mention the ruin of Muscovites (!), the Polish and Lithuanian nations and the devotion of the "Roxolani" (i.e., Ruthenians) to the sovereign with their "affections and

---

17   The Orthodox and Uniate youth of Vilnius who had graduated from their local Orthodox and Uniate grammar schools were often sent to study at the Vilnius Jesuit Academy (Frick, 2013, p. 156). As a consequence, educated Uniates were able to speak and write in different languages used in the region, and clearly they also knew different musical notations. The manuscript, being intended for the Catholic sovereign, was another reason why Western notation was chosen in this case.

Fig. 4: *Se nine blahosłowi hospoda/Ecce nunc benedicite Dominum. Dies Triumphi,* fol. 81v.

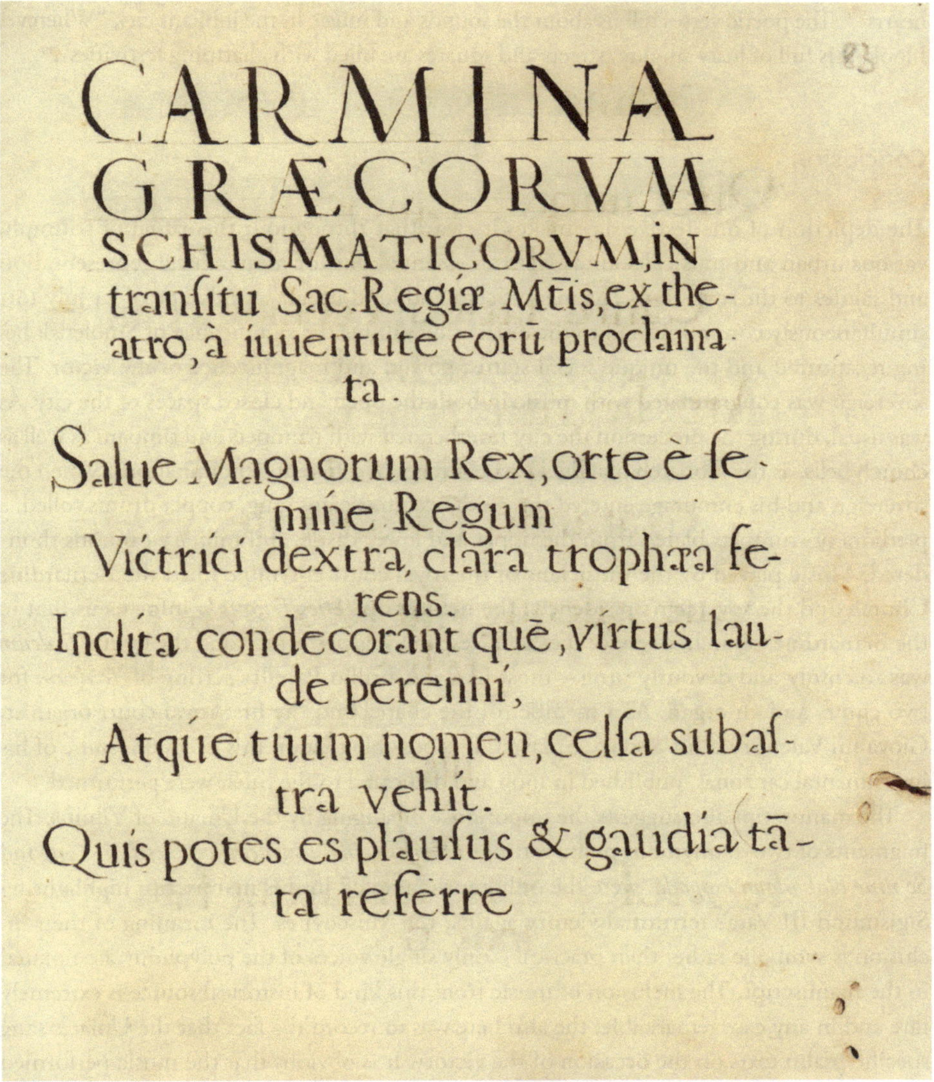

The Sound of Victory

CARMINA GRÆCORVM

SCHISMATICORVM,in transitu Sac.Regiæ M͞tis,ex theatro, à iuuentute eorū proclamata.

Salue Magnorum Rex,orte è semine Regum
Victrici dextra, clara trophæa ferens.
Inclita condecorant quē,virtus laude perenni,
Atque tuum nomen,celsa subastra vehit.
Quis potes es plausus & gaudia tāta referre

Fig. 5: Greek Schismatic verses, recited by young performers on a stage. *Dies Triumphi,* fol. 83r.

hearts".[18] The poetic verses tell us about the sounds and music in the jubilant city, "Wherever I look, it is full of lusty singing, streets and squares are filled with charming festivities".[19]

Conclusion

The depiction of one festive day makes it clear that throughout this ritual of triumph, various urban and musical sounds were an essential part of monarchical representation and salutes to the sovereign. The magnificent and loud urban soundscape of 24 July 1611 simultaneously communicated to the citizens of Vilnius the significance of Smolensk being recaptured and the unique social status, power, and magnificence of the victor. The sovereign was congratulated with music in both the open and closed spaces of the city. As was usual, during the procession the city reverberated with trumpets and timpani as well as church bells, as the monarch marched past churches of different denominations. When the sovereign and his entourage entered the residence, musicians sang, copper drums rolled, a plethora of trumpets blared from the upper and lower castle, and military cannons thundered. Music played by the musicians of the royal court ensemble filled the Bernardine Church and the sovereign's residence. The manuscript *Dies Triumphi* informs us that in the Bernardine Church, a service (perhaps Vespers) was performed and the hymn *Te deum* was solemnly and devoutly sung – most likely, Asprillio Pacelli's setting of *Te deum* for two choirs and an organ. As a member of the chapel and the first royal court organist, Giovanni Valentini must also have played. It is possible that on this occasion, some of his instrumental canzonas, published in 1609 and dedicated to the ruler, were performed.

The manuscript also suggests the importance of singing by the Uniates of Vilnius. The fragments of two anonymous psalm settings *Hospodij, śiloiu twoieiu wozweseli sie Car,* and *Se nine blahosłowi hospoda,* were the only music notated in this manuscript highlighting Sigismund III Vasa's territorial victory against the Muscovites. The meaning of their inclusion is symbolic rather than practical – only single voices of the polyphony are notated in the manuscript. The inclusion of music from this kind of historical source is extremely rare and in any case remarkable; the aim here was to record the fact that the Uniates sang specific psalm texts on the occasion of the victory. It is obvious that the music performed

---

18 "Te Mosci exitio seruarunt fata, Poloni o Nominis & Lithaui ter venerada salus. RoxoLani etiam non vna ab origine quamuis Profecti, affectu subdita turba sumus." (The fate protects thee, dooming the Muscovite to perish, in the name of the Polish and Lithuanians, may thou be venerated thrice. And we Roxolani too, although of different origin, are devoted with our affections and loyal to thee.) (Ulčinaitė & Saviščevas, 2011, pp. 322–323).

19 "Quocunque aspicio, sunt omnia plena sonoro Cantu: laetitiam compita cuncta tenent." (Ulčinaitė & Saviščevas, 2011, pp. 320–321).

reflected the political achievements of the occasion. Differing, even conflicting denominations – such as Uniates and their opponents, the Schismatics – also participated in the official celebration, all demonstrating their devotion to the sovereign.

Bibliography

Manuscripts

Anonymous (1611). *Dies Triumphi in faustissimum reditum Sigismundi Tertii Poloniae et Sueciae Regis de Smolensco ab ipsius Majestate expugnato, Vilnae XXIV Iulii celebrata A. D. M.DC. XI*. MS, SLUB Dresden, Mscr.Dresd.G.258: https://digital.slub-dresden.de/werkansicht/dlf/18313/1. Date of Access: 09.01.2024.

Printed Sources and Source Editions

Pacelli, A. (1608). *Cantus Asprilii Pacelli, Serenissimi ac Invictissimi, Sigismundi III. Poloniea, Suetiae, & c. Regis. Musicae magistri. Sacrae cantiones quae, Quinque, Sex, Septem, Octo, Nouem, Decem. Duodecim, Sexdecim, & Viginti vocibus Concinuntur*. Liber primus. Vnetiis, apud Angelum Gardanum et Fratres.

Ulčinaitė, E. & Saviščevas, E. (Eds.) (2011). *Day of Triumph. The Victory at Smolensk on June 13, 1611, and the Ceremonial Reception of Sigismund Vasa in Vilnius on July 24, 1611*. National Museum – Palace of the Grand Dukes of Lithuania.

Valentini, G. (1609). *Canzoni a IIII, V, VI, VII et VIII voci. Di Giovanni Valentini organista del Sereniss. & Potentiss. Re di Polonia, Svecia. &c. Sigismondo III*. Libro primo. Novamente poste in luce. In Venetia, Apresso Riccardo Amadino.

Valentini, G. (1611). *Motecta IIII, V & VI vocum Ioannis Valentini Organistae. Serenissimi et Potentissimi Regis Poloniae, Suaeciae &c. Sigismundi III*. Liber primus. Venetiis. Apud Angelum Gardanum & Fratres.

Weaver, A. H. (Ed.) (2012). *Motets by Emperor Ferdinand III and Other Musicians from the Habsburg Court, 1637–1657*. A-R Editions, Inc.

Scholarly Literature

Adadurov, V., Almes, I., Baronas, D., Bumblauskas, A., Čiurinskas, M., Duch, O., Jakulis, M., Janonienė, R., Kirkienė, G., Kozakaitė, J., Krečiun, P., Kuncevičius A., Lukšienė, V., Parasiuk, V., Skočilias, I., Tatjanina, J., Teslenka, I., Timošenka, L., Viničenko, O. (2017). *Kultūrų kryžkelė (kolektyvinė monografija): Vilniaus Švč. Trejybės šventovė ir vienuolynas* [At Cultural Crossroads (collective monograph): The Holy Trinity Shrine and Monastery in Vilnius]. Vilniaus University Press.

Federhofer, H., & Saunders, S. (2001/2013). Valentini, Giovanni. *Oxfordmusiconline*: https://doi.org/10.1093/gmo/9781561592630.article.28919. Date of Access: 09.01.2024.

Filipczak-Kocur, A. (2009). The Regaining of Smolensk in 1611 and its Defence in 1634 in the Eyes of Contemporary Lithuanian Prints. In A. Paliušytė, T. Račiūnaitė (Eds.), *Iškilmės ir kasdienybė Lietuvos Didžiojoje Kunigaikštystėje ir jos kontekstuose* [Celebrations and Everyday Live in the Grand Duchy of Lithuania and its Contexts] (pp. 50–60). Vilniaus dailės akademijos leidykla.

Frick, D. (2013). *Kith, Kin, & Neighbors: Communities and Confessions in Seventeenth-Century Wilno*. Cornell University Press.

Janonienė, R. (2010). *Bernardinų bažnyčia ir konventas Vilniuje: pranciškoniškojo dvasingumo atspindžiai ansamblio įrangoje ir puošyboje* [The Church and Friary of Observant Franciscans in Vilnius: The Reflection of the Franciscan Spirituality in the Interior and Décor of the Ensemble]. Aidai.

Kirkienė, G. (2017). Unijos idėja ir jos lietuviškoji recepcija [The Idea of the Union and its Lithuanian Reception]. In V. Adadurov, I. Almes, D. Baronas, A. Bumblauskas, M. Čiurinskas, O. Duch, M. Jakulis, R. Janonienė, G. Kirkienė, J. Kozakaitė, P. Krečiun, A. Kuncevičius, V. Lukšienė, V. Parasiuk, I. Skočilias, J. Tatjanina, I. Teslenka, L. Timošenka, O. Viničenko (Eds.), *Kultūrų kryžkelė. Vilniaus Švč. Trejybės šventovė ir vienuolynas* [At Cultural Crossroads: The Holy Trinity Shrine and Monastery in Vilnius] (pp. 37–48). Vilnius University Press.

Patalas, A. (2021). *De Asprilio Pacello ac illius musica conterfectum adhuc non perfectum*. Wydawnictwo Naukowe Sub Lupa.

Pister, A. (2011). Uniate Chants Glorifying Sigismund Vasa's Triumph: Features of Musical Structure and Notation. In Ulčinaitė, E. & Saviščevas, E. (Eds.), *Day of Triumph, The Victory at Smolensk on June 13, 1611, and the Ceremonial Reception of Sigismund Vasa in Vilnius on July 24, 1611* (pp. 86–89 and pp. 308–317). National Museum – Palace of the Grand Dukes of Lithuania.

Pister, A. (2022). Printed Music as a Medium of International Representation for the Magnates of the Grand Duchy of Lithuania: A Case Study of Music Prints Dedicated to Jan Karol Chodkiewicz and Aleksander Chodkiewicz. *Lietuvos istorijos studijos* 49, 8–29: https://www.journals.vu.lt/lietuvos-istorijos-studijos/article/view/28055. Date of Access: 09.01.2024.

Pister-Gainienė, A. (2020–2022). *Muzika viešųjų ryšių ir kultūros diplomatijos tarnyboje Lietuvos Didžiosios Kunigaikštystės Valdovo ir didikų dvaruose* [Music in the service of public relations and cultural diplomacy at the court of the Grand Duke and nobility of the Grand Duchy of Lithuania]: https://www.if.vu.lt/mokslas/podoktoranturos-stazuotes#dr-aleksandra-pister-gainiene-muzika-viesuju-rysiu-ir-kulturos-diplomatijos-tarnyboje-lietuvos-didziosios-kunigaikstystes-valdovo-ir-didiku-dvaruose. Date of Access: 09.01.2024.

Ragauskienė, R. (2003). Lietuvos Didžiosios Kunigaikštystės valdovų rūmų gyvenimo ritmas. Istoriniai šaltiniai [The Rhythm of Life at the Royal Palace of the Grand Duchy of Lithuania. Historical Sources]. In Ragauskienė, R. (Ed.), *Vilniaus Žemutinė pilis XIV a. – XIX a. pradžioje. 2002–2004 m. istorinių šaltinių Vilniaus Žemutinė pilis XIV a. – XIX a. pradžioje. 2002–2004 m. istorinių šaltinių paieškos* [The Lower Castle of Vilnius in the 14th–Early 19th Century. Search of Historical Sources in 2002–2004] (pp. 304–399). Pilių tyrimo centras "Lietuvos pilys".

The Sound of Victory 415

Rickard, J. (2007). Polish-Muscovite War, 1609–1619, 26 July 2007: http://www.historyofwar. org/articles/wars_polish_muscovite_1609-19.html. Date of Access: 09.01.2024.

Saviščevas, E. (2011). Triumph and Ashes: Circumstances of the Regaining of Smolensk in 1611. In E. Saviščevas & E. Ulčinaitė (Eds.), *Day of Triumph. The Victory at Smolensk on June 13, 1611, and the Ceremonial Reception of Sigismund Vasa in Vilnius on July 24, 1611* (pp. 8–69). National Museum – Palace of the Grand Dukes of Lithuania.

Steinheuer, J. (2020). Valentini, Giovanni. *Dizionario Biografico degli Italiani*, vol. 97: https://www.treccani.it/enciclopedia/giovanni-valentini_%28Dizionario-Biografico%29/. Date of Access: 09.01.2024.

Illustration Credits

Fig. 1: Sigismundus III, D[ei] G[ratia] Rex Polon[iae], M[agnus] Dux Lit[huaniae], Russ[iae], Prus[siae], Mas[oviae], Samo[gitiae], Liv[oniae], Nec Non Suecor[um], Goth[orum], Vand[alorum] Haered[itarius] Rex. Anonymus (17th century), chalcography. Vilnius university library, collection of graphic arts, Sign. Vak.Eur IA-30: https://kolekcijos.biblioteka. vu.lt/islandora/object/kolekcijos:VUB06_000004229. Date of Access: 09.01.2024.

Fig. 2: Map of Vilnius by Johann Georg Maximilian von Fürstenhoff, ca. 1750. Staatsbibliothek zu Berlin, Kartenabteilung, Sign. Kart. X 50203. Ulčinaitė, E. & Saviščevas, E. (Eds.) (2011), *Day of Triumph. The Victory at Smolensk on June 13, 1611, and the Ceremonial Reception of Sigismund Vasa in Vilnius on July 24, 1611*, p. 84. National Museum – Palace of the Grand Dukes of Lithuania. Reprinted with permission.

Fig. 3: Modulatum a Graecis, cum Sancta Romana Ecclesia unitis, dum Sacra Regia Maiestas triumphans transiret. *Hospodij, śiloiu twoieiu wozweseli sie Car/Domine, in virtute tua laetabitur Rex.* Anonymous, *Dies Triumphi in faustissimum reditum Sigismundi Tertii Poloniae et Sueciae Regis de Smolensco ab ipsius Majestate expugnato, Vilnae XXIV Iulii celebrata A. D. M.DC.XI.* Sächsische Landesbibliothek – Staats- und Universitätsbibliothek Dresden, Sign: Mscr.Dresd.G.258, fol. 80r.: https://digital.slub-dresden.de/werkansicht/dlf/18313/167. Date of Access: 09.01.2024.

Fig. 4: *Se nine blahosłowi hospoda/Ecce nunc benedicite Dominum.* Anonymous, *Dies Triumphi in faustissimum reditum Sigismundi Tertii Poloniae et Sueciae Regis de Smolensco ab ipsius Majestate expugnato, Vilnae XXIV Iulii celebrata A. D. M.DC.XI.* Sächsische Landesbibliothek – Staats- und Universitätsbibliothek Dresden, Sign: Mscr.Dresd.G.258, fol. 81v.: https://digital.slub-dresden.de/werkansicht/dlf/18313/170. Date of Access: 09.01.2024.

Fig. 5: Greek Schismatic verses. Anonymous, *Dies Triumphi in faustissimum reditum Sigismundi Tertii Poloniae et Sueciae Regis de Smolensco ab ipsius Majestate expugnato, Vilnae XXIV Iulii celebrata A. D. M.DC.XI.* Sächsische Landesbibliothek – Staats- und Universitätsbibliothek Dresden, Sign: Mscr.Dresd.G.258, fol. 83r.: https://digital.slub-dresden.de/werkansicht/dlf/18313/173. Date of Access: 09.01.2024.

The Soft Sounds of Power

The *Rebecchino* in the Kunsthistorisches Museum Vienna

Thilo Hirsch & Marina Haiduk

"While it is usually the neck that is touched by the palm of the hand, in this case, the hand finds itself resting on the nude legs of a Venus …" What could pass as the beginning of an erotic novel is actually the description of the playing position of the so-called *rebecchino*[1] in the Collection of Historic Musical Instruments of the Kunsthistorisches Museum Vienna (KHM), which according to the description in the catalogue originates from Italy and is dated to the 15th century (Hopfner, 2010, pp. 22–232) (Fig. 1).[2]

In spite of this dating, which would make it one of the earliest preserved European string instruments, the *rebecchino* has attracted very little scientific interest, possibly because it is only a fragment, that is to say, an instrument body without a belly or fingerboard. On the basis of new examinations within the framework of the Swiss National Science Fund research project "Rabab and Rebec" at the Bern Academy of the Arts,[3] Thilo Hirsch, in the first part of this article, presents an organological analysis of the instrument in connection with selected pictorial sources and hypotheses concerning its possible practical musical usage. In the second part, Marina Haiduk discusses an art-historical assessment as well as the hypothesis of the instrument's contextualization in a courtly collection, in which the *rebecchino*, despite its probably rather soft sound, could have served as a representative "instrument of power".[4]

---

1   The instrument name *rebecchino* used at the Kunsthistorisches Museum Vienna was first mentioned in 1619 by Michael Praetorius in the *Syntagma musicum* for the designation of a four-string violin: "Deroselben […] Discantgeig (welche Violino, oder Violetta picciola, auch Rebecchino genennet wird) seynd mit 4. Saiten […] bezogen." / "These […] discant Geigen (which are called violino, violetta picciola and rebecchino) are strung with 4 strings." (Praetorius, 1619, p. 48). However, in the present chapter we do not use *rebecchino* in the sense of Praetorius, but rather generically as the Italian diminutive of the designation rebec.

2   The corresponding illustration of the *rebecchino* is printed laterally reversed there.

3   https://www.hkb-interpretation.ch/projekte/rabab-rebec. Date of Access: 06.01.2024.

4   Apart from the hypothesis of the presentation in the context of a courtly collection, a more detailed German version of this article appeared in the journal *Glareana*: Hirsch & Haiduk, 2020.

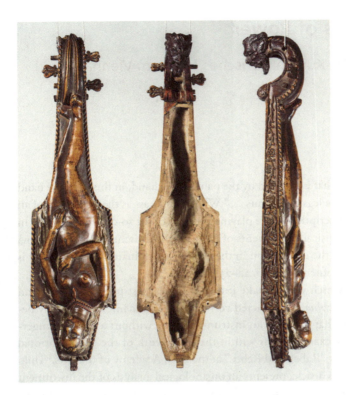

Fig. 1: *Rebecchino*, back, front, and side views.

Organological Analysis in Connection with Pictorial Sources and Hypotheses Concerning Practical Musical Usage

The fact that the *rebecchino* has survived to this day is certainly due to its elaborate carvings. This characteristic was already mentioned in the inventory of the patron and art collector Gustav Benda, from whose estate the instrument came to the KHM in 1932 as part of an extensive bequest. Listed under the "main items of the collection" is found: "A Venetian kit (pochette) with a carved female figure in boxwood" (Kunstkammer-Archiv, 1932, typescript, p. 13).

This female figure, clad only in a necklace and shoes, decorates in high relief nearly the entire back of the instrument. With regard to the material, it is meanwhile assumed to be a fruitwood, probably pear (Hopfner, 2010, p. 22). The edge area of the instrument's back displays a bead and reel framing that continues to the rear corners of the pegbox up to its end. Vegetal ornaments in bas-relief can be recognized on the sides of the body. The fluted, sickle-shaped pegbox displays four peg holes in which three pegs with carved heads are

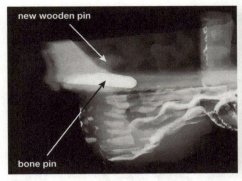 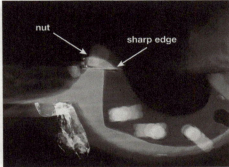

Fig. 2: *Rebecchino*, details of the X-ray image (left: lower end of the body; right: section of the pegbox).

inserted. The end of the pegbox consists of an attached satyr's head, whose style of carving and lacquer differs substantially from the rest of the body. Since the belly and fingerboard are missing, the careful hollowing out of the inside of the instrument is clearly discernible. Visible on the upper edge of the body are eighteen small rectangular notches that were intended as seats for nine crossbars of which only the uppermost has been preserved and to which a small triangular wooden plate is glued.

A carved tailpiece holder, which is fastened by a wooden pin that penetrates the body, is found at the bottom end of the instrument. Surprisingly, under this wooden pin is a second, brighter pin of bone inside the instrument, whose purpose – until now – had remained unclear, but which clearly shows that the instrument was modified over the course of time. Only by means of a newly made X-ray image is it now possible to explain the reason for this alteration. In order to fasten the current tailpiece holder, a new hole was drilled from the outside into the body at the same place where the original, possibly broken-off bone pin had been located. Since the drill channel of the bone pin slants downward (into an area with greater wall thickness), and the new wooden pin points slightly upward, the inner rest of the bone pin remained in the body (Fig. 2).

While the new tailpiece holder seems organologically sensible, this is not the case with the current condition of the nut. The X-ray image clearly shows that the upper end of the nut does not lie on the rim of the pegbox, but juts beyond it and tapers off into a sharp edge which would practically sever any string going to the undermost peg. Without going into too much detail here, it can be said that it is likely that only the body of the instrument (without the satyr's head), the rest of the bone tailpiece pin, the uppermost belly crossbar, and the thin orange-brown (partially worn-away) smooth layer of lacquer as found on the greater part of the body have been preserved from the original substance of the *rebecchino*. But what did the instrument originally look like?

Fig. 3: Circle of Francesco di Giorgio Martini and Neroccio di Bartolomeo de' Landi, *Madonna and Child with music-making Angels*, ca. 1475.

Important information concerning the possible original form is found in two pictorial sources. The first is a *Madonna and Child with music-making Angels*, created ca. 1475, from the circle of the Sienese artists Francesco di Giorgio Martini and Neroccio di Bartolomeo de' Landi, which is in the possession of Siena's Pinacoteca Nazionale (Fig. 3). The other, a southern German pictorial source, is a *Coronation of the Virgin* painted between 1512 and 1516 by Hans Baldung Grien as the middle panel of the high altar in the Cathedral of Freiburg (Fig. 4).

The depicted rebecs clearly display the same body outline as the *rebecchino*. Notable is that the lower part of both instruments, depicted in a lighter colour, is probably parch-

Fig. 4: Hans Baldung Grien, *Coronation of the Virgin*, 1512/1516.

ment. The possibility of such a skin belly for the *rebecchino* had – until now – always seemed improbable, since the edge area on the sides of the instrument in its current state is too thin to function as a gluing surface for a skin belly.

An important part of our examination of the *rebecchino* was the creation of a 3-D model by means of photogrammetry. This model made it possible, on the one hand, to depict the geometry of the instrument much more precisely than by manual measurement and, on the other hand, allowed a subsequent detailed non-contact analysis on the computer. It turned out that the belly edge at the lower part of the belly was very probably subsequently altered, both on the treble as well as on the bass side. A reconstruction of the rim shape from the existing cut edge results in a lengthwise slightly concave belly form that can frequently be observed on instruments with skin bellies, which, however, on the *rebecchino* was probably "levelled" over the course of time in favour of a flat wooden belly. The depth of the reconstructed belly edge would have been entirely sufficient as a lateral gluing surface (black-hatching) for a skin (Fig. 5).

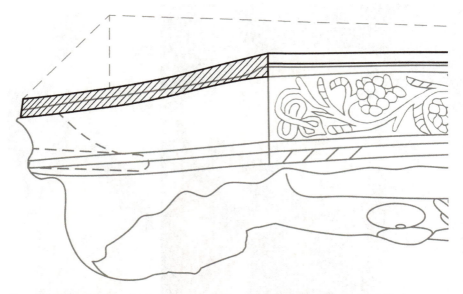

Fig. 5: Plan of the *rebecchino*, detail of the side view with reconstructed belly edge (black-hatching).

Therefore, the *rebecchino* in the KHM could actually be a small version of a rebec with a skin belly as depicted in the abovementioned pictorial sources from the 15th and early 16th centuries (from Italy and southern Germany). While this particular instrument type is not documented by later pictorial sources, a dating to this time period seems sensible from an organological point of view. Moreover, besides Italy, southern Germany would come into question as a possible provenience.

The preparation of the *rebecchino* body with partially extremely thin wall thicknesses is a clear indication of how important it was for the instrument builder to make the acoustically relevant inner resonance space as large as possible. In spite of its intricate external design, it was apparently a functioning musical instrument. But how was it set up? What musical function did it have? And what repertoire could be played on it?

We can only speculate about the tuning of the *rebecchino*, since from the 15th and 16th centuries, only tuning instructions for "normal" treble rebecs have been preserved, but none for the even smaller four-string *rebecchini*. Most likely it was a relatively high tuning in fifths, which could, however, also have been made up of two courses (each two double strings tuned in unison) or two single strings and a course.[5]

---

5   One of the earliest known references to rebec tunings is found in Hans Gerle's 1532 tutor *Musica Teusch*. Mentioned there are both three-string as well as four-string rebecs (called "die kleynen Geigleyn"), which are tuned in two or three consecutive fifths. The tuning there for the treble rebec is: g,

The Rebecchino in the Kunsthistorisches Museum Vienna   423

Johannes Tinctoris mentioned in his treatise *De inventione et usu musicae*, written in 1481/1483 in Naples, that the "rebecum" was a very small instrument invented in France. He emphasized the importance of a skilful artist ("sonitor artifex et expertus")[6] and counted the "rebecum" among his favourite instruments: "I would rather reserve them solely for sacred music and the secret consolations of the soul, than have them sometimes used for profane occasions and public festivities" (Baines, 1950, pp. 23–25).[7] This possible use in a sacred context is certainly also reflected in the pictorial sources shown above, in which the rebecs are played by angels; however, we should not make the mistake of interpreting these concerts of angels as concrete instrumental settings. On the other hand, the frequent appearance of "new" instruments in musical iconography suggests that in many cases it was important to the artists to depict a "contemporary" instrumentarium in order to approximate the lifeworld of the beholders.[8]

The only musical works explicitly notated for a polyphonic rebec ensemble are found in Gerle's *Musica Teusch* of 1532. These are intabulations of so-called tenor songs in which the treble rebec plays the uppermost of the four vocal parts.[9] This is an important indication that rebecs – and probably also *rebecchini* – were used, if anything, for the playing of individual melody lines, which, as the abovementioned sources have shown, could be secular or sacred.

---

 d', a' (Gerle, 1532, fols. Hijv-Jijr; ill. fol. Hiiijr).

6 In 1511 Sebastian Virdung also mentioned in his *Musica getutscht* that, due to the lack of frets, rebec playing can be learned only through "a great deal of practice", for which reason he included it among the "useless instruments" (Virdung, 1511, fol. Biiv).

7 "Extractum est et lyra: aliud instrumentum valde minus: ab allis Gallicorum qui id excogitarunt: rebecum: et ab aliis marionetta nuncupatum. Quod instar leuti testudineum: chordas que vel arculo tanguntur (ut predicta viola) tenet adaptatas. [...] Et quia rebecum (si sonitor artifex et expertus fuerit) modulos illis quam simillimos emittat: quibuslibet affectus spiritus mei (occulta quadam familiaritate) ad leticiam quam simillime excitantur. Hec itaque duo instrumenta mea sunt: mea inquam: hoc est quibus inter cetera: animus meus ad affectum pietatis assurgit: quaeque ad contemplationem gaudiorum supernorum: ardentissime cor meum inflammant. Quo mallem ea potius ad res sacras: et secreta animi solamina semper reservari: quam ad res prophanas et publica festa interdum applicari." / "Also derived from the lyre is a very small instrument called the *rebec* by the French, who invented it, and by others the *marionetta*. This, like the last-mentioned viola, is also strung for bowing, but, like the lute, it is tortoise-shaped. [...] And I am similarly pleased by the rebec, my predilection for which I will not conceal, provided that it is played by a skilful artist, since its strains are very much like those of the viola. Accordingly, the viola and the rebec are my two instruments; I repeat, my chosen instruments, those that induce piety and stir my heart most ardently to the contemplation of heavenly joys. For these reasons I would rather reserve them solely for sacred music and the secret consolations of the soul, than have them sometimes used for profane occasions and public festivities." (Translation: Baines).

8 See also Hammerstein, 1962, pp. 239–257.

9 Gerle, 1532, fols. Jr and Jv.

Art-Historical Analysis and Contextualization of the Instrument Within a Courtly Collection

After these reflections concerning the original form and the musical function of the *re-becchino*, the dating manifested by means of organological criteria will be compared to the style and the iconography of the female nude on the back of the body. Stylistic comparisons with wooden sculptures of the 15th and 16th centuries as well as representational depictions of instruments suggest that the maker of the *rebecchino* was not a first-rate wood carver. At work here was probably an artistically talented instrument maker, who presumably took recourse to a two-dimensional model – a print or even a painting.[10]

The question arises as to the iconographic type on which his depiction is based. Only a few elements can serve for the identification of the figure: its nudity and hairstyle, as well as its jewellery and footwear. In their combination, they do not correspond to any known type. Known, however, is the implied prudish impulse in the gesture of protecting the exposed body from gazes with the hands. This corresponds to the *Venus pudica*, the modest Venus, a traditional type in art since antiquity.[11] Accordingly, we are dealing here with a representation of the goddess of love, which was a very popular subject in the art of the Renaissance and Baroque. Paradoxically, however, the gesture suggesting shame with which the Venus on the *rebecchino* attempts to cover her nakedness underscores the potentially offensive representation of ostentatious nudity inasmuch as both breasts as well as the labia remain clearly visible.

In accordance with her nature as the Goddess of Love, Venus is frequently shown nude in the pictorial sources of antiquity and even predominantly in those of the Renaissance. Along with her nudity, Venus is often depicted barefoot. However, Venus is also shown wearing shoes, for example, while untying her sandals, which in some cases also display raised soles.[12] The footwear of the Venus depiction of the *rebecchino* with high soles and the tied side sections leaving the toes free does not correspond in terms of its design to the

---

10 When the parts are compared with each other, only the oblique view of the right side of the body is convincing in terms of perspective and proportion, which possibly can be explained by a two-dimensional model.

11 In 1873 the Basel archaeologist Johann Jacob Bernoulli coined the term *Venus pudica*, which has commonly been used since then: "Brust und Schooss deckende Aphrodite" (Bernoulli, 1873, p. 220).

12 Footwear with raised platform soles has existed since antiquity. Examples with a connection to the iconography of Aphrodite/Venus are, for example, the sandals of a terracotta statuette from Ephesus: Hellenistic, Aphrodite, removing her sandals, with Eros, clay, 30.8 x 18 x 10 cm (maximum extensions), Selçuk, Efes Müzesi, inv. 34/75/92. The motif likewise appears in connection with the subject known as "Venus at her Toilette". Textual sources such as Lilio Gregorio Giraldi's *De Deis Gentium* also mention, with recourse to antique sources such as Philostrat's *Epistulae* (37, 21), the "sandals" or "slippers of Venus": "sandalia & crepidas Veneris" (Giraldi, 1548, p. 62).

ancient sandal, but rather to a variant of the so-called chopines.[13] In textual and pictorial sources, chopines appear increasingly in Venetian venues where, among other things, they are depicted as footwear for courtesans. The general erotic connotation could however trace back above all to the circumstance that chopines, worn also by socially high-ranking Venetian women under their long skirts, were clothing hidden from view while the wearer was in a dressed state.[14] Accordingly, the chopines in Vittore Carpaccio's painting fragment with the depiction of two Venetian women are not worn by them, but rather seen somewhat away from them in the left margin of the picture.[15] In terms of form and colour, they correspond to the footwear worn by the Venus of the *rebecchino*, and thus a type that was widespread in Italy at least until the end of the 16th century.[16] The chopines of the Venus in a painting made in 1630/1634 by Giovanni Lanfranco provide an iconographical connection to Venus even into the 17th century.[17]

While Venus as a standing nude figure had been popular in Italy since the late 15th century, Lucas Cranach the Elder was the first artist north of the Alps to have realized Venus as an autonomous motif. In 1509 he showed the standing, naked Venus with loosened hair and a double-row pearl necklace along with Cupid wearing a coral necklace (Fig. 6). On the *rebecchino*, Venus is likewise shown with loosened hair that exhibits traces of gilding, which enhances, in equal measure, the material and the depiction. The red colour of her double-row pearl necklace suggests a material imitation of coral. This is confirmed by a pendant on the necklace, which is nothing other than a coral branch. In paintings of the Renaissance, the coral branch is often given to the infant Jesus as an attribute (Brückner, 1994, col. 556);[18] however, as jewellery for Venus, it is not customary. That coral in general is nevertheless probably an attribute of Venus has to do with the myth of the foam-born *Venus Anadyomene* – and thus originating from the sea.

---

13 The multitude of synonyms for the footwear of the Renaissance subsumed under the term chopines can be explained by the long tradition with regional and temporal differences that defy today's attempts at classification. Concerning terminology and history of this type of shoe, see Semmelhack, 2009.

14 Semmelhack, 2009, compares the status of the chopines from the viewpoint of intimacy with that of underwear. They are therefore also absent in the portrait genre, but shown in depictions of women "in various states of undress or *dishabille*" (p. 51).

15 Vittore Carpaccio, *Two Venetian Women*, ca. 1490/1495, tempera and oil on panel (94.5 x 63.5 cm; fragment), Venice, Museo Correr, inv. Cl. I n. 0046 (Fortini Brown, 2004, p. 91; Semmelhack, 2009, p. 55).

16 Italian chopines of red velvet, open in front, with shoelaces, dated to the time between 1580 and 1600, have been preserved in the collection of the Bata Shoe Museum in Toronto (inv. P88.60) (Semmelhack, 2009, p. 55, ill. 40).

17 Concerning the painting made for the harpist Marco Marazzoli, see Haiduk, 2019, pp. 92–93, no. 6.

18 Maurice Saß was able to convincingly show that the symbolic power of the coral as an attribute of the infant Jesus is not limited to its apotropaic effect. Concerning sacrificial-blood, transubstantiation, and resurrection connotations of coral, see Saß, 2012.

Fig. 6: Lucas Cranach the Elder, *Venus and Cupid*, 1509.

Corals belong to the *naturalia* that in their artistic setting were sought-after collectors' items in the courtly *Kunstkammer* of the Renaissance. Even a *Venus Anadyomene* made completely of coral and provided with a pearl necklace, for example, can be seen in the midst of the so-called *Korallenkabinett* of the *Kunstkammer* of Ambras Castle (Hofer, 2019) (Fig. 7). Archduke Ferdinand II of Tyrol collected *mirabilia* of different genres there – alongside *naturalia*, also small-format works of art, the *artificialia*. Common to all items on display was their representative role in a microcosm portraying the macrocosm. This concept had also been pursued by Ferdinand's father (also named Ferdinand), the later Emperor Ferdinand I, who in the 1530s had already established a collection conforming to these considerations in Vienna's Hofburg, while the term *Kunstkammer* is documented for it for the first time in the 1550s (Syndram, 2019, p. 36).

Last but not least, among the objects collected in a *Kunstkammer* were musical items, such as music manuscripts and musical instruments.[19] The latter included those that "were admired as showpieces of the collection rather than played as musical instruments".[20] The precursors of the *Kunstkammer*, above all the *studioli* popular at princely

---

19   The role of illuminated music manuscripts in the *Kunstkammer* is discussed by Gutknecht (2009, p. 47, pp. 55–56). A special case are miniature musical instruments. These were made of more precious materials than the instruments kept in the music chambers for practical use, and correspond, as their miniaturized representations, to the concept of the *Kunstkammer* as the microcosm depicting the macrocosm. Several miniatures likewise from Ambras are partially made of ivory and gilded (for example, Vienna, KHM, SAM 280 and 303) (Hopfner, 2017, pp. 334–335).

20   Beatrix Darmstädter observed this on the example of the natural trumpet by Anton Schnitzer (1581, Vienna, SAM 248), one of twenty-two of the thirty-six musical instruments listed in the inventory of the estate of Ferdinand II from 1596, which were stored together in the fourth cabinet, the so-called "weißer Kasten" (white box), and have been preserved to the present day (Darmstädter, 2017, p. 333,

Fig. 7: Southern Germany, Cabinet with corals, so-called *Korallenkabinett*, second half of the 16th century.

courts of the Early and High Renaissance in northern Italy, also display a close connection to music. The room type of the *studioli* developed out of the medieval studies and often displays intarsia panelling that is presented as an optical illusion in perspective. In this kind of "simulated collection room",[21] even the seemingly open cabinets and their contents remain only in the mode of artistic depiction. With their multifarious references, they mirror not only the world outside the *studiolo*, but also the honoured aspiration to a humanistic education, which is a part of seigneurial representation. Furnished with such a sophisticated pictorial programme are also the two *studioli* made for Federico da Montefeltro, Duke of Urbino, in the palaces of Gubbio and Urbino.

The intarsias of the Gubbio *studiolo* (Fig. 8) display representations of musical instruments, which in interaction with other *instrumentaria* or *scientifica* in this room context could be read as a reference to the quadrivium of the *artes liberales*, namely, arithmetic, geometry, astronomy, and music.[22] This schema also includes the depiction of a rebec with

---

no. 8.13: "eher als Schaustück der Sammlung bewundert denn als Musikinstrument gespielt").

21 "[…] der simulierte Sammlungsraum" (Parmentier, 2009, p. 55).

22 The intarsia with the depiction of square, plumbline, citole, hourglass, and dividers could serve as an example for a compaction of this reference in a single image. Moreover, in 1476/1482 the Flemish painter Justus van Gent made with his workshop a cycle of paintings, today only partially preserved, for the area above the wood panelling, which shows the personifications of the *artes liberales*. In

Fig. 8: Workshop of Giuliano and Benedetto da Maiano after Francesco di Giorgio Martini, intarsia panelling of the Gubbio *studiolo*, ca. 1478/1482.

a skin belly (Fig. 9). In the research literature, it was likewise seen as a part of a reference system in which the depicted musical instruments stand for the nine Muses, as in the *studiolo* conceived already several years previously in Urbino.[23] Finally, a direct link exists with the series of paintings of Apollo and the Muses in the *tempietto delle muse* located right underneath Federico's *studiolo* in Urbino, presumably a *studiolo* established for his son Guidobaldo. There, the Muse Terpsichore plays a rebec (Fig. 10), which belongs to the instrumentarium used during the Renaissance and was understood as a contemporary

---

1473/1476 he had already made such a cycle of paintings for the *studiolo* in Urbino – there with representations of *uomini illustri*, a canon of virtuous men in which Federico da Montefeltro had himself included: Raggio, 1999, pp. 43–44 (Urbino), pp. 157–167 (Gubbio).

23   In Gubbio, the rebec stood for the Muse Thalia. See Kirkbride, 2008, p. 119. In Urbino, where a rebec is not depicted, Thalia is however represented by a fiddle, and Terpsichore by a *lira da braccio* (ibid., p. 117). Concerning the ambiguous attribution of the instruments to each of the Muses, see Salmen, 1998, pp. 79–80.

Fig. 9: Workshop of Giuliano and Benedetto da Maiano after Francesco di Giorgio Martini, bookcase with rebec, bow and horn, intarsia panelling of the Gubbio *studiolo*.

Fig. 10: Giovanni Santi, Terpsichore, ca. 1480/1490.

equivalent of the ancient *cithara*,[24] as shown by the inscription at the picture's bottom edge. Cited here is a poem to the Muses, passed down in various textual sources since antiquity, in which Terpsichore, by playing her *cithara*, moves, dominating and intensifying the affects: "TERPSICHORE AFFECTUS CITHARIS MOVET, I[M]PERAT, AUGET."[25] On a frieze still *in situ* today, everyone entering the room – whoever they might be – are requested to show themselves cheerful and innocent to the Muses, and skilled on the *cithara*, since there is nothing there other than pure beauty: "QUISQUIS ADES LAETUS MUSIS ET CANDIDUS ADSIS FACUNDUS CITHARAE NIL NISI CANDOR INEST."

---

24 Concerning the usual contemporary generic description of string instruments by means of the Latin *cithara*, see Prizer, 1982, p. 107, and Salmen, 1998, p. 82.
25 For example, Ausonius, *Idyllia*, 20, 4, or *Mythographus Vaticanus II*, 24. For an overview of the textual sources, see Strocka, 1977, p. 134, note 471.

Isabella d'Este, the Margravine of Mantua sometimes referred to as the tenth Muse,[26] also employed the term *cithara* in her correspondence (Prizer, 1982, p. 107).[27] Thanks to a visit to the ducal palace of Urbino in 1494, she was familiar with the arrangement and furnishings of the premises there. It is surely no coincidence that also in Mantua, with Isabella's *studiolo* and *grotta*, two rooms similarly oriented in terms of function, reference each other.[28] They are exemplary for the development during the course of the 16th century of the *studiolo* "into a collection room that was also open for selected third parties".[29] For the wood panelling of the *grotta*, in 1506 Isabella commissioned Antonio and Paolo di Mola for the intarsia panels, which this time really function as doors for the cabinets hidden behind them. Among the intarsias, three display a clear reference to music through the depiction of musical instruments and notation. Isabella's affinity for music is also shown by the lively exchange over the course of two decades with Lorenzo Gusnasco da Pavia, her preferred instrument maker, and can be traced back to her training "in which musical knowledge and the study of ancient literature were paramount".[30] Since the *grotta* was also used as a place for music making – not least by Isabella herself – it would be entirely conceivable that musical instruments were actually kept behind the intarsia doors. In fact, no musical instruments are named in the posthumously made inventory of the *grotta*, but there were indeed statues of Venus and corals (Ferrari, 1994). This combination calls to mind the comparison by contemporaries of Isabella with the *Venus pudica*,[31] and leads us back to the *rebecchino*.

---

26 The designation as *decima musa*, used by Battista Guarino (1493), Giulio Cesare Scaligero (Elysium Atestinum, post 1512), and Mario Equicola (Nec spe nec metu, 1513), is with reference to the tenth Muse of antiquity, the poetess Sappho, a sophisticated form of praise of a ruler, honouring Isabella's devoted support of the arts (Campbell, 2004, pp. 199–200).

27 For the letters she exchanged with Lorenzo Gusnasco, see below.

28 A similarly programmatic aspiration as in Urbino can be proclaimed for the sculptured depictions of the Muses on the portal that connects the *studiolo* in the Corte Vecchia of Mantua with the *grotta*. It is only one of many of the works reflecting the origins of the arts that were commissioned by Isabella d'Este. However, the two rooms adjoin one another only since the relocation of Isabella's chambers in 1519/1520. Originally, at their installation in the Castello di San Giorgio in ca. 1500, they were directly above one another – a constellation that Isabella knew from Urbino (Romelli, 2008, p. 74).

29 "[…] zum Sammlungsraum, der auch für ausgesuchte Dritte offen war." (Parmentier, 2009, p. 58).

30 "[…] in der musikalische Kenntnisse und das Studium der antiken Literatur im Vordergrund standen." (Romelli, 2008, p. 37). Concerning Gusnasco, see ibid., p. 111, note 64, and Prizer, 1982.

31 "[…] Venerem sed pudicissimam" (Equicola, 1501, fol. Biir).

Conclusions Concerning Musical and Extra-musical Functional Interaction

Although a small and probably rather soft musical instrument such as the *rebecchino* seems not to have fit into the much better-known courtly context of representative festivities, in all probability it was part of an even more exclusive staging. On the threshold of becoming an autonomous art object, it allowed the humanistic education and knowledge of its owner to be recognized when the instrument was revealed in a seemingly strictly private ritual. It can therefore by all means have fulfilled secular representational requirements within the context of a collection. The possession of such exquisite collectors' items, which go far beyond the fulfilment of their actual purpose as musical instruments, was a part of a courtly competition that potentially enhanced prestige on the one hand. On the other hand, the possibility of viewing with one's own eyes, because of the exclusive custody in an appropriate intimate room in which the collector's items were revealed to only a few insiders, was consciously limited. In the case of the *rebecchino*, the multisensory experience may have been reserved for an even smaller circle of presumably mostly male visitors. Seeing, as the first sensory impression, is joined by the exclusive haptic experience of anyone who wants to elicit audible sound from the instrument by assuming the playing position. The linguistic metaphors of body and neck, anchored in organology, would already have generated erotic connotations which, under the musician's sensual touch, ultimately transformed the Venus into an enticing "resonating body".[32] For this kind of "playing", which serves the eye and the tactile sensation rather than the ear, a "player" would also not necessarily have to have been particularly skilled.

Translation: Howard Weiner

Bibliography

Typescripts

Vienna, Kunsthistorisches Museum Wien, Kunstkammer-Archiv, Akt 11 ex 1932.

Printed Sources and Source Editions

Equicola, M. (1501). *De mulieribus*. Francischus Bruschus.

---

32 Concerning the erotic connotations of the instrument's playing position, see Dennis, 2010, p. 229.

Gerle, H. (1532). *Musica Teusch*. Hieronymus Formschneider.

Giraldi, L. G. (1548). *De Deis Gentivm varia & multiplex Historia*. Johannes Oporinus.

Praetorius, M. (1619). *Syntagma musicum*, vol. 2: *De Organographia,* Elias Holwein.

Virdung, S. (1511). *Musica getutscht*. Michael Furter.

Scholarly Literature

Baines, A. (1950). Fifteenth-Century Instruments in Tinctoris's *De Inventione et Usu Musicae*. *Galpin Society Journal* 3, 19–26.

Bernoulli, J. J. (1873). *Aphrodite. Ein Baustein zur griechischen Kunstmythologie*. Engelmann.

Brückner, W. (1994). Koralle. In E. Kirschbaum & W. Braunfels (Eds.), *Lexikon der christlichen Ikonographie*, vol. 2: *Allgemeine Ikonographie F-K*, col. 556. Herder.

Campbell, S. J. (2004). *The Cabinet of Eros. Renaissance Mythological Painting and the Studiolo of Isabella d'Este*. Yale University Press.

Darmstädter, B. (2017). Naturtrompete, catalogue entry. In S. Haag & V. Sandbichler (Eds.), *Ferdinand II. – 450 Jahre Tiroler Landesfürst* (pp. 333, no. 8.13), exhib.cat., Haymon.

Dennis, F. (2010). Unlocking the Gates of Chastity. Music and the Erotic in the Domestic Sphere in Fifteenth- and Sixteenth-Century Italy. In S. F. Matthews-Grieco, (Ed.), *Erotic Cultures of Renaissance Italy* (pp. 223–245). Routledge.

Ferrari, D. (1994). Das Inventar der Grotta von Odoardo Stivini aus dem Jahr 1542. In W. Seipel (Ed.), *La prima donna del mondo. Isabella d'Este. Fürstin und Mäzenatin der Renaissance* (pp. 263–288), exhib.cat. Wien, Kunsthistorisches Museum.

Fortini Brown, P. (2004). *Private Lives in Renaissance Venice*. Yale University Press.

Gutknecht, D. (2009). Musik als Sammlungsgegenstand. Die Kunstkammer Albrechts V. (1528–1579) in München. In J. Bungardt, M. Helfgott, E. Rathgeber & N. Urbanek (Eds.), *Wiener Musikgeschichte. Annäherungen – Analysen – Ausblicke. Festschrift für Hartmut Krones* (pp. 43–65). Böhlau.

Haiduk, M. (2019). Giovanni Lanfranco. Venus Playing the Harp, catalogue entry. In M. Philipp & O. Westheider (Eds.), *Baroque Pathways. The National Galleries Barberini Corsini in Rome* (pp. 92–93, no. 6), exhib.cat. Prestel.

Hammerstein, R. (1962). *Die Musik der Engel. Untersuchungen zur Musikanschauung des Mittelalters*. Francke.

Hirsch, T. & Haiduk, M. (2020). Mehr Aug' als Ohr? Das Rebecchino im Kunsthistorischen Museum Wien. *Glareana* 2, 7–35.

Hofer, R. (2019). Sie sammeln und sie tauschen. Schloss Ambras als Knotenpunkt eines europäischen Netzwerks kunstaffiner Fürstenhöfe der Spätrenaissance. *historia.scribere* 11, 301–322.

Hopfner, R. (2010). *Meisterwerke der Sammlung alter Musikinstrumente*. Kunsthistorisches Museum Wien.

Hopfner, R. (2017). Neun Modelle von Instrumenten, catalogue entry. In S. Haag & V. Sandbichler (Eds.), *Ferdinand II. – 450 Jahre Tiroler Landesfürst* (pp. 334–335, no. 8.14), exhib.cat., Haymon.

Kirkbride, R. (2008). *Architecture and Memory. The Renaissance studioli of Federico da Montefeltro*. Columbia University Press.

Parmentier, M. (2009). Der Einbruch der Bildungsidee in die Sammlungsgeschichte. Auf der Suche nach den Ursprüngen des modernen Museums. *Zeitschrift für Erziehungswissenschaft* 12, 45–63.

Prizer, W. (1982). Isabella d'Este and Lorenzo da Pavia, 'master instrument-maker'. *Early Music History* 2, 87–127.

Raggio, O. (1999). *The Gubbio Studiolo and Its Conservation*, vol. 1: *Federico da Montefeltro's Palace at Gubbio and Its Studiolo*. Metropolitan Museum of Art.

Romelli, T. (2008). *Bewegendes Sammeln. Das "studiolo" von Isabella d'Este und das "petit cabinet" von Margarete von Österreich im bildungstheoretischen Vergleich* [Doctoral dissertation, Humboldt Universität zu Berlin]: http://edoc.hu-berlin.de/18452/16779. Date of Access: 06.01.2024.

Salmen, W. (1998). The Muse Terpsichore in Pictures and Texts from the 14th to 18th Centuries. *Music in Art* 23, 79–85.

Saß, M. (2012). Gemalte Korallenamulette. Zur Vorstellung eigenwirksamer Bilder bei Piero della Francesca, Andrea Mantegna und Camillo Leonardi. *Kunsttexte* 1, 1–53: https://edoc.hu-berlin.de/bitstream/handle/18452/8299/sass.pdf.

Semmelhack, E. (2009). *On a Pedestal. From Renaissance Chopines to Baroque Heels*, exhib.cat. The Bata Shoe Museum.

Strocka, V. M. (1977). *Die Wandmalerei der Hanghäuser in Ephesos*. Verlag der Österreichischen Akademie der Wissenschaften.

Syndram, D. (2019). Amassing magnificence. The role of the Kunstkammer in princely self-representation. In W. Koeppe (Ed.), *Making Marvels. Science and Splendor at the Courts of Europe* (pp. 34–40), exhib.cat. Yale University Press.

Illustration Credits

Fig. 1: *Rebecchino* (overall length 36.9 cm), back, front, and side views, Vienna, Kunsthistorisches Museum, inv. SAM 433, photos: T. Hirsch 2019.

Fig. 2: *Rebecchino*, details of the X-ray image (left: lower end of the body; right: section of the pegbox). Courtesy of KHM-Museumsverband.

Fig. 3: Circle of Francesco di Giorgio Martini and Neroccio di Bartolomeo de' Landi, Madonna and Child with music-making Angels, ca. 1475, tempera on panel (75 x 52.3 cm), whole painting and instrumental detail (rotated), Siena, Pinacoteca Nazionale, inv. 290. Courtesy of the Ministero della Cultura – Pinacoteca Nazionale di Siena, photo: Archivio Pinacoteca Nazionale di Siena.

Fig. 4: Hans Baldung Grien, Coronation of the Virgin, 1512/1516, tempera on panel (293 x 232.5 cm), whole painting and instrumental details (rotated), Freiburg i. Br., Freiburg Cathedral, photo: Peter Trenkle. Courtesy of the Archbishop's Ordinariate Freiburg i. Br., picture archive.

Fig. 5: Plan of the *rebecchino*, detail of the side view with reconstructed belly edge (black-hatching), image: T. Hirsch.

Fig. 6: Lucas Cranach the Elder, Venus and Cupid, 1509, oil on panel, transferred to canvas (213 x 102 cm), St. Petersburg, The State Hermitage Museum, inv. GE-680, photo: Vladimir Terebenin. Courtesy of the State Hermitage Museum, St. Petersburg.

Fig. 7: Cabinet with corals, the so-called *Korallenkabinett*, second half of the 16th century, wood, pearls, mother of pearl, corals, gypsum, mirror glass, velvet, glass, gold trimmings, bronze, lapis lazuli, gilding (66 x 55 x 56.2 cm), Innsbruck, Ambras Castle, inv. PA 961. Courtesy of KHM-Museumsverband.

Fig. 8: Workshop of Giuliano and Benedetto da Maiano after Francesco di Giorgio Martini, intarsia panelling of the Gubbio *studiolo*, ca. 1478/1482, walnut, beech, rosewood, oak and fruitwoods in walnut base (overall dimensions 485 x 518 x 384 cm), New York, Metropolitan Museum, inv. 39.153. Courtesy of bpk / The Metropolitan Museum of Art.

Fig. 9: Workshop of Giuliano and Benedetto da Maiano after Francesco di Giorgio Martini, bookcase with rebec, bow and horn, intarsia panelling of the Gubbio *studiolo*. Courtesy of bpk / The Metropolitan Museum of Art.

Fig. 10: Giovanni Santi, Terpsichore, ca. 1480/1490, oil on panel (82.7 x 39.8 cm), Florence, Galleria Corsini. Courtesy of Galleria Corsini, Firenze.

Appendix

Biographies

SULEYMAN CABIR ATAMAN is a software developer and earned a Ph.D. in musicology and music theory at Istanbul Technical University. He does research on music, participates in conferences, and writes articles as an independent scholar. He plays baglama, oud, and other string instruments. His areas of interest include traditional Turkish music, music theory, and the concept of *makam* and its applications.

MARTINE CLOUZOT est professeure en histoire du Moyen Âge à l'Université de Bourgogne-Franche-Comté (Dijon). Dans le domaine de l'anthropologie historique, elle étudie les images de la musique dans les manuscrits enluminés du Moyen Âge (XIIIᵉ-XVᵉ s.). En histoire sociale, à partir des textes et des archives, elle s'intéresse aux statuts des joueurs d'instruments dans la société médiévale. Ses recherches sont aussi tournées vers l'interdisciplinarité entre les SHS, les sciences du vivant, mais aussi l'IA (textes et images) dans le cadre de programmes collectifs. Parmi ses principales publications : *Images des musiciens. Figurations, typologies et pratiques sociales*, Turnhout, Brepols, 2008; *Les oiseaux chanteurs. Sciences, pratiques sociales et représentations dans les sociétés et le temps long*, Dijon, Editions Universitaires de Dijon, 2015; *Musique, folie et nature entre le XIIIᵉ et le XVᵉ siècle : les figurations du fou dans les manuscrits enluminés* (Images et textes), Bern, Peter Lang Verlag, 2014.

TIN CUGELJ is a doctoral researcher at the Institute of Musicology, University of Bern. His doctoral project focuses on auditory expressions of the Mass in the Republic of Dubrovnik (1358–1667), with an emphasis on function, meaning, and sound. Cugelj has presented his academic work at conferences across Europe and in publications; he is also a specialist reviewer for the *Early Music Journal*. He is a member of the International Musicological Society, the Croatian Musicological Society, The Hakluyt Society, and Soundscapes in the Early Modern World Network, and is a founding member and co-chair of the IMS Study Group Auditory History. Cugelj is an active musician, performing on historical trombones across Europe and North America. Following the principles of historically informed performance practice, he directs the ensemble Responsorium (Croatia) and co-directs the ensemble canticum trombonorum (Switzerland).

A. Tül Demirbaş is a doctoral researcher at the Institute of Musicology and Interdisciplinary Cultural Studies Doctoral Programme at the University of Bern. After eight years of violin education at the conservatory, she first studied musicology at Mimar Sinan Fine Arts University in Istanbul and later completed her Master's degree in ethnomusicology and folklore studies in 2015 with a thesis on the interaction of migration and music repertoire in the case of Ahıska Turks. She worked as a research assistant and lecturer at the Musicology Department from 2015 to 2019, and studied musicology and music theory at the Istanbul Technical University as a Ph.D. student between 2016 and 2019. From 2019 to 2023, she worked as a scientific researcher in the SNSF-Project "Der Klang der Macht: Klanglichkeit als intermediale Kategorie höfischer Festrituale in interkultureller Perspektive im 15.–17. Jahrhundert" at the University of Bern. Demirbaş is currently completing her Ph.D. dissertation on the sonic aspects of the Ottoman imperial circumcision festival of 1582. In addition to her academic career, she has been involved in concert and festival organization, project management and administration since 2015.

Ali Ergur was born in Athens in 1966. He studied public administration and social sciences at Marmara University, and sociology (Ph.D.) at Middle East Technical University. His main domains of academic interest are the sociology of communication and information, technology, surveillance, post-industrial society, consumption, economic elites, and the sociology of culture. Ergur's second field of research is the sociology of music. He is particularly interested in the process of the modernization of Turkish music. He has published articles in collaboration with musicologists, as well as several essays on the transformation of musical expressions, forms and styles. He is currently Professor in the Department of Sociology at Galatasaray University, Istanbul.

Cenk Güray, born in Ankara in 1973, received a bachelor's degree in 1995, a Master's degree in 1998 and a Ph.D. in 2003 from the Mining Engineering Department of Middle East Technical University. In 2006 he received a Master's degree in musicology from Başkent University and in 2012 he received a Ph.D. in Turkish Religious Music from Ankara University Faculty of Divinity and Institute of Social Sciences. Currently he is working as a Professor of Music Theory in Hacettepe University Ankara State Conservatory, concentrating primarily on Turkish music theory, *Makam* analysis, and the theory of cycles. A performer, composer and researcher, he has participated as a speaker, performer, and director in many symposiums, conferences, concerts, seminars, workshops, masterclasses, TV and radio programmes, and CD projects worldwide, and has written or edited many books, book chapters, papers, stories and poems regarding his areas of concentration. Cenk Güray is also the director of the Ensemble for Anatolian Music Cultures.

Biographies

MARINA HAIDUK studied art history, communication studies and Eastern European studies in Berlin and Vienna and has conducted research on Italian painting and art theory of the 16th and 17th centuries, with a main focus on materiality and material iconology. In the spotlight of this field is painting on stone, which was the subject of both her Master's thesis on Daniele da Volterra's *David and Goliath* and her doctoral thesis "Visibility of Material as Aesthetic Communication. The *pietra di paragone* as a Pictorial Support in Italy around 1600". After earning her doctorate, she dedicated herself to music iconography and its methodology as a postdoctoral researcher in the research project "Rabab & Rebec" at the Bern Academy of the Arts, with a special attention to medial aspects such as the relationship of word, sound, and material culture to the image.

JUDITH I. HAUG studied musicology, medieval history, and German language and literature of the Middle Ages at the University of Augsburg. She received her Master's degree with a thesis on Salomone Rossi's Hebrew psalm motets (1622/1623) in 2005, and her doctorate at the University of Tübingen with a thesis on the dissemination of the Genevan Psalter in Europe and the Ottoman Empire in 2008. Between 2010 and 2012 she was a research assistant at the Virtual Library of Musicology (vifamusik.de), and from 2012 to 2016, she conducted the DFG-funded Habilitation thesis project "Ottoman and European music in the compendium of Alî Ufukî (around 1640): Interpretation, analysis and (trans-)cultural context" at the University of Münster. From 2016 to 2018, she worked as postdoctoral researcher at the Orient-Institut Istanbul/Max Weber Stiftung (OII) in the project "Corpus Musicae Ottomanicae (CMO)" conducted jointly with the University of Münster. She held the position of senior researcher responsible for the research area of musicology at the OII between 2018 and 2023, and Acting Deputy Director between 2020 and 2022. She is currently the grants awarding coordinator of the COST Action "EarlyMuse" and has been an Associate Professor at the University of Oslo since September 2023.

THILO HIRSCH studied viola da gamba and singing at the Schola Cantorum Basiliensis (SCB) and musicology/ethnomusicology at the University of Bern. Concert tours with international ensembles have taken him throughout Europe, North Africa, North and South America and Japan. Between 2007 and 2015, he was co-project leader of several SNSF and SERI research projects at the SCB ("La Grande Écurie", "Transformationen instrumentaler Klanglichkeit" and "Groß Geigen, Vyolen, Rybeben"). The "sounding" results of these projects have been documented in concerts and CDs of the ensemble arcimboldo, which he directs. Since 2019, he has been the head of the SNSF research project "Rabab & Rebec: Research into skin-covered string instruments of the late Middle Ages and early Renaissance and their reconstruction" being conducted at the Bern Academy of the Arts.

GAMZE İLASLAN KOÇ completed her BA at Boğaziçi University in 2013, double majoring in Turkish language and literature and history programmes with an honours degree. During her bachelor studies, she spent one semester at the Freie Universität Berlin in 2011 through the Erasmus Programme. She joined an MA programme in Modern Turkish Studies at Boğaziçi University and completed her MA thesis, titled "Abduction and Elopement in the 19th Century Ottoman Nizamiye Courts". She has contributed to different research projects and worked as a teaching assistant for sociology and history courses. Currently, she is a Ph.D. student at Regensburg University; her dissertation focuses on the material culture of Ottoman and Habsburg diplomacy during the 18th century. İlaslan Koç's research interests include the early modern world, material history, socio-legal studies, and Ottoman-Habsburg relations.

SONGÜL KARAHASANOĞLU is a Professor in the Turkish Music State Conservatory at Istanbul Technical University, where she teaches ethnomusicology and popular music studies. She is the author of *Muş Türküleri ve Oyun Havaları* (Muş Folk Songs and Dances), *Müzikte Araştırma Yöntemleri* (with Elif Damla Yavuz) (Research Methods in Music), and *Mey ve Metodu* (The Mey and Its Method), the only works of their kind currently in publication. She continues her research and publications in the area of Turkish popular music, Islam and music, traditional Turkish music and musical instruments, including the Mey, a Turkish folk instrument.

MORITZ KELBER studied musicology, law, and political science at the University of Munich. In 2016, he received his doctorate from the University of Augsburg with a study on music in the context of the Augsburg Imperial Diets in the 16th century. His thesis was supervised by Franz Körndle and published in 2018. Between 2016 and 2018, Kelber was a research assistant at the University of Salzburg. Between 2018 and 2022, he was an Assistant Professor at the Institute of Musicology in Bern. For the winter semesters 2019/2020 and 2022/2023, he was acting Professor for Early Music History at the University of Munich. Kelber's research focuses on the social history of medieval and early modern music, performance practice, the field of digital humanities, and the history of science. During the summer semester 2023 he is acting Professor of Musicology at the University of Augsburg.

JIEUN KIM, geboren in Seoul, Korea, studierte Musikwissenschaft und Kirchenmusik an der Presbyterian University and Theological Seminary in Seoul, Korea. Die Promotion erfolgte mit einer Arbeit zu Koreanischer Musik und Transkulturalität: Im Spannungsfeld zwischen Verwestlichung und Koreanisierung (Tectum 2022). Im Jahr 2022 war sie Research Associate am Korea Europe Center für Koreastudien der Freien Universität Berlin. Seit 2023 ist sie als Kyujanggak Fellow am International Center for Korean Studies des

Kyujanggak Institute der Seoul National University in Korea tätig. Ihr Forschungsinteresse fokussiert sich auf koreanische Musik und asiatische Einflüsse auf europäische Kunstmusik seit dem 19. Jahrhundert, insbesondere auf transkulturelle Ansätze im Komponieren von traditionellen bis zu populären Musikbereichen, einschließlich der Kunstmusik.

JOSEPH S.C. LAM is Professor of Musicology at the University of Michigan, USA. He studies Chinese music with interdisciplinary methods, probing its sonic expressions of Chinese biography, culture, and history. Lam extensively lectures and publishes in Asia, Europe and the United States. His representative publications include: *State Sacrifices and Music in Ming China (A.D. 1368–1644)* (SUNY, 1998); "Huizong's Dashengyue: A Musical Performance of Emperorship and Officialdom" in *Huizong and the Culture of Northern Song China* (Harvard, 2006); "Ci Songs from the Song Dynasty: A Ménage à Trois of Lyrics, Music, and Performance" (*New Literary History*, 2015), and "A Proposal on Music of Reminiscence/Huaigu yinyue lilun yu shijian di yige chubu ti'an" (*Yinyue yishu*, 2019/2). Lam's latest monograph is his *Kunqu, A Classical Opera of Contemporary China* (Hong Kong University Press, 2022).

JAN-FRIEDRICH MISSFELDER teaches early modern history at the Department of History at the University of Basel. At Basel, he holds an SNSF Professorship and is the Principal Investigator of the collaborative research project "Vocal Power. The Vocality of Early Modern Media and Politics", funded by the Swiss National Science Foundation (SNSF). After studying history, musicology and politics in Göttingen, Berlin, and Leicester, he became an Assistant Professor in Early Modern History and a Senior Researcher at the National Center for Competence in Research (NCCR) "Mediality" at the University of Zurich. His main areas of expertise lie in media history, sensory history, and reformation history, as well as in historical theory and the history of historiography.

ALEKSANDRA PISTER completed her Master's degree in early music theory and composition at the Schola Cantorum Basiliensis. She holds a Ph.D. in musicology from the Lithuanian Academy of Music and Theatre for her dissertation on the Biblical Sonatas of Johann Kuhnau. She has conducted an EU-funded postdoctoral research project at the University of Vilnius on the collections of printed music by Italian composers dedicated to Lithuanian magnates. Her research on music of the Grand Duchy of Lithuania, musical rhetoric, and the doctrine of the affections has been widely published. She is a co-editor (with Marco Bizzarini) of the new edition of Marco Scacchi's book of canons, *Canones nunnulli* (Königsberg, 1649), which has been published by the Palace of the Grand Duchy of Lithuania (2016). She is the leader of the Education Working Group, which is part of the COST-Project: A New Ecosystem of Early Music Studies (EarlyMuse).

BAPTISTE RAMEAU est professeur agrégé d'histoire et actuellement doctorant contractuel à l'Université de Bourgogne. Il travaille depuis 2019 sur les pratiques du don dans la Grande Principauté de Bourgogne et plus particulièrement durant les principats de Jean sans Peur et Philippe le Bon (1404–1467), sous les directions de Martine Clouzot (Université de Bourgogne, UMR 6298 ARTEHIS) et Olivier Mattéoni (Université Paris 1 Panthéon-Sorbonne, UMR 8589 LAMOP). Théorisées depuis l'Antiquité, ces pratiques apparaissent au Moyen Âge comme l'expression de la libéralité princière, visant à la fois à souligner les vertus du prince et à incarner une manière d'exercer le pouvoir. Ses recherches récentes se sont essentiellement focalisées sur les dons en vins ainsi que sur les largesses envers les réseaux bourguignons de la capitale du royaume de France durant la guerre civile entre Armagnacs et Bourguignons (1407–1435).

HARRIET RUDOLPH is Professor of Early Modern History at the University of Regensburg. Her recent publications include: "Zwischen künstlerischer Imagination und visueller Deskription. Materielle Kulturen europäischer Hospitäler bei Adam Elsheimer, Cornelis de Wael und Jan Beerblock (1600–1800)," in *Spitalobjekte. Die materielle Kultur des Spitals in der Vormoderne*, ed. with Artur Dirmeier and Daniel Drascek, Regensburg 2022, 107–140; "Meaningless Spectacles? 18th Century Imperial Coronations in the Holy Roman Empire Reconsidered", in *More than Mere Spectacle: Coronations and Inaugurations in the Habsburg Monarchy, 1700–1848*, ed. Klaas van Gelder, New York 2021, 67–98; *Opfer. Dynamiken der Viktimisierung vom 17. bis 21. Jahrhundert*, ed. with Isabella von Treskow, Heidelberg 2020; and "Material Culture in Modern Diplomacy from the 15th to the 20th Century" (*European History Yearbook* 17), Berlin 2016, ed. with Gregor Metzig.

MARGRET SCHARRER is a postdoctoral researcher at the Institute of Musicology at the University of Bern. From 2019 to 2023 she worked on the SNSF-funded project "The Sound of Power: Sound as an Intermedial Category of Courtly Ceremonial Rituals in an Intercultural Perspective in the 15th–17th Centuries". In 2022/2023, she was a research assistant at the same university. Scharrer studied musicology, history and historical auxiliary sciences in Halle, Lille, and Paris; she earned her MA in 2001 at Martin Luther University Halle-Wittenberg (MLU), with a thesis on the *ars subtilior* at Avignon. She completed her Ph.D. in 2011 at MLU Halle-Wittenberg with a thesis on the reception of French music theatre at German residences in the late 17th and early 18th centuries (*Zur Rezeption des französischen Musiktheaters an deutschen Residenzen im ausgehenden 17. und frühen 18. Jahrhundert*, published in 2014 with Studiopunkt-Verlag). Between 2012 and 2019 she was a lecturer and research assistant at Saarland University. Since 2021 she has been co-editor of the *Swiss Journal of Musicology* and a board member of the Rudolstädter Arbeitskreis zur Residenzkultur. Her research interests lie in the fields of court music between the 14th and

18th centuries, with a special focus on different theatrical forms as well as processes of transfer and reception (also beyond the "Western" world).

ANA CLÁUDIA SILVEIRA holds a Ph.D. in history from the Universidade NOVA de Lisboa (2022). Her dissertation examined the port city of Setúbal, located within the domains of the Portuguese Military Order of Santiago. She is a research member of the Instituto de História Medieval – NOVA, and is a member of the team of the UNESCO Chair "The Cultural Heritage of the Oceans", which operates under the coordination of CHAM – Centro de Humanidades (NOVA). She has been involved as a researcher in several scholarly projects and also coordinated the international project "Tide mills of Western Europe", which was financed by the Culture 2000 Programme. Her research interests are portuary settlements, the exploitation of maritime resources (salt production, fishing resources, harnessing tidal power for milling, maritime connections), military orders, and urban topography and urban civic events as a strategy of political affirmation.

DANIEL TIEMEYER studied musicology and history at the universities of Osnabrück and Vienna, where he graduated in both subjects as Magister artium. He was awarded his Ph.D. in musicology in January 2018 with a dissertation on the early operas of Franz Schreker. From October 2017 to March 2020, he was assistant at the Hochschule für Musik Franz Liszt in Weimar, and from April 2020 to May 2022 he held the same position in the department of musicology at the University of Heidelberg. Since June 2022 he has been coordinator of the German Research Foundation (DFG) project "Digitales Quellen- und Werkverzeichnis Franz Liszt (LQWV)". Tiemeyer's research interests range from late Beethoven music, piano compositions of the 19th century (with an emphasis on Franz Liszt), opera of the early 19th and 20th centuries, to Renaissance music with a specific focus on Marian devotion and music in the Low Countries around 1500.

GRAYSON WAGSTAFF held a full professorship at the Catholic University of America (2000–2020) and is now a faculty affiliate researcher at the University of North Carolina, Chapel Hill. He has published widely on topics in late medieval and early modern music in Spain and music in early Colonial Mexico. His interests in sacred music include the Requiem and Office for the Dead, Marian devotions, the services of Holy Week, and local chant repertories. He is the author of articles and reviews published in such journals as *The Musical Quarterly*, *Journal of the Royal Music Association*, *Heterofonía*, *Notes*, the *Journal of Plainsong and Medieval Music*, *Revista Portuguesa de Musicologia/Portuguese Journal of Musicology*, as well as in several volumes of collected papers, including *The Anatomy of Iberian Polyphony Around 1500* and *Into the Diaspora*.

Tobias C. Weissmann earned his Ph.D. from Humboldt University Berlin in 2019 with a dissertation on the interrelation of music, sound, and visual arts in the festival culture of baroque Rome. The interdisciplinary study was awarded the Rudolf Arnheim Prize 2019, the Hans Janssen Prize 2022 and the Premio Daria Borghese 2023. He held scholarships at the Centro Tedesco di Studi Veneziani, the German Historical Institute Rome, the Bibliotheca Hertziana, the Leibniz Institute for European History and the University of Zurich. Since 2018 he has worked as a postdoc fellow for the research project "CANTORIA – Music and Sacred Architecture" at Mainz University, where he also teaches musicology and art history. He is a member of the Young Academy of Sciences and Literature Mainz and head of the interdisciplinary scientific network "Religious Plurality", funded by the German Research Foundation (DFG).

Online Workshop I

Sonic Rituals: Ottoman, Habsburg & Burgundian Festivities (15th–17th Centuries) from an Intermedial Perspective

4–5 September 2020

Programme

Friday, 4 September 2020

Chair: PD Dr. Judith I. Haug (Orient-Institut Istanbul) & Dr. Margret Scharrer (University of Bern)

14:00   Welcome
(CET)   Prof. Dr. Raoul Motika (Director of the Orient-Institut Istanbul)
        Prof. Dr. Cristina Urchueguía (University of Bern)

14:30   The Discovery of Life's Pleasures in the Tulip Era: The Rise of City Life and a Worldly Perception in the Ottoman Empire
        Prof. Dr. Ali Ergur (Galatasaray University)

15:00   Pro Maximiliano psallite! Carolus, ecce venit! Ritual and Music in Festivities at Habsburg Courts in the Early 16th Century
        Dr. Sonja Tröster (University of Music and Performing Arts Vienna)

15:30   Coffee break

16:00   Sixteenth Century Visual Sources for Ottoman Festivities and Music
        Prof. Dr. Emine Fetvacı (Boston University)

16:30   Performances of La Condemnation du Banquet (around 1500) and Convivii Process (1593). Theatre, Music and Dining in Courtly and Urban Contexts
        PD Dr. Heidy Greco-Kaufmann (University of Bern)

Saturday, 5 September 2020

Chair: Prof. Dr. Cristina Urchueguía & PD Dr. Judith I. Haug

09:30   Performing the Ottoman Power: Music and Space at the Festival of 1582
           M.A. A. Tül Demirbaş (University of Bern)

10:00   Sounding Rituals in Images at the Court of the Valois Dukes of Burgundy,
           Philip the Good and Charles the Bold (1419–1477)
           Prof. Dr. Martine Clouzot (University of Burgundy)

10:30   The Repertoire Choices and the Theoretical Background of Ottoman Urban
           Music in Istanbul during the 15th–17th Centuries
           Prof. Dr. Cenk Güray (Hacettepe University Ankara State Conservatory)

11:00   Coffee break

11:30   Closing discussion

Online Workshop II

Between Court and City: Soundscapes of Power in East and West
(15th–17th Centuries)

5 February 2021

Programme

Chair: Prof. Dr. Cristina Urchueguía & M.A. Tül Demirbaş (University of Bern)

11:00 Welcome
(CET) Prof. Dr. Cristina Urchueguía

11:15 Acoustic Agencies in the Early Modern European City. A Conceptual Approach
Prof. Dr. Jan-Friedrich Missfelder (University of Basel)

11:45 Courts in Motion – The Sound of Power Between Everyday Life and Celebration
Dr. Margret Scharrer (University of Bern)

12:15 Coffee break

12:45 Rituals, Celebrations and Excess – The Imperial Diet in the Age of Emperor Maximilian I, and the Festive Culture of the Holy Roman Empire
Dr. Moritz Kelber (University of Bern)

13:15 Lunch break

Chair: Prof. Dr. Cristina Urchueguía & M.A. Tül Demirbaş

15:00 "Ad sonum campanæ et tubæ": Power-Reflecting Sonic Elements of Renaissance Dubrovnik
M.A. Tin Cugelj (University of Bern)

| 15:30 | "… quando il Gran Signore vuole la musica": Music and the Ottoman State in the 17th Century |
| | PD Dr. Judith I. Haug (Orient-Institut Istanbul) |

| 16:00 | The Soundscape of Istanbul in the 15th-16th Centuries |
| | Dr. Nina Macaraig (Long Beach, CA) |

| 16:30 | Coffee break |

| 17:00 | Closing discussion |

International Conference

Sounds of Power: Sonic Court Rituals In- and Outside Europe in the 15th–17th Centuries

17–19 June 2021

Programme

Thursday, 17 June 2021
Introduction & General Reflections

Chair:	Prof. Dr. Cristina Urchueguía (University of Bern)

14:00 (CET)	Opening
	Prof. Dr. Cristina Urchueguía
	Dr. Margret Scharrer (University of Bern)
	M.A. A. Tül Demirbaş (University of Bern)

14:15	Keynote: Sovereign Power and the Place of Pleasure: Musical Patronage in Mughal India, 1593–1707
	Dr. Katherine Butler Schofield (King's College London)

15:00	What's All This Noise? Exploring the Soundscapes of the Early Modern Court: Chances and Challenges
	Prof. Dr. Harriet Rudolph (University of Regensburg)

15:30	Coffee break

Chair:	PD Dr. Judith I. Haug (Orient-Institut Istanbul)

16:00	Sight and Sound of Power. Communication Strategies of Papal Rituals in Early Modern Rome
	Dr. Tobias C. Weißmann (Johannes Gutenberg University Mainz)

16:30 "Cantiam vittoria, gaudio, honor, trionfo, e pace" – Die Sakralisierung Venedigs mittels der rappresentazioni (1570–1605)
Dr. Evelyn Korsch (University of Erfurt)

Friday, 18 June 2021
Ottoman & Habsburg-Burgundian Court Cultures

Chair: Dr. Margret Scharrer

10:00 "Pour consideracion des bons et aggreables services": dons, musiciens et communication politique à la cour de Bourgogne (1404–1467)
M.A. Baptiste Rameau (University of Burgundy)

10:30 Maximilian I and the Musical Experiences of Bianca Maria Sforza
Dr. Helen Coffey (The Open University)

11:00 Marian Devotion as Expression of Power. Aspects of Repertoire and Political Representation at the Court of Margaret of Austria
Dr. Daniel Tiemeyer (Heidelberg University)

11:30 Lunch

Chair: M.A. A. Tül Demirbaş

13:30 Traces of Modern Ideas in the Music of the Ottoman Empire
Prof. Dr. Songül Karahasanoğlu & Dr. Süleyman Cabir Ataman (Istanbul Technical University)

14:00 The Expression of Awe during the Early Modern Ottoman Carnivals of Animals
Dr. Ido Ben-Ami (Tel Aviv University)

14:30 The Soundscape of Ottoman-Habsburg Diplomacy in the Eighteenth Century
M.A. Gamze İlaslan (University of Regensburg)

15:00 Coffee break

International Conference

Chair: Dr. Margret Scharrer

15:30   Roundtable: Between Ottoman, Habsburg and Burgundy
          Prof. Dr. Markus Koller (Ruhr University Bochum)
          Prof. Dr. Cristina Urchueguía
          Dr. Karolina Zgraja (University of Zurich)

Saturday, 19 June 2021
Other Cultures and Transfers

Chair: PD Dr. Judith I. Haug

09:30   Setúbal Soundscapes: Performing the Power of the House of Aveiro during
          Early Modern Portugal
          M.A. Ana Cláudia Silveira (NOVA University Lisbon)

10:00   "Ein solcher Lärm ..." Der Klang auf den Hochzeiten des Spätmittelalters
          Prof. Dr. Christof Paulus (Ludwig Maximilian University of Munich)

10:30   Coffee break

Chair: Dr. Margret Scharrer

11:00   The Multi-Layered Soundscape of Charles V Entries in Spanish Cities
          Dr. Esperanza Rodríguez-García (University of Tours)

11:30   Die leisen Klänge der Macht – Das Rebecchino im Kunsthistorischen Museum
          in Wien
          M.A. Thilo Hirsch & Dr. Marina Haiduk (University of Bern & Bern Univer-
          sity of Arts)

12:00   Lunch

Chair:	M.A. A. Tül Demirbaş
14:00	Sonorous Spaces of Splendour: Utilization of Sound in the Courtly Culture of the Safavid Empire in the 17th Century Isfahan M.A. Zeynep Çavuşoğlu (Marmara University/Ibn Haldun University)
14:30	Koreanische Hofmusik der Joseon-Dynastie zur Zeit von König Sejong (1418–1450) Dr. des. Jieun Kim (Heidelberg University)
15:00	Coffee break
Chair:	Prof. Dr. Cristina Urchueguía
15:30	Imperial and Far-reaching: State Processional Music of 16th Century China Prof. Dr. Joseph S. C. Lam (University of Michigan)
16:00	The Sound of Habsburg Power in Colonial Mexico: Ritual and Projection of Identity Throughout Music in Exequias and Other Viceregal Events Prof. Dr. Grayson Wagstaff (The Catholic University of America)
16:30	Coffee break
Chair:	Prof. Dr. Songül Karahasanoğlu
17:00	Roundtable: Sound of Power, Sound of Cultures Prof. Dr. François Picard (Paris-Sorbonne University) Prof. Dr. Wolfgang Behr (University of Zurich) Prof. Dr. Britta Sweers (University of Bern)